AFRICAN MIGRATION, HUMAN RIGHTS AND LITERATURE

This innovative book looks at the topic of migration through the prism of law and literature. The author uses a rich mix of novels, short stories, literary realism, human rights and comparative literature to explore the experiences of African migrants and asylum seekers.

The book is divided into two parts.

Part one is conceptual and focuses on art activism and the myriad ways in which people have sought to 'write justice'. Using Mazrui's diasporas of slavery and colonialism, it then considers histories of migration across the centuries before honing in on the recent anti-migration policies of western states. Achiume is used to show how these histories of imposition and exploitation create a bond which bestows on Africans a 'status as co-sovereigns of the First World through citizenship'. The many fictional examples of the schemes used to gain entry are set against the formal legal processes. Attention is paid to life post-arrival which for asylum seekers may include periods in detention. The impact of the increased hostility of receiving states is examined in light of their human rights obligations. Consideration is paid to how Africans navigate their post-migration lives, which includes reconciling themselves to status fracture – taking on jobs for which they are over-qualified, while simultaneously dealing with the resentment borne of status threat on the part of the citizenry.

Part two moves from the general to consider the intersections of gender and status, focusing on women, LGBTI individuals and children. Focusing on their human rights and the fictional literature, chapter four looks at women who have been trafficked as well as domestic workers and hotel maids while chapter five focuses on LGBTI people whose legal and literary stories are only now being told. The final substantive chapter considers the experiences of children who may arrive as unaccompanied minors. Using a mixture of poetry and first person accounts, the chapter examines the post-arrival lives of children, some of whom may be citizens but who are continually made to feel like outsiders. The conclusion follows, starting with two stories about walls by Hadero and Lanchester which are used to illustrate the themes discussed in the book.

Few African lawyers write about literature and few books and articles in Western law and literature look at books by or about Africans, so a book that engages with both is long overdue. This book provides fascinating reading for academics, policy-makers, students of law, literature, gender and migration, and indeed the general public.

African Migration, Human Rights and Literature

Fareda Banda

•HART•
OXFORD • LONDON • NEW YORK • NEW DELHI • SYDNEY

HART PUBLISHING
Bloomsbury Publishing Plc
Kemp House, Chawley Park, Cumnor Hill, Oxford, OX2 9PH, UK
1385 Broadway, New York, NY 10018, USA

HART PUBLISHING, the Hart/Stag logo, BLOOMSBURY and the Diana logo are trademarks of Bloomsbury Publishing Plc

First published in Great Britain 2020

Reprinted 2021

A catalogue record for this book is available from the British Library.

Library of Congress Cataloging-in-Publication data

Names: Banda, Fareda, author.

Title: African migration, human rights and literature / Fareda Banda.

Description: Oxford, UK ; New York, N.Y. Hart Publishing, an imprint of Bloomsbury Publishing, 2020. | Includes bibliographical references and index.

Identifiers: LCCN 2020029899 (print) | LCCN 2020029900 (ebook) | ISBN 9781509938346 (hardback) | ISBN 9781509938353 (Epub)

Subjects: LCSH: Emigration and immigration in literature. | African diaspora in literature. | Law in literature. | Human rights in literature. | Africans—Legal status, laws, etc.—Foreign countries. | African diaspora. | Africa—Emigration and immigration—In literature. | Africa—Emigration and immigration–Social aspects.

Classification: LCC PN56.E59 B36 2020 (print) | LCC PN56.E59 (ebook) | DDC 809.933554—dc23

LC record available at https://lccn.loc.gov/2020029899

LC ebook record available at https://lccn.loc.gov/2020029900

ISBN: HB: 978-1-50993-834-6
ePDF: 978-1-50993-836-0
ePub: 978-1-50993-835-3

Typeset by Compuscript Ltd, Shannon

To Azera and Shamiso, with love

PREFACE

I remember a conversation that I had with my father aged 17. I was filling out university applications and paused on 'programme to be studied'. From the age of nine, he had convinced me that I wanted to be a lawyer. However, in the intervening years, I had developed a love of reading fiction and was now openly saying that I might want to do a degree in English literature instead. His response was withering, 'You can always read books in your own time Fareda. Do something sensible.' Like so many before me, I gave in to demands for a 'practical course' with a pre-determined career path. Studying law had been my father's dream. It was thwarted by a combination of Rhodesian racism and the need to fulfil familial obligations of support.

I have never regretted realising my father's vision – it is hard to begrudge a man who had migrated from his country of birth, then Nyasaland (Malawi) to Southern Rhodesia (Zimbabwe) in a goods train. He had worked his way up from being a clerk in a bakery to running his own accountancy business. Mine was the first generation to go to university. My country, Zimbabwe, had been independent for four years when I started university. Law over English was indeed the 'sensible thing' to do. However, my love of reading remained undimmed. If anything, it was literature and discussing the books that we were reading that bound my father and me until his death in January 2017. Returning to the family home in Harare since his death finds me sitting in his study, scanning his bookshelf and gently weeping over the books that we loved and shared, some of which I discuss later.

Still, as a newcomer to the law and literature field, I have to acknowledge the limitations of my own knowledge and abilities. A passion for reading does not one a literary critic make.[1] I concede my limitations as a literary critic from the outset. Excellence in this field abounds.[2] Lawyers might argue that I should concede my

[1] Posner identifies amateurism as one of the pitfalls that lie before lawyers who wish to write about literature and vice versa. R Posner *Law and Literature*, 3rd edn (Boston MA, Harvard University Press, 2009) 6–7.

[2] A personal favourite is K Osei-Nyame Jnr, 'Images of London in African Literature: Ama Ata Aidoo's *Our Sister Killjoy* and Dambudzo Marachera's *The Black Insider*' in L Phillips (ed), *The Swarming Streets. Twentieth-Century Literary Representations of London* (New York, Rodopi, 2011) 175–97. M Wa Ngugi, *The Rise of the African Novel* (Ann Arbor MI, University of Michigan Press, 2018); E Boehmer, *Postcolonial Poetics: 21st Century Critical Readings* (Cham, Palgrave Macmillan, 2019); M Feldner, *Narrating the African Diaspora: 21st Century Nigerian Literature in Context* (Cham, Palgrave Macmillan, 2019).

ignorance in that field too. Happily, I oblige. I am, however, heartened by the words of Ian Ward in the preface to his book on *Law and Literature:*

> Law and literature scholarship is one of the most exciting of recent interdisciplinary ventures, and its potential is enormous. Whilst embracing the possibilities which it offers, what we must not do is waste that potential by making it too intellectual and above all inaccessible for all but the most conversant in the intricacies of literary or legal theory. Intellectual pretentiousness is the pervasive evil in so much contemporary legal scholarship, and law and literature must seek to avoid falling into this particular trap. What law and literature scholarship must do is to remember that its purpose is to broaden, not merely to deepen. At the same time, importantly, it must strike out and establish its own identity, and it will only do this by returning to and concentrating on the text.[3]

[3] I Ward, *Law and Literature: Possibilities and Perspectives* (Cambridge, CUP, 2008 [first published 1995]) ix–x.

ACKNOWLEDGEMENTS

I have loved writing this book. This is largely due to the company that I have kept – the authors, poets, photographers and musicians cited have taught me so much and also made me laugh. I have also experienced enormous kindness and am grateful to all those who have made this book possible.

My commissioning editor, Kate Whetter, has been kind, responsive, warm and always encouraging. These seem to be common traits amongst the Hart publishing team, who include Rosie Mearns, Emma Platt, Rosamund Jubber, Linda Staniford, Richard Cox and Rebecca Heselton. Jo Choulerton was a meticulous, kind, patient and fun copy-editor. Thank you all so much for your generosity, warmth and patience.

John Eekelaar has read every iteration of this book which started as an experimental draft article. I value your kindness, support, friendship and encouragement over the years. Thank you also to Mavis Maclean for reading an early version of the book and for all that you have done for me. It was with you that I first tried putting a poem in my work (Jenny Joseph's 'When I am an old Woman, I Shall Wear Purple'). Appreciated as always, Mave. I want to remember and honour the life of Don Harris, my first supervisor, whose advice on work, 'six good hours a day and don't count the coffee breaks' has been passed on over the years. Sadly, I have fallen short. Go well and thank you, Don.

Many of the books and poems that I cite were gifts – to the many friends who introduced me to new authors and worlds – endless thanks. Marcelle Akita's gift of Nyarriah Waheed's SALT to honour my father's passing provided both balm and the stimulus to start. Thank you.

My thanks are also due to the three anonymous reviewers whose comments were constructive and helpful. I also appreciate Marie-Benedicte Dembour who kindly, and at short notice, looked over a short extract. The mistakes remain my own but thank you for your insights.

My father has gone on ahead to join the ancestors. I miss him still, but, as in life, I kept up a running conversation with him during the writing of this book. My mother remains the kindest, most selfless woman that I have ever known. The depths of my love for you and gratitude to you and for you are unfathomable. For my brother Adam – chief cheerleader and optimist – thank you. Sue, I always enjoy our mini book-club chats.

To Azera and Shami, our two wonderful daughters who challenge, inspire, tease and make me laugh so much – this book is for you. Thank you for being great co-researchers and book reviewers and for reminding me of the plots of books that we read together. And for Craig, none of this would be possible without you.

CONTENTS

PART II
INTERSECTIONS

AUTHOR'S NOTE

The joy of writing this book has been in the reading of a rich array of fictional literature and poetry. I am grateful to the artists who have enriched my world and my work. While all the works cited fall under the 'fair dealing' principle/exemption, every effort has been made to seek permission. The publishers apologise for any accidental infringement and would be pleased to come to a suitable agreement with the rightful copyright owners in each case.

I would like to acknowledge John Lanchester and Faber and Faber for permission to use short extracts from *Capital* (2013) as well as Jackie Kay and Picador for permission to use a short extract from Red Dust Road (2010) and Sophie Dunsby, Kate Clanchy and Picador for permission to use 'The Path' from *England, Poems from a School.*

TABLE OF CASES

NATIONAL COURTS

Botswana

Canada

England and Wales

Kenya

Malawi

Nigeria

Papua New Guinea

South Africa

Uganda

United States of America

Zambia

Zimbabwe

REGIONAL CASES

Africa

African Commission on Human and Peoples' Rights

African Committee of Experts on the Rights and Welfare of the Child

UN TREATY BODIES

Committee on the Elimination of all Forms of Discrimination against Women (CEDAW)

Human Rights Committee

NATIONAL LEGISLATION

Bostwana

England and Wales

Ethiopia

Kenya

Malawi

Nigeria

Uganda

Scotland

Senegal

South Africa

TABLE OF HUMAN RIGHTS INSTRUMENTS AND DOCUMENTS

UNITED NATIONS HUMAN RIGHTS INSTRUMENTS

Treaties

UN General Assembly Declarations and Resolutions

INTERNATIONAL LABOUR ORGANIZATION

UN TREATY BODIES: *General Recommendations and Comments*

Committee on the Elimination of Racial Discrimination (CERD)

Human Rights Committee (International Covenant on Civil and Political Rights)

Committee on Economic, Social and Cultural Rights (CESCR)

Committee on the Elimination of Discrimination against Women (CEDAW)

Committee on the Rights of the Child (CRC)

Committee on the Elimination of Racial Discrimination (CERD)

UN TREATY BODIES: ***State Reviews–Concluding Observations, Questions & Replies***

Committee on the Elimination of Racial Discrimination (CERD)

Human Rights Committee (CCPR)

Committee on the Elimination of Discrimination against Women (CEDAW)

Committee on the Rights of the Child (CRC)

UN SPECIAL PROCEDURE MECHANISMS

Special Rapporteurs and Independent Experts

Working Groups

Special Procedures Statements, etc

UNITED NATIONS HIGH COMMISSIONER FOR REFUGEES (UNHCR)

Guidelines

UNHCR Case interventions

WEB PAGES

REGIONAL AND SUB-REGIONAL HUMAN RIGHTS DOCUMENTS

Regional: Africa

Treaties

African Commission on Human and Peoples' Rights

General Comments

Resolutions

African Committee of Experts on the Rights and Welfare of the Child (ACERWC)

General Comments

African Union

Notes and Meetings

SUB-REGIONAL INITIATIVES

Economic Community of West African States (ECOWAS)

REGIONAL: EUROPE

Treaties

Directives and Regulations

Parliamentary Assembly Resolutions

Policy, Reports and Recommendations

Introduction

The image was stark: the body of a drowned Eritrean woman had been retrieved after the sinking of a ship off the Italian island of Lampedusa. She was not alone. She was one of many who had died when their overloaded ship caught fire and capsized.[1] The Eritrean woman was different to her fellow passengers: still attached to her by its umbilical cord was her newborn baby; he was dead.[2] I was reminded of Nayyirah Waheed's poem, 'Lands'

> my
> mother
> was
> my first country.
> the first place i ever lived.[3]

This was not the first report about the death of migrants. In June 2013, the BBC had aired a documentary called 'The Man who Fell to Earth'.[4] One Sunday morning, the residents of a quiet street in West London had awoken to find a dead black man on the street. His face was unrecognisable. The police were called. On his body they found Angolan currency and a sim card for a mobile phone. It was locked. Pathologists meticulously reconstructed his face. In the interim, the police had found a second sim card in one of the pockets of his jeans. On this card, they found some telephone numbers, including a Swiss one. This led them to a woman who had once lived in Cape Town, South Africa. She knew the man. He had worked as her gardener and housekeeper. He was not Angolan, but Mozambican, orphaned at an early age. She had promised to send him money to enable him to get a visa to come to Europe. She had kept her word, but he had been duped by some crooks at the visa office who had taken his money and never returned. He made his way

[1] United Against Refugee Deaths – list of deaths documented up to 5 May 2018. To mark World Refugee Day on 20 June, the list was published in *The Guardian* newspaper in a special feature entitled Guardian, '25 Years of the Refugee Crisis', *The Guardian*, London, 20 June 2018. It documents that from 1993 to May 2018, there have been 34,361 deaths recorded. To honour their lives, the list identifies their names and places of origin, where known, as well as the causes of their deaths and the location of their bodies when discovered.

[2] L Davies, 'Lampedusa Victims include Mother and Baby attached by umbilical cord', *The Guardian*, London, Thursday 10 October 2013.

[3] N Waheed, 'Lands' in *Salt* (London, CreateSpace Publishing, 2013) 182.

[4] BBC World Service, *Assignment*, 'The Man who Fell to Earth', *BBC World Service* online, broadcast on Thursday, 13 June 2013. In 2019, yet another man fell from a Kenyan Airways flight coming into land at Heathrow airport in London. BBC, 'Kenyan flight "stowaway" body found in Clapham garden', *BBC News* online, 2 July 2019.

from Mozambique to Angola. Eventually, he paid someone to let him go airside at the airport in Luanda. He tucked himself into the wheel section of a British Airways flight bound for London. After a flight of close to 10 hours, the aeroplane was approaching Heathrow airport, ready to land; the wheels were lowered and he fell out. He became the 'man who fell to earth'. The pathologist who examined him said that the bruising on his organs suggested that he had survived the flight. Through his Swiss-based former employer and friend, we learned his name: Joseph Matada. His mother called him Zuzu. He was buried in Twickenham cemetery. He was one of the lucky ones, given a name and a burial. Another Waheed poem spoke his story, 'Immigrant':

> you broke the ocean in
> half to be here.
> Only to meet nothing that wants you.[5]

In June 2018, a newspaper columnist wrote a short piece about a young boy who had stowed away in the engine of a coach coming from France. The coach had carried the children from the columnist's son's school. The school boys had gone on tour to France to see where the D-Day Normandy landings took place. On their way back to school, the boy had been discovered hiding under the bus. He had been clinging on for 10 hours and his hands were covered in oil. The police took him away.[6] Inequality cannot be more starkly illustrated.

Whether by sea, air or land, people make their way to new lands. These three media reports are just a few examples of the many news features, books, documentaries and human rights reports about what is termed 'the migrant crisis',[7] which, as Kingsley reminds us, 'is only a crisis because of our response rather than one caused by the refugees'.[8] All show that there has been a failure to realise Appiah's Cosmopolitanism: the recognition of the humanity of those not related to us and the importance of seeing difference not as threatening, but as an opportunity to learn about others and oneself.[9] Hanif Kureshi suggests that if, instead of

[5] N Waheed, 'Immigrant' in *Salt* (2013) 5. Wole Soyinka's poem 'Migrations' is inscribed on the graves of unknown migrants who have drowned at sea in Italy. C Bugan, 'Wole Soyinka's Poetry: The insistence on liberty', *English PEN*, 4 June 2015 at: https://www.englishpen.org/pen-atlas/wole-soyinkas-poetry-the-insistence-on-liberty/.

[6] C Edwards, 'Refugee who joined my son's school trip', *Evening Standard*, London, 21 June 2018.

[7] BBC, 'From our Own Correspondent: Migration Special' presented by Kate Adie and Broadcast on *BBC Radio 4* on 9 September, 2015 at 9am: https://www.bbc.co.uk/programmes/b068s1zs. Amnesty International is one organisation that has an ongoing campaign. See Amnesty International "Refugees, Asylum-Seekers and Migrants" at https://www.amnesty.org/en/what-we-do/refugees-asylum-seekers-and-migrants/. J Elgot, 'Family of Syrian Boy washed up on the beach were trying to reach Canada', *The Guardian*, 3 September 2015. See also F Brian and F Lazcko (eds), *Fatal journey tracking lives lost during migration* (Geneva, International Organization for Migration (IOM), 2014), P Kingsley, *The New Odyssey: The Story of Europe's Refugees* (London, Guardian Books and Faber & Faber, 2016); D Trilling, *Lights in the Distance: Exile and Refuge at the Borders of Europe* (London, Picador, 2018).

[8] P Kingsley, *The New Odyssey: The Story of Europe's Refugee Crisis* (London, Guardian Books and Faber and Faber, 2016) 7.

[9] K Appiah, *Cosmopolitanism* (New York, Vintage, 2007) xv. Appiah's vision is captured by K Hosseini, *Sea Prayer* (London, Bloomsbury, 2018). See K Hosseini, 'Refugees are still dying: How do

exclusion, we allowed ourselves to be open to others: 'If it could be, the stranger, with a mixture of naivety and knowing, might be in a position to tell us the truth about ourselves, since he sees more than we know.'[10]

This book, which focuses on migration by people from the African continent, seeks to consider the journeys undertaken to migrate, to focus on what motivates people to leave and to think about what happens to African people when they get to their destinations.[11] What interactions do they have with the law and others within their new societies? What do these interactions reveal about the problems or issues that the migrants face, and what does the response to these problems tell us about the host perceptions of immigrants? What is the impact of migration? In doing this, while maintaining a focus on migration from Africa, the book places this in a global context, drawing on migration events from other locations where they throw light on the general migration experience, and also making reference to conditions prevailing in some of the countries from which migration originates. I am interested here in human rights, comparing and contrasting the rhetorical claims about the inherent value in each human being and the need to offer protection and succour to those in need, with the realities. I am also interested in the mundane – seeing how people live their newly reconstituted lives.

A common theme that emerges from the migration literature is that of the state of 'in-betweenness' experienced by migrants, particularly the undocumented ones. They are described as being in limbo, socially invisible, yet highly sought after by the authorities, and concurrently, by those in search of cheap labour and willing to take a risk. Khosravi's ethnography of undocumented migrants in Sweden captures this liminality well. He illustrates how their enforced 'illegality' makes them the most legally compliant, for they wish to avoid detection. They are also exposed to economic exploitation, contributing to the economy and yet not able to claim any of the benefits. They are the subject of constant (often negative) comment by politicians and the media, and yet they are voiceless, unable to counter untruths or to challenge stereotypes; they are under constant legal surveillance and yet, fearing detection, are unable to avail themselves of any of the remedies that law offers. The emotional and physical costs paid are high. Depression is common.[12] These insights provide rich ground for one with an interest in human rights.

we get over our news fatigue?, *The Guardian*, London, 17 August 2018 at: https://www.theguardian.com/books/2018/aug/17/khaled-hosseini-refugees-migrants-stories.

[10] H Kureshi, 'These Mysterious Strangers: The New Story of the Immigrant' in L Popsescu (ed), *A Country of Refuge* (London, Unbound, 2016) 27–30 at 30. See also M Nussbaum, *Poetic Justice: The Literary Imagination and Public Life* (Boston MA, Beacon Press, 1995) xvi as cited in I Ward, 'Introduction' in I Ward (ed), *Literature and Human Rights: The Law, The Language and the Limitations of Human Rights Discourse* (Berlin, De Gruyter, 2017) 2.

[11] The term African is freighted with meaning. See C Ngwena, *What is Africanness?: Contesting nativism in culture, race and sexualities* (Pretoria, PULP, 2018). See also Appiah on identity, KA Appiah, *The Lies that Bind: Rethinking Identity* (London, Profile Books, 2018). I use it to denote those who self-identify as African and have migrated from the African continent. Science tells us that we are all of African descent.

[12] S Khosravi, 'An Ethnography of Migrant "Illegality" in Sweden: Included yet Excepted' (2010) 6(1) *Journal of International Political Theory* 95–116. See also S Khosravi (2010), n 18 below. H Kureshi

I. My Law and Literature Journey

So how did I come to writing about fiction when I am a lawyer? Truthfully, I found myself reading more novels and poetry than law journal articles and books. I began to weave the insights gained from the novels and poetry into my teaching. My students started to share their recommendations in turn. Still, I knew that I would have to offer an explanation to my employers about what I had been doing with my time. This book is that attempt at an explanation.

Many of the novels that I read had a diasporic theme which often started with departure and the challenges of getting visas before following the character as they make their way in the new place. To a lawyer, it was interesting that many of the novels used law as a backdrop to drive the plot. Their characters navigated the law and the limits it sought to put on their freedom of movement and opportunities. Reading the novels reminded me of the call and response of Black church services: law called and the novelists and poets responded. In *Postcolonial Poetics*, Boehmer notes that our

> position in relation to the text … constantly circles as we read, like radar, so that as we process its meanings we are also repeatedly considering how the book or poem appeals to us, how it solicits our interest, how it may seek to tell us something of ourselves, or our own story.[13]

Clearly my response to the texts was as both lawyer and migrant.

In reflecting on many of the books that I read, I was reminded of Mnookin and Kornhauser's seminal article, 'Bargaining in the Shadow of the Law'.[14] Mnookin and Kornhauser examine the working of out-of-court negotiation processes in divorce. They say that the law and the solution that a court would impose if the parties failed to reach an out-of-court resolution casts a shadow over the parties' negotiation. The shadow cast by the law in negotiation grants each party bargaining counters (endowments). Your position is stronger if the law 'sees you' and frames your claim as legitimate, so for a long time the perception that courts favoured mothers in custody disputes (maternal preference rule) led to men ceding parental rights or agreeing to contact (access) visits because they perceived that the judicial 'audience' would not receive their custody claims favourably.[15]

(2016), n 10 above; M Mengistu, 'This is what the journey does' in VT Nguyen (ed), *The Displaced: Refugee Writers on Refugee Lives* (New York, Abrams Press, 2018) 129–35, 132, 133; NR Tshuma, 'New Lands, New Selves' in VT Nguyen (ed), ibid, 159–73, 166, 167, E Boehmer, *Postcolonial Poetics: 21st Century Critical Readings* (London, Palgrave Macmillan, 2018) 186–88.

[13] E Boehmer (2018) 9. See also 189. See also MC Nussbaum, 'Reading for Life' (1989) 1 *Yale Journal of Law & the Humanities* 165, 170. Nussbaum reviews WC Booth, *The Company we keep: An Ethics of Fiction* (Berkeley CA, University of California Press, 1988).

[14] R Mnookin and L Kornhauser, 'Bargaining in the Shadow of the Law: The Case of Divorce' (1979) 88(5) *Yale Law Journal* 950–97.

[15] R Mnookin and L Kornhauser (1979) 977.

I wondered what bargaining endowments migrants and asylum seekers had. I saw immigration and refugee law as casting a shadow over those who wanted to move. Their bargaining endowments were often limited by their geographic and economic (dis) location. The shadow cast by the law was menacing and unwelcoming. Given its hostility, the law had to be navigated carefully, or more often, circumvented or avoided altogether. The fictional and non-fictional literature explores the means taken to maximise those endowments, or to navigate beyond the shadow's limits to reach their destinations. Law and literature scholar Dolin relies on the insights of Magris on the links between writing and boundaries to note: 'the awareness of boundaries and their effects, especially the realisation of modes of inclusion and exclusion, abounds in traditional and literary representations of law.'[16] He goes on to say: 'it is the ability of literary texts to represent and draw attention to such boundaries and how they function that produces their greatest insights into law.'[17]

I also found that the fictional literature highlighted a key issue in law and dispute processing in general – that of inequality of bargaining power between those from the rich Global North who have unfettered freedom of movement, and those from the poorer south with little to no freedom of movement. In both law and literature, inequalities were further illustrated through the intersectional prisms of class, race, status (age) and gender, including sexual orientation. Those able to pay for 'investor visas', disproportionately rich men, were, and are, treated very differently to those brought to work as domestic maids, invariably women. Those criminalised for their conduct or orientation in their home countries who seek to flee persecution find themselves further ostracised by a sceptical reception to their claims for protection. As they did not belong to the community whose stories are legible in/to law, these others were left out of the narrative, not able to enjoy legal protection.

The diasporic novels also explore how, on arrival, migrants bargain with state institutions and 'citizens' in the shadow of the law. Khosravi explains how citizenship frames entitlements:

> … the loss of citizenship is called '*denaturalization*' becoming unnatural. Citizenship has become the nature of being human. Being outside the realm of citizenship means being outside nature. In the conditions of statelessness, in the absence of citizenship, one becomes dehumanized (unnatural) and can be exposed to necropolitics – violence and death.[18]

[16] K Dolin, *A Critical Introduction to Law and Literature* (Cambridge, CUP, 2007), 8.

[17] K Dolin (2007) 8. He cites (at p 7) Claudio Magris, 'Who is on the Other Side? Considerations about Frontiers' in C MacLehose (ed), *Frontiers* (London, Harper Collins, 1994) 8. Dolin also references Hannah Arendt, *The Human Condition* (Chicago, Chicago University Press, 1958) where she argues that the wall is a 'symbol of law … and insists that its borders are always under pressure, due to action's inherent tendency to establish relations, force open limitations and cut across boundaries.' Dolin at p 6 citing Arendt at pp 63, 90.

[18] See S Khosravi, *'Illegal' Traveller: An Auto-Ethnography of Borders* (Basingstoke, Palgrave Macmillan, 2010) 122. See also 122–27.

Citizenship is complicated by hierarchies of belonging, including within the migrant communities. Some of the novels and short stories expose how those with the 'correct' paperwork sometimes exploit those without. If, as is claimed, human rights inhere in all who belong to the human family, then how is it that they are not enjoyed by all? Are some more human than others; indeed are others not seen as human at all? Khosravi suggests that this is indeed the case for 'loss of citizenship also means loss of human rights.'[19]

And so to the challenges posed by trying to navigate two disciplines, law and literature, which Posner contends are interlinked.[20] Are they equally weighted? Is it law and literature, or law as literature or even law in literature? Rather than thinking about law *and* literature, Ward connects the two disciplines by arguing for law *as* literature.

> In other words, law *as* literature suggests that both teachers and students must be made aware of all the various 'isms' of literary theory, structuralism, post-structuralism, deconstructionism and so on, which can then be used so that as lawyers we can better understand what a text means, both functionally and interpretively.[21]

Manji notes there are competing schools of thought on the history, development and efficacy of the law-literature inter-disciplinary approach.[22] Does law carry a coercive force that literary analysis does not? What do fictional texts and poetry tell us about ourselves and our societies, including the rules by which we choose to live and their application?[23] Who is involved in the construction of these 'community texts'; who is the subject, who is the object, who is an insider, who is an outsider? Reflecting on the work of James Boyd White in the law and literature movement, West notes:

> In fact, those who are not included in the 'textual community' as either readers, writers, or critics occupy an unbreakable circle of objectivity: because they are outside the community, they do not speak; because they do not speak, they are objects; because they are objects, they do not speak, and as non- speakers they are outside the community. They are, or have been in our history, 'slaves,' 'niggers,' 'women,' 'wives,' even endangered species like foxes and whales.[24]

[19] S Khosravi (2010) 122.

[20] R Posner, *Law and Literature*, 3rd edn (Boston MA, Harvard University Press, 2009) 1.

[21] I Ward, *Law and Literature: Possibilities and Perspectives* (Cambridge, CUP, 2008) 15.

[22] A Manji, 'Law, Literature and the Politics of Culture in Kenya' (2003) (2) *Law, Social Justice & Global Development Journal* (LGD): http://www2.warwick.ac.uk/fac/soc/law/elj/lgd/2003_2/manji/; R West, 'Communities, Texts, and Law: Reflections on the Law and Literature Movement' (1989) 1 *Yale Journal of Law & the Humanities* 129.

[23] See M Nussbaum (1989), n 13 above and R West (1989), n 22 above.

[24] R West (1989), n 22 above, 129, 140. West relies here on the work of James Boyd White, cited at 129, fn 2 as: 'J.B. White, The Legal Imagination (1973); When Words Lose Their Meaning (1984); White, *Economics and Law: Two Cultures in Tension*, 54 Tenn. L. Rev. 161 (1987); White, *Is Cultural Criticism Possible?*, 84 Mich. L. Rev. 1373 (1988); White, *Law and Literature: No Manifesto*, 39 Mercer L. Rev. 739 (1988).'

I would add to this list of the excluded, asylum seekers and poor migrants. West urges us to move beyond textual communities. She argues for the creation of an interactive community based on intimacy, nurturance, compassion and friendship. She urges us to continue to engage with cultural and legal texts, but enjoins us to be alive to the stories and subjective experiences of those who are excluded or harmed by their exclusion. Lawyers and academics remain important, but so too do the stories, poems and parables of the excluded.[25]

Yoshino, in his book *A Thousand Times More Fair: What Shakespeare's Plays Teach Us about Justice*,[26] explains why he has always taught a class in law and literature:

> I use this class to keep steadily visible that the law itself is a series of stories – told by legislators and judges, plaintiffs and defendants. As the late law-and-literature scholar Robert Cover put it: 'for every constitution there is an epic, for each decalogue a scripture.' We cannot understand the law unless we see how its formal texts are embedded in the narratives that accord them shape and meaning.[27]

Sociologist Carol Smart describes the job that lawyers do as one of translating problems into legally recognisable categories, which I think of as telling your story so that it will resonate with legal decision-makers and fit into their rules.[28] In his auto-ethnography about his own journey from Iran to Sweden, Khosravi notes how: 'Only those few who could "translate" their local stories into Eurocentric judicial language had a chance' to gain asylum.[29]

There seem to be far fewer analyses of law and literature from an 'African perspective' than of Western literature written in English.[30] I am not aware of a book that casts its gaze on the interaction between African migration and human rights through the prism of stories primarily about Africans. While African lawyers are numerous, and literary theorists and academics sufficient in number as not to be remarkable, lawyers writing about literature are few and far between. I have long admired the work of Ambreena Manji in this field. She has a unique ability to engage with law, politics and the politics of culture.[31] Pertinent to this book is

[25] R West (1989), n 22 above, 129, 156.

[26] K Yoshino, *A Thousand Times More Fair: What Shakespeare's Plays Teach Us about Justice* (New York, Harper Collins, 2012).

[27] K Yoshino (2012) 11.

[28] C Smart, *The Ties that Bind* (London, Routledge, 1984).

[29] S Khosravi (2010), n 18 above, 34.

[30] G Olsen, 'De-Americanizing Law and Literature Narratives: Open Up the Story' (2010) 22 *Law and Literature* 338–64.

[31] Examples include A Manji, '"Like a Mask Dancing": Law and Colonialism in Chinua Achebe's Arrow of God' (2002) 27(4) *Journal of Law and Society* 626–42; A Manji, 'Of the Laws of Kenya and Burials and all That' (2002) 14(3) *Law and Literature* 436–88; A Manji, 'Law, Literature and the Politics of Culture in Kenya' (2003) (2) *Law, Social Justice & Global Development Journal*, at: http://www2.warwick.ac.uk/fac/soc/law/elj/lgd/2003_2/manji/; A Manji, 'Law, Labour and Resistance to French Colonialism in Sembene Ousmane's *Les Bouts de Bois de Dieu*' (2005) 25(2) *Legal Studies* 320–36. See also L Lanzoni, '*The Trial of Jomo Kenyatta*, by Montague Slater: Oral Tradition and Fundamental Rights in the Trial' in I Ward (ed), *Literature and Human Rights* (Berlin, De Gruyter, 2017), 229–34.

her discussion of Chinua Achebe's *Arrow of God*.[32] Her use of Achebe's metaphor of 'like a Mask dancing' highlights the importance of shifting one's gaze to allow for the possibility that there is more to 'law' than the legal centralist approach which focuses only on state generated law.[33] Through her exploration of the mask metaphor and her analysis of legal pluralism, I was able to see how, although relatively powerless, migrants and asylum seekers also find a way to dance around the dominant legal order that would seek to deny them. Outside of state laws on immigration, there are other normative frameworks in play. While the other orders may operate in the shadows, they are real. For Manji, 'The use of literature as a way of understanding issues of law and power is possible because African novelists have shown themselves to be less concerned to restrict themselves to legal centralist conceptions of law.'[34]

It is these other alternative frameworks that many of the novelists discussed in this book explore. An example can be found in Sulaiman Addonia's novel *Silence is My Mother Tongue*, set in a Sudanese refugee camp.[35] In his novel, Addonia introduces us to the norms of the camp. It starts with the trial of a young girl/woman whose 'purity' is the subject of conjecture. She is 'acquitted' after proof of her virginity is adduced. There are festivities:

> to celebrate Saba's rectitude and the camp's, which remained an island of purity in the middle of this bush. How our society kept its sanity even in this wilderness, said the judge, is a testament to our collective awareness. We police each other because we love others as much as ourselves.[36]

In another 'case' a man tries to sell miswak sticks used for cleaning teeth to people in the square. They refuse to pay, pointing out that they cannot afford it. They argue that as he picked the sticks from a tree, they are common property. The vendor argues that he is a businessman and needs to be paid. A fight breaks out, a trial is held. The verdict: 'No one owns anything in the camp … We all share everything.'[37] Clearly the laws of property and commerce do not apply here. Communalism trumps individualism.

I am reminded of Sally Falk Moore's semi-autonomous social fields where state law and other normative orders co-exist. Moore contends:

> the semi-autonomous social field has rule-making capacities, and the means to induce or coerce compliance; but it is simultaneously set in a larger social matrix which can,

[32] A Manji (2002), n 31 above, 626. C Achebe, *Arrow of God* (London, Heinemann, 1964).

[33] She quotes Ezeulu, Achebe's protagonist, '"the world is like a Mask dancing, if you want to see it well, you do not stand in one place"' Achebe at 9; Manji (2002) 626.

[34] A Manji (2002) 642.

[35] S Addonia, *Silence is My Mother Tongue* (London, Indigo Press, 2018).

[36] S Addonia (2018) 30. Addonia's novel is feminist in its outlook, constantly pointing out the 'rules' that are used to police women and their sexuality (ibid, 83). We, the readers, are left longing for the times when, 'tradition closed its eyes, leaving desire free and uninhibited' (at 200). Addonia dedicates the book to 'the girls – my playmates in our refugee camp.'

[37] S Addonia (2018), n 35 above, 64.

> and does, affect and invade it, sometimes at the invitation of persons inside it, sometimes at its own instance.[38]

'State immigration law' and 'smuggler's law'; weak state labour regulation vs employer fiat in the household are some of the social fields explored in the literature and in this book. Khosravi illustrates the interaction between the fields of state vs smuggler law well. He gives the example of Amir, a smuggler, who produced and published online a 48-page guide about the asylum process and how to interact with immigration and airport officials for his 'clients'.[39] This is a 'legal text' for those operating in the shadows. For Amir, there is a connection between his work and that of the refugee lawyer:

> … in fact, I do not smuggle people. I take them to the border where they can seek asylum. When they have sought asylum a refugee lawyer takes care of their cases. Why is my job a crime but not the lawyer's? We both have the same goal.[40]

Legal pluralism and Moore's semi-autonomous social fields do not stop within municipal boundaries but can have transnational application and effect. 'Laws' are as porous and permeable as borders.

The key law and literature texts focus on literature and art by mainly Western writers. Disproportionately, the writers chosen are male, although this is changing very quickly. Manji notes that there is also more diversity that takes us beyond the Western focus.[41] In addition to Manji herself, there is Dolin's exploration of the work of Nobel Laureate Wole Soyinka. Dolin's analysis of Soyinka allows him to see social orders beyond Western-derived law.[42] Books about human rights and literature tend to offer more diversity. Ward includes South African Andre Brink's work written in Afrikaans in his edited collection on *Human Rights and Literature*.[43] Innovative and influential in my writing of this book is Todres and Higinbotham's study of children's literature and human rights. Using article 29 of the United Nations Convention on the Rights of the Child, 1989, they argue that fictional literature can help states to fulfil their obligation to inform and educate children about their rights.[44] They are also alive to issues of race, noting the

[38] SF Moore, 'Law and Social Change: The Semi-Autonomous Social Field as an Appropriate Subject of Study' (1973) 7(4) *Law & Society Review* 719, 720.

[39] S Khosravi (2010), n 18 above, 109.

[40] S Khosravi (2010) 110.

[41] A Manji (2003), n 22 above.

[42] Dolin (2007), n 16 above, 180; Posner (2009), n 20 above, Ward (2008), n 21 above; Yoshino (2012), n 26 above.

[43] M Nicolini, ''n *Droë Wit Seisoen in die Stormkaap*; Andre Brink and the Fundamental Rights of the Afrikaners in Apartheid South Africa' in I Ward (ed), *Literature and Human Rights: The Law, The Language and the Limitations of Human Rights Discourse* (Berlin, De Gruyter, 2017) 235–54. See also L Lanzoni, '*The Trial of Jomo Kenyatta*, by Montague Slater: Oral Tradition and Fundamental Rights in the Trial' in I Ward (ed), *Literature and Human Rights* (Berlin, De Gruyter, 2017) 229–34. See also S McClennen and AS Moore (eds), *The Routledge Companion to Literature and Human Rights* (Abingdon, Routledge, 2020).

[44] United Nations Convention on the Rights of the Child, 1989, GA Res 44/25 of 20 November 1980, 1577 UNTS 3.

importance of literature that reflects the diversity of the learners.[45] The possibility of dissemination via the spoken word and translation suggests that literature can play an important role in democratising human rights knowledge. In repressive states, fictional texts and poetry can be the means by which human rights and states' violations can be exposed and explored in relative safety.[46] If presented and written as fiction, the 'story' can be discussed and the issues analysed with reduced fear of arrest, harassment or imprisonment.[47] Of course fictional books can, and have, been banned for offending the sensibilities of politicians.

While there are few lawyers focusing on Africa-related human rights and literature, looking at developments in fictional literature and poetry, including literary criticism, produces a very different picture.[48] There is an increasing amount written about diasporic accounts of 'home' and also explorations of diasporic literatures.[49] This reflects the trend in writing amongst African-born authors: their stories focus on diasporic communities and their journeys from home to their lives in new lands. The reasons for the plethora of literature by African writers which focuses on migration have themselves been the subject of discussion. Nwaubani contends that the literature is driven by Western publishers and their wish for 'authentic' stories written by African writers in English. There is no appetite for writing in Igbo or other languages. She also identifies that Western publishers have better distribution deals. In order to reach a wider audience, the writer is encouraged to comply. Nwaubani notes how being garlanded with success in the West results in greater interest being taken of one's work 'at home'.[50] It is of course also true to say that the authors may be writing what they know and reflecting on their own diasporic status and experiences.[51]

[45] J Todres and S Higinbotham, *Human Rights in Children's Literature* (Oxford, OUP 2016).

[46] M Feldner, *Narrating the New African Diaspora: 21st Century Nigerian Literature in Context* (Cham, Palgrave Macmillan, 2019) 85–106 on literature depicting 'The Prison of 1990s Nigeria'. See also B Naidoo, *The Other Side of Truth* (London, Puffin, 2000).

[47] Egyptian novels are also good illustrations of this phenomenon. See S Ibrahim (translated by M St Germain), *The Committee* (Cairo, American University in Cairo Press, 2002); M El Bisatie (translated by D Johnson-Davies), *Hunger* (Cairo, American University in Cairo Press, 2014); M Abdelnabi (translated by J Wright), *In the Spider's Room* (Cairo, Hoopoe, 2018). See also K Gqibitole and S Bello, 'Identity, politics and restriction in Athol Fugard's art: Writing and liberalism in apartheid South Africa' (2018) 39(1) *Literator* (online).

[48] See for example E Boehmer (2018), n 12 above.

[49] See generally the papers in E Emenyonu (ed), *African Literature Today* 34, *Diaspora & Returns in Fiction*, African Literature (Oxford, James Currey, 2016), particularly H Oby Okolocha, 'Negotiating Race, Identity & Homecoming in Chimamanda Ngozi Adichie's *Americanah* Pede Hollist's *So the Path Does not Die*' at 143–62. M Wa Ngugi, *The Rise of the African Novel* (Ann Arbor, University of Michigan Press, 2018) 163–88. K Osei-Nyame, 'Images of London in African Literature: Ama Ata Aidoo's *Our Sister Killjoy* and Dambudzo Marechera's *The Black Insider*' in L Phillips (ed), *The Swarming Streets. Twentieth-Century Literary Representations of London* (New York, Rodopi, 2004) 175, 191–95; M Feldner (2019), n 46 above; A Quayson, *Diaspora Literary Studies* (Oxford, Wiley-Blackwell, 2010).

[50] AJ Nwaubani, 'We spoke English to set ourselves apart: how I rediscovered my mother tongue', *The Guardian*, 14 March 2019. On which language to use, Nwaubani acknowledges Achebe's injunction that in wanting to re-engage one's mother tongue, one should not get rid of English, not least because it is now as much 'ours' as it is 'theirs'. M Feldner (2019), n 46 above, 24–29.

[51] M Feldner (2019), n 46 above, 1–11.

It is worth acknowledging that stories about migration, or with migration themes are global. Reading 'beyond Africa(ns)' has shown me that, in the words of Maya Angelou, 'We are more alike than we are unalike, my friend.'[52] Kiran Desai's *Inheritance of Loss* and Sunjeev Sahota's *The Year of the Runaways* on Indian migration illuminated the truth of Angelou's words, not least on the challenges faced to obtain a visa to facilitate migration and then to earn a livelihood.[53] Again, the themes explored in the novels are increasingly picked up and reflected in the academic literature and case law. It is for example, difficult to distinguish the stories of Khosravi's informants in his ethnography, from the fictional characters in Sahota's *The Year of the Runaways*.[54] Sahota also introduced me to issues outside of my personal experience, not least the transportability of caste and the myriad ways that the Dalit seeks to avoid causing offence, but is nevertheless subjected to numerous humiliations.[55] There is the additional dimension of discovering the other – in both Desai and Sahota, the Indians have to reckon with engaging with other people of colour, though most migrants only learn of their raced selves on migration – at home they 'just are.'[56] This in turn calls into question the (British) practice of lumping all people of colour into a category known in Britain

[52] M Angelou, 'Human Family' in M Angelou, *The Complete Collected Poems* (London, Virago, 1997), 224–25. Also available at: Angelou Poems at: https://allpoetry.com/Human-Family.

[53] K Desai, *The Inheritance of Loss* (Hamish Hamilton, 2006); S Sahota, *The Year of the Runaways* (Picador, 2015); cf E Boehmer (2018), n 12 above, 22–23.

[54] S Khosravi (2010), n 18 above; S Sahota (2015). See also, D Pasura, *African Transnational Diasporas: Fractured Communities and Plural Identities of Zimbabweans in Britain* (London, Palgrave Macmillan, 2014); J Bhabha, *Children without a State: A Global Human Rights Challenge* (Cambridge MA, MIT Press, 2011).

[55] Reading Sahota has helped me to make sense of the contentious discussion that followed the British government's proposals to include caste as a protected category. House of Commons Library, 'The Equality Act 2010: caste discrimination' August, 2018 at: http://researchbriefings.parliament.uk/ResearchBriefing/Summary/SN06862. However, see P Shah, *Against Caste in British Law: A Critical Perspective on the Caste Discrimination Provision in the Equality Act 2010* (Basingstoke, Palgrave, 2015). Thornberry highlights the contentiousness of the term 'caste', noting India's resistance to the inclusion of caste within the purview of race discrimination. P Thornberry, *The International Convention on the Elimination of all Forms of Racial Discrimination* (Oxford, OUP, 2016), 122–23. In 2002, CERD adopted UN General Recommendation 29 on Descent-based Discrimination, CERD/C/61/Misc.29/rev.1, 22 August 2002. This covers both caste and other descent-related discrimination, meaning that the Committee is able to address the issue as it arises globally. See International Dalit Solidarity Network, *ICERD Recommendations and Comments on Caste Based Discrimination* (IDSN 2015) (covers the period 1996–2015). Available at: https://idsn.org/wp-content/uploads/2015/11/CERD-Recommendations-and-Comments-on-Caste-Compiled-Nov-2015.pdf. The CERD recommended that the UK change its law to reflect caste discrimination within the race category, at: 'CERD Concluding Observations UK' CERD/C/63/CO/11, 10 December 2003, para 25 and 'CERD Concluding Observations UK' CERD/C/GCR/CO/18-20 (2011), para 30. On a different note, I, like many others, have loved the work of Jumpa Lahiri since her debut, *The Interpreter of Maladies* (Boston MA, Houghton Mifflin, 1999) and *The Namesake* (New York, Harper Perennial, 2004).

[56] See for example, T Cole, 'On the Blackness of the Panther' in N Shukla and C Suleyman (eds), *The Good Immigrant USA* (London, Dialogue Books, 2019), 36, 36–42, 49–51. C Obioma, 'The Naked Man' in N Shukla and C Suleyman (eds), ibid, 155, 162–67. Cf P Chigumadzi, 'Why I am no longer talking to Nigerians about Race', *Africa is a Country*, 7 April 2019, https://africasacountry.com/2019/04/why-im-no-longer-talking-to-nigerians-about-race.

as BAME (Black, Asian and Minority Ethnic) which term obfuscates more than it illuminates.

I have been drawn in by the ways in which many of the authors highlight gender and the transportability of norms from one society to another and of the disproportionate burden borne by women of upholding cultural norms, and by men, of the expectation that they will be breadwinners who are able to support the wider family network. Both are oppressed by these expectations. Women tend to be the ones who end up bearing the heavier burden, being both carers and working outside the home to earn money which is used on the family.[57] Smiling, and in the interests of academic balance, I feel compelled to quote the assessment made of African women by Printer, a character in Mabanckou's *Broken Glass*:

> African women living in France are a tight-arsed lot, stuck-up, affected, unreliable … they think an awful lot of themselves, those girls do, they want you to grovel at their feet, what's more … they're all materialistic, they check out your car, your house, your bank account, your shares on the stock market, you have to pay for their ridiculous hairdos that cost a fortune … you end up paying for this, that and the next thing.[58]

Authors from the 'Global North' have also increased their focus on the issue of migration. In their work, many seek to challenge the dominant narrative of people who have come as 'problems' or 'bogus asylum-seekers', as is sometimes presented by the media.[59] Others make a point of highlighting the economic, emotional and social contributions of their African characters.[60] Added to this has been a concerted effort to present factual information in narrative forms that are comprehensible to the ordinary person.[61]

In concluding this section, I find myself returning to Constitutional law and English scholar Kenji Yoshino who justifies his wish to keep both law and literature in play in his teaching and writing: 'Law wields a brutal coercion literature cannot approximate. Yet literature has a power to get inside us, to transform our hearts and minds, in a way that law cannot.'[62]

[57] Addonia honours the strength of his female companions in the refugee camp within his novel. S Addonia, *Silence Is my Mother Tongue* (London, Indigo Press, 2018).

[58] A Mabanckou, translated by H Stevens, *Broken Glass* (London, Serpent's Tale, 2009) 89. Reader it gets worse, he then moves on to a country by country analysis of women from Congo, Nigeria, Cameroon, Gabon and the Ivory Coast. All I can do is commiserate with my sisters. (89–90).

[59] A particularly good example of this is E Wiles, *The Invisible Crowd* (London, Harper Collins, 2017). She uses newspaper headlines to head each chapter. See also B Zephaniah, 'On Writing *Refugee Boy*' in B Zephaniah, *Refugee Boy* (London, Bloomsbury, 2017).

[60] E Day, *Paradise City* (London, Bloomsbury, 2015); M Gee, *My Cleaner* (London, SAQI, 2005). J Lanchester, *Capital* (London, Faber, 2013); Z Smith, *The Embassy of Cambodia* (London, Hamish Hamilton, 2013).

[61] D Herd and A Pincus (eds), *Refugee Tales* (Manchester, Comma Press, 2016); D Herd and A Pincus, *Refugee Tales II* (Manchester, Comma Press, 2017); D Herd and A Pincus (eds), *Refugee Tales III* (Manchester, Comma Press, 2019).

[62] K Yoshino, *Covering* (New York, Random House, 2007) 26. On the use of film see A Rhoades and D Stein, 'Engaging Audiences through Visual Storytelling', IOM, 14 December 2017, web.log.iom.int.

II. On Migration

When deciding to write this book, I had to confront the fact that the migration literature is vast. It covers a range of disciplines, from economists and development experts arguing the toss about whether the remittances made by migrants to their home countries outstrip the aid budgets of even the most generous states, to legal analyses of refugee and immigration law, to anthropological and geographical accounts of the experiences of migration, to a consideration of the lives of immigrants in their new countries, to historical accounts of the reasons for migration and sociological studies of the impact and consequences of immigration on both those migrating and the communities that they find on arrival.[63] Studies of the role of academics include critical analyses of the role of African intellectuals in the diaspora.[64] The story of migration is not one that only interests academics. It has become an issue that concerns policy-makers. The brain drain has long been an issue of focus. Organisations such as the International Organization for Migration (IOM) run voluntary repatriation programmes designed to encourage migrants who wish to return to their homelands to do so safely.[65]

Important to the migration literature and an inspiration for me, is Khosravi's auto-ethnography, *Illegal*, which documents his own undocumented travel from his native Iran to Sweden where he was eventually given asylum and settled. Khosravi is lyrical about the injustices created by the idea of borders, citizenship and sovereignty which determine how a person's humanity is measured. He notes:

> Through politico-juridical discourse and regulation, this system creates a politicized human being (a citizen of a nation state) but also a by-product, a politically unidentifiable 'left-over', a 'no-longer-human being.' Sent back and forth between sovereign

[63] B Anderson, *Us and Them? The Dangerous Politics of Immigration Control* (Oxford, OUP, 2013); R Anderson, *Illegality Inc.: Clandestine Migration and the Business of Bordering Europe* (Richmond, California University Press, 2014); M-B Dembour, *When Humans Become Migrants* (Oxford, OUP, 2015); P Collier, *Exodus: Immigration and Multiculturalism in the 21st Century* (London, Allen Lane, 2013); E West, *What we got wrong about immigration and how to get it right* (London, Gibson Square, 2015); P Shah, *Refugees, Race and the Concept of Asylum in Britain* (London, Cavendish, 2000). S Khosravi (2010), n 18 above. E Fiddian-Quasmiyeh, G Loescher, K Long and N Sigona (eds), *The Oxford Handbook of Refugee and Forced Migration Studies* (Oxford, OUP, 2016). A Betts and P Collier, *Refuge: Transforming a Broken Refugee System* (London, Penguin, 2017). J Portes, *What do we know and what should we do about immigration?* (London, SAGE, 2019). N El-Enany, *(B)Ordering Britain: Law, Race and Empire* (Manchester, Manchester University Press, 2020).

See also The Migration Observatory at the University of Oxford, at http://www.migrationobservatory.ox.ac.uk; the International Organization for Migration (IOM), at http://www.iom.int and the London international Development Centre Migration Leadership Team, at https://www.soas.ac.uk/lidc-mlt/.

[64] P Zeleza, 'The academic diaspora and knowledge production in and on Africa: what role for CODESRIA?' in T Mkandawira (ed), *African Intellectuals: Rethinking Politics, Language, Gender and Development*, London (London, ZED Books, 2005) 209–34. The collection contains several other interesting chapters.

[65] See the website of the International Organization for Migration section on Migration Flows: Europe at: at www.iom.int.

> states, humiliated and represented as polluted and polluting bodies, stateless asylum seekers and irregular migrants are excluded and become the detritus of humanity, leading wasted lives. The modern nation state has claimed the right to preside over the destruction between useful (legitimate) and wasted (illegitimate) lives.[66]

There has been a flurry of initiatives to address the global movement of people.[67] A Global Compact on Migration was agreed in 2018.[68] It aims to create a global governance initiative on migration, highlighting the centrality of human rights. It emphasises the duty of states to provide their people with the conditions (socio-economic and political) that will enable them to thrive and thus negate the need for them to seek their fortunes elsewhere. For those who leave, countries of transit and destination have obligations to ensure that the new arrivals are treated fairly. Specifically, the receiving states are under a duty to guarantee equal remuneration and conditions of work for migrants, regardless of their paperwork. This is to protect them from exploitation and also to maintain the decent working conditions of the existing workers who will not be undercut by cheaper, exploited labour.[69] Additionally, the Global Compact seeks to get states to ensure that the incomers are given access to health care and education as well as legal aid should they need to access courts or tribunals for remedies for breach of their rights.[70]

Reinforcing the Global Compact are the Sustainable Development Goals (SDGs). Migration is a cross-cutting theme in the 17 Sustainable Development Goals and the 169 targets set for Agenda 2030.[71] States are required to 'Facilitate orderly, safe, regular and responsible migration and mobility of people, including through the implementation of planned and well-managed migration policies'[72]

Those leaving home to seek asylum are covered by the UN Refugee Convention, 1951 and its 1967 Protocol, supplemented by the Guidelines issued by the UN High

[66] S Khosravi (2010), n 18 above, 3 (footnotes omitted). See also P Daley, 'Entangled Spatialities: Immigrants and Worker Citizens in the United Kingdom' in B Anderson and V Hughes (eds), *Citizenship and its Others* (Basingstoke, Palgrave Macmillan, 2015) 65–71.

[67] UN Secretary-General, *In safety and dignity: addressing large movements of refugees and migrants* UN GA decision 70/539 of 22 December 2015.

[68] A lot of work has gone into the preparations for this Compact including the adoption of the New York Declaration for Refugees and Migrants, A/RES/71/1 of 3 October 2016. In December 2018 an Intergovernmental Conference to adopt the Global Compact for Safe, Orderly and Regular Migration was held in Marrakesh, Morocco and confirmed by the UN General Assembly. UN GA *Global Compact for Safe Orderly Migration*, A/RES/73/95, 11 January 2019. For history of meetings and documents, see OHCHR Global Compact for Migration at: https://www.ohchr.org/EN/Issues/Migration/Pages/GlobalCompactforMigration.aspx, and also the official UN Website for the Compact on Migration at: https://refugeesmigrants.un.org/member-states.

[69] See also http://www1.umn.edu/humanrts/iachr/series_A_OC-18.html.

[70] Cf P Melin, 'The Global Compact for Migration: Lessons for the Unity of EU Representation' (2019) 21 *European Journal of Migration and the Law* 194–214 on the lack of co-ordination between European states many of whom pursued individual state interests over the collective European negotiating position.

[71] United Nations, *Transforming our World: The 2030 Agenda for Sustainable Development* A/RES/70/1.

[72] Migration Data Portal, Migration Data for the SDGs' at: https://migrationdataportal.org/sdgs?node=10, 'SDG 10 – Reduced Inequality', target 10.7.

Commission for Refugees (UNHCR).[73] It lists five grounds for claiming asylum for those who have been, or fear that they will be, harmed (or persecuted): race, religion, nationality, political opinion or membership of a particular social group.[74]

Other normative frameworks include the United Nations Convention on Migrant Workers and their Families, 1990.[75] Additionally, there is the work done by United Nations special procedures mandate holders, not least the Special Rapporteur on the human rights of migrants whose mandate requires them:

> To examine ways and means to overcome the obstacles existing to the full and effective protection of the human rights of migrants, recognizing the particular vulnerability of women, children and those undocumented or in an irregular situation.[76]

CEDAW General Recommendation No 26 has been adopted to protect the rights of migrant workers in their countries of destination and indeed their home states.[77] These seek to buttress the existing human rights treaties.

In the conclusion to his commentary on the UN Convention on the Elimination of all Forms of Racial Discrimination, 1966 (CERD), Patrick Thornberry anticipates that, on the basis of the current migration increases, the CERD is bound to focus more of its future work on migrants and non-citizens.[78]

[73] Convention Relating to the Status of Refugees, 1951 and its 1967 Protocol, 189 UNTS 137 (hereafter UN Refugee Convention 1951). Kampala Declaration on Refugees, Returnees and Internally Displaced Persons in Africa, Ext/Assembly/AU/PA/Draft/Decl.(1)Rev. 1. African Union Convention for the Protection of Internally Displaced Persons in Africa, adopted 23October 2009, entered into force 6 December 2012: https://www.internal-displacement.org/publications/african-union-convention-for-the-protection-and-assistance-of-internally-displaced-persons-in-africa.

[74] UN Refugee Convention, 1951 art 1 A(2).

[75] The International Convention on the Protection of the Rights of All Migrant Workers and Members of Their Families, 1990 UN A/RES/45/158. Most of the states ratifying this Convention are 'sending' states whose citizens migrate. See also, UN Committee on the Protection of the Rights of All Migrant Workers and Members of Their Families (CMW), Joint General Comment No 3 (2017) of the Committee on the Protection of the Rights of All Migrant Workers and Members of Their Families and No 22 (2017) of the Committee on the Rights of the Child on the general principles regarding the human rights of children in the context of international migration, 16 November 2017, CMW/C/GC/3-CRC/C/GC/22; UN Committee on the Rights of the Child (CRC), General Comment No 6 (2005): Treatment of Unaccompanied and Separated Children Outside their Country of Origin, 1 September 2005, CRC/GC/2005/6. The UN has a Global Migration Group comprising 14 UN agencies. See OHCHR, 'Migration, A Global Governance Issue', 2010 at: https://ohchr.org/EN/NewsEvents/Pages/MigrationGlobalGovernancelssue.aspx.

[76] Human rights of migrants: mandate of the Special Rapporteur on the human rights of migrants, A/HRC/RES/34/21(2017), para 1(a).

[77] CEDAW General Recommendation No 26 on Women Migrant Workers, CEDAW/C/2009/WP.1/R, 2008.

[78] P Thornberry, *The International Convention on the Elimination of all Forms of Racial Discrimination: A Commentary* (Oxford, OUP, 2016) 497. See also Committee on the Elimination of Racial Discrimination, *Statement on the Current Migration Crises*, A/70/18, Chapter II; 'CERD General Recommendation XXX on Discrimination Against Non-Citizens', CERD/C/64/Misc.11/rev. 3 (1 October 2002) and CERD General Recommendation No 33, Follow up to the Durban Review Conference, CERDC/GC/33, 29 September 2009, para 1(f). See also preamble.

Regional institutions and states are equally invested in the migration debate.[79] The African Union regards the diaspora as its sixth region. Rather than focusing on migration as constituting a loss to the continent, the African Union has chosen to tap into the potential for diaspora citizens to act as global lobbyists and advocates for the continent by their work and remittances.[80] At a meeting of experts to define who is included in the term 'diaspora', held in Addis Ababa in 2005, certain characteristics were identified as guiding principles:

- the bloodline and/or heritage. The Diaspora should consist of people living outside the continent whose ancestral roots or heritage are in Africa;
- migration: The Diaspora should be composed of people of African heritage, who migrated from or are living outside the continent. In this context, three trends of migration were identified – pre-slave trade, slave trade, and post-slave trade or modern migration;
- the principle of inclusiveness. The definition must embrace both ancient and modern Diaspora; and
- the commitment to the African course [sic]. The Diaspora should be people who are willing to be part of the continent (or the African family).[81]

After some discussion, the final definition agreed upon reinforced the importance of reciprocity, noting: 'The African Diaspora consists of peoples of African origin living outside the continent, irrespective of their citizenship and nationality and who are willing to contribute to the development of the continent and the building of the African Union.'[82]

The Ghanaian government has engaged the diaspora link in its tourism policy targeted at African-Americans who wish to re-trace ancestral steps and to visit the homelands of their pre-slavery ancestors to see the point of departure for the trans-Atlantic journeys that they were forced to undertake. Ghana declared 2019 'The Year of Return' to mark 400 years since the arrival of the first slaves in Virginia.[83]

The United Nations has declared a Decade for People of African Descent 2015–2024 with the sub-themes: recognition, justice and development.[84] The justice

[79] The New York Declaration for Refugees and Migrants, 2016 gives the following examples of regional initiatives: 'the European Union-Horn of Africa Migration Route Initiative and the African Union Horn of Africa Initiative on Human Trafficking and Smuggling of Migrants (the Khartoum Process), the Rabat Process, the Valletta Action Plan and the Brazil Declaration and Plan of Action. New York Declaration New York Declaration, 2016, para 19.

[80] F Marini, 'Immigrants and transnational engagement in the diaspora: Ghanaian associations in Italy and the UK' (2013) 6 *African and Black Diaspora: An International Journal* 131, 133–35.

[81] African Union 'Meeting of Experts on the Definition of the African Diaspora 11–12 April 2005 Addis Ababa, Ethiopia', paras 14–16 (at para 11). http://www.dirco.gov.za/diaspora/fr/definition.html.

[82] African Union Meeting of Experts to define diaspora (2005) para 18.

[83] See http://www.yearofreturn.com. N Kleist, 'Flexible Politics of Belonging: Diaspora Mobilisation in Ghana' (2013) 72 *African Studies* 285, 291. A Reed, 'Diaspora Tourism: The Heritage of Slavery in Ghana' in A Quayson and G Daswani (eds), *A Companion to Diaspora and Transnationalism* (Oxford, Wiley Blackwell, 2013) 524.

[84] UN A/RES/68/237 Proclamation of the International Decade for People of African Descent, Resolution adopted by the General Assembly on 23 December 2013.

theme requires acknowledgement of slavery and the negative impact of colonialism on those affected. Also recommended is the provision of equal opportunities together with a guarantee of equality before the law and access to justice for people of African Descent. Development entails fair employment practices, including for migrants as well as access to good quality education for children.[85]

III. On Terminology

The language around migration is often emotive and derogatory. People are often called 'illegal' but, as the Holocaust survivor Elie Wiesel once noted, a human being can never be illegal:

> You, who are so-called illegal aliens, must know that no human being is illegal. That is a contradiction in terms. Human beings can be beautiful or more beautiful, they can be fat or skinny, they can be right or wrong, but illegal? How can a human being be illegal?[86]

Most states have rid their legal systems of the word 'illegitimate' to describe children born out of wedlock, so too, a person who finds themselves outside their country borders remains a human being, entitled to rights, including to dignity. The UN Special Rapporteur on Migrants advocates the use of 'irregular' or 'undocumented' to denote the absence of paperwork, not the lack of humanity.[87] The IOM also works hard to counter the use of pejorative language, which has influenced my decision to eschew terms such as 'illegal immigrants' preferring irregular or undocumented.[88]

Maximilian Feldner draws our attention to the elasticity in the usage of the word diaspora, noting that it is often conflated with, 'a range of related words such as "migration", "exile", "transnationalism", minority, refugee status, and racial and ethnic difference.'[89]

[85] See the website of the UN '2015–2024 International Decade for People of African Descent' at: http://www.un.org/en/events/africandescentdecade/. See also African Union concept note prepared by Citizens and Diaspora Directorate of the AU Commission for the 'African Union Continental Symposium on the Implementation of the International Decade for People of African Descent 18–20 September 2018, Accra/Cape Coast, Ghana' on the African Union website. See also CERD, General Comment No 34, Racial Discrimination against People of African Descent, CERD/GC/34, 3 October, 2011.

[86] Epigraph of E Colfer and A Donkin (with illustrations by G Rigano), *Illegal* (London, Hodder, 2017).

[87] Report of the Special Rapporteur on the human rights of migrants, Mr Francois Crepeau, UN A/71/285, 4 August 2016, para 31. See also Migrant Workers' Convention, 1990, art 5(b) and Committee on the Protection of the Rights of Migrant Workers and Members of their Families, General Comment No 2 on the Rights of Migrant Workers in an Irregular Situation and Members of their Families, CMW/C/GC/2, 28 August 2013, paras 3 and 4.

[88] IOM *International Migration Law: Glossary on Migration No. 34* (Geneva, IOM, 2019) 59, 114.

[89] M Feldner (2019), n 46 above, 14, quoting BH Edwards, 'Diaspora' in B Burgett and G Hendler (eds), *Key Words for American Cultural Studies*, 1st edn (New York, NYU Press, 2007) 82. See also Feldner, ibid, 15.

I must warn that I am not always consistent in my use of language in this book. Lawyers, the IOM and linguistic purists will be infuriated by the language slippage and elision of refugees, asylum-seekers and those who move voluntarily into one term – migrants. Their status and entitlements are different in law. Hirsch and Makumbi raise a different objection. They question why Africans who move north are called immigrants, but people from the Global North who move south are called expatriates or expats.[90] In using the term 'migrant' to denote one who has moved out of their home country, I have absorbed the common every-day usage which is also captured in the fictional literature where the delineations of law are often missing. People move and while they do so, the legal framing of their status shifts and evolves with time and circumstance. Kingsley observes that while people may leave home voluntarily to come to Europe (migrants), their experiences on the journey, which might include abuse and degrading and inhuman treatment (temporary forced labour, sexual assault) meted out to them along the journey, may actually lead to a change of status en route, to that of asylum-seeker based on their experiences of persecution.[91] Costello contends that, even in law, a person may have a shifting identity, moving between legality and being in the shadow of law, or in breach of law before regularisation restores them to a position of formal 'legality'. She observes: 'Taking into account both multi-level legality and the temporal shifts in status reveals the complexity of "illegality"'.[92]

IV. On Coverage

This is a study of Africans abroad. The definition of 'abroad' is of course indeterminate because migration is a global phenomenon. There is, I am given to understand, a booming 'Little Africa' in Guangzhou, China, sometimes called 'Chocolate City'. Here one can find Africans, 'speaking Arabic, Bambara, French, Portuguese, Lingala, Malagasy, Yoruba or Igbo – a reminder of the cultural diversity of this migrant community.'[93]

[90] A Hirsch, 'When is an immigrant not an immigrant? When they're rich', *The Guardian*, 10 April 2019. A Underwood, 'So many ways of knowing: An interview with Jennifer Nansubuga Makumbi, author of "Kintu"', *Los Angelos Review of Books*, 31 August 2017.

[91] P Kingsley (2016), n 8 above, 54, 69–70.

[92] C Costello, *The Human Rights of Migrants and Refugees in European Law* (Oxford, OUP, 2016) 67.

[93] F Kuwonu, 'China's "Little Africa" losing its allure', *Africa Renewal*, August–November 2018. The numbers are going down due to Chinese migration to the African continent which means that the goods that Africans travelled to buy in China can now be obtained on the continent. Other reasons include the impact of the Exit and Entry Administration Law, introduced in 2013, which has led to harsher penalties for overstaying and visa restrictions; racism against darker skinned people and the growth of African economies have resulted in the U-turn. See N Birhanu and B Han, 'Africans in China: The Pivot Back' Council on Foreign Relations, 25 July 2016. See also C Dotto, '"Little Africa" in China', *New Internationalist*, 11 March 2019.

This book focuses on the move to Western states. The idea of Western is not without problems – many now speak of the Global North and South. Nevertheless, Australia for my purpose is constructed as Western, as is New Zealand, but I do not focus on them because of time and space constraints. Of Africans in Australia, the Human Rights Committee noted in its 2017 concluding observations:

> The Committee is concerned about: (a) reports of discrimination on the basis of ethnic, racial, cultural or religious background, with migrants from African countries being particularly targeted by discrimination and racial profiling ...[94]

People who live on borrowed/stolen land should show greater compassion.[95]

The United States also appears sporadically. It is having the same conversation as Europe, only there the 'problem' people wishing to migrate are from South and Central America rather than Africa. There are commonalities between the approach of the Trump regime and that of the Australians and indeed Europeans in seeking to bar people by building legal and physical walls of exclusion. The United States has given up on inviting countries to send their poor, bedraggled masses, preferring to keep them out.[96] Okafor's analyses of Canadian and US refugee policy and practice following the attacks of 9/11 presents an unedifying picture of security concerns trumping and trampling over human rights.[97]

I recognise that migration has gone on for centuries. Black Africans have migrated, both voluntarily and by coercion (slavery), to the place now labelled 'the Middle East' for centuries. The Trans-Atlantic slave trade sees us in the Americas and beyond. Involuntary migration is increasingly as a result of the effects of climate change and poor governance which threaten livelihoods and force people to move. I acknowledge that there is more human mobility and migration within regions and between neighbouring states than there is across continents.[98] I do look at some movement within the region, not least migration to South Africa.

[94] UNCCPR Concluding Observations to the sixth report of Australia, CCPR/C/AUS/CO/6, 1 December, 2017, para 19. See also paras 33–38.

[95] Australia has a long history of racist exclusions and discrimination that go beyond its more recent treatment of Black Africans and other groups. G Martin, 'Stop the boats! Moral panic in Australia over asylum seekers' (2015) 29 *Journal of Media & Cultural Studies* 304–22; J Poon, 'How a body becomes a Boat: The Asylum Seeker in Law and Images' (2018) 30 *Law & Literature* 105–21. NF Tan, 'The Manus Island Regional Processing Centre: A Legal Taxonomy' (2018) 20 *European Journal of Migration* 427–51.

[96] *William P Barr, Attorney-General et al v East Bay Sanctuary Covenant et al*, 588 US 2019 (No 19A230).

[97] O Okafor, *Refugee Law after 9/11: Sanctuary and Security in Canada and the United States* (Vancouver BC, University of British Columbia Press, 2020). See also K Villavicencio, *The Undocumented Americans* (New York, Penguin Random House, 2020).

[98] See data presented in joint report by the Mo Ibrahim Foundation and Afro Barometer, *Updata-ing the Narrative about African Migration* (London, Mo Ibrahim Foundation, 2019). See also World Economic Forum, 'African migration: what the numbers really tell us', *World Economic Forum*, 7 June 2018.

Yet others will say 'why is she looking "overseas" when there are so many problems "at home."?' In chapter three, I do look at the inhospitable environments that cause people to risk their lives to try their luck elsewhere. There is ample evidence to show that in addition to the long-standing normative commitment to offer protection to those in need (both refugees and more recently, Internally Displaced People – IDPs), African states have not always delivered.[99] The xenophobic attacks on foreign migrants remind us that suspicion of 'the other' is not confined to one continent or people.[100] In short, there is no attempt on my part to create a hierarchy or typology of mobility. It is simply that resources – time and human – are in short supply. These are the choices that I have made – but only for now and for this project.

Also worth noting are the limits of the legal coverage in this book. Just as I am not a literary critic or scholar, so too I am not a refugee or immigration lawyer. The subject of migration and asylum-seeking touches on both refugee and immigration law, but they are not the primary focus of this study. I am interested in human rights and what stories and poems tell us about them and how we can better use or learn from fictional literature and art broadly defined, to engage a wider audience. I hope to create a mosaic showing the intesections between human rights, literature and other branches of law.

It is also worth acknowledging that, increasingly, social media is used as an immediate and direct form of expression. It is often the way in which many human rights scholars and institutions now craft a narrative. However, I have chosen to focus on written literature in a traditional format and not social media. Again, this is about capacity.

V. Structure

The book is in two Parts and comprises eight chapters including this Introduction and the Conclusion. The two Parts comprise three chapters each. Given the book's focus on human rights, Chapter one explores the concept of 'artivism' (art activism)

[99] P Daley, 'Refugees, IDPs and Citizenship Rights: the perils of humanitarianism in the African Great Lakes Region' (2013) 34(5) *Third World Quarterly* 893–912. C Beyani, *Protection of the Right to Seek and Obtain Asylum under the African Human Rights System* (Leiden, Brill, 2013); J Crush, A Chikanda and C Skinner, *Mean Streets: Migration, Xenophobia and Informality in South Africa* (South Africa Migration Programme, 2015); P Matthews and T Harley, *Refugees, Regionalism and Responsibility* (Cheltenham, Edward Elgar, 2016); IR Mugisha, 'Deported from Zambia: Former Rwandan Refugees Choose to Stay', *The East African*, 15 September, 2018. In the same newspaper, see J Kanagmugire, 'African Countries in a fix as Rwanda Refugee Status Ends', *The East African*, 20 January, 2018.

[100] P Daley, N Kamata and L Singo, 'Undoing Traceable Beginnings' (2018) 1(1) *Migration and Society* 22–35. S Nyathi, *The Golddiggers* (London, Macmillan, 2018). See also J Mozondidya, 'Migration, Citizenship and Identity among Zimbabweans in South Africa' in J McGregor and R Primorac (eds), *Zimbabwe's New Diaspora: Displacement and the Cultural Politics of Survival* (Oxford, Berghahn, 2010) 37–58; N Kriger, 'The politics of legal status for Zimbabweans in South Africa' in J McGregor and R Primorac (eds), ibid, 77–102.

by looking at the many tools that have been used to educate, advocate and challenge human rights violations.[101] It starts by considering the idea of justice and how it has been conceptualised. Biography and autobiography are explored as a means of excavating history, but also unpacking gender discrimination. The chapter also looks at the use of art specifically in photography and music. The purpose of the chapter is to take us beyond a narrow conception of literature to show that art, more broadly, can play, and has played, a part in human rights education and advocacy. Indeed this is one of the ways in which states can fulfil their obligations to educate their populations; and if more did, then perhaps there would be fewer examples of vilification of those seeking shelter from harm, or those wanting to make a better life for themselves and prepared to work to achieve it.

In light of the definition of diaspora adopted by the African Union discussed above, Chapter two explores the histories of African migration. To challenge the idea that Africans are recent arrivals, I look at multiple sightings of Africans throughout Europe from Roman Times. In *Staying Power* Fryer begins his history of Black people in Britain: 'There were Africans in Britain before the English came here.'[102] I use Ngwena's *What is Africanness?* to explore identity formation before moving on to think about modern migration, noting the links between colonialism and migration – people choose to move to countries with which they feel affinity, even if that comes off the back of a history of oppression. Given the backlash currently in play, I use Achiume's decolonisation thesis. She argues that our shared history creates a common citizenship which entitles those from the former colonies to stake a claim in the other motherland in the Global North.[103] The policies and practices of receiving states suggest that they do not share her vision. The interactions of historical wrong-doing and claims for human rights recognition and reparations are explored through case law. The chapter concludes by examining the ways in which European states are seeking to shift their responsibilities on to other, usually Third World, states.

Chapter three provides a thumbnail sketch of immigration law and policies as well as refugee law through the prism of fictional literature. The academic research shows that there is a marked divide in who is entitled to move freely – those from certain rich, or strategically important states get unfettered access to Europe and beyond, while those from all of Africa are required to apply for visas which are difficult to get. The fictional literature shows how this pushes creativity by forcing people to adopt self-help measures to get to where they need to be. The chapter also looks at the fraudulent elision by states of asylum-seekers, to whom they owe a legal obligation to provide shelter and protection, with migrants, to whom they do not. Despite the fact that both groups are guaranteed human rights in treaties ratified by receiving states, these states are happy to flout their obligations.

[101] A Van Klinken, *Kenyan, Christian, Queer* (Philadelphia PA, Penn State Press, 2019) 6, 64, 188–96.
[102] P Fryer, *Staying Power: The History of Black People in Britain* (London, Pluto Press, 2018 [1984]) 1.
[103] T Achiume, 'Migration as Decolonization' (2019) 71 *Stanford Law Review* 1509–76.

This they do by creating hostile environments, deploying multiple legal and policy tools, including the use of detention. In order to tell this story properly, the chapter also considers the part played by African governments in the movement of their people. Why are so many leaving? They seek relief from inhospitable home environments. Thereafter I consider how Africans live post-migration – they often suffer discrimination, hostility and stereotyping which forces them to accept jobs below their training and abilities. I call this status fracture. After all the gloom, I conclude the chapter on an upbeat note by acknowledging the work done by volunteers, novelists and others to ameliorate the lives of their 'co-citizens'.

Part two consists of Chapters four to six which focus on: women, sexual and gender minorities and children. They look at how the different groups have been treated in literature and case law and legal policies in their countries of arrival. Chapter four on women starts by showing that historically women have waited at home while men travel for work, or have gone as the spouse. Refugee law has also been interpreted in ways that recognise persecution that men face in the public sphere. However, this is changing.[104] Nevertheless, there is still reliance on stereotypes in status determination practice which affects the perception of African women.[105] As a result of their relatively poor education and other structural discrimination, women's migration is linked closely to doing work that Stewart calls 'body work' which includes cleaning, caring and selling sex.[106] Using novels and biography, interspersed with human rights discussion, the rest of the chapter then considers two issues: trafficking of women, and the work of maids and child nannies within the home and as cleaners in hotels. One learns that weak state regulation of this type of labour magnifies the employer's voice or 'law' which can lead to exploitation of the worker. We also learn that the exemptions from state oversight that are given to diplomats also increase the likelihood of abuse of domestic workers.

Chapter five on gender identity and sexual orientation takes a slightly different tack. The journey described is as much a metaphorical 'coming out' and being rendered visible by fictional literature as it is a consideration of the use of law to try to curtail that unfurling. It remains grounded within the African continent, with a brief examination of migration focusing on the application for asylum by sexual minorities. The chapter explores the impact of attempts to erase historical

[104] H Crawley, *Refugees and Gender: Law and Process* (Bristol, Jordan Publishing, 2001); E Arbel, C Dauvergne, J Millbank (eds), *Gender in Refugee Law: From the Margin to the Centre* (Abingdon, Routledge, 2014); CEDAW General recommendation No 32 on the gender-related dimensions of refugee status, asylum, nationality and statelessness of women, 5 November 2014, CEDAW/C/GC/32.

[105] MT Tinarwo and D Pasura, 'Negotiating and Contesting Gendered and Sexual Identities in the Zimbabwean Diaspora' (2014) 40 *Journal of Southern African Studies* 521–38. D Garbin and M Godin, 'Saving the Congo: Transnational social fields and the politics of home in the Congolese diaspora' (2013) 6(2) *Africa and Black Diaspora: An International Journal* 113, 120–24.

[106] A Stewart, *Gender, Law and Justice in a Global Market* (Cambridge, CUP, 2011). See also M Dimova, C Hough, K Kyaa, and A Manji, 'Intimacy and inequality: local care chains and paid childcare in Kenya' (2015) 23(2) *Feminist Legal Studies* 167–79.

pluralities on the continent by invoking externally generated alien laws and religions. I use Yoshino's *Covering* to explore how people are forced to mask or hide their identities, usually by marrying a person of the opposite sex.[107] The tide is turning with an assertion of the humanity of everybody leading to a demand for human rights for all. The demands appear to be getting through, with the African Commission on Human and Peoples' Rights, national courts and governments taking on board the right to dignity and to be free from discrimination in their resolutions, judgments and repeal of repressive laws.

The final substantive chapter, Chapter six, is on children. It utilises the work of Todres and Higginbotham who argue that one of the ways that the right to education can be fulfilled is through the use of literature. Education is broadly defined to include human rights education. Literature, they argue, is an effective tool in teaching children about the contents of their own rights as well as those of others. It helps in building a human rights culture. There is an increasing amount of literature written for children which seeks to engage them in the debates around refugees: who they are (people like us), why they come (because they are fearful), how we should treat them (as we would like to be treated; that is, fairly).[108] In addition to the literature, the chapter explores how the legal protections put in place for unaccompanied minors are sometimes flouted by states which challenge their minority status or detain them in violation of all human rights principles. The second, and longest section, considers the lives of children who arrive with their families, or alone, or indeed who are born here of parents who may have migrated in earlier years. The literature, both literary and non-fiction, suggests that many feel excluded and alienated by being asked where they are from, even though for some this may be the only home they know.

The conclusion follows. This starts by looking at two recent stories, both entitled 'The Wall', one a novel by Lanchester, the other a short story by Hadero (an Ethiopian-American lawyer and fiction writer!).[109] In her auto-fictional story, Hadero looks back fondly at the kindness of an older German professor living in America who, remembering the wall that divided his own city, Berlin, seeks to make her and her family, newly arrived from Ethiopia via Berlin, comfortable and welcome. Lanchester's *The Wall* is more disturbing – he presents a dystopian vision of an island country, surrounded by a wall and permanently guarded to keep the 'Others' out. They offer us two visions of where we are or could be. I explore these two visions while recollecting our journey.

[107] K Yoshino (2007), n 62 above.

[108] A recent example is O Rauf, *The Boy at the Back of the Class* (London, Orion, 2018).

[109] J Lanchester, *The Wall* (London, Faber and Faber, 2019); M Hadero, 'The Wall' in *The Caine Prize for African Writing 2019 Shortlist* (London, New Internationalist, 2019) 41–63. http://caineprize.com/press-releases/2019/5/20/2019-caine-prize-shortlist-announced.

VI. Conclusion

For myself, I have come to a better understanding of the modern migration of Africans, and indeed others, through fictional literature. As a human rights teacher, I assign many readings for my classes. These mainly comprise academic literature. However, if truth be told, the works that have best helped me to understand the causes and consequences of human rights violations such as trafficking and the life of the migrant have been fictional. Reading novels and poetry has opened my eyes to the many human rights violations that are hidden in plain sight. I now notice men in work gear but without helmets standing around corners waiting to be collected for construction work. I also notice men and women at garages and in car parks washing cars in the winter without protective clothing for a pittance. I am more alive to the conditions in hair dressing salons where sharp tongued 'owners' do not bother to hide that workers do not have regular work hours or scheduled breaks for meals or rest. I now notice nail bars where rows of young women, and a few men, sit doing endless manicures and pedicures for a sum that, compared to the level of labour and skill involved, seems unduly small. My nails are unadorned.

While writing this book I have been left wondering what would happen if we were to substitute the vicious, hate-filled headlines about migrants with stories which highlight our common humanity – that show how we all yearn for family, love, dignity and a decent life. Would that change the narrative and thus the treatment of migrants? I believe that literature is not subsidiary to law in this enterprise – it is central.

Finally, as a migrant myself, I have been affirmed by our struggles, moved by our resilience and cheered by our humour – for which many thanks to many of the novelists and poets cited. I bring the book to an end with a note to my late father and children.

This book was going to press as the Covid-19 pandemic was unfolding. A brief afterword reflects on the impact on migrants and the human rights issues raised in relation to some of the issues/topics discussed in the book.

PART I

Plotting Our Journey

1

Artivism, Literature, Law and Justice

Fictional literature and the law both involve story telling: one to entertain the reader, the latter to persuade. To be successful, both require the narration to engage the audience – whether that be reader or court. Both must take the reader on a metaphorical journey.[1] Writers and lawyers are specialist advocates for their clients. A good story sets up characters that we care about, and presents them with a dilemma that finds resolution or provides release at the end. Lawyers are legal ghost writers. They translate the client's story into legally recognisable grounds.[2] For judges, the job involves choosing between two competing and contradictory narratives, sometimes of the events leading the protagonists to the court, sometimes about the interpretation that should (legally) be given to the problem posed. Judges construct their judgments with a keen eye to persuasion and justification of their reading of events.[3] Indeed, many judgments have an elegiac quality in their rendition of a narrative of 'Justice'.[4] Others go so far as to ground decisions in poetry and literature.[5] Richard Posner contends that the two disciplines, law and literature are interlinked.[6]

This chapter explores the many ways that human rights advocacy has been undertaken by various actors including novelists, poets, artists, musicians and even politicians. Some have coined the term 'artivism' which is a merger of art and activism.[7] This can take many forms. Adriaan Van Klinken cites Molefi Asante's definition of an artivist as one who: 'uses her artistic talent to fight and struggle against injustice and oppression – by any *medium* necessary' and 'merges commitment to freedom and justice with the pen, the lens, the brush, the voice, the body, and the imagination.'[8]

[1] K Dolin, *A Critical Introduction to Law and Literature* (Cambridge, CUP, 2007), 8.

[2] C Smart, *The Ties that Bind: Law, Marriage and the Reproduction of Patriarchal Relations* (Abingdon, Routledge, 1984).

[3] J Bruner, *Making Stories: Law, Literature, Life* (Boston MA, Harvard University Press, 2002) 37–62. See also A Sachs, *The Strange Alchemy of Life and Law* (Oxford, OUP, 2011).

[4] Often cited is the US Supreme Court decision in the case that led to de-segregation of education: *Brown v Board of Education*, 347 US 483 (1954). Cited in K Dolin (2007), n 1 above.

[5] Often cited here is the US case of *Plaut v Spendthrift Farm Inc* 514 US 211, 131 L Ed 2d 328. In it, the court uses Robert Frost's poem 'Mending Wall', cited by K Dolin (2007), n 1 above, 1–10.

[6] R Posner, *Law and Literature*, 3rd edn, (Boston MA, Harvard University Press, 2009), 1.

[7] A Van Klinken, *Kenyan, Christian, Queer* (Philadelphia PA, Penn Press, 2019) 6.

[8] M Asante, *It's bigger than hip hop: The rise of the post hip hop generation* (New York, St Martin's Griffin, 2008) 203 as cited by A Van Klinken (2019), n 7 above, 6.

Many of the books and short stories cited in this book point to authors and poets 'writing justice' to challenge human rights violations.[9] As noted in the Introduction, in politically repressive states the violation of human rights is told through allegorical novels.[10] I engage other forms of writing and representation, including autobiography and the use of music, photography and art. Each form speaks to different narrative constructions informed by the intended audience of the creator – an autobiographical account is radically different from reportage; how an asylum seeker frames their claim to a decision-maker may be different to how they would express themselves in a letter to a friend.

I also interrogate what it is lawyers mean when they speak of justice. Is justice merely an aphorism for 'just us' as Charles Mills contends in *The Racial Contract*?[11] Thinking about 'writing justice' also involves the rendering visible of people whose contributions have been lost in the mists of time or who have deliberately been written out of existence. Worthy of mention is the pioneering work of the polymath Sol Plaatje, author, teacher, translator of Shakespeare and founder member of the organisation that later became the South African National Congress.[12] More recent is Tembeka Ngcukaitobi's *The Land is Ours*, tracing the lives of extraordinary black South African men who, the author argues, preceded the Mandelas and Tambos as the pre-eminent lawyers representing black South Africans and challenging unjust laws. He contends that the much lauded South African Constitution relies for its ethos and vision on the work of these early lawyers. Ngcukaitobi goes beyond law to show how music and literature played a part in uplifting morale and also creating transnational solidarity movements including between Black Americans experiencing their own discrimination and South Africans.[13] The fact that it took Ngcukaitobi, a young, black South African lawyer to excavate the contributions of these men and women, speaks to the truth of the old saying, 'until the lion learns to write, the hunter will always be the victor.'

[9] More generally, see S Gikandi (ed), *The Novel in Africa and the Caribbean since 1950* (Oxford, OUP, 2016).

[10] Two Egyptian books come to mind: S Ibrahim (in Arabic *al-Lajna*, 1981) translated by Mary St Germain and Charlene Constable, *The Committee*, (American University in Cairo Press, 2002); Mohamed El-Bisatie (in Arabic as *Ju* 2007) as translated by Denys Johnson-Davies *Hunger* (Cairo, American University in Cairo Press, 2014).

[11] CE Mills, *The Racial Contract* (Ithaca NY, Cornell University Press, 1997) preface.

[12] While Plaatje may have been the first Black South African to write a novel in English, there were many others writing in their mother tongues. M Wa Ngugi, *The Rise of the African Novel: Politics of Language, Identity and Ownership* (Ann Arbor MI, University of Michigan Press, 2018) 'Introduction' 1, 4–8.

[13] T Ngcukaitobi, *The Land is Ours: South Africa's First Black Lawyers and the Birth of Constitutionalism* (Cape Town, Zebra Press, 2018). Sol Plaatje is shown to have been an important figure in articulating injustice (see 133, 246). Uplifting was the visit of the Jubilee Singers from the United States who toured South Africa, leaving behind, 'a legacy that would shape the aspirations of Africans for generations to come' (at 28). This included the establishing of an African Native Choir which set sail for England where they sang. The novelist Dickens is described as contemptuous in his assessment of the 'noble savage' and wrote a patronising account of the choir (31–33). I am grateful to Jason Brickhill for choosing this as one of our Oxford summer masters' reading group book choices for 2019.

It is as well to acknowledge the complexities involved in constructing narratives of justice from the outset. On a related issue of human rights law, Alex de Waal utilises a self-reflexive piece to consider the methodology used in the advocacy efforts of human rights organisations and specifically his own part in the narratives of oppression created by them. In it he shows how well-intentioned people may get things wrong, and identifies the mistakes made by major human rights organisations (and de Waal himself) when trying to 'right justice by writing about injustice.'[14] Contrasting the approaches of two human rights organisations (Amnesty International and Human Rights Watch), he identifies the use of the human-interest story as a driver in advocacy work by the latter. He also shows how the narrative is crafted with a specific end in sight: 'If journalism is the first draft of history, the human rights report is the draft of the prosecutor's indictment.'[15]

The problem with this story-telling, as he later acknowledges, is that the narrative created is often one that replicates what Makau Mutua calls the 'Savages and Saviors' scenario. In de Waal's account: 'In the West, we like morality plays with clearly identified heroes and villains, in which we can play the role of savior. The best tellers of these fairy tales are celebrity activists, the evangelists of the human rights business.'[16] De Waal is also honest about how narratives can be moulded by omission and silence. This can be as a result of state censorship or a carefully thought out strategy by the narrator. Recalling his subsequent silence on Rwanda after he left the organisation that he had co-founded and in which he had worked extensively on Rwanda in 1994 and beyond, he notes:

> Silence can be a deliberate decision. It comes in many forms, including telling partial truths or postponing speaking out, anticipating a more propitious moment. Human rights advocates ration their courage and indignation. As Stanley Cohen observes in his classic investigation of denial, it is not possible to be outraged about every single rights violation; the advocate needs to choose. And that choice often reflects an effort to craft a narrative that will gain attention.[17]

I. Justice in Law and Literature

While the idea of justice is often explored through a legal and philosophical lens, literature also opens up enormous possibilities for its elucidation.[18] Writer Viet

[14] A de Waal, 'Writing Human Rights and Getting it Wrong', *Boston Review*, 6 June 2016, available online at: http://bostonreview.net/world/alex-de-waal-writing-human-rights.

[15] A de Waal (2016), n 14 above.

[16] A de Waal (2016). See M Mutua, 'Savages, Victims and Saviors: The Metaphor of Human Rights' (2001) 42 *Harvard International Law Journal* 201. Aid agencies and some UN agencies who utilise celebrity ambassadors would counter that the engagement of these people can help to amplify their message, can lead to an increase in donations, can raise the profile of the issue which can in turn influence the public to lobby politicians, who may in turn feel compelled to act.

[17] A de Waal (2016).

[18] A Sen, *The Idea of Justice* (Cambridge, Belknap, 2009).

Thanh Nguyen reminds us that, 'justice is not the same as law.' He goes on to note that the demarcation of borders can create laws whose breach may lead to the criminalisation of many migrants and the creation of prisons out of refugee camps. He asks, 'But if borders are legal, are they also just?'. He reminds us, 'our notions of borders have shifted over the centuries, just as our notions of justice and humanity have.'[19]

Kenji Yoshino uses Shakespeare's plays to explore the idea of justice and to discuss US constitutional law and broader international concerns.[20] The plays are alive, Yoshino contends, and still retain the power to provide insights into contemporary concerns.[21] He uses *Othello* to discuss the case of the American Footballer OJ Simpson, who was accused of murdering his former wife and her male friend. It is not solely the race angle that interests Yoshino. Rather, he focuses on the tokens of betrayal. Desdemona is accused of unfaithfulness by Othello because a handkerchief that he had given her is found in the possession of the man, Iago, whom he thinks has cuckolded him. Similarly, the glove that was found at the murder scene in the OJ Simpson case and which formed a central plank of the evidence against Simpson, is one of a pair of gloves that his murdered former wife, Nicole Brown Simpson, had gifted him. Yoshino uses these analogies to explore the nature of evidence and the human bias towards 'ocular proof', or believing the concrete (physical) over the abstract.

> [I]n the assessment of guilt or innocence, the handkerchief and the glove played an inordinately large role. In *Othello*, the question of whether Desdemona is guilty of adultery comes to depend to a staggering degree on whether she has the handkerchief.[22]

We know, in Desdemona's case, that Iago has arranged for both the removal and the 'discovery' of the handkerchief. Othello thus convinces himself of her guilt. On the OJ Simpson case, Yoshino notes that:

> The defense team did not, and could not, argue that the murderer was not wearing gloves. Rather, they argued that the right-handed glove was taken from the scene of the murder and planted on Simpson's Rockingham estate to frame him for the murder. That would require an Iago figure. The defense team cast Mark Fuhrman, a police officer who had repeatedly made racist remarks in the past, in that role.[23]

[19] VT Nguyen, 'Introduction' in VT Nguyen (ed), *The Displaced: Refugee Writers on Refugee Lives* (New York, Abrams Books, 2018) 11–22, 18.

[20] Yoshino uses Shakespeare's *Titus Andronicus* to explore the war in Iraq and Afghanistan which followed the attacks of 9/11 on the US mainland. 'The post-modern war on terror is more like the premodern blood feud than either is like a conventional war.' K Yoshino, *A Thousand Times More Fair: What Shakespeare's Plays Teach us about Justice* (Ecco, Harper Collins, 2012) 3–4. See also P Raffield and G Watt (eds), *Shakespeare and the Law* (Oxford, Hart, 2008); P Raffield, *The Art of Law* (Oxford, Hart, 2017).

[21] There are also contemporary 'updates' of Shakespeare in which leading authors are invited to write stories inspired by his work. See H Jacobson, *Shylock is my name* (London, Penguin, 2016) (on 'The 'Merchant of Venice'); M Atwood, *Hag-Seed* (London, Vintage, 2016) (on 'The Tempest').

[22] K Yoshino (2012), n 20 above, 120.

[23] K Yoshino (2012) 120.

In the OJ Simpson case, the 'ocular proof' was that the glove did not fit OJ's hand. Yoshino gives reasons why this may have been: the blood and dew at the crime scene had shrunk it. Furthermore, OJ Simpson was wearing plastic gloves when he tried it on. The jury, seeing that the glove did not fit, decided to deliver a finding of not guilty, thus complying with the catchy summing up instructions given by Simpson's lawyer, the late Johnnie Cochran, 'if it doesn't fit, you must acquit.' Desdemona, unable to produce the handkerchief given to her as a love token, is found 'guilty' by Othello, but is later vindicated. Yoshino uses Othello and the OJ Simpson case to muse on the reliability of eyewitness testimony, the efficacy of relying on juries and the 'fallibility of collective human factfinding.'[24]

Kieran Dolin's analysis of the Rodney King case, four years before that of OJ Simpson, where an African American man was beaten by the police, echoes Yoshino's analysis on the uses and misuses of eyewitness testimony in the acquittal of the officers involved. 'Their assault had been filmed on a home video, but after minute-by-minute, frame-by-frame analysis, the white jury accepted the defendants' version of events that the force was necessary to subdue the apparent victim.'[25]

Yoshino examines the confirmation hearing (which precedes appointment to the US Supreme Court) of the first Latinx woman, Sonia Sotomayor. Her nomination, by the first African American President, Barack Obama, was challenged, in part, because she was said to have 'biases' which barred her from the role of being a Supreme Court justice. These biases were located in a speech that she had made about the particular insights that those who like her, belong to certain groups, women and minorities may have into the way that discrimination manifests and also the efficacy of law in addressing them. These statements were said to show her prejudice and thus disqualified her from taking on the role of the neutral arbiter. An umpire or judge could not be seen to be partial. Analysing Obama's stated wish for an empathetic judge and Sotomayor's views, Yoshino uses *Measure for Measure* to think about the various ways in which 'judging' is done. He argues that the play puts forward three models:

> … one that values empathy too much leading to an erosion of the rule of law; one that errs in the opposite direction, asking for 'strict construction' of the 'letter of the law'; and finally, one that realizes that judging is much messier than either extreme would indicate.[26]

Reflecting on Sotomayor's confirmation, he argues that the presentation of the role of judges as being value-free vessels for the dispensation of an abstract notion of justice is false. He commends Shakespeare for understanding that 'judges should not choose either pure empathy or pure law',[27] for, as Yoshino notes: 'From

[24] K Yoshino (2012) 120.
[25] Dolin (2007), n 1 above, 201.
[26] K Yoshino (2012), n 20 above, 60.
[27] K Yoshino (2012) 88.

its inception, judging has concerned the question of how fairly to apply general rules to particular circumstances.'[28]

II. On Transplants and Universality

Just as lawyers often talk of the transplantation of law between jurisdictions, so too Shakespeare scholar Edward Wilson-Lee weaves a fascinating narrative of the many uses to which Shakespeare's work has been put once on African soil.[29] Focusing on East Africa, he traces how Shakespearean texts were recited by the early travellers, including Richard Burton, who came to explore the interior of the continent in the nineteenth century. Wilson Lee paints a fascinating picture of tours by Indian theatre companies performing adapted versions of Shakespeare to packed audiences in Mombasa. Equally impressive is his research into how the plays were used for political ends by African elites, many of whom had performed Shakespeare plays in the annual theatrical production staged by Makerere University.

Wilson-Lee gives the example of a British educated Kenyan legislative member, Eliud Wambu Mathu, who used *The Merchant of Venice* as a metaphor to challenge the British wish to impose an unfair tax on the Gikũyu. The British became Shylock who wanted his pound of flesh (tax) irrespective of the cost. However, who would be Portia (arbiter) in the Gikuyu dispute with the British? The inequality of bargaining power was laid bare in the exchange which led the British Minister for African Affairs to remark that he did not 'propose to bandy Shakespeare with my hon. friend.'[30]

Oft told is Mandela's love of Shakespeare. Quoted here is his underlining of the lines on courage from Julius Caesar: 'Cowards die many times before their deaths; The Valiant never taste of death but once.'[31] Less well known is Mandela's letter written while in prison to his wife, Winnie Mandela, on learning of the death of his son (from his first marriage) in a car accident in July 1969. He recalls his son's love for him and his for his son; he sounds regretful for the sacrifices that the family have been made to endure as a result of his stand. He recounts, too, a visit from his son who was on his way to boarding school: 'Somehow the conversation drifted to his studies, and he gave what I considered, in the light of his age at the time, to be an interesting appreciation of Shakespeare's Julius Caesar which I very much enjoyed.'[32]

[28] K Yoshino (2012) 88.
[29] E Wilson-Lee, *Shakespeare in Swahililand* (London, William Collins, 2017).
[30] E Wilson-Lee (2017), n 29 above, 146–47.
[31] Cited in E Wilson-Lee (2017) 148. This was one of my late father's favourite quotes.
[32] N Mandela, *Conversations with Myself* (London, Macmillan, 2010) 166. Poignantly, he dedicates this book to his great-granddaughter Zenani, who died in a car accident in June 2010, aged 13.

III. Literature as Protest in Post-Colonial Settings

When talking of law and justice, the issue of protest is central as it can take many forms. Contemporary student protests about the content of their University curricula and demands that these be 'de-colonised' are represented in the work of Ngugi-Wa-Thiong'o, who, Wilson-Lee notes, challenged the dominance of Shakespeare in the canon in his 1962 play *Black Hermit*.[33] The movement to decolonise thought which led to the 'Africanisation' of the curriculum in Kenya was reversed by Moi in 1988 as part of his attempts to curry favour with Western countries using the export of culture as part of their soft power during the Cold War.[34] Following the lead of Sol Plaatje, who had translated *Julius Caesar* and *The Comedy of Errors* into iXhosa,[35] Julius Nyerere, the first African President of Tanzania, translated *Julius Caesar* into Swahili verse. Wilson-Lee describes the Nyerere translation as a political and cultural act.[36]

In her work, Ambreena Manji, a Kenyan lawyer, has explored the politics of power in law and literature. This she has done by examining the nuances of colonial laws and the 're-creation' of colonial traditional authorities within the legal project.[37] She has also engaged issues of power in her discussion of the work of Ngugi wa Thiongo, and his pointed political decision to write only in Kikuyu. This was, and remains, an act of cultural resistance of the dominance of English.[38] Manji uses Ngugi to explore the uses and misuses of law to enforce linguistic-erasure through the privileging of two languages, English and Swahili, at the expense and to the detriment of other tongues. She bemoans what she sees as an unnecessary return to narrow 'ethno-cultural' interpretations of culture and the resulting violation of the rights of minorities.[39] There are other challenges, such as the translation of 'African' authors from one colonial language (French) to another (English).[40]

[33] E Wilson-Lee (2017), n 29 above, 142, 217–18.

[34] E Wilson-Lee (2017) 215–22.

[35] N Ndana, *Sol Plaatje's Shakespeare: Translation and Transition to Modernity* (Cape Town, Unpublished, PhD Thesis, University of Cape Town, 2005).

[36] E Wilson-Lee (2017), n 29 above, 169–72. Some post-colonial literature reflects the raced and gendered experiences of people during white rule. Famous is T Dangarembga, *Nervous Conditions* (London, The Women's Press, 1988).

[37] A Manji, '"Like a Mask Dancing": Law and Colonialism in Chinua Achebe's Arrow of God' (2002) 27(4) *Journal of Law and Society* 626–42.

[38] Fascinating is the son's take on his father's use of language and the political and cultural considerations around it. M Wa Ngugi (2018), n 12 above, 29–70. See also Wa Thiong'o Ngugi, *Decolonising the Mind: The Politics of Language in African Literature* (Oxford, James Currey, 2009).

[39] A Manji, 'Law, Literature and the Politics of Culture in Kenya' (2003) (2) *Law, Social Justice & Global Development Journal* (LGD) http://www2.warwick.ac.uk/fac/soc/law/elj/lgd/2003_2/manji/ (2003). Appiah notes that Ngugi's decision to write only in Gikuyu has, in his view, been wrongly interpreted as manifestation of Gikuyu imperialism. A Appiah, *In my Father's House: Africa in the Philosophy of Culture* (Oxford, OUP, 1992) 4.

[40] V Steemers, '*Broken Glass* or Broken Text?: The translatability of Alain Mabanckou's *Verre Cassé* (2005) into English' (2014) 45(1) *Research in African Literatures* 107–24.

What if the colonial language has become the language of writing? Cannot the many 'Englishes' belong to us all and be legitimate forms of self-expression?[41] Many of us continue to speak mother tongues that we cannot write.

IV. Music, Art and Photography

In addition to providing a balm for the soul, music and sound (eg beating of pots to alert people to violations of the rights of the disappeared in Argentina) have been a part of human rights protests across the world. Panashe Chigumadzi has written about music, and the human voice being as powerful as a gun, in her essay considering the role of music as a form of politics of resistance and revolution. Chigumadzi also explores the gender politics surrounding women performers who were seen as transgressive. Masuka and her contemporaries were pan-Africanists who fought for an end to both colonialism and its twin, apartheid.[42] She takes the title of her essay 'Voices Powerful as Guns' directly from the legendary musician Dorothy Masuka:

> I never held a gun but my voice was as powerful as a gun. It took me a few moments to send my revolutionary messages home to millions of people when I sang *tinogara musango* (we live in the bush).

On the eve of Zimbabwean independence, my teenage friends and I met Bob Marley who was walking with some of the Wailers (his band) on the streets of Harare. Squealing with delight, we got his autograph. His songs, including 'Zimbabwe' and 'Get up, Stand Up!', are legendary.[43] I am also one for revolutionary songs in Shona, my favourite being 'Mbuya Nehanda' which recounts the story of a female spirit medium who led the first chimurenga (war of liberation) against the British colonialists.[44] At university I danced to Hugh Masekela's anthem 'Bring back Nelson Mandela'[45] and raised defiant fists to Peter Gabriel's anthem, 'Biko'.[46]

[41] AT Nwaubani, 'We spoke English to set ourselves apart: how I rediscovered my mother tongue', *The Guardian*, 14 March 2019. A Hirsch, 'Africa's colonisation of the English language continues apace', *The Guardian*, 29 January 2020.

[42] P Chigumadzi, 'Voices as powerful as guns: Panashe Chigumadzi on Dorothy Masuka's (w)ri(o)ting woman-centred Pan-Africanism', *Johannesburg Review of Books*, May 6, 2019.

[43] Bob Marley and the Wailers, 'Zimbabwe' (album), Island Def Jam Music Group 1979, re-released, Universal Music Group, 2014.

[44] There were of course 'counter narratives' including in music. I remember my disgust at the constant playing, during my childhood which was during the liberation war (my version) or fight against terrorists (white minority regime version) of a song by Clem Tholet called 'Rhodesians Never Die' released in 1973. The song is the inspiration for a group of 'ex-Rhodesians' as they like to call themselves. The lyrics and indeed various versions of the song can be found on the web. I still remember the words 'Coz we are all Rhodesians and we'll fight through thick and thin, to keep our land a free land, stop the enemy coming in.' Trouble is we, the enemy, were already in. In fact, the land was and had always been, ours. For lyrics see: https://sonichits.com/video/Clem_Tholet/Rhodesians_Never_Die.

[45] H Masekela, 'Pure Sounds of Africa', Sony Music, 2015 (copyright belongs to SME Africa (Pty) Ltd 2015).

[46] P Gabriel, 'Biko' Real World Productions 2018, Copyright Peter Gabriel Ltd, 2003.

On the death of Nelson Mandela, I played my Human Rights of Women class a recording of Nina Simone 'I wish I knew how it would feel to be free.'[47] I was reminded of the joy I had felt on the day of his release from prison in 1990 and all the times before that when I had played Julia Fordham's 'Happy Ever After' on a loop.[48] Many years later, my eyes pricked with tears following a dinner in Oxford where a string quartet played the hymn and South African national anthem *Nkosi Sikelela Africa* – God Bless Africa.[49] In Winnie Mandela's biography we learn how the prisoners communicated using song. They shared names and information about other prisoners and relayed vital intelligence to assist each other.[50] Similarly, Nelson Mandela evoked the power of music to elevate and inspire.[51] Reading Warsan Shire's poem, 'Questions for Miriam' I am reminded of the many times we wound our burgeoning hips and sang along lustily (if badly in my case), to the songs of Miriam Makeba.[52] I defy you to not get up and dance to *Pata pata*, or not to listen attentively to her explanations of the political situation in South Africa before she starts to sing *Nonongo.*[53]

Along with music is art and photography. Pablo Picasso's Guernica is a famous 'anti-war' mural which he made as a response to the bombing of the Spanish city Guernica by German and Italian bombers during the Spanish Civil War.[54] Picasso later called the mural a representation of 'every bombed city.' In 1985 the philanthropist Rockefeller donated a tapestry copy of 'Guernica' to the United Nations. It hung outside the Security Council. In 2003, UN staff covered up the tapestry ahead of an address by Colin Powell on the war in Iraq. There could not be an address about war in front of an iconic anti-war image.[55] Subsequent challenges to the legality of the war reinforce that symbolic protest.

[47] N Simone, 'The Very Best of Nina Simone: Sugar in my Bowl 1967–1972' RCA Records Label, 1998.

[48] J Fordham, 'Happy Ever After' on her album *China Blue*, 1988.

[49] Wa Ngugi details how additional revolutionary verses were added to the hymn by author and nationalist, Mqhayi. He adds that Sol Plaatje arranged for it to be recorded in London. M Wa Ngugi (2018), n 12 above, 5.

[50] A du Preez Bezdrop, *Winnie Mandela: A Life* (Cape Town, Zebra Press, 2003) 152.

[51] T Masters, 'Nelson Mandela Death: Film examines power of music', *BBC News*, 6 December 2013.

[52] W Shire, 'Questions for Miriam' in W Shire, *Teaching my mother how to give birth* (London, Mouthmark series (No. 10), 2011) 23.

[53] M Makeba, 'Pata pata', Strut Records, 2019, originally recorded 1967, from the album *Pata Pata*, Reprise Records.

[54] See https/www.pablopicasso.org/Guernica. Listen to: BBC In Our Time: Picasso's Guernica, Picasso is of course also known for having been influenced by African art, although this inspiration is not always acknowledged. See LS Senghor, 'Negritude: A Humanism of the Twentieth Century' in W Carty and M Kilson (eds), *The African Reader. Independent Africa* (New York, Vintage Books, 1970), 179–99, extract reprinted in R Grinker and CB Steiner (eds), *Perspectives on Africa: A Reader in Culture, History and Representation*, 2nd edn (Oxford, Wiley Blackwell, 2010) 477–83, 482.

[55] See D Cohen, 'Hidden Treasures: What's so Controversial about Picasso's Guernica?', *Slate*, 6 February 2003. UN headquarters in New York, the UN Office in Geneva and the UNESCO headquarters in Paris hold some of the world's best artistic treasures. UNESCO has murals by Picasso and Miro. Best of all, the works were given freely by artists and the member states and not looted; thus one's enjoyment of them is not marred by thoughts of their provenance.

Although open to interpretation and manipulation, photographs act as bolts to the conscience. The picture of Hector Pieterson being carried after being shot during what became known as the Soweto Uprisings is one of the defining images of life under apartheid. It highlighted the inequities of apartheid and drew global attention.[56] The picture depicts black students protesting at the enforced use of Afrikaans in schools. It had the same impact as the photograph of the young girl, nine-year-old Kim Phuc, running from the napalm, which also shocked the world and hastened the withdrawal of United States forces from Vietnam.[57] It is important to acknowledge that while photos can be used as consciousness-raising tools, they can also be more open to exploitation of persons. It is doubtful that a picture similar to that of Kim Phuc would have been shared if the girl had been a white child running naked down the street. To mark the fiftieth anniversary of Martin Luther King's assassination, *National Geographic* magazine ran an issue on Race. Publishing in April 2018, the magazine's editor apologised for its racist imagery over the preceding decades. She acknowledged how it had 'exoticised' people from different cultures and reinforced negative stereotypes.[58]

Still, photographs retain the power to uplift. In the week following Mandela's death I gave an assembly at my children's primary school. The theme was human rights. I showed the children a photograph of the Mandelas (Winnie and Nelson) with Rosa Parks. Mandela is clasping Parks's arm and looks delighted.[59] 'Who are these people?', I asked. Hands shot up. They knew about the lady on the bus (Parks) and the man (though not his then wife). I was deeply touched and heartened by the sheer outrage expressed by these young children about the discrimination that both Mandelas and Parks had suffered. They could not fathom it. That gives one hope.

[56] Photo of Hector Pietersen taken by Sam Nzima on 16 June 1976. It is now the image that represents the Hector Pieterson Memorial and Museum, which is in Soweto: https://www.gauteng.net/attractions/hector_pieterson_memorial_and_museum/. See also D Newberry, *Defiant Images: Photography and Apartheid South Africa* (Pretoria, UNISA, 2009). *Drum* magazine had powerful photographs, some of which were taken by Alf Khumalo. See M Cassel, 'Alf Kumalo: the anti-apartheid photographer', *Al Jazeera*, 7 December 2013 at: https://www.aljazeera.com/indepth/features/2013/12/alf-kumalo-anti-apartheid-photographer-201312641847953345.html.

[57] Photograph of 'Napalm Girl' taken by Nick Ut on 8 June 1972, available at AP Images or by entering 'Napalm Girl' into a search engine. The photograph also appears on the subject's autobiography. See Phan Thi Kim Phuc, *The Napalm Girl's Journey through the Horrors of War to Faith, Forgiveness, and Peace* (Illinois IL, Tyndale Momentum, 2017). On a related note, Cohen notes how it was suggested that Picasso's Guernica which was in the US, should be removed from there to protest the US's prosecution of the Vietnam war. D Cohen, 'Hidden Treasures', *Slate*, 6 February, 2003.

[58] S Goldberg (editor in chief), 'For Decades our Coverage was Racist. To Rise Above our Past, We Must Acknowledge it', 233(4) *National Geographic*, April 2018: https://www.nationalgeographic.com/magazine/2018/04/from-the-editor-race-racism-history/.

[59] M Maharaj and A Kathrada, *Mandela: The Authorised Portrait* (London, Bloomsbury, 2006) 247. At 313 there is a picture of Mandela shaking hands with a beaming Betsie Verwoerd, widow of Hendrik Verwoerd, architect of the apartheid state. The book of photographs also contains short essays and tributes by the great and the good. Nadine Gordimer reflects on being a writer and living at the same time 'as this remarkable person.' She recalls her novel *Burger's Daughter* where one of the characters says of living under apartheid 'there was this terrible time, but wasn't it wonderful to be born in a time when there were heroes and heroines?' (Nadine Gordimer at 314).

However, hope is tempered by the memory of the outrage that followed the publication of the photograph of the Turkish policeman cradling the still body of Alan Kurdi.[60] He had drowned while crossing the Mediterranean with his family who had fled the Syrian war to seek shelter. Shocked, politicians and the world in general, declared that meaningless deaths must stop.[61] The phrase 'never again' was uttered several times, and yet, in 2019, we were again confronted by the image of a two-year-old girl lying face down in a river alongside her father who had died while trying to save her. He had taken her across then returned for his wife. However, the little girl panicked and got back in the water. Dad tried to save her; both drowned.[62] The wife/mother watched them drowning from the other (Mexican) side. El Salvadorians, they were on their way to the United States to seek a better life. Their bodies were returned home for burial. Their names were Oscar Alberto Martinez Ramirez and the little girl was Valeria. Mum is Tania Vanessa Avalos. There are questions to be asked about why it is more often than not pictures of children that have the widest response. Is it their vulnerability that forces us to confront the need to protect them? But where does that leave less-emotionally engaging adults who may also be in extremis?

Not all photographs have to be dramatic to be memorable. While I was on sabbatical at NYU in the autumn of 2014, Professor Paulette Caldwell directed me to a photographic exhibition at Grey Art Gallery on Washington Square.[63] It was a retrospective of the photographs of Ernest Cole who had left South Africa in the 1960s and had died of cancer in New York in 1990, aged 49. The photos are stunning. They show black maids interacting with their white employers' children.[64] Sometimes they show photographs of the maid's quarters – one room, with tin cup and plate. She wears a uniform. The 'table' or drawer where she eats is often covered in newspapers. This is contrasted with the lavish lifestyle of the employers. The black and white photographs throw into stark relief the inequalities between master and servant. A photographer for the radical anti-apartheid *Drum* magazine until his move to the United States, Cole documented the daily humiliations of black people (showing passes to policemen, white women sitting

[60] Nilufer Demir, 'Alan Kurdi', *Dogan News Agency*, September 2015. Featured in *Time Magazine*, '100 Photographs: The Most Influential Images of All Time.' At http://www.100photos.time.com.

[61] The photograph also inspired the wonderful children's book *The Boy at the Back of the Class*. O Rauf (London, Orion, 2018).

[62] Image of drowned father and daughter first published by *La Jornada*, Mexico: see J Le Duc, 'Salvadoreno y su hija mueren ahogados en intent por llegal a EU', *La Jornada*, 24 June 2019. See AK Raymond, 'The story behind the viral photo of a migrant father and toddler', *New York* magazine, 26 June 2019 at: https://nymag.com/intelligencer/2019/06/the-story-behind-the-viral-photo-of-drowned-migrants.html. P Timmons, M Hodgson and D Agren, 'Shocking photo of drowned father and daughter highlights migrants' border peril', *The Guardian*, 26 June 2019.

[63] *Ernest Cole: Photographer*, Grey Art Gallery, NYU, Washington Square, organised by the Hasselblad Foundation, Sweden, 2014.

[64] The poignancy of the black women looking after the children of white women while not being able to see their own is captured in Beverley Naidoo's children's novel *Journey to Jo'burg* (London, Harper Collins, 2008). A brother and sister leave their village to travel to Jo'burg in search of their mother who works as a maid.

on 'Europeans-only' benches,) but also their ordinary lives.[65] His photographs, once banned by the apartheid regime, are displayed in the Apartheid Museum in South Africa and provide eloquent testimony to the injustice that was apartheid. In the US Ernest Cole also documented poverty and discrimination there, with photographs of women in the South picking cotton in the 1960s, distinguishable from the days of slavery only by their clothes.[66]

V. On Writing Justice

The writing and political advocacy of Steve Biko, for which he paid with his life, is peerless. In his journalism, speeches and interviews he was always fighting for black consciousness and rights for black people. His work and his words continue to have contemporary resonance.[67] I was reminded of Biko when I read Bernadette Atuahene's *We want what's ours.*[68] Atuahene, a Ghanaian-American lawyer, undertook socio-legal research on the land question in post-apartheid South Africa. She theorised that apartheid had resulted in black people being stripped of their land and dignity (a kind of social death). She called these 'dignity takings'.[69] To make good this loss, there was a need for what she called 'dignity restoration', which went beyond apology. Her three-point plan included process – the use of courts and commissions, communication and restitution awards.[70] She shows how the paying of individual compensation has resulted in socio-economic improvements in the lives of families and communities.[71]

Dolin delves into the long and sustained history of 'writing justice' to right race discrimination by people from William Du Bois, with his short-lived 1920s magazine for black children, *The Brownies Book*, to novelist and playwright James Baldwin, the playwright Loraine Hansberry's *A Raisin in the Sun*, Malcolm X and Martin Luther King and also the Nobel Laureate, Toni Morrison's *Beloved*. As he notes, *Beloved* was inspired by a case of a mother who killed her child rather than see her returned to slavery.[72] Dolin notes that the woman, Margaret Garner, was

[65] E Cole, *House of Bondage* (New York, Random House, 1967). See also the documentary made by J Shaldberg, *Ernest Cole* (Surrey, Journeyman, 2006).

[66] J Sanders and M Campbell, 'Ernest Cole's photographs reveal America's apartheid', *The Sunday Times*, London, 22 October 2017.

[67] S Biko, *Steve Biko 1946–1977: I Write What I Like*, A Stubbs (ed) (Oxford, Heinemann, 1978 (1988 revised edn)). See also A Tambo, *Preparing for Power: Oliver Tambo Speaks* (New York, George Braziller/Heineman, 1987).

[68] B Atuahene, *We Want What's Ours: Learning from South Africa's Land Restitution Program* (Oxford, OUP, 2014). She has an accompanying documentary, Sifuna Okwethu (we want what is ours) see: www.wewantwhatsours.com.

[69] B Atuahene (2014), n 68 above. 'Dignity takings' theory, at 23–34. Application in the South African context, 35–54.

[70] See her criteria for effective communication in dignity restoration: B Atuahene (2014), 107, 108–9.

[71] B Atuahene (2014), 157–63.

[72] In the next chapter, I discuss Morrison's motivation for writing Margaret Garner's story in a fictional voice. See T Morrison, 'Foreword' in *Beloved* (London, Vintage, 2011) ix–xxx, xi.

'not tried for murder, but for stealing the property of her master.'[73] This is also the story of the 'runaway' slave Jim, in Mark Twain's *Huckleberry Finn*.[74] Case law from the civil rights era and beyond is weaved into Dolin's narrative.[75] It also infused Maya Angelou's poetry.[76]

It is worth pausing to consider positionality and the differences in the writing of the slavery story. West distinguishes Twain's *Huckleberry Finn* from Morrison's *Beloved*:

> The greatest contrast between these two books, however, is in point of view. The story of Twain's Jim, the escaped slave, is told from the point of view of the white, free, marginal, critical, but textually included boy. Morrison's *Beloved* is told from the point of view of the excluded and objectified black slave woman. Twain's story gives voice to the critical reflections of the 'textually marginalized': Huck may be marginal to his society, but he is an integral part of it. Morrison's story, in contrast, gives voice to the textually *excluded*. *Beloved* is told from the point of view of the community's object. In Twain's story, the slave is the excluded but sympathetic object: we cannot identify with him but we do sympathize with him. The 'object' of Huck's story becomes the 'subject' of Sethe's story in Morrison's novel. In Twain's *Huckleberry Finn*, Jim is a victim; in Morrison's *Beloved*, Sethe is a heroine.[77]

There is a question to be asked about who is/are the 'we' who cannot identify with Jim the slave. I have always identified with him, as have many others, not only those who experienced the suffering first-hand but also those authors who have chosen to centre the stories of slaves, who are after all their forebears, and make them the subjects. West acknowledges this, noting:

> In *Beloved*, when the textually excluded – those robbed of subjectivity and speech – speak, they speak of the subjective experience of objecthood. They speak of how it feels to be defined as one who is not allowed to feel. They speak of the subjective experience of being the object of a bill of sale.[78]

Through an examination of civil rights case law, Bruner, a psychologist, demonstrates how societies can change their narratives to better reflect a new improved version of themselves. He gives the example of the recognition of Black people in the United States of America as entitled to benefit from the rights accorded to other citizens without discrimination, as reflecting a recalibration of the national

[73] Dolin (2007), n 1 above, 203.

[74] M Twain, *The Adventures of Huckleberry Finn* (London, Penguin Classics, 2003).

[75] See also HL Gates (ed), *'Race,' and Writing, and Difference* (Chicago IL, University of Chicago Press, 1985).

[76] M Angelou, *The Complete Collected Poems* (London, Virago, 1995). There are many memorable poems. See for example, the second section of the book entitled 'Just before the world ends'. See, 'No, No, No, No' (pp 42–44); 'My Guilt' (p 45) and 'When I think about Myself' and in other parts of the book, 'Ailey, Baldwin, Floyd, Killens, and Mayfield' (pp 266–67). Bringing it all together is the poem that she performed at Bill Clinton's inauguration, 'On the Pulse of Morning' (pp 270–73).

[77] R West, 'Communities, Texts, and Law: Reflections on the Law and Literature Movement' (1989) 1 *Yale Journal of Law & the Humanities* 129, 141.

[78] R West (1989), n 77 above, 143.

narrative to reflect a tolerant, just and fair nation. It was the change in culture on the justifiability of segregation in public that led to the *Brown v Board of Education* case, which overturned racial separation in schools. A previous decision, *Plessy v Ferguson*,[79] which had ruled that racial segregation in railway dining cars was, in 1896, defensible under the 'separate but equal doctrine', then had to be re-thought. In the years between *Plessy* and *Brown*, there had been the Second World War, a fight against Nazi racism leading to the association of separation with concentration camps and injustice. Bruner continues:

> Perhaps just as important, there had been enormous literary change as well, an 'inward turn' in narrative. Even for separate-but-equal Jim Crow railroad cars, the question had become a subjective one: How did it feel to be shunted into a separate railroad car, or sent to the back of the bus? What did it do to one's self-respect, and critically, to one's will to learn and develop? The parallel question regarding schools became, what does segregation do to black children's view of themselves, their self-esteem, their readiness to learn? The landscape of consciousness had become part of the narrative of equal protection.[80]

Bruner develops his analysis by showing how the legal-cultural conversation on racial justice continued to be played out in courts with cases on affirmative action. The narrative was reformulated to remedy historical inequalities. However, as Bruner notes, the literary turn towards racial justice was not linear. 'A dialectically contrary one quickly arose: the story of the black being given "unfair advantages."'[81]

VI. Critical Race Feminists

Feminist lawyers and critical race theorists have also taken up the power of story-telling to elucidate the experiences of women and people of colour. Patricia Williams has a collection of books which critique the white liberal constructions of law through stories.[82] A contract lawyer, her discussion of contract involves engaging with the 'contract' enslaving her ancestor. Offer, acceptance and consideration, the foundations of contract in common law, take on a different hue here. What, or who do we mean by 'property'?[83] Her exploration of notions of

[79] *Plessy v Ferguson* 163 US 537 cited in Bruner (2002), n 3 above, 54.

[80] J Bruner (2002), n 3 above, 54. Bruner recounts his own role as a witness in the *Gebhart v Belton*, 33 Del Ch 144, 91 A 2d 137 (1952) case that preceded the *Brown* decision. He had given evidence on the psychological damage that segregation did to black children. He was not cross-examined on his testimony, in part he said because as, the NAACP Legal Defense and Educational Fund lawyer who had coached him on his 'narrative'/testimony noted: 'What was there for them to say that would be palatable?' J Bruner (2002), n 3 above, 55.

[81] J Bruner (2002), n 3 above, 57.

[82] P Williams, *The Alchemy of Race and Rights* (Boston MA, Harvard, 1992); P Williams, *The Rooster's Egg: On the Persistence of Prejudice* (Boston MA, Harvard, 1997); P Williams, *Seeing a Color-Blind Future: The Paradox of Race* (New York, Farrar, Strauss & Giroux, 1997). P Williams, *Open House* (New York, Picador, 2004).

[83] P Williams (1992), n 82 above, 17–19, 216–17. See also R West (1989), n 77 above, 129, 145–46.

freedom of contract includes a story of her seeking to rent an apartment. Her white colleague, a critical legal scholar, does not believe in legal ties and wants to enter into a 'gentlemen's agreement' with the landlord. She, on the other hand, wishes to be bound by the law by entering into a formal contract. For a black woman, this formality is protective rather than oppressive.[84] She argues: 'Although rights may not be ends in themselves, rights rhetoric has been and continues to be an effective form of discourse for blacks.'[85] In another essay she explores the notion of freedom of movement by recounting a story of trying to enter a retail store, Benetton, that used a screening process to decide who should be allowed to enter into the shop. She had been denied entry. One of her solutions was to 'write back' to Benetton by leaving a poster of her views outside the shop that had banned her.[86] However, when she wrote about her experiences in a law journal article and named the shop, she was asked to remove the shop's name because her assertions were potentially defamatory. Also removed was any mention of her race for the purposes of style and to maintain neutrality. And yet, as she notes, this insistence on formal legal neutrality simply masks difference by insisting on uniformity. She then writes: 'Race neutrality in law has become the presumed antidote to race bias in real life.'[87] In their accessibility and use of stories, Williams's books and essays elucidate law more powerfully than many dry legal texts.

A fellow doyenne of the critical race movement is Paulette Caldwell. Caldwell uses her personal experience to elucidate the intersectional discrimination faced by women in general, and black women in particular, in the workplaces where they are expected to conform to a white feminine aesthetic. She uses the different responses that are elicited by her hairstyles, whether straightened or when worn in an afro style or braided. She interweaves the stories of women with case law to illustrate how law has sometimes been a tool of both resistance, and a re-inforcement of the objectification and under valuing of women. Sex, race and intersectional discrimination takes many guises and the failure of law to 'see' that and recognise the resulting harms leaves many women without remedies.[88]

The collection *Telling Stories out of court* is a compendium of personal narratives and cases on employment discrimination faced by women. It recounts the many gendered discriminatory violations that women experience in the workplace and the counter-narratives that employers use to challenge their accounts of discrimination.[89]

[84] P Williams (1992), 145–49.
[85] P Williams (1992), 149.
[86] P Williams (1992), 46.
[87] P Williams (1992), 48.
[88] P Caldwell, 'A Hair Piece: Perspectives on the Intersection of Race and Gender' (1991) *Duke Law Journal* 365–91. See also K Crenshaw, 'Demarginalizing the Intersection of Race and Sex: A Black Feminist Critique of Anti-Discrimination Doctrine, Feminist Theory and Antiracist Politics' (1989) 1 *University of Chicago Legal Forum* 138–69. D Carbado and M Gulati, *Acting White? Rethinking Race in 'Post-Racial' America* (New York, OUP, 2013).
[89] R O'Brien (ed), *Telling Stories Out of Court: Narratives about Women and Workplace Discrimination* (Ithaca NY, ILR Press, 2008). On women and crime see N Lacey, 'Women, Crime and Character in

VII. Literature and Historic Injustice

This section looks first at the work of those not directly affected by injustice but who chose to use their positions to reveal or challenge it from the outside, as it were, then moves to consider how the lives and deeds of those who fought the injustice they suffered from within is conveyed in the literature.

A. Challenges from the Outside

In *White Racism and Black Consciousness*, the anti-apartheid liberation fighter, Steve Biko, argued that White liberals engaged in Black politics to appease their consciences.[90] Nevertheless, Nadine Gordimer and Alan Paton, writing in English, and André Brink, writing in Afrikaans, did much to provoke some White consciences and to publicise the iniquities of apartheid.[91] Recognising the lack of freedom of speech and expression which impacted disproportionately on Black people, some white writers used their positions of privilege to challenge racism.

(i) Doris Lessing

Doris Lessing was one such person. Surprising as it may be to the reader, hers was the first work that I ever read that was located in 'Africa' and specifically Zimbabwe.[92] My 'good education' confined me to early readers whose characters' lives bore no relation to my own, before exposure to the 'great classics of literature' comprising English writers, until we were introduced to Arthur Miller's *Death of*

Twentieth Century Law and Literature: In Search of the Modern Moll Flanders' LSE Legal Studies Working Paper No 20/2017.

[90] S Biko, 'White Racism and Black Consciousness' in *I Write What I Like* (London, Bowerdean Press, 1978) 61, 63–66. His argument is reminiscent of Maya Angelou's poem 'On Working White Liberals'. M Angelou, *The Complete Collected Poems* (London, Virago, 1995) 47. See also Akala, *Natives: Race & Class in the Ruins of* Empire (London, Two Roads, 2019) 214 on the epiphany of the white political classes to the justice of Mandela's fight for freedom of his people ignoring the fact that many had undermined or condemned him for a long time (214–15). Finally, see A de Waal, 'Writing Human Rights and Getting it Wrong', *Boston Review*, 6 June 2016, available online at: http://bostonreview.net//world//alex-de-waal-writing-human-rights. This is on how the reports of human rights organisations may reinforce stereotypes of Western saviors.

[91] N Gordimer, *Burger's* Daughter (London, Penguin, 1981); *July's People* (London, Bloomsbury, 2005). N Gordimer, *The Conservationist* (London, Bloomsbury, 2005); Alan Paton, *Cry the Beloved Country* (London, Vintage, 2002). Andre Brink's, *A Dry White Season* (London, Vintage, 1992). See M Nicolini, ''*n Droë Wit Seisoen in die Stormkaap*: Andre Brink and the Fundamental Rights of the Afrikaners in Apartheid South Africa' in I Ward (ed), *Literature and Human Rights* (Berlin, De Gruyter, 2007). D Lessing, *The Grass is Singing* (London, Fourth Estate, 2013).

[92] The extract was from D Lessing, *The Grass is Singing* (London, Fourth Estate, 2013). Black writers have of course written extensively, not least biographies. M Mathabane, *African Women: Three Generations* (London, Hamish Hamilton, 1994). Another biography detailing the life of a black family during apartheid is L Shuster, *A Burning Hunger* (London, Jonathan Cape, 2004).

a Salesman in my final year of secondary school.[93] To be fair, I enjoyed reading Austen, Chaucer, Hardy and Shakespeare and learning First World War poetry, but it may have been an even more enriching experience had we been introduced to Achebe and the other African greats. In many ways this book speaks to my thirst for literature about and by Africans.[94] I digress.

Doris Lessing wrote for justice and ended up being expelled from Rhodesia for her trouble. She spent her early years in Rhodesia and wrote prescient and biting stories observing the foibles of white colonialists. In the introduction to her short stories, Lessing notes:

'It is a monstrous society. My father's farm was bought by him on a government scheme for "settling the land". Translated, this means "settling it with white men." It was settled by black people already.'[95]

In her novella 'The Antheap' Lessing shows how it was not only land to which white men helped themselves. Set in a rural area on a mine, the novella details the relationship that grows between two boys, Tommy, the son of the white mine manager and Dirk, the unacknowledged 'half-caste' son of Mr Mackintosh, the Scottish mine owner and one of his workers. Dirk has three siblings, two of whom are also fathered by Mr Mackintosh. Mr Mackintosh is unmarried and has no legitimate heir, so dedicates himself to Tommy, ignoring his own progeny. Lessing uses the relationship between the boys to explore the inequities of apartheid and the senseless laws that were used to buttress it. Tommy is sent away to boarding school but, on his return to the mine, teaches Dirk all that he has learned. Eventually he suggests that Dirk, who is intelligent and learns quickly, might like to go to the school for 'coloured' children in town. Dirk, who has said he wants to be an engineer, refuses, explaining:

> 'I wouldn't see my mother again.'
>
> 'Why not?'
>
> 'There's laws, white boy, laws. Anyone who lives with and after the fashion of natives is a native. Therefore I am a native, and I'm not entitled to go to school with the half-castes.'
>
> 'If you went to the town, you'd not be living with natives so you'd be classed as a coloured.'
>
> 'But then I couldn't see my mother, because if she came to town she'd still be a native.'[96]

In her introduction, Lessing speaks of her love for Africa, and notes that many white people came to love the land, but did not think to love its people. Lessing was not a romantic, but clearly understood human nature. Her analysis of the

[93] A Miller, *Death of a Salesman* (London, Penguin, 1989).

[94] See also G Younge, 'My Year of Reading African Women', *The Guardian*, London, 15 December 2018.

[95] D Lessing, 'Introduction' in D Lessing, *Nine African Stories* (London, Longman, 1968 [reprinted 1980]), 1–9. The introduction was written in April 1967.

[96] D Lessing, 'The Antheap' in D Lessing (1968), n 95 above, 182, 214–15. I replicate the language of the era, used by Lessing.

corruption of privilege (white, in her day) and the challenges of fighting oppression are as true of Zimbabwe today as her analyses were of white rule in 1967:

> It is a sad truth that no matter how terrible a society is, there is only a minority who will fight it, or at least, a minority who will provide the leadership that the majority can follow. In Southern Africa the black people who resist are persecuted, imprisoned, exiled or escape. The critical whites are in one way or another silenced or forced out. The opposition has been crushed – except for the few who stay and go on fighting. Braver people than these have never been.[97]

(ii) Ruth First Prison Diaries

Ruth First was an anti-apartheid activist, author, journalist and scholar who fought alongside Mandela, Joe Slovo, the man who became her husband, and other activists.[98] She was also arrested and constantly harassed by the apartheid regime. In a memoir of the 117 days that she spent in state detention in 1963, Ruth First, describes political whites as, 'the errants who would not go into the *laager* of whites against Africans.'[99] First's book details her arrest and detention, a month after Mandela and the co-accused in the Rivonia trial, under the 90-day law which could be 'all things to all police.'[100] As she notes, it was a fishing exercise designed to see if the apartheid regime could find illegal political activity. Despite her imprisonment, she is able to recognise her privilege, noting how she was given hot water to bathe, while the other prisoners were given cold water. She also watches through the bars of her cell as the black prisoners are made to tend the lawns and gardens which are later used and enjoyed by the warders and their friends.[101] There is also a nod to 'sisterhood' of a sort, when she tells how the women prisoners' one-hour exercise had been forfeited because the male warders had commandeered the women's space for use by male prisoners, but the 'women wardresses asserted their (or our) claim.'[102]

In the 1988 introduction to her book, re-released after she had been murdered in Mozambique by a bomb planted by the apartheid regime (which also injured Albie Sachs who sat on the first post-apartheid Constitutional Court), Ruth First's husband, Joe Slovo, shares how in 1965 she had been reluctant to write it so soon after the incarceration of Mandela and his co-accused:

'But she was moved to go ahead in the hope that the narrative would help focus world attention on the plight of a growing number of victims of the regime's physical and mental torture-machines.'[103] Slovo is also keen to emphasise the complicity

[97] D Lessing 'Introduction' (1968) 1–9, 1.
[98] For a thumbnail sketch of her life see J Imel van Allen, *Ruth First South African Activist, Scholar and Journalist*, Encyclopaedia Britannica online.
[99] R First, *117 Days* (London, Bloomsbury, 1988 [first published 1965]) 144.
[100] R First (1988), n 99 above, 14.
[101] R First (1988), 63.
[102] R First (1988), 42.
[103] J Slovo, 'Introduction' to R First, *117 Days* (London, Bloomsbury, 1988 [1965]) 4, 5.

of Western governments in the actions and longevity of the apartheid regime. He shows that violations are not committed without the connivance or knowledge of others who may have the power to intervene, but choose not to. Of his wife's torturers he notes: 'Ruth was among the first batch of detainees on whom the Special branch (straight from refresher courses in Western police academies) began to practise their newly acquired skills of mental torture.'[104] Slovo identifies how the apartheid regime's domestic brutality, coupled with attempts to de-stabilise its newly independent Black-run neighbouring states, went unsanctioned because:

> The Reagans of the world were 'constructively' engaged on the side of thuggery and the Thatchers sabotaged every international attempt to take effective measures against it; arousing a suspicion that the protection of 'kith and kin' overshadowed their concern for 'human rights' and their much-vaunted repudiation of state terrorism. And the rest of the world seemed unready or unable to provide the means.[105]

(iii) Academics

Academics have often used their intellectual capital to write justice. My mentor, John Eekelaar, wrote many reviews and articles challenging the legitimacy of Ian Smith's regime after the latter unilaterally declared (Rhodesia's) independence from Britain in 1965. In a chapter entitled 'Principles of Revolutionary Legality', Eekelaar sets out nine principles that may be relevant to an investigation of whether revolutionary activity should be given legal justification. This article speaks to current debates about the legitimacy of post-Arab Spring dispensations, amongst others. Challenging the idea of academics only being critics without solutions, Eekelaar sought to suggest a possible method of transition from minority to majority rule, trying to take into account the political realities of the time. Going against the grain, he also challenged the lionising of Ian Smith, the rebel Rhodesian leader who had proclaimed a Unilateral Declaration of Independence (UDI) against the British in 1965.[106] There is much that I admire about my mentor and his many achievements. I am moved by his kindness and humility. Of his many achievements, perhaps the one that moves me most is the recognition that at a time when he, a young white man born and raised in Southern Africa, newly ensconced in the comforts of an Oxford college, his feet on the first rung of an academic career that would prove to be stellar, his future set fair, he *chose* to remember those that he had

[104] J Slovo, 'Introduction' (1988), n 103 above, 4, 5.

[105] J Slovo, 'Introduction' (1988), n 103 above, 4, 5.

[106] See J Eekelaar, 'Principles of Revolutionary Legality' in A Simpson (ed), *Oxford Essays in Jurisprudence* (Oxford, OUP, 1973) 22, 39–40. See also J Eekelaar, 'Rhodesia: Constitution-making and Politics' (1967) *Parliamentary Affairs* 120; J Eekelaar, 'Rhodesia: The Abdication of Constitutionalism' (1969) 32 *Modern Law Review* 19. J Eekelaar, 'Review of *Rhodesia and Independence* by Kenneth Young' in (1967) 66 *African Affairs* 270.

See also C Palley's seminal constitutional study, C Palley, *The Constitutional History and Law of Southern Rhodesia 1888–1965* (Oxford, Clarendon Press, 1966).

left behind and, using his best tool, his formidable intellect, proceeded to advocate with them in demanding their human rights. While I do not compare my mentor to Martin Luther King, I can see that the young Eekelaar shared King's understanding that justice required us to challenge unjust laws, whenever and wherever we saw them. Just as King addressed his 'Letter from Birmingham Jail' to those clergy who had urged caution and patience to the civil rights leaders who were marching and demonstrating against segregation, reminding them of the importance of tackling discrimination without delay, so too Eekelaar, 'an insider' tried to ensure that white judges and politicians in Rhodesia and Britain, amongst others, understood that the actions of the rebel Rhodesian regime were simply *wrong*.[107] There could be no defence of 'we didn't know, or we did not understand the consequences' for he was clear and articulate in spelling out the legal, constitutional, and like King, the moral position of their chosen path. That is why I am grateful to have him as my mentor.[108]

Historians and public intellectuals like Simon Schama, Anthony Appiah, Mary Beard and more recently David Olusoga, owe their success, in part, to their ability to animate history by bringing alive the stories and lives of people in years gone by.[109] The cross-pollination between media-historical texts, radio and television helps to enliven the stories of old. By popularising history they democratise learning.[110] Olusoga seeks to re-write the story of Britain by reclaiming the parts and people that have been excised from the national narrative. These include early Roman Africans found through art, text and archaeological excavation and the role played by black servicemen in defence of the colonial motherland during the two world wars.[111] By so doing, Olusoga creates a narrative of continuity of presence and thus a justifiable claim to residence and citizenship. He does this to displace the 'undeserving, new immigrant incomer' of tabloid myth whilst also challenging unpalatable nationalist rhetoric.[112]

Within the African context, social historian Diana Jeater has mined law reports for information about gender in early colonial Rhodesia.[113] One can also excavate

[107] ML King, *Letter from a Birmingham Jail* (London, Penguin, 2018).

[108] That, and the fact that he shares his unpublished work J Eekelaar, 'Moral Failure and the Law'.

[109] Bruner references the work of Schama in J Bruner (2002), n 3 above, 3 n 1; AK Appiah, *The Honour Code: How Moral Revolutions Happen* (New York, Norton, 2011); M Beard, *SPQR A History of Ancient Rome* (London, Profile, 2016). Beard has book-television tie-ins including: M Beard, *Ultimate Rome: Empire without limit* (DVD) (*BBC 2*, 2016); D Olusoga, *A Black History of Britain* (London, Macmillan, 2016). This also had a television tie-in.

[110] Lacey argues that the rise of multi-media may have diluted the impact of literature. N Lacey, *Women, Crime and Character in Twentieth Century Law and Literature: In Search of the Modern Moll Flanders*, LSE Legal Studies Working Paper No 20/2017 at 10.

[111] D Olusoga, *The World's War: Forgotten Soldiers of Empire* (London, Head of Zeus, 2015). See also his history of the Herero Genocide, said to be the precursor to the European genocide of 1939–45, D Olusoga and C Erichsen, *The Kaiser's Holocaust: Germany's Forgotten Genocide and the Colonial Roots of Nazism* (London, Faber and Faber, 2011).

[112] See generally European Network against Racism (ENAR) *Racism and Discrimination in the Context of Migration in Europe* (ENAR, 2016) 9–29.

[113] D Jeater, *Marriage, Perversion and Power: the Construction of Moral Discourse in Southern Rhodesia, 1890–1930* (Oxford, Unpublished D Phil dissertation, University of Oxford 1990). On the use of both

socio-economic, biographical and legal history using cases. I am thinking here of the South African case of *Dadoo Ltd v Krugersdorp Municipality*.[114] Mr Dadoo attempted to circumvent the racist zoning laws which prohibited 'Asiatics' from buying land in areas reserved for commercial activity for white people by registering a company 'Dadoo Ltd'. Through the company he purchased land in the 'whites only' area. On discovering that the shareholders of the company were Indian, the Krugersdorp Municipality sought to have the sale nullified. However, relying on company law and the English case of *Salamon v. Salamon*,[115] it was argued, on Dadoo's behalf, that a company was a separate legal entity that did not and could not have a race. The purchase of the land was therefore lawful. The municipality argued that the land had been acquired fraudulently, the formation of a company being used as a device to circumvent the law. Dadoo was victorious on appeal. In company law speak, there was no need to pierce the corporate veil.

Pending the appeal, the government enacted the Asiatic Land and Trading Act of 1919 to prevent Indians and other 'coloured people' using company law to get around race zoning laws. Gandhi – yes, *that* Gandhi – (he had gone to South Africa and was working as a lawyer) helped with the case. He knew the plaintiff, Yusuf Dadoo's father, Mohammed Dadoo very well because they had worked on the Passive Resistance Campaign initiated by Gandhi. Gandhi was also a prolific letter writer who highlighted what he saw as legislative bad faith in seeking to prevent Indians from trading because they were competing against white businesses.[116]

The Dadoo case formed the leitmotif to my own law degree in Zimbabwe, which, like South Africa, is a Roman-Dutch law jurisdiction. We studied the case in contract, company and property law. The *South West Africa* case which addressed South Africa's misuse of its mandate powers in the former German colony (now Namibia) provided our first introduction to Aristotle's analysis of equality (treating likes alike, and un-alikes unalike – but who is 'like' we wondered?)[117] Studied by some as history, the on-going apartheid in neighbouring states and our own recent past which had involved a civil war of liberation, meant that for us, the *Dadoo* case and South African government's position in the *South West Africa* case elicited visceral reactions against the patent injustices. Fresh from getting our own

missionary archives and Native Commissioner case reports, see E Schmidt, *Peasant, Traders and Wives: Shona Women in the History of Zimbabwe, 1870–*1939 (Oxford, James Currey Ltd, 1992).

[114] *Dadoo Ltd and Others v. Krugersdorp Municipality* 1920 AD 530. Rob McQueen, *The Flowers of Progress: Corporations in the Colonies*, Griffiths Law School, Socio-Legal Research Centre, Research Paper Series 09–14 (2009). I am grateful to Franz Viljoen for passing this paper on to me.

[115] *Salamon v Salamon* & *Co Ltd* [1897] AC 22.

[116] R McQueen (2009), n 114 above, 12–23. There is also a rich bibliographic note on the Dadoo family. See Dr Yusuf Mohamed Dadoo at: sahistory.org.za. It is acknowledged that Gandhi's political awakening came during his time in South Africa where he experienced direct discrimination. Mohandes Karamchand Gandhi on: sahistory.org.za. It is worth noting that Gandhi's race politics while in South Africa sometimes absorbed the racial hierarchies favoured by the apartheid regime so that he regarded Black people as inferior. A Desai and G Vahed, *The South African Gandhi: Stretcher-Bearer of Empire* (Stanford CA, Stanford University Press, 2015).

[117] *South West Africa (Ethiopia v South Africa; Liberia v South Africa)*, 1966 ICJ 6 (July 18).

independence in 1980, we fulminated about the sheer 'cheek' of it all. In my second year of law school, the Nobel Prize was awarded to Ellie Wiesel. In his Nobel Prize winner's speech Wiesel made this historical connection on the delinking of legality from justice:

> How to explain any of it: the outrage of Apartheid which continues unabated. Racism itself is dreadful, but when it pretends to be legal, and therefore just, when a man like Nelson Mandela is imprisoned, it becomes even more repugnant. Without comparing Apartheid to Nazism and to its 'final solution' – for that defies all comparison – one cannot help but assign the two systems, in their supposed legality, to the same camp.[118]

In his much-lauded book *East West Street*, Philippe Sands, an international lawyer and academic, combined a deeply personal family history of persecution by the Nazis with a fascinating legal history of the development of two key principles in international criminal law: genocide and crimes against humanity. Compelling were the links that Sands made between his family who lived in a small Polish town, Lviv,[119] and Lauterpacht and Lemkin, the two international lawyers who were part of the Nuremburg prosecutions at the end of the Second World War and who conceptualised genocide and crimes against humanity, now both enshrined in law as the most heinous of violations. Both these men were, like Sands' family, from Lviv. In a powerfully redemptive section, Sands details his friendship with the son of a Nazi who was involved in the suffering experienced by Sands' family. In detailing their coming together and conversations about their unhappily-interlocking family histories, Sands and his friend come to a new place where they, the sons of two opposing families, fashion a new way of co-existing. One can read any number of books on transitional justice theory and none can match Sands' affecting, intellectually stimulating and – for a book with 'legal themes' – eminently readable and enjoyable book.[120]

Sands is also eloquent about the power of music. In a documentary, he returns to Lviv with Emmanuel Ax, who was born there in 1949 and left in 1956. Ax performs in the Lviv Philharmonic Hall leaving Sands to muse: 'I know from my work in courtrooms, the stories of horror, past and present, are never easily shared. What I've learned over these days is that words can help and that music can help even more.'[121]

[118] E Wiesel, 'Hope, Despair and Memory', Nobel Lecture, 11 December 1986 at: https://www.nobelprize.org/prizes/peace/1986/wiesel/lecture/. See also G Bindman (ed), *South Africa and the Rule of Law* (London, ICJ, Pinter Publishers, 1988). It looks at the entire legal edifice of apartheid laws. For an overview of the legal structures of apartheid, see 11–14.

[119] Lviv has changed name and been under the jurisdiction of different states and is now Ukrainian.

[120] P Sands, *East West Street: On the Origins of Genocide and Crimes against Humanity* (London, Weidenfeld and Nicolson, 2016). Sands also deals sensitively with the issue of sexuality/ sexual orientation and the constraints of the age before gay rights in a 10-part podcast. 'Intrigue: The Ratline', *BBC Radio 4*, 2018.

[121] Sands made a mini-documentary to accompany a *Financial Times* article. The film is at FT, edited by N Whittle and O McGuirk, 'Lviv diary: Philippe Sands on horror, law and music' at: https://www.ft.com/video/30739bf6-d2bc-4bd7-8c5b-b69c2433e45b. The article is *FT*, 'Lviv Diary: Philippe Sands on law, music and a city of history', *Financial Times*, 18 December, 2017.

B. Challenges from Within

(i) Wole Soyinka and Ken Saro-Wiwa

Lawyers sometimes turn their cases into fiction, for example the barrister-novelist, John Mortimer, whose Rumpole of the Old Bailey series has been a global success.[122] One of his cases involved defending Nigerian writer, and later Nobel laureate, Wole Soyinka. Soyinka had entered the radio station that was about to broadcast the (rigged) election results and giving victory to the ruling party in the Western Region of Nigeria. He made his way into the studio and pre-empted the broadcast. He was arrested and charged with robbery and violence. He was put on trial and defended by John Mortimer, who was hired by Amnesty International. Mortimer later recounted the Soyinka case in his autobiography, *Clinging to the Wreckage*, musing that he had probably been 'chosen for this task, ironically, less for my legal expertise than because the man in the dock was a playwright.'[123] Mortimer identifies the transplantation of English law and legal procedure together with 'Shakespeare, Wordsworth, Lord Byron and the herbaceous border, as one of our great contributions to the world.'[124] Valerie Grove, Mortimer's biographer, adds that so impressed was Mortimer by the functioning of the British legal system in 'this ill-governed former colony' that it convinced him not to 'abandon the law, but to try to practise it more interestingly in the future.'[125]

Sometimes, reading a different rendering of the same story, gives one fresh insights. In his autobiography, *You must set forth at Dawn*, Soyinka describes the story of his imprisonment and trial 'as a drama'.[126] Soyinka identifies four lawyers who acted for him pro Deo; 'Tayo Onalajua, Kayoke Somolu, Jide Olatuwura and Dele Ige.'[127] He does not mention Mortimer or the role played by Amnesty International in his case.[128] What are we to make of this omission? Had Soyinka been annoyed by Mortimer's book or perceived attitude towards Africans? Dolin's analysis of the case centres the English barrister naming him, but not the other 'distinguished Nigerian barristers' who worked with him. Might this explain Soyinka's standpoint in refusing to cast Mortimer in the 'saviour' role? Mortimer, Dolin and Soyinka are in agreement in their assessment of the integrity and legal acuity of the judge who freed him.

Discussing a different case, Dolin notes how Soyinka, in his literary writing, used intertextuality, whereby, 'every text is under the jurisdiction of different

[122] J Mortimer, *The Collected Stories of Rumpole* (London, Penguin, 2013).
[123] J Mortimer, *Clinging to the Wreckage: A Part Life* (London, Weidenfeld and Nicolson, 1982) 149.
[124] J Mortimer (1982), n 123 above, 153.
[125] V Grove, *A Voyage Round John Mortimer* (London, Viking, 2007) 193–94 with quotes at 194.
[126] W Soyinka, *You Must Set Forth at Dawn: A Memoir* (London, Random House, 2006) 87.
[127] W Soyinka (2006), 87.
[128] W Soyinka (2006), 87. We gain some insight into his omission of Amnesty International in Soyinka's discussion of the case of Ken Saro-Wiwa and the Ogoni eight. He describes Amnesty International and Human Rights Watch as 'busybodies'. Soyinka at 419. Dolin (2007), n 1 above, 167.

discourses' to challenge injustice. In *The Man Died*, written during another stint in prison (1967–69), Soyinka protested the murder of an Igbo photographer.[129] While two soldiers were charged, they were never tried. The Biafran war that followed, referred to as a genocide by Soyinka, is directly linked to this failure of justice. Of his own detention, Dolin notes that Soyinka:

> draws on the 'golden thread' of Nigerian law to resist his interrogators: 'are you admitting that you presume me guilty already?' … and 'you have accused me of nothing.' These intertexts enable justice to be sought through a specific and answerable demand, not allegorised on a pedestal. Soyinka invokes the fruits of colonial law, however poor the crop, as one element of his post-colonial struggle for justice.[130]

Soyinka's autobiography also yields insights into the case of environmental and political activist Ken Saro-Wiwa and his eight co-accused in the 1990s. They were fighting for the rights of the Ogoni people whose natural resources (oil) were exploited but with little benefit to them. Their land was degraded and polluted. There was also a lack of political representation and their voices and interests were ignored by the centre. Soyinka gives a heart-rending account of the events surrounding the treason trial brought by the Abacha military dictatorship in Nigeria.[131] He describes the process as farcical, before describing the judge as the 'hanging judge Justice Ibrahim Auta.'[132] The unfair trial[133] and the subsequent hanging of the men are embedded within a narrative that focuses on the international lobbying that went on behind the scenes. Soyinka himself travelled to the 1995 Commonwealth Heads of Government Meeting in New Zealand to plead for the life of his friend. While there, he encountered Saro-Wiwa's son who handed him a copy of a statement made by Shell Oil company, whose mining activities had/have led to the environmental pollution in the Ogoni region. The Shell statement was framed in PR speak and sought to absolve Shell of blame. Soyinka's disgust at this exculpatory pleading is evident. He likens it to 'Pontius Pilate washing his hands before handing Christ over to his executioners', before charging Shell with being an accessory to the violations.[134]

[129] In his autobiography, Soyinka mentions that a copy of *The Man had Died* was found beside the body of 'the journalist Baguada Kaltho in the bathroom of the Kaduna Hotel.' W Soyinka (2006), n 126 above, 413.

[130] Dolin (2007), n 1 above, 180.

[131] Communications 37/94, 139/94,154/96, 161/97 (joined) *International PEN and Others (on behalf of Saro-Wiwa) v Nigeria* (2000) AHRLR 212 (ACHPHR 1998) (12th Activity Report). On environmental pollution caused by oil spillages, See also *SERAC and Another v Nigeria* (2001) AHRLR 60 (ACHPHR 2001) (15th Annual Activity Report).

[132] W Soyinka (2006), n 126 above, 418.

[133] Soyinka is clearly affronted by the military regime's failure to uphold even the most basic standards of justice; 'to proceed to hang those victims, even before they had exhausted all avenues of appeal open to them within the provisions of the decree that established "judicial process", was a step that no sensible person ever thought possible' W Soyinka (2006), n 128 above, 421.

[134] W Soyinka (2006), n 126 above, 422–23. Soyinka details how he later wrote a poem invoking the spirit of a dead Russian dissident, to honour his friend. Soyinka, 'Calling Josef Brodsky for Ken Saro-Wiwa' in Soyinka (2006), n 126 above, 428. V Brittain, 'Ken Saro-Wiwa: A Hero for our Times' (2015) 56(3) *Race and Class* 5–17.

Soyinka's words, it turns out, echo those of the condemned Saro-Wiwa in his final address to the military appointed tribunal that sent him to his death by hanging:

> I repeat that we all stand before history. I and my colleagues are not the only ones on trial. Shell is here on trial and it is as well that it is represented by counsel said to be holding a watching brief. The Company has, indeed, ducked this particular trial, but its day will surely come and the lessons learnt here may prove useful to it, for there is no doubt in my mind that the ecological war that the Company has waged in the Delta will be called to question sooner than later and the crimes of that war be duly punished. The crime of the Company's dirty wars against the Ogoni people will also be punished.
>
> On trial also is the Nigerian nation, its present rulers and those who assist them. Any nation which can do to the weak and disadvantaged what the Nigerian nation has done to the Ogoni loses a claim to independence and to freedom from outside influence. I am not one of those who shy away from protesting injustice and oppression, arguing that they are expected in a military regime. The military do not act alone. They are supported by a gaggle of politicians, lawyers, academics and businessmen, all of them hiding under the claim that they are only doing their duty, men and women too afraid to wash their pants of urine.[135]

The significance of Saro-Wiwa's statement is that his analysis went on to found the basis of two legal challenges, one a tort action brought against Shell by Saro-Wiwa's family using the Alien Tort Claims Act (ATCA) and the Torture Victim Protection Act (TVPA) in the United States, and the other, the *SERAC v Nigeria* case cited earlier.[136]

Saro-Wiwa's court oration calls to mind that of one of his international defenders who lobbied hard for his release, President Nelson Mandela of South Africa, at his own trial decades earlier.[137] Autobiographies help to infuse the legal story of

[135] Cited by V Brittain (2015), n 134 above, 5.

[136] See also F Viljoen, *International Human Rights Law in Africa* (Oxford, OUP, 2012) 306–8, 346, 417; F Coomans, 'The Ogoni Case Before the African Commission on Human and Peoples' Rights' (2003) 52(3) *International & Comparative Law Quarterly* 749–60. *Wiwa v Royal Dutch Petroleum*, *Wiwa v Anderson*, and *Wiwa v Shell Petroleum Development Company* are three lawsuits filed by the Center for Constitutional Rights (CCR) and co-counsel from EarthRight International on behalf of relatives of murdered activists who were fighting for human rights and environmental justice in Nigeria. See *Wiwa et al v Royal Dutch Petroleum et al* at: https://ccrjustice.org/home/what-we-do/our-cases/wiwa-et-al-v-royal-dutch-petroleum-et-al. Shell settled the case for US$ 15.5 million.

[137] Nelson Mandela, then President of South Africa implored the Nigerian regime not to execute him but to no avail. N Mandela and M Langa, *Dare not Linger: The Presidential Years* (London, Macmillan, 2017) 200. Soyinka reports Mandela, who was present at the Commonwealth meeting, as having been so outraged by the executions that he promised: 'General Sani Abacha is sitting on a volcano and I am going to make sure that it blows up under him.' W Soyinka (2006), n 126 above, 421. Another biography, this one of Thabo Mbeki by journalist and academic William Gumede, gives a slightly different perspective. He notes that the South African government had been blind-sided by this their first foreign affairs dispute resolution attempt which led them, erroneously, to think that they could 'talk sense' into the Abacha regime. In a stinging rebuke, Mandela is alleged to have been told by one of Saro-Wiwa's lawyers, 'Were quiet diplomacy pursued [in regard to apartheid] I doubt you would be alive today.' This may explain Mandela's volcano comment cited by Soyinka. W Gumede, *Thabo Mbeki and the Battle for the Soul of the ANC* (Cape Town, Zebra Press, 2005) 178.

the trial with the human emotion that accompanied it. Mandela's defiant Rivonia speech – in which he said that he hoped to live to see a democratic and free South Africa, 'But if needs be, it is an ideal for which I am prepared to die'[138] – presents an image of a man who was supremely confident and principled; and yet, in his book, he admits to fear and apprehension: 'And of course, when you are alone in your cell you also thought in terms of yourself and the fact that you are not likely to live and that is … only but human.'[139] This reflection, in which he shares his feelings of vulnerability, is not to be found in the body of the reported case, but it enriches the legal and historical narrative. Mandela is also generous in insisting that his colleagues were far braver than him.[140] Discussing the trial with his fellow Robben Island inmate, Ahmed Kathrada, Mandela seems to have been acutely aware of the need to *perform* courage, whatever their misgivings:

'But all the flourish of trumpets and the hosannas sung by us and our well-wishers in the course of the trial would have been valueless if courage had deserted us when the decisive moment struck.'[141]

(ii) Winnie Mandela

There is a stark contrast between the narratives written about Nelson Mandela and those written about his former wife, Winnie, who also showed courage during her trial and imprisonment where she was represented by the same team of lawyers who had represented her husband.[142] He is revered, but she is often vilified. Generally, she elicits visceral reactions and the narratives constructed around her life reflect this.[143]

While prison may have been difficult for Nelson Mandela, the daily harassment that Winnie Mandela endured from the age of 23 when he was sent to prison

[138] N Mandela (2010), n 32 above, 122.

[139] N Mandela (2010), n 32 above, 123, 124–25. To add to the poignancy, the book contains a photograph of a piece of paper with his key summation points in his own hand. At 122.

[140] N Mandela (2010), n 32 above, 125. Later he recalls emptying the bucket used for human waste that the prisoners had in their cells, of a fellow prisoner who had been taken from Robben Island to Cape Town early that morning. 'I cleaned my bucket every day [*chuckles*]and had no problem, you see, in cleaning the bucket of another.' At 148. In his foreword to Abel's book on the use of law to challenge apartheid, Mandela pays tribute to the work done by lawyers, 'in prying open the ever-widening cracks of apartheid's legal edifice' while also acknowledging, 'the hardships endured and the courage displayed by many ordinary South Africans.' N Mandela, 'Foreword' in R Abel, *Politics by Other Means: Law and the Struggle against Apartheid, 1980–1994* (Abingdon, Routledge, 1995) vii.

[141] N Mandela (2010), n 32 above, 124. There are other powerful biographies including, E Sisulu, *Walter and Albertina Sisulu: In our Lifetime* (Claremont, David Philip, 2002); D Goldberg, *The Mission: A Life for Freedom in South Africa* (Lexington, University of Kentucky Press, 2015). For a 'biography' of Robben Island, see C Smith *Robben Island* (Johannesburg, Struik, 1997).

[142] A Marie du Preez Bezdrop, *Winnie Mandela: A Life* (Cape Town, Zebra Press, 2003).

[143] See for example the positive, award winning film by Pascale Lamche, *Winnie* (Netherlands, Pumpernickel Films, 2017) and contrast with the BBC, *Inside Story* series. Episode TRC 99 'Winnie Mandela and the Missing Witness' (Nicholas Claxton, 2010). It is the same with books. See E Gilbey, *The Lady: Life and Times of Winnie Mandela* (London, Vintage, 1994) (anti) and the more sympathetic du Preez Bezdrop (2003), n 142 above.

(he was 18 years older than her) until his release may have actually been harder than his imprisonment.

One of Winnie Mandela's biographers, Anne Marie Du Preez Bezdorp, describes the legal framing of torture before going on to detail how Winnie Mandela was treated by the apartheid regime during a period of imprisonment. Her house was raided during the night on 12 May 1969, terrifying her two daughters aged nine and ten. Winnie, then aged 35, was charged under the Terrorism Act, No 83 of 1967. She was taken away, leaving her daughters alone. She did not know what they did with her daughters after they took her away. She was held for 17 months, the first 13 months being spent in solitary confinement.

During this time, she slept on a concrete floor with bug infested blankets and a waste bucket which doubled up as a receptacle for the cold bath water she poured over herself. There were times during her menses when blood simply poured between her legs – she fashioned a cloth to use as sanitary protection. She was fed a meagre diet of porridge, morning and night with maize cobs for lunch. All this was punctuated with long periods of interrogation and mental torture including days of sleep deprivation.

One day she was asked who Thembi Mandela was. She replied that he was her stepson, at which point her torturer bluntly told her that he had been killed in a car accident and walked out. It is said to have been the first time that she wept 'for the son who had lost his father and the father who had lost his son.'[144] Ultimately her interrogators wore her down. All this clearly had an impact for she later described herself, as being 'the product of the masses of my country and the product of my enemy.'[145]

Bezdrop finishes the chapter on Winnie's months of imprisonment by detailing how those who have experienced both physical and mental torture identify solitary confinement as particularly difficult. She concludes:

> Nelson Mandela, who had been imprisoned in harsh conditions and forced to perform years of hard labour, said he had found his own brief encounter with solitary confinement – three days – 'the most forbidding aspect of prison life.'
>
> Winnie Mandela had been in solitary confinement for thirteen months.[146]

Here is Winnie's own assessment of her life:

> The years of imprisonment hardened me … Perhaps if you have been given a moment to hold back and wait for the next blow, your emotions wouldn't be blunted as they have been in my case. When it happens every day of your life, when that pain becomes a way

[144] A du Preez Bezdrop (2003), n 142 above, 151. The callousness of her torturer is contrasted with the kindness of the other prisoners who got a note to her offering their condolences and telling her: 'Mother of the Nation, we are with you.' Other notes containing information about betrayals and the state of other prisoners soon followed. Bezdrop (2003) at 151.

[145] A du Preez Bezdrop (2003), n 142 above, 138–56. The quote: 'product of my enemy' is on p 273.

[146] A du Preez Bezdrop (2003), n 142 above, 156. She suffered from post traumatic stress disorder.

> of life … there is no longer anything I can fear. There is nothing the government has not done to me. There isn't any pain I haven't known.[147]

Winnie is also subject to sexual double standards, criticised for allegedly having an affair while her husband was in prison.[148] However, one cannot help but wonder if Nelson would have remained celibate for 27 years had their situations been reversed. I suspect not. The idea of Winnie Mandela and women, who like her are asked to wait for men who have gone to prison or travelled for a lengthy period of time, is explored in novel form by Njabulo Ndebele's *The Cry of Winnie Mandela.*[149] Winnie became the modern-day Penelope waiting for Odysseus to return from the Trojan wars: 'Waiting! It empties out your life. Your thoughts are more with him than with yourself. You become your own after-thought. Your inner life squeezed out by a relentless public concern on his behalf.'[150]

Maya Angelou picks up on the minimisation of the contributions of black women in struggle narratives. In one of my favourite passages from one volume of her autobiography, *The Heart of a Woman*, she recounts a conversation between African women living in exile in London:

> Ruth Thompson, a West Indian journalist, led the conversation as soon as lunch was finished. 'What are we here for? Why are African women sitting, eating, trying to act cute while African men are discussing serious questions and African children are starving? Have we come to London just to convenience our husbands? Have we been brought her as portable pussy?' The Luo woman laughed. 'Sister, you have asked completely my question. We, in Kenya, are women, not just wombs. We have shown during the Mau Mau that we have ideas as well as babies.' Mrs Okala agreed and added, 'At home we fight. Some women have died in the struggle.' A tall wiry lawyer from Sierra Leone stood. 'In all of Africa women have suffered … I have been jailed and beaten. Because I would not tell the whereabouts of my friends, they also shot me … Because I fought against imperialism.'[151]

[147] J Burke, 'Winnie Madikizela-Mandela dies aged 81', *The Guardian*, London, 2 April 2018.

[148] E Gilbey (1994), n 143 above.

[149] N Ndebele, *The Cry of Winnie Mandela* (Banbury, Ayebia, 2003). Echoing the Winnie story about a woman whose husband is unfairly imprisoned and what she does while he is away, see Tayari Jones, *An American Marriage* (London, Oneworld, 2019). Jones said she modelled the book on the Penelope story and a snatch of conversation she heard between a couple, with the woman telling the man that he would not have waited for her for seven years had their situations been reversed. T Jordan, 'The Experiences that Inspired "An American Marriage"', *New York Times*, 23 February 2018.

[150] N Ndebele (2003), n 149 above, 106. Ndebele writes one of the most powerful accounts about anger and its purpose that I have ever read. He links it to global human rights struggles and violations (117–18).

[151] M Angelou, *The Heart of a Woman* (London, Virago, 1986) 135–36. I love this quote so much I included it in my book F Banda, *Women, Law and Human Rights* (Oxford, Hart, 2005), 26. Post independence, some states have chosen to honour women's contributions to their national liberation struggles within their constitutions (25–27).

(iii) Trevor Noah

Autobiographical bridges can be built between the pain of past history and the joyous transcendence that comes from achieving justice. The autobiography written by the comedian and host of the *Daily Show*, Trevor Noah, is that bridge. Born in South Africa to a Swiss German father and a Black South African mother, he was, as the title to his autobiography suggests, *Born a Crime*. This is because interracial relationships were banned under the Immorality Act 1957 and the Mixed Marriages Act 1949. However, this 'Coloured' child of an illicit union is now one of the global standard bearers for the Rainbow Nation as South Africa is often called. He lives and broadcasts his show from New York. He is celebrated as the very embodiment of the global citizen.[152]

(iv) Nelson Mandela's Letters

Letters, like contemporaneous diaries, can shed light on both the person and the time in which they were writing. What was the person thinking and feeling *at that time* and not in hindsight? The audience and the purpose of the letter – intimate letter to a friend, versus a letter to be read by a wider readership – can also be revealing. Mandela's letters which were subsequently published for a general readership provide good examples of letters as documents of advocacy and also intimacy.[153] After his imprisonment following the Rivonia Trial, Mandela engaged in correspondence with the Minister of Justice. Instructive is his letter of 22 April 1969 asking that he and his fellow detainees be released, and, pending release, be given the status of political prisoners and the entitlements associated with this status, which to my delight include a right to 'bioscope' (cinema), and, of course better food, access to books and improved contact with families. The letter reads like a carefully prepared appeal. Mandela invokes as precedent an earlier trial involving a rebellion in the Orange Free State which had resulted in the imprisonment of the white protagonists for treason. He notes that their crimes were worse, having killed many people and yet they had been released from prison after a short sentence. He contrasts the 1914 white rebellion with their liberation cause and argues that the African struggle is not only more legitimate, but also more peaceful. He argues that in committing acts of sabotage, the ANC had been careful to avoid causing a loss of life, 'a fact which was expressly acknowledged by both the trial Judge and the prosecution in the Rivonia case.'[154]

Invoking criminology and the ideas around the purpose of imprisonment, Mandela notes that their treatment has been retributive rather than rehabilitative.

[152] T Noah, *Born a Crime: Stories from a South African childhood* (London, John Murray, 2017).
[153] M Suresh, '"Terrorist" lives in Delhi's courts: An ethnography of the legal worlds of terrorism trials' (Unpublished PhD Thesis, Birkbeck, London, 2016).
[154] N Mandela (2010), n 32 above, 147.

He links this to their being punished for challenging race discrimination. Throughout the letter, Mandela is clear that he is not asking for the mercy of the Minister, he is not a supplicant. He writes in the language of one who understands his legal entitlements; Mandela the lawyer submits the pleadings for the collective case. In modern parlance, this is a claim for his human rights and those of his fellow detainees.[155]

VIII. Conclusion

This chapter began by considering the concept of 'artivism' and the connections between lawyers and writers, both being charged with creating a compelling narrative to engage their audience, whether reader or court, and how the concept of 'justice' has been explored in the literature, including when the literature has crossed cultural boundaries. I then looked at the way protest and injustice has been reflected in music, art and photography before going on to look at the way writers have adopted story-telling to advance justice and to fight for human rights. The chapter concluded by reviewing writing about oppression written, first, by those who were not of the oppressed, and then by those who were from the oppressed communities.

The next chapter starts by exploring 'identity' and 'home' before moving on to look at the history of African migration to what is now the Global North. Using pen portraits of Africans throughout history, I show how this migration to the north is not a recent phenomenon but one that started centuries ago. Using the African Union's definition of diaspora, I consider the movement of what Mazrui calls the diaspora of enslavement through fiction and autobiography before moving on to the diaspora of colonialism and their heirs. The lives of Africans are considered through a prism of case law, novels and poetry and human rights reports. The chapter ends with an examination of the metaphorical drawing up of bridges to prevent the arrival of Africans and others deemed 'undesirable' by European and other governments.

[155] N Mandela (2010), n 32 above, 144–48. There are other examples of Mandela acting as a legal advocate for his fellow detainees. At 216–17.

2

Migration Histories

I. On 'Home' and Identity Formation

The diasporic events detailed in this chapter inevitably raise issues of identity and conflicts over the idea of what is 'home'. There is now a constant traffic of artefacts and body parts being returned from Europe and beyond to their respective African homes for burial. This is in recognition of the importance of rites in all cultures and a belated attempt to make right a colonial wrong and to associate artefacts with a sense of 'place', a 'home' where they belong. In an introductory note to his novel *Woman of the Ashes*, telling, through the eyes of a 15-year-old girl, of the fight mounted by the indigenous people against Portuguese colonialism in Mozambique, Mia Couto notes that the remains of the last Monarch who was banished to the Azores after his defeat in 1895 were returned to Mozambique in 1985.[1] Another example is the return to South Africa of Sara Baartman, a Khoikhoi woman who was taken on tour to Europe in the early nineteenth century and displayed as 'Hottentot Venus.'[2] In a different vein, the Belgians have reconceptualised the Africa Museum in Brussels, to include new art from the post-colonial Democratic Republic of Congo and other (Central) African states. This is an attempt to get the present to address the wrongdoings of the past through artistic expression. The museum has undergone a physical and ideological refit.[3]

The historic 'sightings' and narratives of the Black presence in geographically 'western' settings is not without controversy – the taunt 'foreigner, go home!' can be met with the rejoinder 'I am home.' And yet, where is home? Does a person or a people have only one home? Who are we when we leave home and who do we become when we arrive and settle elsewhere? Who defines who we are? The African Union is keen to define the term 'diaspora' widely to include the descendants of slaves who have new names and who hold the citizenship of their states of arrival, as well as those Africans who have moved permanently or temporarily under different conditions. These are the people that Ali Mazrui has referred

[1] M Couto, 'Introductory Note' in M Couto (translated by D Brookshaw), *Woman of the Ashes* (New York, Farrar, Straus and Giroux, 2018).

[2] C Dunton, 'Sara Baartman and the Ethics of Representation' (2015) 46(2) *Research in African Literatures* 32–51. See also C. Ngwenya, *What is Africanness? Contesting nativism in culture, race and sexualities* (Pretoria, PULP, 2018) 84–94.

[3] See Africa Museum at: http://www.africamuseum.be/en/discover/renovation and also look at the 'mission statement.'

to as the diaspora of colonialism whom he distinguishes from the diaspora of enslavement.[4]

In *We Need New Names* Zimbabwean NoViolet Bulawayo recounts the versions of 'home' that two of her characters carry with them:

> There are three homes inside Mother's and Aunt Fostalina's heads: home before independence, before I was born, when black people and white people were fighting over the country. Home after independence, when black people won the country. And then the home of things falling apart, which made Aunt Fostalina leave and come here (the US). Home one, home two and home three. There are four homes inside of Mother Bones's head: home before the white people came to steal the country, and a king ruled; home when the white people came to steal the country and then there was war; home when black people got our stolen country back after independence; and then home of now. Home one, home two, home three, home four. When someone talks of home, you have to listen carefully so you know exactly which one the person is referring to.[5]

On a return visit 'home' to Bulawayo in Zimbabwe, Novuyo Tshuma finds that while some things have remained the same, neither she, nor the friends that she left behind, are the same people. This forces her to confront the idea of home:

> Though I still yearn for 'home,' I no longer think of it as a place, out there, to go to. It now resides in me, a 'feeling at home' inside of me that I try to cultivate every day, that I can take with me wherever I need to go.[6]

Epaphras Osondu's short story 'Pilgrimage' is about an African-American woman who travels to Nigeria to visit a 'prophet' to be healed (she has breast cancer). It is the market women who heal her as they welcome her 'back home' from the land where she was taken 'screaming and cursing'. They treat her using indigenous medicine.[7]

In *What is Africanness?* Ngwena puts forward two competing narratives on the construction of identity(ies); that of the imperialist forces and the other of 'black/African emancipatory discourses'[8] The former is premised upon establishing racial hierarchy, which has superior whiteness at the top and inferior blackness at

[4] A Mazrui, 'Pan Africanism and the Intellectuals: rise, decline and revival' in T Mkandawira (ed), *African Intellectuals* (London, ZED Books, 2005) 56, 57. In a chapter entitled: 'Non-Western westerners: The Difference Colour Makes', Eisenstein captures well the insider-outsider status of the diaspora of slavery. Z Eisenstein, *Against Empire: Feminism, Racism and the West* (London, ZED Books, 2004) 114–47. See also African Union 'Meeting of Experts on the Definition of the African Diaspora 11–12 April 2005 Addis Ababa, Ethiopia, para 18 at: http://www.dirco.gov.za/diaspora/fr/definition.html.

[5] NV Bulawayo, *We Need New Names* (London, Vintage, 2014) 191–92. See also P Chigumadzi, *These Bones will Rise Again* (London, Indigo Press, 2018).

[6] NR Tshuma, 'New Lands, New Selves' in VT Nguyen, *The Displaced* (New York, Abrams Press, 2018) 159, 173.

[7] E Osondu, *Voice of America* (London, Granta, 2010) 195, 201, 202. See also the poetry of Nayyirah Waheed, 'African American *i, ii, iii*', 'The Secret we Never Say – African American – *iiii*' in N Waheed, *Salt* (London, CreateSpace, 2013) 113–17.

[8] C Ngwena (2018), n 2 above, 6.

the bottom. The middle is filled in by the in-betweens, neither white nor black. The Africanist emancipatory project is one that seeks to reclaim and re-centre African lives and perspectives.[9] Ngwena sees both imperialist and Africanist constructions of identity as based on fictional narratives which 'hypostasise African identity' ignoring the uncertainties and unpredictability that is part of identity creation and re-creation. Ngwena's project seeks to challenge both colonial and Africanist 'nativisms' which he sees as 'shorn of any historical radicalisation or transformative movement.' Instead he wants to theorise African identities in a way that challenges persisting dogmas while creating an African identity built on equality and not hierarchies of race, culture or sexuality, specifically heteronormativity.[10]

In her short story, 'The Master', Chimamanda Adichie, through her eavesdropping servant-protagonist, interrogates identity formation echoing Ngwena's analyses. Ugwu overhears his employer, 'The Master' engaging in debate with his colleagues. He responds to a suggestion that in post-colonial societies, pan-Africanism is the only sensible way forward for Africans, by arguing that in his view:

> [T]he only authentic identity for the African is the tribe … I am a Nigerian because a white man created Nigeria and gave me that identity. I am Black because the white man constructed Black to be as different as possible from his White. But I was Igbo before the white man came.

His colleague and friend counters:

> But you became aware that you were Igbo because of the white man. The pan-Igbo idea itself came only in the face of White domination. You must see that tribe as it is today is as colonial a product as nation and race.

The Master counters: 'The pan-Igbo idea existed long before the white man! … Go and ask the elders in your village about your history.'[11]

Section II of this chapter starts by presenting a snapshot of the multiple sources which show that Africans have been in the northern hemisphere for centuries.[12]

[9] C Ngwena (2018), 6, 7.

[10] C Ngwena (2018), 12, 13.

[11] CN Adichie, 'The Master' (2005) 92 *Granta* 19, 37. 'The Master' is from/was an early extract from CN Adichie, *Half a Yellow Sun* (London, Harper, 2009). See also M Feldner, *Narrating the New African Diaspora: 21st Nigerian Literature in Context* (Cham, Palgrave Macmillan, 2019) 55. Appiah argues that identity formation is a coming together of individual choice, group composition and external recognition. KA Appiah, *The Lies that Bind: Rethinking Identity* (London, Profile Books, 2018), 8–12. Appiah's Reith Lectures for the BBC which form the basis for *The Lies that Bind* can be downloaded from the BBC website. They are worth reading. In the context of Adichie's 'Master', read his Reith lecture on *Country*, delivered in Glasgow, Scotland in October 2016. Available on BBC Radio 4 at: https://www.bbc.co.uk/programmes/b07zz5mf. Also broadcast on the BBC World service on Tuesday 25 and Saturday 29 October 2016.

[12] Feldner acknowledges slavery and colonialism but writes of three waves of African migration to the Global North: 1950s–1970s for education; mid '70s – Africans escaping political upheaval; 21st century — to improve their economic prospects and to share in the global economic prosperity. M. Feldner (2019), n 11 above 15. Feldner's focus is on *modern* migration.

In adopting this approach, I take on board the criticisms made by Odugbemi, Rammala, and wa Kamonji of African Studies courses in London where:

> the class began with 'forgotten' pre-Victorian Africans from London and France who were skilled in European sport, music, and writing. These people were presented as important because their talents were regarded as extraordinary within European societies; they were the exceptions.[13]

I hope my snapshot serves a different purpose and that is to challenge and decentre the current ahistorical (within popular media) view of Europe as having always been an homogenously 'white' continent or indeed of the narrative of powerlessness of Africans, whether in Europe or on the continent.[14] Like any family album, the photos are sometimes haphazard and thus not chronological. I wish also to highlight our inter-connectedness as people. Using the work of E Tendayi Achiume, I hope to show how our sometimes involuntary links through slavery and colonisation create a bond between us as peoples which, Achiume contends, bestows on Africans a 'status as co-sovereigns of the First World through citizenship.'[15] Happily I am able to take up Odugbemi et al's, suggestion for improvement of conceiving African Studies which includes using novels to elaborate the African experience.

Section III of the chapter then moves on to consider contemporary migration patterns and the responses to the changing population mix in the receiving countries before examining, in section IV, the increasingly hostile reception given by states to those who seek refuge or to migrate. The conclusion highlights the journeys that have been travelled historically and the impact that those journeys have had on both those who have left and those in the places of arrival. The story of the methods that states have used to repel new migration is continued in the third chapter.

[13] J Odugbemi, O Rammala, and W wa Kamonji, 'Searching for Africa in African Studies: An open letter to teachers of Africa at UCL.' The short version of this is published as 'Searching for Africa in African Studies' on *Africa is a Country*, 15 August 2019 at: https://africasacountry.com/2019/08/there-is-no-africa-in-african-studies. I am grateful to Eleanor Thompson for sending me a link to this article. The longer version appears on *Medium*, 29 July 2019 at: https://medium.com/@jodugb/searching-for-africa-in-african-studies-an-open-letter-to-teachers-of-africa-at-ucl-29a3a9d20eee.

[14] See for example, Njinga Mbandi, Queen of Ndongo and Matamba (now Angola) who took on the Portuguese invaders. Queen Mbandi also inspired the French writer Jean Louis Castilhon to publish, in 1769, an historical novel about her, *Zingha Reine d'Angola*, which UNESCO describes as the 'first to be written from an anti-colonialist standpoint' which caused 'quite a stir.' Described variously as rich, a cultivated woman of letters, a consummate diplomat paradoxical and complex, Queen Njinga does much to challenge stereotypes of Africans and the powerlessness of African women in particular. UNESCO *Njinga Mbandi: Queen of Ndongo and* Matamba (Paris, UNESCO and Collins, 2015). See 94–95 for a portrait and history of the novel.

[15] T Achiume, 'Migration as Decolonization' (2019) 71 *Stanford Law Review* 1509, 1567.

II. The African Diasporas – Historical Background

A. Africans in Europe

There are, of course, as many starting points as there are academic disciplines involved in telling the stories of how Africans came to be abroad. The scientific consensus is that Africa, which birthed humankind, is the departure point for early human migration.[16] Peter Fryer begins his seminal history of Black people in Britain by noting that the African presence in Britain predates the arrival of the English.[17] He recounts how a division of Moors defended Hadrian's Wall in the third century. The Museum of London has a display of the truncated skeleton of an African man dating from Roman times.[18] The historian David Olusoga details archeological excavations in the North of England which showed that in York, people of Afro-Roman descent made up about 11–12 per cent of the population. They can be found in both poor and wealthier burial sites, meaning that they occupied all strata of society.[19] Bernadine Evaristo's prose poetry romp, *The Emperor's Babe* tells the story of a young Nubian girl, whose parents were 'refugees from the Sudan'[20] who had a relationship with Septimius Severus, the first Libyan Roman Emperor.[21] The Anglo-Saxon ancestors of 'the English' arrived in Britain in the fifth century after the Romans had withdrawn.

In a report written after a visit to Italy in 2015, the UN Working Group on People of African Descent begins by noting the long history of Africans within the territories of Europe. It traces the presence of Africans to the early Renaissance period. Slavery was a part of Italian life before the country reunified in 1861, with city states being actively involved in the slave trade. The report continues:

> Sub-Saharan Africans appeared in northern Italian records as early as in the mid-fourteenth century. Until the mid-fifteenth century, Italian merchants from the northern

[16] D Reich, *Who we are and how we got here: Ancient DNA and the new science of the human past* (New York, Pantheon Books, 2018). Cf J Kahn et al, 'How not to talk about race and genetics', Open letter written by 67 scientists and researchers in response to David Reich's book, on Buzzfeed Opinion 30 March 2018.

[17] P Fryer, *Staying Power: The History of Black People in Britain* (London, Pluto Press, 2018 [1984]). See also A Curry (with photographs by R Benali), 'Who were the first Europeans?' (August 2019) 236(2) *National Geographic* 94, 100, 104.

[18] R Redfern, 'The Surprising Diversity of Roman London', Museum of London Docklands, *Roman Dead Exhibition*, 1 July 2018 at: https://www.museumoflondon.org.uk/discover/surprising-diversity-roman-london-docklands.

[19] D Olusoga, *Black and British: A Forgotten History* (London, Macmillan, 2016) 29–32. The 11–12% figure at 31. Olusoga acknowledges his gratitude to Fryer and sets out on his own journey to write the histories of black people across three continents. D Olusoga, ibid, xix–xxii, 30. A reconstruction of the excavated 'Beachy Head Woman', a woman of African descent who was found in Eastbourne in the Southern part of England, can be seen in his book – plate 2 between pages 138–39. See also 32–33 on her history and discovery. See also D Olusoga, 'Black and British A Forgotten History: First Encounters', *BBC 4*, last aired 23 May 2018.

[20] B Evaristo, *The Emperor's Babe* (London, Hamish Hamilton, 2001) 25.

[21] B Evaristo (2001) 11, 25–26, 41, 128, 154.

> part of the peninsula acquired enslaved Africans mainly from Muslim merchants. Enslaved Africans were present in southern Italy much earlier, owing in part to the commercial and political relations between Sicily and the Kingdom of Aragon and to the proximity of the island to the markets of North Africa. It is estimated that Africans in Sicily accounted for half of the servile population in the sixteenth century. Their numbers decreased sharply thereafter, as slave traders directed their supplies of captive Africans increasingly to the colonies in the Western hemisphere. To replace that source of slaves, traders in Sicily turned to Muslims from the Maghreb.[22]

The Scottish poet William Dunbar records a black lady having appeared in a tournament featuring a black knight and black lady during the reign of James IV. She was among the Africans to be found in Edinburgh in the early sixteenth century.[23] She is not the only 'dark lady'. Literary scholars have argued the toss about whether the dark lady in Shakespeare's sonnets 127–154 was North African, or merely that she had dark hair. Is black here used as a metaphor for a fallen woman or a temptress, or as a literal physical description?[24] (The current bidding is on her being a dark-haired paramour).

Also remembered is the celebrated violin virtuoso George Bridgetower, who lived from 1779 to 1860. Described by Classic fm as 'English',[25] Bridgetower was in fact the son of a Polish mother and an African-Caribbean father, who can thus best be described as Afro-European, perhaps making him one of Johny Pitts' early Afropeans.[26] He was born in Poland but moved around Europe, living in Vienna and Paris as well as London. He was a composer in his own right and played in many prestigious venues. So talented was he, that Beethoven was moved to dedicate the sonata that they had played together to Bridgetower (*Sonata mulattica composta per il mulatto Brischdauer, gran passo e conpositore mulattico*). Unfortunately, they had a falling out and Beethoven withdrew the dedication, naming it after another violinist, Kreutzer, instead. Bridgetower played before royalty and with the renowned composers and musicians of his day. He died penniless in London where he is buried.[27]

[22] Report of the Working Group of Experts on People of African Descent on its mission to Italy, A/HRC/33/61/Add.1, 12 August 2016, para 6. See also paras 5, 7–11. The Working Group cites (at fn 2) TF Earle and KJP Lowe (eds), *Black Africans in Renaissance Europe* (Cambridge, CUP, 2005). The Working Group also identifies the ordination of an Ethiopian and a Congolese priest in 1513. Working Group on people of African descent – Italy para 7. See also Report of the Working Group of Experts on People of African Descent on its sixteenth session – Addendum – Mission to the Netherlands, A/HRC/30/56/Add.1, 27 July 2015, para 6 on Dutch slave history, particularly in the Caribbean.

[23] P Fryer (2018), n 17 above, 3.

[24] H Furness, 'Has Shakespeare's dark lady finally been revealed?', *Daily Telegraph*, 8 January 2013. S Frampton, 'In Search of Shakespeare's dark lady', *The Guardian*, 10 August 2013.

[25] Classic fm, 'George Bridgetower (1779–1860) and Beethoven: a troubled relationship' at: https://www.classicfm.com/composers/beethoven/guides/key-people-beethovens-music-and-life-george-bridge/.

[26] JB Wright, 'George Polgreen Bridgetower: An African Prodigy in England 1789–99' (1980) 66(1) *The Musical* Quarterly 65–82. J Pitts, *Afropean: Notes from Black Europe* (London, Allen Lane, 2019). The poet Rita Dove wrote *Sonata Mulattica* in honour of Bridgetower (New York, WW Norton & Company, 2010).

[27] AfriClassical.com, 'George Augustus Polgreen Bridgetower (1789–1860) at: www.AfriClassical.com. I am indebted to John Eekelaar for alerting me to the Bridgetower biography.

Miranda Kaufmann's book on black Tudors has multiple sightings of black Africans in sixteenth-century England.[28] One of the most famous is the depiction of a trumpeter in the royal court of Henry VIII, known as John Blanke. He is pictured on the Westminster Tournament Roll made to honour the birth of the (ill-fated – he died shortly after) son of Henry VIII and Catherine of Aragon. His is not the only example, for Kaufmann gathers examples of black children, seamstresses and men in artworks across Europe and beyond.[29] A particular favourite of mine is Cattelena of Almondsbury, a village seven miles from Bristol in England. Her name suggests she came by way of Spain. She, an African woman or negra, lived alone, but, Kaufmann insists she was by no means the only African to be found living in the rural areas.[30] She owned a cow which she milked, and produced butter for sale. I am particularly drawn to Cattelena who, Kaufmann tells us,

> was not a wealthy woman, yet neither was she a pauper. Her goods were valuable enough in total to be listed and reckoned by the authorities. At a time when Africans elsewhere in the world were themselves property, it is significant that she was the legal owner of anything at all. Her relative independence as a woman is also significant. Not only was she *free*, as in not enslaved, but she seems to have been free from service or any family obligation. Thanks to her cow, she was able to support herself.[31]

Significantly Kaufmann details that the lives of Tudors revolved around their parish so anyone coming from outside the parish would have been considered a stranger. She notes that Tudors were more likely to judge people by their 'religion or social class than by where they were born or the colour of their skin, though these categories did on occasion intersect.'[32] Indeed Kaufmann argues that the re-construction of Britain as an imperial nation in the nineteenth century may have led to a re-writing of earlier periods of history to fit into a mythical narrative of a country that was always strong, relevant and dominant. Tudor England was 'a small, relatively weak kingdom on the edge of Europe.'[33] Of imperial racial myth-making, she contends: 'These abominations, alongside the imperialism and scientific racism that followed, cast their shadows across almost every discussion of the history of Africans in Britain.'[34] Echoing Kaufmann is Andrew Curry who

[28] In an 'Author's Note' at the end of her book, Miranda Kaufmann identifies the many sources relied on and also the fact that others have also recorded histories of black people in Britain. M Kaufmann, *Black Tudors: The Untold Story* (London, Oneworld, 2017) 265–67. Her introduction also contains an overview of Afro-European stories at 1–6.

[29] M Kaufmann (2017). There are photographs of paintings between pages 184 and 185. See review (and some pictures), by Bidisha, 'Tudor, English and black – and not a slave in sight', *The Guardian*, 29 October 2017. See also A Hirsch on photographs of black women in Victorian Britain. A Hirsch, *Brit-ish: On Race, Identity and Belonging* (London, Jonathan Cape, 2018) Chapter 2 Origins – p 49 with preceding photograph.

[30] M Kaufmann (2017), n 28 above, 243–59.

[31] M Kaufmann (2017) 255, 256.

[32] M Kaufmann (2017) 4.

[33] M Kaufmann (2017) 3.

[34] M Kaufmann (2017) 3.

notes: 'In an era of debate over migration and borders, the science shows that Europe is a continent of immigrants and always has been.'[35]

Kwame Anthony Appiah, the Ghanaian-born philosopher, has uncovered the story of one of his forebears, Amo Afer (Amo the African). He left the African Gold Coast in 1707 on a Dutch West India Company ship.[36] The young boy was a 'gift' for the Duke of Brunswick-Wolfenbüttel who in turn handed Amo over to his son August Wilhelm. There he remained, being educated and cared for. Did Amo become a living experiment? If yes, what was the hypothesis? Appiah says we cannot know for sure, but it may have been: could this boy learn in the European way and contribute to scholarship? The answer was a resounding 'Yes'. Amo gained a first degree in law and then a master's, writing his thesis on the European law on slavery (entitled 'On the Law of the Moors'). He then went on to obtain a doctorate in philosophy, becoming the first black African to do so. His examiners referred to him as having an 'auspicious mind.' (Appiah, now arguably one of the most renowned philosophers and public intellectuals followed in his footsteps). In 1747 Amo returned to the Gold Coast. Appiah offers some thoughts on what might have motivated him to return. He cites the 'early stirring' of European racial tensions, marked in this case by a satirical play in which a young German woman refuses the advances of an African philosophy teacher resembling, and indeed named Amo. Appiah concludes his account with some thoughts of why Amo may have chosen to leave:

> It's impossible to wonder whether his was a flight from color consciousness, a retreat to a place where he would not be defined by his complexion. A place where Amo Afer could just be Amo again; where he didn't need to be *the* African. Indeed his odyssey asks us to imagine what he seems to have yearned for: a world free of racial fixations. It asks if we could ever create a world where color is merely a fact, not a feature and not a fate. It asks if we might not be better off if we managed to give up our racial typologies, abandoning a mistaken way of thinking that took off at just about the moment when Anton Wilhelm Amo was a well-known German philosopher at the height of his intellectual powers.[37]

While European colonialism, in Africa and beyond, is seen by some as central to the *modern* migration story, it is certainly not the only story. In the Persian folk story, 'The King's Ring' we learn: 'Now Queen Shah Banu had a slave girl called Zuhra who was as brown as a date, for she was from Africa.'[38]

[35] A Curry (with photographs by R Benali), 'The first Europeans weren't who you might think' (August 2019) 236(2) *National Geographic* 94, 100: https://www.nationalgeographic.com/culture/2019/07/first-europeans-immigrants-genetic-testing-feature/.

[36] KA Appiah, 'On the Kidnapped African Boy who Became a German Philosopher', *Literary Hub*, 29 August 2018.

[37] KA Appiah (2018).

[38] A Shah, 'The Shah's Ring' in A Shah, *Tales from the Bazaars of Arabia: Folk Stories from the Middle East* (London, Tauris Parke, 2008) 88–93, 89.

B. Slavery and Forced Migration

Slavery, which historically involved people of all ethnicities, but which came to be defined by Blackness, is discussed in books about history, ethics, law and literature, albeit with greater focus on the trans-Atlantic slave trade. One cannot hope to do justice to the vast literature on the trans-Atlantic slave trade. Suffice to note, that the UN Working Group on People of African Descent traces the history of slavery in the United States of America to the early seventeenth Century. Following a visit to the United States in 2016, its report notes that black slaves constituted: 'one fifth of the population of the American colonies by 1775.'[39]

In her novel, *Homegoing*, Yaa Gyasi shows how in what became Ghana, Black African groups raided the villages of other groups and then sold them on as slaves to Europeans. Simultaneously she engages the brutality and cruelty of the holding pens of the slave fortress and slave ships that carried people across the Atlantic. Her two sister protagonists are respectively the mistress of a British slaver at the slave fort while the other is enslaved and sent to the new world. The fates of their families unfurl through the life stories of their respective descendants.[40]

There is a raft of fictional literature on slavery with some of it based on fact. As noted in Chapter one, Toni Morrison's *Beloved* is based on the actual case of Margaret Garner who, having escaped slavery, killed her child, and tried to kill the others, rather than to see them returned to the plantation to suffer in slavery.[41] Her arrest and the challenge to the Fugitive Slave Laws, which said slaves must be returned to their owners, made her famous. In re-imagining Margaret Garner in fiction, Morrison rejected 'the dry legal form' preferring to use the 'imaginative space' of fiction to explore the idea of freedom. Through her heroine Sethe, Morrison is able to explore one of her central themes: how Black slave women were expected to give birth to many children, but were then denied the opportunity to be mothers to them, to parent them.[42]

The film '12 Years a Slave' was based on a non-fiction book of that name written by Solomon Northup, a freeman who was kidnapped and taken to Louisiana

[39] Report of the Working Group of Experts on People of African Descent on its mission to the United States of America, A/HRC/33/61/Add.2, 18 August 2016, para 6. Painter reminds us of the long history of the slave trade (race no object) including in ancient Greece. NI Painter, *The History of White People* (New York, WW Norton, 2010) 12–15.

[40] Y Gyasi, *Homegoing* (London, Vintage, 2017). See also A Mabanckou (translated by S Ardizzone), *Black Bazaar* (London, Serpent's Tail, 2012) 225. Afua Hirsch, herself of British-Ghanaian heritage, visits Elmina, the slave fort and muses on her own history as the descendant of a slaver. Her multi-generational story echoes the structure of Gyasi's novel. A Hirsch, *Brit-ish* (London, Jonathan Cape, 2018) 201 *et seq*. See also I Okojie, *Butterfly Fish* (London, Jacaranda, 2016).

[41] T Morrison, *Beloved* (London, Vintage, 2011). See also E Edugyan's, *Washington Black* (London, Serpent's Tail, 2018).

[42] T Morrison, 'Foreword' (2011) x–xi. Morrison contrasts this absence of choice with the discussions about a woman's right to choose when and whether to have children during the second wave of feminism, when she wrote *Beloved* (at x). See also P Rosenblatt *The Impact of Racism on African American Families: Literature as Social Science* (Abingdon, Routledge, 2014).

where he was enslaved for 12 years. During his enslavement he managed to get word of his fate back to his wife and friends via an abolitionist who visited his farm. They gathered evidence and supporting documents that he was a free man, leading to his release.[43] His first person account of slavery is told with calm detachment. There was an attempt to prosecute his kidnappers. He details how he 'was offered as a witness' but his testimony was said to be inadmissible 'solely on the ground that I was a coloured man – the fact of my being a free citizen of New York not being disputed.'[44] The slave dealers were acquitted. Solomon was reunited with his family, wrote the book and joined the Underground Railroad to help slaves escape to the North and Canada.

In a crowded field, Colson Whitehead's novel *Underground Railroad* stands out. A multi-vocal novel, it takes us from capture, where the slaver expresses a preference for mixing the groups to prevent communication between kin which might foment rebellion; to life on two slave plantations run by brothers with very different temperaments. The novel shows us how the slaves sought to eke out some autonomy and dignity and to build a community in the midst of their misery. At its heart, the book is a tale of freedom and the longing to escape which is manifested through the journeys taken via the titular 'underground railway'. There is a depth and complexity to Whitehead's characterisation which moves beyond 'good' v. 'evil' to show the interactions and motivations of people of different races and indeed class and their inter-mingling in this period. Whitehead also includes allusions to the 'sin' pre-dating slavery; that is of the theft of land from and genocide of the original inhabitants. Far from being an aberration, slavery was yet another manifestation of white supremacy on which, he contends, the United States of America is founded. One of his characters observes: 'This nation shouldn't exist, if there is any justice in the world, for its foundations are murder, theft, and cruelty. Yet here we are.'[45] There is also within this novel an acknowledgement of how the legacy of slavery continues to impact the lives of people of African descent. This includes the transmission of status privilege accorded to lighter skinned Black people who went on to found the Black 'upper class' exemplified by Margo Jefferson in her memoir *Negroland*.[46]

Those familiar with the ending of slavery in the United States will recognise that freed slaves were given 40 acres and a mule. This was as a result of a Special Field Order No 15 given by Union General Sherman in 1865; the land on the Georgia coast, and surplus army mules were to be given to freed slaves to compensate for their unpaid labour during slavery.[47] Those familiar with the work of the

[43] S Northrup, *12 Years a Slave: A True Story of Betrayal, Kidnap and Slavery* (London, Hesperus Press, 2013) 192–93. For the film directed by S McQueen, *Twelve Years a Slave*, Fox Searchlight Pictures, 2013.

[44] S Northup (2013) 195.

[45] C Whitehead, *Underground Railroad* (London, Fleet, 2016) 285.

[46] M Jefferson, *Negroland: A Memoir* (London, Granta, 2016).

[47] HL Gates Jr, 'The Truth Behind "40 Acres and a Mule"', *The Root*, 7 January 2013. The date is given as 1/07/13 which I have 'translated' from American into British dating.

director Spike Lee will recognise that he named his film production company Forty Acres and a Mule Filmworks in tribute to his forebears.[48] In his 2017 novel, *Exit West*, Mohsin Hamid connects the historical narratives of oppression of African Americans during slavery with that of migrants today. The importance of land and the ability to earn a livelihood find expression in Hamid's novel in which he muses about a life where:

> In exchange for their labour in clearing terrain and building infrastructure and assembling dwellings from prefabricated blocks, migrants were promised forty metres and a pipe: a home on forty square metres of land and a connection to all the utilities of modernity.[49]

Hamid's forty metres and a pipe analogy points to the debt owed to both those who were enslaved and also migrants whose labour is used freely but for whom the rewards are few. Hamid also shows the linkages between the dispossession of slavery and ongoing limits to life opportunities of the ancestors of those brought by force.

The report of the UN Working Group of Experts on People of African Descent details the ongoing impact of slavery as manifested by disproportionately high rates of imprisonment of African Americans, particularly men, and the lack of educational and employment opportunities for African Americans as well as poorer health outcomes.[50] The Working Group concludes its report by noting:

> Despite the positive measures, the Working Group remains extremely concerned about the human rights situation of African Americans. In particular, the legacy of colonial history, enslavement, racial subordination and segregation, racial terrorism and racial inequality in the United States remains a serious challenge, as there has been no real commitment to reparations and to truth and reconciliation for people of African descent. Contemporary police killings and the trauma that they create are reminiscent of the past racial terror of lynching. Impunity for State violence has resulted in the current human rights crisis and must be addressed as a matter of urgency.[51]

[48] 40 Acres and a Mule Filmworks, Brooklyn, New York, established 1978 at: http://www.40acres.com. Apparently the assassination of Abraham Lincoln resulted in the land being repossessed and returned to the previous owners.

[49] M Hamid, *Exit West* (London, Penguin, 2017) 167–68.

[50] See Report of UN Working Group of People of African Descent, US visit, 2016, A/HRC/33/61/Add.2, paras 20–35, 43–55. Also damning is the Report of the Special Rapporteur on extreme poverty and human rights, Phillip Alston, on his mission to the United States of America, A/HRC/38/33/Add.1, 4 May 2018, paras 54, 55, 57, 59, 66. See also CERD General Comment 34 on Racial Discrimination against People of African Descent, CERD/C/GC/34, 3 October 2011.

[51] UN Working Group of Experts on People of African Descent, A/HRC/33/61/ Add.2, para 68. While we often focus on the United States it is as well to remember the continued impact of the slave trade on the lives of Afro-Brazilians. N Naro, *A Slave's Place, A Master's World: Fashioning Dependency in Rural Brazil* (London, Bloomsbury, 2016) (new edition), N Naro, R Sansi-Roca, D Treece (eds), *Cultures of the Lusophone Black Atlantic* (London, Palgrave, 2007). *Alyne da Silva Pimentel v Brazil* CEDAW C/49/D/17/2008, 10 August 2011 (on the inadequate hospital treatment afforded to a pregnant Afro-Brazilian woman, which led to her death.)

Disturbingly, slavery continues to exist in twenty-first-century Africa. Mauritania is constantly sanctioned for this.[52] In a report written after a visit to Niger, the UN Special Rapporteur on Contemporary Forms of Slavery identifies the particular vulnerability of refugees, returnees, Malians and Nigerians to slavery. The report also focuses on the continuation of descent-based slavery and the gendered impact of negative stereotypes on women. Issues of access to justice are addressed. The Special Rapporteur recommended that religious leaders issue a fatwa to make clear that slavery is not sanctioned by Islam.[53] In 2017 there was an outcry when CNN showed footage of black African migrants being sold for the purpose of unpaid work in a Libyan market.[54]

Slavery is also discussed in children's books. Popular is the historically accurate series by Caroline Lawrence, *The Roman Mysteries.* Set in Roman times – hence the title – it has 17 scrolls (volumes) and details the lives of four very different children who come together to solve mysteries. One, Nubia, is an African girl whose parents have been killed and who is separated from her brother. She is bought in a slave market by one of the other children, Flavia, assisted by her father. Flavia frees Nubia and they become firm friends. The other two children are Jonathan, a boy whose family have left Jerusalem, and Lupus, an orphan who has had his tongue cut out by his avaricious uncle. The books provide a very good overview of the Roman law of family, property and wills.[55]

Nina Bawden's children's book *Carrie's War* about two siblings evacuated to the countryside during the Second World War, has a narrative about a skull that is on display in 'the big house'. It is said to be the skull of an unhappy African child who was brought to the house as a slave.[56] He died in England within a year of arrival, but not before putting a curse on the house. The myth arose that if anyone ever removed his skull, some ill would occur. Towards the end of the story, the skull is thrown into the river and the house burns down-a metaphor (I think) for the unsettled spirit.[57]

[52] Special Rapporteur on Contemporary forms of Slavery, Mission to Mauritania, A/HRC/15/20/ADD.2, 15 August 2010. See also UN Special Rapporteur on Contemporary forms of Slavery, Report on a Mission to Niger, A/HRC/30/35/Add.1, 30 July 2015 (at para 73).

[53] Special Rapporteur on Slavery, visit to Niger, A/HRC/30/35/Add.1 (2015) paras 73 and 103. The Rapporteur raised the case of *Koraou v The Republic of Niger*, Judgment No ECW/CCJ/JUD/06/08 of 27 October 2008 where Niger was found to have violated the prohibition on slavery by failing to protect a young woman who had been forcibly married and impregnated by her 'owner-master'.

[54] D Kirkpatrick, 'Europe wanted migrants stopped. Now some are being sold as slaves', *New York Times*, 30 November, 2017.

[55] C Lawrence, *The Roman Mysteries* (London, Orion, 2001).

[56] Black African slave children were seen as exotic accoutrements to rich families who sought them out for their households. See UN Working Group on People of African Descent, Italy Report, 2016, para 6 identifying how Isabella d'Este and her family sought out these children who were seen as 'objects of curiosity'. See also the colour plate (plate 8) of Lady Tollemache and her servant, dated 1861, and also another labelled 'Town Miss' (plate 11) in D Olusoga (2016), n 19 above, colour plates between pages 138 and 139.

[57] N Bawden, *Carrie's War* (London, Puffin, 2010 [1973]).

III. Contemporary Migration Patterns and Responses

A. Why do People Migrate and How do they Decide Where to Go?

> We move when it is intolerable to stay where we are. We move because of environmental stresses and physical dangers and the small-mindedness of our neighbors – and to be who we wish to be, to seek what we wish to seek.[58]

Of the many reasons identified by Mohsin Hamid (quotation above) for migration, the one seen as most legitimate is war and the need for safety and security. Climate-induced movement is increasingly recognised as a global challenge, but not always seen as entitling one to protection.[59] There are more prosaic reasons for moving, not least the human urge for self-improvement (via education) and to guarantee a better life for one's children and other dependants.[60] This last one is often disparagingly called 'economic migration' and is seen as less justified, especially for Black and Brown people coming from the Global South. Excoriating people for seeking a better life, ignores the purpose of European colonisation which was an economic project of self-enrichment and, by implication, self-improvement.[61] Amir, who is ethnographer Shahram Khosravi's 'smuggler-informant' makes the link between the West's propping up of corrupt dictators and the assisted plunder of national resources, and people moving to the richer states, 'because they want to come to see where their wealth has ended up.'[62]

Achiume puts forward a theory of migration as decolonisation. She argues that it is time to assert the inter-dependence of the colonisers and their former subjects by reconceptualising sovereignty and self-determination.[63] In the first part of her article she identifies the many ways in which colonialism benefitted the West while eroding any notions of African autonomy or self-determination. Her 'migration as decolonisation' thesis is not a claim for open borders. Rather, she argues for a

[58] M Hamid, 'We are all Migrants' (2019) 236(2) *National Geographic* 15, 16.

[59] OAU Convention Governing Specific Aspects of Refugee Problems in Africa, 1969, OAU Doc CAB/LEG/24.3. T Abebe, A Abebe and M Sharpe, 'After 50 years, Africa's refugee policy still leads', *ISS Today*, 20 June 2019; CEDAW General Recommendation 37 Gender-related dimensions of disaster risk reduction in the context of climate change, CEDAW/C/GC/37, 7 February, 2018, paras 73–78.

[60] D Trilling, *Lights in the Distance: Exile and Refuge at the Borders of Europe* (London, Picador, 2018) 114, 124–26. See also M Hamid (2019), n 58 above, 15–20.

[61] W Rodney, *How Europe Underdeveloped Africa* (Oxford, Pambazuka Press, 2012). P Gatrell, *The Making of the Modern Refugee* (Oxford, OUP, 2015) 226–27 and 294.

[62] S Khosravi, *'Illegal' Traveller: An Auto-Ethnography of Borders* (Basingstoke, Palgrave Macmillan, 2010) 108.

[63] T Achiume, 'Migration as Decolonization' (2019) 71 *Stanford Law Review* 1509–76.

'logic and ethics of imperial interconnection (specifically neo-colonial interconnection.)'[64] She goes on to note that if this stance is adopted then:

> What is widely condemned and reviled as economic migration when undertaken by Third World migrants should instead be understood as radical political action of Third World persons seeking to formalize their status as co-sovereigns of the First World through citizenship.[65]

In short, Achiume seems to be suggesting that the freedom of movement of Third World people has been 'pre-paid'. It is underwritten by 'the beneficiaries of neo-colonial advantages.'[66]

Migration flows reflect past contacts or conquest. The patterns of migration from Africa to Europe reveal what we, as graduate students in Oxford, jokingly referred to as 'the Empire paying a return visit'.[67] My fellow Oxford peer Kwadwo Osei-Nyame quotes from Kwame Nkrumah, addressing Africans in Britain thus:

> You are in Britain not by chance or by choice; you are in Britain for historical reasons; you are in Britain because Britain colonised you and reduced the various countries to which you belong to the level of colonial status. You are in Britain because British neo-colonialism is strangling you in your home countries. Where else can you go to seek survival, except in the 'mother country', which has enslaved you?[68]

The immigrant populations of various European states reflect the reciprocal visits from former colonies: France has a disproportionately large number of North Africans and others from what was Francophone West Africa, while Britain hosts people from the states that now make up the Commonwealth, and Belgium has many Congolese, Rwandan and Burundians.[69] Technology and improved transport links have done much to open up the world, so now even unsuccessful colonising states like Italy end up hosting many Africans from Somalia, Ethiopia and Eritrea.[70] Italy is also host to a high number of Nigerian women who are trafficked for prostitution. There is also the issue of opportunity. Malta, Greece and Spain, by virtue of geographic proximity, have joined Italy as the landing posts of many people coming on boats, ships and coast guard boats after being rescued.

[64] T Achiume (2019) 1509, 1567.

[65] T Achiume (2019) 1509,1567.

[66] T Achiume (2019) 1509, 1567.

[67] P Gatrell, *The Making of the Modern Refugee* (Oxford, OUP, 2015) 226–27 and 294. T Achiume (2019), n 63 above, 1501, 1569. The novelist Alain Mabanckou suggests that his African brothers living in Paris take a different approach to revenge; 'They stripped us of our primary resources, so we've got to steal their treasures, and by that I mean their women!' Rather ungallantly he goes on: 'So ditch that fat-arsed sun-roasted woman of yours and bag a pretty blonde with blue or green eyes …' A Mabanckou (translated by S Ardizzone), *Black Bazaar* (London, Serpent's Tail, 2012) 70.

[68] K Nkurumah, *Revolutionary Path* (London, Panaf, 1973) 431, as cited by K Osei-Nyame Jnr in 'Images of London in African Literature: Ama Ata Aidoo's *Our Sister Killjoy* and Dambudzo Marachera's *The Black Insider*' in L Phillips, (ed), *The Swarming Streets. Twentieth-Century Literary Representations of London* (New York: Rodopi, 2011) 175, at 190.

[69] A Mabanckou (translated by S Ardizzone) (2012) 225–30 (ironic take on colonialism).

[70] Working Group on People of African Descent, Report on Mission to Italy, A/HRC/33/61/Add.1, 2016, para 10. The Working Group also notes that since the 1980s Italy has been the landing post for many African migrants coming on boats (at paras 11, 18,19).

In Ejorh's research on African migration to Ireland, some of his respondents identified the Catholic link and reminded him that there had been Irish missionaries who had converted them. One migrant from Sierra Leone said that, being Catholic, he felt that: 'I would get a good reception … So this spiritual link between the Irish and us was a huge influence for me.' Other 'pull' factors included language – it is easier to migrate to a country where you already speak the language. Finally, safety was said to be a consideration, Ireland not being in the news for violence or terrorist-related activities.[71] There was, for those in the know (until the Irish changed their constitution), the added pull of the granting of citizenship to any child born in Ireland which would then open up an avenue for the mother/parents to bring a claim for the right to family life under article 8 of the European Convention for the Protection of Human Rights and Fundamental Freedoms.[72]

Sometimes new political alliances lead to changed patterns of migration, so after the genocide in 1994, Rwanda asked, and was invited to join the British Commonwealth, leading to an increase in the number of Rwandans in Britain. The Cold War, combined with anti-colonial struggles, led to many Africans heading to China and the Eastern bloc (Soviet Union) and Cuba for education and training.[73] Most returned. China is currently one of the biggest investors' on the African continent, preferred by many governments because it does not indulge in one-way lectures about human rights.[74]

Occasionally one sees a return to colonial patterns of migration so that the collapsing economy of Portugal has contrasted sharply with the vastly improved fortunes of its former colonies, leading many Portuguese to seek work and a better quality of life in Angola and Mozambique. A Portuguese political scientist in Huchu's novel *The Maestro, The Magistrate & The Mathematician* says ruefully:

> I have a special interest in Portugal's African colonies, *ex colonies*. As you know, we were not as successful as the English or the French in Africa, but more successful than the Germans and the Belgians, and equally as barbaric as the rest. We only had a handful of colonies. Now the Mozambicans are leaving us, they want to join the Commonwealth. We have nothing to offer them. Even the Brazilians tower over us, he says with a dry laugh.[75]

There is also irony in the fact that Germany – which, having lost the First World War in 1918, was forced to forfeit its colonies in the Treaty of Versailles, 1919 – has

[71] T Ejorh, 'Modern African Migrations to Ireland: Patterns and Contexts' (2012) 38 *Journal of Ethnic and Migration Studies* 577, 587–91.

[72] European Convention for the Protection of Human Rights and Fundamental Freedoms, 4 November 1950, ETS 5.

[73] Akala, *Race & Class in the Ruins of Empire* (London, Two Roads, 2018) 214. Akala gives an account of the Cuban contribution to liberation struggles and also notes that Cuba was the first foreign country visited by Mandela on his release from prison. He thanked President Castro for his support in the anti-apartheid struggle.

[74] L Hilsum, 'We Love China' (2006) 92 *Granta* 233. See also T Webster, 'China's Human Rights Footprint in Africa' (2013) 50 *Columbia Journal of Transnational Law* 626, available at: http://scholarlycommons.law.case.edu/faculty_publications/620. See also the rejoinder of J Gathi, 'Beyond China's Human Rights Exceptionalism in Africa: Leveraging Science, Technology and Engineering for Long-Term Growth' (2013) 51 *Columbia Journal of Transnational Law* 664.

[75] T Huchu, *The Maestro, the Magistrate & The Mathematician* (Edinburgh, Parthian, 2015) 161.

proved, with states such as Sweden which never colonised Africa, to be the most generous European host of refugees and migrants from the non-European world, including Africa.[76,77] However, like other European states, Germany has proved resistant to the demand for compensation made by the descendants of the Herero and Nama people for the genocide between 1904–08 during the German colonisation of what is now Namibia. This genocide is said to have been the precursor to the 1939–1945 genocide in Europe for which compensation *has* been paid.[78] Statements of regret have been offered by the German government together with a pledge to continue to give 'aid' to the Namibian state.

B. Post-Colonial 'Pick and Mix': Assimilation, Integration/Multi-culturalism and the Issue of Identity

It is interesting to see how the colonial legal method of governing the colonised populations has continued in domestic policy. Using John Berry's typology, Eekelaar identifies the following models that may be followed by minorities:

(i) Assimilation (where the individual abandons his/her cultural values in favour of those of the host community);
(ii) integration, or 'biculturalism' (where the individual retains his/ her cultural values, but also places importance on relations with the host community);
(iii) marginalization (where the individual becomes distant from both sets of values);
(iv) separatism (where the individual identifies with only his/her community and values).[79]

[76] Kunzig, R (with photographs by R Hammond), 'The New Europeans: Voices from a changing continent', *National Geographic*, October 2016: https://www.nationalgeographic.com/magazine/2016/10/ It features a photo gallery with people who have left their countries, voluntarily or to seek asylum, speaking, almost all positively, about their reception (83–99) at: https://www.nationalgeographic.com/magazine/2016/10/europe-immigration-muslim-refugees-portraits/ There is also a feature on Germany which has taken on the most refugees by Robert Kunzig at 100–115.). African states also absorb most of the refugees within the region.

[77] A Betts and P Collier, *Refuge: Transforming a Broken Refugee System* (London, Penguin, 2017) 42. Within Africa, Uganda, Kenya and Chad host large refugee populations. B. Rawlence *City of Thorns: Nine Lives in the World's Largest Refugee Camp* (London, Portobello Books, 2016). It is worth noting that the most generous states are outside the European Union: Jordan, Lebanon, Turkey, Thailand, Nepal.

[78] D Olusoga, *The Kaiser's Holocaust: Germany's Forgotten Genocide and the Colonial Roots of Nazism* (London, Faber and Faber, 2011). See also M Mamdani, *When Victims become killers: Colonialism, Nativism and the Genocide in Rwanda* (Princeton NJ, Princeton University Press, 2001). J Sarkin, *Colonial Genocide and Reparations Claims in the 21st Century. The Socio-Legal Context of Claims under International Law by the Herero against Germany for Genocide in Namibia, 1904–1908* (Santa Barbara, Praeger, 2008). Equally problematic is the Belgian legacy in Congo captured well by Adam Hoschfeld in *King Leopold's Ghost: A Story of Greed, Terror and Heroism in Colonial Africa* (London, Pan, 2012). Barbara Kingsolver's novel, *The Poisonwood Bible* (London, Faber and Faber, 2013) about an American missionary and his wife and daughters in 1950s Congo documents the build-up to independence, relations between the races and the assassination of Patrice Lumumba.

[79] J Eekelaar, 'Children between Cultures', (2004) 18(2) *International Journal of Law, Policy and the Family* 178, 180. J Berry, U Kim, S Power, M Young and M Bujaki, (1989) 'Acculturation attitudes in plural Societies' (1989) 38 *Applied Psychology: An International Review* 185–206, cited by J Eekelaar.

It is of course self-evident that the minority may not be the decision-makers with respect to which approach is acceptable to the majority. Migrants may, and do, take all four positions. There is no 'one' community position, whatever else self-appointed community leaders may assert.

British multi-culturalism, itself a contested term, is in many ways a modified reformulation of its colonial policy of indirect rule.[80] One reading is that indirect rule was the British colonial acknowledgement of the limits of its ability to exercise total power.[81] Under Direct Rule, colonial policy had tried to dictate everything, the familial, social, economic and of course political spheres.[82] Over time it became clear that there were neither the resources nor the will to control everything.[83] Focusing on personal status law, it was decided to allow the governed populations some latitude in running their own courts and regulating family law. This was subject to the proviso that some behaviours – judged by the British to be repugnant to natural justice, morality and good conscience – were not to be permitted.

To varying degrees, the post-colonial British approach to non-indigenes has been to allow limited latitude in customs and practices.[84] This has included permitting the slaughter of animals without stunning to meet religious stipulations, and permitting Sikhs to be exempt from health and safety headwear if it cannot be fitted onto the turban. There are limits to the latitude.[85] In *Akhter v Khan*[86] it was

[80] The literature on the many meanings of multi-culturalism is huge. B Parekh, *Rethinking Multiculturalism: Cultural Diversity and Political Theory* (Boston, Harvard, 2002); S Hall, *They Ain't no Black in the Union Jack: The Cultural Politics of Race and Nation* (Michigan, University of Chicago Press, 1991); T Modood, *Multiculturalism*, 2nd edn (London, Policy, 2013). On personal law and culture in England and Wales, see J Eekelaar, *Family Law and Personal Life* (Oxford, OUP, 2017) 173–78.

[81] Ambreena Manji would argue that indirect rule can be seen as an attempt to amplify colonial power. Relying on the work of Chanock and Hobsbawm and Ranger, Manji explores the creativity of colonial officials in inventing chieftaincies where none had existed before and in refashioning customary law to better serve the needs of the exercise of colonial power during the period of indirect rule. A Manji, '"Like a Mask Dancing": Law and Colonialism in Chinua Achebe's Arrow of God' (2002) 27(4) *Journal of Law and Society* 626, 633–37. T Ranger, 'The Invention of Tradition' in E Hobsbawm and T Ranger, *The Invention of Tradition in Colonial Africa* (Cambridge, CUP, 1983) 211; M Chanock, *Law, Custom and Social Order: The Colonial Experience in Malawi and Zambia* (Cambridge, CUP, 1985).

[82] F Lugard, *The Dual Mandate in British Tropical Africa: Methods of Ruling Native Races* (Edinburgh, Blackwood, 1922) 193–213. T Ranger, 'The Invention of Tradition' in E Hobsbawm and T Ranger, *The Invention of Tradition in Colonial Africa* (Cambridge, CUP, 1983) 211.

[83] HF Morris and JS Read, *Indirect Rule and the Search for Justice* (Oxford, Clarendon Press, 1972).

[84] An early proponent was S Poulter, *English law and Ethnic Minority Customs* (Oxford, Butterworths, 1986). There are multiple perspectives: P Shah and W Menski (eds), *Migration, Diasporas and Legal Systems in Europe* (Abingdon, Routledge-Cavendish, 2006); P Shah, M-C Foblets and M Rohe, *Family Religion and Law. Cultural Encounters in Europe* (Farnham, Ashgate, 2014); M Malik, 'Family law in diverse societies' in J Eekelaar and R George (eds), *Routledge Handbook of Family Law and Policy* (New York, Routledge, 2014) 424–38; F Ahmed, 'Remedying Personal Law Systems' (2016) 30(3) *International Journal of Law, Policy and the Family* 248–73.

[85] Research by Oomen and Chin points to a changed political climate in states that were formerly open to multiculturalism. They now favour a more assimilationist-integration model. Oomen notes how the passing of the Civic Integration Act in the Netherlands meant that immigrants had to pass an exam 3½ years after arrival. Passing the exam is a pre-condition for naturalisation. B Oomen, *Rights for Others: The Slow Home-Coming of Human Rights in the Netherlands* (Cambridge, CUP, 2014) 68–72, 69. See also R Chin, *The Crisis of Multiculturalism in Europe: A History* (Princeton NJ, Princeton University Press, 2017).

[86] *Akhter v. Khan* [2020] EWCA Civ 122.

held that non-registered Sharia marriages would not be recognised in England. Their religious validity in Islam was irrelevant to their legal recognition unless the parties had followed the registration requirements in the Marriage Act 1949.

By way of contrast from British indirect rule, a pillar of French colonial policy was assimilation.[87] To become a French citizen was to learn the language and follow French culture, preferably renouncing African cultural practices. In this way, one could be assimilated and join the elite. Post-colonial France has maintained this myth, so émigrés from former French colonies are invited to give up the ways of the old countries and to embrace the French way of doing things. While the official reason is that it eliminates differences because 'all are one', in reality Delphy notes that the price paid by the immigrant population is much higher.[88] The norms that ostensibly govern all are not, as asserted, culturally, religiously or indeed legally neutral. They are reflective of a white, Catholic heritage. While the British approach makes, or made, a pretence of reciprocity and mutual respect, the French do not.

In 2018, President Macron of France followed through on his predecessor's initiative to remove race from the definition of discrimination in the French Constitution, noting that all citizens, being French, were guaranteed equality.[89]

Also in 2018, the South African-born comedian and host of the Daily Show, Trevor Noah, expressed pleasure that an African team had won the 2018 football World Cup. France had won. Noah was reflecting the fact that the large cohort of players in the French team were of African descent. Noah also tweeted a drawing of a boat full of African migrants handing the World Cup to France. Furious, the French Ambassador to the United States responded that the team were French, as France treated all its citizens equally. He accused Noah of racism in assuming that only white people could be French. Reflecting his own duality, Noah responded: 'When I am saying, "They are African," I am not saying it as a way to exclude them from their Frenchness, but using it as a way to include them in my Africanness.'[90]

[87] H Oludare Idowu, 'Assimilation in 19th Century Senegal' (1969) 34 *Cahiers d'Etudes Africaines* 194–218; F Snyder, 'Colonialism and the Legal Form: The Creation of Customary Law in Senegal' (1981) 19 *Journal of Legal Pluralism* 49. Echoing Ngwena's nativist theory, there was a countervailing movement – Negritude – espoused by Leopold Senghor, seen by many as laying the foundations for post-colonial theory. C Thiam, *Return to the Kingdom of Childhood: Re-envisioning the Legacy and Philosophical Relevance of Negritude* (Columbus OH, Ohio State University Press, 2016).

[88] C Delphy (translated by D Broder), *Separate and Dominate: Feminism and Racism after the war on terror* (London, Verso, 2015) 15–35.

[89] A Lentin and V Amiraux, 'Francois Hollande's Misguided Move: Taking "Race" out of the Constitution', *The Guardian*, London, 12 February 2013. See also R Diallo, 'France's Dangerous Move to Remove "Race" from its Constitution', *Washington Post*, 13 Jul 2018. It is worth noting that perceptions of race/racism and racial identity are contested within migrant communities. E Mudimbe-Boyi, 'Black France: Myth or Reality? Problems of Identity and Identification' in T Keaton, T Denean Sharpley-Whiting and T Stovall (eds), *Black France* (Durham NC, Duke University Press, 2012) 17, 20–27. In the same volume, see also, F Constant, '"Black France" and the National Identity Debate: How Best to be Black and French', 123, 128–38.

[90] BBC News, 'Trevor Noah defends "Africa won the World Cup" joke' *BBC News*, 19 July 2018.

There has been marked growing restiveness among some migrant populations, who are faced with the demands that they should integrate, but find that there is no reciprocity of understanding or indeed equality of opportunities for them or their children. The children of those who migrated are not, like their parents, 'grateful' for the privilege of living in what they consider their homes. If they carry the national passport, then they expect to enjoy full citizenship rights. In *Afropean*, Pitts travels through Europe looking for people like himself – the products of the African diaspora and Europe, whom he calls Afropeans.[91] Pitts contrasts the sadness of the Africans he encounters in Moscow, with the anger he has found amongst those in Clichy-sous-Bois in France and the 'banter' of those in Sweden's Rikeby.[92]

Thoughtfully, Pitts examines his own privilege which leads him to think that perhaps it is he who is Afropean. He comes to the realisation that his African peers in some other European countries were 'more intelligibly *African in Europe*'.[93] They do not share the privilege of freedom of movement and protection that his British passport affords him, or the economic clout of the African sons and daughters of diplomats who attend private schools.[94] He is also insightful about the fact that it is he who inhabits a liminal space. While he seeks blackness as an act of solidarity, for his African peers being black is 'normal' as they are the majority in their homelands. Pitts realises that, for all their apparent misery, the minority status of those in Moscow is short-term, lasting only as long as they need to stay to get their qualifications and return home. He reflects on the slipperiness of identity and community.[95]

Pitts' account of his experience as a Black British male in the twenty-first century must be contrasted with that of Olusoga, who grew up in 1980s Britain and has a Nigerian father and a white British mother, who writes:

> Almost every black or mixed-race person of my generation has a story of racial violence to tell. These stories range from humiliation to hospitalization … This oral history of twentieth century racial violence has never been collected or collated, but it is there and it its shocking. In 1984 my family … were driven out of our home by a sustained campaign of almost nightly attacks. For what seemed like many months, but was in fact only a few weeks, we lived in darkness, as the windows of our home were broken one by one, smashed by bricks and rocks thrown from an old cemetery just across the street.[96]

[91] J Pitts, *Afropean: Notes from Black Europe* (London, Allen Lane, 2019). L Black and S Sinha, 'Stealing a Dream: young migrants living through anti-immigrant times' *Open Democracy* blog, 8 August 2018. See also the book by the same authors, L Black and S Sinha with C Bryan, V Baraku and M Yembi, *Migrant City* (Abingdon, Routledge, 2015). The chapters in N Shukla (ed), *The Good Immigrant* (London, Unbound, 2016) also contain multiple examples of the British children of migrant parents feeling 'othered'. Powerful is Musa Okwongo, 'The Ungrateful Country' in N Shukla (ed), (2016) ibid, 224–34. See also E Eshun, *Black God of the Sun: Searching for Home in England and Africa* (London, Penguin, 2006).

[92] J Pitts (2019), n 91 above, 278.

[93] J Pitts (2019) 279.

[94] J Pitts (2019) 279.

[95] J Pitts (2019) 281.

[96] D Olusoga (2016), n 19 above, xvii.

Fictional literature also explores the multiplicities of migrant identities and communities and how they interact. In his novel, *The Maestro, The Magistrate & The Mathematician* Tendai Huchu shows Edinburgh-based black Zimbabweans clubbing together to pay for the funeral of the Maestro who we learn is a white Zimbabwean who has died in penury.[97] In arranging for his funeral rites, his countrymen claim him as their own and honour their obligations to him. In an interview, Huchu says he wanted to explore the 'indigeneity' question, as the Zimbabwean government had politicised race and belonging, so for the government, The Maestro would have been British and not Zimbabwean. However, although living in Edinburgh, he is disconnected from Scottish society, leaving his Zimbabwean 'kin' to claim him.[98]

In a different context, Alain Mabanckou, in *Black Bazaar*, set in Paris, highlights the inter-connectedness between the Congolese (Brazzaville) protagonist and the shopkeeper at the end of his road whom he refers to throughout as, 'the Arab on the corner.'[99] In turn, 'Arab on the corner', who is very generous and 'comradely', calls him 'my African brother.' Together they put the world to rights, with the 'Arab on the corner' declaiming that Africans are the only people who are not migrants, as they originated humanity.[100] In the face of challenges from Chinese and Pakistani incomers whom he perceives as a threat to his livelihood, the 'Arab on the corner' asserts the debt owed to them (Arab and African) by France. He recounts the many ways in which Africans and Arabs have helped the French, including by fighting in their armies when they did not have to. France, he proclaims, would collapse without them.[101] The 'Arab on the corner' reinforces

[97] T Huchu (2015), n 75 above.

[98] H Cousins and P Dodson-Katiyo, 'Zimbabweanness Today: An Interview with Tendai Huchu' in E Emenyonu (ed), *Diaspora & Returns in Fiction, African Literature Today 34* (Oxford, James Currey, 2016) 200, 202–3. T Huchu (2015), n 75 above, 271.

[99] A Mabanckou (translated by Sarah Ardizzone), *The Black Bazaar* (London, Serpent's Tail, 2012) 105. It is worth noting the very funny explanation, and colonial insight, into how the two Congos came to be after the Berlin Conference of 1884 where European powers carved Africa up between them. The disastrous impact, and African complicity, is also explored. At 232–39. On the failure and foibles of politicians see 72–76, 176–77 193, 207–16.

[100] A Mabanckou (translated by S Ardizanne) (2012) 108–9.

[101] A Mabanckou (translated by S Ardizanne) (2012) 114–15. The issue of Africans serving in colonial armies that discriminated against them is also explored in a short story by Makumbi. J Makumbi, 'Our Allies the Colonies' in JN Makumbi, *Manchester Happened* (London, Oneworld, 2019) 31–61. See also N Mohamed, *Black Mamba Boy* (London, Harper Collins, 2010); B Phillips, *Another Man's War: The Story of a Burma Boy in Britain's Forgotten Army* (London, Oneworld, 2014). Phillips' account of the service of Nigerian Isaac Fadoyebo in Burma and the reasons that he joined the British war effort remind me of my father's attempts to join the King's African Rifles to fight Hitler, who, he was told, had called black people 'baboons'. My father and his young peers were invited to help King George to defeat him. My grandfather who was illiterate, refused to signal his consent with a thumbprint. He pointed out the stupidity of fighting wars to defend the sovereignty of the people who were denying you your own. He was proved right – after the war black soldiers returned to poverty and discrimination. Even the war graves were classified into 'A' and 'B' sections, with the 'A' white graves, well-tended and the 'B' neglected. The contribution of black soldiers has until recently, been written out of history including in many of the remembrance celebrations held on 11 November every year. See also D Smith, 'They fought for Britain. In return they were given £10.', *The Guardian*, 2 September 2006.

the importance of strengthening solidarity between the Maghreb and Sub-Saharan Africa, but in so doing seeks to elide over difficult history:

> We are strangers to one another, which is why there are fools who claim that in the old days the Arabs forced their black African brothers into slavery. Can you believe lies like that? … But I say to Westerners that slavery is the West's story, it is not about us Arabs. We are all brothers and no one forces their own brothers into slavery …[102]

In a different conversation, the wonderfully named Hippocratic reminds his interlocutor that African chiefs sold other Africans, and also that Arabs were involved in slavery. Colonialism is painted as an act of benevolence, not exploitation.[103] Mabanckou cleverly shows the sensitivities still engaged by some subjects. He also challenges the idea of an homogenous 'African' or diasporic viewpoint. There are, he observes, other intra-ethnic tensions, including between people who are black. The differences can be because of colourism – a concept denoting the socio-cultural and economic privileges accorded to those with lighter coloured skins, such as the Franco-Ivorian character in whom the protagonist sees unearned privilege. Mabanckou also explains tensions linked to geography through the words and attitudes of the man from Martinique who is not keen on his African brothers. There are also hierarchies based on the length of migration, so the longer-term inhabitants look down on the new arrivals.[104] Mabanckou is an astute commentator on the changing tides of dominance and on the failures of the political classes. He references the political theories of Franz Fanon and weaves them into his satire, noting at one point that on the arrival of the Europeans in Africa, Africans, 'had to choose for their survival: a black skin or a white mask. And the cleverest amongst them chose the white mask because black skin is the curse of Ham.'[105]

While the leaders of some former colonising states have often tried to paint colonialism as benign, 'not that bad', or 'in the past', or indeed argued that colonialism had been positive,[106] those who were subjected to violence or dispossession have been more vocal in their disagreement and in seeking to demand that the colonial debt be acknowledged. Ranger identifies a tension between the claims of those from former colonies who look to Britain as a haven of human rights, bound to provide safety, with the practice of the Labour Government led by Tony Blair: 'As far as it was concerned colonialism was over and left no obligations.' He goes

[102] A Mabanckou (translated by S Ardizanne) (2012), n 99 above, 145.
[103] A Mabanckou (translated by S Ardizanne) (2012) 221–24, 225–29.
[104] A Mabanckou (translated by S Ardizanne) (2012) 8, 144. The intolerant Hippocratic is, like Fanon, from Martinique echoing Fanon's own analyses of intra-group tensions: ibid at 89. Like Mabanckou, Makumbi also picks up on intra-black differences with those settled for longer, usually West-Indians, perceiving themselves as 'more Western'. J Makumbi (2019), n 101 above, 'Our Allies the Colonies' 47.
[105] A Mabanckou (translated by S Ardizonne) (2012), n 99 above, 229. See also A Mabanckou (translated by H Stevenson), *Broken Glass* (London, Serpent's Tail, 2009/2011) 44. See also L Gordon, *What Fanon said: A Philosophical Introduction to his Life and Thought* (New York, Fordham University Press, 2015). D Olusoga (2016), n 19 above, 29.
[106] F Sevenzo, 'Viewpoint: Boris Johnson and his 'colonial views' on Africa', *BBC News*, 14 July 2016.

on that this repudiation includes the application of asylum policy, meaning that '"no special responsibility" is accepted for Zimbabwe or former Commonwealth colonies', leaving them to rely on human rights treaties and refugee law and not 'an unequally shared colonial history.'[107] Dembour highlights how, 'the institutional resistance to finding anything wrong with a colonial power abandoning or turning away from its former colonial subjects is of central importance when thinking about the human rights of immigrants.'[108]

The next section considers the resistance by the British state to addressing certain aspects of its imperial legacy. It starts with the case law brought in an attempt to right historic wrongs.

IV. Resistance and the Imperial Legacy

A. Encounters between British Hypocrisy and Claims for Restorative Justice and Dignity Restoration

The concepts of dignity takings and dignity restoration were developed by Bernadette Atuahene to explain the challenges of making right the wrongs of apartheid. She argues that apartheid stripped people of both their land and their dignity by dehumanising and infantilising them, which she calls 'dignity takings'. This created the need for 'dignity restoration' which requires both material compensation and processes that are affirming of people's humanity and which reinforce their agency.[109] Atuahene asks us to consider how the dignity of a group can be restored.[110] The cases that follow show how those affected have tried to demand dignity restoration.

(i) The Mau Mau *Case*

A claim for compensation was filed in 2011 in the London High Court by Kenyans who alleged that they had been sexually assaulted and tortured, including by

[107] T Ranger, 'The Narratives and Counter-narratives of Zimbabwean Asylum: female voices' (2005) 26 *Third World Quarterly* 405, 409.

[108] M-B Dembour, *When Humans become migrants* (Oxford, OUP, 2015) 94. See also 95. Much of Dembour's book focuses on how these colonial connections have been explicitly excluded from European human rights discourse and case law. See also N El-Nany, *(B)Ordering Britain: Law, Race and* Empire (Manchester, Manchester University Press, 2020). P Gopal, *Insurgent Empire: Anti Colonial Resistance and British Dissent* (London, Verso, 2019) vii–x, 1–32, 406–441 and M Goodfellow, *Hostile Environment: How Immigrants became Scapegoats* (London, Verso, 2019).

[109] B Atuahene, 'Dignity Takings and Dignity Restoration: Creating a New Theoretical Framework for Understanding Involuntary Property Loss and the Remedies Required' (2016) 41(4) *Law and Social Inquiry* 796.

[110] V Hans, 'Dignity Takings, Dignity Restoration: A Tort Law Perspective' (2017) 92 *Chicago-Kent Law Review* 715, 716.

castration, by British forces during the pro-independence, Mau-Mau resistance.[111] Their claims were supported by extensive archival material found and kept in British Foreign Office storage and in the Kew Gardens documentation centre.[112] Despite this, the British government tried to get the case dismissed before the merits could be considered. It argued that the international law of succession meant that the British government's legal liability had been expunged at the hand-over of power at independence. This stance was challenged on both legal and moral grounds. Archbishop Desmond Tutu berated the government for its reliance on legal technicalities: 'Responding with generosity to the plea of Kenyan victims is not a matter of legal niceties. No, it is about morality, about magnanimity and humanness, about compassion.'[113] The High Court ordered that the case should be heard, leading the British government to settle the claims.[114] It was unedifying to see a government which regularly lectures African states about the importance of upholding human rights and not torturing citizens itself trying to wriggle out of its obligations. The Foreign Secretary did eventually issue a statement in Parliament in which he expressed regret that the abuses had taken place. He acknowledged that Kenya's independence had been delayed. A memorial has since been constructed in Kenya.[115]

Adam Foulds has captured the brutality of the British Home Guard in Kenya at the time of the Mau Mau. His prose poem *The Broken Word* is told from the perspective of a young man-boy on the cusp of going to University, but spending a year with the Home Guard serving in Kenya.[116] It details the casual and vicious violence meted out to the Kenyans, including the rape of women and girls.[117] Those Mau Mau who have sworn the 'oath' are particularly brutalised. Five are sent for 'further interrogation' which is code for torture.

> Three weeks later two of the men came back,
> Wordless and unsteady, heavily edited. Between them:
> Nine fingers, two ears, three eyes, no testicles.

[111] *Mutua, Nzili, Nyingi, Mara and Ngondi v Foreign and Commonwealth Office* [2011] EWHC 1913.

[112] See also C Elkins, *Imperial Reckoning: The untold story of Britain's Gulag in Kenya* (New York, Henry Holt, 2005).

[113] Archbishop Tutu, quoted by Leigh Day, 'Historic judgment as UK Government loses court battle on Kenyan colonial torture', 21 July 2011, at: https://www.leighday.co.uk/News/2011/July-2011/Historic-judgment-as-UK-Government-loses-court-battle'. The French acknowledged that they had used torture during the Algerian war which lasted from 1954–1962. In 2018, President Macron issued an apology to the widow of Maurice Audin, a French dissenter who died in French detention in Algiers while formally acknowledging the use of systematic torture. A Chrisafis, 'France admits systematic torture during Algeria war for first time', *The Guardian*, London, 13 September 2018. K Willsher, 'My father's murder shaped my life. That's why Macron's apology is so important', *The Observer*, London, 16 September 2018. A Hussey, 'Macron should be praised for facing France's last great taboo – torture in Algeria', *The Observer*, London, 16 September 2018.

[114] *Ndiki Mutua & Others v The Foreign and Commonwealth Office* [2012] EWHC 2678.

[115] D Leader, 'The Mau Mau Litigation-Justice at Last' (OxHRH Blog, 3 November 2015).

[116] A Foulds, *The Broken Word: An Epic Poem of the British Empire in Kenya, and the Mau Mau Uprising against it*, (London, Penguin, 2011).

[117] A Foulds (2011) 25, 26.

No good to anyone, they were let out
to wander briefly as mayflies
and die as a warning.[118]

(ii) East African Asians Try to Come 'Home' to Britain

East Africans seem to be particularly affected by British reluctance to honour obligations generated by colonial policy. The response of the British government to the indigenisation programmes in East Africa which led to the exodus of people of Asian descent was to change the nationality law and to deny them hitherto granted rights to enter Britain freely under the Commonwealth Immigrants Act 1962, rendering their immigration status precarious – neither Ugandan or Kenyan, nor British.[119] In 1968 the government passed the Commonwealth Immigrants Act which curtailed the rights of Commonwealth citizens to come to live in Britain. It was targeted at East African Asians and the 'Coloured' populations of the Commonwealth.[120] Using the European Convention on Human Rights, 1950, a number of East African Asian applicants challenged the new law and the restrictions on travel.[121] The European Commission held that there was no need for further action, since they had eventually been allowed in. (The government had created a voucher system).[122] However, the Commission did say that it would still hear the case. On the claim that the group had been subjected to degrading and inhuman treatment in violation of article 3 of the Convention, the Commission was of the view that they had indeed been treated as 'second class citizens'.[123] It is also noteworthy that while the admissibility findings were published, the East African Asian report was kept secret (officially confidential) for more than 20 years and was made public after the intervention of the young lawyer who had argued the original case and who was now an influential member of the establishment sitting in the House of Lords.[124] One loses count of the number of times that

[118] A Foulds (2011), n 116 above, 39. See also P Gopal (2019), n 108 above, 414–15.

[119] Commonwealth Immigrants Act 1968. See M-B Dembour (2015), n 108 above, 62–95.

[120] See P Shah, *Refugees, Race and the Concept of Asylum in Britain* (London, Cavendish, 2000). See also N El-Nany (2020), n 108 above, 103–15.

[121] *East African Asians v The United Kingdom*, Application 4403/70 and Others, decision of 10 and 18 October 1970 (Report of the Commission, 14 December 1973) (1974) 78A DR 5. Dembour has accessed the full version of the decision. M-B Dembour (2015), n 108 above, 63 fn 4.

[122] Shah makes the point that the government's policies were racist. He further argues that by treating them as protected persons (and not the citizens that they were) and by failing to see that they had been or were being persecuted, the government sought to avoid its humanitarian responsibility. P Shah (2000), n 120 above, 77–88.

[123] It took until 2002 and the passing of the passing of the British Nationality, Immigration and Asylum Act for the situation to be remedied. M-B Dembour (2015), n 108 above, 64. See also 87–88. See further 89–91.

[124] A Lester, '*East-African Asians v The United Kingdom*: The Inside Story', Odysseus Trust, Lectures, 23 October 2003 at: http://www.odysseustrust.org/lectures/221_east_african_asians-sharma.pdf.
M-B Dembour (2015), n 108 above, 63 fn 7, 87. With some exceptions, most UK government documents which are labelled secret are opened after 30 years.

the African Commission was criticised for its practice, in its early life, of keeping its findings confidential.[125]

Reading the case now and learning about the background negotiations in the government that led to the passing, in 1968, of the Commonwealth Immigrants Act, one is struck by how the 'migrant swamp panic' of yesteryear is echoed in current discourse. It came as a shock to read that East African Asians were often detained on arrival. They were put in prison.[126] The post-millennial approach, in Britain and elsewhere, is to use detention centres for some asylum applicants and for those whose original claims have failed and who are in the process of appealing.[127] In a Commonwealth Immigration Committee meeting, the Attorney-General in 1968 had tried to caution against passing the Act, noting that the government's proposals 'did not spell out the difficulties which legislation of the kind proposed would entail for us in the context of a number of international instruments dealing with human rights and racial discrimination.'[128] The Minister of State for Foreign Affairs had already warned of a breach of the 'Universal Declaration of Human Rights, the Fourth Protocol of the ECHR as well as customary international law.'[129] The Labour Prime Minster argued that limiting immigration was, in current parlance, to ensure good community relations and to protect people of Asian and other origin (the word 'coloured' was no longer to be used) from race discrimination. With this in mind, he proposed a Race Relations Bill, which was passed.[130]

The impact on East African Asians of the 1968 Act is captured well in Bawden's children's book *The Runaway Summer*, published in 1969. Two English children are playing at the seaside when a boat comes ashore discharging two Asian men and a young boy. The men run away leaving the boy. The two children, Mary and Simon, take Krishna under their wing. Krishna's parents based in Kenya, anticipating the change in the law, had sent him on ahead to live with his uncle in England. His flight from Nairobi to London is diverted to Paris due to engine problems. He cannot get a connecting flight to London as the flights are all fully booked

[125] F Viljoen, *International Human Rights Law in Africa*, 2nd edn (Oxford, OUP, 2012) 416–17.

[126] M-B Dembour (2015), n 108 above, 63, 87.

[127] C Costello, *The Human Rights of Migrants and Refugees in European Law* (Oxford, OUP, 2016) 285–87. D Taylor and N McIntyre, 'Revealed: sick, tortured immigrants locked up for months in Britain', *The Guardian*, London, 10 October 2018.

[128] In M-B Dembour (2015), n 108 above, 85.

[129] Cited in M-B Dembour (2015) 84. It is of course ironic that the Universal Declaration on Human Rights, 1948, which Britain had helped to draft, was then less than 20 years old and yet its founding principles were already being breached. Universal Declaration of Human Rights (UDHR), GA Res. 217 A, 10 December 1948. There have been many iterations of the Race Relations Act in England, 1965, 1968, 1976 and latterly, its repeal and incorporation of race as a protected ground into the Equality Act 2010.

[130] Ibid. 'Community cohesion' is a theme which runs through many government departments in England, including The Department for Communities and Local Government, the Home Office (ministry of the interior) and the education department to name but three. See Commission on integration *Our shared future, the final report*, London, Commission on Integration, 2007 available at: http://www.integrationandcohesion.org. See also Communities and Local Government (CLG), *The government's response to the Commission on Integration and Cohesion* (London, HMSO, 2008).

with people who want to arrive before the change in immigration law comes into force.[131] He is approached by men who offer him alternative passage to Britain, hence the arrival by boat. Krishna tells Mary and Simon that he wants to join his uncle in London and gives them the uncle's address in an up-market part of London close to Buckingham Palace. They are sceptical. Tired of Mary and Simon speculating about his origins and thinking he cannot speak English, Krishna corrects them by saying he is not from Pakistan: 'I am from Kenya. My name is Krishna Patel. I am a British Subject.'[132] Simon, the son of a policeman, had raised the issue of Krishna's legality before saying that, as Krishna was an 'illegal immigrant', he would be, 'put in prison, if their papers are not right and then sent back where they came from.'[133] Concerned, Mary asks her grandfather and aunt, hypothetically, whether children do get sent to prison for helping a burglar, and then, tentatively, an 'illegal immigrant' child; 'an Indian from Kenya, or someone like that.'[134] Her aunt distinguishes illegal immigrants from criminals, before her grandfather explains:

> 'Indians from Kenya are rather a special kind of immigrant. Kenya used to belong to England … When Kenya became independent, the Indians who lived there were afraid they would be badly treated under an African government. So they were offered British Passports, just in case. And now things *have* gone wrong – they're not being ill-treated by the Africans, exactly, but things are being made difficult for them in the way of jobs and schools for their children, and so on – a lot of them have decided to use their British Passports and come to live in England. But *our* government has just passed a new law saying they can't come, after all. At least, not of right. They've got to take their turn with all the other people who want to come.'
>
> 'It's disgraceful' Aunt Alice said. 'Going back on our word.'[135]

Aunt Alice's sentiment is shared by journalist Yasmin Alibhai Brown, one of the people whose family were expelled from Uganda by Idi Amin in 1972.[136]

[131] Nina Bawden, *The Runaway Summer* (London, Penguin, 1969) 83.

[132] N Bawden (1969), n 131 above, 63.

[133] N Bawden (1969) 59–60.

[134] N Bawden (1969) 79. For a 21st-century version of that conversation see O Rauf (illustrated by P Curnick), *Boy at the Back of the Class* (London, Orion, 2018) 49–50.

[135] N Bawden (1969) 80.

[136] Y Alibhai Brown, *Who do we think we are?* (London, Penguin, 2001) 72–79. Her autobiography *No Place Like Home* (London, Virago, 1995) is also insightful about the sense of alienation that many felt on arrival in the UK. There is also the rare acknowledgement that the poor treatment of black Africans by 'Asians' (who were themselves African by birth or migration) may have been in part responsible for the expulsions. Alibhai Brown observes that the lack of warmth and support by many of their fellow Africans towards their expelled employers was because the employees had felt exploited by them. Alibhai Brown writes about how people tried to dissuade her from documenting this particular pain. See A Nuzhat book review of Y Alibhai Brown, '*There is no Place Like Home*' (1998) 26 (1/2) *Resources for Feminist Research*, 1 January 1998 at: https://www.questia.com/read/1P3-704806721/no-place-like-home.

(iii) The Right of Return: The Chagos Islanders Ask to Go Home

The Chagos Islands had been considered to form part of Mauritius, which itself was a British colony. Anticipating the granting of independence to Mauritius in 1968, in 1965 the British Colonial Office severed the Chagos from Mauritius and created the British Indian Ocean Territory (BIOT). In 1966, the British and American governments entered into a secret arrangement where the US gave the British '5 million [pounds sterling] to be written off by waiving the UK payments in respect of joint missile development programmes' for setting up the BIOT (three islands comprising the Chagos).[137] The reason for the deal soon became clear. By 1971 the British would clear the island of its inhabitants, permitting the Americans to have exclusive use. Renamed Diego Garcia, the island became a US military base. The islanders were taken off the island and sent to Mauritius and the Seychelles. The British government mendaciously declared the islands 'uninhabited'. They said that the islanders were merely migrant workers and not residents. Some compensation was later given for the islanders sent to Mauritius but not those sent to the Seychelles. Bancoult, one of the islanders who had found their way to Britain, launched a successful claim in the High Court asking to return to their homeland and for compensation. The government disputed their claim and appealed to the House of Lords which reversed the decision of the original court, noting that any right of return was now nominal. A 2012 claim to the ECHR was found to be inadmissible for jurisdiction reasons. Further, the Court noted that by accepting the compensation (and in some cases British citizenship) the islanders had renounced their claim to a right to return.[138] Other cases followed.

Meanwhile in 2010 the British government had set up a Maritime Protection Area (MPA), ostensibly to protect the environment. Mauritius launched arbitral proceedings under the International Convention on the Law of the Sea, arguing that it did not have the authority to do so. Without going into issues of sovereignty of the islands, the Court of Arbitration found in favour of the Mauritian government to the extent that it had not been consulted about the setting up of the MPA and also that it had been deprived of fishing rights. In 2017, Mauritius won a UN vote authorising it to seek an advisory opinion from the International Court of Justice on the issue of sovereignty, which it linked to the right of return of the Chagossians.[139] This was heard in September 2018, with Philippe Sands QC

[137] O Bowcott and S Jones, 'UN ruling raises hope of return for exiled Chagos islanders', *The Guardian*, London, 19 March 2015.

[138] *Chagos Islanders v Attorney General* [2003] EWHC 2222 (QBD); on appeal, *Commonweath and Foreign Affairs Secretary v R (on the application of Bancault)* [2007] EWCA Civ 498 (CA) on further appeal, *R (on the application of Bancault) v Commonwealth and Foreign Affairs Secretary* [2008] UKHL 61. *Chagos Islanders v United Kingdom* (Application no 35622/04) ECtHR, 11 December 2012.

[139] *Chagos Marine Protected Area Arbitration v UK*, Case 2011-03, *Final Award*, ICGJ 486 (PCA 2015), 18th March 2015; UN A/RES/71/292, *Request for an advisory opinion of the International Court of Justice on the legal consequences of the separation of the Chagos Archipelago from Mauritius in 1965*, A/RE/71/292, 22 June 2017.

appearing on behalf of the Chagos Islanders/Mauritius.[140] In February 2019, the ICJ issued its advisory opinion in favour of the right to return of the Chagossians. The court recommended that the UK should bring its control of the Chagos Islands to an end 'as rapidly as possible.'[141] It is worth noting that the UK had been told, more than once, by the UN Committee on the Elimination of all Forms of Racial Discrimination, that it needed to consult the Chagossians about returning and to facilitate this.[142] In May 2019 the UN General Assembly affirmed the decision of the ICJ by a vote of 116 in favour with six against and 56 abstentions.[143] The British government has remained obstinate in its refusal to yield: it will not let people out to return home; nor, as the final section of this chapter will show, will it let them in.

B. Testing 'European' Values of Tolerance and Equality

(i) Stereotyping

Many of the diaspora of colonisation, and their children, have been disappointed by their reception and treatment in the 'motherlands', finding themselves excluded from enjoying equal employment opportunities, often as a result of poor-quality education, housing and structural discrimination.[144] Growing immigrant confidence in their entitlements has coincided with governments worried about domestic 'indigenous' discontent blamed on migrants 'taking our jobs, women and houses, spreading disease and fomenting terrorism.'[145]

In recent years, the rightward and nationalist social and political turns in both British and French policy have resulted in significant shifts in policy. The latitude given to people of ethnic minority origin in Britain has been slowly narrowing, not least with respect to practices seen has harmful or discriminatory on grounds

[140] International Court of Justice, Legal consequences of the separation of the Chagos Archipelago from Mauritius in 1964 (Request for Advisory Opinion), Press Release No 2018/39, 1 August 2018.

[141] BBC, 'Chagos Islands dispute: UK obliged to end control – UN', *BBC News*, 25 February, 2019.

[142] CERD/C/GBR/CO/21-23, (3 October 2016) paras 40 and 41. The Committee references its previous recommendation to withdraw all discriminatory restrictions on the Chagossians and to end the forcible evictions of Chagossians from Diego Garcia, at para 40. The previous recommendation is CERD/C/GBR/CO/18-20, para 12.

[143] UN Meetings Coverage and Press Releases, 'General Assembly welcomes International Court of Justice Opinion on Chagos Archipelago, Adopts text calling for Mauritius's complete Decolonization' GA Plenary, GA/12146, 22 May 2019.

[144] T Keaton *et al* (eds) (2012), n 89 above; O Imoagene, 'Being British v. Being American: Identification among second-generation adults of Nigerian descent in the US and UK' (2012) 35(12) *Ethnic and Racial Studies* 2153, 2160–64. There appeared to be little sense of 'belonging to' Britain. Respondents cited racism and a lack of equal opportunities in employment when compared to white citizens. The British passport was seen a guarantee of non-deportation but not as a marker of allegiance.

[145] Bracing is Akala's autobiographical-historical riposte in *Natives: Race & Class in the Ruins of Empire* (Two Roads, 2019).

of gender.[146] In many ways this tightening is itself a reflection of the colonial approach for, as Claire Palley noted, the 'repugnancy clause' in colonial times was used to protect women and girls from forced and early marriage.[147] It is of course important to note that these practices are also outlawed by the African human rights system and many national laws.[148]

Some groups have come under greater scrutiny from states. The post-9/11 linking of Muslims with terrorism has resulted in a spotlight being shone on this community and its practices which, echoing the period of indirect rule, are sometimes labelled as 'antithetical to British or European values' or repugnant. In his 2009 report on gender, the UN Special Rapporteur on the promotion and protection of human rights while countering terrorism, Martin Scheinin, highlighted that one of the ways in which French police and security services sought to ascertain if a man had terrorist leanings was to ask him about his views on gender equality, thus reinforcing a stereotype of religion-specific misogyny. Women were asked to justify their reasons for wearing the veil.[149] He also identifies a problem with the UK anti-radicalisation strategies which sought: 'to include Muslim women as counter-terrorism agents on the basis of their position "at the heart not only of their communities but also of their families"', leading the Special Rapporteur to note that this approach may 'reinforce stereotypical gender norms about roles of women within the family.'[150]

These are not the only stereotypes that have arisen as a direct result of the British government's 'Prevent' strategy, ostensibly set up to tackle terrorism and radicalisation, but widely perceived to be targeted at Muslims.[151] Ben Emmerson,

[146] Forced Marriages Act 2007. R Gaffney-Rhys, 'From the Offences against the Persons Act 1861 to the Serious Crime Act 2015 – the development of the law relating to female genital mutilation in England and Wales' (2017) 39(4) *Journal of Social Welfare and Family Law* 417–34. See also B Oomen (2014), n 85 above and R Chin (2017), n 85 above.

[147] C Palley, *The Constitutional History and Law of Southern Rhodesia* (Oxford, OUP, 1966) 511. Oyewumi contests this benevolent view of the impact of colonialism. O Oyewumi, *The Invention of Women: Making an African Sense of Western Gender Discourses* (Minneapolis MN, University of Minnesota, 1997) 127–28.

[148] See for example, African Charter on the Rights and Welfare of the Child, 1990, CAB/LEG/24.9/49 (1990), art 21; Protocol to the African Charter on the Rights and Welfare of the Child on the Rights of Women in Africa, 2003, OAU, AHG/Res.240, arts 5 and 6(a), (b).

[149] UN Special Rapporteur Martin Scheinin, *Report on the Protection of human rights and fundamental freedoms while countering terrorism*, Section III 'A gender perspective on countering terrorism', A/64/211, 3 August 2009, para 37. See also CERD Concluding Observations, Canada, CERD/C/CAN/CO/18, 25 May 2007, para 14. The Committee noted that the state had already been found wanting by its Constitutional Court in *Charkaoui v Canada*, 23 February 2007. See also CERD Concluding Observations, Australia, CERD/C/AUS/CO/15-17, 27 August 2010, para 12.

[150] Special Rapporteur on Countering Terrorism, A/64/211, 3 August 2009, *Report on the Protection of human rights and fundamental freedoms while countering terrorism*, Section III at para 34.

[151] HM Government, Revised Prevent Duty Guidance: England and Wales, HMSO, 2015 plus updates. See also Counter-Terrorism and Security Act 2015. For a challenge to 'Prevent' see, *R (on the application of Butt) v Secretary of State for the Home Department*, [2019] EWCA Civ 256. OHCHR, 'End of Mission Statement of the Special Rapporteur on Contemporary Forms of Racism, Racial Discrimination,

another UN Special Rapporteur on countering terrorism, has also reflected on the negative impact of stereotyping on migrants and asylum-seekers from certain regions or groups.[152]

This stereotyping is not confined to states. In their book, *Refuge*, Betts and Collier engage with the duties of the refugee. Focusing on Syrians in Germany, they ask:

> Should all refugees be expected to attend language classes? Should they be required to succeed? Most controversially, should refugees be expected to participate in attempts to change those aspects of Syrian cultural values that are radically out of step with German society? For example, *should extreme religious attitudes to women*, infidels, and apostates be challenged?[153] (emphasis added).

In the same year that *Refuge* was published, 2017, the UN Women's Committee concluded its examination of the German state report by noting, in the section headed 'Stereotypes', its concerns about three issues,

> (a) Prevailing stereotypes about the roles and responsibilities of women and men in the family and in society continue to impede progress in advancing gender equality;
> (b) Stereotyped and sexualized images of women continue to appear in the media and advertisements;
> (c) Stereotyped media portrayals and negative images of ethnic minority women and migrant women undermine their ability to become better integrated into society.[154]

Gender stereotyping is a universal phenomenon it would appear; it is only particular in its manifestation.[155] The societal impact of stereotyping has been captured in fictional literature. This can help to build understanding between strangers.

Xenophobia and Related Intolerance at the Conclusion of Her Mission to the United Kingdom of Great Britain and Northern Ireland', 2018, paras 40–48: https://www.ohchr.org/EN/NewsEvents/Pages/DisplayNews.aspx?NewsID=23073&LangID=E.
The government has strenuously denied that Prevent targets Muslims, arguing that those from the far right have also been included in the Prevent agenda. United Kingdom Mission to the United Nations, 'UN Human Rights Council 41: UK Response to the UK Special Rapporteur's Report on Racism', 8 July 2019, reproduced at: https://www.gov.uk/government/news/un-human-rights-council-41-uk-response-to-the-special-rapporteurs-report-on-racism. Site visited 15 August 2019. See also Comments by the State following presentation of the formal report, A/HRC/41/54/Add.4, 3 July 2019, paras 56–58.

[152] UN Special Rapporteur on the Promotion and Protection of Human Rights and Fundamental Freedoms While Countering Terrorism – Ben Emmerson, *General Assembly report on Impact of counter-terrorism measures on the human rights of migrants and refugees*, A/71/384, 13 September 2016. See also O Okafor, *Refugee Law after 9/11: Sanctuary and Security in Canada and the United States* (Vancouver, University of British Columbia Press, 2020).

[153] A Betts and P Collier (2017), n 77 above. Moreover, the questions also leave one wondering if a person can be compelled to succeed, how success is measured and whether there is an element of reciprocity in the host nation being required to create the conditions for one to succeed.

[154] CEDAW Concluding Observations, Germany, CEDAW/C/DEU/CO/7-8, 9 March 2017, para 21.

[155] R Cook and S Cusack, *Gender Stereotyping* (Philadelphia PA, Penn Press, 2010).

Katherine Applegate's *Wishtree* is a children's story, told through the perspective of a red oak tree which provides shade and shelter for the people and animals living on a suburban street. Red, the tree, records the various comings and goings of families who: 'spoke Chinese and Spanish, Yoruba and English and French Creole. They ate tamales and pani puri, dim sum and fufu and grilled cheese sandwiches … That's our neighbourhood: wild and tangled and colourful. Like the best kind of garden.'[156] Red goes on to note that things changed when a Muslim family moved in. They were not welcomed warmly, eggs were thrown at their house and: 'One afternoon, a car passed by, filled with angry men yelling things, like "Muslims, get out!"'[157] Red is perplexed by this behaviour: 'Our neighbourhood had welcomed many families from faraway. What was different this time? The headscarf Samar's mother wore? Or was it something else?'.[158] The book concludes with Red telling us that as the story is not a fairy tale, things have not magically fallen into place. While two of the boys (Samar being one) sometimes do their homework together, 'Their parents still don't talk to one another. I'm not sure they ever will.'[159]

A counterpoint to the intolerance described in the *Wishtree* is to be found in the folk tale of the 'The Queen of Saba and the Infidel' included in Amina Shah's *Tales from the Bazaars of Arabia*.[160] The 'infidel' is a European traveller who finds himself in the court of a curious queen. Her courtiers are suspicious of the man but she engages him in conversation, asking about his people and their ways. She asks him if he would like to: 'embrace our wonderful religion and become one of the jewels of Islam?'.[161] He replies 'No, oh Queen, I have made my own arrangements and I have made my peace with my own God.' She tries to persuade him to listen to her courtiers but he resists: 'No, great Queen, I would rather be put to death than change my religion …'. His answer pleases the Queen who proclaims: 'We've been told by our book that people who have another book are also to be honoured. Do you have a book?'.[162] He assures her that his people *do* have a book, which satisfies her.[163] Perhaps this is what Abdullai An-Na'im meant by cross-cultural dialogue.[164]

[156] K Applegate, *Wishtree* (New York, Feiwel and Friends, 2017) 54.
[157] K Applegate (2017) 55.
[158] K Applegate (2017) 55–56.
[159] K Applegate (2017) 210.
[160] A Shah, 'The Queen of Saba and the Infidel' in A Shah, *Tales from the Bazaar of Arabia: Folk Stories from the Middle* East (London, Tauris Parke, 2008) 26–31.
[161] A Shah (2008) 27.
[162] A Shah (2008) 27.
[163] A Shah (2008) 27.
[164] A An Na'im, 'State Responsibility under International Human Rights Law to Change Religious and Customary Laws' in R Cook (ed), *Human Rights of Women: National and International Perspectives* (Philadelphia PA, Penn Press, 1994) 167. See also P Gopal (2019), n 108 above, 27.

(ii) Discrimination

Increasingly academics have started to interrogate the treatment of migrants and to conclude that there is dissonance between the claims made about equality and tolerance in European societies and the widespread and often politically sanctioned discrimination experienced by immigrants.[165] In a gendered analysis of French policy, Christine Delphy excoriates both the political class and civil society in France for preaching equality while denying Black and Muslim immigrants decent housing and equal opportunities to enter into employment. This goes to the root of who is a 'citizen' and who is constructed as the 'Other'. The construction of the 'Other' is as the one with alien values who wishes to destroy the French Republic. She notes that those whom she calls 'the Ones', who deny their own history and cannot see their privilege and dominance, condemn the 'Others': 'for being different, for not being "the same", and exhort them to be more "similar" if they want to obtain their rights.'[166] She then goes on to ask: 'But how could the Others be like the Ones, when the Ones are only the Ones because they oppress the Others?'.[167] Her answer is that it is not possible, not least because the privilege of the dominant group is built on the suffering of the Others, hence:

> The Others will never manage to fit into what is presented as a universal norm that goes for everyone and which everyone can live up to. Something which results from the One's othering and alteration of these people is interpreted as these 'Others'' own failing, and in any case their responsibility. Meanwhile, the One's privileges – won on the backs of the Others – instead appear as the proper recompense for their capacity to live up to the norm.[168]

Delphy's analysis also highlights the disproportionate impact on immigrant women of this denial of true citizenship. She targets a particular strain of French feminism whose response to the ban on the wearing of the veil has been to express solidarity with Muslim women, while banning them from attending meetings if they are wearing the veil. She also identifies the policy of *laïcité* (the separation of church and state) as just a mask for discrimination against people who are not Christian, for Catholicism is seen as the neutral, normative, unacknowledged

[165] M Dembour (2015), n 108 above; B Oomen (2014), n 85 above, T Keaton *et al* (eds) (2012), n 89 above. K Hosseini, 'Refugees are still dying. How do we get over our news fatigue?', *The Guardian*, London, 17 August, 2018.

[166] C (Delphy translated by D Broder), *Separate and Dominate: Feminism and Racism after the war on terror* (London, Verso, 2015) 15.

[167] C Delphy (2015) 19.

[168] C Delphy (2015) 20. See also Z Eisenstein (2004), n 4 above. Further, see L Sawyer and Y Habel, 'Refracting African and Black Diaspora through the Nordic region' (2014) 7 *African and Black Diaspora: An International Journal* 1–6, 3–4. J Lanchester's dystopian novel, *The Wall* (London, Faber and Faber, 2019) echoes Delphy's analysis. In it a wall is built around a country to protect those within the boundaries of the wall from the approaching 'Others' who must be repelled at all costs. M Goodfellow (2019), n 108 above, 176.

default.[169] Before moving on, it is as well to acknowledge that the veil issue in France is complex. Some Muslim women were pleased about the ban. This is not, of course, to excuse banning fellow women from feminist meetings.[170]

It is also worth noting that not all people who racially qualify to be 'ones' enjoy the privileges associated with dominance. Class is an important intersector. Moreover, Sabrina Mahfouz's discussion of race amongst people from the Middle East and North Africa suggests that many would like to regard themselves as 'white' because they are alive to the privileges that being raced in that way allow, but also because they perceive 'blackness' as speaking to a state of inferiority with which they do not wish to associate.[171] The internal racisms and colourist hierarchies among and between migrants often remain undiscussed.[172] There is a conversation to be had about our collective psychological damage that propels some to claim pale skins as badges of honour and achievement and thus to internalise hatred of self and to construct as 'other', those who could be allies in life's journey.[173] Priya Minhas, who with her Indian origin family, moved from the UK to the USA, describes the pursuit of whiteness as her own 'Sisyphean task'.[174] She had earlier explained:

> Whiteness – in pigment, not behaviour – is celebrated in my community, and 'You don't look Indian' was the 'You're not like other girls' for brown people. I chased it and accepted all those scraps of 'Pretty for a brown girl' and 'you could be mixed' that always left me feeling empty.[175]

[169] Confirmed in *SAS v France* [2014] ECHR 695. Cf *Mariana Hebbadj v France* CCPR/C/123/D/2807/2016, 17 October 2018. In *Hebbadj*, the majority found articles 18 on religion and 26 on equality, to have been violated. There were three concurring opinions given. However there were two dissents. See in particular the dissenting opinion of Jose Manuel Santos Pais and in particular his focus on the duties of people who are implicitly constructed as incomers at para 7. His reference to terrorist incidents in France and the link to Islam call to mind the observation by the protagonist in Mohsin Hamid in *The Reluctant Fundamentalist* (London, Penguin, 2007) where he, a Princeton educated, Pakistani broker working for a high end valuation firm in the United States, notes how he, 'had heard tales of the discrimination Muslims were beginning to experience in the business world – stories of rescinded job offers and groundless dismissals …' (at 137).

[170] K Bennoune, 'Law of the Republic vs. Law of the "Brothers": A Story of France's Law Banning Religious Symbols in Public Schools' in D Hurwitz, M Satterthwaite and D Ford (eds), *Human Rights Advocacy Stories* (New York, Foundation Press, 2009) 155–90 (Reprinted in Women Living Under Muslim Laws (WLUML), *Dossier 30–31, The Struggle for Secularism in Europe and North America* (July 2011) 11–42.

[171] S Mahfouz, 'Wearing Where you're at: Immigration and UK Fashion' in N Shukla (ed), *The Good Immigrant* (London, Unbound, 2016) 141, 144–45.

[172] Mabanckou turns the colourist discussion into farce, talking about acquiring and selling de-negrifying products (skin-lightening creams) because 'we will never give up trying to lighten our skin as long as we're convinced that the curse hanging over us is simply a matter of colour …' A Mabanckou (2012), n 99 above, 76. See also 79.

[173] See also R Eddo-Lodge, 'Forming Blackness through a screen' in N Shukla (ed), *The Good Immigrant* (London, Unbound, 2016) 77–83. R Eddo-Lodge, *Why I'm no Longer talking to White People about Race* (London, Bloomsbury, 2017). See also NI Painter (2010), n 39 above.

[174] P Minhas, 'How not to be' in N Shukla and C Suleyman, *The Good Immigrant USA* (London, Dialogue Books, 2019) 52–66, 61.

[175] P Minhas (2019) 52, 59.

From the perspective of the 'The Ones' in Delphy's analyses, one needs also to consider issues of class. In Britain, there is a view that the reason that the working class are so ambivalent about an increased refugee intake and immigration, is not, as is sometimes asserted by the liberal elite, because they are racist, but because the limited resources that they enjoy (and which continue to be cut) cannot sustain additions without their already precarious livelihoods being further threatened. Musa Okwongo acknowledges the undercutting of white working-class wages by cheaper European labour, but, he goes on: 'It's remarkable how many of the country's economic problems were blamed, not on the misfiring calculations of the financial sector, but instead on the ills of mass migration.'[176] This view is supported by Kenan Malik who observes that those in positions of power that enable them to marginalise the working class – including politicians, bankers and company bosses – tend to be disproportionately white. There is no homogenous 'white identity'; nor are the privileges associated with whiteness evenly distributed or enjoyed. For Malik, the problem is not race but the collapse of class solidarity:

> The idea of 'white interests' obscures the real problems facing the working class. It transforms solidarity from a sense of commonality with those sharing my values and aspirations, though not necessarily my skin colour or culture, to an identity with those who do not share my political hopes and may undermine my interests, but whose skin colour or cultural background is similar. There's little dignity in that.[177]

Farai Sevenzo also notes how some black Africans voted for Britain to leave the European Union in the 2016 referendum. He argues that the Africans had seen the impact of European freedom of movement and the ease of access of Europeans to the labour market as a threat their own livelihoods. The prospect of the expansion of the EU to take in poorer Balkan states meant that Africans saw themselves as even more likely to be pushed out of all work, including low-skilled work which many had come to rely on. They therefore made common cause with their 'indigenous' British neighbours who were also fearful of being further squeezed out of the crowded job and housing market and voted to leave.[178]

Post Charlie Hebdo,[179] Delphy identifies a concerted shutting down of any dissent, including, and indeed especially, if that dissent comes from people of Muslim or Black origin. The French claims to *liberté, egalité and fraternité*, have, like the British claims of fairness and tolerance, been found wanting when put against the lived realities of black and minority populations.

[176] M Okwongo (2016), n 91 above 224, 230. See also R Eddo-Lodge (2017), n 173 above, 189–211 addressing racialised class prejudice.

[177] K Malik, 'White Identity is meaningless. Real dignity is found in shared hopes', *The Observer*, London, 21 October 2018. Cf E Kaufmann, *Whiteshift: Populism, immigration and the future of white majorities* (London, Penguin, 2018).

[178] F Sevenzo, 'Britain's African Migrants who backed Brexit', *BBC News*, 28 June 2016.

[179] Journalists working on a satirical magazine called Charlie Hebdo were targeted and murdered for re-publishing religiously sensitive cartoons.

Post-millennial Britain has seen the government threaten to exit the European human rights system and to repeal the Human Rights Act 1998 to counteract the perceived interference of Strasbourg institutions on national policy.

The failures of claims of fairness and indeed moral behaviour are no better illustrated than in what has become known in Britain as the 'Windrush scandal', where the children of first-generation migrants from the Caribbean, who were brought to Britain at the end of the Second World War to help to re-build the country, were told that they were not 'British' and were thus not entitled to any of the benefits of citizenship, including the right to remain in the territory.[180] Some were detained and then summarily deported.[181] Although subsequently widely recognised as a 'scandal', the pursuit of the policy was seen to be endemic in the culture of the Home Office, and is in keeping with current European trends.

(iii) Playing 'Pass the Parcel' with Asylum Seekers

The legal regime for seeking refuge is well established. The Refugee Convention of 1951 initially only covered Europeans. It was designed to address the post-Second World War displacement of people and specifically to give sanctuary to people of Jewish origin, who, along with others including the Roma, had been persecuted during the war. For some the Convention also served an ideological purpose, offering assistance to those seeking to escape from behind the Iron Curtain during the Cold War. In 1967, the Refugee Convention was expanded and now covers the globe. There have also been regional developments, which have seen the development of region-specific norms and the expansion of the protection regime to include internally displaced people.[182] The challenge, then, is not the absence of a legal framework for responding to asylum seekers, but the conflation

[180] In many ways, the East Asian case was the canary in the mine – flagging up the fact that successive British governments had deliberately changed nationality laws to exclude 'Coloured and Asian' colonial subjects otherwise entitled to British citizenship, and to limit entitlement to citizenship to those from the White Commonwealth or to those who were White. M-B Dembour (2015), n 108 above, 83–85, 91. See also KH Perry, *London is the Place for Me: Black Britons, Citizenship and the Politics of Race* (Oxford, OUP, 2018).

[181] The story was broken by *The Guardian* journalist Amelia Gentleman. A Gentleman, *The Windrush Betrayal: Exposing the Hostile Environment* (London, Guardian, Faber, 2019). It became a national scandal and generated political and popular outcry. See *The Guardian*, 'The Windrush Scandal' (2018) at: https://www.theguardian.com/uk-news/windrush-scandal'; see also BBC 'Windrush Scandal', 12 October 2018 at: https://www.bbc.co.uk/news/topics/c9vwmzw7n7lt/windrush-scandal. To mitigate the fall out, the Government set up a Windrush review chaired by Wendy Williams and also set up a Windrush page with various policies on compensation and guidance for landlords, employers and National Health Staff. Gov.UK *Collection Windrush* at: http://www.gov.uk/government/collections/windrush. See also M Goodfellow (2019), n 108 above. For final report see, Home Office *Windrush lessons learned review: independent review by Wendy Williams* (London, Home Office, 2020). Also available on www.gov.uk

[182] M-B Dembour (2015), n 108 above; C Costello (2016), n 127 above; C Beyani, *Protection of the Right to Seek and Obtain Asylum under the African Human Rights System* (Leiden, Brill, 2013).

of immigration with refugee law and policy.[183] As we will see in the following chapter, the scope for documented migration has narrowed considerably in the last decade. States have tightened migration criteria and introduced ever-more stringent visa regimes, making it difficult for many to move. This has resulted in the starting position being to assume that the person seeking entry is not entitled and must therefore be 'illegal', which has in turn resulted in states taking a harsh immigration control and criminal law approach rather than the prescribed and agreed, human rights approach. Sadly, along with compassion, solidarity between states has also dissipated. There is no longer co-operation between states, with each government taking a NIMBY (not in my back yard) approach.[184]

Despite several European initiatives on managing migration, which include 'burden sharing' (the burden being the asylum seekers), the arrangements invariably break down due to the resistance of those states which are not the countries of arrival.[185] They insist on the upholding of the Dublin arrangements whereby a person is required to seek asylum in the first country of arrival.[186] Those with coastlines (Italy, Greece, Spain, Cyprus, and Malta) are thus forced to manage alone.[187] However, some use the principle of the freedom of movement with its open borders within the European Union to allow non-entitled migrants to cross over into other states.[188]

The preferred approach of most European states is to push the 'problem' elsewhere, preferably out of Europe, or by maintaining porous borders with neighbouring states if necessary.[189] The 'out of Europe' option involves a multiple

[183] Ayan Hirsi-Ali, herself the beneficiary of the Refugee Convention, 1951 argues that it is no longer fit for purpose. She says that the distinction between asylum seeker and migrant has blurred to the point of incomprehensibility. A Hirsi-Ali, 'We need a better definition of "refugee"', *Washington Post*, 18 December 2018.

[184] L Martin and S Penasa, 'Migration Crises and the Principle of Solidarity in Times of Sovereignism: Challenges for EU Law and Polity' (2020) 22(1) *European Journal of Migration and Law* 1. The whole volume, a special issue, is on this topic.

[185] T Gammeltoft-Hansen, 'International Cooperation on Migration Control: Towards a Research Agenda for Refugee Law' (2018) 20 *European Journal of Migration* 373–95.

[186] Regulation (EU) No 604/2013 of the European Parliament and of the Council of 26 June 2013 establishing the criteria and mechanisms for determining the Member State responsible for examining an application for international protection lodged in one of the Member States by a third-country national or a stateless person. An evaluation of Dublin III found that it was not working because of the number of migrants and asylum seekers arriving in European states and the refusal of some states to follow the procedural requirements of Dublin III. European Commission, DG Migration and Home Affairs, prepared by ICF International for the European Commission, *Evaluation of Dublin III Regulation*, 4 December 2015. See also H Wilkins and M Macdonald 'What is the Dublin III Regulation? Will it be affected by Brexit?' House of Commons Library, 4 November 2019.

[187] E Koka and D Veshi, 'Irregular Migration by Sea: Interception and Rescue Interventions in light of International Law and the EU Sea Borders Regulation' (2019) 21 *European Journal of Migration and Law* 26, 43–51.

[188] A Betts and P Collier (2017), n 77 above, 68–71.

[189] The smuggler in Sunjeev Sahota's *Year of the Runaways* arranges for a flight to Turkey and then onward travel by truck to Paris. The driver of the truck suggests that for an extra payment, he could arrange for Tochi, the protagonist, to go to England, where work is easier to get than France. 'For the ferry to England, he hid in the back of the lorry. Europe was no problem, Deniz had said, but these

strategy of offering non-European states money to take the people deported from Europe, to build 'holding' (read 'detention') facilities and the plain bribery of increased 'aid' or 'budget support'.[190] They also offer to assist with 'processing' the migrants offshore.[191] Intra-European tensions have seen Italy blaming France's colonial history for the influx of migrants while also accusing France of refusing to take responsibility for the problems it has created.[192]

In 2015, the UN Working Group on People of African Descent engaged the Italian government about the arrangement that it had made with Libya to take back migrants and also to prevent them from trying to make their way to Italy at all. The treatment of migrants by Libya was well known – they were detained in unsanitary conditions and often subjected to abuse and other human rights violations.[193] Kiri Santer details how Italy has continued to divert boats to the jurisdiction of the Libyan authorities rather than allowing NGO rescue ships and others to intervene. In this way, Italy, by a process of what Santer calls indirect rule, manages to evade its responsibilities.[194] Santer describes the Libyan Coast Guard as acting like a '"legalised lawless" agent functioning as an exceptional police force, acting beyond public knowledge and review and operating between national and supranational levels of governance.'[195]

The Italian government has been censured by the Grand Chamber of the European Court of Human Rights in the case of *Hirsi Jamaa and Others v Italy*.[196]

English types could be very difficult.' S Sahota, *Year of the Runaways* (London, Picador, 2015) 80. See also the Concluding observations of the UN Human Rights Committee to the sixth periodic report of Hungary, CCPR/C/HUN/CO/6 (9 May 2018) paras 47–48. See also Report of the Commissioner for Human Rights of the Council of Europe following her visit to Hungary from 4 to 8 February 2019, Council of Europe, CommDH (2009) 13, Strasbourg, 21 May, 2019, paras 10–27.

[190] D Howden, A Fotiadis, Z Campbell, 'Revealed: The secret European plot to keep migrants out.', *The Guardian*, 13 March 2020. See also J Rankin, 'Migrants on Greek Islands to be offered €2000 to go home', *The Guardian*, 13 March 2020: https://www.theguardian.com/world/2020/mar/12/eu-to-offer-2000-to-migrants-willing-to-go-home-from-greek-islands.

[191] Looking at the website for the European Union on migration is instructive – there are many initiatives and agreements listed, see: https://ec.europa.eu/commission/priorities/migration_en; See also Fourth EU-Africa Summit, 2–3 April 2014, Brussels, Roadmap 2014–17, where a Joint Declaration on Migration and Mobility was made and an Action Plan for the period 2014–2017 was agreed (para 36); European Commission, *Partnership Frameworks with Third Countries under the European Agenda on Migration* (Brussels, European Council, 20–21 October 2016). The Rwandan government was forced to deny that it had agreed to accept, in return for payment, the removal of mainly Sudanese asylum seekers from Israel to Rwanda. Haaretz Editorial, 'Israel's African Asylum seekers can't go 'home' to Rwanda', *Haaretz*, 25 January 2018. Israel had threatened to detain for a prolonged or indefinite period, Sudanese and Eritrean asylum seekers who did not agree to leave the territory. Human Rights Watch, 'Israel: Detained Asylum seekers pressured to leave', *Human Rights Watch*, 13 March 2013.

[192] M Johnson, 'Matteo Salvini accuses France of 'stealing' Africa's wealth', *Financial Times*, London, 22 January 2019. See also BBC, 'France summons Italian envoy over Africa remarks', 22 January 2019.

[193] UN High Commissioner for Refugees (UNHCR), *UNHCR Position on Returns to Libya – Update I*, October 2015, available at: http://www.refworld.org/docid/561cd8804.html.

[194] K Santer, 'Governing the Central Mediterranean through Indirect Rule: Tracing the Effects of the Recognition of Joint Rescue Coordination Centre Tripoli' (2019) 21 *European Journal of Migration*, 141–65.

[195] K Santer (2019), 141, 164.

[196] *Hirsi Jamaa and Others v Italy*, (Application No 27765/09), ECtHR (Grand Chamber) 23 February 2012.

A ship containing Somali and Eritrean migrants had been intercepted within Italian waters by the Italian authorities, who took the passengers back to Libya. The Italians passed the migrants to Libya without informing them of their nautical location or rights or giving them an option to claim asylum. This was in violation of both refugee law against refoulement and also the principle contained in article 4 of Protocol 4 of the ECHR prohibiting the transfer of third-party aliens to the country of departure. Although not removed from Italian soil, the nature of migration which involved sea travel and maritime boundaries meant that the passengers were considered to be within Italian jurisdiction. Italy should not have engaged in unlawful expulsion of third-party aliens.[197] The Grand Chamber noted that there was abundant evidence that any returnees faced a risk of ill-treatment in both Libya and also their own countries of origin, and yet this had been ignored. It was foreseeable that Libya would seek to return them to their own countries of origin and yet that risk was also ignored. There was therefore a finding of a violation of article 3 of the ECHR on degrading and inhuman treatment and also article 13 on the failure to provide the migrants with information about their right to a remedy. Under article 46 of the Convention, the Grand Chamber held that the Italian government was required to seek assurances from the Libyan government that the remaining claimants (two had died, some had disappeared and others had been resettled by the UNHCR) would not be sent back to their countries of origin or treated badly. The migrants were also to receive €15,000 each in non-pecuniary damages.

However, in practice there seems to have been little change to the policy.[198] Indeed the case of *ND and NT v Spain*[199] appears to have rolled back some of the gains made in the *Jamaa* decision. Spain was allowed to return to Morocco people who had sought to breach the three fences enclosing its North African enclave, Melilla, without giving them the right to seek asylum, or indeed even

[197] The *Hirsi* reasoning prohibiting collective expulsions from an area controlled by a state has been incorporated into the Committee on the Protection of the Rights of all Migrant Workers and Members of their Families, General Comment No 2 on the Rights of Migrant Workers in an Irregular Situation and Members of their Families, 28 August 2013, CMW/C/GC/2, para 51 (expanding on art 22(1) of the Migrant Workers' Convention).

[198] This is confirmed by K Santer (2019), n 194 above, 141, 163–64. See also, T Gammeltoft-Hansen (2018), n 185 above, 373, 393.

[199] *Case ND, and NT v Spain* (Applications Nos 8675/15 and 8697/15) (Grand Chamber) together with the intervention of the UNHCR, UN High Commissioner for Refugees (UNHCR), *Supplementary observations by the Office of the United Nations High Commissioner for Refugees in the case of N.D. and N.T. v Spain before the Grand Chamber of the European Court of Human Rights*, 5 April 2018, 8675/15 and 8697/15, available at: https://www.refworld.org/docid/5b92533f4.html. See Migreurop and others statement on 'European Court of Human Rights: Spain and the European Union will prevail the protection of European borders over the right to asylum.', *Migreurop*, 21 February 2020. Better was the original 'Chamber judgment' decision: Case of *ND and NT v Spain* (Applications No 8675/15 and 8697/15), 3 October 2017. Spain was found to have violated article 13 on the need to provide a remedy read with article 4 of Protocol 4 prohibiting collective expulsion of aliens. The two applicants were to be paid damages of €5000 each. There was one dissent on damages. Referred to the Grand Chamber with the result discussed in the text.

ascertaining their identities, in part because it was said that Spanish jurisdiction was not engaged. They should not have attempted to enter 'illegally'. The principle of non-refoulement appears to have been abandoned.

It is worth noting that the EU-African state initiatives may have contributed to a slowing of the traffic, but it can never be eradicated. Journalist Patrick Kingsley recounts how after they were told about the EU threat to use their navies to intercept Libyan smugglers, one of the most prolific smugglers, a 33-year-old law graduate named Hajj, dismissed the idea:

> 'What are they going to do, put two frigates here?' Hajj chortles, 'Two warships? In Libyan waters? That's an invasion.' They all scratch their heads. What on earth would military operations look like against such a tangled, complex trade? His haulier friend continues: 'Who? Where? … No one has the name "smuggler" written on their chest.'[200]

Kingsley notes that smuggling takes place from many places across the huge African coast. The chaos that followed the 2011 Libyan revolution has also created a constantly shifting landscape of informal networks that 'emerge, morph and fade by the week.'[201]

Hajj's analysis is reminiscent of the views of Somali-Canadian rapper K'naan, challenging the Western media narrative that Somali 'pirates' were illegally capturing and detaining Western ships and crew. He notes that Somali considered the so-called 'pirates' to be their coastguard, protecting Somali waters from illegal fishing which has decimated the fishing stock for local fisherman. He also speaks to the dumping of nuclear waste by Western companies who take advantage of the political chaos in Somalia and resultant lack of regulation to act with impunity. K'naan argues that the companies have the protection of their states who shield them from censure even while they send their navies to challenge the pirates.[202]

Similarly, one of Khosravi's informants, Amir, a smuggler, speaks of 'humane law' which does not recognise any borders. For him, borders are made by 'inhumane minds', so he chooses to ignore them.[203] Amir describes himself as:

> my own migration board. I work for those who are declined visas and passports. I work for anyone who has no passport, and with pleasure help them to go wherever they want. You see birds and animals go everywhere they want. They do not have passports so why should human beings? My thesis is to make the world more international. When the world is globalized, it is foolish for human beings not to be globalized as well.[204]

[200] P Kingsley, *The New Odyssey: The Story of Europe's Refugees* (London, Guardian Books and Faber & Faber, 2016) 60.

[201] P Kingsley (2016) 60.

[202] K'Naan, 'Somalia', *Current Media*, 2009. Watch Hard knock TV, 'K'naan on Somali Pirates – There is a Reason why this started', *Hard knock TV*, 30 December 2008. Available at:. https://www.bing.com/videos/search?q=k%27naan+on+somali+pirates&&view=detail&mid=ECF363CCBA3C9E140A2D ECF363CCBA3C9E140A2D&&FORM=VRDGAR See also J Gettleman, 'Somalia, Pirates tell their story: They only want money', *New York Times*, 30 September 2008. However, K'naan does acknowledge that the element of greed may have led to a widening of the 'turf' outwith Somali waters and interests.

[203] S Khosravi (2010), n 62 above, 108.

[204] S Khosravi (2010) 109.

European leaders will also not be easily deterred, not least those who have staked their political careers on 'stopping migration'. In 2018, the Italian Minister of the Interior, Matteo Salvini sought to restrict voluntary agencies from rescuing or assisting migrants stranded at sea.[205] A mayor of a town which has welcomed migrants has also been arrested for aiding and abetting illegal migration by arranging marriages of convenience.[206] Some, not least the UN Special Rapporteur on extrajudicial, summary or arbitrary executions, see this as harassment designed to put off any other 'do gooders' or allies. In a 2018 report entitled 'Saving Lives is not a Crime', the Special Rapporteur, Agnes Callamard, acknowledges the humanitarian work being undertaken to look after migrants and others belonging to vulnerable groups. However, she goes on to express her concern that some states have criminalised these 'acts of solidarity and compassion', which actions she regards as constituting a violation of the obligations of states to uphold the right to life.[207] Poignantly, her report cites a 2017 statement made by Holocaust survivors in which they acknowledge that their very survival is testament to the decisions made to break the law by those who chose to shelter and protect them during transit to safety. They concluded by noting:

> But this duty of solidarity also applies today, and we call for an end to these intimidating procedures We proclaim the legitimacy of citizens' right to scrutinize administrative, judicial or police practices. We stand with those who show solidarity with people in precarious situations without regard to the legality of their residency status. We pass the torch of solidarity to whistle-blowers, to citizens critical of xenophobic policies, to those in solidarity with everyday life.[208]

Perhaps one of the most cynical moves was the agreement entered into between the European Union and the Sudanese government under former President Al Bashir to manage and contain migrants. The EU was prepared to overlook the genocide allegations made against him. Indeed, the EU had previously pushed for the UN Security Council to refer him (Bashir) to the International Criminal Court to be indicted for genocide in Darfur, but was prepared to enter into an agreement with him which required Sudan to respect the human rights of returned

[205] BBC, 'Italy's Matteo Salvini Shuts Ports to Migrant Rescue Ships', BBC, London, 11 June 2018. In the *Hirsi Jamaa* case, the Grand Chamber of the ECtHR had listed a raft of instruments requiring states to assist those in distress at sea and yet these were ignored by Salvini. See *Hirsi Jamaa and Others v. Italy* (Application No 27765), paras 22–27. See also reports and soft law cited at: paras. 33–42. Human Rights Watch, 'EU/Italy/Libya: Disputes Over Rescues Put Lives at Risk', *Human Rights Watch*, 25 July 2018; UN High Commissioner for Refugees (UNHCR), *UNHCR Position on Returns to Libya – Update II*, September 2018, available at: http://www.refworld.org/docid/5b8d02314.html.

[206] T Kington, 'Italian Mayor who welcomed migrants is Arrested', *The Times*, London, 3 October 2018.

[207] Special Rapporteur of the Human Rights Council on extrajudicial, summary or arbitrary executions, Agnes Callamard, *Saving Lives is Not a Crime*, A/73/314, 7 August 2018, paras 9–13;53–75.

[208] UN Special Rapporteur on extrajudicial, summary and arbitrary executions, A/73/314, para 8. Citing Union Juive Francaise pour la Paix, '*Manifeste des enfants caches*', 6 April 2017.

migrants/asylum seekers.[209] This is akin to putting the fox in with the hens to guard them. In preparation for its constructive dialogue with Sudan in October 2018, the Human Rights Committee prepared a list of questions which included asking after its last recommendations on the treatment of asylum seekers.[210] The Committee also asked for information on the number of Eritrean and Ethiopian asylum seekers who had been summarily deported without access to lawyers, the treatment of Sudanese deported by Jordanian authorities and also answers to allegations that many asylum seekers had been subjected to degrading and inhuman treatment including by the use of leather whips to beat them.[211]

The Sudanese government produced a classic 'statist response' denying that it had deported any asylum seekers, while simultaneously acknowledging that those who had entered the country illegally had been expelled. It also notified the Committee that it had passed a new Immigration Act which was on all fours with both the UN Refugee Convention and the regional African one – thus compliance all round.[212] In the course of the people's revolution in 2019 which overthrew the Bashir regime, the EU suspended its arrangement with Sudan.[213]

While the focus has been on the EU, this regional bloc is not alone in the way it treats those seeking to move, whether as migrants or asylum seekers. There are commonalities between the approach of the Trump regime in the United States and that of the Australians and indeed Europeans. In 2016 the Supreme Court of Papua New Guinea found that Australia's practice of 'off-shoring' asylum seekers was unconstitutional and in breach of their human rights. Denying them their liberty and freedom of movement and holding them in indefinite detention was egregious.[214] Despite this ruling and many other interventions, including by the UN Special Rapporteur on Torture, the Australian government announced that it would not be moving the asylum seekers to Australia or accepting anyone arriving by boat.[215]

[209] L Oette and M Abdelsalam Babiker, 'Migration Control á la Khartoum: EU external engagement and human rights protection in the Horn of Africa' (2017) 36(4) *Refugee Survey Quarterly* 64–89.

[210] CCPR/C/SDN/CO/4, 19 August 2014, para 23.

[211] UN Human Rights Committee, 'List of issues in relation to the fifth periodic report of the Sudan, CCPR/C/SDN/Q/5, 3 May 2018, para 22. See also para 23.

[212] Replies of the State of Sudan on the List of Issues, CCPR/C/SDN/Q/5/Add1, 13 August, 2018. However, see a submission made to the Committee by civil society: SOAS, Centre for Human Rights Law, together with the International Refugee Rights Initiative and WagingPeace, 'Sudan's compliance with its obligations under the International Covenant on Civil and Political Rights in the context of mixed migration from, and to Sudan 124th session of the Human Rights Committee – Review of Sudan's State Party report.': https://tbinternet.ohchr.org/Treaties/CCPR/Shared%20Documents/SDN/INT_CCPR_CSS_SDN_32358_E.pdf.

[213] F Lindsay, 'Sudan Unrest Led EU to Suspend Funds for Migration Control, but Khartoum Process Should End for Good', *Forbes Magazine*, 6 August 2019.

[214] *Namah v Pato* [2016] PGSC 13; SC1497, 26 April 2016.

[215] Report of the Special Rapporteur on torture and other cruel, inhuman or degrading treatment or punishment, Juan E Mendez, Observations on communications transmitted to Governments and replies received, A/HRC/28/68/Add.1, 6 March 2015, paras 16–31. The Australian Prime Minister Tony Abbott hit back, saying that Australia 'was sick of being lectured to by the United Nations' (in the past

The United States has given up on presenting itself as a country of and built by immigrants. It is no longer open to and welcoming of those facing persecution. In 2019, the Supreme Court granted the Attorney-General's application requiring that people apply for asylum in their first country of arrival. This, as the joint dissent of Justices Sotomayor and Ginsberg noted, overturned US policy which had always allowed people to apply for asylum irrespective of how many countries they had traversed.[216] The aim was clear – to make the 'problem' that of Mexico the entry point of many, not that of the United States. That, and the increased security on the US-Mexican border, coupled with the persistent threat to build a wall to 'keep the problem out' has created a hostile environment.[217]

V. Conclusion

This chapter began by interrogating the meanings of home, belonging and identity. It then provided snapshots of African peoples who have lived in what is now 'the West' over the ages. Their contributions may not always have been acknowledged, but their presence is incontestable. It then moved on to look at the impact of the colonial project on patterns of migration. It looked at the lives of the people that Ali Mazrui calls the diaspora of colonisation in their 'colonial homes' and the issues that arose around their perceptions of identity within these new spaces, as well as the hosts' reception of them. Bernadette Atuahene's theory of dignity takings and dignity restoration was used to frame three contemporary legal claims brought by groups who had been dispossessed of land or dignity, or both. As the chapter progressed, it became clear that there is a distinction between first and subsequent generations of diaspora with regard to their views on citizenship and entitlements. The older generations seem more resigned to their in-between status. The younger abhor the racism and discrimination that they see as limiting their opportunities and want to claim their rights as full citizens of the states whose passports they carry. The chapter ended by looking at the growing resistance and resentment towards (African) attempts to move, whether it be to seek refuge or to settle down.

Using fictional literature, the next chapter focuses on the challenges that must be overcome to move, including obtaining visas or seeking refugee status. It looks at the reception given to incomers by focusing on state policies. It then moves on to consider the increasingly draconian measures taken to remove people who are

it has been criticism of Australia's treatment of Aboriginal people that has resulted in anger). B Doherty and D Hurst, 'UN accuses Australia of systematically violating torture convention', *The Guardian*, 10 March 2015. See also Australia Human Rights Commission, 'Information for List of Issues Prior to Reporting – Australia: Submission to Committee against Torture (2016)', 27 June 2016.

[216] *William P Barr, Attorney-General et al v East Bay Sanctuary Covenant et al*, 588 US ___ (2019) (No 19A230).

[217] See also O Okafor (2020), n 152 above.

seen as undocumented and thus unentitled to remain. The final section turns its gaze to the experiences of those who do get to stay, regularised or unregularised. How do they navigate living in increasingly hostile environments? Chapter three ends by paying homage to the goodness and kindness of allies whether they be writers or photographers using their craft as tools of advocacy, or those working and volunteering in NGOs or religious groups providing shelter and spiritual comfort. In a globalised world, stories and poetry are used to remind us of our common humanity.[218]

[218] See for example, VT Nguyen, *The Refugees* (London, Corsair, 2017).

3

Of Visas and Visions of a Better Life

I. By any Means Necessary

As any person from the Third World who has ever had to get a visa will tell you, freedom of movement is a nice idea, a human right to aspire to, but hard to achieve in practice. Writing about visa requirements in Europe, Maarten den Heijer shows how race, income and geography are central to the determination of who is required to get visas before travel. On a map he shows that all African countries are listed as requiring visas and most Asian and Arab ones. The exceptions to the Asian and Arab states are those deemed 'rich' or strategically important.[1] Den Heijer highlights that because of specific exemptions in some EU equality directives, states are not under any obligation to guarantee equal treatment to third country nationals from outside the European Union.[2] This severely limits the scope for challenging discriminatory decision-making. For Shahram Khosravi, these differences show that we live in an 'era of world-apartheid; where borders differentiate individuals. While for some, the border confers a "surplus of rights"; for others it is a "colour bar"'.[3] He goes on to highlight the enforced territoriality of the global underclasses, which he contrasts with the elites who are allowed to exercise unfettered freedom of movement or extraterritoriality.[4]

The restrictions around freedom of movement lead to creativity on the part of those who are excluded. It is not surprising that people resort to self-help measures: paying smugglers to enter without the right paperwork; entering into marriages of convenience; and using short-stay permits (visitor or tourist visas) for long-stay residence.[5] The term 'bargaining in the shadow of the law' was developed in the context of dispute processing to show how litigants framed their claims taking into account the way in which the law courts would rule, or had previously ruled on a

[1] M den Heijer, 'Visas and Non-discrimination' (2018) 20 *European Journal of Migration and Law* 470, 480–82. African countries fare particularly badly in the Henley Passport Index which ranks passports by ease of travel. Henley Global, *2020 Henley Passport Index*, 7 January, 2020.

[2] M den Heijer (2018) 480, 478.

[3] S Khosravi, *'Illegal' Traveller: An Auto-Ethnography of Borders* (Basingstoke, Palgrave Macmillan, 2010) 66 (footnotes omitted).

[4] S Khosravi (2010) 66.

[5] E Anyangwe, 'Why is travelling with an African passport so difficult?', *The Guardian*, London, 11 September 2015. K Dawes 'Passport Control: 'please can I be a Jamaican?' (2005) 92 *Granta* 61–75.

particular issue.[6] It can be seen that asylum seekers and migrants also do the same; they engage in creative auto-fictional biography-writing in the shadow of immigration or refugee law. Narratives are fashioned and stories refined to fit into the legally and politically acceptable migrant/asylum seeker moulds.[7]

It is this closed-ness and lack of flexibility of the immigration system, that leads Cathryn Costello to say of the European system: 'When the state or the EU act to prevent 'illegal immigration' by making migration subject to greater legal and practical barriers, those moves may well create further impediments to legal migration, and thus more illegal migration.'[8] Powerfully, Tendayi Achiume calls for a reconceptualisation of international law and specifically the concept of sovereignty. She argues that there is a need to take on a decolonial approach when confronted with economic migration from former colonial states. Rather than exclude these migrants, she argues that there is a continuity of obligations born of the historical links where colonising states have been the economic beneficiaries of that colonising process. This means that ex-colonial subjects, now migrants, are not strangers but co-dependents who should work together to make and remake their societies and international law.[9]

To capture the near impossibility of legal migration, Mohsin Hamid, in his novel *Exit West*, resorts to the use of a literary device whereby his characters simply walk through doors to the next point of arrival: Myknos in Greece, London in the UK and California in the United States. The narrator observes:

> Doors out to the richer destinations were heavily guarded, but the doors in, the doors from poorer places, were mostly left unsecured, perhaps in the hope that the people would go back to where they came from – although almost no one ever did – or perhaps there were simply too many doors from too many poorer places to guard them all.[10]

Writing about the work he did as an expert in asylum cases, Terence Ranger underscored the competing stories of the asylum seeker, the text of the Home Office interview and the refusal letter. These, he says,

> reveal asylum-seeker narratives about two things – the political situation in contemporary Zimbabwe, and the refugee's vision of Britain. They reveal Home Office and judicial counter-narratives both about Zimbabwe and about the limits of Britain's commitment either to human rights or to its postcolonial obligations.[11]

[6] RH Mnookin and L Kornhauser, 'Bargaining in the Shadow of the Law: The Case of Divorce' (1979) 88 *Yale Law Journal* 950–97.

[7] A Woolley, 'Narrating the "Asylum Story": Between Literary and Legal Storytelling' (2017) 19(3) *Interventions: International Journal of Postcolonial Studies* 376–94.

[8] C Costello, *The Human Rights of Migrants and Refugees in European Law* (Oxford, OUP, 2016) 67.

[9] T Achiume, 'Reimagining International Law for Global Migration: Migration as Decolonization?' (2017) 111 *AJIL Unbound* 142–46.

[10] M Hamid, *Exit West* (London, Penguin, 2017) 101.

[11] T Ranger, 'The Narratives and Counter-narratives of Zimbabwean Asylum: female voices' (2005) 26 *Third World Quarterly* 405, 407.

This chapter utilises Ranger's narrative analogy to explore the story told by the migrant and asylum seeker to gain both entry and the right to remain (self-narrative); the stories told about contact with the state via immigration and asylum processes and the outcomes (external narrative which can include the decision-maker's account as well as reportage).[12] The impact of the measures introduced by governments seeking to limit migration by creating hostile environments is explored as are the reasons that migrants give for leaving their own inhospitable countries. The chapter also considers the impact of what John Lanchester, in the novel *Capital*, calls 'the state of not-ness' on those who find themselves living outside the law, but firmly embedded in the economy.[13] I also explore the 'status fracture' of migrants who find that, far from having a better life in Europe and abroad, their lives may in fact become more challenging. I end by focusing on those who show kindness and compassion to migrants and asylum seekers in the face of state and sometimes citizen hostility.

II. Fictional Strategies for Gaining Entry

The reason that so much literature produced by writers living in the diaspora reflects the challenges of migration and 'getting by', is that stories of 'getting in and getting on' dominate social intercourse within migrant communities. While it has been argued that the literary imaginations of diasporic writers are constrained by commercial pressures to tell the stories that appeal to Western publishers, it is equally true that following the adage, 'write about what you know' lends itself to the production of migrant-story literature.[14] To be clear, this is not to suggest that migrant-focused literature is all that diaspora writers do or indeed, can do. The 'migration story' also draws in non-African writers and poets.

Fictional-legal creativity is captured with humour and insight in Imbolo Mbue's novel *Behold the Dreamers*.[15] A Cameroonian couple and their son find their way to the United States on temporary visas. Once in the United States, the aim is to find a way to prolong their stay so that the wife and son can go to school and they can make money to build a better life in Cameroon. In their quest, a cousin introduces them to a Nigerian lawyer, who runs through the legal immigration options and concludes that claiming asylum is the only one that is feasible for the husband. His cousin had already told him that the choice was between asylum and marrying 'an old white woman in Mississippi with no teeth.'[16] Alive to the fact that the

[12] T Ranger (2005) 407.

[13] J Lanchester, *Capital* (London, Faber, 2013) 134.

[14] M Feldner, *Narrating the New African Diaspora: 21st Century Nigerian Literature in Context* (Cham, Palgrave Macmillan, 2019). See also A Nwaubani, 'We spoke English to set ourselves apart', *The Guardian*, 14 March 2019).

[15] I Mbue, *Behold the Dreamers* (London, 4th Estate, 2016).

[16] I Mbue (2016) 19.

deck is stacked against an applicant, the lawyer, Babukar, sees the asylum-seeking process with its in-built appeals as the best way of achieving his client's wishes – a prolonged stay.

Behold the Dreamers captures the fact that migrants become immigration specialists. Early on in the book, we are told about all the evidence that Jende, the protagonist, needed to produce before he could get a short-stay visa. It resonates with anyone who has ever had to present themselves in a Western embassy, leaving little to distinguish fiction from the lived realities of many black migrants. Jende's cousin, Winston, working as a lawyer in New York, helps with the preparations and the air fare. Asked at his interview, how long he plans to stay in America, he says three months. To reinforce this, he is required to submit evidence:

> … his work supervisor's letter describing him as a diligent employee who loved his job so much he would never abandon it to go roam around aimlessly in America; his son's birth certificate, to show he would never remain in America and desert his child; the title on a piece of land his father had given him, to show he intended to return and build on the land; a letter from the town planning office, which he'd paid a distant uncle who worked in the office to get for him, stating that he had applied for permission to build a house; a letter from a friend who swore under oath that Jende wasn't going to remain in America because they were going to open a drinking spot together when he returned.[17]

Given the rigmarole, it is not surprising that he notes his intention to leave Cameroon, returning only when he has made good, which he defines as coming back with a Green Card or US passport and lots of money. He understands that getting this visa is a once in a lifetime opportunity.[18]

The fictional literature points to a variety of schemes used to try to access visas. These include: paying the manager of a band to apply for a visa for someone to travel as part of the band's entourage; agreeing to carry 'parcels' which turn out to contain drugs and obtaining a passport in a new name (if you have been deported).[19]

A. Smuggling and Self-help

In *Black Bazaar*, Alain Mabanckou's character from Congo-Brazzaville simply heads off to Luanda in Angola where there are many smugglers. He pays his

[17] I Mbue (2016) 18.

[18] I Mbue (2016) 19. See also CN Adichie, *Americanah* (London, Fourth Estate, 2014) where the protagonist, a Nigerian woman, announces that she is returning to Nigeria only to be met with a confused and incredulous 'Why?' by the Senegalese woman who is plaiting her hair. Having made it in, why would anybody leave?, she asks, especially after a 15-year residence which is what the protagonist has claimed. CN Adichie (2014) 16–17.

[19] P Gappah, 'My Cousin-Sister Rambanai' in P Gappah, *An Elegy for Easterly* (London, Faber and Faber, 2009) 207, 227–31 (deported, buys new passport with a new name to evade detection following previous deportation – Zimbabwe). E Osundu, 'Stars in my mother's eyes, stripes on my back' in *Voice of America* (London, Granta, 2010) 131, 135 (School – Nigeria – USA); See also E Osundu 'Going Back

300,000 CFA francs, travels to Portugal before moving on to Belgium and finally France, 'with the ID of a long-dead compatriot whose brother sold his residency card to Angolan traffickers.'[20] The protagonist takes the names on the ID card. Phlegmatically he notes that when he dies, his younger brother will sell on the stolen ID to Angolan traffickers; thus the circle will continue unbroken. Tochi in Sunjeev Sahota's novel *The Year of the Runaways*, who flies to Europe from India, takes the longer route by road to England because his smuggler notes that there are fewer checks when leaving from Dieppe than the much more heavily policed Calais, both ports in France.[21] One of the characters in Tendai Huchu's *The Maestro, The Magistrate and The Mathematician* applies for a passport using the stolen birth certificate of a Scottish boy who has died. He struggles with the split identity that follows – is his name Scott or Tamuka? Who is he, the same affable person as before the theft, or a new, more conflicted one after?[22]

In literary fiction and indeed in 'real life' everyone knows that getting married to a citizen is the best way to continue to live in a country.

B. The Marriage Visa

The marriage visa is the premier route as it entitles one to enter the territory and to work.[23] The ECHR case of *Coman v Romania* reinforced the entitlement of third country spouses of EU citizens to live with their spouses anywhere within the EU.[24] In his ethnography, Adriaan Van Klinken notes how he was often asked to find spouses or partners for his queer Kenyan informants many of whom were very keen on moving to North America and Europe, especially Amsterdam in the Netherlands, 'because same sex marriage is legal, because of the vibrant gay scene, and because of the liberal culture and the anonymity in which sex can be enjoyed.'[25]

West' (2010) 67–78 (band membership, drugs, alternate route); 'Welcome to America' (2010) 155–63. I Mbue (2016), n 15 above (school enrolment to keep legal). Getting work on a ship as a means of getting a work visa to get to the United States is also mooted in K Desai, *The Inheritance of Loss* (London, Hamish Hamilton, 2006) 179.

[20] A Mabanckou (translated by S Ardizzone), *Black Bazaar* (London, Serpent's Tail, 2012) 192.

[21] S Sahota, *The Year of the Runaways* (London, Picador, 2016) 80.

[22] T Huchu, *The Maestro, The Magistrate & The Mathematician* (Edinburgh, Parthian Books, 2015) 212–15.

[23] See generally, Home Office, UK Visa and Immigration, *Family Life (as a Partner or Family) Private Life and Exceptional Circumstances*, Home Office, 2019, at: https://www.gov.uk/government/publications/family-life-as-a-partner-or-parent-private-life-and-exceptional-circumstance.

[24] *Coman v Romania* C-673/16. The Coman case concerned two gay men, one an EU citizen married to a citizen of the USA. The CJEU appeared to suggest that for same sex people the status of spouse was the one that led to automatic entitlement to freedom of movement within the union. The recognition of registered partnerships was to be determined by whether the Member state treats registered partnerships the same as marriage. O Marzocchi, 'EU Fact Sheet on the Freedom of Movement of Persons 2019' at: https://www.europarl.europa.eu/ftu/pdf/en/FTU_4.1.3.pdf.

[25] A Van Klinken, *Kenyan, Christian, Queer* (Pennsylvania, Penn Press, 2019) 122. Van Klinken is sceptical about their rosy view of Europe (at 123).

Randeep in Sahota's novel *The Year of the Runaways* is roundly cheered for having a spousal visa: '"You've hit the jackpot," they said.'[26] However, a spousal visa is difficult to obtain.[27] Some states have immigration rules on the minimum age of third country spouses (to prevent or limit early and forced marriage). These may provide for an age higher than the national age of marriage and may bind both citizens and residents wishing to marry someone outside the EU. Moreover, some states may have language requirements before allowing entry.[28]

If you do not have someone to marry, then you have to arrange for a fixer to find you someone. Katula, in Jennifer Makumbi's short story 'Malik's Door' wants to regularise her stay in Manchester. She adopts a two-strand approach; she puts in an appeal and sends her passport back to the Home Office while in search of a husband with a British passport. Rather than risk discovery, she uses her friend's address.[29] Written for comic effect, the search for said husband seems, again, to involve finding, 'white pensioners, whom, she had heard, had a penchant for young African women.'[30] Eventually she marries her age-mate Malik, who it turns out, needs her as much as she needs him to regularise her stay. An observant Muslim, Malik feels compelled to cover his homosexuality and his love for a male 'friend'. Marrying a woman is the best decoy.

Hilarious is Chimamanda Adichie's short story 'The Arranger of Marriages'.[31] A Nigerian woman joins her Nigerian husband in America only to discover he is bigamous, having paid someone to marry him for papers and not yet having obtained a divorce. He is also a buffoon, an immigrant who has tried to become even more American than the Americans, despite saying he wanted a Nigerian wife (preferably a virgin) who was light-skinned because 'light skinned blacks fare better in America.'[32] He asks her to take on an English name to better fit in and spends all his time explaining the ways in which America is better than home. She plots her escape.

The theme of marriage for papers also comes up often in Mbue's *Behold the Dreamers*. In an amusing story, the protagonist Jende recalls how his friend Sapeur (a word used for a dandy) got his papers by marrying a woman he met in a nightclub

[26] S Sahota (2016), n 21 above, 203.

[27] *Ngambi and Nebol v France* CCPR/C/81/D1179/2003, UN Human Rights Committee, 16 July 2004 (on criteria for establishing family life under art.23 of the ICCPR). Discussed in F Banda and J Eekelaar, 'International Conceptions of the Family' (2017) 66 *International and Comparative Law Quarterly* 833, 842.

[28] *R (Quila and another) v Secretary of State for the Home Department* [2011] UKSC 45 challenging the Immigration regulations that set the minimum age for a non-EU foreign spouse at 21. The age of marriage in England and Wales is 16 with parental consent or 18 and above without. The guidelines now state that both parties must be over the age of 18. See Home Office, UK Visa and Immigration, *Family Life (as a Partner or Family) Private Life and Exceptional Circumstances*, Version 5.0, Home Office, December 2019, 22.

[29] JN Makumbi, 'Malik's Door' in JN Makumbi, *Manchester Happened* (London, Oneworld, 2019) 123, 127.

[30] JN Makumbi (2019) 123, 127.

[31] CN Adichie, 'The Arranger of Marriages' in CN Adichie, *That Thing around your neck* (London, Fourth Estate, 2009) 167–86.

[32] CN Adichie (2009) 185.

while 'dressed in a three-piece orange suit and a red fedora.'[33] The importance of targeting the right marriage partner is discussed in the context of convincing the immigration officials that the marriage is genuine. They are mistrustful of unlikely inter-generational romantic liaisons where: 'beautiful young women proclaim endless love to ninety-year old men for the sake of green cards.'[34]

Even those playing by the rule book find that marrying a foreigner raises suspicion. You are required to furnish proof of the romance: cards, letters, emails, texts, photographs, all to prove that the marriage is 'genuine'. To circumvent proxy marriage, the British rules now specify that the parties must have met face to face.[35] The British partner must prove that they have adequate means to support their foreign partner, meaning that the system denies the article 8 ECHR right to family life to those deemed 'too poor' to marry a foreigner.[36] Applicants can be subject to arbitrary decision-making. A British woman recounted how they had tried to get a tourist visa to enable her Moroccan fiancé to travel to be with her at the birth of their child. She had £5000 in the bank so he would not be dependent on state funds (to which he would not have been entitled in any event) and a return ticket. His visa was refused on the basis that he would not be able to pay for his flight home, despite submission of the return ticket.[37]

In the prologue to his autobiography, *The Jive Talker or, How to Get a British Passport*, Malawian Samson Kambalu writes:

> When my Scottish fiancée and I decided to get married, the consul at the High Commission in Malawi asked me: 'Are you marrying Susan to get a British passport?' My reply to that was deliberate. 'Not really,' I said. The consul regarded me for a moment and filled in 'No.'
>
> 'The answer is NO, OK? The answer is NO,' he said.[38]

[33] I Mbue (2016), n 15 above, 82. See also the stories in C Unigwe, *Better Never Than Late* (London, Cassava Press, 2019) especially 'The Transfiguration of Rapu'; 'Cunny Man Die, Cunny Man Bury Am' and 'Love of a Fat Woman'.

[34] I Mbue (2016), n 15 above, 225.

[35] Home Office (2019), n 23 above, 24.

[36] C Berneri, 'Family Reunification between Static EU Citizens and Third World Country Nationals' (2018) 20 *European Journal of Migration* 289–313. In 2012 the British government introduced a minimum income requirement (MIR) of £18,600 for those wishing to bring non-EU spouses into the UK. The rule was upheld by the Supreme Court: *R (on the application of MM (Lebanon) (Appellant) v Secretary of State for the Home Department and others* [2017] UKSC 10. The court considered the MIR, the presence of children and the availability of other income. It upheld the MIR at paras 77–87. One of the appellants was a Congolese woman, SS, who had married a fellow Congolese man who was given refugee status in Britain. He subsequently became a naturalised citizen. However, he could not meet the MIR requirement – paras 35–36, 102–108 – appeal allowed in part (availability of other income and pre-rule considerations.) At 105 the court acknowledged the challenges facing refugees who may not be able to go to live in their partner's home country. Children were dealt with differently. The court noted that leave to remain (but not to enter) was permissible if exceptional circumstances exist, including the applicant having a 'genuine and subsisting' parental relationship with a child who is under the age of 18, is British, has lived in the UK continuously for seven years and cannot be expected to leave the UK (para 21). See also paras 22–26, 88–92.

[37] J Dorward, 'Families torn apart as visa misery hits Britons with foreign spouses', *The Observer*, London, 19 August 2018. See also C Berneri (2018), n 36 above, 289.

[38] S Kambalu *The Jive Talker or, How to Get a British Passport* (London, Jonathan Cape, 2008) Prologue. See also C Berneri (2018) 289–313.

Sahota's *Runaways* shows that even if a spousal visa is given, once both are in Britain, the couple still have to 'perform' marital life to prove that it is genuine. In Sahota's story, the young man from India moves his clothes and belongings into the flat of the British wife pending the visit of the immigration officials there to check that the couple are 'real'. In scenes reminiscent of the film *Green Card* she shows him where to find pots, pans and tea because others have been caught out by not knowing, thus revealing that the couple is not really co-habiting.[39]

C. On Getting Education Visas and Visas for the Educated

The student visa is also desirable as it enables one to work, ostensibly for a limited number of hours. However, it is getting harder to obtain one. Moreover, a student visa necessitates proficiency in English, attendance at college, the payment of often prohibitively high fees and the need to make time to study to sit exams, all of which distract from working to make money to send home. This leaves the short-term tourist visa, which does not allow one to work at all. It also explains the 'problem' of over-stayers, who in practice comprise the largest group of irregular migrants.[40] Were the system more flexible, then more migrants might return to their countries of origin.

There is a sharp contrast drawn between those who are highly skilled and can get visas with the rest. This is cast into stark relief by the young narrator, Sade, in Beverley Naidoo's *Web of Lies*. Her uncle Dele is an academic and thus has a work permit which his employers apply for on his behalf, while her father, his older brother, is a journalist seeking asylum and thus left to his own devices. The uncle is entitled to apply to become a permanent resident; her father has to report to the police on a monthly basis to show that he has not absconded. She muses, 'Isn't it crazy that Papa is treated so differently?'[41] The reality is not so clear cut.[42]

In practice, it is difficult for highly qualified professionals to get visas to travel to the Global North for conferences or for short visits. Typing 'Africans denied visas for travel to conferences' into Google search engine yields news of denials from the UK, Canada and the US.[43] Research undertaken on behalf of three All Parliamentary Groups in the Westminster Parliament highlighted that African

[39] S Sahota (2016), n 21 above, 22–23 (photographic proof), 223 (language, check they have one in common), 229 (notice of visit from Immigration), 230 (flat familiarisation – one guy caught out because he did not know where the glasses were kept to get the inspector a glass of water), 243 (creating communal life, toiletries and hanging photos), 244 (the visit – ostensibly not an inspection, more a courtesy call to check if help needed with language lessons and so on.) One of the two inspectors is suspicious and returns, at a later date. Peter Weir (director) *Green Card*, Touchstone Pictures, 1990.

[40] BBC World Service, The Real Story 'Who Should be Let in?', BBC, Broadcast 22 June 2018.

[41] B Naidoo, *Web of Lies* (London, Penguin, 2004) 212.

[42] A Fazackerly, 'UK to deport academic to the Democratic Republic of the Congo which she has never visited', *The Guardian*, 19 October 2019. See also A Islam, 'The UK used to be attractive to us academics. Now it is just hostile.' *The Guardian*, 28 November 2019.

[43] One example is M Grounds, 'Systemic prejudice in the UK, and visa refusals for African academics', *Mail and Guardian*, Johannesburg, 10 July 2019.

applicants were twice as likely to have their visa applications denied as those from other parts of the world.[44] Moreover, the *Financial Times* reported that the Home Office had introduced an algorithm traffic lights scheme, green, amber or red, where it graded 'risk' – meaning the likelihood that a person would stay on after the expiration of the visa.[45] Africans did not fare well.

Scottish immigration lawyer Iain Halliday gave evidence to the three All Parliamentary Groups that were examining the unfair treatment of Africans in the visa determination process. He identified a catalogue of challenges. These included the fact that there were only 32 visa application centres to service the whole continent. This necessitated travelling long distances, adding to the already prohibitive costs of obtaining a visa. If one had to travel to another country, then a visa might be required to enter to apply for the other visa. He also identified the problems of having to prove that one had enough maintenance money, even if a sponsor had already provided their bank details and guaranteed their willingness to meet all your expenses. Halliday identified women as being particularly disadvantaged. Unlike men, they were also asked to show that they were married, had children or property – some 'extra links' to show that they would not abscond. Racial biases identified included the assumption that African academics could only be travelling for training and not because they had anything to contribute to conferences or learning. Delays in visa processing were common. The wide discretion given to visa determination officials was often abused and irrational decisions were made which were difficult and costly to challenge.[46]

III. Processes

A. The Visa Interview: Demeanour

Whichever visa one is applying for, an issue that causes particular difficulty is that of presenting the correct 'demeanour', otherwise known as passing the visa interview. It is not as simple as it sounds. There is a document entitled, 'Top Mistakes to avoid during a visa interview' prepared by a Schengen visa service. Helpfully, it suggests that the guidance can be applied to other visa applications. The mistakes listed are, in order: lateness; inappropriate answers; skipping questions or false answers; inappropriate appearance (too much perfume is a no-no, apparently);

[44] See the joint report of the All-Party Parliamentary Groups on Africa, Diaspora, Development and Migration and Malawi on Africa, 'Visa Problems for African Visitors to the UK', APPG Africa, APPG Malawi, APPG for Diaspora, Development and Migration with the Royal African Society, ASA UK, AFFORD, Scotland Malawi Partnership, 16 July 2019. Available on: http://www.royalafricansociety.org.

[45] H Warrell and D Pilling, 'Africans twice as likely to be refused UK visa, say MPs', *The Financial Times*, 16 July 2019.

[46] I Halliday, 'MPs publish damning indictment of UK visa process for African visa' on http://www.freemovement.org, These criticisms are all contained in the APPG report, 2019, section 3, 21–30.

incomplete supporting documentation; offering unnecessary information; nervousness, and, finally, disagreeing with the visa official. Here is the section on demeanour:

> Another important component of the Schengen visa interview is the body posture and mimics you make during the question-answers session. A face that expresses fear and uncertainty, as well as a body that is not sitting properly, might lead visa officials to consider you a worthless and dishonest candidate. If you lean back you might be considered arrogant, leaning forward – aggressive, if too laid-back you will be perceived as a lazy individual, while arms-crossed tells you are trying to resist and defend yourself from the questions.
>
> In its place, try holding a neutral body position by sitting tall and keeping your arms open to show you are open and ready for a fair interview.
>
> Avoiding the eye contact with the embassy official during the interview also does not help at all. This is also one of the things that make you an inappropriate candidate to be given a visa, as it is usually perceived as a lack of seriousness.
>
> Instead, keep the normal eye contact when listening questions or giving answers, by avoiding odd and consistent eyeing (sic).[47]

The aim of publishing the advice is to be helpful. However, the recommendations on the 'correct demeanour' reveal the potentially very subjective nature of the decisions made. Moreover, they are culturally loaded. Not all cultures think direct eye contact is a sign of trustworthiness; some may perceive it as challenging, aggressive or just disrespectful. Perhaps this is why Amir, one of Khosravi's informants, prepared his own guide, including a section on demeanour, for those whom he was assisting to cross borders in the shadow of the law.[48]

B. Cost and Generating the Right Paperwork

In their novels Kiran Desai and Sunjeev Sahota both detail the cost (financial and emotional) involved in the process of trying to get a visa. Fiction mirrors reality. In Sahota's *The Year of the Runaways*, one of the characters sells his kidney to enable him to get some of the money to travel. Extortionate money lenders are used and family businesses are employed as collateral for loans to facilitate the acquisition of visas. In Stephen Kelman's *Pigeon English*, a Ghanaian woman who has borrowed money to pay fixers to get to London is phlegmatic:

> How else would I have made it here? Should I have planted a plane ticket? I'd still be at home putting my coins in a Milo tin, ten pesewa here, fifty there. I made the choice, nobody forced me. I did it for me, for these children. As long as I pay my debt they're safe and sound.[49]

[47] Schengen Visa Info 'Top Mistakes to avoid during a visa interview' 22 July 2016 at: https://www.schengenvisainfo.com/top-mistakes-to-avoid-during-a-visa-interview/.

[48] S Khosravi (2010), n 3 above, 109.

[49] S Kelman, *Pigeon English* (London, Bloomsbury, 2012) 232.

The protagonist in NoViolet Bulawayo's *We Need New Names* recounts the challenge of getting to America:

> How hard was it to get to America – harder than crawling through the anus of a needle. For the visas and passports, we begged, despaired, lied, grovelled, promised, charmed, bribed – anything to get us out of the country. For his passport and travel, Tshaka Zulu sold all his father's cows, against the old man's wishes. Perseverance had to take his sister Netsai out of school. Nqo worked the fields of Botswana for nine months. Nozipho, like Primrose and Sicelokhule and Maidei, slept with that fat, black pig Banyile Khoza from the passport office. Girls flat on their backs, Banyile between their legs, America on their minds.[50]

Desai's *The Inheritance of Loss* shows that there is a visa market involving a network of fixers who include doctors who will falsify medical information, lawyers who will act as brokers, including of marriage, and corrupt airline officials who will take a cut for onward transmission of the 'cargo'. There are many people involved in the creation of the exit narrative.[51]

> Sometimes every single paper the applicants brought with them was fake: birth certificates, vaccination records from doctors, offers of monetary support. There was a lovely place you could go, clerks by the hundred sitting cross-legged before typewriters, ready to help with stamps and the correct legal language for every conceivable requirement ...[52]

Standing in the line for a visa to the United States, the characters in Desai's *Inheritance* discuss the many hurdles to be overcome, not least ensuring that you have enough money in your bank account to show that you are not the kind of person likely to abscond. The answer to the question 'How do you find so much money?' shows initiative and the importance of family networks:

> 'My whole family' he explained, 'uncles from all over, Dubai, New Zealand, Singapore, wired money into my cousin's account in Tulsa, the bank printed the statement, my cousin sent a notarized letter of support, and then he sent the money back to where it had come from. How else can you find enough to please them?'[53]

I have a cousin who takes out a bank loan three to six months before applying for the visa. This is to show that she is financially stable. She leaves the money in her account until after the interview because the criteria often require one to present one's bank accounts for a minimum of three months. After the interview she repays the loan 'early' to avoid incurring interest.

[50] NV Bulawayo, *We Need New Names* (London, Vintage, 2014) 240.

[51] K Desai (2006), n 19 above. See also S Khosravi (2010), n 3 above, 30.

[52] K Desai (2006), n 19 above, 183. Rambanai in Gappah's short story 'My Cousin-Sister Rambanai' bribes government officials and buys herself (or has bought for her) a new birth certificate, ID and passport in order to allow her to travel. She had been deported for over-staying her original visa. P Gappah (2009), n 19 above, 153–72, 229.

[53] K Desai (2006), n 19 above, 183.

Visa problems do not end on gaining entry into one's chosen country. In their socio-legal study of migrants in Belgium, Jean-Baptiste Farcy and Sarah Smit show how even, for those who start off living within the law, time and money considerations can lead to periods of irregularity. The renewals of visas for oneself and one's family and attendant costs, such as the need to pay for health insurance and renewal fees, may push one into a state of temporary irregularity for want of funds. The irregularity can then count against one when applying for settled status after a period of legal residence. Their research also shows how even those who do have the right paperwork to move to a different country to take up employment opportunities may find themselves constrained by fear of losing their entitlement to apply for residence by moving and thus 'stopping the clock' in the country of primary residence. Most states require a continual period of residence and the years required are increasing – Belgium in 2013 increased its requirement from three to five years.[54]

Staying with money, the issue of the fees for processing documents, including for those lawfully in a country who need to renew their immigration paperwork, is also becoming a subject of focus in Britain. As noted, without money, the family may not be able to extend their leave to remain, which impacts on other entitlements. This can include the child's ability to take part in school trips to other countries, or indeed to apply for loans to attend university as a home student, a right enjoyed by their peers.[55] The prohibitive cost of applying for citizenship for children has been challenged in the courts. The Project for the Registration of Children as British Citizens (supported by Amnesty International), together with two children, brought a case to the High Court challenging the Home Office for charging a fee of £1012 for registration as a citizen when the administrative cost of processing the claim was only £372, meaning the Home Office was profiting by £640.[56] The effect was to exclude many who could not afford the fee, with the result that in some families, some children had British citizenship, while others did not, because the parents were still saving to pay the fee. The High Court found for the applicants, noting that the high fee prevented registration. The Home Office had failed to factor in the best interest of children. The Court further ruled that the fee

[54] J-B Farcy and S Smit, 'Status (Im)Mobility and the Legal Production of Irregularity: A Socio-legal Analysis of Temporary Migrants' Lived Experiences' (2019) XX (X) *Social and Legal Studies* 1–21. See also *Rhuppiah v Secretary of State for the Home Department* [2018] UKSC 58.

[55] G Greenwood, 'Home Office citizenship fees "scandalous"', BBC, 13 February 2018; J Grierson and S Marsh, 'Slash "obscene" Home Office fees, say MPs and campaigners', *The Guardian*, London, 24 June 2018; S Joiner, A Lombardi, S O'Neill, 'Hostile environment: Home Office makes 500m (sterling) from immigration fees', *The Times*, London, 11 August 2019. The denial of student loans for university to young people whose immigration status was either irregular or in the process of being resolved, was addressed by the Supreme Court in *R (on the application of Tigere) v Secretary of State for Business, Innovation and Skills*, [2015] UKSC 57.

[56] Project for the Registration of Children as British Citizens (PRCBC) '*R (PRCBC & Others) v Secretary of State for the Home Department: Strategic litigation seeking to challenge the fee for children's registration of British citizenship*' PRCBC, October 2019 at: https://prcbc.files.wordpress.com/2019/10/note_fees_litigation_-oct_-2019.pdf.

had the effect of making children feel alienated and not part of the society. It did not reach a conclusion about whether it was right that the Home Office should seek to make a profit.[57]

Meanwhile, in South Africa, the High Court has declared that schools must register children in school irrespective of the undocumented immigration status of their parents.[58] The Court was considering the exclusions contained in sections 39 and 42 of the Immigration Act 13 of 2002, which prohibited training institutions from providing instruction to undocumented foreigners or those whose status disentitled them from receiving training.[59] The Court ordered schools to admit children who did not have birth certificates and to accept alternative proof of identity such as affidavits, or sworn statements deposed by the parents or carers of the child. The Court was of the view that the Immigration Act could not be seen to be targeting or hampering basic education for children. This interpretation, it argued, was in keeping with South Africa's international obligations and with maintaining the best interests of children. It also honoured and reflected South Africa's constitutional values.[60]

Freedom of movement and the visa problem is not confined to people wanting to go to the Global North. Sue Nyathi's novel *The Gold Diggers* details how in the years before visa requirements were abolished, Zimbabweans were smuggled into South Africa. This involved crossing the crocodile-infested Limpopo, 'also known as the River of Death', aided by a smuggler who had to be paid.[61] After the relaxation of the visa regime a new line of work emerged – the trade in taking the passports back to the border to be stamped with fresh dates to ensure that the owners were keeping themselves within the law by showing that they had not over-stayed their allotted time. The going rate in the *Gold Diggers* was R1000, but R2000 for those who had overstayed because: 'In such instances you needed a stamp that could be backdated and that service invariably cost a lot more.'[62] Obtaining legitimate papers to stay in South Africa also involved bribing officials at the Department for Home Affairs, which required substantial savings.[63]

IV. The Moral Economy of Smuggling

In journalist Kingsley's investigation of migration across the Mediterranean, we learn of a different economy – that of the smuggler. In Libya, Kingsley meets a

[57] *Project for the Registration of Children as British Citizens and others v Secretary of State for the Home Department* [2019] EWHC 3536 (Admin).

[58] *Centre for Child Law and Others v Minister of Basic Education and Others* (2840/2017) [2019] ZAECGHC 126 (12 December 2019).

[59] *Centre for Child Law* (2019) para 104.

[60] *Centre for Child Law* (2019) para 135.

[61] S Nyathi, *The Gold Diggers: A Novel* (London, Macmillan, 2018) 19 for quote and 20–30 for story of crossing.

[62] S Nyathi (2018) 267.

[63] S Nyathi (2018) 111.

haulier who tells him that smuggling is an option for many; you can write your own rags to riches story:

> Anyone here who has no money can sell their apartment, buy a boat and organise a smuggling trip. By the time of the next trip you'd already have regained half the cost of the apartment. It's a very easy formula.[64]

Smuggling also becomes a part of the local economy, with the cost of bribing the local coastguard to turn a blind eye factored into the cost of buying a boat.[65] Financial hierarchies also impact on the level of service given to the smuggled, so that those who have little money (Africans) find themselves in the hold where they may suffocate. If the ship sinks, they are the likely ones to drown. 'Since they pay more, Syrians travel on boats with slightly fewer people.'[66] The below-decks analogy with earlier slave trades is inescapable.

The perils of smuggling are captured in fictional literature by Aunt Sonia in Kelman's *Pigeon English* who muses that if she had to do it again:

> … this time I'll pay the extra fifty dollars to get a boat with a driver (who) knows the difference between fishermen and the coastguard. I tell you, you don't want to know what a Libyan jail smells like, I still dream about that smell.[67]

A BBC documentary featuring the first-person account of 'the undercover migrant' is harrowing. A young Ghanaian man decided to investigate the migration route taken by his countrymen to get to Europe. The child of a policeman, he bought himself a pair of spectacles with a hidden camera with which to record his journey. The documentary that followed is extraordinary – bodies scattered over the Sahara, thirst and violence including, disturbingly, the multiple rapes of the women in the group.[68]

In his auto-ethnography, Khosravi discusses the moral economy of smuggling. Rather than seeing smuggling as always constituting an act of illegality or immorality, Khosravi says that there is a need to distinguish between traffickers and those locals who may help the traveller in order to supplement their meagre incomes. They guide people to cross over borders without detection. He includes within this group of benign smugglers the person who facilitated his escape from Iran to Afghanistan.[69] Khosravi subsequently made his way to Sweden. We have met Amir Heidari, one of Khosravi's informants, who in addition to being well-read and thoughtful, paints himself as a man of honour seeking to facilitate

[64] P Kingsley, *The New Odyssey: The Story of Europe's Refugees* (London, Guardian Books and Faber & Faber, 2016) 61.

[65] P Kingsley (2016) 61.

[66] P Kingsley (2016) 71.

[67] S Kelman (2012), n 49 above, 233.

[68] BBC World Service, Assignment, 'The Undercover Migrant', BBC, 26 May 2019. The programme is also available as a Documentary podcast also on the BBC website, dated 23 May 2019. See also Channel 4 News, 'Underage girls sex trafficked into Italy', *Channel 4 News*, London, aired Monday, 19 August 2019.

[69] S. Khosravi (2010), n 3 above, 26.

freedom of movement in an unjust world.[70] He concedes that there are examples of 'poor practice' or smugglers who do exploit people. Khosravi contends that while authorities blame smugglers for the deaths of travellers, it is often the acts of the authorities – for example the Spanish attempts to deflect ships carrying people in the Mediterranean – which have produced a higher death toll. He also shows how the very act of deportation makes it difficult for a person to re-enter a country legally, thus necessitating the use of smugglers.[71]

V. You can Buy Your Way in Legitimately – Wealth and Visa Waivers

It is worth noting that there is a different visa market or racket carried out by states which offer residence permits and the possibility of naturalisation to those rich enough to get what are called investment visas. There is a lucrative market in advising people on how to obtain investor visas, comprising lawyers, bankers and even academics.[72] These are given out to people who can show that they can invest a lot of money in a state.[73] It is only recently that the security implications of allowing lightly vetted citizenship purchasers (not all states seek to ascertain how the person came about their wealth) to roam freely across European and other international borders are being considered.[74] The distinction between these rich economic migrants and the less desirable 'other' economic migrants is hard to fathom. There is, however, a distinct disdain and refusal to contemplate allowing less well-resourced people who want to move for a better life to migrate, thus the use of alternative routes.

Den Heijer shows how Europe's focus on giving visa waivers only to the citizens of countries that are seen as economically or strategically valuable, 'perpetuates global economic inequalities.' He contends that giving 'unfavoured' countries the opportunity to become visa free may actually incentivise them to meet the 'EU's benchmarks on public order and illegal migration so that visa free travel can become a possibility.'[75] Achiume supports this, noting that the contention that open borders will lead to uncontrolled migration is not proven. Specifically, she notes that many people from the Third World are happy to stay within their

[70] S Khosravi (2010) 105–11.
[71] S Khosravi (2010) 21–27.
[72] See the website of the Investment Migration Forum at: http://www.investmentmigrationforum.org and Henley Global which has lists of countries offering investment visas and the criteria at Henley & Partners Holdings Ltd. See henleyglobal.com.
[73] J Henley, 'Citizenship for sale: how tycoons can go shopping for a new passport', *The Guardian*, London, 2 June 2018.
[74] J Garside and H Osborne, '"Golden Passports" threaten European Security, warns EU Commissioner', *The Guardian*, London, 16 October 2018.
[75] M den Heijer (2018), n 1 above, 470, 489. All quotes on p 489.

countries or regions. Citing research on migration, she further contends that it is the restrictive immigration policies in Western states that lead to people not feeling able to return to their homelands. Were there fewer restrictions on re-entry, more would leave.[76]

VI. On Slippery Categorisations: 'Illegal' Migrant v ('Bogus') Asylum Seeker?

In his book *The New Odyssey*, journalist Patrick Kingsley notes that, for many, the distinction between the deserving asylum seeker/refugee fleeing war and the 'undeserving' economic migrant fleeing poverty, is merely semantic. Moreover, Kingsley observes that it is ironic that characteristics that would be considered admirable in 'indigenous Europeans', including grit and determination, are in the migrant, not valued. Far from being 'benefit scroungers' who want to come to the West to avail themselves of state welfare payments, these are people who want to work hard for themselves and their families.

Kingsley also notes that the abuse and degradation encountered by black African migrants in Libya may mean that their flight from there to Europe is fuelled by a fear of persecution, thus tipping them into the refugee category.[77] He then identifies the cost and danger of attempting to return to one's home country from Libya as being much higher than that of undertaking a perilous journey across the sea to Europe. Kingsley concludes his analyses by quoting a Nigerian pastor and plumber called Ohioyah whom he meets in Libya:

> 'You have to issue us with papers,' he says. 'You need to tell us that we can have a future.' And, if not, Ohioyah promises a stark alternative: 'You can't escape us immigrants. We won't stop trying. We won't stop taking risks.'[78]

In Kelman's *Pigeon English* the 11-year-old protagonist's Ghanaian aunt, who has made it to England takes drastic action to avoid detection or interaction with state authorities – she simply burns her fingertips to remove her fingerprints:[79]

> Auntie Sonja says she'll stop burning them when she finds the perfect place. When she can stay in that place forever and there's nobody there to ruin it or send her away, then she'll let her fingerprints grow back for good.[80]

One could argue that her self-harm is in response to the psychological violence meted out to her by the state whose policies keep in her in a state of anxiety. We learn too that she has a violent boyfriend who beats her. Given her irregular status,

[76] T Achiume (2019) 1509, 1571–73.
[77] P Kingsley (2016), n 64 above, 54, 69–70.
[78] P Kingsley (2016), n 64 above, 55.
[79] A Kelman (2012), n 49 above, 93.
[80] A Kelman (2012) 93.

she is unlikely to report him to the authorities. She is reliant on him and thus her economic vulnerability completes the full spectrum of physical, sexual, psychological and economic violence.[81]

A. Resettlement and Corruption

For those forced to flee their homes to neighbouring states, there is the possibility of resettlement to a third country, which may include one in the Global North, via the UNHCR Resettlement scheme. This is equivalent to winning the golden ticket in Roald Dahl's children's book, *Charlie and the Chocolate Factory*.[82] The camp refugee is the mirror of poor Charlie Bucket who manages to get a ticket to visit the chocolate factory along with four other children, one of whose parents has in effect paid for hers in a manner mirroring the investment visa scheme. However, just as with other visas, there is also the possibility of corruption within the UNHCR system and the host state. There are also delays occasioned by receiving states, which can take years to organise the move. In his book on the Dadaab Refugee camp in Kenya, *City of Thorns*, Ben Rawlence recounts how Kenyan officials were fired for selling passports; how in a separate camp, there were over 15,000 people awaiting repatriation to the United States which, 'at the current rate, … will take 15 years before all of them make their way there.'[83] Meanwhile a couple promised repatriation to Australia learned, after years of waiting, that there had been a change of government 'with a very hard line on immigration that was going slow on all resettlement cases'.[84] This couple's plight is contrasted with that of a UN cleaner who having claimed to a supervisor, that she was being harassed and had nearly been raped by guards and G4 Security, was fast-tracked to America. It ends by observing that the informant, 'was not so well connected.'[85]

VII. Refugee Law and Literature

Fictional literature often gives an accurate account of refugee law. Ellen Wiles, a barrister who works in immigration law, cites a case of an Eritrean asylum seeker who shared the same birthday as her, as the source of the inspiration for the novel, *The Invisible Crowd*. She imagined what it would have been like, had

[81] See Protocol to the African Charter on Human and Peoples' Rights on the Rights of Women in Africa, 2003 (Maputo), Assembly/AU/Dec.14 (II), arts 1(j), 4, 10, 11. Council of Europe Convention on Preventing and combating violence against women and domestic violence, 2011, CETS 210, arts 3(a); 33, 35, 59–61.

[82] R Dahl, *Charlie and the Chocolate Factory* (London, Puffin, 2016).

[83] B Rawlence, *City of Thorns: Nine Lives in the World's Largest Refugee Camp* (London, Portobello Books, 2016) 347–57. Quote at 353.

[84] B Rawlence (2016) 354. See also 355–56.

[85] B Rawlence (2016) 355.

their circumstances been reversed.[86] Her two protagonists, Yonas and Gebre, had left home because of the repressive Eritrean regime which enforced absolute obedience under pain of torture. Both had been imprisoned by the regime, Yonas for emailing negative human rights reports outside the country. On their journey towards the UK, their passports were taken from them. On arrival, they were forced to work unpaid in a seafood processing factory until, separately, they escaped. Hungry and penniless, Gebre is caught stealing bread from a supermarket on the first day that he arrives in London after escaping. He is arrested and put in an immigration removals centre. He claims asylum.

As in refugee law, so too in diasporic literature, there is discussion of the need to prove persecution. This requires you to show that the state that you are fleeing is unable or unwilling to protect you from harm. Without explicitly citing the United Nations Refugee Convention 1951, the characters in fictional literature are aware of the grounds for claiming refugee status. Discussions around which of the five UN Refugee Convention grounds of persecution to claim (race, religion, nationality, membership in a particular social group and political opinion) form part of the literary narrative.[87] Recounting his release from a detention centre, Brian Chikwava's protagonist in *Harare North* explains his use of political opinion as the source of his persecution:

> The story that I tell the immigration people is tighter than a thief's anus. Me I tell them I have been harass by them boys in dark glasses because I am a youth member of the opposition party. This is not trying to shame our government in any way, but if you don't spin them smooth jazz numbers then the immigration people is never to give you chance to even sniff first step into Queen's land. That is they style, I have hear.[88]

Stereotypes also play a role in how claims are framed. The madam who is in charge of the trafficked women in Chika Unigwe's novel *On Black Sisters' Street*, sends Sisi, a new arrival, to apply for asylum. The story she is to tell is that she is Liberian and that her father, a Mandingo Chief, was killed by Charles Taylor's soldiers along with the rest of her family. She is to say that she witnessed the slaughter and only survived by hiding in the kitchen cupboard. While there she heard one of the soldiers say someone was missing. He said that they would return to make sure that they had killed the whole family as they had been instructed. She managed to leave her village and escape, without a passport, with the help of a white man who took pity on her.[89] The advice on demeanour is revealing:

> Look sad. Cry. Wail. Tear your hair out. White people enjoy sob stories. They love to hear about us killing each other, about us hacking each other's heads off in senseless ethnic conflicts. The more macabre the story the better.[90]

[86] E Wiles, *The Invisible Crowd* (London, Harper Collins 2017). Ellen Wiles at: https://www.ellenwiles.com/.

[87] UN Convention relating to the Status of Refugees, 1951, 189 UNTS 137. For the European Regime, See C Costello (2016). See I Mbue (2016), n 15 above, 20–25.

[88] B Chikwava, *Harare North* (London, Vintage, 2010) 4.

[89] C Unigwe, *On Black Sisters' Street* (London, Vintage, 2010) 120.

[90] C Unigwe (2010) 121. See also S Khosravi (2010), n 3 above, 72–73.

Sisi's claim is rejected, showing that far from being pushovers, those in charge of asylum determination err on the side of cynicism, not sympathy.[91]

In Mbue's *Behold the Dreamers*, the lawyer who guides and advises the protagonist through his dealings with bureaucracy provides different storylines that have succeeded in refugee claims. For him, it is about trying one, or more, on for size – the correct fit is that which will be held to be sufficiently plausible to allow one to stay living in the United States. He is also partial to using process – that is appealing immigration decision-makers' decisions – as a means of prolonging one's stay. The lawyer advises that appealing stays deportation so one cannot be removed while one's appeal is in train.[92] He is a consummate player of the legal game to boost his clients' endowments.

Research undertaken by Theophilus Ejorh in Ireland shows that it is the absence of options that leads to creativity. The near impossibility of migrating legally means that people are forced to resort to self-help measures including the visa switch – applying for a tourist or student visa when you have no intention of returning home. The delineation with refugee law also becomes blurred. Ejorh gives the example of one of his interviewees who was given a visa to come to Ireland for medical treatment. She decided to claim asylum so that they could stay on, reasoning: 'There was no other choice left for me and I didn't know the system.'[93] This in turn creates a culture of scepticism which leads to mistrust on both sides. The people who suffer are those who are trying to do the right thing and tell the truth.

In his auto-ethnography, Khosravi rues his mistake in refusing to buy an asylum story from a broker for US$100. The broker had guaranteed success. Khosravi's story about fearing death and injury from war was not considered strong enough to meet the persecution threshold and he was turned down. Recalling how the broker had laughed at him on learning that he had been refused, he notes: 'He was probably right that there was no use telling the UNHCR the truth.'[94] He recounts how UNHCR refused to consider him a political refugee from Iran because he did not fit into the mould of previous claimants whose stories were now used as the template.[95] Citing Kafka's short story, 'Before the Law' he describes the UNHCR and international protections for those seeking refuge as 'available but not accessible or reachable.'[96]

[91] See H Cheikh Ali, C Querton and E Soulard, *Gender Related Asylum Claims in Europe: A Comparative analysis of law, policies and practices in nine EU Member States*, European Parliament, Directorate for Internal Policies, 2012. On credibility in general, see 60–69. See also 39–40, singling out France for not believing rape and sexual assault allegations because they are so frequently mentioned. Meanwhile Spain is said not to recognise trafficking and forced prostitution as a form of persecution (at 41, 42).

[92] I Mbue (2016), n 15 above, 24, 57–59, 224–226.

[93] T Ejorh, 'Modern African Migrations to Ireland: Patterns and Contexts' (2012) 38 *Journal of Ethnic and Migration Studies* 577, 585.

[94] S Khosravi (2010), n 3 above, 33.

[95] S Khosravi (2010) 33–35.

[96] S Khosravi (2010) 36.

One of the characters in Lanchester's multi-vocal novel, *Capital* is a Zimbabwean woman, Quentina Mksfesi, who had been arrested and beaten so badly by the police that she had to be hospitalised. Before getting to hospital, she had been waylaid by some 'goons' who gave her 72 hours to leave the country. Aided by a missionary, she escaped and came to England on a student visa:

> To make a long story short, she had overstayed on purpose, applied for asylum, been rejected, been arrested and sentenced to deportation, but the judge at the final appeal had ruled that she could not be sent back to Zimbabwe because there were grounds for thinking that if she was she would be killed. At that point Quentina had entered a legal state of semi-existence. She had no right to work and could claim only subsistence-level benefits, but she couldn't be imprisoned and deported. She was not a citizen of the UK but she could not go anywhere else. She was a non-person.[97]

Quentina is not alone in discovering that she is a 'non-person'. In her autobiography, *Infidel*, Ayan Hirsi Ali recalls how she received a letter voiding her naturalisation as a Dutch citizen because 'of the use of incorrect personal data'.[98] When she first arrived in the Netherlands and claimed asylum, she had used the name Hirsi Magan, not Hirsi Ali. The story that follows is instructive. She is accused of having given a different name – she says she has previously freely admitted this: 'Yes, I should have told the whole truth in 1992 when I arrived in Holland, even though I was frightened of being sent home. In time, as I learned not to be afraid, I learned that it was wrong not to tell the truth.'[99]

She had another problem, the person to whom she had said she was forcibly married denied it. The Dutch parliament discussed her case (she was after all a Member of Parliament and a prominent one at that, having made a film denouncing Islam which led to the murder of Theo van Gogh the film-maker). The minister in charge insisted that rules needed to be adhered to and ordered that Ali be stripped of citizenship. She meanwhile had been invited to the United States where

[97] J Lanchester (2013), n 13 above, 131–32. See also T Ranger (2005), n 11 above, 405, 420–21 who recounts the *real* stories of women with similar fact situations. See also *AA (Involuntary Returns to Zimbabwe)* [2005] UKAIT 00144 in which Ranger gave evidence that a dishonest Zimbabwean asylum seeker should not be returned to Zimbabwe because the government would persecute him for having sought to claim asylum. While clearly uncomfortable with the misrepresentations made by the appellant in his originating claim, the tribunal did grant him and other Zimbabweans who had claimed asylum, a stay relying on the evidence of Professor Ranger, NGOs and others who were familiar with the workings of the Zimbabwean government. However, see R Ford, 'Zimbabwe asylum seekers can be sent back after ruling on persecution risk', *The Times*, London, 3 August 2006, uplifting the blanket ban on removals to Zimbabwe and urging a case by case approach. The case law went back and forth until in 2019 following a change of government in Harare, the Home Office was found to be inviting Zimbabwean officials to sit in on asylum interviews in the United Kingdom which has itself generated legal action. F Perraudin, 'Home Office held 'illegal interview' with asylum seeker', *The Guardian*, 20 March 2019; F Perraudin, 'Home Office faces legal cases over Zimbabwean asylum seekers', *The Guardian*, 5 January 2020.

[98] A Hirsi Ali, *Infidel: My Life* (London, Simon and Schuster, 2008) 338.

[99] A Hirsi Ali (2008) 342. She says that she had disclosed her lie in the past to the minister now seeking to deport her (at 341).

she had a job offer. She noted the irony of her position: she could not get a US visa if she was not a Dutch citizen – she would be stateless. Eventually the matter was resolved in her favour: 'I found a lawyer, who told me that because I used the name Ali, which was the birth name of my grandfather known as Magan, I hadn't in fact fraudulently filled in any forms.' She also filed a document analysing Somali law, which showed that:

> I had a right to use any name in the long list of my male ancestors as my family name. (I hadn't known that.) Because I was unable to procure birth certificates for my grandfather, father, and mother, as requested, I obtained a statement from my brother confirming that my grandfather Magan was named Ali at his birth.

Were it not for her class, profile and resources, which enabled her to get expert help, would she have had her citizenship restored?

Narrative is particularly important in refugee status decision-making, where applicants are sometimes disbelieved if they do not present a coherent narrative of their reasons for fleeing.

VIII. Credibility

The leitmotif of the asylum seeker's narrative centres on credibility and the frustration of not being believed. The default starting point of the immigration system is to assume that the person is lying. It articulates the dilemma identified by Carol Bohmer and Amy Shuman in their study of deception within the asylum system, which is that sometimes people *do* lie or embellish facts in the hope that this will strengthen their case. They are then caught out in the lie. Ironically, the perceived need to tell a coherent story may also count against them.[100] Similarly, there is also evidence that scepticism is the starting point in status determination proceedings.[101]

Noo Saro Wiwa relies on the work of Beneduce, a professor of Medical and Psychological Anthropology in Turin. She cites his paper on the 'The Moral Economy of Lying' to show how there is a disconnect between what immigration and asylum officers *think* a migrant should be able to prove, and the ability of the supplicant to furnish the required evidence. In part, this is because of a difference

[100] C Bohmer and A Shuman, *Political Asylum Deceptions: The Culture of Suspicion* (London, Palgrave Macmillan, 2018) 27. They also identify patterns in the narratives of persecution put forward by asylum seekers, which patterns are linked to the perceived success of a particular ground at the time of application.

[101] McDonald identifies three credibility flags in status determination proceedings: internal inconsistencies, applicants' demeanour and presentation, and apparent implausibility. D McDonald, 'Credibility Assessment in Refugee Status Determination' (2014) 26 *National Law School of India* 116–26.

in emphasis on what constitutes 'proof' and their different experiences of bureaucracy and paperwork:

> The asylum seeker born out of shoddy bureaucracy often struggles to prove not only their identity but their ill-treatment too. The policeman who dragged them into African prison cells don't always fill out paperwork. Those same police might not maintain records of gang rape reported to them by a distraught girl.[102]

Saro Wiwa's observations are captured in Adichie's story 'The American Embassy'. The protagonist, who is at the embassy to claim asylum after a failed attempt on her journalist husband's life (they killed her son instead while the husband escaped and fled), recounts her interview with the embassy official, who on hearing that she is claiming political asylum, requests proof. The protagonist answers that she buried her son the day before. She sees her son's death as the 'proof'. The embassy official, who must be aware of widespread violations of human rights, this being set during the notorious Abacha regime which ruled in Nigeria from 1993–98, seeks to maintain a 'neutral' position. She offers her condolences for the woman's loss of her son before going to say that while she is aware of inter-group conflict, what she requires is proof that the government has been directly involved in the violation. Further, the protagonist is asked to show that she will be harmed if she stays in Nigeria.[103]

The visa official is met by silence, as, perplexed, the protagonist wonders if the embassy official truly understands what is going on, or indeed what life is like for the ordinary Nigerian. She cannot bring herself to pollute the memory of her son for the sake of a visa. She will not tell her story so as to fit the victim mould required by the refugee process. The embassy official continues: 'Ma'am? The United States offers a new life to victims of political persecution but there needs to be proof ….'[104]

The impact of arbitrary decision-making is captured in a three-volume edited collection, *Refugee Tales*,[105] which are real life accounts told by asylum seekers and those who assist them. It is based on Chaucer's *Canterbury Tales* and the words of the speaker are told as a 'tale' by the writer assigned to them. In the original, Chaucer recounts the stories told by his various characters on their pilgrimage to Canterbury. The twenty-first-century rendition makes those involved in the asylum process the pilgrims, so in lieu of the Wife of Bath and the Knight, we hear

[102] N Saro Wiwa, 'A Time to Lie' in L Popescu (ed), *A Country of Refuge. An Anthology of Writing on Asylum Seekers* (London, Unbound, 2016, 128. See also T Ranger (2005), n 11 above, 411–18 and S Khosravi (2010), n 3 above, 34.

[103] C Adichie, 'The American Embassy' in C Adichie, *The Thing around your neck* (London, Fourth Estate, 2009) 128, 140. For the 'real-life' version, see T Ranger (2005), n 11 above, 405, 413.

[104] C Adichie (2009) 128, 141. See also A Wooley, 'Narrating the "Asylum Story": Between Literary and Legal Storytelling' (2017) 19 *Interventions: International Journal of Postcolonial Studies* 376, 386–91.

[105] D Herd and A Pincus (eds), *Refugee Tales* (Manchester, Comma Press, 2016); D Herd and A Pincus (eds), *Refugee Tales II* (Manchester, Comma Press, 2017); D Herd and A Pincus, *Refugee Tales III* (Manchester, Comma Press, 2019). The proceeds from the sale of the books benefit the Gatwick Detention Centre.

the tales of the migrant, the lorry driver, the chaplain, the translator, the barrister, the detainee and the appellant amongst others. These real-life every-day accounts of the perils faced are rendered more powerful and accessible by the use of this fictional device. In the prologue to the first *Refugee Tales*, the narrator contrasts the camaraderie in Chaucer's tales, which painted a positive picture of England, with the current situation where 'sweete England' has been:

> Rendered hostile by act of law
> So that even friendship is barely possible.[106]

The other tales are replete with examples of the arbitrariness of the legal process and the absence of natural justice and basic fairness.[107] In The Interpreter's Tale from the *Refugee Tales*, the narrator observes:

> Word for word.
> I am not believed.
> I am believed when she is not.
> You need to understand, I tell her.
> This is how it works here.
> They will not believe you more if you shout louder.[108]

The UNHCR refugee status determination guidelines for those interviewing asylum seekers call for greater cultural sensitivity and an understanding that trauma may result in altered behaviour.[109] That is what *should* happen. However, state practice can differ, meaning there is no 'right demeanour' or narrative.[110] Khosravi notes that: 'Only those few who could "translate" their local stories into Eurocentric language had a chance.'[111] Writing about the UK process, David Herd captures how language can be used to 'lock' an asylum seeker out of the process. He details the ways in which the person is thwarted in their attempts to express or convey what has happened to them, to share details of their lives that they may not

[106] D Herd, 'Prologue' in D Herd and A Pincus, *Refugee Tales* (2016) v–x at viii–ix.

[107] The UNHCR Guidelines on interviewing asylum seekers and its general advice on processes is generally disregarded. UN High Commissioner for Refugees (UNHCR), *Handbook on Procedures and Criteria for Determining Refugee Status and Guidelines on International Protection Under the 1951 Convention and the 1967 Protocol Relating to the Status of Refugees*, April 2019, HCR/1P/4/ENG/REV. 4, available at: https://www.refworld.org/docid/5cb474b27.html. See also, UNHCR, 'Refugee Status Determination' at: https://www.refworld.org/rsd.html.

[108] C Watts, 'The Interpreter's Tale' in D Herd and A Pincus (eds) (2016), n 105 above, 63–68, 64. See also S Collis, 'The Lawyer's Tale' ibid 107, 111, 119.

[109] UN High Commissioner for Refugees (UNHCR), *Handbook and Guidelines on Procedures and Criteria for Determining Refugee Status under the 1951 Convention and the 1967 Protocol Relating to the Status of Refugees*, December 2011, HCR/1P/4/ENG/REV. 3. It is linked to other guidelines identifying particular groups or situations. Some states also have national guidelines. UK Border Agency, *Asylum Instruction: Considering the Protection (Asylum) Claim and Assessing Credibility*, Home Office, 2012. Judges in the UK are also issued with judicial Bench books identifying good practice when dealing with different groups. Judicial College, *Equal Treatment Bench Book 2018* (London, Judicial College, 2018).

[110] S Khosravi (2010), n 3 above, 33.

[111] S Khosravi (2010) 34.

have shared with those closest to them and which they may themselves not have processed, in a system built on scepticism and disbelief.[112]

> What one sees repeatedly, in other words, and with an intensity that increases year on year, is the fact that, in a way that simply isn't metaphorical, the language is the border. It isn't the whole of the border, nor its most manifest aspect, but it is absolutely a medium in which the border takes effect.[113]

This leads to the frustration identified so well by two of Wiles's characters in *The Invisible Crowd*. Yonas, the Eritrean protagonist asks his peers in the squat about claiming asylum.[114] Two recount their experiences in which they both regret ever having bothered to apply for asylum:

> I claim at the airport, when I get 'ere, like I was advise and am told I am *lying*. But still they make me tell my story so many times more, and if I say *one thing* differently they say to me: Ha! This *prove* you are lying. Even after they say I was *lying* from the start. And after that I am kept waiting. I cannot work, and I no get any decision for six years after.[115] (Histoire)

Another, Michel, recalls how he had to wait for four years to get a decision. He was not believed despite telling them that he had been tortured along with his family. The interviewer had accused him of making it up, calling his story a fairy tale and leaving Michel wondering what kind of person would make up a story of torture. Both identify the problem faced by those who, like Quentina in Lanchester's *Capital*, are not given recognition, but cannot be refused: they are left in limbo, not entitled to work or to claim benefits leaving him (Michel) having to live ''ere like an animal for my 'ole life.'[116]

[112] D Herd, 'Afterword: Calling for an End to Indefinite Detention' in D Herd and A Pincus (eds), *Refugee Tales II* (2017), n 105 above, 113, 119. See also S Khosravi (2010), n 3 above, 34.

[113] D Herd (ed), *Refugee Tales II* (2017), n 105 above, 113, 120.

[114] There is a plethora of reports from civil society and government agencies which detail the widespread human rights violations in Eritrea. Clearly it is not a lack of information that leads to refusals; more a lack of empathy and the correct application of the rules. See: United Kingdom: Home Office, *Country Policy and Information Note – Eritrea: National service and illegal exit*, July 2018, Version 5.0; United Kingdom: Foreign and Commonwealth Office, *Human Rights and Democracy Report 2017 – Eritrea*, 16 July 2018; United States Department of State, *2018 Trafficking in Persons Report – Eritrea*, 28 June 2018; Human Rights Watch, *Human Rights Abuses of Eritreans, At Home and Abroad*, 18 April 2018; L Oette and L Hovil, 'Tackling the root causes of human trafficking and smuggling from Eritrea: The need for an empirically grounded EU policy on mixed migration in the Horn of Africa' in IRRI, SIHA, SOAS Centre for Human Rights Law *Tackling the root causes of human trafficking and smuggling from Eritrea: The need for an empirically grounded EU policy on mixed migration in the Horn of Africa* (November 2017).

[115] E Wiles (2017), n 86 above, 84. S Khosravi gives an account of how he left out information about his imprisonment and father that he thought irrelevant. When he later added it, he was met with scepticism by the interviewing officer. Khosravi (2010), n 3 above, 34.

[116] E Wiles (2017), n 86 above, 84. See also C Adichie (2009), n 103 above, 128, 134. N Saro Wiwa gives the real-life example of a Malian man who tells the truth but is refused leaving him to rue his disregard of advice given on the boat to Lampedusa, telling him to lie and say he was from the Cote d'Ivoire. '… they would have believed me. Instead I am still here, without a job, without a thing! Oh, Doctor, this does not work.' Saro Wiwa details how women who have been gang raped, may point to their caesarean scars and pretend that they have been stabbed. N Saro Wiwa (2016), n 102 above, 125, 130.

Histoire and Michel, advise Yonas not to bother wasting his time and effort applying for asylum because his application would not be properly considered and all he would get is a refusal: 'in one letter which is like copy and paste from all the other letters from all the other fuckers who try to live their life 'ere.'[117]

Encouraged by a British friend, Yonas does apply, citing the torture that he endured when it was discovered that he had been writing and publishing anti-government material. He is unsuccessful. Research shows that the refusals often ignore compelling evidence of systematic human rights violations in the countries from which asylum claimants originate.[118] The scepticism expressed in the rejection letter reads like the 'copy-paste' homogeneity alluded to by Yonas's fellow squatters. It also reflects the literature on the failure of asylum decision-makers to give due care and attention to the claims made.[119] In 2014 a scandal broke out after it was revealed that the British Home Office had incentivised staff by giving shopping vouchers to those who turned down the most applications.[120] This points to the pressures that they are put under to meet impossible decision quotas within unfeasibly short timeframes.[121]

Echoing research on Home Office status determination practice,[122] Lanchester's *Capital* captures well the arbitrariness of the decision-making process by contrasting two tribunal judges. One is a liberal female judge who reads, for contextual information, novels and reportage like the *Kite Runner* and *We Wish to Inform you that Tomorrow we will be killed with our Families* to assist her in case determination.[123] The other judge, a man, is a sceptic, believing that many of the people before him

[117] E Wiles (2017), n 86 above, 84.

[118] Eritrea which has sometimes been referred to as the 'North Korea of Africa' receives poor human rights ratings and yet there is still equivocation in the allocation of asylum to those who manage to flee. UNHCR, 2009 *Eligibility Guidelines for Assessing the International Protection Needs of Asylum Seekers from Eritrea.* Refugee Council *Between a rock and a hard place: the dilemma facing refused asylum seekers* (London, Refugee Council, 2012) 13–17. See n 114 above. M. Wrong *I didn't do it for you: how the world used and abused a small African nation,* Harper, 2005.

[119] T Ranger (2005), n 11 above.

[120] D Taylor and R Mason, 'Home Office staff rewarded with gift vouchers for fighting off asylum cases', *The Guardian*, London, 14 January 2014.

[121] See the first-person account of a former Home Office decision maker, Anonymous 'I worry asylum caseworkers are failing people in their darkest hour', *The Guardian*, London, 8 April 2017. J. Souter 'Asylum decision-making in the UK: disbelief or denial?' Open Democracy, 4 April 2011 at: http://www.opendemocracy.net. CJ McKinney, 'Home Office loses a quarter of asylum decision-makers in six months', Free movement, 28 November 2017 at www.freemovement.org.uk.

[122] D Bogner, CR Brewin and J Herlihy, 'Refugees' Experiences of Home Office Interviews. A Qualitative Study on the Disclosure of Sensitive Personal Information' (2014) 36 *Journal of Ethnic and Migration Studies*, 519. The credibility issue is not unique to the UK. See T Luker, 'Decision-making Conditioned by Radical Uncertainty: Credibility Assessment at the Australian Refugee Review Tribunal' at: https://opus.lib.uts.edu.au/bitstream/10453/27042/4/Trish%20Luker%2c%20Decision-making%20and%20Radical%20Uncertainty%20-%20FINAL%20.pdf.

I Mighetto, 'The Contingency of Credibility: Gender Related Persecution, Traumatic Memory and Home Office Interviews' (2016) 3 *SOAS Law Journal* 1–37.

[123] *Kite Runner*, a novel by Khaled Hosseini (London, Bloomsbury, 2011) is set in Afghanistan, while *We Wish to Inform you* was written by a Canadian General after the Rwandan genocide to tell the stories of those who waited, in vain, for the international community to intervene. P Gourevitch, *We Wish to Inform you that tomorrow we will be killed with our families* (London, Picador, 2015).

have invented stories to enable them to stay.[124] The female judge muses on the limbo status that often befalls failed asylum seekers because of the impact of the Human Rights Act 1998 which means that failed asylum seekers cannot be sent back to countries where they are likely to be tortured or disappeared. However, they are also forbidden to work and cannot claim state benefits, leaving her to muse: 'Even from the most realistic, least idealistic perspective, it could not be seen as an ideal solution.'[125] Quentina gets the sceptic at her hearing and finds herself sent to a detention centre.[126] Here again, the description of the conditions are in keeping with reports made by academics, NGOs and television news exposés.[127]

Beverley Naidoo in *Web of Lies*, identifies, through the young narrator, how there is bias against people from certain countries, in this case Nigeria. Writing in her diary, she recounts how her father had told her and her brother that the claims of thousands of Nigerians have been refused. She is distressed, and worries whether the authorities will take the time to properly consider her father's claim. She is keen that they listen so that they can understand his truthfulness about the reasons for their flight from home.[128] Her anxiety is well founded. Her father had been to one interview conducted at Heathrow Airport to ascertain if he and his family were entitled to asylum. He waited for the outcome for a year. When a letter finally came from the Immigration Department, it had been to tell him that they had lost his file and interview and to alert him that he would have to make a fresh application.[129] She describes her turbulent feelings as being like a small boat on a rough sea being tossed about, fearing being broken on the rocks.[130]

By way of contrast, there is sometimes a perception that those who come from the LGBTI community who are fleeing persecution from a continent seen as 'homophobic' will be welcomed with open arms in the more 'enlightened' North. In Chapter five I show that this is misconceived.

IX. Access to Justice

The UN Special Rapporteur on the Human Rights of Migrants suggests that states should seek to improve access to justice by providing legal aid and making people

[124] C Bohmer and A Shuman (2018), n 100 above.

[125] J Lanchester (2013), n 13 above, 484, 485. See also B Zephaniah, *Refugee* Boy (London, Bloomsbury, 2017) 120–21, 134. H McDonald, 'The Student's Tale' in D Herd and A Pincus (eds), *Refugee Tales II* (2017), n 105 above, 3, 8–9 (features an epidemiologist sitting in a hostel anxiously, but impatiently, waiting for a decision on his application so that he can work and contribute to society.)

[126] J Lanchester (2013), n 13 above, 525–28.

[127] A Lindley, *Injustice in Immigration Detention: Perspectives from Legal Professionals* (London, Bar Council, 2017); Women for Refugee Women *Detained* (London, Women for Refugee Women, 2014); Women for Refugee Women, *I am Human* (London, Women for Refugee Women, 2015); *Channel 4 News*, 'Yarl's Wood interactive: inside the immigration centre', 2 March 2015. D Herd, 'Afterword' (2017), n 112 above, 113, 114–122.

[128] B Naidoo, *Web of Lies* (London, Puffin, 2004) 211.

[129] B Naidoo (2004) 13, 14

[130] B Naidoo (2004) 211.

aware of the remedies available while ensuring that these remedies can be effectively engaged.[131] The reality, as identified by Mavis Maclean and John Eekelaar in their study of England and Wales, is that states are rolling back on legal aid provision in all branches of the law.[132]

Migrants find themselves in a bind – fearing detection and yet needing to regularise their status which involves engaging with the authorities. More than that, it requires a knowledge of how to navigate the immigration system and a lot of money to pay lawyers and the necessary visa and other processing fees to the Home Office. Those who cannot pay lawyers, the majority, have to rely on a shrinking and chronically underfunded voluntary sector. Common to most of the stories set in Britain is the contact with legal advice-giving agencies or charities which provide support and accommodation, such as *Refuge* or the Refugee Council.[133]

In 2018, it was revealed that in the UK, the immigration regulations and policies had been amended 5,700 times since 2010, doubling in length to 375,000 words, or four PhD theses. The report reveals that in the year of the introduction of the 'hostile environment' policy in Britain, there were 1300 changes. A leading immigration and asylum barrister, Colin Yeo, is quoted as saying:

> The frequency of the changes mean it's very difficult to keep on top of them … You have to read everything that's coming out and it's very hard to be certain you've captured every single change that might be relevant to your clients. The changes are often hurried out, which means they can be badly written. They can be very difficult to understand, even for judges and lawyers. We've seen a number of errors in drafting that have to be corrected in later versions.[134]

The process is not helped by the removal of discretion in decision-making and the narrowing of the grounds and time-scale for lodging appeals.[135] The applicant and their advisors are required to keep up with rule changes and paperwork; the Home Office is not. In Beverley Naidoo's *Web of Lies*, the journalist father is told to reapply after the immigration service loses his paperwork. He is only told this after a year of waiting for a determination. His lawyer expresses frustration but notes that there is nothing to be done about it. Another year passes.[136]

It is not only the fictional literature that points to arbitrary usurpation of the right to a remedy, countless reviews and human rights advocates' interventions

[131] UN Special Rapporteur on Migrants A/71/285 paras 79–81, paras 79–81.

[132] M Maclean and J Eekelaar, *After the Act: Access to Family Justice after LASPO* (Oxford, Hart, 2019). LASPO stands for the Legal Aid, Sentencing and Punishment of Offenders Act 2012.

[133] E Wiles (2017), n 86 above, 86, 94–96. J Lanchester (2013), n 13 above, 132.

[134] M Bozic, C Barr, N McIntyre and P Noor, 'Revealed: immigration rules in UK more than double in length', *The Guardian*, London, 27 August 2018. At the start of 2020 the British government overhauled its immigration system to adopt a points-based system akin to the one used in Australia. Home Office, 'The UK's points-based immigration system: policy statement', Home Office, 19 February 2020.

[135] A Travis, 'Tory immigration bill to curb right of appeal against deportation', *The Guardian*, London, 2013. The outcome was the promulgation of the 2014 Immigration Act, where a person can be removed before appeal, meaning that the appeal would be filed after they have left the jurisdiction; a clear intent to frustrate.

[136] B Naidoo (2004), n 128 above, 14.

do the same.[137] Equally important have been the first-person accounts of the arbitrariness of detention schemes. These have brought to our attention the injustices that are locked away and out of sight.

X. Detention

In 2018–19 Behrouz Boochani, an Iranian-Kurdish journalist, author and asylum seeker, won several of the most prestigious literary prizes in Australia. The accolades were for his book *No Friend but the Mountain*, which he wrote in Farsi on his mobile phone and sent to be translated while he was imprisoned (his word) on Manus Island by the Australian government.[138] He was one of the many caught up in Australia's 'deterrence-based' immigration policy which refuses to permit asylum seekers to live in Australia, putting them in detention facilities on outlying islands, bribing or bullying its smaller island neighbours to take on its responsibilities.[139] Boochani's book is both a moving account of his attempts to hold on to a sense of dignity and worth, and a scathing denunciation of the inhumanity of the Manus detention centre, ostensibly dismantled in 2017. One of Boochani's prizes, the Victoria Premier Literary Award, is awarded to honour the best in 'Australian' writing. Perhaps holding a mirror up to Australia is the best service that Boochani may have performed.[140] Boochani reminds us that it is our collective task to ensure that 'out of sight' does not mean, 'out of mind'.[141]

It is telling that detention features so extensively in the fictional literature. In Naidoo's *The Other Side of Truth*, the Nigerian journalist father of two children who had been smuggled into Britain after their mother was shot, is also detained on arrival. Protests and a media campaign eventually secure his release.[142]

[137] Human Rights Committee Concluding Observations to the sixth report of Australia, CCPR/C/CO/AUS/6, (1 December 2017), para 38. The Committee also points to its General Comment No 35 on Article 9 on Liberty and Security of the Person, CCPR/C/GC/35, 16 December 2014, para 18. See also *Arf v Secretary of State for the Home Department* [2017] EWHC 10 (on the breach of article 3 of the ECHR resulting from the unlawful detention of a mentally ill woman who had been trafficked).

[138] B Boochani (translated by O Tofighian), *No Friend but the Mountains: The True Story of an Illegally Imprisoned Refugee* (London, Picador, 2019).

[139] The Supreme Court of Papua New Guinea struck down this arrangement: *Namah v Pato (Minister for Foreign Affairs and Immigration) and others* [2016] PJSC 13. Discussed in NF Tan, 'The Manus island Regional Processing Centre: A Legal Taxonomy' (2018) 20 *European Journal of Migration and Law* 427, 434–39. Tan explores the many other examples of 'off-shoring' including by European states – discussed in Chapter two of this volume.

[140] K Allahyari and P Rae, 'Behrouz Boochani's literary prize cements his status as an Australian writer', *The Conversation*, 1 February 2019. His translator has explained the process that they went through to get the book from Farsi mobile texts into a book in English. O Tofighian, 'Truth to Power: my time translating Behrouz Boochani's masterpiece', *The Conversation*, 15 August 2018.

[141] See J Wittenberg (2019), n 149 below.

[142] B Naidoo, *The Other Side of Truth* (London, Puffin, 2000) 147. See also B Chikwava, *Harare North* (London, Vintage, 2010), 4. Although the issue of the efficacy and fairness of detaining people is regularly discussed in the media, there seems to be little appetite to close detention centres by the government. A Sarkar, 'By demeaning refugees, Tories have caused a hunger strike', *The Guardian*, 1 March 2018.

Some of the protagonists in Helon Habila's novel *Travellers* find themselves in a migrant 'centre' in Basel which is described as remote. To reinforce their isolation, the inhabitants are not allowed to engage in every-day activities including visiting the library or going to church. The aim of the law is clear; it is designed to limit migration by making conditions difficult and also to assuage the anxieties of the locals.[143]

John Lanchester's *Capital* depicts mental illness amongst detainees and casual cruelty by the guards. It provides an accurate reflection of detention conditions as recorded in hidden filming by a news programme, *Channel 4 News*, and newspaper reports.[144] In 2018 the UN Working Group on People of African Descent enjoined Spain to consider the deleterious mental health impact of detention. It highlighted the failure to provide specialist care for minors and for trafficked and pregnant women in detention. The Working Group noted that there was, in effect, little to distinguish the detention centres from prison and noted that asylum seekers and migrants were sometimes being mixed with convicted criminals or those awaiting deportation having served their sentences.[145] Reflecting on her detention, Quentina, in Lanchester's *Capital*, muses that the only thing distinguishing those released from prison compared to those deported was that the former, 'went somewhere better' while the detainees, 'were sent back to the place they had done everything to escape.'[146]

Detention draws many into its net. The use of detention creates ethical dilemmas for those in the medical profession who have to decide whether working within the system compounds the problem and provides cover for a state, or whether they are doing the right thing by treating those in need.[147]

The use of detention and the observation by Lanchester that it was like being in a prison, echoes the treatment of East African Asians in 1968 who sought refuge in what they thought was their home, Britain, but found themselves in prison.[148] In a lecture delivered in 2003, Lord Lester, who as a young lawyer successfully represented the group when they were denied citizenship warned that the same mistake could be made:

> What was done to British citizens of Asian descent in 1968 is not a remote chapter of history. In times of populist hysteria, racism and xenophobia, it could happen again

[143] H Habila, *Travellers* (London, Penguin, 2019) 106.

[144] J Lanchester (2013), n 13 above, 525–28. *Channel 4 News*, 'Yarl's Wood: Undercover in the Secret Immigration Centre', 2 March 2015 at: https://www.channel4.com/news/yarls-wood-immigration-removal-detention-centre-investigation; A Gentleman, 'Yarl's Wood Women feel Desperate Says Diane Abbott', *The Guardian*, 23 February, 2018. See also Human Rights Watch, *Fast-Tracked Unfairness: Detention and Denial of Women Asylum Seekers in the UK*, Human Rights Watch, 2010.

[145] Report of the Working Group of Experts on People of African Descent on its mission to Spain, A/HRC/39/69/Add.2, 14 August, 2018, paras 33–38. See also CEDAW General Recommendation No 32 on the gender dimensions of refugee status, asylum, nationality and statelessness of women, CEDW/C/GC/32, paras 34, 49.

[146] J Lanchester (2013), n 13 above, 528.

[147] British Medical Association, *Locked up, locked out: health and human rights in immigration detention* (London, BMA, 2018). See in particular part 2.

[148] *East African Asians v United Kingdom* (Application No 4403/70) (ECtHR). Discussed in chapter 2.

> if a future Government decided to deprive some other vulnerable minority of their common humanity and their basic rights and freedoms.[149]

Lester has, yet again, been vindicated.[150] In its General Comment on Aliens, the Human Rights Committee which oversees the International Covenant on Civil and Political Rights, distinguishes between aliens who are in a territory legally and others, but still requires that the principle of equal protection before the law be upheld:

> The particular rights of article 13 only protect those aliens who are lawfully in the territory of a State party. This means that national law concerning the requirements for entry and stay must be taken into account in determining the scope of that protection, and that illegal entrants and aliens who have stayed longer than the law or their permits allow, in particular, are not covered by its provisions. *However, if the legality of an alien's entry or stay is in dispute, any decision on this point leading to his expulsion or deportation ought to be taken in accordance with article 13.* It is for the competent authorities of the State party, in good faith and in the exercise of their powers, to apply and interpret the domestic law, observing, however, such requirements under the Covenant as equality before the law (art. 26)' (emphasis added).[151]

Moreover, in its General Comment 30 on Non-Citizens, the UN Race Committee reiterates the importance of non-discrimination and asks states to report using gender and race disaggregated data. Detention facilities are more likely to hold black and brown people from the Global South. The CERD General Comment also calls on states to tackle hate speech and to refrain from stereotyping. States are enjoined to ensure that there are routes to naturalisation for long-term stayers and to reduce statelessness for children. Non-citizens, broadly defined, are to be given opportunities to participate in employment and to access other socio-economic rights. In common with the Human Rights Committee's comment, states are required to ensure equality for all before the law and to make sure that the administration of justice is conducted fairly and to facilitate access to justice.[152]

[149] A Lester, '*East-African Asians v The United Kingdom*: The Inside Story', Odysseus Trust, Lectures, 23 October 2003 at: http://www.odysseustrust.org/lectures/221_east_african_asians-sharma.pdf, at 18. The use of detention is also contentious in the 21st Century. See J Wittenberg 'You have no voice in there', *The Guardian*, London, 28 June 2019. Reproduced in Pincus and Herd (eds), *Refugee Tales III* (2019), n 105 above.

[150] European Union Agency for Fundamental Rights, *European Legal and Policy Framework on immigration detention of children* (Brussels, Office of the European Union, 2017).

[151] Human Rights Committee, *CCPR General Comment No 15: The Position of Aliens Under the Covenant*, 11 April 1986, para 9.

[152] CERD General Recommendation XXX on Discrimination Against Non-Citizens, CERD/C/64/Misc.11/rev.3. See also P Thornberry, *The International Convention on the Elimination of all Forms of Racial Discrimination: A Commentary* (Oxford, OUP, 2016) 145–59. The Committee cited its General Recommendation 30 in its concluding observations to the report of the UK where it enjoined the state to ensure that children were not detained and also to use detention only as a 'measure of last resort.' Further, the state was to ensure that detained individuals had 'effective access to justice, including legal aid.' CERD/C/GBR/CO/21–23, (2016) para 39. See also para 38. See also CERD General Comment No 34 on Racial discrimination against people of African descent, CERD/GC/34, paras 47–49, 53, 58.

Meanwhile in its General Comment No 2 on Migrants in an Irregular Situation and their Families, the Committee on Migrant Workers cautions states not to use detention, especially of families. Children should not be detained and the state should avoid the use of private detention facilities. States should keep in mind the importance of ensuring that there is a right to be contacted and seen. Detention should, if used, be for a short specified period and not indeterminate. The state should facilitate access to legal assistance and ensure due process. Compensation should be paid if breaches have occurred or the detention is ruled unlawful. Special consideration should be given to vulnerable groups, including those who are HIV positive. The system should ensure that detention facilities separate men and women. Particular attention should be paid to women who may have been sexually assaulted and those who may be pregnant.[153]

The Committee on the Rights of the Child has adopted General Comment 6 on the Treatment of Unaccompanied and Separated Children outside their country of origin and also a joint General Comment 3 with the Committee on Migrant Workers and Members of their Family, both of which make extensive recommendations on the obligations of states to avoid placing children in detention, to provide them with access to adequate health care, counselling, education and legal services, and to expedite applications for residence or asylum speedily.[154]

It is also worth noting the environment within which these detentions take place. There is a tension between doing the right thing by unaccompanied minors while also facing down the negative and hostile response to their presence by those who feel that their children are deprived of opportunities that are rightfully theirs because resources are being diverted to look after 'foreigners'. It is trite but remains true to say that children demand our compassion and generosity.

XI. Hostile Environments

The global mobility of people has led to greater heterogeneity but not necessarily an increase in empathy. Many states have responded by abrogating their human rights obligations. They have done this by limiting the scope and space for migrants to arrive, or, having arrived, to regularise themselves. The means taken have been varied.

[153] CMW/C/GC/2 (2013) paras 31–48.

[154] UN Committee on the Rights of the Child (CRC), *General Comment No 6 (2005): Treatment of Unaccompanied and Separated Children Outside their Country of Origin*, 1 September 2005, CRC/GC/2005/6; UN Committee on the Protection of the Rights of All Migrant Workers and Members of Their Families (CMW), *Joint general comment No 3 (2017) of the Committee on the Protection of the Rights of All Migrant Workers and Members of Their Families and No 22 (2017) of the Committee on the Rights of the Child on the general principles regarding the human rights of children in the context of international migration*, 16 November 2017, CMW/C/GC/3–CRC/C/GC/22. See also CRC/C/NOR/CO/7 (2018) para 32.

A. Creating a Hostile Environment

The term 'hostile environment' was coined by the British Home Secretary (equivalent to a Minister of the Interior), later Prime Minister, Theresa May. The goal of this policy was to make life unbearable for those perceived to be unentitled to live in the jurisdiction.[155] The means employed were to make it difficult for irregular migrants to access services including banking, health and housing. This was done by passing two restrictive Immigration Acts in 2014 and 2016. A strict enforcement regime was operationalised. It was supplemented by high-profile campaigns, including the 'go home' advertising hoardings urging undocumented people to leave the UK voluntarily or face detention and deportation.

Additionally, the British government deployed vans with the slogan: 'In the UK Illegally? Go Home or Face Arrest.' On the side of the vans were listed phone numbers that those wishing to report those whom they perceived to be 'illegal' (undocumented) could contact the authorities.[156] The decision to place adverts in 'eight minority ethnic newspapers, postcards in shop windows, and leaflets and posters advertising immigration surgeries used by faith and charity groups' gave an indication of who was being targeted.[157] In this way, the hostile environment moved from rhetoric to official government policy.

I have yet to hear of groups of white Australians, Canadians, South Africans or New Zealanders being held in detention in the United Kingdom, even if they have overstayed their visas. In 'Luck of the Irish', Maeve Higgins documents her experiences as an overstayer in the United States. She is clear that she benefitted from white privilege, which she shows has historically been enshrined in immigration laws that encouraged 'white migration' but excluded migration from certain 'undesirable groups' like the Chinese.[158] She contrasts her sense of entitlement with the fear of other, 'non-white' immigrants who are consumed by the need to have the correct paperwork. Explaining her decision to breach her visa conditions, she states simply, 'It was because I felt like it.'[159] She understood that the chances of her being profiled by immigration services were minimal because the target groups tended to be people of colour.[160] Unlike many who overstay their visas,

[155] D Herd, 'Afterword' (2017), n 112 above, 113, 115–18.

[156] Yonas, in Wiles's *Invisible Crowd* (2017), n 86 above, 54–55, comes across one of these vans, which proclaims '106 arrests in your area last week' (at 54). It terrifies him and leaves him petrified that he will be the 107th.

[157] A Travis, '"Go home" vans resulted in 11 people leaving Britain, says report', *The Guardian*, London, 31 October 2013. See also H Jones, Y Gunaratnam, G Bhatacharya, W Davies, S Dhaliwal, K Forkert, E Jackson and R Saltus, *Go Home? The Politics of Immigration Controversies* (Manchester, Manchester University Press, 2017). This was a 'living research' project undertaken by a collective of academics, civil society and community activists to document the impact of the hostile environment on migrants.

[158] M Higgins, 'Luck of the Irish' in N Shukla and C Suleyman (eds), *The Good Immigrant USA*, (London, Dialogue Books, 2019) 104, 109.

[159] M Higgins (2019) 106.

[160] M Higgins (2019) 104, 107, 113.

Higgins has been able to re-enter the United States on a visa for 'extraordinary aliens'. She lives and works unhindered by her irregular immigration history, leaving her to conclude:

> I am not extraordinary at all. It's dumb luck that I was born white and Irish. And that luck, combined with a history of racialized immigration policies, mean that I was allowed to move here, to a country whose leaders look at me and see themselves, and welcome me with open arms as they push others away.[161]

It is her 'dumb Irish luck' that emboldens her to write about her past immigration irregularities, confident that there will not be any repercussions.

One of the consequences of the British government's hostile environment policy, as the UN Special Rapporteur on contemporary forms of racism, racial discrimination, xenophobia and related intolerance, Professor Achiume, has noted, is that it has caught many in its net, including those who are Black British citizens or lawfully resident and therefore entitled to access services. There has been a marked increase in suspicion of minorities, which has resulted in a reported increase in complaints about race discrimination and racial profiling. The renaming of the policy as 'the compliant environment' following the *Windrush* scandal, where the government was found to have systematically discriminated against British citizens with Caribbean heritage, has not blunted the effects of the hostile environment policy which continue to be felt by minorities.[162]

It is worth noting that the British government is not alone in adopting a hostile policy.[163] In 2015 Hungary used prisoners to erect a wall to stop largely Syrian asylum seekers from crossing over from Serbia at the height of the flow of people seeking protection. The Hungarian government is impervious to criticism about racist, anti-migrant rhetoric and its effects. This may be because it focuses on the domestic political scene where government xenophobia is popular with many, but by no means all, Hungarians. The justification given by Hungary for its stance is that it is upholding the international refugee protection system by insisting that assistance should be provided close to people's states of origin. Hungary is insistent that it does not want to become a corridor for migration. In its dialogue with the

[161] M Higgins (2019) 104, 115.

[162] UN Special Rapporteur on contemporary forms of racism, racial discrimination, xenophobia and related intolerance, *Visit to the United Kingdom of Great Britain and Northern Ireland*, A/HRC/41/54/Add.2, 27 May 2019, para 52. See also M Goodfellow, *Hostile Environment: How Immigrants became Scapegoats* (London, Verso, 2019) 5.

[163] Indeed the government has vehemently challenged the UN Special Rapporteur's account of her visit to the UK and her interpretation of government policies including the hostile environment. See Report of the Special Rapporteur on contemporary forms of racism, racial discrimination, xenophobia and related intolerance on his (sic) [her] visit to the United Kingdom of Great Britain and Northern Ireland – Comments by the State, A/HRC/41/54/Add.4, 3 July 2019. See also A Gentleman, *The Windrush Betrayal: Exposing the Hostile Environment* (London, Guardian, Faber, 2019). *The Times*, 'Home Office is "institutionally racist" said report into Windrush scandal'. The headline went on to say 'Incendiary claim dropped as review watered down', *The Times*, London, 21 February 2020.

UN Race Committee, the Hungarian delegation described 'transit zones' which had reception centres that sound not unlike detention centres.[164]

Maya Goodfellow describes how the 'Hungarian fear' of mass migration was weaponised by the right-wing British politician Nigel Farage during the 2016 referendum about the UK's membership of the EU which eventually led to BREXIT. His then party, the UK Independence Party (UKIP), produced posters showing lines of mostly brown men crossing the Croatia-Slovenia border. It was a warning: if Britain stays in the EU, these people will be coming to live here.[165]

Juan Pablo Aris Escarcena notes that in France, the hostile policy is played out using administrative orders. This involves moving people from camps – such as the Calais camp which housed many asylum seekers, many of whom were trying to make their way to the UK – to other parts of France far from the British border.[166] This dispersal policy involved the use of many strategies, including fining organisations who provided food for violating health regulations after camp inhabitants fled in a hurry and left their food containers behind. Other methods included disturbing sleep by shining lights or using loud noises.[167] Escarcena labels these strategies, 'the politics of exhaustion' which,

> manifest themselves in the construction of a hostile environment where certain forms of extreme, physical and symbolic violence take place, whose fundamental objective is not to discipline bodies, but to reduce the possibilities of exercising vital autonomy as political autonomy.[168]

Hostility is not confined to the Global North. Loren Landau and Roni Amit reflect on amendments made by the South African government to the Refugee Act No 130 of 1998.[169] Using regulations, the government has sought to restrict the rights of refugees to work and others to claim asylum. In common with refugees in other states, refugees were never allowed to vote in South African elections, but have now been warned that they may be stripped of their refugee status if they engage in political activism, including campaigning for political change in their countries of origin. This is a violation of the South African Constitution, 1996, which grants rights to all who live in South Africa. It seems incongruous to strip someone of their refugee status for engaging in political activity if they have been granted

[164] CERD, Summary record of the 2720th meeting, Consideration of reports, comments and information submitted by States parties under article 9 of the Convention, Combined eighteenth to twenty-fifth periodic reports of Hungary, CERD/C/SR/2720, 3 May 2019, paras 22–27. (Transit zones, para 25).

[165] M Goodfellow (2019), n 162 above, 177.

[166] JP Aris Escarcena, 'Expulsions: The Construction of a Hostile Environment in Calais' (2019) 21 *European Journal of Migration and Law* 215–37.

[167] JP Aris Escarcena (2019) 215, 230–33.

[168] JP Aris Escarcena (2019) 215, 234.

[169] L Landau and R Amit, 'Decolonization's Borders', *Africa is a Country*, 21 February 2020. At: https://africasacountry.com/2020/02/decolonizations-borders. See also N Nyoka, 'Amended Refugee Act restricts fundamental rights', *Mail and Guardian*, Johannesburg, 20 February 2020.

asylum on grounds of political status.[170] Landau and Amit note that complaining about conditions in South Africa will likely lead to loss of status. Disturbingly, Landau and Amit trace the state-sanctioned xenophobic action, 'closing borders, workplaces and public services to non-nationals', to an attempt to appeal to a South African population which has long displayed intolerance to outsiders, including those from the African continent. They note how the local population distinguishes xenophobia as legitimate hate, from racism which is not.[171]

B. The Impact of the Hostile Environment: State-Driven Exclusion

Following a visit to the United Kingdom in 2018, the UN Special Rapporteur on anti-racism issued a statement in which she noted that the restrictive immigration policy had turned private individuals and civil servants into immigration officials. She further noted that the effect was to turn places of safety and support, 'hospitals, banks and private residences into border checkpoints.'[172] The direct result of this was heightened racial discrimination. Khosravi explains how for the undocumented, a state of 'deportability' is created whether or not one is detained. There is a constant fear of being found out. Every day activities are 'illegalised'. Moreover, undocumented migrants are not only excluded from access to basic services including health care, but, 'also the right to social relations and freedom of movement in public spaces.'[173]

Until a successful High Court challenge brought by the Joint Council for the Welfare of Immigrants (JCWI) in 2019, one could not rent a house without proving one's right of abode in the United Kingdom.[174] Proof usually involved showing

[170] Arguably the South African government is within its regional rights as the African Charter on Human and Peoples' Rights, 1981, art 23(2) and the OAU Convention Governing the Specific Aspects of Refugee Problems in Africa, 1969, 1001 UNTS 45, makes it a condition that the asylum seeker should not engage in 'subversive activities' widely interpreted as including the host state to prohibit 'refugees residing in their respective territories from attacking any State Members of the OAU, by any activity likely to cause tension between Member States, and in particular by use of arms, through the press, or by radio.' (Art.3 of the OAU Refugee Convention)

[171] L Landau and R Amit (2020). See also S Msimang, 'Belonging – Why South Africans Refuse to let Africa in', *Africa is a Country*, 15 April 2014.

[172] OHCHR, 'United Kingdom: UN expert condemns entrenched racial discrimination and inequality' OHCHR, Geneva, 14 June 2019 at: https://www.ohchr.org/EN/NewsEvents/Pages/DisplayNews.aspx?NewsID=24698&LangID=E. For the full report see Report of the Special Rapporteur on Contemporary Forms of Racism, racial discrimination, xenophobia and related intolerance, A/HRC/41/54/Add.2, 27 May 2019, paras 52–61. It is worth noting that the Special Rapporteur contrasted the draconian policies of the English government with that of the devolved states in the UK highlighting more human rights compliant policies and practices in Wales and Scotland (at paras 58, 59).

[173] S Khosravi (2010), n 3 above, 90.

[174] *Joint Council for the Welfare of Immigrants (JCWI) v. Secretary of State for Home Affairs and the Residential Landlords Association* [2019] EWHC 452 (Admin). The court struck down the offending provisions (sections 20–37) of the Immigration Act 2014, as being in breach of articles 8 on private and

one's passport. Migrants, especially those that 'look foreign', were, and indeed still are, less likely to secure housing even if they have paperwork. British minorities are also negatively impacted. The UN Special Rapporteur on race cited research which showed that 48 per cent of landlords said they were unlikely to rent to someone who did not have a British passport.[175]

In *Goloshvili v Secretary of State for Home Affairs* landlords sought a judicial review of Home Office rules on letting. Landlords who suspected that they had inadvertently let their properties to someone who was ineligible had to issue a notice to the tenant and alert the Home Office. The landlords argued that they were caught between a rock and a hard place – issue the notice and they may face a challenge for race/nationality discrimination under the Equality Act 2010; fail to issue the notice and they may face penalties for breach of section 33D duties (checking immigration status of any tenant before letting to them) under the Immigration Act 2014. Following the *JCWI* case findings above, the court found no need for review, but did, in *obiter dicta*, identify the potential difficulties faced by landlords.[176]

Employers are obliged to check workers' eligibility to work, under pain of paying heavy fines of thousands.[177] This includes *all* work that is paid. For academics in the United Kingdom, this means that even if you are examining a PhD at another university, a one-off event, you have to bring, or send proof of, eligibility to work. In my institution this requires the host academic (me) to collect and photocopy the hard copies of the passports and then certify that you have seen the originals. If you do not do this, the examiner will not be paid. It is a deeply embarrassing process which makes border guards of us all.[178]

In the wider world, employers are also less likely to employ people with 'foreign-sounding names' because they do not have the administrative capacity to undertake the checks and so simply choose not to employ migrants, or indeed legally entitled minorities. Those prepared to 'overlook' the paperwork checks know they run risks and so feel entitled to exploit.

Undocumented migrants also cannot get bank accounts because of the identity checks so they have to rely on cash-in-hand payments. They also cannot get National Insurance (social security) numbers so have to 'borrow' one from someone to whom they pay a fee, or use a fake one. I once sat through an employment

family life and 14 prohibiting discrimination of the ECHR. However, this was reversed on appeal. See *Secretary of State for the Home Department v JCWI and Others* [2020] EWCA Civ 542.

[175] UN Special Rapporteur on Contemporary Forms of Racism, A/HRC/41/54/Add.2, 27 May 2019, para 55.

[176] *Goloshvili v Secretary of State for Home Affairs* [2019] EWHC 614 (Admin). However, see the appeal from the JCWI decision, *Secretary of State for the Home Department v JCWI and Others* [2020] EWCA Civ 542.

[177] GovUK, 'View a Job Applicant's Right to Work Details' at: https://www.gov.uk/view-right-to-work.

[178] A Mckie, 'British Professor quits as external examiner over passport check', *The Times Higher Education Supplement*, 21 January 2020. See also S Inge, 'Academics asked to check visas of international visitors', *Times Higher Education Supplement*, 8 March 2018.

tribunal case involving a Nigerian woman who had worked as a cleaner. She sued her boss for not paying her the minimum wage (he under-counted her hours worked). He countered that she had misled him about her right to work, noting that she had used someone else's national insurance details. He had known. The tribunal referred him to Inland Revenue and threw her case out on the basis of *ex turpi causa* – you cannot come to court with dirty hands. The boss was chastened, she was furious – neither won. This was in 2004. Had this been in 2020, they would have faced more sanctions.

In fictional literature we learn that some, like Quentina in John Lanchester's *Capital*, secure employment in someone else's name.[179] She works as a traffic warden. She is paid by cheque, which she takes to a fixer who cashes it, but takes a cut. Although the face value on the cheque is £227, she is given £150 by the man with whom she deposits the cheque. He tells her, 'I am happy to take this risk for you.'[180] Earlier in the novel, Quentina reflects on the amount of money that she makes for the council for doing 250 days' work a year – £375,000. She is only paid £12,000 'in theory' but does not get any pension or health benefits.[181] In short, Quentina contributes to the system, but cannot benefit from her contribution.

Another conundrum facing the undocumented migrant is that of limited access to health care. Doctors and hospitals are now under a duty to check entitlement before treatment. While many have objected that this breaches professional ethics, undocumented migrants tend to keep away, thus exacerbating existing medical conditions. Sahota's *Runaways* shows how even those who are entitled to care may be afraid to deal with bureaucracy. Avtar, one of the male protagonists, seems to have contracted a sexually transmitted infection which leaves him in pain. He is on a student visa, but is not studying in London as per the visa requirements, but working elsewhere. His boss informs him of his entitlement to free health care while friends at the gurdwara urge him to go to the doctor. Avtar does find a doctor's surgery. He tells the receptionist that he is away from his London home and would like to see a doctor. She gives him a form to fill but he is stumped: 'Address. Current doctor. Non-UK national status (if applicable). Medical card number. He didn't know what to put for any of these.'[182]

The kind receptionist tries to guide him through the form. He writes his name but then worries that he can be traced. He leaves without seeing a doctor, relying on friends. A private visit from a doctor at home is arranged. The doctor counsels Avtar to go to hospital, noting the possibility of septicaemia. He reinforces Avtar's entitlement to treatment without fear of arrest.[183] At the end of the novel, we learn

[179] J Lanchester (2013), n 13 above, 133.

[180] J Lanchester (2013), n 13 above, 129, 131. Dialogue at 131 – sum on face of cheque 129. Fictional literature is replete with these examples of 'helping out.' In *Black Bazaar*, 'Sylvio would draw the money out from his bank and hand it over to Centre Forward, after taking ten per cent commission for the use of his identity card.' A Mabanckou and S Ardizzone (2012), n 20 above, 87.

[181] J Lanchester (2013), n 13 above, 52.

[182] S Sahota (2016), n 21 above, 435.

[183] S Sahota (2016) 450.

that Avtar has sustained long-term damage – he delayed his treatment until it was too late.[184]

Avtar's reluctance to access health care, despite being entitled to it, echoes the findings of the UN Special Rapporteur on Race's report where she found that many women, including those who were entitled, eschewed accessing hospitals and maternity treatment. Many elect to give birth at home. The reluctance has been driven, in part, by a policy (since withdrawn) whereby the National Health Service digital section (data) would share information with the Home Office regarding the immigration status of patients.[185] In her contribution to the drafting of the UN Compact on Migration, the Special Rapporteur on contemporary racism asked states to ensure that there were firewalls in place which prevented immigration sections sharing data with public and social welfare providers.[186]

In Britain there is a discourse around 'health tourism'. There are frequent assertions that the National Health Service (NHS) is rapidly turning into the International Health Service, because of undeserving users. To curb these alleged abuses, de facto immigration checks were introduced, requiring one to prove entitlement to access the health services before treatment was given. The other trope is the overly fecund asylum seekers and 'foreigners' having so many children that the schools are 'full'.[187]

For migrants, complaining about conditions is not an option. They understand their obligations of support to the wider family left at home.[188] Their focus is on kin and group, even if, as identified by Huchu, the family sometimes let you down by mis-spending the money remitted.[189] Already seen as the 'lucky ones' by virtue of their 'escape', they are loath to draw attention to themselves by complaining. And anyway, to whom would they complain given the precarity of their status?

[184] S Sahota (2016) 461, 464.

[185] UN Special Rapporteur on contemporary racism, A/HRC.41/54/Add.2, 27 May 2019, para 30.

[186] OHCHR, 'Open Letter from the Special Rapporteur on Contemporary Forms of Racism, Racial Discrimination, Xenophobia and Related Intolerance on Draft Rev 2 of the Global Compact on Migration', 6 June 2018. Available at: https://www.ohchr.org/Documents/Issues/Racism/SR/OpenLettertoGCM_EN.pdf.

[187] Chapter 25 of Ellen Wiles's *Invisible Crowd* (2017), n 86 above, 255, has this heading. R Slater and J Knowsley, 'Struggling schools "swamped with asylum seekers"', *Mail on Sunday*, available on website: www.dailymail.co.uk.news.

[188] H Breant, 'What if diasporas didn't think about development? a critical approach of the international discourse on migration and development' (2013) 6(2) *Africa and Black Diaspora: An International Journal* 99, 108–109. Emphasising that for the migrant development is more personalised than the statist model of development. See also JN Makumbi, 'Author's Note' in JN Makumbi, *Manchester Happened* (2019), n 29 above, xi–xii. In her short story 'Manchester Happened' Makumbi talks about the pressures of working hard in England so that they could 'perform success and perpetuate the dream' while 'Inside we were dying.' JN Makumbi (2019) 62, 69.

[189] T Huchu (2015), n 23 above, 107–8. The protagonist returns home to Harare where he finds that his brother had misappropriated the money that he had been sending to facilitate the building of a house. Instead he finds an empty plot overgrown with grass. The people in the neighbouring house tell him that his brother often came to take photographs of their house as they were building it. The brother had been sending pictures of someone else's house construction. This is a popular anecdote that I have heard told in Western Union sending queues.

XII. Irregularity and Employment

The Convention on Migrant Workers and their Families, 1990 enjoins states who find undocumented migrant workers to consider taking 'appropriate measures to ensure that such a situation does not persist,'[190] while also providing that:

> States of employment shall take all adequate and effective measures to eliminate employment in their territory of migrant workers in an irregular situation, including, whenever appropriate, sanctions on employers of such workers. The rights of migrant workers vis-a-vis their employer arising from employment shall not be impaired by these measures.[191]

The Convention appears to want to balance protection of the migrant worker and their family, with a recognition of the state's right to control its borders and domestic labour market.[192] States, including non-ratifying ones, seem more focused on the control than on the use of pro-worker discretion or the granting of what many perceive to be 'unearned' or undeserved rights. While giving some protections to all, the Convention distinguishes between the documented and undocumented.[193] The impact on the undocumented is that they feel caught between the devil and the deep blue sea. Yes, the Migrant Worker's Convention enjoins states to ensure that they are entitled to the same working conditions as the rest of the labour force, that they are free from torture and degrading and inhuman treatment, that they are not subjected to slavery and slave-like conditions or to forced labour, and also that they have access to remedies, but in practice, self-disclosure by way of

[190] Convention on the Rights of Migrant Workers and their Families, 1990, art 69(1). It is worth noting that the Convention has not been ratified by most of the states discussed in this book. Sending states are more likely to ratify than receiving states.

[191] Convention on the Rights of Migrant Workers and their Families, 1990, art 68(2). See also Inter-American Court of Human Rights, *Advisory Opinion on Juridical Condition and Rights of Undocumented Migrant Workers*, OC-18/03, 17 September 2003, Inter-Am Ct HR, (Series A) No 18 2003. The court affirmed that migrant workers, including those without papers, were entitled to equality before the law including in employment. It was for the benefit of both those with and without papers to require employers to treat all workers equally because violation of the rights including to equal pay and decent conditions of service impacted on both undocumented and documented workers. The latter would suffer if employers chose to employ easily exploitable undocumented workers. See also CERD Concluding Observations Italy, CERD/C/ITA/CO/19-20, 17 February 2017, paras 23, 24.

[192] See for example arts 35 and 79.

[193] By way of contrast, the Human Rights Committee, in its General Comment 31 on the nature of state obligations under article 2(1) of the International Covenant on Civil and Political Rights clarifies entitlement: 'the enjoyment of Covenant rights is not limited to citizens of States Parties but must also be available to all individuals, regardless of nationality or statelessness, such as asylum seekers, refugees, migrant workers and other persons, who may find themselves in the territory or subject to the jurisdiction of the State Party.' UN Human Rights Committee (HRC), *General comment no 31 [80], The nature of the general legal obligation imposed on States Parties to the Covenant*, 26 May 2004, CCPR/C/21/Rev.1/Add.13, para 10. The Committee refers to its earlier General Comment No 15 on the Rights of Aliens, and acknowledges that while the Convention does not apply in all cases to aliens (including the right of entry or residence, except in some instances), there are provisions which cannot be derogated from, not least the discrimination provisions. Human Rights General Comment No 15 para 2. The Committee on Migrant Workers acknowledges this higher standard in its General Comment on Irregular Migrant Workers and their Families, CMW/C/GC/2 paras 9–10. See also paras 18–20.

claiming these rights is more likely to lead to removal than vindication, so they continue their lives of drudgery and penury.[194]

The Committee on Migrant Workers and their Families (CMW) has adopted a comprehensive General Recommendation No 2, focusing on and reiterating the rights of migrant workers and their families who are in an irregular situation. The Committee is clear that these workers are entitled to equal treatment by both private and public employers, that they should not be exploited, that routes of regularisation should be made available to reduce vulnerability and that there should not be any humiliating and degrading treatment. The Committee cites many ILO Conventions on good work practices as well as the provisions prohibiting discrimination found in the ICCPR, the ICESCR and regional conventions, and enjoins states to abide by these as well. The Committee enjoins states to ensure that workers can access benefits to which they have contributed. The CMW is clear in requiring states to provide urgent medical care as well as ante-natal and obstetric services. The children of irregular migrants are to be provided with education that is on the same terms as other children. The General Comment concludes by reinforcing the importance of legal identity and requiring states to ensure that all children born within the jurisdiction are given birth certificates regardless of the immigration status of their parents[195]

XIII. Irregularity and the Exposure to Exploitation by Non-State Actors

Faced with state-generated hostile environments, it is the undocumented migrant who pays the highest price. Good businesses should, according to the UN Special Rapporteur on Contemporary Slavery, uphold

> the ILO Declaration on Fundamental Principles and Rights at Work, undertake ongoing human rights due diligence and put in place processes to enable remediation for any negative human rights impact they cause or contribute to, in accordance with the Guiding Principles on Business and Human Rights: Implementing the United Nations 'Protect, Respect and Remedy' Framework.[196]

Many do not.

Both Khosravi's research and the novels of Desai and Sahota suggest that the exploitation by 'like' people may be linked to community networks which

[194] Convention on the Rights of Migrant Workers and their Families, 1990 arts 70 and 25 (same working conditions); art 11(1); art 11(2) (slavery or servitude).

[195] CMW/C/GC/2. On equal pay and the right to be free from discrimination, see also http://www1.umn.edu/humanrts/iachr/series_A_OC-18.html, paras 82–110. This decision is reflected in para 64 of the Committee's General Comment.

[196] UN Special Rapporteur on Contemporary Slavery, Niger report, A/HRC/30/35/Add.1, para 105. See also UN Special Rapporteur on Contemporary forms of Slavery, Report on eradicating contemporary forms of slavery from supply chains, A/HRC/30/35, 8 July 2015.

lead people without papers to look for work and assistance from people like themselves.[197] Their properly papered countrymen and women in turn take advantage of the vulnerability of the undocumented migrant. In Sahota's *The Year of the Runaways*, set in Britain, two female Sikh women are sitting in the cramped room of one of them. One explains that they (with her husband) rent the room from a pious man at the gurdwara, who, 'To look at him, you would think he shat pearls. You won't believe how much rent he charges.' She then goes on to say: 'Our own people are the worst at bleeding us dry.'[198] In her short story 'Manchester Happened' Makumbi identifies: 'the ruthless aunt who picked you up, found you a job, registered you in her name, her National Insurance number and bank account.' The aunt would then refuse to hand over your wages pointing out that she was providing for you. Said aunt may also point you to a man who had papers who might marry you.[199]

Learning of the working conditions, especially the psychological and economic abuse, experienced by some undocumented workers, calls to mind the workhouses documented in the literature of Charles Dickens.[200] In Desai's *Inheritance of Loss*, the protagonist slips on a dirty floor and is injured at work. When he reminds his boss that the injury occurred under his watch and is therefore his responsibility, the employer is outraged and rails at what he perceives to be ingratitude. The employer says he has taken them in and allowed them to live rent-free. Undeterred, Biju, the employee, tells the boss that he is exploiting them and asks why the boss has not applied for Green Cards to enable them to remain lawfully in the United States. The boss's response is described as a volcanic explosion which leads him to point out his own dilemma – with so many undocumented workers, how can he be expected to apply for paperwork for all of them? Who should he prioritise? The boss explains the complexity of applying for papers and underlines risk that he is taking by employing them at all:

> I have to go to the INS and say that no American can do the job. I have to prove it. I have to prove I advertised it. They will look at my restaurant. They will study and ask questions. And the way they have it, it's the owner who gets put in jail for hiring illegal staff.[201]

He knows he has his workers over a barrel. He tells Biju that if they do not like the conditions then they should leave. He reminds them that there are hundreds of others just like them desperate for jobs. All he has to do is snap his fingers and they will flock to him.

[197] S Khosravi, 'An Ethnography of Migrant "Illegality" in Sweden: Included yet Excepted' (2010) 6(1) *Journal of International Political Theory* 95–116 (Khosravi (2010a). Desai (2006), n 19 above; Sahota (2016), n 21 above.

[198] S Sahota (2016) 340.

[199] JN Makumbi, 'Manchester Happened' (2019), n 29 above, 69.

[200] For example, C Dickens, *Oliver Twist* (London, Penguin Classics, 2012).

[201] K Desai (2006), n 19 above, 188. See also M Jordan, 'The Overlooked undocumented immigrants from India, China, Brazil', *New York Times*, 1 December 2019.

Equally powerful and poignant is NoViolet Bulawayo's fictional account of working in violation of the conditions of one's student visa and finding oneself, a law-abiding person, ashamed because:

> ... we were no longer people; we were now illegals. When they debated what to do with illegals, we stopped breathing, stopped laughing, stopped everything, and listened. We heard: exploiting America, broken borders, war on the middle class, invasion, deportation, illegals, illegals, illegals. We bit our tongues until we tasted blood.[202]

This realisation leads to self-segregation grounded in fear of detection and rejection:

> We did not meet stares and avoided gazes. We hid our real names, gave false ones when asked. We built mountains between us and them, we dug rivers, we planted thorns – we had paid so much to be in America and we did not want to lose it all.[203]

Bulawayo details the fear that rises up when one hears about immigration checks. She says their blood ran cold: 'and when at work they asked for our papers, we scurried like startled hens and flocked to unwanted jobs, where we met the others, many others.'[204] Ever cognisant of the suffering that they left at home, they do not feel that they have any other options.

These extracts, which are US based, could apply equally in most European states. Three of the male characters in Sahota's *Runaways*, based in Britain, are all housed together with others from the Indian Sub-Continent by a fixer who picks them up in the mornings to ferry them to the construction sites that they will work at without papers. In *Harare North*, Chikwava also details both the precarity of the work, which can be cancelled at a moment's notice, and the exploitative wages which may not be paid in full when the work is complete.[205]

It is important to acknowledge that the stories of migrants are replete with examples of solidarity between those who find themselves far from home. In Elizabeth Day's *Paradise City*, Beatrice from Uganda is befriended by the Somali newsagent who is a 'fund of information about housing benefits, community grant applications and government welfare schemes over the years.' Hamid's *Exit West* is also moving in its descriptions of the communities that form when the people in flight come together and seek to co-exist.[206]

The journalist Trilling highlights how even countries, such as Italy, that do allow asylum seekers to work pending the completion of their status determination process, do not ensure that they are paid the minimum wage. He gives the example of a Gambian man named Alimamo who had, 15 months previously, left a

[202] NV Bulawayo (2014), n 50 above, 242.

[203] NV Bulawayo (2014), n 50 above, 242. Khosravi details the same phenomenon in Sweden where the undocumented were the most law abiding, including avoiding jay walking, for fear of detection. S Khosravi (2010), n 3 above, 91.

[204] NV Bulawayo (2014), n 50 above, 242–43.

[205] B Chikwava (2010), n 142 above, 49–54.

[206] E Day, *Paradise* City (London, Bloomsbury, 2015) 84. M Hamid (2017) 17.

wife and two children at home, and was earning €250 a month doing 'work experience' in a shop. The downside was that the reception centre that housed him then stopped his allowance.[207]

Relying on UK data from 2010–16, economists Isabel Ruiz and Carlos Vargas-Silva confirm that refugees earn less than long-term voluntary migrants and natives in the labour market. This they attribute to mental health challenges and poorer language facilities, amongst other things. It may also be because voluntary migrants may have higher levels of education. However, they point out that it is possible for refugees to reach parity and indeed exceed the earnings of voluntary migrants.[208]

XIV. Public Perception and Prejudice

It is clear that even those workers with papers face discrimination. Migrants, especially black African migrants, suffer from higher rates of unemployment and are to be found lower down the hierarchy.[209] Those who seem to have 'made it' soon discover that they are paid considerably less than less qualified white colleagues. To challenge this state of affairs is to be seen as 'difficult'. A black African is expected to be grateful not questioning.[210] One must tread a careful line, for as noted by Iranian-American author Dina Nayeri in her piece, 'The Ungrateful Refugee':

> The refugee has to be less capable than the native, needier; he must stay in his place. That's the only way gratitude will be accepted. Once he escapes control, he confirms his identity as the devil … You're not enough until you're too much. You're lazy until you're a greedy interloper.[211]

In a short autobiographical piece entitled 'The Ungrateful Country' Musa Okwonga recounts how, despite getting a prestigious scholarship to Eton and graduating with a first-class degree from Oxford University, he still faces discrimination. He tells how he grew weary of always having to explain himself and, as a journalist, being pigeon-holed as a 'Race Commentator'. He bemoans the ignorance of the local

[207] D Trilling, *Lights in the Distance: Exile and Refuge at the Borders of Europe* (London, Picador, 2018) 113.

[208] I Ruiz and C Vargas-Silva, *Differences in labour market outcomes between natives, refugees and other migrants in the UK*, COMPAS, Working Paper No 137 of 2018. https://www.compas.ox.ac.uk/2018/differences-in-labour-market-outcomes-between-natives-refugees-and-other-migrants-in-the-uk-2/.

[209] See CERD Concluding Observations Norway, CERD/C/NOR/CO/23–24 (2 January 2019) paras 17(a) and 18(a).

[210] O Imoagene, 'Being British vs. Being American: identification among second-generation adults of Nigerian descent in the US and UK' (2012) 35(12) *Ethnic and Racial Studies* 2153, 2162–63.

[211] D Nayeri, 'The Ungrateful Refugee' in VT Nguyen (ed), *The Displaced: Refugee Writers on Refugee Lives* (New York, Abrams Press, 2018) 137, 149–50. Nayeri also speaks about the constant demand for gratitude: 'From then on we sensed the ongoing expectation that we would shed our old skin, give up our former identities – every quirk and desire that made us – that we would imply at every opportunity that America was better, that we were so lucky, so humbled to be here.' Nayeri at 137, 142. See also S Khosravi (2010), n 3 above, 94.

population about the history of the British Empire and also how and why so many immigrants come to the United Kingdom.[212] His piece ends with a move to Berlin.

In his book on African novels, Wa Ngugi notes how the reviews of Bulawayo's *We Need New Names* laud the 'authenticity' of the first part of the novel, set in Zimbabwe, while simultaneously criticising her for the second half, set in the United States, where it is said there is lack of gratitude for the opportunities that America has granted immigrants in general and her in particular. Listing her academic achievements in the US, the *New York Times* critic Michiko Kakutani says her (Ndebele's) story 'sounds very much like a dream achieved.'[213]

Reading Jamaican-American poet Claudia Rankine's *Citizen*, I was struck by her sentiment of being tired of 'overachieving oneself to death.'[214] That line, and Musa Okwonga's chapter in *The Good Immigrant*, resonated with me. The relentless proof of 'excellence', often a place-holder for the plaintive cry, 'accept me',[215] is also captured by Novuyo Tshuma, a Zimbabwean writer, who migrated to America:

> Even now, living as an immigrant in America, where I came to through a notion of 'exceptionalism' … I am ever working, overworking, because I'm aware of the potential, as a non-white body and passport holder from 'Africa,' without the safety of 'being at home' of my easy disposal from the political imagination of the world.[216]

She goes on:

> It is an implicit understanding that only through this exceptionalism can one 'earn' one's place in the new society, earn one's right to the humanity which, for those in their *proper place*, is normal. Exceptionalism, then, is really an aspiration towards safety, human rights, access to food, to water, to resources, to an edifying life, to the free pursuit of one's endeavors, to support from the state.[217]

[212] M Okwonga, 'The Ungrateful Country' in N Shukla, *The Good Immigrant* (London, Unbound, 2017) 224, 233. Listen to the podcast by A Hirsch, 'We need to talk about the British empire' (Podcast, Audible, 2020) at: https://www.audible.co.uk/pd/We-Need-to-Talk-About-the-British-Empire-Audiobook/B081581253?qid=1582546112&sr=1-2&pf_rd_p=c6e316b8-14da-418d-8f91-b3cad83c5183&pf_rd_r=EY3575FB6V2GPQZYDD7S&ref=a_search_c3_lProduct_1_2.

[213] M Wa Ngugi (2018) 172. Quote from M Kakutani, 'A Child of Two Lands', *New York Times* book review, 15 May 2013 cited by Wa Ngugi (2018) 172.

[214] C Rankine, *Citizen* (London, Penguin, 2015) 15. Explaining the book's title, Rankine noted: 'I called it *Citizen* because I wanted to ask: who gets to hold that status – despite everyone technically having it? How is it embodied and honoured? The title contains a question.' From an interview by K Kellaway, 'Claudia Rankine: "Blackness in the white imagination has nothing to do with black people"', *The Guardian*, London, 27 December 2015.

[215] Dina Nayeri captures how this acceptance is premised on distinguishing you from other 'less worthy' immigrants, who have not, like you, 'made something of themselves and taken the opportunities afforded by the new society.' She notes how even liberals take this line of 'your success, proves our generosity,' while simultaneously ignoring all the structural barriers that confront most migrants. Nayeri also challenges the 'we did you a favour' narrative, noting that 'What America did was a basic human obligation.' D Nayeri (2018), n 211 above, 137, 146–48. Quote at 148.

[216] NR Tshuma, 'New Lands, New Selves' in VT Nguyen (ed), *The Displaced: Refugee Writers on Refugee Lives* (New York, Abrams Press, 2018) 159, 167.

[217] NR Tshuma (2018) 159, 168. Chigumadzi calls this being the model migrant. P Chigumadzi, 'Why I am no longer talking to Nigerians about race' in *Africa is a Country*, 7 April 2019.

It is not surprising that Tshuma details her mental health 'episode'. Like other migrants, Tshuma recognises the disconnect between the 'old self' and the arrived self.[218] Sitting in a café in Florence watching an Eritrean refugee man unravel in broad daylight in the street outside, leaves Maaza Mengiste to write in her notebook: 'You do not leave home like this. This is what the journey does.'[219]

XV. On Dignity

The issue of dignity is important when considering migration and the lives of migrants in receiving states. What do lawyers mean when they say all human beings have a right to dignity?[220] Is Amartya Sen's human capability approach – arguing that each person has, or should have, the freedom to make decisions which enable them to live lives of dignity with sufficient food and shelter – not for migrants?[221] Discussing the Sen approach, Eekelaar notes that the idea of an individual having rights:

> *presupposes* a moral system in the same way as Hart showed that claims to legal rights presuppose the existence of a legal system. The moral system will fashion the values that individuals hold and it is the task of that system to promote virtuous values. It is therefore evident that the present account of rights does not in itself tell us what rights people should have.[222]

Despite not being citizens, or legally resident, it is of course arguable that migrants may have a moral claim to dignity which is capable of being a right deserving of respect.[223] Here we may try to conceive of a metaphorical poverty of spirit which attaches to those who require 'proof of suffering' as a pre-condition to seeing the humanity of another and judging whether they are in 'genuine' need. Asylum seekers should not, as Khosravi has detailed, have to perform 'refugee-ness' which requires them to become victims without history or agency, ever reliant on the goodness of others for their very being.[224]

[218] NR Tshuma (2018) 159, 171–73. See also S Khosravi (2010), n 3 above, 86.
[219] M Mengiste, 'This is what the journey does' in VT Nguyen (ed), *The Displaced: Refugee Writers on Refugee Lives* (New York, Abrams Press, 2018) 129, 133.
[220] D Cornell *et al* (eds), *The Dignity Jurisprudence of the Constitutional Court of South Africa Volumes I & II* (New York, Fordham University Press, 2013).
[221] A Sen, 'Human Rights and Capabilities' (2005) 6 *Journal of Human Development* 151; A Sen *Justice* (Belknap Press, Boston, 2009) See also M Nussbaum, 'Women's Capabilities and Social Justice' 1 (2000) *Journal of Human Development* 219 and M Nussbaum, *Women and Human Development: The Capabilities Approach* (Cambridge, CUP, 2000).
[222] J Eekelaar, *Family Law and Personal Life*, 2nd edn (OUP, 2017) 37. Also pertinent is Eekelaar's later discussion of the concepts of friendship and brotherly love at 95–102.
[223] See further J Eekelaar (2017) 37–40.
[224] S Khosravi (2010), n 3 above, 70–75.

It is important to acknowledge that the hostile environment is not only to be found in receiving states. Arguably some of the drivers of migration are to be found 'at home' where governments have abrogated their responsibilities to deliver political stability and socio-economic and cultural living conditions that are conducive to a person living a decent life.

XVI. 'Home' and the Inhospitable Human Rights Environment

Listening to interviews with African migrants who are rescued from sinking or unseaworthy vessels on the Mediterranean yields a consistent narrative about why they left home: they felt that they had no means of making a livelihood, that they had no future in the countries of their birth. This is a damning indictment of the failure of African governments to guarantee basic human rights to their citizens. Zimbabwean Belinda Zhawi captures the myriad reasons that force Zimbabwean people to migrate in her poem 'Reasons for leaving home' which include, along with potholes, high bread prices, the impact of sanctions as a result of the land redistribution programme, and separation of families, '*Mugabe, innit.*'[225]

In her first-person account of migration from Zimbabwe to South Africa, Tshuma details the deterioration in living standards which are mirrored in the seeping of joy and spirit from her teacher mother, forced to take up market-gardening to supplement the family coffers and diet. Of herself the author notes: 'I, a formerly middle-class kid with city sensibilities, became a mini subsistence farmer.'[226] Even after the move, Tshuma expresses great resentment that Mugabe, whom she calls 'Grandfather' has, by his actions, forced this change on her and her family.[227] Tshuma also highlights the xenophobia, violence and threats faced by many migrants in South Africa, reminding us that the suspicion of the 'other' is not confined to one place or people.[228]

The former Zimbabwean President, Robert Mugabe, acknowledged the population flight, but referred, patronisingly, to Zimbabweans working in Britain by the acronym BBC (British Bum Cleaners), a deliberate put-down which ignored the President's own role in making life so difficult for citizens that they were forced to migrate and to undertake care work.[229]

[225] B Zhawi, 'Reasons for leaving home' in B Zhawi, *Small Inheritances* (Oxford, Ignitonpress, 2018) 6, 7.

[226] NR Tshuma, 'New Lands, New Selves', n 216 above, 159, 162.

[227] NR Tshuma (2018) 159, 163. See also P Chigumadzi, *These Bones will not rise* again (London, Indigo Press, 2018).

[228] See also Human Rights Watch, *Neighbours in Need: Zimbabweans Seeking Refuge in South Africa* (New York, Human Rights Watch, 2008). See also HJ Golakai, 'Fugee' in E Wakatama Allfrey, *Safe House: Explorations in Creative Non-Fiction* (London, Cassava Republic, 2016) 25, 25–33.

[229] J McGregor, 'Diaspora and Dignity: Navigating and Contesting Civic Exclusion in Britain' in J McGregor and R Primorac (eds), *Zimbabwe's new diaspora: Displacement and the cultural politics of*

The journalist Patrick Kingsley attributes the exodus of people from Eritrea mainly to the compulsory and indefinite conscription into the Eritrean army.[230] The two Eritrean protagonists in Ellen Wiles's *Invisible Crowd* flee the system that leads to one experiencing sexual assault in the military and the general lack of freedoms. Similarly, the father in Benjamin Zephaniah's *Refugee Boy* brings his son to England to escape the tensions and mistrust that confront the family, caused in part by the parental mixed Ethiopian-Eritrean marriage which elicits suspicion in both countries in a time of conflict and tension between the two neighbouring states.[231]

In his satirical style, Mabanckou, in *Black Bazaar*, has his protagonist from the 'small Congo' explore under-development caused by corrupt politicians who steal money that they then come to spend in France, and the seemingly never-ending tensions between ethnic groups. He also discusses the on-going influence, or political meddling, of France and the US.[232] Simultaneously, Mabanckou incisively skewers the patronising treatment meted out to diasporic Africans in his protagonist's conversation with a neighbour, who incidentally, is himself from Martinique: 'Dearie me, the poor Congolese, we've got to do something for them! There are diseases, there is famine, they have many wives, and they are always fighting all the time, poor things.'[233] This neighbour from Martinique acts as a useful foil to discuss intra-group tensions between people from the African continent and other migrants. Wiles also uses the musings of her Polish security guard at the detention centre to show how he distinguishes the arrival of his Polish parents – his father was a translator – from that of the detention centre inhabitants: 'My parents took risks too, but theirs didn't involve breaking the law.'[234] He goes on to say that his parents' contribution to the country which has included paying taxes, entitles them to stay, but that not 'everyone from everywhere does.'[235]

In his novel *The Maestro, the Magistrate & the Mathematician*, Huchu explores the migrant's dilemma: wanting to criticise one's government but also being aware of misrepresentation. He explores the reinforcement of stereotypes of 'Africa' via the use of 'experts' who appear on a news bulletin to talk about Zimbabwe:

> 2 experts, a professor from the School of Oriental and African Studies and another man from Oxfam, comment on THE SITUATION. Manufacturing consent. They use key words, BASKET CASE, HUMAN RIGHTS, WHITE FARMERS, REGIME. There is no

survival (Berghan Books, 2010) 122, 129–30. J McGregor, '"Joining the BBC (British Bottom Cleaners)": Zimbabwean Migrants and the UK Care Industry' (2007) 33 *Journal of Ethnic and Migration Studies* 801–24.

[230] P Kingsley (2016), n 64 above, 44–52. See also L Oette and M Babiker 'Migration Control á la Khartoum: EU external engagement and human rights protection in the Horn of Africa' (2017) 36(4) *Refugee Survey Quarterly* 64.

[231] B Zephaniah, *Refugee Boy* (London, Bloomsbury, 2017).

[232] A Mabanckou (translated by S Ardizzone) (2012), n 20 above, 8, 71–3.

[233] A Mabanckou 9translated by S Ardizzone) (2012) 32. The litany of complaints is hilarious and endless eg (at 30–31) printing fake money, dealing drugs or smoking them.

[234] E Wiles (2017), n 86 above, 271.

[235] E Wiles (2017) 271.

historical context to the issues upon which they air their expert opinions, broadcast to millions of viewers across the globe. The picture of a nameless, starving African child next to a skinny dog is superimposed onto the screen behind them. They have followed THE SITUATION closely from London.[236]

XVII. Status Fracture v. Status Threat

While my peers and I were lucky to have scholarships that freed us from the need to work, in truth, the reality for most migrants is that they are unable to study at all, or if studying, to do so on a full-time basis. Indeed many experience '*status fracture*', meaning that they find themselves in a hierarchically inferior position to the one that they enjoyed 'at home'. The assumptions of their inferiority are made manifest from their arrival at the port of entry. The Nobel laureate Amartya Sen starts his book *Identity and Violence* with this anecdote:

> Some years ago when I was returning to England from a short trip abroad (I was then Master of Trinity College in Cambridge), the immigration officer at Heathrow, who scrutinized my Indian passport rather thoroughly, posed a philosophical question of some intricacy. Looking at my home address on the immigration form (Master's Lodge, Trinity College, Cambridge), he asked me whether the Master, whose hospitality I evidently enjoyed, was a close friend of mine. This gave me pause since it was not altogether clear to me whether I could claim to be a friend of myself ... Since all this took some time to work out, the immigration officer wanted to know why exactly did I hesitate, and in particular whether there was some irregularity in my being in Britain.[237]

Nigerian author Chigozie Obioma recounts how, returning to his home in the United States, he was quizzed by the immigration official about where he had been. His answer, that he was returning from the Booker prize ceremony in London because his book *The Fishermen* had been on the shortlist, led to him being detained for longer to enable the sceptical immigration official to check out his story, which clearly seemed improbable. His fellow temporary detainees included, 'a man from some Arab country who was being sent back' despite having a visa. Of him Obioma simply states: 'The man was in distress.'[238]

[236] T Huchu (2015), n 23 above, 97. See also 96.

[237] A Sen, *Identity and Violence: The Illusion of Destiny* (London, Allen Lane, 2006) xi. In another, very funny passage, he recounts arriving in Britain as a student in 1953 and having to assure his landlady that his skin colour would not rub off in the bath; 'I had to assure her that my hue was agreeably sturdy and durable.' At 152. Hirsch also recounts how as a young child in London, she witnessed a young white child wiping her Ghanaian mother's face to see if her colour would rub off, 'like paint or melted chocolate'. A Hirsch, *Brit(ish)* (London, Jonathan Cape, 2018) 33 at 34. Khosravi argues that the function of airports is to screen out 'undesirables' which requires a system of profiling. S Khosravi (2010), n 3 above, 66.

[238] C Obioma, 'The Naked Man' in N Shukla and C Suleyman, *The Good Immigrant USA* (London, Dialogue Books, 2019) 155, 165–68 with quotes at 167.

The fictional literature on African migrants picks up on the status downgrade. In *Capital* Lanchester introduces his female Zimbabwean protagonist as 'Quentina Mkfesi BSc MSc (Political Science, University of Zimbabwe, thesis subject: Post-Conflict Resolution in Non-Post-Colonial Societies, with special reference to Northern Ireland, Spain and Chile).'[239] This introduction comes as she is at work, as a traffic warden.

In his ethnographic research on Zimbabweans living in Britain, Dominic Pasura encountered many people like Quentina. Two of his interviewees who were working in care homes explained that at home they had been a loss adjustor and a mechanical engineer respectively. The loss adjustor who said he worked with his brother-in-law, an Ethiopian who had been a military attache, acknowledged the status downgrade, but said pragmatically: 'but when you are faced with the reality of life, what is the point in being a loss adjustor if you can't feed yourself?'. Meanwhile, the one who had been a mechanical engineer acknowledged:

> It's a bit disheartening! For many times I had second thoughts about what I was doing. You ask yourself, who am I to wash a white person's bum? Some shout at you abuses. Because of being black and the inferiority complex, you think if I shout back at the person they will fire me the job (sic)'.[240]

Their stories are echoed in Segun Afolabi's fictional story 'Monday Morning'. The father and his family with whom he is seeking asylum and who are housed in bed and breakfast accommodation is approached by a fellow asylum seeker and encouraged to work in violation of the rules: 'The man had been an architect in his own country, but now did the slightest thing in order to help himself.'[241] Commenting on his friend's inability to secure a job in law (he had worked as a magistrate at home), Alfonso, in Huchu's *Maestro*, suggests that the magistrate try nursing, by which he means care work, reasoning: 'Only nursing is the same, because no matter where you go in the world, wiping bums is still wiping bums.'[242]

The men in Sahota's *The Year of the Runaways* spend most of their time looking for work. Like many men, undocumented migrants in literature seem to end up in construction or security or, in the Sahota book, working in 'chippies' (fast food outlets) and helping in small corner shops.[243] The women are also sometimes

[239] J Lanchester (2013), n 13 above, 51. Hirsch, writing about what it means to be British also recounts the experiences of African migrants who are forced by racism and the lack of equal opportunities in the labour market to take jobs that do not align with their qualifications. These jobs are 'the jobs that white people were willing to throw away.' A Hirsch (2018), n 237 above, 40. It is worth noting that the other African in Lanchester's *Capital* (2013) comes to play premiership football and is cushioned by agents and lawyers. He is unusual.

[240] D Pasura, 'Towards a Multisided Ethnography of the Zimbabwean Diaspora in Britain' (2011) 18 *Identities: Global Studies in Culture and Power* 250, 258.

[241] S Afolabi, 'Monday Morning' in S Afolabi, *A Life Elsewhere* (London, Jonathan Cape, 2006) 1, 6. Key to the decision to work is the need to supplement the meagre state allowance and also to continue to support the family that has remained at home (at 8). This must be counter-balanced with the possibility of detection which would lead to deportation (at 12).

[242] T Huchu (2015), n 23 above, 38–39.

[243] S Sahota (2016), n 21 above, 10, 12, 82, 236. A Mabanckou (translated by S Ardizzone) (2012) 87.

compelled to work in brothels.[244] Huchu's well off Mathematician frequents night-clubs where he notices that Africans seemed to have a monopoly on the toilet attendant jobs.[245] Along with other migrants, the two Ugandan women in the novels of Elizabeth Day and Maggie Gee do cleaning jobs in offices (an unseen, invisible army), hotels and private homes.[246] Beatrice, in Day's *Paradise City* muses on the difference in circumstance between her experience of London and that of the character in the Virginia Woolf book, *Mrs Dalloway* that she had read while in Uganda.

> She wonders what had happened to her copy of Mrs Dalloway. She'd had to leave it behind, like everything else. She had been good at school. She wishes she had been able to stay at university. Hard to remember now but she was studying to be a lawyer.[247]

Day captures the sting of the life of compromise, status diminution and its attendant abuse in the character of Beatrice.

In Gee's *My Cleaner*, Mary Tendo, the protagonist, muses on the lives that their parents wished for them as they urged them to leave: 'They saw us as teachers, lawyers, dentists, doctors, even presidents. Did they not see we might be porters and cleaners, taxi drivers, parking attendants? Despite our degrees and certificates.'[248]

The last (fictional) word should go to Adichie's *Americanah*. Ifemelu, an Igbo woman living in Princeton, travels by train to Philadelphia to get her hair braided. Emerging from the station, she contemplates taking a taxi with some foreboding:

> She hoped her driver would not be a Nigerian, because he, once he heard her accent, would either be aggressively eager to tell her that he had a master's degree, the taxi was a second job and his daughter was on the dean's list at Rutgers; or he would drive in sullen silence … nursing humiliation, that this fellow Nigerian, a small girl at that, who perhaps was a nurse or an accountant or even a doctor, was looking down on him.'[249]

The flip-side of status fracture is *status threat*. This is embodied by sections of the 'native population' who feel that their values and livelihoods are threatened by migration. The UN Special Rapporteur on the Rights of Migrants identifies the reasons for these attitudes:

> Unregulated migration in host countries has led to rising anti-migration sentiment, discrimination and violence, as migrants are portrayed as 'stealing' jobs and draining social services. Against the backdrop of a poor economic climate, the rise in nationalist populist parties and the tragic terrorist attacks around the world, xenophobia and hate speech have increased, causing a significant upward trend in negative perceptions of

[244] S Sahota (2016), n 21 above.
[245] T Huchu (2015), n 23 above, 260.
[246] E Day (2015), n 206 above, 44. M Gee, *My Cleaner* (London, SAQI, 2005).
[247] E Day (2015), n 206 above, 43. We later learn that Beatrice's home in Uganda was filled with books including the African classics, Achebe, Adichie, Mpange. At 293.
[248] M Gee, (2005), n 246 above, 19.
[249] CN Adichie (2014), n 103 above, 8.

migrants and creating a stumbling block in the development of more efficient evidence-based and human rights-based policies.[250]

Research undertaken in the United Kingdom by the organisation Hope not Hate suggests that there has been a rise in far-right organisations. Their focus is on attacking Muslims. Moreover, 'In the language of these movements, immigration is rephrased as "the great displacement" and segregation re-styled as "ethno-pluralism".'[251] The picture on views on immigration tends to be more complex depending on who is polled, how (face to face, on the phone, or in an anonymous internet survey) and when. The perception of migration as negative seems to have shifted since the United Kingdom voted to leave the European Union (Brexit).[252] Ford identifies that fewer people identify immigration as a problem or as a top priority requiring attention; there is also a more positive outlook on the cultural and economic benefits of migration (higher among groups that have university education).[253]

It is also worth reiterating that anti-migrant feeling is not confined to the West.[254] In her novel *The Gold Diggers*, Nyathi describes the violence that is meted out to 'foreigners' called *makwerekwere* (rubbish bags), by South Africans angered by the 'theft' by foreigners of jobs and opportunities which they think are rightfully for South Africans. In one scene, Chamunorwa, a Zimbabwean, is confronted by Kgosi, the former partner of Leratso, the woman to whom he, Chamunorwa, gave shelter after Kgosi beat and mistreated her. Kgosi, incensed, confronts them, calling Chamunorwa a 'piece of shit.'[255] He goads him knowing that the police will take his side as a fellow South African. Kgosi leaves, but not before issuing a threat: 'You come into our country and disrespect us. I will teach you a lesson *kwerekwere*.'[256] He is as good as his word and later returns with others, to raze the home that Chamunorwa and Leratso share.

The litany of complaints against the foreigners echoes those of right-wing populists in Western states; in addition to taking jobs and women, the foreigners

[250] UN Special Rapporteur on the Rights of Migrants A/71/285 (2016) para 18. UN Working Group People of African Descent, Mission to Italy, A/HRC/33/61/Add.1, 2016, para 74.

[251] N Lowles, 'Overview' in Hope not Hate, *The State of Hate 2018*, Hope not Hate, available at: https://www.hopenothate.org.uk/research/state-of-hate-2018/overview/

[252] On the effect of Brexit and the rise in antipathy towards minorities and people perceived to be 'foreign' see, Special Rapporteur on contemporary racism report on a visit to the UK, A/HRC/41/54/Add.2, 27 May 2019, paras 62–71.

[253] R Ford, 'How have attitudes to immigration changed since Brexit' at The UK in a Changing Europe, 1 June 2018 at: ukandeu.ac.uk/how-have-attitudes-to-immigration-changed-since-brexit/. See also *The Observer*, reporting 'The Audit; Attitudes to Immigration', *The Observer*, London, 21 October 2018, citing Hope not Hate research showing 60% of people think immigration has been good for Britain with a higher proportion (76%) of people holding that view compared to 45% of those who left school at 16. J Portes, *What do we know and what should we know about immigration?* (London, SAGE, 2019). Cf M Goodfellow (2019), n 162 above, 169–76.

[254] Khosravi details the poor treatment of Afghan refugees in Iran in the 1990s. S Khosravi (2010), n 3 above, 91–92.

[255] S Nyathi (2018), n 61 above, 144.

[256] S Nyathi (2018) 144.

also take housing and fail to learn 'our' languages.[257] They are ingrates who need to put in their place by being taught an unforgettable lesson.[258] Chamunorwa is burned alive. Reflecting what actually took place in South Africa, the novel then describes the chain effects of this xenophobia:

> Somali and Pakistani businesses were looted before being razed to the ground. Conspicuous foreigners resident in the area were beaten to a pulp and robbed of their belongings. Unsuspecting women were raped. Many were forced to flee to camps which started to sprout up in response to the scorching campaign of discontent against foreigners.[259]

It does not stop there:

> Ethiopians, Malawians, Mozambicans, Nigerians, Somalians and Zimbabweans were drowned in the frenzy of madness. The deep south was not spared either. Violence broke out in Soweto. Black-on-black violence; brother against brother. It was a rising tide of enmity ready to sink any foreigner that stood in its path.[260]

While Kgosi and his violent troupe are the most extreme manifestation of the hatred, they are not alone in their resentment. Other characters also manifest their dislike of foreigners. These include South African maids on a break who, discussing one of their fellow maids, a Zimbabwean, also bemoan the foreign incursion and the taking of opportunities. They are sceptical of the Zimbabwean woman's claim that she had once worked as a teacher at home, questioning why she would now be working as a maid if she had indeed had a high-status job before.[261]

[257] Huchu remarks drily that Westerners have themselves moved freely to settle in other people's countries and not bothered to integrate or learn the local languages. H Cousins and P Dodgson-Katiyo, '"Zimbabweanness Today" An Interview with Tendai Huchu' in *African Literature Today 34, Diaspora & Returns in Fiction* (Oxford, James Currey, 2016) 200, 204.

[258] For many of South Africa's neighbours, it is the South Africans who are behaving like ingrates who have forgotten the collective regional effort to resist apartheid and to support the anti-apartheid struggle, often at great cost to their own citizens. See also S Msimang (2014), n 171 above.

[259] S Nyathi (2018), n 61 above, 204.

[260] S Nyathi (2018) 204. There is little to distinguish Nyathi's fictional account from actual research data gathered for monitoring purposes. S Mlilo and JP Misago, Xenowatch, *Xenophobic Violence in South Africa: 1994–2018 An Overview*, The African Centre for Migration and Society (2018). Available at www.xenowatch.ac.za. See also, J Turkewitz, 'South African Riots Kill Five and Spur Cries of Xenophobia', *New York Times*, 3 September 2019. South Africa is not unique. For the treatment of Sierra Leonean refugees, see Communication 249/02, *African Institute for Human Rights and Development (on behalf of Sierra Leonean Refugees in Guinea) v Guinea* (2004) AHRL 57 (ACHPR 2004) (20th Activity Report). UN Treaty bodies and Special Procedure mandate-holders have also taken Angola to task for its treatment of refugees and migrants from neighbouring African states. Report of the Special Rapporteur on the human rights of migrants on his mission to Angola, A/HRC/35/25/Add.1, 25 April 2017. Key issues in paras 9, 11, 12. Human Rights Committee, Concluding Observations, Angola, CCPR/C/AGO/CO/2, 8 May 2019, paras 39, 40. Finally in his novel *Hiding in Plain Sight*, Naruddin Farrah's protagonist flies in to Nairobi from Italy. Somali by birth, she decides to use her Italian passport because, 'Kenya has lately been a problem country for Somalis, who are harassed from the moment they present their papers to the immigration officials and are asked relentlessly embarrassing questions.' N Farrah, *Hiding in Plain Sight* (New York, Riverhead Books, 2014) 33. She reasons that if she tells Kenyan immigration that she is a photographer coming as a tourist they will address her respectfully as 'madam' and 'stamp her in' (at p 34).

[261] S Nyathi (2018), n 61 above, 99–100.

Nyathi's novel also identifies a different form of gendered exploitation that follows from foreigner vulnerability, not least the rape of one Zimbabwean female maid by the white South African male boss on her first day at work while his wife is out. He had caught her trying on the wife's clothes and raped her in exchange for his silence. She leaves that day and never returns.[262]

All this points to the fact that xenophobia can very quickly be normalised and become 'mainstream'. It is not the preserve of extremists.[263] It may be this sense of those with little, feeling further pushed back, that is the catalyst for the discontent. It is also worth noting the possibility that 'foreigners' are easy scapegoats for the failure of the state to live up to its promise to deliver radical post-Apartheid change which includes better lives (socio-economically) for those who have suffered historic exclusions and injustice. There has been a rise in social differentiation not only in terms of foreigner – South African, but also by other categories including ethnicity and economic status.[264] It appears to be irrelevant, indeed it can be an exacerbating factor, that the migrants, many of whom are undocumented, do not occupy jobs in the formal sector, but rather take on informal work, sometimes being seen to depress wages or set up their own informal businesses.[265] All these factors contributed to earlier expulsions of Nigerians from Ghana and then Ghanaians from Nigeria. The latter expulsion brought to the fore 'Ghana must go bags', sturdy carriers purchased at markets by fleeing Ghanaians. *Ghana must go* is also the title of Taiye Selasi's much celebrated inter-continental novel of a wealthy Ghanaian family who move easily between the United States and Ghana.[266]

National and regional case law shows that judges can play an important role in upholding the principle of equal protection before the law and the right to freedom from discrimination including on grounds of status.[267] This includes the right to participate in the economy. The South African case of *Somali Association of South Africa v Limpopo Department of Economic Development, Environment and Tourism*

[262] S Nyathi (2018), n 61 above, 118–21.

[263] Amnesty International, 'South Africa: Ten years after xenophobic killings, refugees and migrants still living in fear' (London, Amnesty International, 2018).

[264] Research commissioned by the International Organization for Migration (IOM) showed that the triggers and explanations for the violence were far more complex than the foreigner bashing narratives that dominated. IOM, *Towards Tolerance, Law, and Dignity: Addressing Violence against Foreign Nationals in South Africa* (Pretoria, IOM, 2009). See also L Laundau (ed), *Exorcising the Demons Within: Xenophobia, Violence and Statecraft* (Tokyo, UN University Press, 2012).

[265] J Crush, G Tawodzera, S Ramchandran and R Tengeh, 'Refugee Entrepreneurial Economies in Urban South Africa', Research Gate, September, 2017, 783, 796–97.

[266] T Selasi, *Ghana must go* (London, Penguin, 2014). S Lawal, 'Ghana Must Go: The ugly history of Africa's most famous bag', *Mail & Guardian*, Johannesburg, 4 April 2019.

[267] *Lawyers for Human Rights v Minister of Home Affairs and Others* 2017 (5) SA 480 (CC). Successful Constitutional challenge of the failure to give adequate notice for detention and failing to bring detainee before a court when applying for extension under the Immigration Act, 2002. The Inter-American Court of Human Rights *Advisory Opinion on Juridical Condition and Rights of Undocumented Migrant Workers* OC-18/03 of September 17 2003.

2015 (1) SA 151 (SCA) reaffirmed the right of asylum seekers and refugees to apply for trade licences.[268]

In the midst of a seemingly never-ending stream of bad news stories about migrants and refugees, coupled with the abrogation by many states of their human rights obligations, we must remember the extraordinary work and kindness of those who step into the breach and offer advice and material and emotional support to asylum seekers, the undocumented and those that are just struggling. Writing about South Africa, Landau enjoins us to remember that even within the narratives of violence and persecution of migrants, it must be recognised that for the most part, the 'locals' and the incomers live peaceably.[269]

XVIII. On Kindness: Refugee and Migrant Organisations and Volunteers

The idea of co-operatives now seems dated, and yet one sees a pooling of expertise to help migrants. Lawyers give free advice; doctors volunteer in walk-in clinics where no paperwork is requested; churches, mosques, gurdwaras and synagogues offer shelter and emotional and spiritual succour; charities offer warm clothes and food. In their manifestation of their belief in our common humanity, volunteers offer a counter-narrative to the 'we all hate migrants' line pushed by some media outlets. Their compassion acts as a rebuke to state cynicism and the rolling back of human rights protections.[270] Counter-intuitively, it may also result in the state continuing to cut back on services that it should provide because it knows that the gap will be filled by the voluntary sector.

On its visit to Italy, the UN Working Group on Persons of African Descent acknowledged the work done by civil society, highlighting the assistance provided to newly arrived migrants. It also commended the inter-cultural and religious work done to promote integration and acceptance.[271]

Writers have also made efforts to challenge the anti-migrant rhetoric. This they have done through their art. There are collections that have advocacy and

[268] *Somali Association of South Africa v Limpopo Department of Economic Development, Environment and Tourism* 2015 (1) SA 151 (SCA). It will be interesting to see if the amendment to the Refugee Act, 1998 discussed earlier will have any impact on this aspect of refugee life. See Landau and Amit (2020).

[269] LB Landau, 'Xenophobia in South Africa: why it's time to unsettle narratives about migrants', *The Conversation*, 6 September 2018.

[270] Not all states have abrogated their responsibilities. Some have signed up to UNESCO'S Coalition of Inclusive and Sustainable Cities, launched in 2004. The network of interested cities aims to 'share experiences in order to improve their policies to fight racism, discrimination, xenophobia and exclusion' a:t http://www.unesco.org, Site visited 20 August 2019. UN Women also participates in a Safe Cities initiative to minimise violence against women. UN Women, *Safe City and Safe Public Spaces: Global Results Report* (New York, UN Women, 2017).

[271] Statement to the media by the United Nations' Working Group of Experts on People of African Descent, on the conclusion of its official visit to Italy, 1–5 June 2015. At: https://www.ohchr.org/EN/NewsEvents/Pages/DisplayNews.aspx?NewsID=16047&LangID=E.

fundraising as their object. These include *Refugee Tales* and *A Country of Refuge.*[272] Warsan Shire's poem 'Conversations about Home' has gained the status of global anthem for refugees and migrants.[273] If fiction reflects the concerns of the time, then many of the books discussed so far reflect the wish of the authors to use their craft to contribute to raising the profile of migrants while challenging their treatment. This social realism is reflected in lawyer, Ellen Wiles's *The Invisible Crowd.* In an afterword, she recounts how her life as a practising barrister showed her that the dry language of law failed to capture the drama and texture of her clients' stories. She goes on to say how angered she was by lurid tabloid headlines about migrants and asylum seekers, which in no way reflected the people that she met; hence her decision to 'write back' in the form of a novel.[274]

Wiles seeks to confront the hateful newspaper headlines by using them as the chapter headings in her story. This acts as a particularly effective counterpoint which confronts the reader with a sharp emotional contrast between the 'real world' and their growing attachment to the characters. Your sympathies are firmly with the characters. In her acknowledgements, Wiles also pays tribute to the work of other writers including Benjamin Zephaniah, whose novel *Refugee Boy* was one of the first examples of post-millennial fictional writing on unaccompanied refugee children.

In a foreword to *Refugee Boy*, Zephaniah explains that he wrote the book because he grew tired of the stereotyping and scapegoating of refugees. Having visited refugee camps around the world and spoken to many refugees, he had come to understand that 'each of them had a unique and usually terrifying story to tell.' His book is a compendium of the stories that he has heard. Zephaniah speaks to universal human needs: 'We all want to live in peace, we all want the best for our families.' He reminds the reader: 'The Celts, the Angles, the Saxons, the Jamaicans are all refugees of one sort or another.' He ends provocatively: 'What kind of refugee are you? And what are you scared of?'.[275]

In her afterword, Wiles also commends Sahota's *The Year of the Runaways.* Reading Sahota's novel, I was struck by how often the characters retreated to the gurdwara. Whenever they arrived in a new town, they went first to the gurdwara. They were fed, sheltered and networked as needed. They invoked kinship and religious ties and these came through for them, even if the help was sometimes delivered at arm's length. In Lanchester's *Capital* and Zadie's Smith's *The Embassy of Cambodia*, going to church enables the protagonists to meet up with other

[272] D Herd and A Pincus (eds), *Refugee Tales* (2016); *Refugee Tales II* (2017); *Refugee Tales III* (2019), all at n 105 above, and L Popescu, *A Country of Refuge* (2016), n 102 above. All the profits from *The Refugee Tales* series go to Gatwick Detainees Welfare Group and Kent Refugee Help. See also the charity Music in Detention which uses music in detention centres to uplift the spirits of detainees, at: www.musicindetention.org.uk.

[273] W Shire, *Teaching my mother how to give birth* (London, Flipped Eye, Mouthmark series (No 10), 2011) 24–27.

[274] E Wiles (2017), n 86 above, 'Afterword' – no page number, but immediately after p 328.

[275] B Zephaniah, 'On Writing *Refugee Boy*' in B Zephaniah, *Refugee Boy* (London, Bloomsbury, 2017).

Africans. This is the only time that they feel a sense of community.[276] For Quentina in *Capital*, she also sees the church as a place where she can get a date. The protagonist in Smith's *The Embassy of Cambodia* finds her partner at church. Research confirms the importance of church networks. In a survey of Ghanaians in Canada, the researchers asked why the participants had joined that particular church. The reason that had the highest response (45 per cent men and 32.6 per cent women) was 'Opportunity to worship and socialize with Ghanaians.'[277] Church provides a place of solace and solidarity and a break from racism, so much so that the women are said to be prepared to overlook the internal gender discrimination within the group in the name of racial solidarity.[278]

While many novels speak of the solace of community networks, not all seek the companionship of fellow nationals. In Nyathi's *Gold Diggers*, Portia considers going to the central Methodist church but decides against it, because it is: 'overflowing with Zimbabwean refugees who poured into Johannesburg like heavy rain. The church sheltered thousands who slept on its floors. Portia preferred to distance herself from kith and kin.'[279]

Yonas, in Wiles's *Invisible Crowd*, finding himself alone when he first gets to London, decides against looking out for fellow Eritreans for he would 'be dragged' to church and also have to engage in political conversations with people whose political allegiances he did not know. His preference is to spend time with British people who would show him the way of life and who would not interrogate him about his past or force him to reflect on all that he had left behind.[280]

The denouement to Huchu's *The Maestro, The Magistrate & the Mathematician* reveals the double life of Alphonso, who, although masquerading as an opposition party organiser in Edinburgh, is actually (*spoiler alert! Skip paragraph*) an agent of the Zimbabwean government, who are using him to spy on opposition members overseas.[281] Interviewed about the book and this narrative turn, Huchu notes that he was keen to show that his Zimbabwean protagonists were not victims. He describes Alphonso as a 'player in the great game', the game being politics.[282]

[276] Z Smith, *The Embassy of Cambodia* (London, Hamish Hamilton, 2013). In *Exit West* (2017), n 10 above Hamid shows the many ways in which communities are formed and co-exist. In the refugee camp in Myknos, Greece, 'everyone was foreign, and so in a sense, no one was.' (at 100). In the London squat the disparate groups form a community with rules and obligations (at 120, 124). A different need for community of people 'like one' leads to the creation of community of kind (national or religious) 128, 152. J Lanchester (2013) n 13 above, 143.

[277] J Mensah, C Williams and E Aryee, 'Gender, Power and Religious Transnationalism among the African Diaspora in Canada' (2013) 32 *African Geographical Review* 157, 165.

[278] J Mensah *et al* (2013) 157,166. This phenomenon is also identified in b hooks *From Margin to Centre* (Southend press, 1984) 14–15.

[279] S Nyathi (2018), n 61 above, 127.

[280] E Wiles (2017), n 86 above, 48. Makumbi's Ugandans are sometimes also suspicious of each other's political affiliations. Makumbi, 'Manchester Happened' (2019), n 29 above, 67.

[281] T Huchu (2015), n 23 above, 296–98.

[282] H Cousins and P Dodgson-Katiyo (2016) 200, 209.

There are other reasons for self-exclusion from community life. Research undertaken by Anderson and Doyal showed how African women migrants with HIV are reluctant to share information or to join support groups because of the fear of exposure and stigmatisation. However, many relied on their faith to carry them through difficult times.[283] Doyal also identifies that a decade-long study involving migrant women, heterosexual men and men who have sex with men (MSM) also revealed a shrinking from, rather than a reaching out for community. For heterosexual men, there was the challenge of reconciling masculinist concepts of breadwinner, provider and virility, with the impact of the illness, while MSM understood and feared the stigma associated with behaviour that many in the community would regard as outside the accepted norms. 'Indeed, a number talked to us about what they saw as the existential impossibility of being both gay and an African.'[284]

It is of course true to say that church and religion can have a malign influence, so that in Uzodinma Iweala's *Speak No Evil*, Niru, the gay son of two conservative Nigerian parents living in Washington, is subjected to what can only be described as gay conversion therapy by the family priest. The trip back to Nigeria also yields a well meant (from the parental perspective), but deeply disturbing 'demon casting out' scenario at the hands of a different religious leader.[285] Iweala dedicates his book 'To those who lack voice.'

On a lighter note, the nine-year-old protagonist in Makumbi's 'Christmas is Coming' provides a hilarious post-mortem of his parents' conversation on the way home from a party with fellow Ugandans which explains why one may want to keep away from compatriots:

> So-and-so is getting deported ... so-and-so has bought a Mercedes and yet lives like a rat ... they are on benefits ... so-and-so married for the visa ... so-and-so's children have turned into British brats ... that daughter of theirs must be a lezibian; did you see her haircut ... so-and-so are same clan, same totem but cohabiting, spit, spit.[286]

There is a stereotype, in Britain, of the kind of person one finds staffing charity shops and doing voluntary work: she is white (although this is changing), middle aged or older and middle class. She is sometimes assisted by high school students performing civic tasks to achieve a badge or accreditation (as in the Duke of Edinburgh scheme), or increasingly, by asylum seekers and others who cannot find work or are not allowed to work. Research undertaken in six European countries, including the UK, showed the positive benefits that accrued to women asylum

[283] J Anderson & L Doyal (2004) 'Women from Africa living with HIV in London: a descriptive study' (2004) 16:1 *AIDS Care* 95–105.

[284] L Doyal, 'A Decade of Researching the Social Aspects of HIV and AIDS' (2014) 384 *The Lancet* 2102–03. Quote at 2102. See also a mid-term review at L Doyal, 'Challenges in researching life with HIV/AIDS: an intersectional analysis of black African migrants in London' (2009) 11 *Culture, Health & Sexuality* 173–88.

[285] U Iweala, *Speak no Evil* (London, John Murray, 2018) 78–79.

[286] JN Makumbi, 'Christmas is Coming' in JN Makumbi, *Manchester Happened* (2019), n 29 above, 1–28, 4.

seekers from volunteering. The psychological benefits were said to include greater confidence and feelings of being valued and recognised. Coming into contact with a diverse range of people helped with integration and provided skills and networking opportunities, which would enhance the opportunities for securing future employment.[287]

It is important to recognise and acknowledge the myriad ways in which migrants help each other. The second half of Sylvia Ofili's graphic novel *German Calendar, No December* looks at a different community. This involves a diverse group of migrants who work at a Hamburg train station as cleaners, cooks and sellers. They have coffee together in the morning and quietly hide and provide shelter for migrants and other homeless people by allowing them to sleep in the toilets and hiding them when immigration officials raid. This international family is united in its humanity and care for others more desperate than themselves.[288]

Volunteers who give of their time generously and for no financial reward perform an invaluable service. In the *Invisible Crowd*, one such woman volunteers to teach English to asylum seekers at the Refugee Council. However, she soon finds that her class time is taken in responding to student requests for help:

> But then Padma said could I help her understand a letter she'd got from her son's school? And Rabah piped up-could I help explain his solicitor's letter? And so on. I didn't have the heart to refuse. So my class ended up involving a vocab lesson for the first half hour, and then a problem-sharing session for the second half hour, followed by about three hours after class helping people individually with some issue or other.[289]

Quentina, in Lanchester's *Capital*, finding herself without papers, accommodation, or ability to work (though she resolves this by working anyway), seeks shelter from a charity, Refuge. She is told about the charity by her lawyer and finds herself:

> living in a terraced house in Tooting with six other stateless women and a house manager. The charity splits nationalities up because it didn't like the idea of national cliques developing in the different houses and it thought that refugees learned English more quickly if they weren't with their own language group. This was a mistake in Quentina's view, but it was their charity, not hers.[290]

The charity, Refuge, has also worked with the lawyer-turned-photographer Bill Knight to produce a stunning photographic exhibition entitled 'Refugee's Gift'.[291]

[287] SMART Volunteering for Migrant Women, 'Volunteering: Perceptions, Experience and Barriers among Migrant Women, NGOs and Private Sector in Six European Countries' (Brussels, SMART Volunteering for Migrant Women, 2018). The countries included were: Belgium, Cyprus, France, Italy, Spain, UK.

[288] S Ofili (with illustrations by B Weyhe), *German Calendar, No December* (London, Cassava Republic, 2018) 140–47.

[289] E Wiles (2017), n 86 above, 95. In B Zephaniah's *Refugee Boy*, Alem, the unaccompanied minor seeking asylum is told: 'the Refugee Council will be backing you one hundred percent' (at 122).

[290] J Lanchester (2013), n 13 above, 132.

[291] B Knight, 'The Refugee's Gift.' Bill Knight – see https://www.knightsight.co.uk. A photo gallery can also be found at: Amnesty International, 'The refugee's gift – online exhibition' at: https://www.amnesty.org.uk/files/the_refugees_gift.pdf.

The aim of the project was to challenge the stereotyping of refugees including in photographs that denuded them of their dignity. Knight's photographs challenge the erasure of refugees' characters and their history. He shows them as ordinary human beings and highlights the fact that they had, and indeed continue to have, professions and interests beyond their status as refugees. They are not broken or bowed but engaged and willing to contribute to their new communities. The photographs and the accompanying text provide testimony of the enormous contributions that refugees have made and continue to make to British society. If the popular media refugee narratives remove their dignity from them, then Knight's photographs are a pictorial example of the power of Bernadette Atuahene's dignity restoration thesis, discussed in Chapters one and two.[292] The photographs leave one feeling uplifted. Importantly, by providing alternative stories about refugees, they achieve their aim of challenging stereotypes.

An often forgotten and underappreciated group is foster carers. These are private individuals who offer to look after children who are unaccompanied, or whose families may not be able to look after them, or pending adoption. In the UK they are paid an allowance by the local authorities under which they live. However, the literature highlights that, for many, this is a work of love and compassion, not driven by the relatively small payments made. The foster carers in Naidoo's *The Other Side of Truth* do so much to make their two Nigerian charges feel at home, cooking food that is familiar and providing love, support and warmth at all times. Similarly, the Fitzgeralds, the foster carers in Zephaniah's *Refugee Boy*, take the time to explain to their young charge that discrimination and prejudice against incomers is cyclical. They explain that, as Irish people, they too were once the objects of suspicion during what is known as 'The Troubles'. The perception then was that all Irish people must support and belong to the Irish Republican Army (IRA), which was labelled a terrorist organisation by the British government.

> Now they want to tell us that the blacks and refugees are causing all our problems … And you know, if people didn't come from abroad, we wouldn't have a health service, or a bus service, and most of the great big British corner shops would be gone. And guess what, mate – don't just take it from me, check up on it – even the royal family, yes, even that lot, they came from abroad. These politicians make me sick!'[293]

And finally, on to lawyers. While it is true that the line from Shakespeare that most lawyers have quoted at them is, 'The first thing we do, let's kill all the lawyers',[294] it is also true that both in real and fictional life, lawyers play an important role. The

[292] B Atuahene, 'Dignity Takings and Dignity Restoration: Creating a New Theoretical Framework for Understanding Involuntary Property Loss and the Remedies Required' (2016) 41(4) *Law and Social Inquiry* 796.

[293] B Zephaniah (2017), n 231 above, 122.

[294] Said by Dick the Butcher in 'Henry VI, Part 2', Act IV, Scene II, Line 73. Apparently, it was only corrupt lawyers that were a problem. Shakespeare is said to have admired lawyers and judges for administering and ensuring justice. See D Vogel, '"Kill the Lawyers", A Line Misinterpreted', *New York Times*, 17 June, 1990.

cutbacks in legal aid, the growth in complexity of rules and regulations, the rise in asylum applicants, together with a hostile and often mendacious media, means that immigration and refugee lawyers work in trying conditions. That they continue is a testament to their tenacity and strong belief in that much used, but little practised, word, 'justice'. From Lanchester's *Capital*, to Imbue's *Behold the Dreamers*, to Wiles's *Invisible Crowd*, to Zephaniah's *Refugee Child*, lawyers are information gatekeepers, translators of norms, psychologists, friends and champions.[295]

XIX. Conclusion

This chapter started by considering how difficult it is for Africans to migrate legally. This forces them to make alternative arrangements to facilitate their freedom of movement. The fictional literature is replete with examples of ingenuity reflecting the fact that 'they cannot close all the doors of the world.'[296] Sadly, the legal literature is equally well-armed with examples of state counter-insurgency to thwart the movement of those considered 'undesirable'. The chapter considered the means used by the state to enforce compliance with often unjust or inequitably applied immigration and refugee law and their impact on those on the receiving end. This includes the use of detention. The scepticism of decision-makers creates the conditions for asylum applicants to embellish their stories in an effort to be heard and believed. The economic challenges faced by African migrants and the status fracture that they experience were examined. The chapter concluded by focusing on the many positive examples of kindness and generosity of writers, volunteers and lawyers.

Part II, comprising three chapters follows. I look at the fictional and legal lives of African migrants, starting with women, before moving on to look at people belonging to the LGBTI community, and finally exploring the migration stories of children, both as unaccompanied minors and within the diaspora as the children of migrants. In taking this intersectional approach, one is better able to tease out the specificities of the social and legal experiences of the three groups. The final chapter is the Conclusion.

[295] Within the UK context, one is struck by the similarities between the challenges facing those working in immigration and family law. See for example, J Eekelaar and M Maclean, *Family Justice: The Work of Family Judges in Uncertain Times* (Oxford, Hart Publishing, 2013); M Maclean and J Eekelaar, *Lawyers and Mediators: The Brave New World of Services for Separating Families*' (Oxford, Hart Publishing, 2016). Huchu offers an alternative view of lawyers as beneficiaries of human rights violations for their services are in greater demand T Huchu (2015), n 23 above, 167.

[296] S Khosravi (2010), n 3 above, 108.

PART II

Intersections

4

Women's Lives

From the ancient Greek myth of Odysseus who went to fight the Trojan wars, we learn that historically it has been women's role to wait. Odysseus's wife, Penelope, waited for him for 17 years; she refused to believe he was dead, or that he would have abandoned her; she scorned all advances and faithfully waited for her man to return. And he did. Njabulo Ndebele used the Odysseus myth in his novel *The Cry of Winnie Mandela*.[1] The muse, Winnie, also waited for 27 years for Mandela to be released from prison. Similarly, the other women in the novel, whom Ndebele calls Penelope's descendants, wait for men to return from studying abroad or working away from home.[2]

I. Historical Reasons for Restrictions on Women's Freedom of Movement

The 'women at home' framework is rooted in both (heteronormative) gendered notions of the public and private which reinforced stratified gender roles involving women being homemakers, and men the breadwinners, working in the public sphere.[3] While there has been progress, there is still a gendered divide of labour, status and prestige in most societies. The policing of women, and specifically their sexual expression and reproductive functions, has reinforced the notion that a woman should be monitored by being kept under the jurisdiction of her husband or a trusted agent, usually a member of his family.[4] This, and in some societies, economic dependence coupled with the need for male permission to obtain a

[1] There seems to be some contestation over the exact length of time that Penelope waited. Figures range from 10 to 20 years. Classicist Mary Beard says 'decades'. M Beard, *Women and* Power (London, Profile Books, 2017), 3. Novelist and academic Njabulo Ndebele veers between 17 and 19. N Ndebele, *The Cry of Winnie Mandela* (Banbury, Ayebia Clarke, 2003).

[2] Two excellent feminist-infused Penelope-inspired and -focused novels are M Atwood, *The Penelopiad* (London, Canongate, 2018) and T Jones, *An American Marriage* (London, Oneworld, 2019).

[3] Clearly this division is less pronounced in some societies which claim to operate a non-hierarchical dual sex model of gender relations. N Nzegwu, 'Gender Equality in a Dual Sex System: The Case of Onitsha' (1994) 7 *Canadian Journal of Law and Jurisprudence* 73–95.

[4] In Atwood's *Penelopiad*, this policing role is played by Eurycleia, the woman who nursed Odysseus and then stayed on to nurse his son Telemachus. As he grew into adulthood, Telemachus also policed his mother. M Atwood (2018), n 2 above, 121, 157–60.

passport or to travel, has further constrained women's ability to leave home to look for paid work.[5] Gender stereotypes are also in play. This is well captured by Sue Nyathi in her novel *The Gold Diggers*. Dumisani, the husband in Nyathi's novel, rails against his wife's decision to leave their children (his word is 'dumping') in Zimbabwe to go to Britain to look for work. For him, her actions, 'felt like she had taken a knife and cut his balls off and thrown them out the window.' He describes her lacking faith in him. He feels emasculated and cannot bring himself to acknowledge his failure to provide for the family. His own migration to South Africa in search of work has not been successful.[6] When he left, no one accused him of 'dumping' the family.

Additionally, the framing of many countries' nationality laws has reinforced the gendered idea of patrilocality whereby a woman, once married, 'followed her husband.' Historically, she was expected to live with him or his family. If the marriage involved two people of different nationalities, then it was expected that the woman would relinquish her nationality because she would take on that of her husband. It was rare for a woman to be permitted to pass on nationality to her husband, or indeed for foreign husbands to be permitted to move to live in the wife's country of citizenship and residence, leading to many cases challenging the discriminatory effects of these laws.[7] Women as wives were bound even more tightly to their husbands by the failure of nationality laws to recognise a mother's right to pass on her nationality to her children because they only recognised the patrilineal line of descent. It was for this reason that one of the first women's rights-oriented treaties adopted by the UN was the Convention on the Nationality of Married Women, 1958 which finds echo in article 9(1) of CEDAW and the African Protocol on Women's Rights, article 6(g).[8]

While it is true that gender-based discrimination continues to permeate the lives of women globally, women are starting to move across borders. Moreover,

[5] CEDAW, General Recommendation No 26 on Women Migrant Workers, CEDAW/C/2009/WP.1/R, 5 December 2008, para 24(a) where the Committee recommends that States remove the discriminatory laws and address the discriminatory practices that lead to checks on women's voluntary migration.

[6] S Nyathi, *The Golddiggers* (London, Macmillan, 2018) 166.

[7] *Attorney-General of Botswana v Unity Dow* [1992] LRC (Const) 623; *Abdulaziz Cabales Balkandi v UK* (1985) 7 EHRR 471 (28 May 1985); Proposed Amendments to the Naturalization Provisions of the Political Constitution of Costa Rica Inter Am Ct HR, Advisory Opinion OC-4/84 of 19 January1984, Series A No 4; *Aumeeruddy Cziffra v Mauritius* (2000) AHRLR 3 (HRC 1981). In 2017 Nigeria was censured by the Migrant Workers' Committee for its discriminatory nationality laws. CMW/C/NGA/CO/1 (2017) para 27 (c).

[8] UN Convention on the Nationality of Married Women, 1957, 309 UNTS 65. CEDAW art 9(2) allows mothers to pass on their nationality to their children, while art 6(h) of the African Protocol is more equivocal, leaving it to national law. See CEDAW General Recommendation No 32 on the gender-related dimensions of refugee status, asylum, nationality and statelessness of women, CEDAW/C/GC/32, 5 November 2014, paras 54, 60, 61. K Knop and C Chinkin, 'Remembering Chrystal Macmillan: Women's Equality and Nationality in International Law' (2001) 22 *Michigan Journal of International Law* 523–85; S Goonesekere, 'Article 9' in M Freeman, C Chinkin and B Rudolph (eds), *CEDAW: A Commentary* (Oxford, OUP, 2013) 233–49. D Brennan, 'Statelessness and the Feminist Toolbox: Another Man-made Problem with a Feminist Solution?' (2019) 24 *Tilburg Law Review* 170.

not all are marrying. They are not reliant on men for their livelihoods. In 2018, the International Labour Organization reported that between 2013 and 2017, there were 96 million male migrants, composing 58 per cent of the total, and 68 million women migrants who made up the remaining 42 per cent. More often than not, they leave in search of work and better opportunities. Unsurprisingly, the majority of migrant workers congregate in the richer parts of the world, with North America and Europe having the highest proportion at 46.9 per cent.[9]

Within this global movement, migrant women are particularly disadvantaged. They often come as dependants because the structural disadvantages that they have experienced means that they do not have the education or skills which would enable them to migrate as experts or in the skilled categories.[10] When women do travel in their own right, they often come to do 'women's work', including working as domestic help.[11] They have limited autonomy, as their immigration status is often dependent on the employer who is tasked with the responsibility of ensuring compliance with immigration laws and policies. It also opens the women up to abuse.[12] The limited regulation of domestic work by states leaves women open to the unregulated and often exploitative 'law' of the employer. If employed by a diplomat or in an embassy, a woman may find herself truly in 'no man's land'. Women are also often caught up in the immigration quagmire of the shifting legality of their family members who may have periods of irregularity.[13]

In this chapter, I explore the experiences of migrant women, focusing on trafficking and domestic work. Ann Stewart has coined the phrase 'body work' for work that women do. She argues that in a globalised world, Third World migrant bodies perform caring, cleaning and sex work. These women sometimes experience economic and physical violence.[14] Stewart's focus is on the economy of the body primarily as worker.[15] But first, a brief look at women in refugee law.

[9] ILO, 'New ILO Figures show 164 Million people are migrant workers' ILO, News, 5 December 2018 at: https://www.ilo.org/global/about-the-ilo/newsroom/news/WCMS_652106/lang--en/index.htm. These figures are contained in the report: ILO, *Global Estimates on International Migrant Workers – Results and Methodology* (ILO, 2018).

[10] CEDAW, General Recommendation No 26 Workers, CEDAW/C/2009/WP.1/R, 5 December 2008 para 5. Even when coming as skilled workers, gender assumptions lead to officials assuming that they are accompanying their husbands who are regarded as the head of the household for purposes of family immigration. M Coker, 'Can a Woman Head a Household in Dubai? Our Reporter Ventures to Find Out', *New York Times*, 21 August 2018.

[11] H Lutz, *Migration and Domestic Work: A European Perspective on a Global Theme* (Routledge, 2008). See also UNGA, 'Note by the Secretary-General on Contemporary Forms of Slavery, including its causes and consequences' UN Doc A/73/139, 10 July 2018, paras 19, 24, 48.

[12] B Anderson, *Us and Them? The Dangerous Politics of Immigration Control* (Oxford, OUP, 2013) 159–76. See also CEDAW General Recommendation No 26 on Migrant women workers.

[13] International Convention on the Protection of the Rights of All Migrant Workers and Members of Their Families, UN GA Res 45/158 of 18 December 1990.

[14] A Stewart, 'Who do we care about? Reflections on Gender Justice in a Global Market' (2007) 58(3) *Northern Ireland Legal Quarterly* 358–74.

[15] In her book Stewart also considers the work that women in Kenya do to ease the lives of Western consumers (flower and vegetable picking and packing). A Stewart, *Gender, Law and Justice in a Global Market* (Cambridge, CUP, 2011). See also H Lutz, *The New Maids: Transnational Women and the Care Economy* (New York, ZED Books, 2011).

II. Women and Refugee Law

The framing of persecution and the grounds for claiming within refugee law favour the experiences of men. In the UN Convention on the Status of Refugees, 1951 grounds for claiming refugee status do not include sex or gender as a reason for persecution, nor does the discrimination provision encompass sex.[16] They focus on public sphere violations and on the actions of the state as an actor working against the individual. Women tend to be discriminated against by non-state actors and those violations occur disproportionately within the private sphere.[17] While much work has gone into seeking to make women normatively visible, in practice, women continue to be disadvantaged at home and beyond.[18]

The body and fear for its violation also frames many of the claims of African women seeking asylum. When asking for asylum, the African woman is required to confirm the view that there is an inherent violence and lack of respect for human rights and 'civilised values' in African societies. There is no space for drawing comparisons with the practices of discrimination that are experienced by white women in Western societies, or indeed for describing discrimination against women as a global problem. The more brutish and less protective she is able to paint the country that she has just left, the better her chances of legal recognition. Stereotypes abound.

Migrant and asylum-seeking women are constantly treading a fine line, between wishing to talk about issues that are important to the community that one comes from, without simultaneously reinforcing stereotypes about 'backwardness' and inherent misogyny.[19] Peroni argues that even the Council of Europe

[16] UN Convention Relating to the Status of Refugees, 1951, 189 UNTS 137, art 1A(2), art 3. This is a point made also by Hale LJ in *Fornah (FC) v Secretary of State for the Home Department* [2006] UKHL 46, paras 84–86, 94–103, 108–15. UNHCR Guidelines on International Protection: Gender-Related Persecution within the context of Article 1A(2) of the 1951 Convention and/or its 1967 Protocol relating to the Status of Refugees, HCR/GIP/02/01, 7 May 2002; Some states also have national guidelines on gender and the asylum process. H Cheikh Ali, C Querton and E Soulard, *Gender Related Asylum Claims in Europe: A Comparative analysis of law, policies and practices in nine EU Member States*, European Parliament, Directorate for Internal Policies, 2012; A Edwards, CEDAW 'Summary of background paper entitled "Displacement, statelessness and questions of gender equality and the Convention on the Elimination of All Forms of Discrimination against Women".' CEDAW/C/2009/II/WP.3, 11 July 2009. CEDAW, General Recommendation No 32 on the gender-related dimensions of refugee status, asylum, nationality and statelessness of women, 5 November 2014, CEDAW/C/GC/32. Council of Europe, Resolution 2159 (2017) Protecting refugee women and girls from gender-based violence, available at: https://assembly.coe.int/nw/xml/XRef/Xref-XML2HTML-en.asp?fileid=23700&lang=en. Council Directive 2004/83/EC of 29 April 2004 on minimum standards for the qualification and status of third country nationals or stateless persons as refugees or as persons who otherwise need international protection and the content of the protection granted.

[17] C Chinkin and M Freeman, 'Introduction' in M Freeman, C Chinkin and B Rudolph (eds), *Commentary on the Convention on the Elimination of all Forms of Discrimination against Women* (Oxford, OUP, 2013), 1–33.

[18] Council of Europe, *Gender Based Asylum Claims and Non-Refoulement: Articles 60 and 61 of the Istanbul Convention* (COE, 2019), 12.

[19] U Narayan, *Dislocating Cultures: Identities, Traditions and Third World Feminism* (New York, Routledge, 1997) 121–57.

Protocol on the Prevention of Violence against Women pathologises violence that is labelled as particular to certain migrant groups. These practices, which include so-called honour crimes (a justificatory name given to gendered murder) and female genital mutilation (FGM), are labelled 'cultural', and thus distinguishable from the ordinary violence experienced by European women.[20] One could argue that gender-based violence is underpinned by culture so that the type of violence may reflect the framing of gender in any one society.[21]

The leading United Kingdom Supreme Court case, *Fornah v Secretary of State for Home Affairs*,[22] is on female genital mutilation. Fornah was a young woman from Sierra Leone. She had arrived in the country in March 2003, aged 15. Her flight had been arranged by an uncle. She claimed asylum, saying she feared female genital cutting. (She also disclosed that she had been raped during the civil war). FGM is practised extensively in Sierra Leone. After initial success, her claim was overturned on appeal, hence her appeal to the Supreme Court.

The Supreme Court considered this to be a straightforward case. Using the vast literature, comparative case law and UNHCR Gender Guidelines on the interpretation of the Refugee Convention, they found that she did have a claim to refugee status. They placed her within the social group category which: 'might best be defined as Sierra Leonean women belonging to those ethnic groups where FGM is practised: then it is quite clear that the reason for the persecution is membership of that group.'[23] Telling was the assessment by Lord Bingham of Sierra Leonean society's propensity to discriminate against women.[24] There is no recognition that women in England (the Global North) experience different forms of violence or discrimination frequently. This is not to discount that women in Sierra Leone *do* suffer from discrimination, FGM being one manifestation of that, but rather that it would have been preferable to have framed discrimination as a global phenomenon before homing in on the particularities of the discrimination faced by women in Sierra Leone.[25]

Equally interesting is the way in which the other judges express their surprise that they should even be entertaining this case, for 'The United Kingdom is apparently alone in the *civilised world* in rejecting such a claim. Nor do we reject them all …'

[20] L Peroni, 'Violence against Women: The Istanbul Convention through a Post-Colonial Feminist Lens' (2016) 24 *Feminist Legal Studies* 49–67. Migrant women do not always get the protections offered to those from within the EU. See J Wessels, 'The Boundaries of Universality – Migrant Women and Domestic Violence before the Strasbourg Court' (2019) 37 *Netherlands Quarterly of Human Rights* 336–58.

[21] A Simon-Butler and B McSherry, 'Defining Sexual and Gender-Based Violence in the Refugee Context', *IRIS Working Paper Series*, No 2/2018, Birmingham: Institute for Research into Superdiversity.

[22] *Fornah v Secretary of State for Home Affairs* [2006] UKHL 46.

[23] *Fornah v Secretary of State for Home Affairs* [2006] UKHL 46, para 114.

[24] *Fornah*, para 7.

[25] H Crawley, *Refugees and Gender: Law and Process* (Bristol, Jordan Publishing, 2001). Cf E Brems, "Strong Women don't need Asylum" (The European Court on FGM)', *Strasbourg Observers*, 19 August 2010: https://strasbourgobservers.com/2010/08/19/%E2%80%98strong-women-don%E2%80%99t-need-asylum%E2%80%99-the-european-court-on-fgm/.

and 'It would be most unfortunate if the jurisprudence of the United Kingdom (out of step with that of most *enlightened* countries) were available to support a narrow view of the Convention's protective reach'[26] (emphasis added). Lady Hale does acknowledge the impact of tradition and continuity, noting that, like fagging (senior boys getting junior boys to undertake tasks for them) in the novel *Tom Brown's School Days*, painful practices are likely to be continued by those who have themselves been victimised.

David Garbin and Marie Godin show how Congolese women living in Europe (Belgium and England) have challenged sexism within their own communities whilst also providing counter-narratives to explain sexual violence in their home country. Echoing Gayatri Spivak, they challenge the 'beastly African men exploiting weak women' explanation commonly advanced to explain the high rate of violence against women. Giving evidence to a Parliamentary committee in the Westminster parliament, one Congolese woman noted:

> They rape Congolese women [in the East of the DRC] to intimidate them, because they *resist* the presence of the rebels, not because they are powerless. Women are not passive victims. We oppose this image. African women are very powerful, contrary to what the media are saying.[27]

III. Trafficking in Law and Literature

Chika Unigwe's *On Black Sisters' Street* focuses on the trafficking of Nigerian women to Belgium.[28] We meet each of the four women in their homes on the continent. Sisi, a Sudanese woman whose family was murdered during the war and who was herself raped, was taken to Nigeria by one of the ECOWAS peacekeeping soldiers deployed to Sudan. The soldier does not marry her because she is not of his group and his family would not approve. Like the other three women, she is introduced to a man called 'Chief', or Oga Dele, who facilitates her trafficking to Belgium, where she ends up living in a communal house run by the madam who collects the money from their sexual exploitation. As we have seen in Chapter three, the madam gives her a story to tell the immigration interview panel

[26] *Fornah*, paras 108 (Lady Hale) and 121 (Lord Brown) respectively.

[27] D Garbin and M Godin, '"Saving the Congo": Transnational Social Fields and the Politics of Home in the Congolese Diaspora' (2013) 6(2) *African and Black Diaspora: An International Journal* 113, 122. G Spivak, 'Can the Subaltern Speak?' in Cary Nelson and Lawrence Grossberg (eds), *Marxism and the Interpretation of Culture* (Urbana IL, University of Illinois Press, 1987). Finally, see S DasGupta, '"Your women are oppressed, but ours are awesome": How Nicholas Kristoff and *Half the Sky* use women against each other' at: http://www.racialicious.com, 8 October 2012, site visited 23 September 2015. I arrived in New York in August 2009 to find the N Kristoff and S WuDunn, *Half the Sky* (New York, Virago, 2009) book featured extensively. I read it and renamed it 'It takes an American'. I appreciated its intent – to raise the profile of women globally, but was frustrated by the Western saviour approach, already extensively critiqued, not least by Mutua. M Mutua, 'Savages, Victims and Saviors: The metaphor of human rights' (2001) 42 *Harvard International Law Journal* 201.

[28] C Unigwe, *On Black Sisters' Street* (London, Vintage, 2010).

who are to assess the asylum application that has been made. She is not believed, thus rendering her 'irregular'. The madam takes her passport knowing that she is now completely within her control. Telling Sisi that she no longer exists as she is 'persona non grata', in Belgium, the madam goes on: 'Now you belong to me. It costs us a lot of money for us to organise all this for you.'[29] Madam then goes on to lay out the terms of the 'contract' to which Sisi is expected to adhere:

> 'Now, until you have paid every single kobo,' she pointed the cigarette at Sisi, 'every single cent of what you owe us, you will not have your passport back. Every month we expect five hundred euros from you. That should be easy if you are dedicated. But I understand that sometimes you may not be able to, so we have set a minimum repayment of one hundred euros. Every month you go to the Western Union and transfer the money to Dele. Any month you do not pay up …' She let the threat hang, unspoken, yet menacing, her left hand plucking at a tuft of hair under her chin.[30]

The story line captures well the bind facing women who may have agreed to be smuggled, but who find themselves trafficked. The reality, as the journalist Daniel Trilling documents, is equally grim.[31] Girls and women are often encouraged by family members who see other people's children returning with riches, to take up the offer to travel to Europe to work.[32] Before leaving they are taken to shrines and made to swear oaths. They are told that if they run away or do not follow instructions, their families will be harmed. On arrival, they are collected from reception centres and disappear. Research done on Nigerian organised crime by Stephen Ellis notes that the movement of women for sexual exploitation is part of a network of organised crime. Sisi, in Unigwe's novel cited above, is part of sophisticated criminal networks with links in Nigeria and also all over Europe and beyond. The madams are often women who have themselves been trafficked and have worked off their debts or are now seen as too old to work in the sex trade.[33]

The two United Nation's Protocols on Smuggling and Trafficking make a distinction in their treatment of the two categories of people: the smuggled and the trafficked.[34] Smuggling is treated as a crime and an immigration offence which

[29] C Unigwe (2010) 182.

[30] C.Unigwe (2010) 183.

[31] D Trilling, *Lights in the Distance: Exile and Refuge at the Borders of Europe* (London, Picador, 2018) 137–40. See also Plan International, London School of Health and Tropical Medicine (LSHTM) and IOM, *The Trafficking of Girls and Young Women in Nigeria* (London, PLAN, 2019) (PLAN (2019)). J Jones, 'The BAWSO Diogel Project. An Interview with Imogen Gunner, BAWSO Trafficking Senior Support Worker' (2018) 8(1) *Onati Socio-Legal Series* 71, 81–82.

[32] J Sarson and L McDonald, 'No Longer Invisible: Families that Torture, Traffic and Exploit their Girl Child' (2018) 8(1) *Onati Socio-Legal Series* 81–105. PLAN (2019) 13.

[33] S Ellis, *This Present Darkness: A History of Nigerian Organised Crime* (London, HURST, 2016) 180–87.

[34] Protocol to Prevent, Suppress and Punish Trafficking in Persons Especially Women and Children, supplementing the United Nations Convention against Transnational Organized Crime, UN GA Res 55/25 of 15 November 2000, 2237 UNTS 319 (Palermo Protocol); Protocol against the Smuggling of Migrants by Land, Sea and Air, supplementing the United Nations Convention against Transnational Organized Crime UNGA Res 55/25 of 15 November 2000. As of May 2019, 49 African States have acceded to the Palermo Protocol and two have signed.

should lead to punishment and deportation. Trafficking, which is marked by a lack of consent on the part of the victim, is regarded as a human rights violation that should lead to the compassionate treatment of the trafficked person.[35] It may even require that they be given residence.[36] In practice, states do not always distinguish the two modes of arrival, taking a criminal and immigration-focused approach for both.[37] Ellis makes the point that the women and girls cannot be said to be trafficked, 'meaning taken against their will'[38] but concedes that they are, 'socially obligated to take part in a very exploitative business.'[39] He notes that the women, sponsors, traffickers and even police all from the same region, are all involved, thus further cementing the social bonds and sense of obligation. Ellis mischaracterises consent – the fact that one goes along is not the same as saying that one has consented. This is recognised in the definition of trafficking:

> (a) 'Trafficking in persons' shall mean the recruitment, transportation, transfer, harbouring or receipt of persons, by means of the threat or use of force or other forms of coercion, of abduction, *of fraud, of deception, of the abuse of power or of a position of vulnerability or of the giving or receiving of payments or benefits to achieve the consent of a person having control over another person, for the purpose of exploitation.* Exploitation shall include, at a minimum, *the exploitation of the prostitution of others or other forms of sexual exploitation*, forced labour or services, slavery or practices similar to slavery, servitude or the removal of organs;
>
> (b) *The consent of a victim of trafficking in persons to the intended exploitation* set forth in subparagraph (a) of this article *shall be irrelevant* where any of the means set forth in subparagraph (a) have been used; (emphasis added).[40]

Research undertaken by Liz Hales and Loraine Gelsthorpe on trafficked migrant women in prison in England and Wales showed that most had been victimised and threats made against them or members of their family. One of the largest groups comprised Nigerian women. The research also showed that even if they

[35] A Gallagher, 'Human Rights and the New UN Protocols on Trafficking and Migrant Smuggling: A Preliminary Analysis' (2001) 23(4) *Human Rights Quarterly* 975–1004, at: https://muse.jhu.edu/article/13800; A Gallagher, *The International Law of Trafficking* (Cambridge, CUP, 2012).

[36] Council of Europe Convention on Action against Trafficking in Human Beings, 2005, CETS No 197.

[37] Detention Action, *Trafficked into Detention: How Victims of Trafficking are Missed in Detention*, Detention Action, November 2017.

[38] S Ellis (2016), n 33 above, 183.

[39] S Ellis (2016) 184. Ellis contends that the girls and women moved out of the country may be no different to the many children forced to work in Nigeria selling goods for other people for little or no reward. They too may have been moved from their homes. Ellis also discusses 'baby farms' where young women are forcibly impregnated and held against their will until they give birth. The children are then sold to prospective 'adopters'. S Ellis (2016), 187. On the sale of children see the case *London Borough of Hackney v Mrs E and Mr E* [2006] EWHC 1620. 'Kenyan Pastor Extradited from the UK to face child theft charges' (4 August 2017) at: http://home.bt.com/news/world-news/kenyan-pastor-extradited-from-uk-to-face-child-theft-charges-11364201241492. See also the short story by EC Osundu, 'Miracle Baby' in EC Osundu, *Voice of America* (London, Granta, 2010) 117, 120–22.

[40] Trafficking Protocol, art 3.

had managed to escape, the women lacked papers and thus could not work or claim state benefits, thus pushing them back to the traffickers.[41]

The difficulties confronting women such as those in the Unigwe novel are captured in the CEDAW case of *Zheng Zheng v The Netherlands* brought by a woman who argued that the Netherlands had unfairly refused to recognise that she had been trafficked. She had been brought into the Netherlands as a minor and been forced to work in the sex trade until she became pregnant and was thrown out on the street where she was taken in by someone who used her to do their heavy domestic work. Immigration caught up with her. She was challenging her deportation order. The state noted that she had originally claimed asylum, and since the trafficking claim had not been litigated in the domestic legal system the CEDAW petition was inadmissible. The Committee agreed that the claim was inadmissible due to failure to exhaust domestic remedies. However, in a dissenting opinion, three Committee members reasoned:

> In light of the nature of the crime of trafficking and the difficulty for victims, who are often uneducated and traumatized, to report precisely and with great details their experience, we are of the view that [the Immigration and Naturalization Service] did not act with the due diligence that the author's situation required by failing to recognize that she might have been a victim of trafficking in human beings and accordingly inform her of her rights … Under the Palermo Protocol, such a duty is clearly established under article 6.[42]

The dissenting opinion is important in that it identifies the woman's poverty and illiteracy as drivers for the trafficking and also as the explanation for her failure to seek help.[43] Given these factors, it was incumbent on the Dutch state to offer help, as is provided in Dutch law.

The Unigwe book also acts as a positive jumping off point for discussing the issue of state responsibility to prevent trafficking and also to detect and protect trafficking victims.[44] It calls to mind the European case of *Rantsev v Cyprus and Russia*,[45] which followed the death of a Russian woman who had been trafficked from Russia to Cyprus. Russian women were promised bar work in Cyprus, but ended up being compelled to work in the sex industry. This was known to the Russian government which did nothing to put in deterrent measures or to warn Russian women of the dangers that lay ahead. The Cypriot government failed to monitor the migration and work of women known to be vulnerable to trafficking. This was a failure of due diligence on the part of both states.

[41] L Hales, 'The Criminalisation and Imprisonment of Migrant Victims of Trafficking' (2018) 8(1) *Onati Socio-Legal Series* 50, 56, 58.

[42] Communication No 15/2007, UN Doc CEDAW/C/42/D/15/2007 (26 October 2009), para 9.1. See generally J Chuang, 'Article 6' in M Freeman, C Chinkin and B Rudolph (eds), *Commentary to CEDAW* (Oxford, OUP, 2013) 169, 174–75.

[43] See also CEDAW, Concluding Observations South Africa, CEDAW/C/ZAF/CO/4, 4 April 2011, para 27.

[44] See also UNODC, *The Global Report on Trafficking in Persons 2018* (Vienna, UNODC, 2018).

[45] *Rantsev v Cyprus and Russia* (Application no 25965/04) ECtHR, 7 January 2010.

The due diligence obligations were clearly articulated in the follow up case of *Chowdury and Others v Greece*[46] on forced labour. These included adopting preventative measures, protecting victims and investigating if a violation was identified, criminalising the act and punishing the perpetrators.[47] In addition to calling for the enactment of laws criminalising sexual exploitation of children and urging intercountry cooperation to stem trafficking, the UN Children's Rights Committee has also enjoined states to provide health and rehabilitation services for children who have been exploited and asked that the state ensure that such children are treated as victims and not offenders.[48]

Unigwe's book and the *Rantsev* case are illustrative of a disregard for the lives of women. It is well known that Nigerian women, particularly from Edo State, are regularly trafficked to Italy and beyond for sexual exploitation, and yet little is done, either by the Nigerian authorities or the receiving Italian state, thus rendering the findings in the *Rantsev* decision meaningless. In 2019 the British government was criticised for suggesting that trafficked women who returned to Nigeria were lauded, thus seemingly dismissing the state's own due diligence obligations.[49] In 2017, the Committee on the Elimination of all Forms of Discrimination against Women (CEDAW) enjoined Nigeria to:

> Step up efforts aimed at bilateral, regional and international cooperation to prevent trafficking, including by exchanging information and harmonizing legal procedures to prosecute traffickers, in particular with countries in the Economic Community of West African States and the European Union.[50]

[46] *Chowdury and Others v Greece* (Application no 21884/15), ECtHR, 30 March 2017.

[47] *Chowdury and Others v Greece*, para 104. See V Stoyanova, '*Chowdury and Others v Greece*: Further Integration of the Positive Obligations under Article 4 of the ECHR and the CoE Convention on Action against Trafficking' at: http://strasbourgobservers.com, 28 April 2017. For other proposals to strengthen the anti-trafficking regime, see J Jones and J Winterdyk, 'Human Trafficking: Challenges and Opportunities for the 21st Century. Outcomes and Proposals' (2018) 8(1) *Onati Socio-Legal Series* 165–73. See also CEDAW, General Recommendation No 35 on gender-based violence against women, updating General Recommendation No 19, CEDAW/C/GC/35, 26 July 2017, paras 24–35.

[48] UN Committee on the Rights of the Child (CRC), General Comment No 4 (2003): Adolescent Health and Development in the Context of the Convention on the Rights of the Child, 1 July 2003, CRC/GC/2003/4, para 33, reflecting and reinforcing articles 34 and 35 of the UN CRC, 1989 and articles 8 and 10 of the UN Optional Protocol on the sale of children, child prostitution and child pornography, GA Res A/RES/54/263 of 25 May 2000. See also UN Committee on the Rights of the Child (CRC), General Comment No 13 (2011): The right of the child to freedom from all forms of violence, 18 April 2011, CRC/C/GC/13, paras 25 and 26.

[49] Home Office, *Country Policy and Information Note Nigeria: Trafficking of Women*, Version 5.0, Home Office, July 2019. Sections 8:1 to 8.6 rely on various sources including the Australian government to assert that women are not ostracised or looked down upon by their families or society. The difficulty is that the preceding sections have highlighted the many ways in which women do face difficulties. Some are arrested on arrival and held for days even if there is no proof of criminality on their part, others are terrified of meeting their debtors if they have not finished paying off their traffickers, few if any return to their homes of origin and a significant number seek to make the return journey to Europe. The Nigerian government has not put in place an adequate return package or made any real efforts to properly support those who have been trafficked and returned.

[50] CEDAW, Concluding Observations Nigeria, CEDAW/C/NGA/CO/7–8, 2017, para 28(c).

Tom Obokota's survey of trafficking laws on the continent shows the African states have both adopted international protocols and initiatives on trafficking and also entered into regional and sub-regional arrangements to cooperate to curtail the practice.[51] This is in addition to enacting domestic laws, some of which even offer temporary or permanent residence permits to trafficked people.[52] Nigeria has ratified CEDAW, the Palermo Protocol and the African Protocol on Women's Rights all of which proscribe trafficking.[53] It is also bound by the ECOWAS Plan of Action on Trafficking, especially women and girls, and has enacted an anti-trafficking statute.[54] It is therefore not the absence of law that is the problem but a lack of political will, which creates an environment of impunity.[55]

Trilling shows how Nigerian women have been coming to Italy and Europe[56] for decades and yet there is little in the way of employment creation in Edo State or warnings of the true impact of life as a trafficked woman. Receiving states complain but do little to actively protect the young girls who are trafficked. Trilling identifies the disappearances of girls from asylum centres with little or no follow up by state authorities.[57] Instead, all that seems to happen is that there is increased stereotyping of African women in general and Nigerian women in particular.[58]

A. On Stereotyping

The case of *BS v Spain* illustrates the issue of stereotyping.[59] A Nigerian woman, legally resident in Mallorca, Spain, found herself the object of particular attention of the local police. She was engaged in sex work and was regularly arrested and taken to the police station. While there, she was humiliated and called a 'black

[51] T Obokota, 'Human Trafficking in Africa: Opportunities and Challenges for the African Court of Justice and Human Rights' in C Jalloh, K Clarke and V Nmehielle, *The African Court of Justice and Human and Peoples' Rights in Context: Developments and Challenges* (Cambridge, CUP, 2019) 529–52.

[52] T Obokota (2019) 529, 544.

[53] African Protocol on Women's Rights, 2003, art 4(2)(g).

[54] A Sowale, 'Economic Community of West African States' Protocol on Free Movement and the Challenges of Human Trafficking in West Africa' (2018) 10(2) *Insight on Africa* 215–25; ECOWAS, 'ECOWAS moves to promote free movement to tackle trafficking in persons in the region' http://www.ecowas.int, 29 April 2019; ECOWAS 'Initial Plan of Action against Trafficking in Persons 2002–2003' at: http://www.unodc.org/documents/treaties/trafficking/Minimum_Plano_CEDEAO.pdf.

19. Finally, see OHCHR, 'Fostering Cooperation between National Rapporteurs and Equivalent Mechanisms and Cooperation with International and Regional Organizations', Consultative meeting on strengthening partnerships with national rapporteurs on trafficking in persons and equivalent mechanisms 23–24 May 2013, at: https://www.ohchr.org/EN/Issues/Trafficking/Pages/Consultative-MeetingonStrengtheningPartnershipswithNationalRapporteursonTrafficking.aspx.

[55] UNODC, *Global Trafficking Report 2018* (Vienna, UNODC, 2018) 8.

[56] D Trilling (2018), n 31 above, 140.

[57] UNHRC, Report of the Special Rapporteur on Trafficking in Persons, especially women and children, UN Doc A/HRC/38/45, 14 May, 2018, paras 16, 35. D Trilling (2018), 138.

[58] D Garbin and M Godin (2013), n 27 above. CERD Concluding Observations Italy, CERD/C/ITA/CO/19-20, 2017, para 14.

[59] *BS v Spain* (Application no 47159/08), ECtHR, 24 October 2012, [2012] ECHR 1904.

whore'. When she asked the police why they singled her out, they said because her behaviour was immoral.[60] However, she pointed out that they did not arrest the white women who were also selling sex in Mallorca. Selling sex was legal in Mallorca. She eventually brought a claim which made its way to the ECtHR which found in her favour. There was a breach of article 6 on due process and also article 14 on discrimination. The Court acknowledged that the woman had been targeted because of her race. There had also been stereotyping because she was a migrant.[61] This was a welcome recognition of the concept of intersectionality within the European human rights system.[62] It provides a good example of the UN Race Committee's General Comment No 25 on race and gender. This provides a four-point typology for analysing intersectional discrimination: form and manifestation of the racial discrimination, context within which it arose, consequences for the victim/survivor and availability and accessibility of remedies.[63]

The case also illustrates the stereotyping faced by some women out in public on their own.[64] Specifically, the assumption is that women who are unaccompanied by men are soliciting for sex. They are also not believed whatever they say.

It is important to note that the attitude of the Spanish police in the *BS v Spain* case is to be found in other countries, including Nigeria. In her autobiography, Jackie Kay recounts sitting on the terrace of the hotel where she was staying in Abuja. She was waiting to meet her birth father for the first time. She was approached by a man who informed her that he was a banker and asked if she was a call girl. She said no, and he explained that he assumed she was, as the other women who had joined her briefly were call girls. Undeterred, he assured her that he would not give her AIDS and suggested that they retire to her room. Horrified, she got up and went to her room, alone. Her female companions had also 'tried it on' before asking her for money.[65]

[60] On a visit to Spain in 2018, the UN Working Group on Peoples of African Descent, 'collected numerous testimonies that women of African descent were being associated with sex workers which led to harassment and multiple forms of discrimination.' A/HRC/39/69/Add.2, 2018, para 28.

[61] The UN Working Group on Peoples of African Descent, identified racial profiling of people of African descent as 'endemic'. The assumption made was that they were all undocumented migrants which resulted in their being disproportionately targeted and stopped in the street compared to other groups. A/HRC/39/69/Add.2, 2018, para 19. Spain had already been sanctioned by the UN Human Rights Committee for stopping a black Spanish woman without cause. The policeman stereotyped her as an 'illegal' immigrant: *Rosalind Williams Lecraft v Spain* UN CCPR /C/96/D/1493/2006, 27 July 2009.

[62] K Yoshida, 'Towards Intersectionality in the European Court of Human Rights: The Case of *BS v Spain*' (2013) 23 *Feminist Legal Studies* 195–204. Council of Europe (2020), n 18 above, 9. CRPD, General Comment No 3 on Article 6: Women and girls with disabilities, CRPD/C/GC/3, 2 September 2016, para 16. See also *RPB v Philippines*, CEDAW/C/57/D/34/2011, paras 3.7–3.17, 8.3, 8.5, 9.

[63] CERD, General Recommendation No 25 on Gender Related Dimensions of Racial Discrimination, A/55/18. Annex V, 20 March 2000, para 5.

[64] On stereotyping see R Cook and S Cusack, *Gender Stereotyping* (Philadelphia PA, Penn Press, 2010). S Cusack, Gender Stereotyping as a Human Rights Violation, Research report submitted to OHCHR, 14 October 2013. R Holtmaat, 'Article 5' in M Freeman, C Chinkin and B Rudolph (eds) (2013), n 17 above, 141–67.

[65] J Kay (2010), n 92 below, 171–72.

In *Dorothy Njemanze & 3 Others v Federal Republic of Nigeria*[66] four women, including a 'Nollywood' actress who was the lead applicant, challenged their detention. The women had each been picked up while out at night by the Abuja Environmental Protection Board and by the Society against Prostitution and Child Labour (SAPCLN). They had been detained under vagrancy laws. Each of them was among other women and girls caught up in a 'round up'. The stereotyped assumption was that they were engaged in prostitution.[67] Why else would women be out after dusk on their own – meaning unaccompanied by men?[68] Attempts to challenge the detention at the time had led to their being beaten. There were further instances of harassment.

In bringing this challenge to the regional ECOWAS Court of Justice,[69] the women invoked all of Nigeria's international and regional treaty obligations, including the African Charter and the Women's Protocol thereto, CEDAW, the ICCPR and the Torture Convention. They said that their treatment constituted discrimination on grounds of sex and gender. It violated their right to dignity and freedom of movement and breached their right to equality. The women also claimed that they had a right to be free from gender-based violence and to an effective remedy for the multiple breaches of their rights.[70] They also called for effective police training, and the provision of female-only police stations as well as refuges. Echoing the ECtHR in the *BS v Spain* case discussed above, the African Commission on Human and Peoples' Rights case of *Egyptian Initiative for Personal Rights and Interights v Egypt* and the CEDAW Committee in various cases including *Vertido v Philippines* and *Jallow v Bulgaria*, they called for education to eradicate stereotyped views of women.[71]

In what can only be described, colloquially, as a car crash defence, the state denied that there had been any state involvement, before saying that if indeed

[66] *Dorothy Njemanze & 3 Others v Federal Republic of Nigeria*: SUIT NO: ECW/CCJ/APP/17/14 (ECOWAS Court, Abuja, Nigeria): http://www.courtecowas.org/site2012/pdf_files/decisions/judgements/2017/ECW_CCJ_JUD_08_17.pdf. Discussed by B Chakaya, 'ECOWAS Court challenges vagrancy laws that target women' Reproductive health blog, 2017 at: https://reprohealthlaw.wordpress.com/2017/11/30/africa-nigeria-ecowas-court-challenges-vagrancy-laws-that-target-women. See also *Lucy Nyambura & Another v Town Clerk, Municipal Council of Mombasa & Others* [2011] eKLR, Petition No 286 of 2009 Kenya, High Court.

[67] The officer in charge at one police station said that he agreed with the actions of his colleagues because they 'looked like prostitutes': *Dorothy Njemanze*, n 66 above, at para 5(1).

[68] This was also the starting point in the case of *Sarah Longwe v Intercontinental Hotels* [1993] 4 LRC 221.

[69] ECOWAS is the Economic Community of West African States. It comprises 15 states within the West African region. See www.ecowas.int.

[70] *Dorothy Njemanze and Others v Nigeria*, n 66 above, at paras 4 and 5(1) I–XII. See also the African Commission case: Communication 323/06 – *Egyptian Initiative for Personal Rights and Interights v Arab Republic of Egypt*, at: http://www.achpr.org/files/sessions/10th-eo/comunications/323.06/achpreos10_232_06_eng.pdf, where similar issues were raised.

[71] *Dorothy Njemanze*, n 66 above, at para 5(1) XI. *Jallow v Bulgaria*, CEDAW/C/52/D/32/2011, para 8(6); *Vertido v Philippines*, CEDAW/C/46/D/18/2008, para 8.9(b). Communication 323/06 – *Egyptian Initiative for Personal Rights and Interights v Arab Republic of Egypt*, 16 December 2011.

police had arrested people, the defendants were not amongst them. It then moved on to argue that it was a well-known 'fact' that the first plaintiff was a prostitute. Prostitution was illegal in Nigeria and its practice violated African culture and therefore any arrests that followed could not be a breach of the right to liberty or, indeed any human rights provisions. Adding insult to injury, the state claimed that the plaintiffs ran a grooming ring known as 'Big Aunty', bringing in young girls whom they trained to be prostitutes,[72] who then harassed willing and unwilling men in the streets. The state said that the prostitution inference was justified because only prostitutes would be out at midnight. In their rejoinder, the plaintiffs challenged these characterisations and noted that the case was not about prostitution.[73]

The Court found for the plaintiffs on all counts. Using a range of comparative jurisprudence, the Court found that the state had not proved that the women were working as prostitutes. Its assumption that any woman out at night must be a prostitute violated the women's dignity and also reinforced gendered stereotypes. It noted that prostitution needs two participants and focusing on women constituted discrimination. Moreover, the Court held that the state had unjustly and arbitrarily detained the women. Furthermore, the state was held to have failed in its due diligence obligations to prevent, investigate and prosecute violations. It had failed to offer a remedy. It ordered the state to pay each 6 million Nigerian Naira with costs of suit to be met by the state.[74]

Bridget Anderson identifies the ambivalence of states on the issue of sex, noting that even in a neo-liberal individualised economy, there is a morality (moral economy) which trafficking or sex work is seen to transgress.[75]

There have been those who have challenged the conflation of trafficking with exploitative sex, which is always classed as oppressive and violative of the woman's rights. They say it speaks to a lack of agency for the women involved and that it patronises women and denies them agency.[76] Just because one would not make the *same* choice, does not mean that the decision made is the wrong one.[77]

[72] One is reminded here of Efe's story in Unigwe's *On Black Sisters' Street*. Violated from the age of 16, she has a baby with a married man whose wife calls her a prostitute, an '*ashawo*', the same word used in the *Dorothy Njemanze* case, and tells her to go away. C Unigwe (2010) 70. Efe ends up in Belgium, working under the supervision of the older Madam who takes away the passports of the women whom she has helped to traffic. They are required to earn €500 a month, and a minimum of 100 when things are difficult for them. C Unigwe (2010) 182–83.

[73] *Dorothy Njemanze*, n 66 above, para 6:1 pp 15–19.

[74] *Dorothy Njemanze* 6:1 and Court Decision – pp 19–43. Prostitution allegation – degrading in violation of art 5 of ACHPR at p 37. CEDAW cited at p 38.

[75] B Anderson (2013), n 12 above, 137, 145–55.

[76] J O'Connell Davidson, 'Gender, Migration, "Trafficking" and the Troublesome Relationship between Agency and Force', *Border Criminologies* blog, 19 June 2015. Available at: http://bordercriminologies.law.ox.ac.uk/gender-migration-trafficking/. S Tamale, 'Exploring the Contours of African Sexualities: Religion, Law and Power' (2014) 1 *African Human Rights Law Journal* 150–77.

[77] J Halley, P Kotiswaran, H Shamir, and C Thomas, 'From the International to the Local in Feminist Legal Responses to Rape, Prostitution/Sex Work and Sex Trafficking: Four Studies in Contemporary Governance Feminism' (2006) 29 *Harvard Journal of Law and Gender* 335. For a critique of the approach of the US Government zero tolerance approach see J Chuang, 'Exploitation Creep and the

B. Sex Work in Fictional Literature

Fictional literature provides examples of women who do voluntarily agree to sex work: Wafa, a young Moroccan woman in Leila Slimani's novel *Lullaby*, tells how she was brought to France by an older man to whom she used to give massages in a 'seedy hotel in Casablanca'.[78] The man's children forced her to leave his apartment whereupon 'she was recruited by a woman who signed her up for dating sites aimed at young Muslim women who were illegal immigrants.'[79] One of the clients offered to marry her for €20,000, telling her, 'That's cheap for getting your French papers.'[80]

Epaphras Osondu's story 'A letter from home' is a letter from a disappointed mother in Nigeria to her son in the United States. He has failed to look after her as other children in the diaspora look after their parents and families left at home. She writes:

> I am sure you remember Obi's daughter. She went to Italy to work as a prostitute after you left for America. Just last year she came back with lots of goodies for her parents and has even married a boy from a responsible family. They had their wedding in the church and the priest said that though her sins were like scarlet she had been washed clean by the blood of Jesus (after she made a huge donation for the repair of the church roof). She has gone on to bear a son and now nobody remembers that she was once a prostitute in Italy.[81]

In another Osundu story, 'A Simple Case' a man goes to look for his girlfriend whom he met in a brothel and who had continued to work there. He is told she is has gone to Italy because, 'something good has happened to her.' Asking what she has gone to do in Italy, the lost lover is met with impatient incredulity being told that she has gone to do the same thing that she was doing in the brothel, but this time she will be earning US dollars.[82]

C. State Failure to Prevent Harm and to Support Returnees

Media reports indicate that there has been an increase in Nigerian women being forced into prostitution once they arrive in Italy by boat. Young girls arrive and disappear from the state reception centres, never to be seen again.[83] Some

Unmaking of Human Trafficking Law' (2014–15) 108 *American Journal of International Law* 610. See also A Ahmed '"Exploitation Creep" and Development: A Response to Janie Chuang' (2014–15) 108 *AJIL Unbound* 268, 11 June, 2015.

[78] L Slimani (translated by S Taylor), *Lullaby* (London, Faber & Faber, 2018) 98.

[79] L Slimani (2018) 99.

[80] L Slimani (2018) 99.

[81] EC Osondu, 'A Letter from Home' in *Voice of America* (London, Granta, 2010) 45, 46.

[82] EC Osundu, 'A Simple Case' in *Voice of America* (London, Granta, 2010) 141, 153.

[83] A Kelly and LO Tondo, 'Trafficking of Nigerian Women into prostitution in Europe "at crisis level"', London, *The Guardian*, Monday 8 August 2016; K Hyland (Anti-slavery commissioner), 'Britain

advocates argue that women, and specifically migrant women, tend to be involved in working in the sex industry under duress.[84] They are exploited. Passports are confiscated, wages not paid, the women are subjected to violence from clients and those in control, and, crucially, they are unable to leave.[85]

The 2017 concluding observations of the CEDAW to the Nigerian report show that although Nigeria has updated its Trafficking in Persons (Prohibition) Law Enforcement and Administration Act, and also established a trust fund for victims, the fund is inadequately financed due to budget constraints. Moreover, there are few shelters for trafficked women and even fewer job opportunities, so their exit or return options are severely constrained.[86]

Meanwhile, in its Concluding Observations on Nigeria, also issued in 2017, the Committee on Migrant Workers acknowledges the efforts that Nigeria is making to combat trafficking. However, it goes on to note that judges are more likely to issue fines in lieu of terms of imprisonment.[87] The Committee also observes that 'trafficking related corruption and complicity at all levels remains pervasive.'[88]

In 2019 Human Rights Watch produced a report focusing on what happens to Nigerian women and girls who are repatriated. It showed that many were housed in state-run shelters which were inadequately funded meaning that there was insufficient food. The women were confined to the centres with little or no rehabilitation support.[89]

There has been a renewed interest in trafficking with a focus on sexual exploitation since the adoption of the Palermo Protocol. However, the normative developments and promises of human rights protections have not kept pace with the lived realities of those who live in the shadows of legality. The failure of states to honour their human rights obligations by offering protection to trafficked women exacerbates the situation. A focus on bringing an end to the suffering of trafficked women rather than on immigration control and criminalisation would go a long way toward fulfilling the promises of human rights protection.

The focus on sex trafficking may have served to obscure the other ways in which women who move across borders can have their rights violated.

must address the root causes of sex trafficking from Nigeria to Europe', London, *The Guardian*, Friday 12 August 2016. See also D Trilling (2018), n 31 above, 137–41.

[84] Research by Trilling indicated that many women passing through Libya en route to Europe experienced sexual violence. D Trilling (2018), n 31 above, 124.

[85] J Bindel, *The Pimping of Prostitution: Abolishing the Sex Work Myth* (London, Palgrave Macmillan, 2017). Cf B Magnanti, *Sex, Lies and Statistics: The Truth Julie Bindel Doesn't Want you to See* (London, Self-published, 2017). An academic, Magnanti worked as an escort to fund her PhD.

[86] CEDAW, Concluding Observations Nigeria, CEDAW/C/NGA/CO/7-8, 24 July 2017, paras 27 and 28.

[87] CMW Concluding Observations on Nigeria in the absence of a report, CMW/C/NGA/CO/1, 2017, para 55(c).

[88] CMW/C/NGA/CO/1, para 55(f). See also para 56. It is worth recording that Nigeria failed to submit a report so the Committee proceeded without it.

[89] Human Rights Watch, *You Pray for Death* (New York, Human Rights Watch, 2019).

The next section moves on to look at the other work that migrant women do: cleaning, cooking and caring. These are often the only means of making a livelihood open to women. In 2018, the UN Special Rapporteur on Contemporary forms of Slavery documented that in the private sector women and girls comprised 92 per cent of people in forced labour in accommodation and food services and 61 per cent in domestic work.[90] She also notes that:

> In *Global Estimates of Modern Slavery*, it is noted that 24 per cent of domestic workers are subjected to forced labour and many more experience situations of debt bondage. ILO estimates that women account for 81 per cent of national domestic workers and 73 per cent of all migrant domestic workers.[91]

IV. Whither Sisterhood? Race and Class in Cleaning Work

The pressures faced by middle classes in Europe and abroad have meant that there is a 'domestic labour gap' which more often than not is filled by migrant workers, most of whom are women.[92] The work, often performed in the informal, unregulated economy, is in the shadow of state surveillance. There is complicity between employer and employee – the employer does not want to report, or indeed acknowledge, that they are using irregular labour because they like the flexibility and also because it allows them to evade employment and tax laws; for the employee, this cash in hand work enables them to make money without coming under the surveillance of state authorities who are more likely to focus on public-facing private and public employers. This in turn minimises detection for breaches of immigration conditions. It also leaves the worker vulnerable to exploitation.[93]

However, immigration status is not entirely irrelevant. In *Lullaby*, Paul and Myriam, the young Parisian couple with two young children, consider hiring a nanny to facilitate Myriam's return to work as a lawyer. Paul cautions against hiring undocumented women because he fears that in the event of an accident, they would be reluctant to summon help from the police or to go to the hospital.

[90] UN Special Rapporteur on Contemporary Slavery: Gender, A/73/139, 2018, para 25.

[91] UN Special Rapporteur on Contemporary Slavery, A/73/139 at para 43. She relies on ILO and Walk Free Foundation, *Global Estimates of Modern Slavery* (Geneva, ILO, 2017) p 11; and Asia Pacific Forum on Women, Law and Development, 'Briefing paper on the gender dimension of contemporary forms of slavery, its causes and consequences' Estimates of activities that are criminal are difficult to do and contested.

[92] In her autobiography, Scottish writer and poet laureate, Jackie Kay recounts how the nurse discharging her mother assumed that Jackie, who has Scottish-Nigerian heritage, but was adopted by a white couple, was the mother's carer from the nursing home. J Kay, *Red Dust Road: An Autobiographical Journey* (London, Picador, 2010) 242. The nurse is also ageist referring to Jackie's mother as an 'old biddy' (at. 242).

[93] These vulnerabilities were identified in a case involving the exploitation of two Nigerian migrant domestic workers by Lady Hale in *Taiyo v Oliagbe* [2016] UKSC 31, para 25.

He is not against hiring undocumented people to do other work such as cleaning or decorating, reasoning that they need to live, but hiring an undocumented nanny for his children is his red line. He is however clear that the nanny should be 'energetic and available' because this will free them up to do their work.[94]

To this, Myriam's friend adds that she should avoid a woman with her own children, unless they are in her homeland. Of her own nanny, Emma, Myriam's friend complains that as she has two sons, 'she can never stay late or babysit for us. It's really not practical.'[95]

We learn that the nannies on the books of the agency that Myriam approaches to help her to find a nanny are: 'Dozens of photographs of women, most of them African or Filipino'.[96] The women who come to interview for the job include 'Grace, a smiling, undocumented immigrant from the Ivory Coast … Malika, a Moroccan woman of a certain age who stresses her 20 years of experience and her love of children.'[97]

Myriam decides against hiring a fellow North African as a nanny. Wanting intimate-distance, Paul and Myriam hire Louise, a white French nanny, great with their children, eager to take on extra chores, unencumbered by other caring responsibilities but, unbeknownst to them, with untold, deep trauma. Always available to stay on late, sometimes over-night and on weekends, she is 'the perfect nanny.' In a flashback later in the book, we learn that, when alive, Louise's pugnacious, litigious and unemployed husband had been scornful of her work: '"I'm not a doormat, a slave content to clean up the shit and puke of little brats. Only black women do work like that now." He thought his wife excessively docile.'[98]

The relationship of maid and madam may not be directly comparable with the book of that name,[99] which looked at the relationship between white women and their black maids during the Apartheid era, but the new 'domestic help' relationships do throw up issues of class, race and of course gender. The pretence of a lack of hierarchy and the 'friendship' rhetorically insisted upon by the employers, mask the inequalities between the employer and the carer. Often they also reflect the global structural inequalities which led the migrant women to move. This is beautifully realised in Maggie Gee's *My Cleaner* about a white British woman asking her Ugandan maid to return to help with her depressive son. The cleaner explores the contradictions in the employer's words and actions.[100] It creates feminist tensions because in outsourcing their boredom and undervalued work, the employing

[94] L Slimani (2018), n 78 above, 4.
[95] L Slimani (2018) 4.
[96] L Slimani (2018) 13.
[97] L Slimani (2018) 15.
[98] L Slimani (2018) 83.
[99] J Cock, *Maids and Madams: Domestic Workers Under Apartheid* (London, The Women's Press, 1989). For a fun 'write back' see also the satirical post-apartheid cartoon series by S Francis, H Rugmore and Rico, *The Madam and Eve Collection* (Cape Town, David Phillips, 1998).
[100] M Gee, *My Cleaner* (London, SAQI, 2005). E Gutierrez-Rodriguez (ed), *Migration, Domestic Work and Affect: A Decolonial Approach on Value and the Feminization of Labor* (Abingdon, Routledge, 2010).

women are seen to replicate patriarchal patterns of oppression, a conundrum identified by bell hooks in *From Margin to Centre.*[101]

Despite the inequalities, affective relationships do develop. This is well captured by the relationship between the two wives in Mbue's *Behold the Dreamers.* The wife of the American banker seeks the domestic help of the Cameroonian driver's wife during the family's summer sojourn at their home in the Hamptons. The banker's wife shares her marital concerns with her 'maid-friend' and plies her with expensive and impractical cast-offs. Here labour transforms into affective work with the worker being drawn into the life of the employer as confidante and carer.[102] However, the structural inequalities remain. In her autobiography *Slave*, the brutalised Mende, enslaved in Sudan since the age of 12, goes to kiss the children of her enslavers before they take her to the airport in Khartoum to board a flight to her next job in London.[103] In *Lullaby*, Slimani captures the conditionality of the affection through Wafa, an undocumented Moroccan nanny whom Louise, Paul and Myriam's nanny, befriends while looking after her own charges in the park. Wafa is grateful to the French-American couple for whom she works. She sees them as having treated her kindly and mentions that they rent a bedsit for her just around the corner from their own home. However there is a sting in the tale: 'They pay my rent, but in exchange I can never say no them.'[104] Enforcement or performance here is not as understood in lawyers' (labour) law, but rather reflects the unwritten 'law' of private gratitude and obligation owed by one who relies on another for their livelihood.

The exchange – labour for opportunity is one that has the potential to benefit both employer and the migrant. Belinda, the house-help in Donkor's novel *Hold*, is asked to move from Ghana to England to help the family of her current employers. In return she is promised that she will receive an education while money will be sent back to her mother in Ghana to help her.[105] Belinda, who is acutely aware of the hardships endured by her mother who is parenting alone and trying to eke out a living working in a bar, agrees to move.

[101] See b hooks, *From Margin to Centre* (Boston MA, South End Press, 1984) 1–15 in which hooks notes that the boredom complained of by white, middle-class American women living in the suburbs was not universal. Indeed, she notes that African-American and Latina women who worked in cleaning and other jobs to maintain their families would have welcomed the boredom described by Friedan. B Friedan, *Feminist Mystique* (London, Penguin, 2010). Originally published in 1963, Friedan wrote about the 'problem that has no name' or the constraints of suburban wifely confinement. A Oakley, *Housewife* (London, Pelican, 1976) railed about unpaid women's work in the home starting a 'wages for housework' campaign.

[102] See also N Bulawayo, *We need new names* (London, Vintage, 2014).

[103] M Nazer and D Lewis, *Slave: The True Story of a Girl's Lost Childhood and her Fight for Survival* (London, Virago, 2004). J Ewins, *Independent Review of the Overseas Domestic Worker Visa*, Final report presented to the Home Office, 6 November 2015.

[104] L Slimani (2018), n 78 above, 99.

[105] M Donkor, *Hold* (London, Fourth Estate, 2018) 11.

V. Norm Development and the Challenges of Implementation

Many migrant women are exposed to poor conditions of work. This is despite the recognition by the International Labour Organization and the Committee on the Rights of Migrant Workers of the rights of domestic workers.[106] The ILO acknowledges that women are over-represented in domestic service and thus seeks to protect them from exploitation, not least by encouraging states to ratify its Convention and Recommendation for Decent work for Domestic Workers (Domestic Workers' Convention).[107] In this it is echoed by CEDAW and its General Recommendation No 26 on women migrant workers. Both the ILO and CEDAW see the potential exploitation in the very organisation of the system of migration, not least the system of tying domestic workers to employers.[108] Female domestic workers – the majority – are further exposed to rape and sexual violence by employers and members of their family.[109] The CEDAW Committee identifies the discriminations faced by migrant domestic workers as including dismissal from work for pregnancy. It also flags up immigration rules that do not permit migrant domestic workers to apply for family reunification – a right often granted to high-income migrants.[110]

The Committee joins the ILO in condemning the practice of removing passports from employees and the lack of regulation of hours of work or provision of sick leave or holiday entitlement. The ILO shows that few states have laws regulating domestic work. In its report on Tanzanian domestic workers in the Middle

[106] ILO, *Domestic workers across the world: Global and regional statistics and the extent of legal protection* (Geneva, ILO, 2013). The first General Comment elaborated by the Committee on the Rights of Migrant Workers and their Families is on the rights of domestic workers. CMW, *General Comment No 1 on migrant domestic workers*, 23 February 2011, CMW/C/GC/1. See also OHCHR, *Protecting and Promoting the Human Rights of Domestic Workers in an Irregular Situation*, HR/PUB/15/4 (2015).

[107] ILO Domestic Workers Convention, 2011 (No 189) & Recommendation 201 on Decent Work for Domestic Workers, 2011.

[108] CEDAW, General Recommendation no 26 on Migrant women workers, paras 13–15. ILO *Employer–Migrant Worker Relationships in the Middle East: Exploring scope for internal labour market mobility and fair migration* (Geneva, ILO, 2017) 3, 6–8. The challenges faced by migrant domestic workers are documented on p 8. See also UN Committee on the Protection of the Rights of All Migrant Workers and Members of Their Families (CMW), *General Comment No 1 on migrant domestic workers*, 23 February 2011, CMW/CGC/1 (2011) para 12.

[109] R Begum, '#MeToo, Say Domestic Workers in the Middle East', Human Rights Watch, 8 December 2017. See also CEDAW, General Recommendation No 26 on migrant workers, para 20. These issues were identified as needing attention in the UN Race Committee's dialogue with Saudi Arabia, CERD/C/SAU/CO/4–9, 8 June 2018, paras 17–21. See also Migrant Workers' Committee General Comment No 1 on domestic workers, CMW/C/GC/1 (2011) paras 60, 61.

[110] CEDAW General Recommendation No 26 on migrant women, paras 18 and 19. See also the recommendations made by the Special Rapporteur on the Human Rights of Migrants report on The Impact of migration on migrant women and girls: A Gender perspective, A/HRC/41/38, 15 April 2019, para 80. See also Migrant Workers' Committee General Comment No 1 on domestic workers, CMW/C/GC/1 (2011) paras 54, 55.

East, Human Rights Watch demonstrated how poorer countries felt compelled to permit migration of their citizens without any guarantee of good working conditions.[111] Given the individualised, private sphere, nature and location of the work done by domestic workers, there is little scope for trade union organisation or resistance, thus making imperative state regulation and enforcement of rules and laws.[112] Special attention is given by the ILO to migrant domestic workers whom it says, should, before departure, be issued with employment contracts that can be enforced in the destination country where the work is to be performed.[113] The British government has now made employment contracts a pre-condition for the issuance of domestic worker visas.[114]

However, the experience of Mende Nazer, whose first-person account of being a slave for a family in Khartoum who then pass her on to relatives at the Sudanese Embassy in London, shows that in practice evasion of the rules is possible. After obtaining a passport for her, they prepare her for a visa interview at the British consulate. She is to say that she is well-treated by her current employers. She is to say that for her work, she will do: 'cleaning, cooking and washing. Don't tell them you'll be looking after the children as well.'[115] She is to give the name of a different person than the one she will work for in London. It later transpires that the real employer, a diplomat, has a mark against him because his last employee has run away due to ill-treatment.[116] It is what transpires at the consulate that is of interest. Mende is asked several questions about her future work and employers, to which questions she replies 'I don't know.' The visa officer, who jokingly refers to her as 'I don't know', queries:

> 'You mean to tell me that you don't know how much you'll be paid, you don't know how many days off you'll have, and you don't know how many hours you'll work each day?' He was laughing at me now, but not in an unkind way.[117]

She is twice sent away with written questions. It was only on her third visit to the consulate that the visa was issued. There is an admirable persistence in the

[111] Human Rights Watch, *Working like a Robot: Abuse of Tanzanian Domestic Workers in Oman and the United Arab Emirates* (New York, Human Rights Watch, 2017). Had the women been given pre-departure information as envisaged in CEDAW General Recommendation 26 on migrant workers para 23, perhaps they would not have gone or would have been better prepared. Similarly, the receiving states failed in their obligations to the women–see para.26. On the importance of inter-state co-operation-para 27. See also CMW/C/GC/1 (2011).

[112] See art 3 of the ILO Domestic Workers Convention–focusing on the right to freedom of association, to form trade unions and to engage in collective bargaining. See also art 15(2). See also UN Special Rapporteur on Contemporary Slavery, A/73/139, paras 13–14, 43–45, 54. See also the Sustainable Development Goals, target 8.7, on the eradication of forced labour and contemporary forms of slavery.

[113] ILO Domestic Workers Convention, art 8(1). See also art 15. 'Immigration Rules, Appendix 7 Overseas Workers in Private Households' at: https://www.gov.uk/guidance/immigration–rules/immigration-rules-appendix-7-overseas-workers-in-private-households.

[114] 'Immigration Rules, Appendix 7 Overseas Workers in Private Households' at: https://www.gov.uk/guidance/immigration-rules/immigration-rules-appendix-7-overseas-workers-in-private-households.

[115] M Nazer and D Lewis, *Slave* (2004), n 103 above, 221.

[116] M Nazer and D Lewis (2004) 317.

[117] M Nazer and D Lewis (2004) 222.

visa official, but one wonders why further investigations were not carried out in the UK given the interviewee's total ignorance of issues about which she would be expected to have some detailed knowledge. In its General Comment No 1 on Migrant Domestic Workers, the Committee on Migrant Workers and their Families recommends that states have a duty to ensure decent conditions of work and to stipulate terms that address all the issues raised by the visa official in Mende's case.[118] It also recommends the provision of social security and that the employee has access to adequate health care.[119] Importantly, the employee is supposed to be fully schooled in their rights before departure.[120]

The UK Supreme Court case of *Taiwo v Olaigbe* about the exploitation of domestic workers shows that contract rules can be evaded.[121] In that case the employer applicants simply lied, including about the terms of the employment. The visas were granted but they never fulfilled any of the contractual guarantees. Indeed, one of the two maids involved said that she had never been shown the contract. In addition, her passport had been taken from her on arrival from Nigeria.[122]

In its Concluding Observations on Nigeria, which was reviewed despite Nigeria's failure to submit a report, the Committee on Migrant Workers rights expressed concern that Nigerian domestic workers face exploitation and harassment. Referencing its General Comment No 1 on Domestic Workers, the Committee enjoined the state to include standard form contracts in all its bilateral agreements specifying basic conditions of work including effective remedies. It also asked the state to ensure that its citizens could access consular assistance at its embassies, which should provide shelter, legal assistance, medical and psychological care as well as interpreters.[123] The problem, as we will soon see, is that often diplomats are themselves the exploiters.

The case of *Siliadin v France* provides an example of exploitation. Siliadin was brought to France from Togo by a relative. She was aged 15 years and seven months. Her father had given his consent. The agreement was that the girl would live with, and work for, the relative for a few months to 'pay for her ticket'. She would help out in the home and the relative would arrange for her to go to school and also regularise her stay. She arrived on a three-month tourist visa.

A few months after arriving, the relative 'lent' the girl to her friends, the 'B' family. They had three children and shortly after, a fourth child was born. The girl was expected to work from 7am to 10pm at night. She had to take the older children to school and nursery and to their extra-curricular activities while also looking

[118] CMW General Comment No 1 on migrant domestic workers. CMW/C/GC/1 (2011) paras 37–41.
[119] CMW/C/GC/1 (2011) paras 42, 43.
[120] CMW/C/GC/1 (2011) para 19.
[121] *Taiwo v Olaigbe and another; Onu v Akwiwu and another* [2016] UKSC 31 (hereafter *Taiwo v Olaigbe*).
[122] *Taiwo v Olaigbe* [2016] UKSC 31, para 3.
[123] CMW/C/NGA/CO/1 (2017) para 50 On consular assistance see CMW/C/GC/1 (2011) paras 62–64.

after the baby and keeping the house clean. Her other duty included cleaning Mr B's office. She slept on a mattress in the baby's room. Her passport was taken from her and she was not given a salary, although the Bs' grandmother gave her occasional cash gifts. She attempted to leave twice – once by going to work for a Haitian woman whom she met in a supermarket. The Haitian woman paid her properly and did not exploit her. Her uncle persuaded her to return to the Bs. Eventually she told a neighbour about her situation and the neighbour contacted the authorities. The Bs were convicted but appealed and had part of the conviction quashed.

The girl, Siliadin, brought a case to the European Court of Human Rights claiming a violation by France of article 4 of the ECHR on the prohibition of slavery and forced labour. The Court gave a detailed overview of Council of Europe initiatives to ban modern slavery-like practices and also considered international treaties and conventions on slavery. It also examined ILO regulations on forced labour. It noted that while she was not a slave in that she had not been 'owned' by the B's, her situation did meet the threshold for servitude. Summarising her situation, the Court started by noting the she had not been given any choice about whether she would go to France. Furthermore, as a minor she was wholly dependent on a couple who confiscated her papers, restricted her freedom of movement, made her work excessively, and broke their promise to regularise her immigration status, send her to school and pay her. In these circumstances, she would be afraid to seek police assistance and, without resources, did not have the option of moving to live elsewhere.[124]

The Court found that France had failed to live up to its positive obligations under article 4 in that 'the criminal-law legislation in force at the material time did not afford the applicant, a minor, practical and effective protection against the actions of which she was a victim.'[125] Siliadin's situation is the norm for the treatment of many migrant domestic workers.

Government attempts to outlaw modern slavery do not always capture the vulnerable, including children trafficked by family members.[126] It is difficult to separate family obligation from exploitation. In the *Siliadin* case the girl's uncle had given evidence for the Bs in the criminal case. He denied that she had been exploited by them, arguing that they had been keeping her money in a trust fund so that they could give her a lump sum when she was older. He also noted that she rang him from phone booths, thus her freedom of movement was not impeded and also that she must have had money to enable her to call him.[127]

Following on was the case of *CN v United Kingdom*,[128] which involved a Ugandan woman, CN, who had come to Britain in 2002 on forged documents.

[124] *Siliadin v France* (Application No 73316/01), ECtHR, 26 July 2005, paras 126–128. On the pressures put on undocumented women, see CEDAW General Recommendation No 26 on migrant workers, para 22. On the challenges of accessing justice see para 21.

[125] *Siliadin v France* (ECtHR), paras 148 and 149.

[126] *Osman v Denmark* (Application No 38058/09) ECtHR, 14 June 2011.

[127] *Siliadin v France* (ECtHR), para 39.

[128] *CN v United Kingdom* (Application No 4239/08), ECtHR, 13 November 2012.

Her original visa application had been unsuccessful, so her father and uncle had paid for false documents to enable her to come to Britain. She wanted to escape the trauma of rape. It was assumed that she would work to get the money to save to continue her education. On arrival, her relative, KS, introduced her to Mohamed, the owner of a company which provided care workers. He in turn arranged for her to work as an in-house carer for an elderly Iranian couple. They paid Mohamed £1600 monthly for her services. Mohamed in turn deducted 'his fee' before passing on the remainder to KS, who, it was assumed, would ensure that the woman doing the work would get the money. She did not. She was never paid. She had her passport taken away from her and was picked up on her monthly free afternoon and taken to KS's home where she was warned against going out.

The Iranian couple travelled to Egypt, and their carer went to KS. She then found herself in a bank and told the staff of her situation. She collapsed and was hospitalised. KS's wife visited her and cautioned her against revealing her situation, noting that the immigration officials would be informed and she would be deported. The police were informed. They asked the UK Trafficking Centre to investigate her story. The Trafficking Centre said that her story failed to meet the criteria for trafficking for the purposes of exploitation as laid out in section 4 of the Asylum and Immigration (Treatment of Claimants etc.) Act 2004.[129] Moreover, they did not find her credible.

In the interim, the woman made an unsuccessful claim for asylum. Again, the Immigration Tribunal found her story to lack credibility. The police wrote to her lawyers to let them know that they would not be pursuing the case. In their view, the issue arose out of one party, the relative, KS, failing to hand over money to his female relative. It was the view of the police that the third-party payments had been made to evade detection. As the woman had arrived on false documents, she could not get a real national insurance number to facilitate her working, so her uncle acted as 'her front'.[130] There was an appeal.

At the ECtHR it was argued that the UK had failed to properly investigate and to provide adequate remedies. The focus on trafficking and exploitation missed the domestic servitude experienced by CN. Significantly, the Poppy Project, an independent organisation funded by the government, had found that her story about the domestic servitude was credible. They noted that she met five of the six indicators for forced labour set out by the ILO:

> In particular, her movement had been restricted to the workplace, her wages were withheld to pay a debt she did not know about, her salary was withheld for four years, her passport was retained, and she was subjected to threats of denunciation to the authorities.[131]

[129] These were laid out by the court in para 32.

[130] *CN v United Kingdom*, n 128 above, para 25. On states' responsibility to protect undocumented workers, see CEDAW General Recommendation No 26 on migrant workers, para 26(l). See also para 26(h) on recruitment agents.

[131] *CN v United Kingdom*, para 20. The ECtHR reproduced these in para 35. See also OHCHR (2015), n 106 above, 26, 28.

Similarly, a clinical psychologist who specialised in violence against women also found her account of domestic servitude and her claim that she had been raped, credible.

The UK was said not to have had laws in place that addressed domestic servitude as anticipated by article 4 of the ECHR prohibiting slavery and forced labour. The UK countered that there were other offences, including kidnap, which could have covered the situation faced by CN. CN had not complained about her non-payment and had continued to work. It added that it had since made provision for an offence of holding a person in slavery or servitude or requiring a person to perform forced or compulsory labour.[132]

While acknowledging the change of the law, the Court did find a violation of article 4 of the ECHR, noting that the facts of the CN case were, with the exception of the ages of the parties (CN being older than Siliadin who had been a minor), almost identical to those of Siliadin. The UK had failed in its duty to properly investigate the complaints made by CN. The fact that there was no law directly on the point of domestic servitude meant that the investigations that were undertaken were done without benchmarks, and so were ineffective. The Court also referenced with approval the evidence of the Poppy Project and the clinical psychologist in querying the dismissal of CN's credibility. The UK was ordered to pay her €8000 in damages.[133]

VI. Legislative and Judicial Responses to Modern Slavery

The British government has attempted to address these problems through legislation. The Modern Slavery Act 2015 makes it criminal to force someone to work or to hold them in servitude.[134] It also prohibits trafficking.[135] It tries to take a human rights, rather than criminal law, approach in its assessment of the victim. It uses article 4 of the ECHR as the starting point, reinforcing the prohibition of slavery, servitude and forced labour. It recognises the vulnerability of those who are often tricked or trafficked into migrating, including being a child, having a family relationship with the perpetrator, and mental illness. Even if a person did consent to undertaking compulsory labour or undertaking other activities that are illegal – such as growing cannabis – this will not protect the perpetrator. This is in recognition of the power differentials between the 'master' and the 'servant'. Section 53 of the Act focuses on domestic workers and provides that those who

[132] Section 71 of the Coroners and Justice Act 2009, which came into force on 6 April 2010.This was later repealed. See Modern Slavery Act 2015.
[133] *CN v United Kingdom*, paras 70–82.
[134] Modern Slavery Act 2015, s 1.
[135] Modern Slavery Act 2015, s 2.

have been trafficked or are found to be victims of slavery may apply to be granted leave to remain for a period to be specified. Given the case law just discussed, the Act includes within its protective remit, not only those who have worked in private households, but also those who have worked as 'a private servant in a diplomatic household.'[136] While criminal prosecution awaits perpetrators, the Act adds two new civil preventative orders: the Slavery and Trafficking Prevention Order and the Slavery and Trafficking Risk Order. An Anti-Slavery Commissioner is also established.

Migrant women are still caught between disclosure of abuse, the fear of deportation and the disbelief that meets many victims. The addition of a fear of letting the family down and of shame all point to silence. In July 2018, there was a report of a Kenyan maid working in Lebanon who, on complaining of her working conditions, was beaten and then issued with a deportation notice.[137] In the *Kahn* case a Pakistani-born woman who had married a doctor based in Tanzania and moved to live there, before relocating to London on his death, was convicted of exploiting a Tanzanian woman, Ms Mruke, whom she had brought from Tanzania to work for her, cooking, cleaning and caring for her two adult disabled children. Despite promises to deposit a paltry monthly salary of £21 in Tanzania and to give her £10 pocket money in London, she was not paid, did not have clear working hours and did not have a day off for four years. Ms Mruke had agreed to come to try to save money for her child's education. Nevertheless, she was threatened, made to sleep on the floor and poorly fed. At one point she was said to have been given two slices of bread a day. She met an interpreter at the doctor's surgery who, seeing her distress, contacted Kalayan, the domestic workers' NGO, who facilitated her leaving the Khan household and tipped off the police. This slavery prosecution led to a conviction which was later overturned on appeal.

Ms Mruke then took her case to an employment tribunal where she argued that she had been subjected to: unfair withholding of wages, lack of holiday pay, working without rest breaks, race discrimination and unfair dismissal. The tribunal upheld the first three claims but not the race and unfair dismissal claims. Ms Mruke appealed to the Court of Appeal, which agreed that a claim for race discrimination had not been made out. The Court was of the view that it was not her race or nationality that was in issue but her socio-economic status which had resulted in the poor treatment. However, they did find that there had been constructive dismissal because Ms Kahn had paid her the equivalent of 33pence per hour, which was many times below the minimum wage. This was an egregious violation which justified Ms Mruke leaving her employment.[138]

[136] Modern Slavery Act 2015, s 53(7)(b).

[137] R Hall, 'Kenyan domestic worker assaulted by mob in Lebanon faces deportation', *The Guardian*, London, 6 July 2018. R Hall, 'Deportation reprieve for Kenyan domestic worker attacked in Lebanon', *The Guardian*, London, 6 July 2018. R Hall, 'The secret networks saving Lebanon's migrant maids from abuse', *The Guardian*, London, 1 August, 2018.

[138] *Mruke v Khan* [2018] EWCA Civ 280.

The Court of Appeal in *Mruke v Kahn* relied on the Supreme Court decision in *Onu v Akwiwu and Taiwo v. Olaigbe*[139] for its finding that there was no racial discrimination or discrimination on grounds of nationality. In that case two women were brought from Nigeria to the UK to work as domestic servants by two Nigerian couples (one spouse was Ugandan). The two women were treated as poorly as Ms Mruke in the *Kahn* case – they were made to work interminably, poorly paid or not paid at all, subjected to degrading and inhuman treatment and not afforded their human dignity. Both were able to leave their situations because of the kindness of people they had met at a playgroup and at church. While both won their cases for the violations of their employment rights and were awarded compensation, the employment tribunals denied that there had been discrimination on grounds of race. The matter came before the Supreme Court which confirmed the race findings. The Supreme Court examined the protected characteristics found in the Equality Act 2010 and the Race Relations Act 1976 which had preceded it. Race was a protected characteristic, as was nationality. But did that then mean that immigration status was also a protected characteristic? Put differently, did discrimination on grounds of immigration status amount to discrimination on grounds of nationality?[140] The Supreme Court found not. The two women were not discriminated against because they were Nigerian; indeed their employers were themselves non-UK nationals. Rather their vulnerability arose from being migrant domestic workers, tied to employers, whom the Court noted, treated them disgracefully. The two exploited women deserved better.[141] However, the Court explained:

> Clearly, however, there are many non-British nationals living and working here who do not share this vulnerability. No doubt, if these employers had employed British nationals to work for them in their homes, they would not have treated them so badly. They would probably not have been given the opportunity to do so. But equally, if they had employed non-British nationals who had the right to live and work here, they would not have treated them so badly. The reason why these employees were treated so badly was their particular vulnerability arising, at least in part, from their particular immigration status.[142]

There was reluctance in the Court's decision not least because it recognised the inadequacy of the law and specifically section 8 of the Modern Slavery Act 2015 which provided for compensation after a conviction or a confiscation order had been obtained. In this case there had been no conviction or confiscation order, meaning that, as explained by the Court at the start of the judgment, the Court could not:

> make a slavery and trafficking reparation order under section 8 of the Act, requiring him to pay compensation to the victim for any harm resulting from the offence.

[139] *Taiwo v Olaigbe* [2016] UKSC 31, n 121 above.
[140] *Taiwo v Olaigbe* [2016] UKSC 31 para.14.
[141] *Taiwo v Olaigbe* [2016] UKSC 31, para 34.
[142] *Taiwo v Olaigbe* [2016] UKSC 31 at para 26.

> (But such orders can only be made after a conviction and confiscation order); and remedies under the law of contract or tort do not provide compensation for the humiliation, fear and severe distress which such mistreatment can cause.[143]

The *Siliadin*, *CN* and *Taiwo* cases throw up another uncomfortable fact: mistreatment in domestic service is often at the hands of fellow Africans and indeed, the victims' relatives. Unfortunately, this helps to reinforce the stereotype of Africans as inherent violators of human rights. There appears to be an 'us' and 'them' approach to domestic workers by those who are legally settled. The reluctance of Leila Slimani's protagonist, Myriam, to hire a fellow North African as a nanny for her children is illuminating:

> She fears that a tacit complicity and familiarity would grow between her and the nanny. That the woman would start speaking to her in Arabic. Telling Myriam her life story and, soon, asking her all sorts of favours in the name of their shared language and religion. She has always been wary of what she calls immigrant solidarity.[144]

The treatment of women in domestic service is more often than not exploitative. The maids are in an invidious position being embedded within the family and yet treated with disdain and suspicion. The case law finds echo in fiction.

VII. Fictional Maids

In Brian Chikwava's *Harare North*, about Zimbabweans living in London, he meets a young 17-year-old woman/girl, Tsitsi, whose visa has expired. The narrator explains: 'She have run away from tyrant aunty who is married to a doctor.'[145] He then goes on to recount the 'usual story' of the poor, rural girl who is brought from the village to be 'uplifted' by town relatives. Instead they exploit her and eventually the man of the house sexually violates her, leading to a baby and family scandal. In this case, it is the narrator's friend who takes the girl in who is the sexual exploiter.

It is not all doom and gloom. Donkor's *Hold* provides us with a wonderful example of a couple who honour the pledge they made to the mother of the girl that they brought to England as a companion for their daughter. Belinda, the 17-year-old Ghanaian girl living with this diasporic British-Ghanaian family, is treated like a member of the family, sent to school, bought clothes which she is allowed to choose, and discouraged from doing the domestic chores. Nana, the mother, starts by acknowledging that since Belinda's arrival her house is now so clean that she could eat off the floor. However, she pleads with Belinda not to clean, telling her that she has brought her to Britain to study and to be a friend and

[143] *Taiwo v Olaigbe* [2016] UKSC 31 at para 1. See also para 34.
[144] L Slimani (2018), n 78 above, 16.
[145] B Chikwava, *Harare North* (London, Vintage, 2010) 30.

companion to her daughter Amma. Nana insists that she can do her own laundry and cleaning.[146]

Belinda continues to clean on the sly. She finds it therapeutic. One night, unable to sleep, she encounters Amma and encourages her to help clean the kitchen. This, she hopes, will also be therapeutic for Amma. However, Amma is outraged and in a wonderful explosion asks:

> 'Be, this is like some fucking slave labour shit. It's out-rage-ous. Has Mum got you doing this? Or, was it Dad? Did Dad make you? Is this you, like, paying your way? Like the level of exploitation is un-'.[147]

Belinda reassures her that she is not being exploited and encourages Amma to clean the fridge as this may help to soothe her, to which suggestion she retorts, 'I doubt domestic chores will work love.'[148]

Faced with the 'humiliation' of having to clean his own toilet, the magistrate in Huchu's *The Maestro, The Magistrate & The Mathematician*, who is now living in Edinburgh with his wife and daughter, remembers the cavalier way in which they had treated their maid 'back at home'. He ruminates that of all the things and people that he misses, she is first on his list. She cleaned, cooked and looked after their daughter without complaint. They in turn felt able to cancel her one day off with little or no notice. The magistrate asks himself:

> Why did I never question this before – an injustice in my own house, yet there I was dispensing justice every day while I kept a virtual slave in my own house? How could this have seemed normal?[149]

In stark contrast to Belinda's story in the novel *Hold* is the case of *Hounga v Allen*.[150] Aged 14, Hounga was persuaded to leave Nigeria to come to the UK by the family of the woman who became her employer. A false identity was provided and a tourist visa obtained. This soon expired but she continued to live with and look after Hounga, her husband and their two children. The promise of payment and schooling never materialised. Instead she was assaulted and threatened with arrest. She made her escape and sued her employer in the Employment Tribunal. Like the *Taiwo* case discussed above, the case was won and then lost on appeal, before coming before the Supreme Court. The Supreme Court was asked to decide if it was indeed correct that, by participating in the immigration fraud, Hounga had disqualified herself from bringing a claim for discrimination and unfair work conditions. The Supreme Court held not. She was entitled to bring the claim and her own part in the illegal behaviour did not cancel her ability to seek a remedy in tort. Public policy was a consideration, but it pointed to offering a remedy rather

[146] M Donkor (2018), n 105 above, 134.
[147] M Donkor (2018) 208.
[148] M Donkor (2018) 208.
[149] T Huchu, *The Maestro, The Magistrate & The Mathematician* (Edinburgh, Parthian Books, 2015) 8.
[150] *Hounga v Allen* [2014] UKSC 47.

than rewarding poor behaviour by denying one. The Supreme Court surveyed a wide range of jurisprudence on trafficking but decided against pursuing the evidence, not least because they said that young though Ms Hounga was, she knew right from wrong. With respect, the Court may have missed the vulnerability and desperation that leads young women in Ms Hounga's situation to 'agree' to deceive to facilitate migration.[151]

Ending this section on a lighter note, in her short story, *The Maid from Lalapanzi*, Pettina Gappah identifies the criteria for a good maid:

> 'Housemaids should not eat too much,' said my mother …
>
> 'Housemaids should not be too pretty,' all the women agreed. 'Housemaids should not enjoy themselves too much,' my mother declared.[152]

VIII. Undiplomatic Exploitation and Abuse

The jurisprudence of the Migrant Workers Committee seems to see consulates as a source of information and protection for migrant workers who find themselves in trouble.[153] However, disturbingly, the worst employers seem to be diplomats who seek to hide behind the privileges accorded to them by diplomatic immunity.[154] It is here worth giving the full backstory for Mende whom we have already met via her autobiography *Slave*. Mende was 12 when she was captured in the Nuba mountains and sold to a woman in Khartoum. She lived as their domestic slave for seven years, being given scraps of food, severely beaten until she learned to comply, while

[151] See UN Committee on the Protection of the Rights of All Migrant Workers and Members of Their Families (CMW), Joint General Comment No 4 (2017) of the Committee on the Protection of the Rights of All Migrant Workers and Members of Their Families and No 23 (2017) of the Committee on the Rights of the Child on State obligations regarding the human rights of children in the context of international migration in countries of origin, transit, destination and return, 16 November 2017, CMW/C/GC/4-CRC/C/GC/23. See also Concluding Observations on Nigeria CMW/C/NGA/CO/1 (2017) para 55(b) recommending that Nigeria remove the exception to the prohibition on child labour that allows children to undertake 'light work' for family members at home and in agriculture, noting that this makes children vulnerable to trafficking.

[152] P Gappah, 'The Housemaid from Lalapanzi' in P Gappah, *An Elegy for Easterly* (London, Faber and Faber, 2009) 153, 159. There is a rich literature on domestic workers. See E Jansen, 'Black authors, maids and madams', *Africa is a Country*, 1 August 2019; E Jansen, 'Like Family', *Africa is a Country*, 30 July 2019. The latter is an extract from her book, E Jansen, *Like Family: Domestic Workers in South African History and Literature* (Johannesburg, Wits University Press, 2019).

[153] General Comment No 1 on migrant domestic workers CMW/C/GC/1 (2011) paras 62–64.

[154] This was noted in the *Reyes* case, n 163 below, where evidence from the UK charity Kalayaan to this effect was accepted (n 170 below). See also Report to the Committee on Equal Opportunities for Women and Men for the Council of Europe (18th sitting), dated 17 May 2001 (Doc 9102),citing the findings of the French organisation where it is noted that 95% of domestic workers are women and also that 20% of violators are diplomats. See also the Committee's Recommendation 1663 of 22 June 2004 (19th sitting) on: 'Domestic Slavery, Servitude, Au Pairs and Mail-order Brides' in response to a Report dated 19 April 2004 on the same (Doc 10144).

always sleeping on the floor of a shed at night.[155] On the eve of the millennium and now mature and catching the attention of male visitors and the woman's husband, she was then 'given' to a relative in London, a diplomat. In a chilling exchange between her 'owner' and the man who supplied her, the two discuss how difficult it is to get servants in England. They speak of her and her replacements like chattels. Will the slave dealer be able to supply her with another 'girl' who is just as good? Mende describes her replacement as a: 'little black girl standing nervously behind them. She looked about the same age as I had been when I first arrived. She looked so young and scared and confused … Here was my replacement slave.'[156]

These were not the only similarities. The new girl, Nanu, tells Mende how she came to be captured:

> From then on, Nanu's story was pretty much a repeat of my own. She was taken away from the village by the Arab raider, along with lots of boys and girls. He put her on his horse and then raped her repeatedly when they were in the forest. After that, the raiders took Nanu and the rest of the children to an army camp, which sounded like the same one that I'd been taken to.[157]

Mende's London life, spent working for the Sudanese embassy in London makes for unedifying reading.[158] Her owner's sister, for whom she works initially, treats her relatively well, given what she had become used to. In addition to cooking, cleaning, washing and looking after five children under 10 years, including twin boys aged two, she is also required to wash two big cars. Eventually she discovers from the children that their father, who treats her in a very high-handed manner, is the acting ambassador at the Sudanese embassy. Mende makes the mistake of asking the wife if she knows whether a phone number that she had been given in Khartoum of a fellow from her area is an English one. The paper with the number is torn and Mende's passport is confiscated as she cannot be trusted with it.[159] The relationship sours and her new 'employer' starts to treat her very badly. Mende is warned against going outside, being told that London is a dangerous place and that the girl before her had disappeared without a trace.[160]

[155] M Nazer and D Lewis (2004), n 103 above, 246. Her description of her treatment, which required her to use separate cutlery and crockery from the family, reminds one of the photographs taken by Ernest Cole of the living and working conditions of black maids during the Apartheid era. E Cole, *House of Bondage* (New York, Random House, 1967).

[156] M Nazer and D Lewis (2004) 225. See also, the African Committee of Experts on the Rights and Welfare of the Child (ACERWC), No 007/Com/003/2015 *Decision on the Communication Submitted by Minority Rights Group International and SOS-Enclaves on Behalf of Said Ould Salem and Yarg Ould Salem against the Government of the Republic of Mauritania.* 15 December 2017. In a case challenging the enslavement of two boys, the Committee found Mauritania to have violated several provisions of the African Charter on the Rights and Welfare of the Child, including those prohibiting torture, child labour and discrimination. Furthermore the state was found to have failed to meet its obligations and to ensure that the best interests of the children were protected.

[157] M Nazer and D Lewis (2004), n 103 above, 230.

[158] M Nazer and D Lewis (2004).

[159] M Nazer c and D Lewis (2004) 257.

[160] M Nazer and D Lewis (2004) 260.

Like a game of 'pass the parcel', Mende is left in the care of a married couple with two young daughters who also work at the embassy, while the diplomat and his family travel home to Sudan. They treat her with kindness and when one of the children finds her crying, the husband convinces her to tell him what has happened to her. By asking about her conditions of work, he ascertains that she has no set hours and more importantly that she is not paid. He tells her that this is against the law.[161]

Mende ended up running away with the help of a fellow Sudanese that she had met at the mall while staying with the 'kind diplomat'. She waged a battle with the Home Office for asylum which was eventually granted, freeing her from a life of degrading and inhuman treatment.

In Zadie Smith's novella *The Embassy of Cambodia*, Fatou, the Ivorienne maid to the Cambodian ambassador in London and his family, finds a newspaper report recounting a story similar to that of Mende Nazer, author of *Slave*. She ponders her own situation and wonders if she is also a slave. She discounts this as she reminisces that it was her father who had arranged and paid for her passage to Italy, before she made her way to London. She thinks that she cannot be a slave because, unlike the girl in the story, she has not been beaten, although the mother of the family has slapped her twice and the children treat her disrespectfully. On the other hand, she muses:

> just like the girl in the newspaper, she had not seen her passport with her own eyes since she arrived at the Derawals', and she had been told from the start that her wages were to be retained by the Derawals to pay for the food and water and heat she would require during her stay, as well as to cover for the room she slept in.[162]

Fatou concludes her deliberations by deciding that she cannot be a slave because she is allowed out to church and to do the shopping. Through church she meets a Nigerian friend, Andrew, who works as a night security guard to fund his studies. It is to him that she turns when the Derawals evict her without notice. Giving an insight into the experiences of low-paid migrant workers living in an expensive city, Andrew informs her that he and his roommates sleep in shifts, meaning that when one is out working, the one who is at home can rest, vacating the bed for the incomer when they go out to work.

IX. Called to Account: Maids Confront Diplomats in Court

On Anti-slavery day in 2017, the UK Supreme Court handed down a decision (*Reyes*) involving diplomats from Saudi Arabia.[163] A separate Supreme Court

[161] M Nazer and D Lewis (2004) 277–80.
[162] Z Smith, *The Embassy of Cambodia* (London, Hamish Hamilton, 2013) 16.
[163] *Reyes v Al-Malki and another* [2017] UKSC 61.

case (*Janah* and *Benkharbouche*) had involved a challenge to the Foreign and Commonwealth Office which claimed that immunity from suit should apply to diplomats from Sudan and Libya.[164] The three diplomats had employed domestic workers from the Philippines (Saudi Arabia – *Reyes*) and two Moroccans (Libya and Sudan) whom they, and members of their families, had treated appallingly, including by failing to pay them the required wages and making them work unregulated hours. One claimed that she had been unfairly dismissed. Allegations of racism were also made. The complainant in the Saudi case, Ms Reyes, also noted that, while she had entered the country using a Tier 5 visa applied for by her Saudi employers in Manila, she had been trafficked. The diplomats all claimed Diplomatic Immunity under the Vienna Convention on Diplomatic Relations 1961, incorporated into UK law by section 2(1) of the Diplomatic Privileges Act 1964. Also considered in the Libya and Sudan case was state immunity under the State Immunity Act 1977.

In both cases, the Supreme Court emphasised that there had to be a distinction made between the work done by a diplomat as a state function which would be covered by immunity,[165] and anything outside of that, which would not. The Court was of the view that the employment of domestic workers, while helpful to diplomats and their families, could not be regarded as diplomatic work directly linked to the work done on behalf of the sending state. Furthermore, the claim for an exemption on grounds of 'professional or commercial activity undertaken by the diplomat outside their official duties', did not, in the case of the employment of domestic servants, give protection in this instance.[166]

Moreover, it was noted in the case involving Reyes against her Saudi employer that, as the diplomatic posting had ended, the diplomat would not be covered by diplomatic immunity. In *Janah* and *Benkharbouche* the Supreme Court further noted that employment rights were derived from European law. According to article 47 of the Charter of Fundamental Rights of the European Union and article 6 of the ECHR, the women could not be denied their right to access to justice and a fair trial. The cases were returned to the Employment Tribunal which had initially granted the diplomats immunity.[167]

[164] *Janah v Secretary of State for Foreign and Commonwealth Affairs and Libya*, and *Benkharbouche v Secretary of State for Foreign and Commonwealth Affairs* [2017] UKSC 62.

[165] In *Taiwo v Olaigbe* [2016] UKSC 31, Hale LJ had, in a section on the many ways in which domestic workers are exploited, raised the use by diplomats of diplomatic immunity as a defence – at para 25.

[166] *Reyes*, n 163 above, para 3, citing Article 31(1)(c) of the Vienna Convention on Diplomatic Relations, 1961, 500 UNTS 95.

[167] The Supreme Court decisions join an increasingly long line of decisions at both the European and national level seeking to limit diplomatic immunity being used to frustrate claims brought against embassies, by often relatively powerless employees. In *Reyes*, the Supreme Court looked at US decisions – see para 47. See also *Cudak v Lithuania* (23 March 2010) ECtHR (Application 15869/02), *Sabeh El Leil v France* (29 June 2011) ECtHR (Application 34869/05) and Case C-154/11 *Mahamdia v Peoples Democratic Republic of Algeria* (19 July 2012) CJEU. McCann Fitzgerald, 'Diplomatic/Sovereign Immunity in Employment law' (Ireland), 31 March 2015 at: https://www.lexology.com/library/detail.aspx?g=4ed4c788-44cc-483a-86f3-d028946705ef.

In the *Reyes* case the Supreme Court considered the obligations of both the UK and Saudi Arabia under the Palermo Protocol, which they had both ratified. Palermo, the Court noted at paragraph 60:

> contains elaborate commitments by each state party to criminalise trafficking; to make material provision for victims in aid of their physical, psychological and social recovery; by article 6(6), to 'ensure that its domestic legal system contains measures that offer victims of trafficking in persons the possibility of obtaining compensation for damage suffered'… and so on.

It further noted that the UK was also a state party to the Council of Europe Protocol on Trafficking, discussed earlier. It was clear that there were obligations owed to Reyes, whom the Court agreed had been trafficked. Also worthy of note was the Court's invocation of Saudi Arabia's ratification of the Arab Charter on Human Rights, 2004 which contained, in article 10, a clear prohibition against slavery and servitude.[168] The Court further considered the role of the person who receives the migrant worker and considered that they may be said to be part of the chain of exploitation which is anticipated in the definition of the multiple elements of trafficking.[169]

The three women were supported by two non-government organisations: the Kalayaan organisation, set up in 1987 to assist people in domestic service, and the Anti-Trafficking and Labour Exploitation Unit (ATLEU), which provides legal representation to victims of trafficking and labour exploitation. Given the relative power of the diplomatic community and their connections to the political elites within their sending states, one wonders what, if any, action is ever taken against those found to have violated the rights of workers when posted abroad. In *Reyes*, the Supreme Court observed that diplomats were overrepresented in cases involving in the mistreatment of domestic workers. It accepted the evidence given by Kalayaan that:

> (1) Between about 200 and 250 domestic workers enter the UK each year under a diplomatic overseas domestic worker's visa.
> (2) The proportion of domestic workers who are the victims of trafficking is considerably higher in diplomatic households than in other households.
> (3) Thus, in one representative period, 17 out of 55 referrals to the government agency set up to identify the trafficking of domestic workers related to diplomatic households whereas, had such referrals been in proportion to the number of workers in other households, there would have just been one.
> (4) The explanation for the high ratio of trafficked workers in diplomatic households is largely because perceived immunity from claims for compensation leads diplomats to consider that they can exploit them with impunity.
> (5) The perceived immunity makes trafficking with a view to domestic servitude a low risk, high reward activity for diplomats.[170]

[168] *Reyes*, n 163 above, para 60.
[169] *Reyes*, paras 61–62.
[170] *Reyes*, para 59.

While noting the findings of the *Taiwo v Olaigbe*[171] case discussed earlier in this chapter, dismissing race discrimination claims, it is hard to shake off the feeling that Mende's treatment recounted in her autobiography, *Slave*, and indeed that of others employed by diplomats, was not a direct result of racism in addition to socio-economic status. In one of the most racist passages that I have ever read, Mende recounts a conversation between her owner and her friend while she was still in Khartoum. The owner tells her friend that she does not pay Mende a wage because she has already bought her.[172] The owner then goes on to marvel at Mende's pliability: 'She never causes any trouble. I think these blacks are just sort of made for it. I suppose their people have been slaves for generations. They never complain. They just get on with it.'[173] This comes as a shock to Mende who recounts:

> When I was locked in my shed that night, I was unable to sleep for hours. I couldn't believe that this was my fate – that I had been sold as a slave and would remain a slave for the rest of my life. It all seemed so final.[174]

Worth reading is Sulaiman Addonia's novel, *The Consequences of Love*, about migrant workers set in Saudi Arabia, which seems to echo many of the experiences of migrant workers explored in Nazer's autobiography and detailed in the 'diplomatic' case law. To tempt you, it also has a love story at its heart.[175]

X. Other Forms of Labour

Barbara Ehrenreich's sociological study of the work done by low-paid workers in the USA is a searing account of legalised oppression and exploitation of poor working-class people, many of whom were migrants. Ehrenreich provides detailed accounts of the nature of the work that she did as a hotel maid, a contracted cleaner for home cleaning companies and as a waitress. This included cleaning faeces from toilets, picking out pubic hairs from plug holes, getting skin infections from cleaning products, walking miles as a waitress while experiencing abuse from diners and sometimes from management. She identifies a high dependency on over-the-counter medication to 'keep going', the long-term health impacts of repetitive strains left untreated and the general morale-sapping nature of work for which there is no status, little thanks, and even less pay.[176]

[171] *Taiwo v Olaigbe* [2016] UKSC 31.
[172] M Nazer and D Lewis (2004), n 103 above, 192.
[173] M Nazer and D Lewis (2004) 193.
[174] M Nazer and D Lewis (2004) 193.
[175] S Addonia, *The Consequences of Love* (London, Vintage, 2009).
[176] B Ehrenreich, *Nickel and Dimed: On (Not) Getting by in America* (New York, Metropolitan Books, 2001). More recently Ehrenreich wrote the foreword to a first-person account of a woman who had worked as a cleaner while balancing sole care of her child. S Land, *Maid: Hard Work, Low Pay and a Mother's will to Survive* (London, Trapeze, 2019).

It is difficult to separate out the empirically grounded findings of Ehrenreich from the equally powerful insights in the novel *We need New Names* by NoViolet Bulawayo which touches on the lives of students and undocumented workers doing difficult jobs in the United States:

> And the jobs we worked, Jesus – Jesus – Jesus, the jobs we worked. Low-paying jobs. Backbreaking jobs. Jobs that gnawed at the bones of our dignity, devoured the meat, tongued the marrow. We took scalding irons and ironed our pride flat. We cleaned toilets. We picked tobacco and fruit under the boiling sun until we hung our tongues and panted like lost hounds. We butchered animals, slit throats, drained blood.[177]

The next section looks at hotel maids in fiction.

XI. Hotel Maids Wanted: Abuse Included

The novels of Zadie Smith and Elizabeth Day explore a darker element of cleaning work, specifically the abuse of hotel maids. Smith's Fatou from the Ivory Coast explains how her father had sent for her to leave Togo to join him in Ghana. He had secured a job for her in the hotel that he worked in as a waiter. She was to be a maid cleaning rooms. In a matter of fact way she sets out the many ways in which hotel maids were assaulted and abused by the male guests,[178] but also how the young male workers 'entertained' English women by dancing with them in the ballroom and then going with them to their cabins. Beatrice, in Day's *Paradise City* sounds resigned:

> It is part of the job, she has come to realise. Bitter experience has taught her that it is better not to resist but to be pliant, to allow them to do their silly business and get it over with. All the maids have the same problem: oversexed businessmen and adulterous foreigners. They tend to clean in pairs now, each one doing an adjoining room, so that if anything ever gets nasty or goes further than you want it to, you can scream out and otherwise bang the walls.[179]

Some maids occasionally managed to get some money for the sexual encounters, whether consensual (a way to supplement a meagre wage) or not. In Smith's *Embassy of Cambodia*, Fatou details how she was raped by a Russian guest while working at a beach hotel in Ghana, and says that she did not bother to report to the police because they would not have believed her. Beatrice in Day's *Paradise City* is also violated while cleaning, but she leverages her attack by blackmailing her assailant into giving her a job in his firm.

Lest this sound far-fetched, one need only remember the Dominique Strauss-Kahn affair, when the head of the International Monetary Fund was

[177] N Bulawayo (2014), n 102 above, 240–44.
[178] Z Smith (2013), n 162 above, 42–45.
[179] E Day, *Paradise City* (London, Bloomsbury, 2015) 42.

charged with sexually assaulting Ms Diallo, a Senegalese hotel maid, in the room of an expensive hotel in New York. After initial resistance, and indeed scepticism that the story could possibly be true, Strauss-Kahn, denied rape, but agreed that there had been 'moral failing' on his part, and resigned his job at the IMF. He was prosecuted in New York but the charges were dropped with reasons given including the 'unreliability' of Ms Diallo's testimony and history.[180] He counter-sued her for US$1 million, later settling a civil suit brought by Ms Diallo.[181] This one event triggered an avalanche of more exposure revealing that Strauss Khan had a history of paying for prostitutes in France and taking part in orgies. His loyal wife who had supported him during the Diallo accusations lost patience and divorced him. The last news heard of Ms Diallo is that she had bought and opened an African-themed restaurant in the Bronx.[182]

XII. The Ache: Missing those Left Behind

The UN Women's Committee in its General Recommendation No 26 on Migrant Women notes that families are more likely to stay intact when women stay behind than when men do. It is equally true that when families move together, it is mainly women who fight to keep the family together, who seek to keep alive memories of people and food of the mother country. Gogol's mother in Jumpa Lahiri's novel *The Namesake* is the exemplar of this woman. The representations of gender in the fictional literature show disruption and transformation but also resistance and attempted continuity of gender relations transported from 'home.' Women's resilience and ability to adapt, survive and often thrive in what can sometimes be a hostile environment is marked by authors including Gappah.

In her short story 'Before Tonde, After Tonde', Gappah notes how the protagonist's father, a University graduate who used to have a good job in a brewery, finds himself unemployed despite sending out many applications. He becomes increasingly angry in England and explodes when his wife suggests that he register with her agency so that he can do care work. He struggles with his inability to provide and with the role reversal.[183] Dominic Pasura also explores the impact of gender in the demands made on men to continue to work because they need to continue to provide for the family.[184]

[180] *The People of the State of New York v Dominique Strauss-Kahn* (Indictment No 02526/2011): *Recommendations for Dismissal.*

[181] J Ax, 'Strauss-Kahn countersues NY hotel maid for $1million', *Reuters*, 15 May 2012; BBC, 'Strauss-Kahn reaches legal settlement with hotel maid', *BBC News*, 10 December 2012.

[182] P Sherwell, 'Dominque Strauss-Kahn accuser builds restaurant and a new life in New York', *The Telegraph*, 12 June 2015.

[183] P Gappah, 'Before Tonde, After Tonde' in *One World: A Global Anthology of Short Stories* (London, New Internationalist, 2008), 115–25.

[184] D Pasura, 'Towards a Multisited Ethnography of the Zimbabwean Diaspora in Britain' (2011) 18 *Identities: Global Studies in Culture and Power* 250, 259.

However, in this penultimate section I would like to focus on women who migrate alone and the ache that they feel for those left behind, not least their children. Earlier in this chapter, we saw how Myriam, in Slimani's *Lullaby*, was advised not to hire a woman with children because of their lack of flexibility and inability to stay late to look after the employer's children. The legal reality is that migrant domestic workers are unlikely to be issued with visas which enable them to bring their families, not least because of the minimum income thresholds and because they would not be able to house and feed the entire family on their salaries.[185] Indeed for many domestic workers, living 'in-house' with the family is a condition of service. As the cases showed, often they are not even provided with a room, let alone a bed for themselves.[186]

In December 2018, *National Geographic* magazine ran a special feature on migration. It looked at the lives of Filipino workers abroad;[187] at the sadness of women who migrate as domestic workers to look after other people's children, leaving their own children to be brought up by their grandmothers and other relatives. They do this as a form of intergenerational aspiration building and social engineering. They suffer and sacrifice so that the generation that will come after will not have to. In remitting money, they pay for their children to attend 'good schools' with the aim of one day getting a 'professional job'. They are called the *bagong bayani*, the new heroes. The material gains are counter weighed by the emotional and psychological stress of both the working-abroad mother, whose only solace is seeing her child growing up on a telephone screen, and the child, who is materially provided for, but must also ache for the mother's presence. Instead they paper over their pain and distress and continue.

In her novel, Slimani describes the secret lives of the nannies who meet daily in the playground with their young charges:

> They all have shameful secrets. They hide awful memories of bent knees, humiliations, lies. Memories of barely audible voices on the other end of the line, of conversations cut off, of people who die and are never seen again, of money needed day after day for a sick child who no longer recognises you and who has forgotten the sound of your voice.[188]

The heartache does not end there, for as we later learn in *Lullaby*, the nannies move on to new families as the charges become independent. The children forget all the loving endearments whispered to them in 'Baoulé, Dyula, Arabic and Hindi, sweet nothings whispered in Filipino or Russian.'[189] While the nannies never forget their charges, the children sometimes no longer recognise them in the street as they grow into adulthood, adding a further layer of pain.[190]

[185] The CMW enjoins states to facilitate family unity and to protect children, CMW/C/GC/1 (2011) paras 54–59.

[186] CEDAW General Recommendation No 26, paras 17, 19.

[187] A Almendral, 'Heroes of the Philippines', *National Geographic*, December 2018, 138–49.

[188] L Slimani (as translated by S Taylor) (2018), n 78 above, 179.

[189] L Slimani (2018) 178.

[190] L Slimani (2018) 179.

In their semi-autobiographical novel *Freshwater*, Akwaeke Emezi describes how their Malaysian mother (who trained as a nurse, and married their father, a Nigerian doctor whom she met in London and with whom she returned to Nigeria) is forced to leave the family to look for work to supplement the family income as the father is no longer able to practise and is not willing to 'lower himself' to look for other work.

> Saachi looked at his prideful back, then she looked at their bank accounts and at their family and she made a choice. It was easier to get free for the sake of her children than for the sake of herself – she did things for the Ada that Saul would never have lifted a finger to do.[191]

We learn:

> By the time her last contract ended, the human mother had spent ten years there, from Riyadh to Jeddah and, finally, the mountains of Ta'if. She returned to Nigeria once or twice a year with suitcases that smelled cool and foreign. She left behind the sacrifice of three children fastened to an altar with thin sinews, and she would pay the costs of that for the rest of her life.
>
> And this is how you break a child, you know. Step one, take the mother away.[192]

XIII. Conclusion

Over the past decade I have taken to telling my students that it is not the absence of law that is the problem, rather it is failures of compassion, empathy, will, humanity and imagination. In this chapter I have deliberately focused on the case law to show the myriad ways in which poverty and vulnerability are exploited. The gendered inequalities faced by women mean that they are over-represented in trafficking for sex and domestic service which leaves them more open to abuse. The cases present a shaft of light in that the women find solace and firm friends and advocates in those who refuse to look away, but choose to confront the abuse and provide practical help to facilitate escape.

The fictional literature confirms the many ways in which women as workers are exploited. But it does more than this. The fictional literature gives the women agency. The directness of Unigwe's novel, *On Black Sisters' Street*, confronts us with what feels like the reality of the lives of trafficked women. It helps us better contextualise and understand the lived realities of the woman in the *BS v Spain* case discussed earlier. Leila Slimani's *Lullaby* offers a penetrating analysis of middle-class hypocrisies and the politics of class and gender. These novels and others discussed in this chapter, lift women from the cold, abstract statistics, which can often leave one feeling helpless and hopeless, and draw us out, make us see and

[191] A Emezi, *Freshwater* (London, Faber & Faber, 2018) 30–31.
[192] A Emezi (2018) 32.

think about our own privilege. One feels empathy and outrage simultaneously. As one reads the novels and case law, the mind takes flight and one starts to imagine that if placed in the centre of the narrative, you, the reader, would be the interpreter who picked up on Tanzanian Ms Mruke's distress and alerted the authorities; that you would be the friend in the child-minding group who staged an intervention in the *Taiwo v Olaigbe* case; that you would be the Haitian woman in the *Siliadin* case who saw a distressed young woman in the supermarket and offered her shelter and proper pay; that, in *Slave*, you would be the diplomat who told the truth about what pay and conditions of work *should be* or the Sudanese man who planned and arranged for Mende's flight from her brutal employers; that you would be the journalist who wrote her story and forced the Home Office to back down and grant her asylum; that you would be the lawyer, Alison Stanley, who reassures Mende that: 'They're not sending you back to Sudan, Mende … Don't worry. It'll be over my dead body.'[193] Would you be that person? More importantly, for those who are themselves the employers of nannies and maids, what kind of legal regime do you run in your household: a compassionate, human rights compliant one, or a bullying and exploitative one?

The novels of Day and Smith, depicting the lives of women who have worked as hotel maids, open our eyes to abuses that we do not think of as we check in and out of hotels, grateful for clean sheets, but pleased that we will not have to make the bed; little thinking that the women who will do this may be raped within the course of their workday on those very beds. One can only cheer that there are people who had the insight, compassion and strength of will to set up Kalayan, the NGO that represents domestic workers in Britain – and all the others like them. Cliché though it is, in reading law and literature together, our minds and our hearts are both opened.

For all the perspicacity of trans-continental novels, there is one area in which they have, until fairly recently, fallen short and that is in dealing with sexual orientation. The next chapter marks the evolution from invisibility to hyper-visibility of sexuality and gender identity discourse in literature.

[193] M Nazer and D Lewis (2004), n 103 above, 308.

5

Sexual Orientation and Gender Identities

Until very recently, the lives of gay, lesbian, bisexual, transgender and intersex people (LGBTI) were rarely ever reflected in fictional works. Where they were, they were cardboard cut-outs, mere stereotypes. In two recent offerings by Tendai Huchu (*The Hairdresser of Harare*) and Epaphras Osondu (*Voice of America*), gay men are hairdressers who are fastidious about appearance and are empathetic and sympathetic to women. In short, they defy boorish stereotypes of a masculinity grounded in machismo. However some might argue that they do so only by reinforcing stereotypes of the 'effeminate homosexual'. Conversely, that observation may lead to a charge of asking gay people to 'pass' or to cover or mute their identities.[1]

In Brian Chikwava's *Harare North*, a satire, the protagonist adopts a slightly mocking tone when talking about gay people, referring to 'them gays' and describing the demeanour of a friend with whom he is having an argument about politics thus: 'Aleck recover, fold his arms, shift his weight to one leg in fancy homosexual kind of way …'.[2] Meanwhile, in *Broken Glass*, another satire, Alain Mabanckou ponders on a character, 'he was quite a nice guy, he might have been gay, from the way he wiggled his behind like a woman when he walked …'.[3]

The boss and kingpin of a 419 operation (fraud) in Adaobi Nwaubani's *I do not come to you by chance*, asks the protagonist about his relationships, or more accurately sex life. On being told that he does not have a girlfriend, or indeed any women (the boss cannot understand how any man would only want one) the boss asks him: 'Are you having some problems with your machete?'. On being reassured that the machete is working just fine, the boss probes: 'Or are you a homo?' On being told that he is not, the boss expresses relief: 'I have enough problems on my hands. I do not want to add the one of having a homo brother.'[4] In case you were wondering, his other problems include the fact that his wife has just discovered that he has been

[1] T Huchu, *The Hairdresser of Harare* (Harare, Weaver Press, 2010) (London, Freight Press, 2013). (Set in Harare, the story documents the protagonist's attempt to hide his sexuality and ends with the hero's uncovering as gay and he flees to England to seek asylum). A Chitando and M Manyonganise, 'Saying the Unsaid: Probing Homosexuality in *The Hairdresser of Harare*' (2016) 63(4) *Journal of Homosexuality* 559–74. K Yoshino, *Covering: The Hidden Assault on our Civil Rights* (New York, Random House, 2007) 91–93.
EC Osondu, 'I will lend you my wife' in Osundu, *Voice of America* (London, Granta, 2010) 107–16. (The wife marries her Nigerian husband's gay friend to facilitate a visa marriage in America).

[2] B Chikwava, *Harare North* (London, Vintage, 2010) 122.

[3] A Mabanckou (translated by H Stevenson), *Broken Glass* (2009) 112.

[4] A Nwaubani, *I do not come to you by chance* (London, Phoenix, 2009) 224–25.

renting a flat for his mistress on the same road as the marital home in Belgravia, London. This conversation comes after she had just beaten him in his office.

This chapter looks at the challenges that have confronted people belonging to the LGBTI community in their journeys through life on the continent. It is a metaphorical exploration of internal migration from a place of fear to one where one is able to live, 'fully seen', as one truly is and not as society dictates.[5] It looks at the increased visibility of LGBTI people in both fictional literature and popular discourse. The cultural roadblocks that are put in their way are uncovered and examined. It also traces the legal journey from criminalisation for people with the same sex orientation, to erasure and invisibility for others, including transgender and intersex individuals, to limited legal recognition and protection from discrimination and violence. There is a brief detour to consider migration, and specifically, the response to asylum claims made on grounds of sexual orientation. Through an examination of fictional literature, art and legal change, the last section seeks to offer a picture of a more hopeful and less distressing future. This seems a good place to pause and rest from the journey, while recognising that there is still some way to go to change attitudes before we are able to all arrive at the end point – justice for all, not just us/justice for some.[6]

I. History, Context and Continuities

Discussing her classroom method in her sexualities course, Sylvia Tamale highlights the importance of taking an historical approach for three reasons: first, to show the impact of 'colonialism, religion and culture in shaping sexuality on the continent'. Secondly, she notes that an historical approach, 'reveals the dynamism of the phenomenon of sexuality and how it has continued to unfold over the years.' Finally, taking an historical perspective helps students to better understand contemporary 'sexual controversies, placing them in their proper contexts.'[7]

[5] Kenji Yoshino cites Donald Winnicott's typology of the 'True self' which is contrasted with the 'False self'. 'The True self is the self that gives an individual the feeling of being real, which is "more than existing; it is finding a way to exist as oneself, and to relate to objects as oneself, and to have a self into which to retreat for relaxation." … "Only the True self can be creative and only the True self can feel real." The False self in contrast, gives an individual a sense of being unreal, a sense of futility. It mediates the relationship between the True self and the world.' Yoshino also notes how, 'The False Self has one positive and very important function: to hide the True Self which it does by compliance with environmental demands.' K Yoshino, *Covering: The Hidden Assault on our Civil Rights* (New York, Random House, 2007) 185 (footnotes omitted).

[6] Charles Mills recounts one of my favourite aphorisms which he attributes to the African-American community. It can be applied to take in other communities who feel disenfranchised. 'When white people say of justice, they mean just us.' C Mills, *The Racial Contract* (Ithaca NY, Cornell University Press, 1997) epigraph.

[7] S Tamale, 'Interrogating the link between gendered sexualities, power and legal mechanisms: experiences from the lecture room' in S Tamale (ed), *African Sexualities: A Reader* (Capetown/Nairobi/Oxford, Pambazuka Press, 2011) 606, 608–9. See also, Human Rights Watch, *This Alien Legacy: The Origins of 'Sodomy' Laws in British Colonialism* (New York, Human Rights Watch, 2008).

Meanwhile, Rahul Rao has presented evidence showing that in pre-colonial Uganda, the Kabaka (ruler) of the Baganda was gay. He is said to have ordered the murder of his pages after they refused his sexual advances because they had converted to Christianity which forbade same sex relations. The Catholic Church proclaimed them martyrs. Rao explores how the commemoration of their martyrdom has conveniently excluded the history of sexuality with which they are intimately linked. He uses this partial remembrance to challenge the religious–state narrative that says homosexuality is alien to Uganda.[8]

Writing about the commemoration of the martyrs, J Osogo Ambani identifies that there was an attempt by the Ugandan President, Museveni, to 'blame' Islam and Arabs for introducing homosexuality and misleading the Kabaka and some in his court into homosexuality. Although a problematic premise, there is, within the attempt to explain-away the gay, a grudging acknowledgment of pre-colonial sexual pluralism.[9]

Charles Ngwena provides a useful roadmap for challenging the dominance of an a-historical, heteronormative narrative that has displaced and indeed rendered invisible the pluralism and heterogeneity of sexualities and identities that has always existed on the continent.[10] He attributes the enforced homogeneity to a combination of the mis-use of religion and a reclamation of a 'pure' (meaning heterosexual) African cultural heritage by politicians. Religious and traditional leaders, as well as politicians, are able to use their extraordinary influence to regulate the lives of those seen as 'dissident' or transgressive. For Ngwena these religious and 'nativist' claims are dangerous and undemocratic for, 'The narrative not only disenfranchises sexual minorities of equal citizenship but also sets them up as just targets for oppression, vilification and harm.'[11]

It is true to say that there is ample evidence to indicate that, whatever politicians or so-called cultural purists would like to claim, African societies, like

[8] R Rao, Re-membering Mwanga: same-sex intimacy, memory and belonging in post-colonial Uganda' (2015) 9 *Journal of Eastern African Studies* 1, 1–19. Discussing her novel *Kintu*, Makumbi is clear that she wanted to engage with the political amnesia and erasure of homosexuality in (pre-colonial) Ugandan society by including it. A Underwood, 'So many ways of knowing: An interview with Jennifer Nansubuga Makumbi, author of 'Kintu', *Los Angelos Review of Books*, 31 August 2017.

[9] JO Ambani, 'A Triple Heritage of Sexuality? Regulation of Sexual Orientation in Africa in Historical Perspective' in S Namwase and A Jjuuko (eds), *Protecting the Human Rights of Sexual Minorities in Contemporary Africa* (Pretoria, PULP, 2017) 14–50, 21. M Epprecht, *Hungochani: The History of a Dissident Sexuality in Southern Africa*, 2nd edn (Montreal, McGill-Queen's University Press, 2013); On Nigeria, see VO Ayeni, 'Human Rights and the Criminalisation of Same-Sex Relationships in Nigeria: A Critique of the Same-Sex Marriage (Prohibition) Act' in S Nwamase and A Jjuko (eds), (2017), ibid 203, 209–15.

[10] C Ngwena, *What is Africanness?: Contesting nativism in race, culture and sexualities* (Pretoria, PULP, 2018). See generally, 197–268.

[11] C Ngwena (2018) 201. See also A Van Klinken, *Kenyan, Christian, Queer* (Philadelphia PA, Penn Press, 2019) 4–7.

all human societies, have always had diversity in gender identities and sexual practice.[12] In Bernadine Evaristo's poetic novel, *The Emperor's Babe* set in Roman London, Zuleika, the protagonist whose parents migrated from Sudan, reminisces about how she and her friend would often spy on people having sex by, 'peeping through candle-lit shutters.'[13] This is what they saw: 'Men and women, women and women, men and men, multiples of all sorts.'[14]

It is also important to recognise that the 'Western enlightenment' on issues of sexuality is itself fairly recent. The lesbian classic, Radclyffe Hall's *The Well of Loneliness*, was labelled 'obscene, corrupt and depraved' and, following a trial, was banned in England in 1928. The defence of free speech led to a different outcome in the United States.[15]

II. On Erasure and the Demand for Visibility

In their ground-breaking first-person account interviews with queer women in Nigeria, Azeenarh Mohammed, Chitra Nagarajan and Rafeeat Aliyu identify three types of erasure. The first is 'the erasure of queer people from the discussion of their own lives.'[16] The second involves the importance of addressing historical erasure by re-writing the histories and culture of Nigeria to show that these are not new phenomena – diversity has always been there, even before European colonialism. The final erasure involves the constructed ignorance of many who deny their own experiences or who say that they do not know anyone who is queer.[17] The challenge of rendering visible that which has been hidden is apparent in their decision to use initials rather than the names of the interviewees. This is because many

[12] See for example, S Arnfred, '"African Sexuality"/Sexuality in Africa: Tales and Silences' in S Arnfred (ed), *Rethinking Sexualities in Africa* (Uppsala, Nordiska Afrikainstitutet, 2004) 59–77. M Epprecht, *Hungochani: The History of a Dissident Sexuality in Southern Africa*, 2nd edn (Montreal, McGill-Queen's University Press, 2013). Z Matebeni, S Monro and V Reddy (eds), *Queer in Africa: LGBTI Identities, Citizenship, and Activism* (Routledge, 2018). E Han and J O'Mahoney, *British Colonialism and the Criminalisation of Homosexuality: Queens, Crime and Empire* (Abingdon, Routledge, 2018).

[13] B Evaristo, *The Emperor's Babe* (London, Hamish Hamilton, 2001) 11.

[14] B Evaristo (2001) 11.

[15] D Soushami, 'Introduction' in R Hall, *The Well of Loneliness* (London, Quality Paperbacks Direct, 1998) introduced by QPD, 1998, v–xix, xiii–xi. See also British Newspaper Archive Blog, 'The Obscenity Trial of Miss Radclyffe Hall's novel, 'The Well of Loneliness – 16 November 1928' in Headlines from History, 15 November 2013 at: https://blog.britishnewspaperarchive.co.uk/2013/11/15/the-obscenity-trial-of-miss-radclyffe-halls-novel-the-well-of-loneliness-16-november-1928/. There are two reports cited *Sheffield Independent*, 17 November 1928 and *Hull Daily Mail*, 'The Banned Book. Magistrate Decides it is an Obscene Libel', *Hull Daily Mail*, 16 November 1928.

[16] A Mohammed, C Nagarajan and R Aliyu, 'Introduction' in A Mohammed, C Nagarajan and R Aliyu (eds), *She Called me Woman: Nigeria's Queer Women Speak* Out (London, Cassava Republic, 2018) 1–20.

[17] A Mohammed *et al* (2018) 1, 2.

of their interviewees would only participate on condition of anonymity. Despite this, they regard it as important to record these voices, for: 'the writing of experience and documenting of lives at least ensures that the lived experiences, if not the people of experience themselves, enter history.'[18]

In the introduction to *Safe House*, the book that she edited on creative non-fiction on the African continent, Ellah Wakatama-Allfrey notes how she invited submissions on any topic of interest to the writer, but *commissioned* pieces on LGBTI and the Ebola crisis. For Wakatama-Allfrey, the LGBTI debate 'has become a bellwether, in that expression of sexuality seems to articulate a particular tension between tradition and modernity on the African continent.'[19]

However, knowing that African societies have always had human diversity does not translate into positive lived realities for those seen as on the margins. The reality is sobering. First-person accounts of being gay such as that of Binyavanga Wainaina, or intersex, like Julius Kaggwa and Sally Gross, throw light on the physical and emotional turmoil foisted upon the authors by societal denial of difference. Equally powerful is Audrey Mbugua's account of life as a transsexual woman.[20]

III. On Intersectionality

The Committee on the Rights of Persons with Disabilities (CRPD) says that 'intersectional discrimination recognizes that individuals do not experience discrimination as members of a homogenous group, but rather, as individuals with multiple layers of identities, statuses and life circumstances.' The Committee goes on to require states to recognise 'the lived realities and experiences of heightened disadvantage of individuals caused by multiple and intersecting forms of discrimination.'[21]

In *The Lies that Bind*, on the constructions of identities in society, Kwame Appiah discusses how challenged many people feel by issues of gender and sexuality.

[18] A Mohammed *et al* (2018) 1, 7. See also Van Klinken's account of the creation of a queer anthology called *Stories of Our Lives* by a group called The Nest. A Van Klinken, *Kenyan, Christian, Queer* (Pennsylvania, Penn Press, 2019) 98 et seq. The Nest expressed its aim as including making room 'for Kenyans and Africans in that space of queerness' (at 99).

[19] E Wakatama Allfrey, 'Introduction' in E Wakatama Allfrey (ed), *Safe House: Explorations in Creative Non-Fiction* (London, Cassava Republic, 2016) 19. See also A Jama, *Being Queer and Somali. LGBT Somalis at Home and Abroad* (Oracle Releasing, 2015).

[20] B Wanaina, 'I am a homosexual, mum', *The Guardian*, London, 21 January 2014; J Kaggwa, 'Intersex: the forgotten constituency' in S Tamale (ed), *African Sexualities: A Reader* (Oxford, Pambazuka Press, 2011) 231–34; S Gross, 'The chronicle of an intersexed activist's journey' in S Tamale (ed), (2011) 235–37; A Mbugua, 'Gender dynamics: A transsexual overview' in S Tamale (ed), (2011) 238–46.

[21] CRPD, General Comment No 3 on Article 6: Women and girls with disabilities, CRPD/C/GC/3, 2 September 2016, para 16. See also CEDAW General Recommendation No 28 on State Obligations, CEDAW/C/GC/28, 16 December 2010 para 18 and CEDAW General Recommendation No 35 on gender based violence, CEDAW/C/GC/35, 14 July 2017, para 12.

This has resulted in movements that seek to address the exclusion and subordination of groups outside of the binaries of man and woman.[22] Using intersectionality, Appiah points out how differently gay men and lesbian women are treated. Clearly to both these groups one would have to add a further ground of differentiation, that of race. It is black gay men and lesbians who suffer disproportionately.[23]

The UN Race Committee enjoins us to engage intersectionality by thinking of the form of the violation, the context in which it occurs, the consequences of the violation for the victim/survivor and finally to consider the availability of remedies.[24] An example of this is provided by Siya Khumalo who presents a harrowing account of the murder of Duduzile Zozo, a black South African lesbian woman found with a toilet brush stuck in her vagina. He explains the misogynist rationale for the brutality:

> Putting a toilet brush in Zozo's vagina was her rapist's way of saying unless it was offered to hetero-patriarchy, it was no better than a dirty toilet to be cleaned, a 'drain' down which she'd flushed her obligations and so her right to protection as society's woman. Instead of using her vagina to expand the tribe, she had insisted on first experiencing it as her own sexual property to be shared at her discretion – taking other women out of the cultural system to make them *her* lovers. Who did she think she was – the founder of a new system that could only reproduce by feeding off the old one?[25]

Adriaan Van Klinken recounts a different form of gendered violence – that of procreative rape. It involved a transgender man whose mother, anxious to be a grandmother, arranged for them to have sex with a male family friend. Through this rape, they conceived a child to whom they gave birth. Van Klinken argues that while the focus has been on 'corrective rape', this 'procreative rape' is inspired,

> not by homo or transphobic motivation per se but by the socio-cultural pressure to procreate, if not voluntarily, then by force. Both forms of sexual violence, as well as the dehumanization of childless women … are of course driven by similar patriarchal and heteronormative prejudices.[26]

[22] KA Appiah, *The Lies that Bind: Rethinking Identity* (London, Profile, 2018) 11–20. See also CRPD General Comment No 3 on Women with Disabilities, CRPD/C/GC/3, 25 November 2016, paras 4(c) and 5. R Mahadew and D Raumnauth note how one of their interviewees had observed that in Mauritius, a white homosexual was more likely to be accepted than an Asian one. R Mahadew and D Raumnauth, 'A Psycho-Legal Reflection on issues Surrounding the LGBTI Community in Mauritius' in S Namwase and A Jjuko (eds), *Protecting the Human Rights of Sexual Minorities in Contemporary Africa* (Pretoria, PULP, 2017) 159, 176. See also A Van Klinken (2019), n 18 above, 20 on intersections between 'queer sexualities, Kenyan and African identities, and Christian symbols, belief, and practices.'

[23] KA Appiah (2018) 19.

[24] CERD General Comment No 25 on Gender Related Dimensions of Racial Discrimination, A/55/18. Annex V, (20 March 2000) race and gender, para 5.

[25] S Khumalo, *You have to be Gay to know God* (Cape Town, Kwela Books, 2018) 148. The Committee on the Elimination of all Forms of Discrimination against Women sanctioned South Africa for having good constitutional provisions on sexual orientation while failing to ensure that lesbian women were actually protected from violence. CEDAW/C/ZAF/CO/4, 5 April 2011, paras 39 and 40.

[26] A Van Klinken (2019), n 18 above, 136–37.

Another intersecting factor is that of age. Mohammed et al note that they tried and failed to get older queer Nigerian women to speak to them, hence their respondents are all aged under 42.[27] In her inter-generational novel, *Girl, Woman, Other*, Evaristo has two older women who are both widowed and attend church together. Gradually a friendship develops which morphs into a warm sexual relationship where they move from church to worshipping each other at home. It is heart-warming and wonderfully rendered.[28]

Barbara Wanjala, Mark Gevisser and Frankie Edozien also identify class and specifically poverty as another important intersecting factor.[29] Poor people have fewer opportunities to be private; thus they run higher risks of arrest and harassment than wealthier members of the community.[30] Poor people's access to justice and specifically their ability to pay for lawyers to help when they are arrested or harassed is also compromised. There is no guarantee of assistance even if one does make it to the police station. An example is Peter, a gay asylum seeker from Uganda, living in Kenya. He was lured to meet someone whom he thought was gay. There he was held against his will, beaten until he coughed blood and subjected to other degrading and inhuman treatment. He went to the police, who responded by shouting at his lawyer: 'You human rights organisations are helping gays!', leaving Peter further traumatised, especially when one of his assailants was released on bail and a group showed up at Peter's door.[31]

Gevisser also shows how leaving one's country to seek asylum can lead to a status decline. Furthermore, he identifies a political economy of identity, noting of his chief interviewee, Peter, the Ugandan living in Nairobi while awaiting resettlement by the UN High Commission for Refugees (UNHCR):

> Peter's homosexuality is manifestly not a strategy for getting out of poverty. But perhaps it could be said that his identity as an LGBTI – which is what he and all other refugees call themselves – is connected to the capital this label carries in a new global economy where the wealthy West values such identities and understands them as vulnerable.[32]

[27] Inter-generational change is well observed in B Evaristo, *Mr Loverman* (London, Hamish Hamilton, 2013) on the lives of two Antiguan born men who have a life-long (teens to old age) relationship starting in Antigua and continuing when they move to Britain. The marriage of one to a woman does not dim their love. The marriage to a formidable 'God fearing, church going woman' reflects societal expectations.

[28] B Evaristo, *Girl, Woman, Other* (London, Hamish Hamilton, 2019) Bunmi's story.

[29] B Wanjala, 'A Woman's Smile' in E Wakatama Allfrey (ed), *Safe House: Explorations in Creative Non-Fiction* (London, Cassava Republic, 2016) 205, 211; M Gevisser, 'Walking Girly in Nairobi' in E Wakatama Allfrey (ed) (2016) 103–25; CF Edozien, 'Forgetting Lamido' in E Wakatama Allfrey (ed), (2016), 289–307. See also RA Mahadew and DS Raumnauth (2017), n 22 above, 159, 175–76.

[30] Writing about Cameroon, Togue notes how the attitude of the President changed once members of the elite were named in media reports outing alleged homosexuals. President Biya became more vocal in his support of the right to privacy. Togue notes that the arrest and prosecution for homosexuality of 32 individuals following a raid on a nightclub had not yielded any calls for respect for privacy – quite the contrary. M Togue, 'The Status of Sexual Minority Rights in Cameroon' in S Namwase and A Jjuko (eds), *Protecting the Human Rights of Sexual Minorities in Contemporary Africa* (Pretoria, PULP, 2017) 245, 245–47, 249.

[31] M Gevisser (2016) 103, 112.

[32] M Gevisser (2016), n 29 above, 106, 117,

Edozien identifies how poverty and need may lead to transactional sex, when he reflects on how his friend, who is married to a woman, keeps a man, who works as a gardener, on the side for sex. 'I gather that he earns little and has a wife and young son. He helps Lamido out sexually, and Lamido helps him out financially.'[33] This is said after the author and his friend, Lamido, have enjoyed a threesome with said nameless gardener (the others are given pseudonyms). We are told that he is Yoruba. (Nigerians seem very keen on identification by group).

IV. Plural Identities or 'Naming'

Gevisser shows how the lumping together of all into the 'gay' category, may miss gender pluralism. In 'Walking Girly' Peter, who is awaiting resettlement by the UNHCR, has a mentor in Nairobi who tells Gevisser:

> 'Since he has come to Nairobi, he is so much more comfortable with himself. He is realising that he is not gay, but actually transgender. That is why he gets slapped so often in the streets for 'walking girly.' Peter agreed with this assessment and had even chosen a female name for himself. But this would have to wait until he is resettled in the West he told me. For now, he would have to hold his femininity in check.[34]

Meanwhile, on a visit to Senegal, Wanjala learns of the arrest of seven *goorjigeen* (Wolof for man-woman) accused of 'homosexual tendencies.' Wanjala details how the *goorjigeen* were an established part of Wolof society even before colonialism. They participated in community activities, assisted female leaders and even welcomed Senegal's first post-independence president, Senghor, to the city of St Louis. The association of the *goorjigeen* with homosexuality and the link with homosexuality and the spread of HIV have led to a new prejudice and stigmatisation.[35]

Elnathan John explores the concept of '*dan daudu*' (singular) or '*yan daudu*' (plural) amongst the Hausa of Nigeria. The meaning ascribed to their gender non-conformist behaviour (doing things done by women such as selling food in the market) leads some to consider them male homosexuals and others to call them 'transgendering men.'[36]

[33] CF Edozien (2016), n 29 above, 289, 299. See also M Gevisser (2016), n 29 above, 103, 111 about Peter, an asylum seeker in Nairobi who 'hooked up with a series of dodgy benefactors including one who pimped him.' See also E John, 'The Keepers of Secrets', in E Wakatama Allfrey, *Safe House: Explorations in Creative Non-Fiction* (London, Cassava Republic, 2016), 129–50. He meets a man called Tukur who tells him that he sells sex to other men. Indeed he says that he moved from Kano to Abuja for the express purpose of doing 'harka' male-to-male sex.

[34] M Gevisser (2016), n 29 above, 103, 109. For a definition of gender, incorporating sexual orientation and gender identity, see UN Special Rapporteur on the Protection of human rights and fundamental freedoms while countering terrorism, Martin Scheinin, *General Assembly report on a gender perspective on countering terrorism*, A/64/211, 3 August 2009: https://www2.ohchr.org/english/issues/terrorism/rapporteur/docs/A-64-211.pdf, para 20.

[35] B Wanjala (2016), n 29 above, 205, 214–15.

[36] E John (2016), n 33 above, 130, at 133 and 131–32.

While collectively these disparate people fall under the umbrella LGBTI, it is important to acknowledge that their interests do not always coalesce; nor is there agreement about strategies for challenging discrimination; nor should one expect unity of purpose or perspective from any diverse group. Van Klinken gives as examples the disagreement between the trans activist Mbugua who objected to a song billed as being about 'LGBTI struggles', which she felt annexed 'trans people into gay activism' and reinforced the 'practice of homosexualizing transgender people', which she viewed as a form of 'irresponsible activism.' There were also disagreements over a court challenge of the refusal to register the National Gay and Lesbian Human Rights Organisation as an NGO. It had as its mandate, advocacy on behalf of the LGBTI community. Mbugua thought the transgender community could 'articulate its own issues.'[37] In an earlier piece, Mbugua also addresses the tensions within the LGBTI community, noting that while LGB people have made 'significant contributions to the transgender movement … we cannot ignore the marginalisation and abuse some LGB individuals and organisations have imposed on transgender people.'[38]

V. On Fear and Curiosity

The phobia – or fear, for that is what it is – of same sex intimacy is linked in part to concern over conduct and the prurience of wanting to know what people who engage in intercourse actually *do*.[39] In her autobiography *Red Dust Road*, Scottish Jackie Kay, who was adopted by Scottish parents, recounts meeting her Nigerian biological father for the first time. She had returned to Nigeria to meet him. On telling him that she is a lesbian, he is perplexed and asks a series of questions:

> 'Oh-oh, oh-oh, oh-oh you mean you are a lesbian?' He credits the word lesbian with three syllables with emphasis on the last. *Les be an*. 'You mean you are *les be AN*?'
>
> 'Yes, that's rights. (right?) I'm a lesbian.' Despite myself, I'm agog to see how he will take this news.
>
> 'OK-OK-OK-OK, OK-OK-OK-OK' he says a string of OKs like prayer beads. Then very quickly he says, 'OK, OK. Which one of you is the man?'
>
> 'Sorry?' I say.
>
> 'I've often wondered about this' he says. 'And I have never understood. How does it work? Which one of you is the man?' He is clearly having more fun than he's had all day.

[37] A Van Klinken (2019), n 18 above, 62–64.

[38] A Mbugua (2011) 238, 343.

[39] S Tamale, 'Interrogating the link between gendered sexualities, power and legal mechanisms: experiences from the lecture room' in S Tamale (ed) (2011), n 7 above, 606, 608, 614. Writing about the United States, Yoshino notes how courts have often used civil rights laws 'to protect statuses but not behaviors, *being* but not *doing*.' Later he identifies the assimilationist model of civil rights as one that 'protects *being* a member of a group, but not *doing* things associated with that group.' K Yoshino (2007), n 5 above, 24 and 173 respectively.

> 'How is it possible for two women to have sex?' he asks me, asking me perhaps the most un-fatherly question I've ever heard.
>
> 'Neither of us is the man. It doesn't work like that.' I say, embarrassed. I down half a glass of wine. 'It's not like that.'
>
> 'So how do you have sex?' he asks. 'You can tell me now.' He leans forward.
>
> I don't believe this: now the preacher wants a sermon on lesbian sex. It is too much. You never expect to talk to your father about sex, any father, adoptive or birth, about any sex, heterosexual or lesbian. But he won't let the matter drop. He keeps on. He reaches into the depths of his imagination for one final image. 'So what do you do? You squeeze each other's titties and so on and so forth?'
>
> 'And the rest,' I say under my breath, sweating now.[40]

We learn that Kay's father doesn't mind lesbianism after all. However, he cannot abide homosexuality, especially among the clergy. It is his view that God's injunction against same-sex activity was never supposed to apply to women. He counsels his daughter to avoid men who will only give her AIDS. She is to focus on her career instead.[41]

The prurient interest of Kay's father is reflected in the Malawian case of *R v. Soko and Another*[42] where two people were charged and convicted with performing acts against the order of nature. In this context this is legalese for having sex with a person of the same sex.[43] They were reported after entering into a traditional engagement ceremony at the tourist lodge where one of them worked. Giving evidence, many of the witnesses, including the lodge owner who had attended the engagement, spoke of how they, the witnesses, had asked one to strip to see their genitals because one had acted like a woman. They also gave evidence about having sought to ascertain how the two engaged in intimacy.

Summing up, the magistrate was scathing, noting that although there was no medical or eye witness proof of anal intercourse, the engagement, photographs of the engagement, the couple's cohabitation, the gendered behaviour (with one adopting the 'female role') all pointed to the likelihood that the two had engaged in 'acts against nature' or, in the alternative, gross indecency. The prosecution called for a stiff deterrent sentence, pointing to cases where people had been sentenced to 14 years in prison. This was to protect society and to send a strong message that Malawians would not tolerate such conduct. The court agreed and convicted

[40] J Kay, *Red Dust Road: An Autobiographical Journey* (London, Picador, 2010) 104–5. In M Donkor, *Hold* (London, 4th Estate, 2018) 188, one of the two girls is horrified at the thought of what her friend Amma who has just come out as lesbian, does with her girlfriend. Van Klinken recounts a similar prurient encounter with one of the people he interviewed and who offered him accommodation. A Van Klinken (2019), n 18 above, 93.

[41] J Kay (2010) 106.

[42] *Rv Soko and Another* (Criminal Case No 359 of 2009) [2010] MWHC 2.

[43] Demone contends that Kachepa, the other defendant identified as a transgender woman while Soko, identified as male. Their assigned birth status was as men. B Demone, 'LGBTI Rights in Malawi: One Step Back, Two Steps Forward? The Case of *R v Steven Monjeza Soko and Tiwonge Chimlanaga Kachepa*' (2016) 60(3) *Journal of African Law* 365, 366.

the two of buggery and gross indecency under the Penal Code. This, despite the magistrate recording that he found the two accused eloquent, and their testimony, moving. Sentencing them to 14 years in prison each, he said that it was not only the first case of its kind, and thus to him, 'that becomes "the worst of its kind"'. He found it abhorrent that the two had not seemed ashamed. For this he thought he needed to pass a 'scaring sentence so that the public must also be protected from others who may be tempted to emulate their [horrendous] example.' The judgment was given in open court thus ensuring maximum publicity and heaping humiliation on the two accused who were 'guilty' of loving each other and seeking to honour their relationship by way of public affirmation.[44] The law criminalised both their being and their (alleged) doing.

While a combination of a visit from the UN Secretary-General, Ban Ki-Moon, cuts in aid, and international pressure, led to a Presidential pardon and their release, the damage to the LGBTI community had been done.[45] Enforced 'covering' was the order of the day.

VI. Fictional Literature

The rising demand for visibility is mirrored in fictional literature, not least Chinelo Okparanta's *Under the Udala Trees*, Elizabeth Day's *Paradise City*, Nuruddin Farah's *Hiding in Plain Sight*, Olumide Popoola's *When we Speak of Nothing*, Ellen Wiles's *The Invisible Crowd*, Udzodinma Iweala's *Speak No Evil* and Michael Donkor's *Hold* among many others.[46] Moving is Muhammad Abdelnabi's *In the Spider's Room* which seeks to tell the fictional story of men arrested following the now infamous Egyptian 'gay boat party' that led to the arrest of 52 men who had allegedly been celebrating a gay wedding on a Nile cruise. It recounts their trial and imprisonment.[47] Akwaeke Emezi's *Freshwater* lives in an in-between place of autobiographical fiction.[48]

[44] *R v Soko and Kachepa* 2010 [MWHC] 2 – not paginated. (19 May 2010). See also E Mandipa, 'The Suppression of Sexual Minority Rights: A Case Study of Zimbabwe' in S Namwase and A Jjuko (eds), *Protecting the Human Rights of Sexual Minorities in Contemporary Africa* (Pretoria, PULP, 2017) 151, 155–158.

[45] See also Human Rights Watch, 'Malawi: Arrests, Violence against LGBT people. Repeal Laws; Moratorium is not enough', Human Rights Watch, 26 October 2018.

[46] C Okparanta, *Under the Udala Trees* (London, Granta, 2015); E Day, *Paradise City* (2015); O Popoola, *When we Speak of Nothing* (London, Cassava Republic, 2017); E Wiles, *The Invisible Crowd* (London, Harper Collins, 2017); U Iweala, *Speak No Evil* (London, John Murray, 2014); M Donkor (2018), n 40 above.

[47] M Abdelnabi (translated by J Wright), *In the Spider's Room* (Cairo, Hoppoe, 2018). Human Rights Watch, *In a Time of Torture: The Assault on Justice in Egypt's Crackdown on Homosexual Conduct* (New York, Human Rights Watch, 2004).

[48] A Emezi, *Freshwater* (London, Faber and Faber, 2018). See also B Evaristo, *Girl, Woman, Other: A Novel* (London, Hamish Hamilton, 2019) – the chapter on Megan/Morgan who is the 'other' in the title. Evaristo engages a currently contentious topic with humanity and insight.

The experiences of transgender or intersex people are less frequently reflected in this literature, although this too is changing.[49] Discussing their novel *Freshwater*, author Akwaeke Emezi, self-described as a 'non-binary trans and plural person', notes that Ada, the protagonist, is (in Igbo) an *ogbanje*, or spirit child. 'She is not possessed by spirits; people think in binaries a lot, so that one thing has to be possessed by another. But with *ogbanje* these things are collapsed.' This appears to be a multi-layered metaphor, for, as the author notes, 'I describe Ada as a singular collective and plural individual. Ada is described as a "girl" but is not, actually. "She" has gender-affirming surgery and it is not said but she is trans.'[50]

Nana, the mother in Donkor's *Hold* recounts the visit of a *Kwadwo besia* (translated as an effeminate man) to the family compound to ask for change:

> I never knew anything such as this, Belinda. More than six feet and with a dress for a nightclub with sparkles, only covering his buttocks and let you see all of the big legs – and his hair? A wig like he has fetched it from the roadside. Trampled. And a massive one of these dolls strapped to his back in our normal way as if he is normal. We laughed! We laughed.[51]

Belinda, freshly arrived from Ghana and now living with Nana and her family in London, is intrigued and regretful that she had not been there to witness the spectacle. Amma, Nana's teenage daughter, who is a closeted lesbian, is discomfited.

Evaristo's prose-poem *The Emperor's Babe*, about a Sudanese refugee girl living in Roman London with her parents, reminds us that gender fluid people were always there. Zuleika the protagonist describes how she befriended Venus, 'nee Rufus', who tells Zuleika that as a child she had liked to dress up in her sister's clothes which amused her family. However, when they found out that Rufus/Venus snuck out at night to meet a local shepherd boy dressed as a girl, they had been thrown out of the family home. Aged 14 Venus found herself alone in London. There Venus worked as a rent boy near Spitalfields cemetery at night.[52]

The LGBTI literature speaks mainly of abnegation, rejection, persecution and suffering.[53] In the Caine prize award-winning short story *Jambula Tree*, Monica Arac de Nyeko writes about two girls who are friends and later lovers. They are discovered by the gossipy neighbour, leading one to be sent away to London by her father.[54]

[49] Until recently, the same could be said of the legal literature. B Deyi, 'First class Constitution, second class citizen: Exploring the adoption of the third-gender category in South Africa' in S Namwase and A Jjuko, *Protecting the Human rights of Sexual Minorities in Contemporary Africa* (Pretoria, PULP, 2017) 128–50, Deyi identifies a confusion between gender identity and sexual orientation (at 134).

[50] A Akbar, 'Akwaeke Emezi "I read everything, even the cereal box"', *The Observer*, London, 21 October 2018. A Emezi (2018), n 48 above. Emezi has also written a young adult novel exploring similar themes using a dystopian lens. A Emezi, *Pet* (London, Faber and Faber, 2019).

[51] M Donkor, *Hold* (2018), n 40 above, 58.

[52] B Evaristo, *The Emperor's Babe* (2001), n 13 above, 48.

[53] Cf B Smith, 'The Truth that Never Hurts: Black Lesbians in Fiction in the 1980s' in C Mohanty, A Russo and L Torres, *Third World Women and the Politics of Feminism* (Bloomington IN, Indiana University Press, 1991) 101–29.

[54] M Arac de Nyeko, 'Jambula Tree' in *Jambula Tree and Other Stories: The Caine Prize for African Writing, 8th Annual Collection* (London, New Internationalist, 2008) 9–19.

Ukamaka Olisakwe's short story 'This is how I remember it' traces the friendship that develops between two female university students. One confesses her erotic love for the other: 'I love you like a boy loves a girl.'[55] The friend, who had been holding her hands, dropped them and called her mad. The narrator tells us that her friend 'grew into someone else. Someone scary.'[56] Then, this interaction:

> 'You are homosexual,' you said.
> 'I am different sexual,' I whispered.
> 'What the fuck is – When did this begin?'
> Your voice, it was cold, cold, cold. I stared at my palms and the words would not come.[57]

The short story 'Sew my Mouth' by 2019 Caine Prize finalist, Cherrie Kandie, is a moving tale of the love of two women who live together in plain sight. The mother of one knows that they are intimates, but refuses to acknowledge it, causing great pain. The pain is transferred into self-harm by their daughter. Adding to the women's challenge is the male neighbour who is keen on one of them. To hide their relationship, they have to re-arrange themselves and their living arrangements (messing up the unused single bed in the second bedroom to hide the fact that they sleep together in the double bed.) It is an affecting story of the price of having to 'sew one's mouth'.[58]

Amma, in Donkor's *Hold*, is a 17-year-old lesbian girl, and although London born and privately educated, she is aware that identifying as a lesbian is likely to be perceived as a problem:

> Because Amma knew the unwieldly truth: no one likes a black girl who likes girls. Friends would wriggle: their liberalism tested by something they couldn't *quite* get on board with. Mum would die. *Ghanaofoo* would explode in a shower of Jollof.[59]

Hold traces her emotional journey, from suppression to limited sexual expression, to an attempt to date a boy to conform. The novel has Amma conducting an internal monologue, and, after she reveals her true self to her friend Belinda, a dialogue of opposites ensues. Amma's fears of rejection are confirmed, for Belinda is scandalised. Belinda loves her friend, but is clear that she cannot 'condone' or indeed understand Amma's behaviour. For Belinda it is too much for her to deal with her friend's 'homosexual lesbian problem'.[60] In her worldview, the only time that one

[55] U Olisakwe, 'This is how I remember it' in E Wakatama Allfrey, *Africa 39, New Writing from Africa South of the Sahara* (London, Bloomsbury, 2016) 250, 258.
[56] U Olisakwe (2016) 250, 258.
[57] U Olisakwe (2018) 250, 258.
[58] C Kandie, 'Sew my Mouth' in *The Caine Prize for African Writing* (London, New Internationalist, 2019) 65–80.
[59] M Donkor (2018), n 40 above, 108. See also 118–19, 173–74. Ghanaofoo are the Ghanaian community.
[60] M Donkor (2018), n 40 above, 191. Belinda cannot conceive of two girls together and cannot fathom why anyone would want to contemplate 'down there' (at. 189).

needs to engage with 'down there' is when one is menstruating. It takes a return trip to Ghana for Belinda to see that it may be more important to live an authentic life than an unhappy one that fulfils societal expectations of propriety.

Violence and exile are the leitmotif in writing about lesbian women. This can be seen in Elizabeth Day's *Paradise City* where Ugandan Beatrice, the protagonist, finds herself in London having fled her homeland after she is raped by her girlfriend's brother who finds the two women naked in bed. The police beat her and her mother calls her a 'devil-child'. The trafficker who helps her to leave and to whom she pays £21,000 after selling her inherited land, is unable to take them both at the same time. The unrealised plan is that the girlfriend will follow later.[61]

Beatrice's story reflects the charged political atmosphere that followed the tabling of the Anti-Homosexuality Bill in Uganda in 2009. It was subsequently promulgated in 2014.[62] In *Paradise City*, Beatrice observes: 'They couldn't be together in Uganda. They'd be arrested or murdered before the year was out.'[63] There is also a realisation of the pressure that the law put on all those associated with the lesbian person, so before discovery, Beatrice had been alive to the importance of not disclosing her sexuality to her mother who had been pressuring her to find a man to marry: 'The law said it was an offence not to report a gay person to the authorities if you knew they were homosexual. She didn't want to put her mother through that.'[64] In a moving passage, Day captures the cost of forcing women to hide their sexuality: 'So the lies started to accumulate, like a pile of stones that soon become a wall and then an edifice of fabricated rooms and a maze of corridors that Beatrice could no longer see her way through.'[65]

In his satire *Broken Glass* set in a Congolese bar, Mabanckou shows the impact of sexual abuse on one of the characters. After he returned home drunk one day and nearly burned the house down, his wife had falsely accused him of having abused their daughter. The police threw him in prison where he remained for two

[61] E Day (2015), n 46 above, 48–49; 162–67.

[62] However, the Anti-Homosexuality Act was successfully challenged on a procedural point (non-quorate passage) in the Supreme Court. *Oloka-Onyango & 9 Others v Attorney-General* (Constitutional Petition No. 08 of 2014) [2014] UGCC 14. See also J Oloka-Onyango, 'Debating love, human rights and identity politics in East Africa: The case of Uganda and Kenya' (2015) 15 *African Human Rights Law Journal* 28–57.

[63] E Day (2015), n 46 above, 48.

[64] E Day (2015) 291. This passage reflects a clause in the 2009 Anti-Homosexuality Bill. S Tamale, 'A human rights impact assessment of the Anti-Homosexuality Bill' (2009) 15 *East African Journal of Peace and Human Rights* 509–19. See also CEDAW Concluding Observations, Uganda, CEDAW/C/CO/UGA/7, 22 October 2010, paras 43, 44.

[65] E Day (2015), n 46 above, 291. The negative psychological impact of enforced covering or erasure is high. See M Mitchell Waldrop, 'Diversity: Pride in Science' (2014) 513 *Nature* 297–300 (18 September 2014). Moving is Khumalo's account of the shock and distress of the mother of Duduzile Zozo, who was murdered for being lesbian; '… she felt hurt because Duduzile "was not aware that her sexuality affected other people", while the family didn't have any problem with her choices. She loved herself the way she was. "I don't know what it is that disgusted them when they looked at her."' S Khumalo (2018), n 25 above, 148.

and a half years without a trial. The character, Pampers, is so called because he is rendered incontinent by being repeatedly sodomised by both prison guards and inmates while in prison.[66] Pampers, as the reader knows, is the brand name of a type of nappy or diaper. The narrator writes: 'then I got a close up of his backside, bulging with four layers of Pampers, a damp backside, bulging with flies ….'[67] While Mabanckou initially writes him as a humorous drunk, Pampers' recollection of his time in prison left me in tears. Gender based violence against men is often denied or erased. In Pampers' story, I was reminded of the many challenges facing prisoners, men who have sex with men and other groups who may be at higher risk of contracting HIV but who are denied condoms. The availability and distribution of anti-retrovirals is patchy at best.[68]

The compulsion to hide oneself is a phenomenon that impacts disproportionately on less powerful groups who feel pressured to conform to whatever the dominant norms demand. Kenji Yoshino calls this 'covering'.[69]

VII. On Covering

Research undertaken by the Human Dignity Trust shows that one of the ways that lesbian women seek to hide their sexuality and to 'blend in' is by marrying someone of the opposite sex. By 'conforming' they hope to have anonymity and to be free from prejudice and violence.[70] The pressure put on women to marry impacts even those who may be straight but agree to 'overlook' the fact that the man they are marrying is gay. These are the other covering demands placed on women in hetero-patriarchal societies that see women's roles as being limited to wife and mother. This is captured in Abdelnabi's novel *In the Spider's Room* where the gay protagonist details why Shireen, his friend and colleague, sees their pending marriage as offering her freedom:

> She would finally leave her uncle's house and be free from her mother harassing her. She would dress up as a bride and have a husband, a house and a family … Marriage for her was a necessity, a means to achieve fulfilment and a normal life now that she was over thirty and had started to put on more weight than she should. Above all, my status was an opportunity she shouldn't miss.[71]

[66] M Mabanckou (translated by H Stevenson) (2009), n 3 above, 33–34. U Iweala, 'Alain Mabanckou's Masterfully Unstructured Novel of Addiction', *The Paris Review*, 1 October 2018.

[67] M Mabanckou and H Stevenson (2009), n 3 above, 34.

[68] UN AIDS, *Update on HIV in Prisons and other Closed Settings* (Vienna, UNODC, 2017) Written by M Beg, The United Nations Standard Minimum Rules for the Treatment of Prisoners (The Nelson Mandela Rules) A/RES/70/175, 17 December 2015.

[69] K Yoshino (2011), n 5 above.

[70] Human Dignity Trust, *Breaking the Silence: Criminalisation of Lesbians and Bisexual Women and its Impacts* (London, Human Dignity Trust, 2016) 15–29.

[71] M Abdelnabi (translated by J Wright) (2018), n 47 above, 130. She doesn't know he is gay.

Gay men are also subjected to compulsory covering. In *In the Spider's Room* the putative groom also carries a weight on his shoulders; 'I felt like a calf being fattened for slaughter on the altar of its mother and society for the sake of appearances.'[72]

Similarly, the Lamido who must be forgotten in Edozien's autobiographical essay 'Forgetting Lamido', is his first true love who has, in the interim, married. However, he is happy to re-ignite their sexual relationship when they meet. Lamido is not alone. Edozien details how all the boys with whom he had relations while in boarding school have since married. He speaks to a married friend at a party who points out that while in Nigeria he tries to refrain from same-sex relations, but, on his business travels, meets other men for 'coffee and a chat.' The chapter finishes with the businessman saying that he has met a fellow married man who works in Lagos during the week before returning to his family at the weekend, and confides that the two are having a discrete relationship. Respectability is seen as important. Although Lamido's family know that he is gay, they pretend not to know, or do not engage with it. We learn that Lamido had made his *Hajj* pilgrimage to Mecca and had a lovely wedding and children and then carried on his secret life with the nameless gardener and other men, including Edozien.

This is not confined to men living in Nigeria. Edozien recounts meeting a Delta-Ibo man in a gay bar in London, they flirt, kiss and then his countryman tells him that he is preparing to return home for his wedding. African American slang terms this 'being on the down low.' Keeping up appearances and saving face are all important, even if they involve industrial strength quantities of hypocrisy. Edozien who has a cosmopolitan life moving between continents and is openly gay, shares how his family has come to accept him and concludes: 'Sharing a life with someone you don't love can't be easy.'[73]

Chinedu, the male character in Chimamanda Adichie's short story 'The Shivering', having come out to his friend Ukamaka, tells her the story of his own Lamido-type relationship while still living in Nigeria (they are now in New Jersey). In his case, his lover, Abidemi was also wealthy and controlling. He took Chinedu to a private gay bar where 'they shook hands with a former head of state.'[74] Chinedu shares the pain that followed Abidemi's engagement to a woman. While both had always understood the inevitability of marriage, Chinedu was particularly upset by Abidemi's behaviour at his engagement party and his lack of regret about his decision to marry:

> I watched him that day, the way he was with both of us there, drinking stout and making jokes about me to her and about her to me, and I knew he would go to bed and sleep

[72] M Abdelnabi (translated by J Wright) (2018) 133.

[73] CF Edozien (2016), n 29 above, 289, 301. 'Forgetting Lamido' forms the first chapter of C Edozien, *The Lives of Great Men* (London,Team Angelica, 2017) 1–17. See also A Jama (2018), n 19 above, 77–78.

[74] CN Adichie, 'The Shivering' in E Wakatama Allfrey, *Africa 39, New Writing from Africa South of the Sahara* (Bloomsbury, 2016), 1–14, 10. This reminds one of the prosecution brought against the former ceremonial President of Zimbabwe Reverend Canaan Banana for sodomy. *Banana v State* [2000] 4 LRC 621.

> well that night. If we continued, he would come to me and then go home to her and sleep well every night. I wanted him not to sleep well sometimes.[75]

Chinedu ends the relationship, angering Abidemi: 'He did not understand why I would not do what he wanted.'[76]

It is the sense of loneliness and alienation that leads Amma, in Donkor's *Hold*, to agree to go on a date with the jheri-curled 'good' Ghanaian boy. He is on course to obtain a first-class degree from the prestigious Imperial College in London and has the added advantage of being liked by her mother.[77] Sceptical, her friend Belinda challenges her on this turn. 'Amma sniffed. "I have nobody. I'm just like, this fucking half-of-a-person skulking about with absolutely no one, no hint that it might, at some point, get a tiny bit better. I'm just me. I'm only me."'[78]

In his non-fiction piece, 'The Keepers of Secrets', Elnathan John discusses how the Hausa regard homosexuality as something that you *do*, rather than something that you *are*.[79] The outcome seems to be the equivalent of the old 'don't ask, don't tell' philosophy, a form of enforced 'passing'.[80] To show respect to their families, many who sell sex to other men move to other towns where they are not known. Tukur, one of the few men prepared to admit selling sex to men, also speaks to the hypocrisy of the community and married men in particular: 'There is an alhaji in my neighbourhood in Kano who has four wives and many children and wallahi, there is no day he does not do harka with many boys.'[81]

Again Evaristo's *Emperor's Babe*, set in Roman Britain, reminds us that it was ever thus. She tells how our old friend Venus, born Rufus, is in love with a married lawyer who has six children. They are intimate but the lawyer will not take Venus out to public places for fear of discovery, 'He professes love but won't act on it.'[82]

It may well be that in societies where segregation on gender lines is the norm, intimacy with people of the same assigned gender may be the only option. Writing about the life of poor migrants in contemporary Saudi Arabia, Sulaiman Addonia's novel *Consequences of Love* identifies many examples of the workers being compelled to have sex with Saudi men. One, a waiter, confides in his Eritrean friend, who has endured the same treatment:

> I spent last night over at Fawwaz's house. His parents are not here. He told me the usual thing: 'What we are doing is *haram*. But in this country it is like we are in the biggest prison in the world, and people in prison do things to each other they wouldn't

[75] CN Adichie (2016)1, 11.
[76] CN Adichie (2016) 1,11.
[77] M Donkor (2018), n 40 above, 232.
[78] M Donkor (2018), n 40 above, 232.
[79] E John (2016), n 29 above, 129, 134–35.
[80] Again Yoshino bemoans the impact of the 'don't ask, don't tell policy' used by the US military during the Clinton presidency. He argues; 'So long as there is a *right to be* a particular kind of person I believe it logically and morally follows that there is a *right to say what one is*.', K Yoshino (2007), n 5 above, 70. The problem is that there is no right to either in the Nigerian context.
[81] E John (2016), n 29 above, 129, 135.
[82] B Evaristo (2001), n 13 above, 122.

> otherwise do.' He asked me to be his boy until he gets married. Anyway, the café will shut soon for prayer time and so he will take me on a date to the shopping mall.[83]

The story reminds one of the prosecution for murder of a Saudi Prince at the Old Bailey in London. He had beaten his servant to death. While claiming to be heterosexual, all the evidence pointed to the fact that the two had been intimates. It was clear that the servant-companion was beaten often.[84]

VIII. Religion

It is not only community peer-policing that constrains behaviour and choices, but also religion.[85] Elnathan John shows how the adoption of the Sharia Penal Code from 2000 made many *yan dauda* go underground or modify their behaviour.[86] More interesting is the use of religion as a shield. One of John's interviewees tells him that he deflects attention by ensuring that he goes to the mosque to pray five times a day, like a good Muslim should. He is also exceedingly deferential to the elders. He reasons that any allegations of homosexuality would be met with scepticism because of his pious behaviour.[87]

Edozien shares how after his first sexual experience in high school he went to confession to repent. The family priest names his 'sin' as homosexuality. He is sympathetic, but urges Edozien to stop, warning of dire consequences. However, Edozien, 'relapses' often, concluding 'No number of Hail Marys will work.'[88] The Catholic priest is positively muted compared to his colleagues on the Pentecostal wing of Christianity. In Iweala's novel *Speak No Evil*, the gay son of two Washington-based doctors is, on the advice of their Washington-based Nigerian priest, taken 'home' to Nigeria where they connect with Bishop Okereke, who comes highly recommended, and his helpers.[89] He is seen as a conversion specialist.[90] The Bishop intones:

> We ask you to banish the spirit of homosexuality and perversity from this young man, bind it and cast it out in the name of your son, Jesus Christ, Amen. Father almighty

[83] S Addonia, *The Consequences of Love* (London,Vintage, 2009) 15. See also 44, 63, 67 Forced sex is common – see p 28. *Haram* means forbidden. The justification for separating the sexes is: '*Allah* is trying to protect us for our own good.' (at p 20).

[84] Reuters, 'Saudi prince killed servant at luxury London hotel', London, 5 October 2010.

[85] Almost all the papers in S. Namwase and A. Jjuuko (eds) *Protecting the Human Rights of Sexual Minorities in Contemporary Africa* (Pretoria, PULP, 2017), make reference to the pernicious effect of religious leaders and interpretations of religious texts on social and political discourse, which leads to the ostracization of people in LGBT communities. Siya Khumalo engages the uses and misuses of religion in a bracing book, S Khumalo (2018), n 25 above. See also A Van Klinken (2019), n 18 above.

[86] E John (2016), n 33 above, 129, 136–37.

[87] E John (2016) 129, 143.

[88] CF Edozien (2016), n 29 above, 289, 293.

[89] U Iweala (2014), n 46 above, 48.

[90] Yoshino details the many ways in which society has sought 'to convert' gay people, including by the use of electro-shock therapy. K Yoshino (2007), n 5 above, 32–46.

> destroy each and every unclean thought, untoward desire and abominable noting in the corners of this young mind and heart, refill him with the love of your Word and reverence for your teachings … Return your child to the spirit of obedience to his parent so that he may hear their direction and heed their advice, the Bishop shouts.[91]

The protagonist, Niru, has already been hit by his father in frustration at the son's supposed intransigence.[92] Niru is sorry to be such a 'disappointment' and so heavy is his burden that he longs, 'to be normal, for my father to say my name with pride … for him to look at me without disgust, for me to look at him without fear.'[93]

Equally frustrated is Katula, the protagonist in Jennifer Makumbi's fictional story 'Malik's Door'. They married out of mutual need; she needed papers, Malik needed to hide his sexuality. She was not aware that he was gay when they married but soon cottons on when they start living together. Although he treats her with kindness and generosity, she becomes frustrated on his behalf and is aware of the high cost of covering. He is very pious, praying five times a day. She thinks he is trying to pray the gay away: 'She would clench her fists to stop herself from screaming *How can God create you the way you are and then say, "hmm, if you pray hard and I fancy it, I can change you?"*'[94]

Physical violence and rejection are two constant themes. Draconian is the response of many states, which label anyone who is perceived to be gay, or who seeks to assist gay people, as a terrorist or perverted and thus polluting.[95] On a familial level, Gevisser recounts how Peter, the young Ugandan awaiting his refugee status determination in Kenya, was thrown out by his father who refused to pay his fees, leaving him homeless. He finds a church boarding school that takes him in, only for his father to confront the pastors with a knife, accusing them of 'teaching his son homosexuality.'[96] Shocked, the pastors expel Peter. They are contacted on Facebook to ask about how this can be 'a Christian' response. The head pastor answers: 'We could not be with someone who was a gay person: there was a fear that he will spread it among other students.'[97]

[91] U Iweala (2014), n 46 above, 78–79. In her short story 'The Shivering' Adichie's protagonist, Ukamaka, considers this 'particularly Nigerian Pentecostal' way of praying as being unnecessarily pugilistic. CN Adichie, 'Shivering' in E Wakatama Allfrey, *Africa 39, New Writing from Africa South of the Sahara* (London, Bloomsbury, 2016), 1–14, 2. Van Klinken has a section entitled 'A queer satire of Pentecostal Demonology' in which he recounts his experiences of visiting Pentecostal churches alongside the late Wainaina's trenchant critiques of Pentecostalism's fascination with demonology. A Van Klinken (2019), n 18 above, 47–52.

[92] U Iweala (2014), n 46 above, 55.

[93] U Iweala (2014) 79.

[94] JN Makumbi, 'Malik's Door' in JN Makumbi, *Manchester Happened* (2019) 123, 139. See also C. Okparanta (2015), n 46 above, 228–229.

[95] M Scheinin, UN Special Rapporteur on Countering Terrorism, A/64/211, 2009, n 34 above, paras 27 and 36.

[96] M Gevisser (2016), n 29 above, 103, 111.

[97] M Gevisser (2016) 103, 111. In a chapter entitled 'The Church and I', Khumalo takes on scriptures that are regularly cited to justify homophobia. S Khumalo (2018), n 25 above, 150–67. Yoshino allies this thinking to seeing homosexuality as being like a 'contagion' in which homosexuals seek to 'infect' waverers. K Yoshino (2007) 45–6.

Research undertaken by Mahadew and Raumnauth highlights how even in legally tolerant countries such as Mauritius, societal opprobrium still constrains behaviour. They give examples of forced confinement of girls to keep them away from their lesbian loves, suicide of boys considered effeminate, public mocking, ostracisation and other oppressive behaviours.[98]

The fear of 'contagion' is a constant refrain of those opposed to the humanity of others. Reflecting on the 'recruitment' fears expressed by the pastor and later by the Ugandan ethics minister who argues that the lure is money, Gevisser considers that it may be easier for a parent to rationalise their child's homosexuality as being about need or greed. To accept it as something innate may lead to a crisis of faith. There is the additional fear about the future of the family bloodlines and wealth.[99]

There is another dimension to religion that is thrown up by Iweala – the dissonance between a branch of 'Western' Christianity seen as tolerant and inclusive by some, and lost and without biblical foundations by its critics. Reverend Okereke commends Niru's father for bringing him back 'home' to Nigeria. Praising the Washington-based Nigerian priest who referred him, Reverend Okereke says:

> He is right, this demon of homosexuality has become so entrenched in America that you can't really fight it there, some churches are preaching that love of any kind is good while some of them have lost their way and are appointing gays as clergy. You are right to bring him here, this is a place where the faith is strong and has not been infiltrated by the devil.[100]

This reads like a verbatim account of the exchanges that one has read about in the discussions of the Anglican church about the inclusion of gay clergy within the church's ministry.[101] African churches in Western towns and cities sometimes see themselves as the vanguards of professing and protecting the 'true' word of God, in societies that are increasingly secular (in Europe at least). Research undertaken by Moreblessing Tinarwo and Dominic Pasura shows that often Zimbabwean church-goers in London distinguished themselves from the majority population by their rejection of homosexuality, seeing it as a manifestation of the 'fall' in the Sodom and Gomorrah story in the bible.[102]

Chinelo Okparanta's 2015 novel, *Under the Udala Trees*, explores lesbian love in Nigeria. Religion, and specifically a robust, anti-homosexuality strain of Christianity, forms the leitmotif to this novel. It is shot through with the pressures of gendered cultural expectation, to marry, to conform, not to 'shame one's family' or to bring disgrace upon it. The protagonist battles with her orientation, marrying and having a child in an effort to conform. Eventually, she is no longer able to continue this duplicitous, emotionally empty life and so returns to the mother who

[98] RA Mahadew and DS Raumnauth (2017), n 22 above, 159, 167, 169–70, 173.
[99] M Gevisser (2016), n 29 above, 103, 117.
[100] U Iweala (2014), n 46 above, 72.
[101] BBC, 'Ugandan archbishop responds to Welby on anti-gay laws', BBC, 1 February, 2014.
[102] M Tinarwo and D Pasura (2014), n 159 below, 521, 537.

had insisted on marriage, but who now accepts her back with the insight: 'God, who created you, must have known what He did. Enough is enough.'[103]

Echoing this is Kaggwa's autobiographical reflection on their emotional and religious journey as a person born intersex. Kaggwa no longer prayed for deliverance:

> While I still believe in the supremacy and omnipotence of God and I still strongly subscribe to prayer, I realise that back then my belief was premised upon a false conviction that I was abnormal, haunted by generational curses, with a questionable future and in need of divine deliverance from the sins of my ancestors. I had no idea that my sexuality was simply a diversion from what was popular and furthermore that it happened more often than acknowledged.[104]

Van Klinken cautions against the presentation of the debate as being solely about repressive religions vs. secular norms of equality. He sees the two discourses as being in a symbiotic relationship. Van Klinken does not seek to downplay or scorn religion, noting that it is an important part of African public and private life. He is critical of Western queer literature, which he says seeks to downplay or diminish religion.[105] Throughout the book Van Klinken cites the work of African scholars such as Ezra Chitando and Masiiwa Gunda who argue that African culture and religious texts point to a liberatory reading which can accommodate diversity. Also cited is Cameroonian Bongmba who invokes *ubuntu* to 'interrogate discourses of othering around sexuality in Africa.'[106] He also shows how LGBTI people themselves rely on and deploy religion to buttress their claims and to provide emotional and psychological support to each other within the community. This has included forming their own inclusive religious community or church.[107] On leaving Kenya, one of his informants enjoins him to be an ambassador who gives a more nuanced picture of the lives of queer people.[108]

IX. Changing People, Changing Laws[109]

Human rights organisations and human rights committees have all worked hard to challenge and change anti-LGBTI legislation and to press for states to meet their obligations to promote and protect the rights of all people. The focus has

[103] C Okparanta (2015), n 46 above, 323.
[104] J Kaggwa (2011), n 20 above, 231, 232. See also S Khumalo (2018), n 25 above. A Van Klinken (2019), n 18 above, 129.
[105] See A Van Klinken (2019), n 18 above, generally.
[106] A Van Klinken (2019), n 18 above, 22.
[107] A Van Klinken (2019) 143–84
[108] A Van Klinken (2019) 184–87.
[109] Heading borrowed from, and used in tribute to the late Joan May, *Changing People, Changing Laws* (Gweru, Mambo Press, 1987). Remembered with affection and gratitude for helping a lost 22-year-old with her doctoral fieldwork.

been on preventing violence against LGBTI communities.[110] In its fourth General Comment, on torture, the African Commission includes sexual orientation in its protected grounds for discrimination. It explicitly addresses so called 'corrective rape' of lesbian women and enjoins states to adequately address: 'Acts of sexual violence against men and boys, persons with psychosocial disabilities, and lesbian, gay, bisexual, transgender and intersex persons.'[111] This General Comment provides further reinforcement of the Commission's Resolution 275 on 'Protection against Violence and other Human Rights Violations against Persons on the basis of their real or imputed Sexual Orientation or Gender Identity'.

The Commission has been supported by the work of novelists and other advocates. However, like all movements, there have been setbacks and resistance along the way.

In a note at the end of the *Under the Udala Trees*, the author identifies her purpose as being her attempt 'to give Nigeria's marginalized LGBTQ citizens a more powerful voice, and a place in the nation's history.'[112] Discussing the advocacy campaign of the US evangelist Scott Lively who went to Uganda to persuade the government not to 'allow' homosexuality into the country from the West, Marc Epprecht argues: 'the idea [that] "homosexuality is un-African" owes a great deal to European and North American authors and propagandists who had their own interests in promoting that sweeping generalization, regardless of what Africans themselves had to say.'[113]

Van Klinken offers the example of Tolton, an African-American gay Pentecostal preacher who said he was aligning himself with the African gay Christian movement to preach a 'radical gospel of social justice' in opposition to people like Lively and his like, who were seen as the agents of a spiritual colonising agenda which

[110] Amnesty International, *Mapping anti-gay laws in Africa* (London, Amnesty International, 31 May 2018); W Isaack, 'African Commission tackles sexual orientation, gender identity', Pambazuka News, 1 June 2017; Human Rights Watch, 'No Longer Alone: LGBT Voices from the Middle East and North Africa at: https://www.hrw.org/no-longer-alone; See also, S Namwase, A Jjuuko and I Nyarango, 'Sexual minorities' rights in Africa: What does it mean to be human; and who gets to decide?' in S Namwase and A Jjuko (eds), *Protecting the Human Rights of Sexual Minorities in Contemporary Africa* (Pretoria, PULP, 2017) 2–12, 5–9.

[111] African Commission on Human and Peoples' Rights, General Comment No 4 on the African Charter on Human and Peoples' Rights: The Right to Redress for Victims of Torture and other Cruel, Inhuman or Degrading Punishment or Treatment (Article 5), Adopted at the 21st Extra-Ordinary Session of the African Commission on Human and Peoples' Rights, held from 23 February to 4 March 2017 in Banjul, The Gambia, at: http://www.achpr.org/files/instruments/general-comment-right-to-redress/achpr_general_comment_no._4_english.pdf, paras 20 (non-discrimination) and paras 57–61 on Sex and Gender Based Violence para 58 ('corrective rape') and para 59 (other types of violence). African Commissions Resolution 275 on 'Protection against Violence and other Human Rights Violations against Persons on the basis of their real or imputed Sexual Orientation or Gender Identity' The African Commission on Human and Peoples' Rights (the African Commission), meeting at its 55th Ordinary Session held in Luanda, Angola, from 28 April to 12 May 2014: at: http://www.achpr.org/sessions/55th/resolutions/275/.

[112] C Okparanta (2015), n 46 above, Author's Note.

[113] M Epprecht, *Sexuality and Social Justice in Africa: Rethinking Homophobia and Forging Resistance* (London, ZED, 2013) 10.

was happy to challenge homosexuality, but not the capitalist framework which reinforced socio-economic inequalities. He also argued that there was a failure to tackle racism which impacted both Africans and African Americans.[114] To counter criticism that he was also an outsider, Tolton emphasised that the local leadership was in charge.[115]

It is important to acknowledge that homophobia is not the preserve of religions or the religiously observant. Nagarajan engages the fraught issue of homophobia and transphobia in the Nigerian women's rights activist community. She recounts:

> I have facilitated VAWG (anti-violence) workshops where activists have labelled lesbianism as a form of violence, spoken of homosexuality as synonymous with paedophilia and talked of the need to address 'sexual initiation practices' of 'lesbian cults'. Reports of 'lesbianism' in IDP camps are seen as symbolic of the immorality to which people have degenerated. Referral services are likely to be staffed with people of discriminatory attitudes and queer women needed to be warned to be selective about details they reveal.[116]

In Nigeria, the push for cultural-religious purification led to a demand for legal 'clarity' which resulted in the promulgation of an unnecessary law on marriage, titled Same Sex Marriage (Prohibition) Act, 2013 (SSMPA). It was not needed because marriage had always been conceived of in heterosexual terms in statute law, although customary laws of various groups had always recognised the possibility of woman to woman marriages.[117] The reach of the Act goes beyond marriage, to prohibit rights of association by banning LGBTI organisations. It also breaches rights to freedom of expression, conscience and belief.[118]

The Nigerian law, which came into force in 2014, has had a pernicious effect, with Human Rights Watch noting that the Act has led to violence and extortion against LGBTQ individuals, or those perceived to belong to this community, whether or not they do.[119] The law, which criminalises homosexuality and anyone who seeks to promote it or run an organisation which advocates for same sex rights, clearly breaches human rights norms outlawing discrimination, while eroding rights to freedom of expression and assembly, all of which are guaranteed in

[114] A Van Klinken (2019), n 18 above, 155–56.
[115] A Van Klinken (2019) 154.
[116] C Nagarajan, 'Culture/Religion/Tradition v. Modern/Secular/Foreign' (2018) 3 *Feminist Dissent* 114, 133–34. She also identifies splits on religious grounds – Muslim women advocates and Christian women advocates sometimes treat each other with suspicion. See also Zahrah Devji on exclusion of transgender people ZZ Devji, 'Forging Paths for the African Queer: Is There an "African" Mechanism for Realizing LGBTIQ Rights?' (2016) 60(3) *Journal of African Law* 343, 353.
[117] The banning of same sex marriages in states such as Kenya and Nigeria, which allow customary law woman to woman marriages throws up potential conflicts.

F Banda, 'Changing the Constitution and Challenging Attitudes: Recent Developments in Kenyan Family Law' in B Atkin (ed), *International Survey of Family law* (2014) 255–72. See also M Karethi and F Viljoen, 'An argument for the continued validity of woman to woman marriage in post-2010 Kenya' (2019) 63(3) *Journal of African Law* 303–28; VO Ayeni (2017), n 9 above, 203, 210–13.
[118] VO Ayeni (2017), n 9 above, 203, 218–32.
[119] Human Rights Watch, 'Tell me where I can be safe: The Impact of Nigeria's Same Sex Marriage (Prohibition) Act' (New York, Human Rights Watch, 2016).

Nigeria's constitution and in international and regional human rights instruments ratified by the state.[120]

In the same year that it was promulgated, there was an attempt to challenge the same-sex marriage prohibition law. In *Teriah Joseph Ebah v Federal Government of Nigeria*,[121] the plaintiff challenged the law on grounds that it breached constitutional and human rights principles in the African Charter on the right to be free from discrimination as well as the right of freedom of association. The plaintiff also invoked article 28 of the Charter, which lists duties of each individual as including the duty to show and promote mutual respect and tolerance to fellow citizens. The government argued that the applicant did not have the capacity to bring a claim on behalf of 'the gay community' in Nigeria because said community did not exist. As he had not declared his own sexuality (not surprisingly given the circumstances), he could not prove that he had any interest in the case and therefore he could not prosecute it. Onoura-Oguno criticises this narrow reading of capacity and notes that the procedural rules governing the bringing of human rights cases encourage public interest litigation. The decision thus goes against the spirit of these rules.[122]

However, echoing Sandra Burman's article 'First World Solutions for Third World Problems' where she warned about transplanting laws and policies that had worked in the West onto other soils, so too Tukur in John's non-fiction 'The Keepers of Secrets' is reticent about calling lawyers to deal with arrests. Tukur is also wary of NGOs, because he 'fears that the matter will be unduly escalated if it is treated as a human rights issue.'[123] He prefers to deal with a discretely supportive politician who can quietly use his leverage to help the *yan dauda*.

Responses to the passing of the SSMPA were not uniform. Edozien notes, 'The stunt unleashed a manhunt of suspected gays among the *hoi pololloi*. But folks of means simply retreated indoors and carried on. Or went abroad.'[124] Meanwhile Elnathan John notes that although Tukur was identified as the leader of the association of Men who have Sex with Men (MSM) and interrogated by the Department of State Security, nothing more came of it because they realised: 'that no one in the area was [concerned with] outing us as homosexuals or complaining about our existence, they did not bother us much.' He distinguishes the Hausa MSM community from the English-speaking one, noting that the Hausa community 'don't have problems [of outing].'[125] However, John does recount that there have been raids in

[120] Human Rights Watch, 'Nigeria: Anti-LGBT law Threatens Basic Rights', Abuja, 14 January 2014. See also VO Ayeni (2017), n 9 above.

[121] *Teriah Joseph Ebah v Federal Government of Nigeria (FGN)* (*Ebah's* case) SUIT FHC/ABJ/CS/197/2014.

[122] AC Onuora-Oguno, 'Protecting Same-Sex Rights in Nigeria: Case Note on *Teriah Joseph Ebah v. Federal Government of Nigeria*' in S Namwase and A Jjuko (eds), *Protecting the Human Rights of Sexual Minorities in Contemporary Africa* (Pretoria, PULP, 2017) 238–42.

[123] E John (2016), n 33 above, 129, 144. See also S Burman, 'First World Solutions for Third World Problems' in L Weitzman and M Maclean, *Economic Consequences of Divorce: International Perspectives* (Oxford, Clarendon Press, 1992) 367–80.

[124] C Edozien (2016), n 29 above, 289, 307.

[125] E John (2016), n 33 above, 129, 142.

Abuja and that a gay man was found stabbed.[126] Speaking to a law student in Kano, he learns that there have been convictions, largely of men who have propositioned 'blind' men.[127] On the effect of the 2014 Act in Kano, his interviewee tells him that 'Everyone became more cautious.'[128] There is a further, health, impact – there is reluctance to get treatment or to engage in HIV prevention activities, which has disproportionately impacted MSM.[129]

Wanjala reflects on Senegal, which outlaws 'improper acts' or acts 'against nature' which are committed by people of the same sex.[130] Clearly the intent is to target gay people. The focus on the parties being of the same sex confirms this. This interpretation is supported by the events reported by Wanjala, who interviewed Ndeye Kebe, the head of *Sourire de Femme*, an LGBTI Non-Government Organisation, who told her that they deal with the arrest of gay people who are charged with 'crimes against nature' on a monthly basis.[131] (As an aside Kebe notes that hers is the only lesbian advocacy group, while 17 other organisations focus on gay men,[132] thus further reinforcing the feminist challenge to the invisibility of women's interests, including amongst human rights advocates.)

The President of Senegal, Macky Sall, challenged President Obama's plea for human rights and compassion during the latter's visit to Senegal in 2013 noting:

> Senegal, as far as it is concerned, is a very tolerant country which does not discriminate in terms of the inalienable rights of the human being. We do not tell anybody that he will not be recruited because he is gay or he will not access a job because his sexual orientation is different. But we are still not ready to decriminalise homosexuality … It is Senegal's position, for the time being … But of course this does not mean that we are all homophobic. But the society has to absolve these issues. It has to take time to digest them, bringing pressure to bear upon them, on such issues.[133]

[126] E John (2016) 129, 143.

[127] Ayeni defines 'blind' thus '"Yan Daudu" who do not engage in homosexual sex are referred to as *mahaho* (meaning "blind men"). Those who do engage in homosexual sex refer to themselves as *masubarka* (meaning "those who do the business").' VO Ayeni (2017), n 9 above, 203, 214.

[128] E John (2016), n 33 above, 129, 148.

[129] E John (2016) 129, 145, 146. R Mahadew and D Raumnauth identify how blood donor services in Mauritius give potential donors a questionnaire to complete before accepting the donation. It asks if the person has had sex with persons of the same sex. If the answer is yes, they are refused. R Mahadew and D Raumnauth, (2017), n 22 above, 159, 166. Some other countries such as the UK and the US have restrictions (listed in the pre-donation questionnaire) on donation by men who have had sex with another man within particular time periods prior to donation, the reasoning being that such men are at higher risk of having contracted HIV than other donors. https://www.redcrossblood.org/donate-blood/how-to-donate/eligibility-requirements/eligibility-criteria-alphabetical.html (see HIV Aids) (US); https://www.blood.co.uk/who-can-give-blood/men-who-have-sex-with-men/ (UK).

[130] Wanjala cites article 319 of the Penal Code on this point. B Wanjala (2016), n 29 above, 205, 209. See also Civil Code of Ethiopia, 2004 which provides as a ground for annulling a marriage, 'error in the behaviour of the spouse who has the habit of performing sexual acts with persons of the same sex.' Revised Family Code 2004 art 13(3)(d).

[131] B Wanjala (2016), n 29 above, 205, 206, 208.

[132] B Wanjala (2016) 205, 218.

[133] B Wanjala, citing White House Press Office, 23 June 2013, at B Wanjala (2016) 205, 217. Cf R Maloney, 'Trudeau on defensive for not publicly calling out Senegal's anti-gay law', *Huffington Post*, 14 February 2020.

The argument that 'society' is not ready for or happy with a human rights issue is used to justify discrimination against women, hate speech against migrants and other 'unpopular groups'.[134] In the case of *RM v Attorney General*, the Kenyan High Court refused to make a finding of discrimination on grounds of sex in a case brought by an intersex person who had been put in a male prison where they had been harassed and humiliated. RM had also argued that the Births and Deaths Registration Act discriminated against them because it only allowed two categories: male or female but did not recognise the intersex group. They requested that the Act be amended to recognise intersex people and to register them as citizens of Kenya. This would remedy the discriminatory effect of the legislation. Furthermore, RM's attempts to marry had been frustrated because of the heteronormative requirements for penetrative sex to evidence consummation. Inability to consummate is a ground for annulling a marriage. Despite these clearly argued violations, the Kenyan High Court simply said that Kenyan society was not ready for a 'third gender' and so refused to grant relief on the claim of discrimination on grounds of sex. It did, however, allow the claim against the state for failing to protect RM from degrading and inhuman treatment in prison.[135]

In 2019 the Kenyan High Court also rejected a claim that the Penal Code which prohibited same-sex relations was a breach of privacy, equality, the right to dignity, health and non-discrimination, and thus unconstitutional. Denying the petition, the High Court noted that it was tasked with interpreting the statute in line with constitutional provisions. With this in mind the many rules of interpretation required the Court to give meaning to the words as used in the statute – these were clear and had to be given weight. They prohibited certain conduct, including same-sex relations. Despite the petitioners having expressly said that they were not asking for the recognition of same-sex marriages, the Court said recognising same-sex relationships would open the door to the recognition of same-sex marriages or cohabitation. The Court cited article 45(2) of the Constitution which provides: 'Every adult has the right to marry a person of the opposite sex, based on the free consent of the parties' and noted that this precluded the recognition of same-sex relationships. The Marriage Act 2014 also so provided in section 3(1).[136] The ban on same-sex marriage had come from the people of Kenya, who had clearly expressed their views during the nation-wide consultations that preceded the adoption of the Constitution in 2010.[137] The Court went further to say that

[134] LC Olebile, 'The Status of LGBTI rights in Botswana and its implications for social justice' in S Namwase and A Jjuko, *Protecting the Human Rights of Sexual Minorities in Contemporary Africa* (Pretoria, PULP, 2017) 190, 192–94.

[135] S.Wekesa and K Murithi, 'Intersexuals in Kenya: Case Review; *RM v. Attorney General and 4 Others* [2010] eKLR':https://www.academia.edu/9400959/INTERSEXUALS_IN_KENYA_CASE_REVIEW_R.M_v_ATTORNEY_GENERAL_and_4_others_2010_eKLR.

[136] *EG and 7 Others v Attorney General; DKM and 9 Others (interested)* n 139 below.

[137] The values argument was also raised by the Orthodox Church and the Minister of Justice, unsuccessfully in the ECtHR case of *Vallianatos and Others v Greece* (Applications No 29381/09 and 32684/09), ECtHR (Grand Chamber), 7 November 2013, paras 11 and 14.

there was not any scientific proof that LGBTIQ identity was in any way innate. It conceded that there had been an earlier Kenyan Court of Appeal case recognising LGBTI human rights defenders, but this did not mean that the recognition had to apply in every instance.[138] It was on a case-by-case basis. In this case, recognition would lead to a breach of article 45(2) of the Kenyan Constitution and was thus not permissible. While acknowledging the comparative jurisprudence that pointed to legal and social change elsewhere, the Kenyan Court noted that it was not bound to follow these global trends. Moreover, the Court noted the absence of consensus in decisions of other courts around the world. Furthermore, it noted that there had not been an example of a country with mirroring provisions to the Kenyan Penal Code. Societal reasons were again cited in defence of the prohibition.[139]

It is because of these societal justifications for on-going discrimination that UN Committees, such as the Women's Committee, call for transformative equality which requires states to act to ensure that laws are equal and that they are applied. Moreover, transformative equality requires the state to act to change attitudes. To throw our metaphorical hands up in the air and say 'what can we, the state, do? we are waiting on the people', will no longer do.[140] To buttress this, there has been a restatement of the Yogyakarta Principles+10, reiterating that LGBTI rights are human rights and not dependent on the goodwill or approval of 'society'.[141]

That said, resistance to recognition of LGBTI rights remains strong in parts of the continent. The President of Tanzania is the latest to take up the homophobic baton with relish and vitriol towards the LGBTI community.[142]

The father of the politics of state-sponsored homophobia is the former Zimbabwean President, Robert Mugabe. His views are captured in Pettina Gappah's short story *Before Tonde, After Tonde.*[143] Set in the home of a Zimbabwean family who have moved to England, the story is told by Patience, the 12-year-old sister

[138] *Non-Governmental Organizations Co-ordination Board v EG and 5 Others* [2019] eKLR (Kenya Court of Appeal): http://kenyalaw.org/caselaw/cases/view/170057/.

[139] See *EG and 7 Others v Attorney General; DKM and 9 Others (interested)* Consolidated Petitions 150 of 2016 and 234 of 2016, (High Court of Kenya), available at: http://kenyalaw.org/caselaw/cases/view/173946/, paras 402–403 (on society). Human Rights Watch, 'Kenya Upholds Archaic Anti-Homosexuality Laws: Activists plan to appeal', Human Rights Watch, 24 May 2019.

[140] R Holtmaat, Article 5 in M Freeman, C Chinkin and B Rudolph (eds), *CEDAW: A Commmentary* (Oxford. OUP, 2013) 141–67.

[141] *Yogyakarta Principles plus 10, Additional Principles and State Obligations on the Application of International Human Rights law in Relation to Sexual Orientation, Gender Identify, Gender Expression and Sex Characteristics to Complement the Yogyakarta Principles*, adopted Geneva, 10 November 2017, available at: www.yogyarkataprinciples.org.

[142] S O'Grady, 'Tanzania walked back on a claim that it was going after LGBT people. Now Amnesty says 10 men have already been arrested', *The Washington Post*, 6 November 2018. The 'walk back' came after Tanzania's second biggest aid donor, Denmark, cut its aid in protest at the homophobic and threatening comments made by the President. Associated Press, 'Denmark withholds aid to Tanzania over gay rights', 16 November, 2018, at news.24.com. In Abdelnabi's *In the Spider's Room*, the protagonist recounts how they spoke to the foreign western media as a way of getting their story out and influencing the decision of the court. M Abdelnabi (2018), n 47 above, 230.

[143] P Gappah, 'Before Tonde, After Tonde' in C Brazier (ed), *One World: A Global Anthology of Short Stories* (London, New Internationalist, 2009) 115–25.

of 17-year-old Tonde. When the story opens, Tonde has been thrown out of the family home by his angry father. At the end, Tonde returns briefly and a confrontation ensues between father and son. The rift, it turns out, has been caused by the son's homosexuality. Tonde taunts the father who tells him he does not speak to animals: 'Animals, Dhedi (daddy), animals? But you can do better than that surely. Pigs and dogs, isn't that the phrase you are looking for? Isn't that what your President calls us, pigs and dogs?'.[144]

The President is Mugabe, who developed a penchant for giving public speeches, including at funerals, on the evils of homosexuality, likening gay people to 'pigs and dogs'.[145] Ayeni cites similar animal analogies made by the Nigerian Primate of the Anglican Communion and head of the African Anglican Bishops' Group. The then President of Nigeria, President Obasanjo, described homosexuality as 'un-Biblical, un-natural, and definitely un-African.' Ayeni also documents how at the country's Universal Peer Review at the United Nations in Geneva, the Nigerian Foreign Minister denied that there were any LGBT people in Nigeria, concluding that this meant that there was no need for rights for this group, a claim that was rejected.[146]

Tonde's story, as well as Udzodinma Iweala's *Speak No Evil*[147] about the gay son of well-to-do Nigerian immigrants living in Washington, are both timely reminders that both cultural pride and prejudice are brought on the journey, including when a family migrates. In Gappah's story, Tonde reminds his father that they are no longer 'at home'. Graphically he tells him: 'This is England Dhedi, England … I can suck dick and no one cares. I can take it up the ass and no one cares. I can even get married if I want to. No. One. Cares.'[148]

When Tonde asserts that no one cares about one's sexuality, who is included in 'no one?' Is he including other members of the diaspora? Clearly their attitudes to same-sex orientation are complex and more than likely to reflect the views expressed by his father. As noted, the research shows ambivalence, if not outright hostility, to same-sex relationships, with religious leaders speaking out against adopting the 'questionable' practices of the local communities.[149] Moreover, is Tonde's assessment of England accurate? Does the state honour its promise to protect all irrespective of orientation or origin? The actions and policies of some states in the Global North seem to be at odds with their professed adherence to human rights and advocacy for same-sex rights globally.

[144] P Gappah (2009) 124.

[145] T Shoko, '"Worse than dogs and pigs?" Attitudes towards homosexual practice in Zimbabwe' (2010) 57(5) *Journal of Homosexuality* 634–49. M Epprecht, 'Black skin, "cowboy" masculinity: A genealogy of homophobia in the African nationalist movement in Zimbabwe to 1983' (2006) 7(3) *Culture, Health and Sexuality* 253–66. Typing in 'Mugabe dogs and pigs' into the google search engine yields several pages including video clips of the former President. See also C Ngwena (2018), n 10 above, 199–200 and E Lopes, 'The Legal Status of sexual minorities in Mozambique' in S Namwase and A Jjuko (eds), *Protecting the Human Rights of Sexual Minorities in Contemporary Africa* (Pretoria, PULP, 2017) 183, 187.

[146] VO Ayeni (2017), n 9 above, 203, 207.

[147] U Iweala, *Speak no Evil* (London, John Murray, 2018).

[148] P Gappah (2009), n 143 above, 125.

[149] M Tinarwo and D Pasura (2014), n 159 below, 521, 537.

X. Migration and Sexuality

A. African Homophobia Meets Western Enlightenment: A Fairytale

Speaking at the Commonwealth Heads of Government conference held in Canberra, Australia in 2011, the then Prime Minister of the United Kingdom, David Cameron, reiterated British values of tolerance and equality. He abhorred discrimination, including that based on sexual orientation, and enjoined his fellow heads of government to remove any discriminatory laws on their books. He followed this up with a threat to withhold aid, which resulted in a backlash.[150] In the previous year Cameron had said that Africans seeking refuge from persecution because of their sexual orientation should be allowed to stay in the UK.[151]

By 2018, his successor, Theresa May, had softened the hectoring tone. Also speaking at a Commonwealth Heads of Government meeting, this time hosted by the UK in London, she noted Britain's historical legacy of exporting homophobic laws around the world and hence to Commonwealth States. Nevertheless, she enjoined these now independent states to repeal these laws and to respect the rights of *all* their citizens.[152]

An exhibition on LGBTI rights at the 2014 Commonwealth Games held in Glasgow, Scotland, showed that homosexuality was criminalised in 42 out of 53 Commonwealth nations. The research showed that most of the 18 African states in the Commonwealth criminalised homosexuality. However, even in those states which permitted homosexual conduct, such as Rwanda, there were strong social taboos which led to stigmatisation and therefore silencing. South Africa, which was the first country in the world to include in section 9 of its Constitution sexual orientation as a ground on which one could not discriminate, also reports prejudice and violence against some members of the LGBTI community.[153]

[150] Agence France-Presse, 'I will never support legalizing homosexuality, Ghana's President Says', *National Post*, Accra, 2 November 2011. While threats to withhold aid may result in the result desired by the economically powerful state, the gain is temporary and usually triggers resentment, does not lead to cultural or attitudinal change and generates greater problems for the affected communities. See B Demone, 'LGBT Rights in Malawi: One Step Back, Two Steps Forward? The Case of *R v. Steven Monjeza Soko and Tiwonge Chimbalanga Kachepa*' (2016) 60(3) *Journal of African Law* 365–387. The UN Independent expert on protection against violence and discrimination based on sexual orientation and gender identity, Viti Muntarbhorn, recognises that there are sensitivities that have to be managed, and also that the national context of states is crucial. While reiterating that human rights are non-negotiable, he is alive to the importance of strategic sensitivity and of engaging all sectors. *Report of the Independent Expert on protection against violence and discrimination based on sexual orientation and gender identity*, UN A/72/172, 19 July 2017 at paras 5, 6, 8–11.

[151] M Tandeka and D Pasura (2014), n 159 below, 521, 535.

[152] P Crerar, 'Theresa May says she deeply regrets Britain's legacy of anti-gay laws', *The Guardian*, London, 17 April 2018.

[153] Equality Network, Kaleidoscope Trust, University of Glasgow Human Rights Network, *LGBTI People of the Commonwealth* (Equality Network, 2014) 9–44. See also Kaleidoscope Trust, *Speaking*

One would imagine that Britain and other Western states that advocate for recognition and protection of LGBTI human rights around the globe would be the first to welcome LGBTI people from the Commonwealth and beyond who are fleeing persecution. In practice this is not so; indeed, the reality is unedifying.[154]

In 2017, the Home Office, which is responsible for immigration and asylum policy, published a set of 'experimental' statistics. These are not definitive, but an attempt to get an idea of the volume of applications. In total 6 per cent of all claims brought cited sexual orientation or gender issues. The countries with the highest number of claims on LGBTI grounds were, in order: Pakistan, Bangladesh and Nigeria. However, the countries with the highest proportion of claims using orientation as the chief ground for claiming asylum were Uganda (67 per cent), Cameroon (38 per cent) and Tanzania (18 per cent). Ugandans were most likely to be successful in both initial claims and on appeal.[155] The high rate of success of Ugandans can be linked to the passing by the Ugandan government of the draconian Anti-Homosexuality Law of 2014.[156]

In writing its country guidance, the Home Office scrupulously goes over the guidance issued by the UNHCR and also considers the country reports issued by other governments as well as NGO accounts, including from LGBTI advocacy groups such as ILGA.[157] While this thoroughness is welcome, it is not always applied consistently, hence the high success rate of cases initially denied when taken to appeal. It is also worth noting that until 2008, the Home Office was more likely than not to refuse to grant an orientation-based asylum claim.[158]

It is worth noting that well-publicised state homophobia will not necessarily result in a positive hearing. Tinarwo and Pasura identify two decisions on Zimbabweans claiming asylum on the basis of persecution because of their orientation.[159] In 2009, a lesbian woman was denied asylum because while she

Out (London, Kaleidoscope Trust, 2013); Human Dignity Trust, *The Criminalisation of Consensual Same-Sex Sexual Relations Across the Commonwealth-Developments and Opportunities* (London, Human Dignity Trust, 2015).

[154] N Duffy, 'The UK has rejected thousands of gay asylum seekers', *Pink News*, 30 November 2017. This despite the guidance provided by the UNHCR: UN High Commissioner for Refugees (UNHCR), *Guidelines on International Protection No 9: Claims to Refugee Status based on Sexual Orientation and/or Gender Identity within the context of Article 1A(2) of the 1951 Convention and/or its 1967 Protocol relating to the Status of Refugees*, 23 October 2012, HCR/GIP/12/01.

[155] Home Office, *Asylum claims on the basis of sexual orientation: Experimental Statistics* (London, Home Office, 2017).

[156] *Oloka-Onyango & 9 Others v. Attorney General* [2014] UGCC 14, which invalidated the law due to it having been passed when Parliament was not quorate.

[157] Home Office, Country Policy and Information Note: Uganda Sexual Orientation and Gender Identity and Expression (London, Home Office, 2019), available at: https://assets.publishing.service.gov.uk/government/uploads/system/uploads/attachment_data/file/792036/CPIN_Uganda_SOGIE_EXT_April_2019.pdf. (London, Home Office, 2016 updated 2019). Hereafter cited as Home Office Uganda (2019).

[158] 'In the country guidance case of JM (homosexuality risk) Uganda CG [2008] UKAIT 00065 (11 June 2008), heard 30 November 2007, the Asylum and Immigration Tribunal found that in general the evidence did not establish that there was 'persecution of homosexuality' (paragraph 171).' Home Office -Uganda (2017) para 2.3.18.

[159] MT Tinarwo and D Pasura, 'Negotiating and Contesting Gendered and Sexual Identities in the Zimbabwean Diaspora' (2014) 40 *Journal of Southern African Studies* 521, 536.

might be ostracised by her family 'this would not constitute persecution'. It further noted that: 'there is a homosexual scene in Zimbabwe, especially in urban areas.' However, by 2014, the Upper Tribunal noted that there was a high risk that unsuccessful asylum applicants would be at risk if returned to Zimbabwe. They reiterated the standard line (tribunal and Home Office), that each case would have to be evaluated on its facts.

It is this lack of consistency that has been the cause of much of the criticism of decision-making in asylum cases. As noted earlier, the default position of the Home Office seems to be 'no' and evidence provided by those in the system, as well as independent research, points to a culture of scepticism and disbelief of the asylum seeker.[160] The evidentiary hurdles that are put in the way of a claimant are high. If coming from a place where same-sex conduct is banned, it is unlikely that one would have kept detailed photographic or written evidence in the way of cards or letters. Similarly, the fear of discovery would also militate against putting one's life on social media or indeed exchanging intimate texts, emails or personal messages. Without this 'concrete' evidence, it becomes a matter of credibility – with the Home Office holding all the cards.

Stereotypes of what is 'normal' or acceptable within the community from which the claimant comes abound, as do questions about what 'evasive action' the claimant took to avoid detection either by relocating internally or behaving differently, in effect, hiding one's true identity or 'covering'.[161] Sometimes psychiatric tests are used to disprove the claim that the person is gay.[162] If navigating this bureaucratic nightmare is difficult, it is made more so by the lack of legal aid and other sources of information to guide asylum seekers who now sometimes find themselves in detention. The organisations able to offer support are under enormous strain and cannot cope with the demand for their help and intervention.

B. On 'Playing the 'Gay' Card'

It is sometimes asserted that once word gets out that 'papers' can be obtained by claiming to be a member of a persecuted group under the 'social group' ground in the Refugee Convention, 1951, there is some abuse, with people claiming to be gay or lesbian when they are not.[163] Gevisser's account of LGBTI Ugandan asylum

[160] Jenni Millbank, 'From Discretion to Disbelief: Recent Trends in Refugee Determinations on the Basis of Sexual Orientation in Australia and the United Kingdom' (2009) 13(2/3) *International Journal of Human Rights* 2–4.

[161] K Yoshino (2007), n 5 above.

[162] A-M Konsta, 'Is there a right to human dignity? The Example of the Right to Education of Refugees' (2019) 21 *European Journal of Migration and the Law* 261, 276–78, examining European case law on the evidence that national authorities have sought in European states.

[163] M Tinarwo and D Pasura (2014), n 159 above, 521, 536. See also T Batchelor, '"Guilty until proved Innocent": The trial of LGBT Asylum Seekers' Detained in the UK', *The New Statesman*, London, 10 March 2015.

seekers living in Nairobi while awaiting resettlement by the UNHCR provides many examples of accusations of 'playing the gay card' as a means to get to the West. 'Even Nairobi's own LGBTI community viewed them with suspicion: one Kenyan friend referred to them contemptuously as "professional gay-fugees."'[164] Here one is again reminded of the Robert Mnookin and Lewis Kornhauser thesis on 'bargaining in the shadow of the law': that being recognised as gay gives one more bargaining endowments that one can leverage to one's advantage. The claimant fashions their narrative in response to the shadow cast by the law – in this case the decision-maker sees being gay as a form of persecution that requires quick evacuation to a place of safety. 'Cashing in' your endowments gets you a seat on the plane.[165]

Gevisser identifies two 'pull factors' to choosing the ground of social origin into which LGBTI claims generally fall as the basis for seeking asylum: the first being the fast-tracking of gay applications for resettlement and the other being the payment of stipends to gay asylum seekers to enable them to live anonymously in Nairobi. The numbers applying went from 13 in December 2013, to 500 in 2015. The UNHCR and its partners estimated that at least 100 of these were fraudulent, and indeed some traffickers were recommending 'acting gay' as a means of migration. The result was a reversal of the fast-track procedure.[166]

One of the two main characters in Wiles's *Invisible Crowd*, Gebre, is gay. He finds himself in detention and facing deportation after being caught stealing food because he was hungry and did not have any money. Wiles gives a detailed account of both the asylum application process and the interview.

At the interview, Gebre details the torture that he endured at the hands of the Eritrean regime. He also reveals that he was sexually assaulted by the prison guards who discovered that he was gay. Rather than follow the Home Office and UNHCR guidelines which say that a person can rely on more than one ground to claim asylum, the interviewer responds incredulously: '"So now you are *gay* as well?" And laughed.' Relying on the protection that he has heard is given to gay people in Britain, Gebre decides to open up about his sexuality, only to be met with: '*And* you've been *sexually abused*? Sounds to me like a convenient, erotic little story you have come up with for this interview! Right?'[167] The interview proceeds on that sceptical note with the interviewer asking wholly unjustified questions about how Gebre enjoyed sex. Again, the disbelief creeps in, 'Well, this seems like a neat way to add a bonus human rights layer to your asylum claim. Did your lawyer tell you to say this?' They then move on to religion and to Gebre's disclosure that he is an Orthodox Christian, the interviewer asks; 'So how can you justify being a homosexual? The Bible says it is a sin, correct? Orthodox Christians are very strict about that sort of thing.' By now Gebre realises that the interview has taken a turn. The interviewer continues: 'So

[164] M Gevisser (2016), n 29 above, 103, 107.

[165] RH Mnookin and L Kornhauser, 'Bargaining in the Shadow of the Law: The Case of Divorce' (1979) 88 *Yale Law Journal* 950–97.

[166] M Gevisser (2016), n 29 above, 103, 105–6.

[167] E Wiles (2017), n 46 above, 237.

how am I supposed to believe that you defied your entire culture and religion to have all this twisted gay sex you are now claiming you had?' Wryly Gebre muses: 'He had not even got onto asking why I left Eritrea yet.'[168]

While this is a fictional account, it bears going into in detail, as it reflects much of the research and first-hand accounts of people who have claimed asylum because of their orientation. It also highlights that, however detailed guidelines or legal protections on processing asylum claims may be, those in charge can and often do, ignore them.[169] The novel also follows the process for Yonas, the second Eritrean. He too is initially denied asylum. His decision letter from the Home Office bears all the hallmarks of having been cut and pasted – another criticism made of the Home Office's rejection letter.[170] Yonas's appeal hearing highlights the inequality of arms between the inexperienced barrister representing Yonas, and the more experienced Home Office presenting officer, both appearing before a jaded judge.[171]

The demand to 'cover' is one that was addressed by the Supreme Court in the case of *HJ (Iran) and HT (Cameroon) v Secretary of State for the Home Department*.[172] This was an appeal brought by two gay men, one from Iran and the other from Cameroon. They had been denied asylum sought on the ground of persecution because of social origin. The reasons given amounted to an insistence that they could return to their countries of origin if they agreed to cover, or, in Home Office parlance 'to be discreet'.[173] However, the Supreme Court found for the men, noting that it was unreasonable to expect a person to live a life of self-suppression. It also found that re-location – that is internal movement to another part of the country to avoid persecution – was not an option.

Despite the *HJ* case, it is worth noting that the UK country advice for Uganda still states:

> LGBT persons who live discreetly for fear of persecution cannot be said to have a real choice and they are likely to have a well-founded fear of persecution. However, LGBT persons who choose to conceal their sexuality or gender identity because of social or family pressures or for cultural or religious reasons of their own choosing may not have a well-founded fear of persecution.[174]

[168] E Wiles (2017), n 46 above, 238.

[169] Refworld, the UNHCR database, has a Sexual and Gender Orientation section (SOGI) which is replete with its guidelines, national guidelines, guidelines drawn up by civil society organisations and case law from around the world. It is therefore not a lack of information that leads to poor decision making. UNHCR Refworld 'Sexual Orientation and Gender Identity' at: www.refworld.org/sogi.html.

[170] The novel reproduces a prototype rejection letter for Yonas: E Wiles (2017) at 249–53. Earlier his lawyer had decided not to tell him that 90% of asylum applications were refused at the first instance and the majority also failed on appeal. She had mused about the difficulties that were posed by the requirements for credibility when one did not have documents to prove one's story. Wiles (2017), n 46 above, 156.

[171] E Wiles (2017), n 46 above, 315–19.

[172] *HJ (Iran) and HT (Cameroon) v SSHD* [2010] UKSC 31. See also UK Lesbian & Gay Immigration Group, 'Applying *HJ (Iran) and HT (Cameroon) to Asylum Claims Based on Sexual Orientation* (2018) at: https://uklgig.org.uk/wp-content/uploads/2018/06/UKLGIG-on-HJ-Iran.pdf. See also K Yoshino (2007), n 5 above, 101.

[173] UNHCR Sexual Orientation Guidelines (2012) paras 30–33.

[174] Home Office Uganda Guidance (2017) para 3.1.2. (policy summary).

The distinction between discreet living and concealment is a fine and, one may argue, imperceptible one.[175] Both the Supreme Court in *HJ* and the UNHCR confirm that:

> A proper analysis as to whether a LGBTI applicant is a refugee under the 1951 Convention needs to start from the premise that applicants are entitled to live in a society as who they are and need not hide that.[176]

However, highlighting the threat faced by gay people is the advice given to gay Ugandan asylum seekers living in Kenya, which shows that there are times when even the UNHCR does not follow its own Guidelines. Gevisser notes how, in Nairobi, Peter and his friends had been told by the UNHCR: 'to act in an inconspicuous and discreet manner for their own security … It is therefore of utmost importance that applicants keep a low profile.' For Peter, this was a challenge for, '… nature obeys no law.'[177] The UNHCR prescribes covering to save oneself from harm.

In the penultimate section, I consider the advances that have been made and suggest that while there is still some way to go, there are signs that point to a hopeful future.

XI. Reasons to be Hopeful

While societies the world over have tried very hard to render LGBTIQ people invisible or to compel covering, change is slowly underway. Van Klinken highlights the use of 'artivism' and identifies how music videos showing same-sex love have been used to proclaim the existence of gay love. He also speaks of storytelling and the documenting of life stories as both celebration and resistance.[178] Manifestations of the growing confidence of the LGBTI community and their allies can be seen in the increase in literature and in case law fighting for legal rights as well as the right to live as their 'true selves', not their compromised and cowed 'false selves'. This is captured in the African LGBTI Declaration adopted in Kenya in 2010.[179]

In 2018/19 the Kenyan government found itself in a bind – it had banned the 'lesbian' film *Rafiki* 'due to its homosexual theme and clear intent to promote lesbianism in Kenya contrary to the law and dominant values of the Kenyans'.[180]

[175] *HJ (Iran) and HT (Cameroon) v. SSHD* [2010] UKSC 31, at para 63. See also, *LC (Albania) v SSHD* [2017] EWCA Civ 351. https://uklgig.org.uk/wp-content/uploads/2018/06/UKLGIG-on-HJ-Iran.pdf. See in particular the Recommendations, specifically A enjoining the Home Office to update its policies and country guidance at p. 17.

[176] UNHCR Guidelines, 2012, para 12.

[177] M Gevisser (2016), n 29 above, 103, 109.

[178] A Van Klinken (2019), n 18 above, 16–18, 57–92. See also the epigraphs to the book.

[179] African LGBTI Declaration, Kenya, Nairobi, 18 April 2018 reproduced in S Tamale (ed) (2011) 182.

[180] G Mumford, 'Rafiki review – ground breaking lesbian romance aims to change Kenyan hearts and minds', *The Guardian*, 9 May 2018. W Kahiu, *Rafiki*, released 23 September 2018, Kenya.

But then the film was nominated for an Oscar, so was allowed to be shown briefly because a showing in the home country was a requirement of the Oscar nomination.[181] While not happy with the content, the Kenyan judge who heard the challenge to the ban understood the historic significance of Kenya's first Oscar film nomination. He allowed it to be shown with some stipulations. The film, which is based on de Nyeko's Caine prize-winning short story 'Jambula Tree',[182] discussed earlier, was the first Kenyan film to show at Cannes Film Festival.

Nuruddin Farah's *Hiding in Plain Sight* is a good literary example of the attitudinal transition underway in some quarters. After a father is killed in Mogadishu, his Italian-Somali sister, Bella, returns from Italy to look after his two teenage children who are living in Nairobi. Their mother, Valerie, left many years ago to live with her (Ugandan-Indian) female lover, Padmini. There is a custody tussle between mother and aunt. The title of the book, *Hiding in Plain Sight*, comes up in conversation between the two lovers preparing to meet Bella. They muse on Bella's sexual preferences:

> 'Some women who hide in plain sight?' says Valerie.
> 'You reckon she is in the closet?' says Padmini.[183]

Later in the book Dahaba, the daughter, comes downstairs to find her mother and Padmini making love. She is discomfited by the idea of the two women together.[184] She tells her brother, Salif, who says he already knew because a cousin had sent him a YouTube video of his mother and Padmini together.

There follows a discussion between brother and sister on the mother's breach of etiquette, with both agreeing that the mother's partner should have slept on the couch made up for her and that the couple should have waited until they had their own private hotel room. Dahaba then says: 'After they went to jail for it, you would think that they would be more careful next time.'[185] The children say it is not their mother's lesbianism that they object to, but agree that they have been shocked by 'seeing them and all.'[186] The aunt intervenes:

> In much of Africa, being gay is considered an abomination. I hope you are more advanced in your own views and are more tolerant of other people's choices. What people do and who they do it with is their own private affair.[187]

Salif reiterates that he does not mind that his mother is lesbian, but does mind that she has lied by describing her partner as being akin to her sister. Dahaba also says

[181] Reuters, 'Director of banned Kenyan film about lesbian romance sues government', *The Guardian*, 14 September 2018. *NBC News*, 'Kenya lifts ban on lesbian film, making it eligible for Oscars.', 21 September 2018.
[182] M de Nyeko (2008), n 54 above.
[183] N Farah, *Hiding in Plain Sight* (New York, Riverhead Books, 2014) 123.
[184] N Farah (2014), n 183 above, 190–91.
[185] N Farah (2014) 193.
[186] N Farah (2014) 193.
[187] N Farah (2014) 194.

she does not mind, but then sounds hesitant, leading Salif to ask his aunt's opinion, to which Dahaba notes that their aunt lives in Europe where being gay is accepted.[188] The aunt reiterates her argument about personal freedom before saying: 'We Africans lag behind the rest of the world, and we waste valuable energy putting our noses in people's private lives. We have no business there.'[189] Salif wonders whether she has always believed that or that is a view she has come to as a result of living in Europe. Bella replies that she has always appreciated difference. Dahaba wonders why most people do not appear to share this perspective, to which her aunt replies:

> 'We are ill informed about the world, ill-educated, intolerant of the views of others when they do not agree with ours,' Bella says. 'We are undemocratic, just like our governments. But sex is a personal matter that our societies and governments have no business with.'[190]

The children are said to be very proud of her statement, with the girl looking like she might applaud.[191] In this somewhat didactic account, the focus on individual happiness over communal and familial responsibility may not sit well with all. Privacy and family life may be linked in European human rights, but may not resonate elsewhere. Nevertheless, Farah, an influential and much-read novelist and scholar, does engage the reader in a novel about the lives and choices of ordinary people – well, upper middle class elites.

Pasura's research on Zimbabweans living in England indicates that attitudes to sexual diversity are informed by the attitudes of those around them. While there may still be disapproval of homosexuality as 'wrong', usually grounded in religious belief, there is greater acceptance of these differences. Indeed, the research indicates that sexual minorities may be more willing to live their lives more freely and openly than if they had remained at home.[192]

Popoola's novel *When we Speak of Nothing* speaks of the alienation and exclusion of black youth in London. Karl, one of the protagonists, moves to Nigeria to get away from riots and disruption in London. There follows a meeting and a burgeoning friendship with 18-year-old Janoma. They are clearly drawn to each other, but first there is something that Karl needs to tell her:

> 'I'm trans.' Karl paused. 'Transgender. Some say I was born a girl. I don't agree with that, but anyway, it's complicated.'
> 'And?' She kept looking.
> 'So?'
> 'What's your real question?'
> 'Are you still interested?'[193]

[188] N Farah (2014) 194.
[189] N Farah (2014) 194–95.
[190] N Farah (2014) 195.
[191] N Farah (2014) 195.
[192] M Tinarwo and D Pasura, 2014, n 159 above 521, 537.
[193] O Popoola (2017), n 46 above 172.

They both are. The two continue their relationship after Karl returns to London. She comes to visit London and meets Karl's mother and friends. Their relationship continues and plans are made for Karl to move to Nigeria. Similarly, in Hamid's *Exit West* the transition from heterosexual marriage to a lesbian relationship is seamless. Evaristo's Booker Prize-winning *Girl, Woman, Other* explores the gamut of sexualities without being 'preachy'.[194] Two older women (one widowed) who meet at church form a firm friendship, which eventually evolves into an intimate one, enabling them to sing praises and make sweet music together. The 'other' character described in the book's title, is transgender. Their interaction with their older grandmother and society is described in a very human way, reflecting both the acceptance and resistance of sections of society to difference. It is a prescient piece of work.

The lesbian couple in Cherrie Kandie's 'Sew your Mouth' are parted by the mental illness and self-harm of one, Magda, but come together at the end:

> It is the way Magda squeezes my hand under tables when I have sewn my mouth so tightly that I can hardly breathe. It is the certainty that is the great big engine that is her heart: how it runs on butter and Baringo honey, how it warms me, melting open my stitches.[195]

The inter-generational changes in attitude are also captured in Okparanta's *Under the Udala Trees*. The protagonist finally reveals to her 14-year-old daughter that her female friend is more than 'just a friend': 'It turned out to be an underwhelming kind of revelation, almost a non-revelation, because unbeknownst to me, the girl already knew. And somehow, it did not matter to her.'[196] In this the epilogue, her lover muses about a place (different places in Nigeria) where men and women can love each other, irrespective of gender, where different ethnicities can live together peaceably. It is Lennon-esque in its invocation of an imagined place of peaceable co-existence, love and harmony.[197] Alive to the role that religion has played in denying them love until the very end, the protagonist meditates on a biblical verse found in the book of Hebrews, Chapter eight – where God makes a new covenant with the houses of Israel and Judah – and notes: 'This, it seem to me, is the lesson of the Bible: this affirmation of the importance of reflection, and of revision, enough revision to do away with tired, old, even faulty laws.'[198]

The first-person accounts and the desire of writers such as Frankie Edozien and Afdhere Jama, from Nigeria and Somalia respectively, to document their openly gay and happy lives are powerful ripostes to those who would seek to silence them

[194] B Evaristo (2019).
[195] C Kandie (2019), n 58 above, 65, 79.
[196] C Okparanta (2015), n 46 above, 320.
[197] The epilogue echoes John Lennon's song 'Imagine'. Lyrics at http://www.genius.com. The lyrics are also used in a picture book for children aged 3–5, John Lennon, Yoko Ono Lennon, Amnesty International (illustrated by Jean Jullien), *Imagine* (London, Frances Lincoln Children's Books with Amnesty International, 2017).
[198] C Okparanta (2015), n 46 above, 321. See also 322.

or to keep them in the closet.[199] The love and support of their families is also another reason to be hopeful. It is true that their stories also reflect the ongoing self – and societal – repression that keeps others closeted, but their testimony and their lives are testament to the changes underway. With the novels of their peers, one is left optimistic that the legacy of James Baldwin's *Giovanni's Room* and his own advocacy, by example, lives on.[200]

These changes can be seen in case law. While in *RM v Attorney General*[201] the Kenyan Court of Appeal refused to recognise the rights of intersexual people as a group that were discriminated against (including by not being able to register births and marriages because the statutes only recognised male and female categories), the situation is improving. In the *Baby 'A'* case in 2014, the court was prepared to recognise the right of a baby born with intersex features to recognition.[202]

The courts in Botswana have held that a transgender person should be given the right to have identity papers issued in their chosen gender. The ban on registering LGBTI organisations was also overthrown.[203] The importance of recognising these organisations is not only linked to their freedom of association and of speech, but also speaks to their ability to fundraise. To be able to raise donor funds, one must be able to prove that the organisation is a registered civil society organisation. The denial of registration impacts on the ability of the group to do its work.[204]

In the landmark decision of *Letsweletese Motshidiemang v Attorney General*[205] in June 2019, the Botswana High Court ruled that the provisions in the Penal Code that prohibited consensual same-sex relations were unconstitutional. Specifically, the Court agreed with the petitioners that the Penal Code was a colonial relic imposed on the country by the British, who imposed the transplanted article 377 of the Indian Penal Code into Botswana law. The Penal Code breached Constitutional provisions on equality, non-discrimination, dignity and privacy.[206] Discussing the case, Frans Viljoen notes the importance of civil society in seeking to 'mainstream' LGBTI rights within society; the importance of influential advocates such as the former High Court judge Unity Dow, who herself made history when she challenged discriminatory nationality laws. Furthermore, Viljoen identifies the

[199] C Edozien (2016), n 29 above; A Jama (2018), n 19 above.

[200] AJ Williams, 'James Baldwin's Black Queer Legacy', 23 March 2017, at: www.electric literature.com.

[201] *RM v Attorney General* [2010] eKLR paras,118, 130. S Wekesa and K Murithi, 'Intersexuals in Kenya: Case Review; *RM v Attorney General and 4 Others* [2010] eKLR', available at: https://www.academia.edu/9400959/INTERSEXUALS_IN_KENYA_CASE_REVIEW_R.M_v_ATTORNEY_GENERAL_and_4_others_2010_eKLR.

[202] *Baby 'A' (Suing through the Mother EA) & another v Attorney General & 6 Others* [2014] eKLR.

[203] G Reid, 'Victory for Gender Identity in Botswana: Country's High Court Rules in Favour of Transgender Man,' Human Rights Watch, 3 October 2017.

[204] M Tabengwa, 'Dispatches: Judgment Day Looms for Botswana LGBT Group', Human Rights Watch, 13 November 2014.

[205] *Letsweletse Motshidiemang v Attorney General* MAHGB-000591-16.

[206] For a short case commentary, see P de Vos, 'A Brilliant Court Victory for LGBTI people in Botswana Lays the Ground for Further Legal Activism', *Constitutionally Speaking*, 12 June 2019 at: http://www.constitutionallyspeaking.co.za.

transformative equality stance taken by the Botswana government which had not only repealed discriminatory laws, including in employment, but also emphasised the dignity of people belonging to LGBTI communities.[207]

Increasingly one sees a breakdown in consensus about whether it is 'un-African' to support LGBTI rights. This is best exemplified by the rebuke issued to Egypt when it sought to speak on behalf of the Africa Group in denouncing the mandate and appointment of the UN Expert on LGBTI.[208] The reissued Yogyakarta Principles plus 10, restating the inclusion of LGBTI persons within the protections offered by human rights norms, includes seven Africans amongst its 33 signatories.[209] Some countries have moved to repeal their discriminatory laws, while scientists have published research refuting the idea that homosexuality is alien to Africans.[210]

XII. Conclusion

This chapter began by looking at fictional stereotypes of gay people.

While it is true that many of the laws that prop up anti-gay prejudice are colonial in origin (British especially),[211] the blame for the rise in homophobic rhetoric can no longer be laid entirely on colonialism, but must factor in sheer political expediency and the adoption of alien religions like Christianity and Islam while negating African cosmologies. The current trend for silencing or rendering invisible these histories of diversity is part of a conscious socio-cultural and political attempt to 'reinvent' the African narrative, 'untainted' by the stain of 'Western debauchery'. This myth-making has not gone unchallenged.

The chapter then considered the histories of sexuality and the pluralities within the term LGBTI. The challenges to being in the LGBTI community and the resulting enforced 'covering' were explored. We learned that far from being received sympathetically, those seeking asylum on grounds of persecution because of their sexual orientation were often met with scepticism and suspicion. The chapter concluded by seeing positive shoots in case law. Through the imaginations of extraordinary novelists and short story writers we were asked to imagine an equal

[207] F Viljoen, 'Botswana court ruling is a ray of hope for LGBT people across Africa' in *The Conversation*, 12 June 2019. The *Dow* nationality case is *Attorney-General of Botswana v Unity Dow* [1992] LRC (Const) 623.

[208] G Reid, 'Egypt Doesn't Speak for Africa on LGBT Issues', Human Rights Watch, 1 November 2017. Egypt misrepresents the African position, but also neglects its own more tolerant history. See S El Feki, *Sex and the Citadel: Intimate Life in a Changing Arab World* (Chatto and Windus, 2013). Above all, read M Abdelnabi (2018), n 47 above.

[209] The Yogyakarta Principle plus 10 (2017) at http://www.yogyarkartaprinciples.org.

[210] L Nordling, 'African academics challenge homophobic laws' 522 *Nature* 135–36 (11 June 2015). See also the editorial on 'Sex and the Law' in the same volume at p 127.

[211] Human Rights Watch, *This Alien Legacy: The Origins of 'Sodomy' Laws in British Colonialism* (New York, Human Rights Watch, 2008).

future for all. Ngwenya asks us to conceive of an Africanness that is inclusive; which is one that:

> should seek constantly to disrupt the discourse of sexual essentialism in order to secure a heterogeneous sexual domain of non-exhaustive benign variations. Sexuality should be understood not for its sameness, but for its relational and non-hierarchical difference and capacity to evolve and assume newer forms. Accepting this argument first requires accepting a democratic understanding of equality which cannot be achieved without a concern for plurality in which claimants at the equality table are able to articulate different needs without being required to assimilate to a normalised paradigm, precisely because normalisation without equal participation lacks democratic legitimacy as it speaks only to hegemonic or structural power. It side-steps the 'human condition.'[212]

We now move on to look at the lives of children.

[212] C Ngwena (2018), n 10 above, 208.

6

Children in Literature

Like many before me, it was reading Harper Lee's *To Kill a Mockingbird* at the age of 14 that opened my eyes to the possibility of law as a useful career. Until then, the law dream had been my father's. For a child who had been born in the apartheid era, the story of racial injustice and the redemption, through law, of the Black man who was unjustly accused, spoke to me in a profound and hope-giving way. Justice was possible and law was one of the means by which one could achieve it. Well, of late the world has not been kind to its children.

This last substantive chapter explores the ways in which we have failed. It is divided into three. The first section acknowledges the influence on my thinking of Jonathan Todres and Sarah Higinbotham's *Human Rights in Children's Literature* on why it is important to look at children in law and literature. They highlight how literature can be used to disseminate knowledge about the UN Convention on the Rights of the Child, 1989. Specifically, they identify that using stories can help states to fulfil their obligation to promote children's rights and to educate children about their rights. I give an overview of some children's literature – including that written by a child – that speaks about what it means to be a refugee or migrant. The second section is a consideration of migration and the young body. It looks at literature exploring why children leave, before alighting on how unaccompanied minors are treated in law. This section also examines how children as family members are treated: are they seen as dependants whose fates are bound to the adults in their families, or are they independent bearers of rights, which means that their claim can lead to family-life-giving entitlements for their parents and carers? This section focuses on the interactions of human rights treaty bodies with governments and national and regional case law. The final section is a consideration of the lives of children who arrive as dependants or who are born to migrants. It explores the challenges of liminality: they are caught between parental demands to remember 'home' while simultaneously navigating integration into their new home. What do home and belonging mean in this context?[1] This section relies on both fiction and first-person accounts to show how children experience their liminality, and the toll it takes on them to feel that they do not belong anywhere.

[1] *Re M (Child's Upbringing)* [1996] 2 FLR 441. J Eekelaar, 'Children Between Cultures' (2004) 18 *International Journal of Law, Policy and the Family* 178, 181–82. H Lee, *To Kill a Mockingbird* (Philadelphia PA, Lippincott & Co, 1960).

It ends by looking at legal responses to what are sometimes considered 'cultural issues'; that is, the practice of female genital mutilation and also early marriage.

I. The Role of Literature

Writing on children's rights and literature, Todres and Higinbotham contend that while much has been written about the content of children's rights and the obligations of states, there has not been the same engagement with the question of how children come to 'know and understand their rights.'[2] Just as Hunt says that literature for children has been ignored or not considered important in literary criticism, so too Todres and Higinbotham make a further point about the invisibility of children in law – historically they have been seen as the appendages of adults who represented their interests.[3] It is clear that stories can help to fulfil the goals of the United Nations Convention on the Rights of the Child ('the Children's Rights Convention'): to educate and inform children and adults about the Convention, their rights and indeed, the rights of others.[4] Echoing the goals of the UNICEF Rights-respecting Programme for schools, Todres and Higinbotham also argue that children's literature can help to foster a human rights culture in compliance with article 29(1) of the Children's Rights Convention.[5]

> Stories give expression to human rights in a way that is more accessible to children and more relatable to their lives. In this regard, children's literature has the potential to contribute to human rights *culture* – a rights fulfilling and rights-respecting culture – that ultimately is the goal of international human rights law.[6]

In short, children's literature can assist a state to meet its promotional duties under the Children's Rights Convention. Children's literature can also elicit empathy and greater understanding about the lives of other children. Better yet, it does not have to be written by adults; an excellent example of the genre being *There's a Boy Just*

[2] J Todres and S Higinbotham, *Human Rights in Children's Literature: Imagination and the Narrative of Law* (Oxford, OUP, 2016) 2.

[3] P Hunt, 'Introduction' in P Hunt (ed), *Literature for Children: Contemporary Criticism* (Abingdon, Routledge, 1992) 1, 2. J Todres and S Higinbotham (2016) 190.

[4] UN Convention of the Rights of the Child, 1989, 1577 UNTS 3, arts 42, 28, 29. UN Committee on the Rights of the Child (CRC), General Comment No 5 (2003): General measures of implementation of the Convention on the Rights of the Child, 27 November 2003, CRC/GC/2003/5, paras 66, 68, 69. See also paras 28, 33, 53.

[5] J Todres and S Higinbotham (2016), n 2 above, 3. See also the Preface to the book written by Carol Bellamy, former head of UNICEF. For the UNICEF Rights Respecting Programme, see: https://www.unicef.org.uk/rights-respecting-schools/. See also CRC, General comment No 1 (2001), Article 29(1), The aims of education, 17 April 2001, CRC/GC/2001/1, paras 15, 16, 18, 19, 21, 22.

[6] Todres and Higinbotham (2016) 3. See also, African Committee of Experts on the Rights and Welfare of the Child (ACERWC), General Comment No 5 on Article 1 of the ACRWC: https://www.acerwc.africa/wp-content/uploads/2018/08/Website_Joint_GC_ACERWC-ACHPR_Ending_Child_Marriage_20_January_2018.pdf, ACERWC/C/05 (2018), sections 4.4; 5.3.3; 6.5.

Like Me, written by nine-year-old Fraser Cox and used by Save the Children in its advocacy work.[7] Cox's book draws on the similarities between him, a British boy, and another nine-year-old boy and imagines all the things that they both enjoy doing. However, they are not the same, for his book friend is displaced, a refugee from the war which destroyed his home and forced him to move with his family. He goes on:

> We're strangers and each have a different life,
> He faces worry, and sadness, and strife.

Showing an understanding of the negative portrayal of refugees, Fraser makes a human connection:

> As humans we share an incredible link,
> And, although we are different, I definitely think
> His family and people are misunderstood.
> If we could find friendship, our world would be good.

The book ends by returning us to childhood pleasures:

> I wish he could come and be
> best friends with me,
> So we could eat sweets and climb high in the trees.[8]

The simplicity of the language and the rhyming speaks to children of a younger age. The moral arch is very clearly delineated in literature for younger children.

Also about a nine-year-old boy, but written by an adult, is the award-winning and much enjoyed (by my younger daughter and chief critic) Rauf's *Boy at the Back of the Class.*[9] This is about a Syrian boy, Ahmet, who arrives at an English school where he is bullied by one boy, but befriended by other children. One of his friends narrates how he had shown Ahmet his *Tintin* book. Seeing the pictures of Captain Haddock on a raft in the ocean had led him to recall his family crossing of the Mediterranean. He says his sister is in the sea, his father is missing, maybe in France, his cat is in the mountains and 'flicking to another page, he pointed to a tent and said, "Mum sick. Last time I see her."'[10] After some campaigning by the

[7] F Cox (with illustrations by A Brown), *There's a boy just like me* (London, Little Tiger Press, 2018). Stunning is the collection of poems by children who have come as migrants or whose parents are migrants in a secondary school, Oxford Spires School in Oxford, Britain. K Clanchy, *England Poems from a School* (London, Picador, 2018). See also the first person accounts of girls in M Yousafzai, *We are Displaced: My Journey and Stories from Refugee Girls around the World* (London, Weidenfeld & Nicolson, 2019). UNICEF, *A Right to be Heard: Young Migrants and Refugee Girls*, UNICEF, 2018.

[8] F Cox (with illustrations by A Brown) (2018), n 7 above, not paginated. O Rauf (illustrated by P Curnick), *Boy at the Back of the Class* (London, Orion, 2018).

[9] O Rauf (illustrated by P Curnick), *Boy at the Back of the Class* (London, Orion, 2018).

[10] O Rauf (with P Cunick) (2018) 139. The young narrator also learns that his late grandma Jo saved lots of Jewish people running away from the Nazis in Germany. She lived in Austria. O Rauf (with P Cunick) (2018) 131–32.

children, their teachers and parents, the book ends as well as one could expect. Ahmet's family is reunited (missing the sister who drowned) and given asylum in England.[11] Significantly, the author adds a note explaining her stimulus for writing the book – it was seeing the picture of young Alan Kurdi, the boy whose body was pictured on a Turkish beach, which moved her to act. At the end of the book one also finds questions for the reader, as well as information about refugees challenging the official narrative that there are 'too many' and that Britain has taken a lot of people in. The author explains that some of the royalties will be given to organisations that help refugees. She also dedicates the book to a baby who was born in the Calais camp but who disappeared when the French government dismantled the camp. The book is both educational and a call to arms. It leaves the child-reader with a sense of agency and urgency – they can act and make a difference, if only by showing kindness to others who are unalike.

Writing about children's literature, Ian Ward argues that as they get older, children are capable of understanding more complex stories. He cites Piaget and Tucker on how age impacts on the child's reasoning and their framing of right and wrong. He notes that between the ages of 11 and 14:

> children are capable of thinking in the abstract and … that they are also capable of making moral judgments … Rather than just accepting good and evil they begin to ask why certain people are good or evil, so the literature for these ages and beyond is laced with moral dilemmas, and situates these dilemmas in realistic conditions. Happy endings are no longer guaranteed.[12]

This idea of a moral dilemma is captured well in Nina Bawden's *The Runaway Summer* where two children, Mary and Simon, watch an Asian boy, Krishna, clambering out of a boat with two older men who run away. The boy, who turns out to be from Kenya, needs help to find his uncle who lives in London. The boy has been sent ahead by his parents who fear that the Commonwealth Immigrants Act enacted in 1968 will mean that they are no longer entitled to come to Britain. The child needs to enter before the law comes into force. Simon, one of the two English

[11] O Rauf (with P Cunick) (2018) 294–95. A powerful autobiographical account is that of children's rights author, Judith Kerr, *When Hitler Stole Pink Rabbit* (London, Harper Collins, 2017). Other stories include A Gratz, *Refugee* (London, Scholastic, 2017). This looks at three migration waves focusing on Josef, a Jewish boy leaving Germany to escape Nazism, Isabel, a Cuban girl taking to a boat to escape to the United States and, Mahmoud, leaving war-torn Syria for Europe in 2015. Books about internal migration focusing on the evacuation of British children during the Second World War have also resonated with children over the years. Key amongst these are Nina Bawden's *Carrie's War* (London, Puffin, 2014 [1973]); and M Magorian, *Goodnight Mr Tom* (London, Puffin, 2014 [1981]). All four children in the popular children's series, *The Roman Mysteries* do not have their mothers living with them, two mothers having died. Two of the four protagonists are 'migrants': Nubia, is an orphaned slave girl while Jonathan is the son of a Jewish doctor and secret convert to the new religion of Christianity, who has been forced to leave Jerusalem after the razing of the temple by the Romans. C Lawrence, *The Thieves of Ostia* (London, Orion, 2002). This, the first of the series, details the children's backgrounds. There are 15 books, or scrolls as they are called, in the series.

[12] I Ward, *Law and Literature* (Cambridge, CUP, 2008) 97–98.

children is the son of a policeman. Mary thinks they should help the new arrival, to which Simon explains that he cannot help to conceal the boy because his father is a policeman. He continues: 'He's breaking the law … He's an-illegal immigrant …' He goes on: 'My father says there is no point in being sentimental … It's just the law. People have to stick to the law'.[13]

The Runaway Summer was first published in 1969 and yet it still resonates. Simon details how people are smuggled in from France. Echoing his father, he is of the view that the country cannot accommodate everyone and that it is just bad luck that they have spent so much money to get to Britain. He assumes that Krishna is from Pakistan or India because that is where 'most of the ones who land here come from'.[14] The book is studded with philosophical discussions about law and morality: should one ignore a law if it seems to be unjust? The children befriend Krishna, the new arrival and help him.

Beverley Naidoo's *The Other Side of Truth* tells the story of a Nigerian journalist critical of the Nigerian government for its human rights violations and poor governance. (The story is set during the Abacha regime, which ruled Nigeria from 1993 to 1998 following a coup.) The journalist's children come to London for safety after their mother is killed in a botched murder (the father being the intended target). Abandoned at a train station in central London by the woman paid to bring them to England, and unable to find the uncle who is supposed to act as their guardian, they are left to fend for themselves until the social services catch up. The story is a poignant study of the impact of living in the shadows of the law, neither properly documented, nor granted refugee status (until the end). It also explores the meaning of childhood and highlights the dissonance between the ideological positioning of childhood in Western societies – as being about protection and facilitation of the child's development with a focus on happiness and emotional nurture – and the experiences of unaccompanied minors who enjoy none of the protections or emotional support ordinarily afforded to the child, but who also do not have the legal or social capacity or means to live the lives of adults.

The Other Side of Truth champions courage and tenacity. It also speaks to the importance of a free media. The opening sections of the book about the journalist father's campaigning and harassment by the government call to mind the many cases brought to the African Commission challenging Nigeria's violations, during the Abacha regime, of the right to fair trial and the presumption of innocence, unjust ouster of the jurisdiction of courts by use of military decree, and the issue

[13] N Bawden, *The Runaway Summer* (London, Puffin, 1969), 60. At 83, Krishna, the boy explains the effect of the 1968 law. Dembour highlights that 11 of the 25 applicants whose cases were admitted in *East African Asians v United Kingdom* (Application 4403/70) were unaccompanied minors. M-B Dembour, *When Humans become migrants* (Oxford, OUP, 2015) 64. The book and the case are discussed in Chapter 2 of this volume.

[14] N Bawden (1969), n 13 above, 60.

of unjust imprisonment occasioning writs of habeas corpus.[15] The book starts with the violation of the father's right to freedom of speech in Nigeria and the terrible price paid by the family (including the father going into hiding and ultimately escaping to England, where he is put in the Oxfordshire detention centre) and culminates with the children approaching a television news anchor (who bears a remarkable similarity to British *Channel 4*'s Jon Snow) for help to tell their story. The father is vindicated and freed. The family rebuild their lives, still mourning the loss of their mother who is present throughout the book to mark the permanence of loss. We actually meet them again in the follow up, *Web of Lies*,[16] where we learn more about the family's lives and challenges.

Illegal is a graphic novel that traces the story of a young orphan boy called Ibo. It is a fictionalised account grounded in a compendium of life-like stories, designed to explain the issue of migration to children and young adults. Its publication coincided with many media stories detailing the Mediterranean crossings.[17] The epigraph to the book contains a quotation from Jewish Holocaust survivor Elie Wiesel, repeated in the Introduction to this book, that a person can be many things, but not illegal. This is why the book is called *Illegal*. Ibo lives in a village (location unidentified) with his alcoholic and neglectful grandfather.[18] His brother leaves for Libya and Ibo follows him in a bus and a truck across the desert to Libya. They are reunited in Libya and take odd jobs to earn the money to pay the smugglers who will take them to Europe. They undertake the perilous sea journey together. His brother drowns when their dinghy fills with water, but he survives and is rescued along with the baby that he had been asked to hold by its mother. We see him sitting alone on a bed in an Italian rescue centre. At the end of the book is an explainer written by the authors where they note that all the stories are true. For the reader, there are within the text, pictures of different people on the boat, explaining why they are prepared to put themselves in peril. These reasons include escaping from war, wanting a better life for one's children, the prospects of a job and a better life.[19]

[15] Communications 105/93, 128/94, 130/94, 152/96 (joined) *Media Rights Agenda and Others v Nigeria* (2000) AHRLR 235 (ACHPR 1998) (12th Annual Activity Report) (military decrees and ouster clauses); Communication 87/93, *Constitutional Rights Project (in respect of Lekwot and Others) v Nigeria* (2000) AHRLR 183 (ACHPR 1995) (8th Annual Activity Report) (access to lawyers); Communication 224/98 *Media Rights Agenda v Nigeria* (2000) AHRLR 262 (ACHPR 2000) (14th Annual Activity Report) (Malaolu case) (trial within a reasonable time). All discussed in F Viljoen, *International Human Rights Law in Africa* (Oxford, OUP, 2012) 215–16.

[16] B Naidoo, *Web of Lies* (London, Puffin, 2004).

[17] The tale of the Unaccompanied Minor in the Chaucer-inspired *Refugee Tales* follows a similar trajectory but is more graphic and direct in its descriptions of death. I Ellams, 'The Unaccompanied Minor's Tale' in D Herd and A Pincus (eds), *Refugee Tales* (Manchester, Comma Press, 2016) 17–24.

[18] E Colfer and A Donkin (with illustrations by G Rigano), *Illegal* (London, Hodder, 2017). The title is deliberately provocative.

[19] E Colfer and A Donkin (2017) 72. There is a bonus feature added to the book which is the story of a young Eritrean woman trafficked to Europe. The boat gets into trouble, they are rescued, she ends up in a lorry from Calais in France to England. She is discovered by the driver and the story ends with her in a hostel for asylum seekers in the north of England, safe but unable to work. 'Helen' as told to *Women for Refugee Women* adapted by Colfer/Donkin/Rigano, addendum to Colfer, Donkin and Rigano, *Illegal* (2017). See also UNICEF, *Harrowing Journeys* (New York, UNICEF, 2017).

Equally compelling is David Eggers' *What the What.*[20] It is the factually based account of one the lost boys from Sudan, Achak Deng and his journey to America which was preceded by war and life in refugee and squatter camps. Here one is forced to recall the United Nations Optional Protocol to the Convention on the Rights of the Child on the Involvement of Children in Armed Conflict, 2000 (OPAC) which raises the age of combat from the 15 given in the Children's Rights Convention, to 18.[21] Similarly, the African Charter on the Rights and Welfare of the Child, 1990, prohibits recruitment of children as soldiers.[22] Eggers' book shows us the gap between that which is promised by law and human rights treaties and the lived realities of many children. The good news is that Achak Deng has made a good life for himself in the United States as have many of the other 'lost boys'.

Osondu's short story compilation begins with a story called 'Waiting' of children in a camp. They are reliant on the Red Cross for provisions. Food is always in short supply and those who do not have parents or relatives to fend for them are constantly hungry and fighting over food when it is there. The children long to be adopted by American families. The story hints at the violence they have seen. The children, who have given each other the names printed on their donated T shirts: London, Acapulco, Orlando, Paris, Lousy – because his shirt says 'My dad went to Yellowstone and Got me this Lousy T-Shirt' – have suffered trauma. In the case of one boy, Acapulco, this trauma was watching his parents being murdered by militia. Desperate though their lives are, they are also aware of the fate of other children who have been recruited into militia and forced to fight: 'Sometimes I want to join the Youth Brigade, but I am afraid; they say they give them we-we to smoke, and they drink blood and swear an oath to have no mercy on the soul, including their parents.'[23]

The children are also alive to the fact that the Red Cross is trying to arrange for them to get to America to avoid them joining the Youth Brigade because of the human rights violations that they commit and also because the children's life chances are harmed by not getting an education. One is left unsettled by Osondu's 'Waiting', because it is not at all clear that there will be a happy ending for most of the children.

NoViolet Bulawayo's *We Need New Names* offers up an ironic account of the work of Non-government organisations (NGOs). The children need to be photographed for the donor pamphlets that will be used to raise money for the NGO. In turn the children receive packages of gifts. The photographer is drawn to their dirty and bedraggled clothes. This makes the photographs look grittier and more

[20] D Eggers, *What is the What* (London, Penguin, 2008). See also LS Park, *A Long Walk to Water* (New York, Clarion Books, 2010) and M and E De Prince, *Ballerina Dreams: From Orphan to Dancer* (London, Random House, 2014).

[21] The Optional Protocol to the Convention on the Rights of the Child on the Involvement of Children in Armed Conflict (OPAC) General Assembly resolution A/RES/54/263 of 25 May 2000.

[22] African Charter on the Rights and Welfare of the Child, 1990, art 22.

[23] EC Osundu, 'Waiting' in *Voice of America* (London, Granta, 2010) 1, 7.

authentic. The children know this and play up to the camera. They also long to escape their desperate lives and move overseas to America and England, the lands of milk and honey. In Osondu's 'Waiting', the children wonder which poses are most likely to get them noticed by the American families who will pick them for adoption, as one picks from a shopping catalogue. The children operate on the basis of stereotype. Americans like dogs, therefore one child says, he wants to pose with a dog as this will make him more attractive. The stories of the lives of children dependent on humanitarian aid, particularly those of Osondu and Bulawayo are prescient, reflecting the debates about the pornographisation of poverty.[24] Osondu's 'Waiting' and Egger's 'What is the What' both force us to confront the failure of African states to protect which is promised to children.

II. Children in Migration

A. Children Alone

Often forgotten in the discussion of the global movement of people is the increasing number of unaccompanied minors, sent by families desperate to protect them from the ravages of war and the vagaries of life at home. Both the UN Children's Rights Convention, 1979 and the African Charter on the Rights and Welfare of the Child, 1990 (ACRWC) are clear that states owe a special duty of protection and assistance to unaccompanied minors.[25] However, the UN Children's rights organisation UNICEF notes:

> Many children move alone and face particularly grave risks. In parts of the world, the number of children moving on their own has skyrocketed. On the dangerous Central Mediterranean Sea passage from North Africa to Europe, 92 per cent of children who arrived in Italy in 2016 and the first two months of 2017 were unaccompanied, up from 75 per cent in 2015. At least 300,000 unaccompanied and separated children moving across borders were registered in 80 countries in 2015–2016 – a near fivefold increase from 66,000 in 2010–2011. The total number of unaccompanied and separated children on the move worldwide is likely much higher.[26]

UNICEF has conducted research with children who have crossed the Mediterranean on their own. The children recount the challenging conditions that forced them to

[24] N Bulawayo, *We need new names* (London, Vintage, 2014), 51–57. S Edwin, '(Un) solving global challenges: African short stories, literary awards and the question of audience.' (2016) 28 *Journal of African Cultural Studies* 359–71.

[25] UN Convention of the Rights of the Child, 1989, 1577 UNTS 3. art 22. See also art 20 on children deprived of a family environment; African Charter on the Rights and Welfare of the Child, 1990, CAB/LEG/24.9/49 (1990), art 23.

[26] UNICEF, *A Child is a Child: Protecting Children on the Move from Violence, Abuse and Exploitation* (New York, UNICEF, 2017) 6. See also E de Oliveira, 'Myths about Migrants', *First News*, issue 656, 11–17 January 2019, p 11.

leave while expressing pride in their survival.[27] Bhabha and her co-authors investigate the impact of migration on children, focusing on statelessness and the failure to protect.[28] Migration, especially as an unaccompanied minor, often marks the end of 'childhood'. While one may remain classified chronologically, as a child, experientially, the child is forced to take on adult responsibilities. Life is difficult for the unaccompanied minor.[29] Legal and bureaucratic processes are difficult to navigate in breach of UNHCR guidelines.[30]

The story of the 'Deportee's Tale' in the *Refugee Tales* tells of the fate of a 14-year-old boy who is detained with adults. It reminds us of the gap between the promise of special protection for vulnerable children and the practice. It also highlights the compassion of fellow detainees:

> 'This is a prison! For men! What are you doing here!'
> 'He needs a lawyer!'
> 'Do you have a lawyer?'
> 'This isn't human rights!'
> It took prisoners to claim his human rights. His being human.
> It took prisoners to do that.
> It took prisoners to rally around and find him a lawyer.
> It took prisoners to pay his fees so a letter could be written.
> Another court, another judge.
> The same stock solution grasped at blindly, because no one dare take off their blindfolds.[31]

The unaccompanied minor must face the possibility that they will be disbelieved, not least about their age.[32] Some may also be detained. They suffer discrimination and abuse. In 2008, the United Kingdom was criticised for detaining children

[27] UNICEF, *Harrowing Journeys* (New York, UNICEF, 2017).

[28] J Bhabha (ed), *Children without a State* (Cambridge MA, MIT, 2011). Bhabha's introduction is particularly instructive. J Bhabha, 'From Citizen to Migrant: The Scope of Child Statelessness in the Twenty-First Century' (ibid) 1–39, 22–23. See also UNHCR, 'Guidelines on statelessness No 4: ensuring every child's right to acquire a nationality through articles 1–4 of the 1961 Convention on the Reduction of Statelessness' (HCR/GS/12/04). See also J Bhabha, *Child Migration and Human Rights in a Global Age* (Princeton NJ, Princeton University Press, 2014). J Bhabha, J Kanics and D Senovilla-Hernandez (eds), *Handbook on Childhood Migration* (Cheltenham, Edward Elgar, 2018).

[29] UNICEF, *A Right to be Heard: Listening to young people on the move*, UNICEF, 2018.

[30] UNHCR, Guidelines on Determining the Best Interests of the Child (UNHCR, 2008). UN CRC *General Comment No 6 on the Treatment of Unaccompanied and Separated Children outside their Country of Origin*, CRC/GC/2005/6 (1 September, 2005). These were cited by the UK Supreme Court in the case of *ZH v Secretary for Home Affairs* [2011] UKSC 4 at paras 25, 27,28. The court also noted that the obligations of the CRC were partially reflected in the duties of Secretary of State under s 55 of the Borders, Citizenship and Immigration Act 2009. *ZH v Tanzania*, n 59 below, at para 12.

[31] A Mohammad, 'The Deportee's Tale' in D Herd and A Pincus (eds), *Refugee Tales* (2016) 99, 105.

[32] In its concluding observations to the fourth UK report, the CRC recommended that the state: 'give the benefit of the doubt in age-disputed cases of unaccompanied minors seeking asylum, and seek expert guidance on how to determine age.' CRC/C/GBR/CO/4 (20 October 2008) para 71(e). The Committee also recommended specialist training of Border agency officials who interview with children (para 71(b)).

by the UN Committee on the Rights of the Child (CRC): 'as also acknowledged recently by the Human Rights Committee, asylum seeking children continue to be detained, including those undergoing an age assessment, who may be kept in detention for weeks until the assessment is completed.'[33] The CRC also criticised France for:

> The situation of unaccompanied migrant children automatically placed in waiting zones of airports or hotels, and other administrative detention facilities (locaux de rétention administrative), sometimes detained with adults, and reports of their removal, even before speaking to an ad-hoc administrator.[34]

By 2016, the UK was commended for ending detention of children in 2010.[35] Nevertheless, the Committee continued to express concern about the fact that: 'Children can be detained in the course of asylum processes, including in short-term holding facilities at the entry into the State party, and age disputed children seeking asylum can be detained in adult facilities.'[36]

Not having proof of age, children may be asked to undergo questionable dentistry or bone tests to ascertain their age.[37] There is little legal aid, meaning that the children and their families do not have effective advocates.[38] Reviewing the UK's fifth report in 2016, the CRC expressed concern that:

> The Immigration Act (2016) removed the entitlement of unaccompanied children in care with an irregular or unresolved immigration status to leaving care support and adopted the 'deport first, appeal later' scheme which allows migrants to appeal against

[33] CRC/C/GBR/CO/4 (20 October 2008) para 70(a). See also CCPR/C/HUN/CO/6 (9 May 2018) para 46(f).

[34] CRC/C/FRA/CO/5 (29 January, 2016) para 73(a). France was also censured for its treatment of child refugees and their families in Calais and Grande-Synthe, and specifically 'the refusal by the authorities to register children and the insufficiency of venues and services to provide them with appropriate and adapted protection.' CRC/C/FRA/CO/5 (2016) para 75(a). The Committee recommended the provision of adequate health and education facilities, access to legal services, training for officials as well as social assistance and vocational training for unaccompanied minors (at paras 74 and 76).

[35] However there are still cases where children have been wrongly assessed as adults and put in detention such as this one involving a young Sudanese man: *The Queen (on the application of Abdul-Muttelab Awed Ali) v Secretary of State for the Home Department and Another* [2017] EWCA Civ 138.

[36] CRC/C/GBR/CO/5 (3 June 2016) para 74(d). It recommended an end to this practice at para 75(d). See the British government's updated guidelines for its staff, Home Office, 'Assessing age: Version 3.0' Home Office, 23 May 2019.

[37] CRC/C/FRA/CO/5 (2016) para 73(b). The Human Rights Committee also queried the practice of the Hungarian government of relying on visual assessments of child asylum seekers to ascertain their age. It recommended that these assessments be done by qualified experts and that decisions be made in the best interests of the child. The State was also to ensure 'adequate education, social and psychological services and legal aid are provided with a legal representative and/or guardian without delay.' CCPR/C/HUN/CO/6 (9 May 2018) paras 49 and 50.

[38] D Wenke, *Age assessment: Council of Europe member states' policies, procedures and practices respectful of children's rights in the context of migration* (Brussels, Council of Europe Children's Rights Division, 2017). There are attempts to ensure that children are given adequate support and information. Council of Europe, *How to convey child-friendly information to children in migration* (Brussels, Council of Europe, 2018).

> the refusal of their stay only from outside the UK, including in cases where such deportation might undermine family unity for migrant children.[39]

It is through the prism of Benjamin Zephaniah's novel *Refugee Boy* that we can properly see what it must be like for an unaccompanied child to navigate the immigration and asylum system. Alem, Zephaniah's protagonist, has the good fortune to have caring foster parents and access to a lawyer provided by the organisation Refuge. They give him a suit to wear to the hearing but he is not clear why what he wears matters. He asks when he will meet his lawyer, and is surprised to discover that he will only meet the barrister representing him at the door of the tribunal. Zephaniah's depiction of the boy's wonderment at the court process and its rituals (everyone stands for the judge but the boy does not) reminds us how alienating the legal system is at the best of times – imagine being a child within it.[40] The case is adjourned. At the second hearing, the boy faints when his barrister recalls how his mother was 'hacked to death.'[41] That is not the only shock, for the adjudicator, having heard evidence of the impact of the continuing war between Eritrea and Ethiopia, and having had explained the difficulty of a mixed Ethiopian-Eritrean family returning in the circumstances, goes on to note the reuniting of father and son:

> When this case first came to my attention last month, my major consideration was the well-being of the juvenile. Being separated from his family was a more important matter. But things are somewhat different now. Now that your family is reunited, albeit with one member of the family missing, the issue of the juvenile not having anyone to turn to and not having a legal guardian is no longer relevant.[42]

Alem does not understand so asks his barrister, described earlier as, 'tired, but smiling'[43] thus reflecting the relentless pressure on the few barristers still assisting those without resources, what the adjudicator means.

> The adjudicator responded. 'It means that you must try and make a life with your father in your own country. It is possible. You now have your father with you so you will not be alone. Your barrister will explain. We do have a very fair system of justice here so you do have the right to appeal.'[44]

Alem does finally get asylum, but only because he suffers yet another catastrophic trauma in his life.[45]

Not believed, and without access to state support, it is not surprising that many children simply disappear. In its concluding observations to the Norwegian

[39] CRC/GBR/CO/5 (3 June, 2016) para 75(g). It recommended that children be given sufficient support to access services (para 75(f)) and also suggested that the state 'Establish statutory independent guardians for all unaccompanied and separated children throughout the State Party.' (para 75(b))
[40] B Zephaniah, *Refugee Boy* (London, Bloomsbury, 2017) 131–45.
[41] B Zephaniah (2017) 223.
[42] B Zephaniah (2017) 225.
[43] B Zephaniah (2017), n 40 above, 219.
[44] B Zephaniah (2017) 226.
[45] B Zephaniah (2017) 282.

report, the CRC identified the issuance of temporary residence permits as one of the reasons that children, fearing that their applications for permanent residence will be denied, choose to disappear instead. This, the Committee noted, explained why so many children went missing from reception centres.[46]

Migrant children often find themselves caught in a state of liminality. The unaccompanied minors are not accorded the consideration that accompanies their minority. This forces them to take on adult roles and demeanours. They have to navigate alien justice systems and contend with under-funded social services departments that seek to 'move them on' out of their jurisdiction so that they become someone else's 'problem'. This creates uncertainty and instability and opens up the risk, especially for girls, of being tricked into working in the sex industry.[47] Both boys and girls can also find themselves being made to participate in other coerced work or activities.

As noted in Chapter three, the CRC has adopted General Comment 6 on the Treatment of Unaccompanied and Separated Children Outside their Country of Origin and also a Joint General Comment 3 with the Committee on Migrant Workers and Members of their Family, both of which make extensive recommendations on the obligations of states to avoid placing children in detention, to provide them with access to adequate health care, counselling, education and legal services, and to expedite applications for residence or asylum.[48]

I am reminded of Philippe Sands' *East West Street* where he recalls the indifference of European governments to the plight of Jewish people in Germany prior to, and during, the Second World War. He notes how the international lawyer, Hersch Lauterpacht, himself a Polish Jew who came to live in England,

> wrote a paper titled 'The Persecution of Jews in Germany', proposing action by the League of Nations to prevent discrimination on grounds of race or religion ... He hoped Spain, Ireland, or Norway might act on an issue of political morality. They didn't, and the paper had no discernible impact.[49]

[46] CRC/C/NOR/CO/5–6 (4 July 2018) para 31(a). The Human Rights Committee echoed this point and also identified the distinction in treatment meted out to children over 15 who were cared for 'by reception centres with lower levels of care, staffing and accommodation conditions, while other children are cared for by the Child Welfare Services, ensuring higher levels of care.' CCPR/C/NOR/CO/7 (25 April 2018) para 30.

[47] Noted in the CRC Concluding Observations to Norway's report, CRC/C/NOR/CO/5–6 (2018) para 31(b).

[48] UN Committee on the Rights of the Child (CRC), *General Comment No 6 (2005): Treatment of Unaccompanied and Separated Children Outside their Country of Origin*, 1 September 2005, CRC/GC/2005/6; UN Committee on the Protection of the Rights of All Migrant Workers and Members of Their Families (CMW), *Joint general comment No 3 (2017) of the Committee on the Protection of the Rights of All Migrant Workers and Members of Their Families and No 22 (2017) of the Committee on the Rights of the Child on the general principles regarding the human rights of children in the context of international migration*, 16 November 2017, CMW/C/GC/3-CRC/C/GC/22. See also CRC/C/NOR/CO/7 (2018) para 32.

[49] P Sands, *East West Street: On the Origins of Genocide and Crimes against Humanity* (London, Weidenfeld, 2016) 86. See also R Abel, *Politics by Other Means: Law and the Struggle Against Apartheid* (Abingdon, Routledge, 2002).

Despite this history, little seems to have been learned. Spain has been censured for summarily expelling children from its territory.[50] One could also point to the failure of the British government to honour its promise to bring 480 unaccompanied children living in the Calais camps to Britain. This pledge had been made in remembrance of and to replicate an earlier era where Britain had welcomed Jewish children fleeing persecution. The initiative was called Dubs in honour of Lord Dubs, himself a former *Kindertransport* beneficiary and advocate of ensuring that unaccompanied minors receive help and support. Actually, in the original law passed, section 67 of the Immigration Act 2016, which came to be known as the Dubs Amendment, the pledge had been to take 3,000 children but the government had reneged and decided on only 480.[51] In the period of two years to 2018, only 240 children had been settled in the UK.[52]

There has since 1945 been a greater appetite for creating norms that should, technically, offer protection, but which norms are not honoured. International and regional human rights instruments all guarantee children a right to a nationality, from which flows entitlement to other basic rights and services. There are Statelessness Conventions designed to catch those who fall between the cracks. There is international recognition of the need to ensure that all rights are enjoyed without discrimination, including on grounds of nationality or origin and irrespective of status.[53] However, states are determined to limit what they perceive to be the cynical use of children to gain the right to stay, or indeed to enter the country using the 'family reunification' route. In 2004 an Irish referendum led to an amendment to its Constitution which hitherto had granted automatic Irish citizenship to any child born in Ireland irrespective of their parents' legal status; from 2005 at least one of the child's parents must have, or be entitled to, Irish citizenship for citizenship to be conferred on the child.[54] An examination of ECHR article 8 'right to family life' case law of the European Court of Human Rights suggests

[50] CRC Spain, CRC/C/C/15 Add 185, (13 June 2002) para 45(e). See also Human Rights Committee, Concluding Observations for Hungary, CCPR/C/HUN/CO/6 (9 May 2018) paras 47 and 48.

[51] Home Office, 'Policy Statement: Section 67 of the Immigration Act 2016', 10 March 2017, updated 17 February 2020. Home Office, 'Detailed Process Transfer of Minors to the UK from France under section 67 of the Immigration Act 2016' (December 2018).

[52] Y Cooper, 'On the anniversary of the Kindertransport, we should reflect on why we're failing child refugees today', *The Independent*, London, 21 November 2018.

[53] BK Blitz, 'Neither Seen nor Heard: Compound Deprivation among Stateless Children' in J Bhabha (ed), *Children Without a State* (2011), n 28 above, 44–66. Convention Relating to the Status of Stateless Persons, in force 22 April 1954, 360 UNTS 117: http://treaties.un.org/doc/Publication/UNTS/Volume%20360/v360.pdf (p 117); UN Convention on the Reduction of Statelessness, in force 30 August 1961, 989 UNTS 175: http://treaties.un.org/doc/Publication/UNTS/Volume%20989/v989.pdf (p 175); CRC art 7. See also ACERWC *Decision on the communication submitted by the Institute for Human Rights and Development in Africa and the Open Society Justice Initiative (on behalf of children of Nubian descent in Kenya) v. the Government of Kenya*, No Com/002/2009; African Committee of Experts on the Rights and Welfare of the Child (ACERWC), General Comment No 2 on Article 6 of the ACRWC: 'The Right to a Name, Registration at Birth, and to Acquire a Nationality', 16 April 2014, ACERWC/GC/02 (2014). B Manby, *Citizenship Law in Africa* (Oxford, Hart, 2018).

[54] C Costello, *The Human Rights of Migrants and Refugees in European Law* (Oxford, OUP, 2016) 77.

that Norway is frequently challenged on the right to remain of children whose parent(s) may be classified as irregular.[55]

We now turn to some of the fictional literature which may throw light on the reasons for such state reluctance before alighting on national and European case law on family unity.

In EC Osundu's 'Teeth' the narrator, a student from Nigeria, recounts how his wife persuaded him that they should have a baby while they were living in America. She explained the concept of 'anchor babies' to him; that all children born on American soil were entitled to citizenship and with it earned the right to become President of the country. His reluctance was overcome by her pointing out that there had been a young Kenyan man who had come to America to study. He met and married an American woman with whom he had a son, who was now a Senator. He is not named, but the reference is to Obama.

> But that is not even the best part – the best part is that when our son is eighteen, he can file for a green card for us, his parents, to join him here in America, and you know what that means, it means we can spend our old age in this beautiful country.[56]

In Ellen Wiles's *The Invisible Crowd* a Nigerian man who shares a squat with the Eritrean protagonist in London explains how his church attendance is part of his plan to get the right to remain:

> One day I will choose a nice woman from there – who has British citizenship and a curvy ass – and then I will marry her and have kids. At least six kids … I know one guy who did that and the judge said he had family life. That is what I am going for.[57]

This next section looks at national and European case law on the rights of children to stay within the jurisdiction irrespective of the irregularity of the status of their parents.

B. Citizenship, the Right to Remain and Family Life

Generally states are reluctant to grant citizenship to the children of third-country nationals born in the jurisdiction, especially if they perceive that the creation of a

[55] *Omoregie v Norway* [2008] ECHR 761; *Nunez v Norway* (Application No 55597/09) (ECtHR, 28 June 2011); *Antwi and Others v Norway* (Application No 26940/10) (ECtHR, 14 February, 2012); *Kaplan and Others v Norway* (Application No 32504/11) (ECtHR, 24 July 2014). Discussed in C Costello (2016), n 54 above, 122, 124–26. See also the response of the Norwegian government to questions from the Committee on the Rights of the Child, CRC/C/NOR/Q/4/Add.1 (6 January, 2010) in response to the 4th Periodic report of Norway (CRC/C/NORW/Q/4) In its response, Norway identified amendments to its Immigration Law which reinforced its commitment to the application of the welfare test in immigration law, to removal of a minimum salary for family reunification, to changes to the regulations to include 'A provision in section 14-1 (of the Immigration Regulations) to state that 'a foreigner who has a child in Norway, shall not, as a general rule, be expelled if the reason for expulsion is illegal stay.' It CRC/C/NOR/Q/4/Add.1 at p 6.

[56] E Osundu, 'Teeth' in *Voice of America* (London, Granta, 2010) 165, 166.

[57] E Wiles, *The Invisible Crowd* (London, Harper Collins, 2017) 85.

family was designed to evade deportation.[58] The UK Supreme Court case of *ZH v Tanzania* is a good example of this. The Home Office was seeking to deport a Tanzanian woman whose immigration history was referred to as 'appalling'.[59] She countered that she should be allowed to stay because she had two children aged 12 and 9. The Home Office argued that she could take the children back to Tanzania with her. It was the Home Office's contention that she should not be able to 'use' the children and the ECHR article 8 right to family life to evade the consequences of her misuse of the asylum system. The mother had arrived in the UK in 1995 aged 20. She had made three unsuccessful asylum claims, one in her own name and two using false identities. In 1997 she met the man who would become father of her children, married him and had the two children before they separated in 2005. Their father was a British citizen and the children had acquired citizenship through him. He saw the children but the mother argued that he was not in a position to look after them on a long-term basis. His HIV status was mentioned.

In any event, the Supreme Court focused on the children and allowed her appeal. Specifically, Baroness Hale noted that the children were British citizens and, as such, they were entitled to remain in the country of their birth. It further noted that the UK was a State party to the UN Children's Rights Convention whose guiding principle, in article 3, was in looking out for the child's best interests. It was in these children's best interests to remain in the country of their birth, with their mother, who had been their primary care-giver since birth. It was also important to ascertain the children's wishes, and, where possible, to accommodate them.

Depending on one's viewpoint, the mother's actions may be seen as 'proving the point that all asylum claims are bogus and so-called asylum seekers liars', or as reflecting the challenge of legal entry and valid pathways to continued legal residence.[60] The *Daily Mail*, a right-of-centre newspaper which is published in

[58] B Anderson, *Us and Them? The Dangerous Politics of Immigration Control* (Oxford, OUP, 2015) 122. Anderson cites research showing that in 2010, there were 155,000 under-19 children who did not have the right paperwork. Of these 85,000 were UK-born. See *Omoregie v Norway* (Application No 265/07) [2008] ECHR 761, 31 July 2008. British citizens who have children abroad may also find that their children are not entitled to British citizenship. In February 2019, the British Home Secretary announced his intention to strip the citizenship from a British-born 19-year-old woman who was a British citizen because she had left the country aged 15 to join the proscribed group ISIS in Syria. He reasoned that she was entitled to Bangladeshi citizenship by descent from her parents. The Home Secretary was prepared to overlook the fact that the woman had never been to Bangladesh, having spent all of the first 15 years of her life in Britain. He also stripped her of citizenship a few days after the birth of her third child, the other two having died while she was in Syria. Bangladesh refused to accept responsibility for her. At the time of writing, the woman's family had launched an appeal to challenge the Home Secretary's decision. Her third child also died. K Rawlinson and V Dodd, 'Shamima Begum: Isis Briton faces move to revoke citizenship', *The Guardian*, London, 19 February 2019. P Noor, 'What do experts think of revoking Shamima Begum's Citizenship?', *The Guardian*, London, 20 February 2019.

[59] *ZH (Tanzania) (FC) v Secretary of State for the Home Department* [2011] UKSC 4 at para 5.

[60] C Costello (2016), n 54 above, 65 notes that, 'Many migrants find themselves from time to time in semi-compliance with immigration law. Taking this "dynamic, processual perspective" reveals that migrants often drift between different statuses. Importantly, they often lack control over their legal status.'

London and has one of the highest national circulations, ran the following headline following the *ZH* case: 'Lying asylum-seeker can stay here – because she had two children by an HIV alcoholic'.[61]

A more edifying account of this case has been published in a child-friendly biography called *Equal to Everything* written by Afua Hirsch. It celebrates the life and achievements of Brenda Hale ('Judge Brenda'), who was the first woman Supreme Court Justice and its first female President. Judge Brenda also wrote the lead judgment in the *ZH v Tanzania* case. The 'story' is told from the perspective of a group of seven-year-old children going to visit the Supreme Court on a school trip. There they meet Judge Brenda – or Lady Hale, which they learn is her formal title – who grew up in their town, thus making a connection and showing that they too can grow up and become judges if they want to and are prepared to work hard. She also talks about being the first woman on the Supreme Court. Lady Hale answers their questions and tells them about some of the cases that she has decided. In the Todres and Higinbotham mould, the book also seeks to introduce children to the work of the Supreme Court, providing both information about and photographs of the court, and also a longer biography of Judge Brenda at the end. Noteworthy is the child-friendly explanation of the *ZH v Tanzania* case, which is markedly different in tone to the *Daily Mail* version:

> There was a mum from Tanzania, her children were British like you. When she asked to stay in this country, what she said wasn't always true.
>
> She was told she would be sent away. Her family was terribly sad.
>
> Her kids would've had to go with her, leaving their friends and even their Dad?
>
> But we changed the law by deciding it wasn't fair to make her leave. Children shouldn't suffer for adults' mistakes. *That* is what I believe.[62]

Also worth examination is the decision of the ECtHR Grand Chamber in the case of *Biao v Denmark.*[63] It involved a man who, although born in Togo, had spent his formative years in Ghana. In 1993, aged 22, he had immigrated from Ghana to Denmark. He was given citizenship in 2002. He travelled to Ghana where he met and married a Ghanaian woman. In 2004 she applied to join him in Denmark. They had a son. Her application for family reunification was denied, forcing the family to move to Sweden. It was from there that they launched an appeal alleging discrimination in violation of article 14 of the ECHR, read with article 8 on the right to family life. The Danish government had in 2003 put in place an Aliens'

[61] J Doyle and C Fernandez, 'Lying asylum seeker can stay here-because she had two children by an HIV alcoholic', London, *Daily Mail*, 1 February 2011. The online comments that follow the article are almost all critical of the decision. This headline is used by Wiles in her novel *The Invisible Crowd* (2017), n 57 above, as the header to chapter 12.

[62] A Hirsch and H Beaumont, *Equal to Everything: Judge Brenda and the Supreme Court* (London, Legal Action Group Education and Service Trust Ltd, 2019).

[63] *Biao v Denmark* (Application No 38590/10), ECtHR (Grand Chamber), 24 May 2016.

Act. The law specified that to be granted reunification, a couple had to show that their ties to Denmark were stronger than ties to any other country. There was a rule which required that one spouse had to be a Danish national for at least 28 years, or, in case of 'non-Danish nationality, has been born and/or raised in Denmark and has lived there lawfully for 28 years.' The Biaos were stumped: their application for reunification was dated 2004 and so did not meet the 28-year rule; Mrs Biao had never visited Denmark, did not speak Danish and had married in Ghana, so did not qualify. The Biaos successfully claimed before the ECtHR that the law constituted indirect discrimination on grounds of race as the 28-year rule was more likely to be met by white Danes than by people of other ethnicities who had acquired Danish nationality by means other than birth.[64] While the outcome is laudable, de Vries argues that it is limited in scope, protecting naturalised citizens but not non-nationals. Moreover, the judgment failed to engage with the underlying stereotypes.[65]

The willingness of states to deport children, including child-citizens, shows the determination of states to 'seal all routes' of entry. The proportionality of the means taken to prevent this, refusing to recognise the entitlement of children born in the jurisdiction to access resources given to other 'recognised' children, can exacerbate inequalities which will have to be addressed further down the line. Deprived of state benefits, including adequate housing, help with school meals or trips, undocumented children may have poorer life chances.[66]

A good example of this is the English High Court case *of R (on the application of O) v London Borough of Lambeth* [2016] EWHC 937 (Admin). The case was brought by a six-year-old child assisted by her mother. The child claimed that they were homeless and asked that their local authority provide them with housing. The child's advocates cited section 17 of the Children Act 1989 which requires a local authority to make provision for any child in need. The family did not have recourse to public funds because the mother was in breach of immigration rules and was not an asylum seeker. They were destitute and needed assistance. The mother refused to name the father of the child. Despite the mother's immigration status, the family contended that the local authority retained a

[64] See the view of the dissenting judges in the original case *Biao v Denmark* (Application no 38590/10) (ECtHR, 25 March 2014) who noted that taken to its logical conclusion, the family would not be able to reunite until 2030. They regarded this as disproportionate, drastic and an unjust interference with their right to pursue happiness. Discussed in C Costello (2016), n 54 above, 109, 118–21.

[65] See KM de Vries, 'Rewriting Abdulaziz: The ECtHR Grand Chamber's Ruling in *Biao v. Denmark*' (2016) 18(4) *European Journal of Migration and Law* 467–79. See also A Schlüter, '*Biao v Denmark*: Grand Chamber Ruling on Ethnic Discrimination Might Leave Couples Seeking Family Reunification Worse Off.' Guest blog *Strasbourg Observers*, 13 June 2016. *Abdulaziz, Cabales and Balkandali v United Kingdom* (Applications No 9214/80, 9473/81 and 9474/81), ECtHR, 28 May 1985. Following this case, the British government levelled down, something Schlüter argues could happen post *Biao*.

[66] A Mohdin, 'Destitute Children 'Unlawfully denied aid' because of focus on parents' status', *The Guardian*, London, 27 May 2019.

duty to the child, whose immigration status was not material. Further, if accommodation was to be provided to the child, then she should not be separated from her primary care-giver, as this might constitute a breach of her article 8 of the European Convention right to family life.[67] The local authority challenged this, arguing that the mother had arrived on a visitor's visa in 2007 and had overstayed. She had worked in breach of the law and in fact had accommodation, including with friends and relatives. The authority had ascertained that the mother's attempts to extend her stay in the country had been unsuccessful. The local authority, which had provided emergency accommodation to the two, further noted that even if it was found that the pair was in need, they could move to live in Nigeria. The judge sided with the local authority and held that it was not under any duty to provide the family with housing, as the mother had alternative sources of accommodation with friends. The mother was said to have hidden her income. The High Court found therefore there was no section 17 need for the local authority to meet.[68] In *obiter dicta*, the Court further noted that the local authority had agreed to extend the availability of the temporary accommodation if the mother agreed to a local-authority-facilitated return to Nigeria. Perhaps this was a way of showing 'reasonableness' on the part of the authority.

The next section looks at the lives and experiences of those children who stay on, or indeed, who are born as citizens. Their 'in-betweenness' is captured in the last stanza of a poem, 'The Path', by 17-year-old Sophie Dunsby, who is described as coming from a mixed Filipino-British family:

> I know what it's like
> to only half-understand
> the words people say, to half-
> belong in a room. I know
> what it is to be in between.[69]

[67] *R (on the application of O) v London Borough of Lambeth* [2016] EWHC 937 (Admin) paras 9–14.

[68] See also *RL and Others v London Borough of Croydon* [2018] EWCA Civ 726, paras 28, 35–42. London Borough of Croydon, Freedom of Information Team, 'Response to a Freedom of Information Request made by Ms Anna Mulchay, Our REF: F/10009648, 10 July 2018' available from http://www.whatdotheyknow.com.The letter includes the number of requests for help made under section 17 of the Children Act 1989 and responses thereto. The original request had also asked for the number of requests made in the preceding six months by those excluded from seeking public help because of the Nationality Asylum and Immigration Act 2002, and the answer was 130. The challenge of providing housing to a high number of children assessed under section 17 of the Children Act was identified in *RL v* Croydon[2018] EWCA Civ 726, para 40 citing the leading case of *R (G) v Barnet London Borough Council* [2004] 2 AC 208, paras 92, 93. Cf *Ekaterina Abdoellaevna, on behalf of herself and her minor daughter Y v The Netherlands*, CCPR/C/125/D/2498/2014, 15 April, 2019, paras 7.2–7.10, 8–10, plus Annex I (finding a violation of art 24(1) of the ICCPR on the child's right 'without discrimination … the right to such measures of protection as are required by his status as a minor, on the part of his family, society and the State.'

[69] S Dunsby, 'The Path' in K Clanchy (ed), *England, Poems from a School* (London, Picador, 2018) 67.

III. Citizen or Migrant?

From Nina Bawden's 1969 *Runaway Summer* to the more recent offerings, children whose families come from 'Africa' have to contend with crude stereotypes involving lions which roam everywhere and of course the idea that all people in the 'country' called 'Africa' are poor.[70] Starting his new school in Hawaii, the man who became America's first black president, Barack Obama, told his peers that his father was Kenyan. He was taunted, with one girl asking if she could touch his hair, while another boy asked if his father ate people.[71] In a moving letter to his daughter, David Chariandy, whose parents moved from Trinidad to Canada – his mother on a domestic worker visa, the one route definitely open to migrants of colour – recounts both their experiences of racism and his own, which included being called a spear-thrower and being told to go back whence he came. While he survives, his friend is broken.[72] The irony is of course that most migrants must have resources to enable them to migrate in the first place; thus some, but by no means all, are more likely to have left comfortable homes. Similarly, having parents born elsewhere results in even those children born in the new country being seen as not fully belonging. The alienation of black children is compounded by their absence in literature.[73] It could be argued that the very absence of black children in literature adds an additional dimension of erasure.

In his poem 'Kung'anda', Chingonyi captures a different kind of alienation faced by the migrant child – the media depictions of their parental homeland as backward, which they must weigh up against the more positive and uplifting image of home painted by their parents.[74] Meanwhile in her auto-fictional account, *What we Lose*, South-African-American Zinzi Clemmons says of her fellow students: 'They thought that in Africa we lived in huts and played with elephants. I did nothing to disabuse them of that notion.'[75]

[70] N Bawden (1969), n 13 above, 86, 95, 101. Katharine Rundell's *Girl Savage* offers an alternative to these negative views. It transposes 'savagery' to the English boarding school to which the protagonist is sent from Zimbabwe. The school seems to her zoo-like in its wish to contain its captives. The city is described in ways that remind one of a concrete jungle – another inversion of a stereotype of the African continent with its jungles where animals roam wild. Freedom and joy are to be found in the Zimbabwean veld, and misery and oppression in the English city. K Rundell, *The Girl Savage* (London, Faber and Faber, 2011).

[71] B Obama, *Dreams from my Father: A Story of Race and Inheritance* (Edinburgh, Canongate, 2007) 60.

[72] D Chariandy, *I've Been Meaning to tell you: a letter to my daughter* (London, Bloomsbury, 2018) 12–14; 19–20; 46–51; 57.

[73] In 2018 the trade magazine *The Bookseller* revealed that only 4% of the books published in the UK in 2017 featured any Black, Asian or minority ethnic (BAME) characters. This despite the fact that 32% of pupils of compulsory school age in England were minorities. It was ever thus. N Onwwuemezi, 'Alarming Study reveals only 4% of books feature a BAME character', *Bookseller*, July 2018, at: https://www.thebookseller.com/news/representation-childrens-literature-827841.

[74] K Chingonyi, 'Kung'anda' in *Kumukanda* (London, Chatto and Windus, 2017) 45.

[75] Z Clemmons, *What we Lose* (London, 4th Estate, 2017) 81. I think it important to say that some children *do* grow up in huts. I was one such child whose formative years were spent happily living in my grandmother's village, chasing chickens, helping to milk the cows, ploughing the fields, collecting firewood and eating sweet potatoes. It was wonderful. I remember it as a joyous time filled with love.

Migrant parents also face their own challenges. They sacrifice a great deal, often taking a status downgrade so that their children can have better opportunities. Janus faced, they look forward to a better future for their children, while looking back longingly at 'home' and all that it represents. They try very hard to ensure that their children can integrate into the new home while simultaneously trying to keep alive the best of the old home.[76] In her short story, 'Christmas is Coming', Jennifer Makumbi replays snatches of conversation between Ugandans at a Christmas party which reveal the strategies that they employ to ensure that their children remain grounded in their Ugandan culture. This includes an insistence that they only speak Luganda within the home, or the more radical option of leaving them 'at home' until they know their culture sufficiently that their heads will not be turned when they come to the UK.[77] Some Africans are known to send their children back to the parental homes on the continent when they reach their teenage years. This may be a protective measure, not least for boys whose parents fear that they may experience violence if they stay.

Kayo Chingonyi's award-winning collection of poems, *Kumukanda*, also highlights what is missed by migrant children, including those who have the right paperwork.[78] In the poem entitled 'Kumukanda', Chingonyi reflects on how the failure to participate in the initiation ceremonies like his peers at home has left him neither man nor boy: he is 'unfinished'.[79]

Black children go to school and seldom see themselves represented in books. White children take their 'normativity' for granted – they are everywhere. Books are about them and these books cover every genre imaginable. We were reminded of this when a row erupted over the casting of a Black actor to play Hermione in the stage version of *Harry Potter*. JK Rowling, the author, was forced to say that she had never described Hermione as belonging to any racial group and affirm that she was delighted with the casting.[80]

For Black and Brown children, it is more complex – where they appear in stories they are side-kicks or accessories to the main white character. It is not a surprise that black children sometimes report wishing they were white – why would they not when white people always get to be the heroes and do the fun stuff? In an essay about the recurring nightmares in which he re-experiences childhood traumas, the writer Ekow Eshun remembers:

> My racist friends. I loved them. I also envied the freedom their colour bestowed. Whiteness meant a lack of self-consciousness. No one pointed or laughed or sneered.

[76] Priya Minhas gives a moving account of the burden of being the child for whom many sacrifices have been made, P Minhas, 'How Not to Be' in N Shukla and C Suleyman (eds), *The Good Immigrant USA* (London, Dialogue Books, 2019) 51–66.

[77] JN Makumbi, 'Christmas is Coming' in *Manchester Happened* (London, Oneworld Publications, 2019) 1–28, 19.

[78] K Chingonyi (2017), n 74 above.

[79] K Chingonyi (2017) 33.

[80] R Ratcliffe, 'JK Rowling tells of anger at attacks on casting of black Hermione', *The Observer*, 5 July 2016.

> No one made monkey noises or mimed the throwing of spears. It meant you could lose yourself in a game of war or British Bulldog in the playground without being yanked from fantasy by a shout of 'wog'![81]

It gets worse. He goes on to recount how:

> Home from school one afternoon, aged nine, I stood in front of the bathroom mirror. I had a Brillo pad in my hand and I started to scrub my face. My forehead reddened. The wire fibres of the pad tugged at my skin. It stung terribly but I continued. The skin began to tear and little beads of blood prickled their way to the surface. I went at it harder, until my forehead was grazed and red and raw to the touch. It was soon too painful to continue. But I also knew there was no point in carrying on. I wanted to scrub the blackness off my face. But I couldn't erase what I saw in the mirror.[82]

One cannot help but recall Toni Morrison's *The Bluest Eye* about the young girl who longs for blue eyes as these are a marker of beauty, along with a white skin. In an Afterword to a later edition of the book, Morrison reveals that she based the story on the memory of a friend who had said at the start of primary school that she wanted blue eyes. Morrison recounts how this stayed with her and inspired the book:

> *The Bluest Eye* was my effort to say something about that; to say something about why she had not, or possibly ever would have, the experience of what she possessed and also why she prayed for so radical an alteration. Implicit in her desire was racial self-loathing. And twenty years later I was still wondering about how one learns that. Who told her? Who made her feel it was better to be a freak than what she was? Who had looked at her and found her so wanting, so small a weight on the beauty scale? The novel pecks away at the gaze that condemned her.[83]

Todres and Higinbotham note that the issue of race and representation is one of both a child's right to equality and to be free from negative stereotyping. They go on to identify that values are formed early on, and hence how we perceive certain groups colours our future interactions, including in making decisions about who to hire.[84] Worth quoting in full are the CRC General Comment No 1 views on state obligations to use education to tackle racism:

> The Committee also wishes to highlight the links between article 29 (1) and the struggle against racism, racial discrimination, xenophobia and related intolerance. Racism and related phenomena thrive where there is ignorance, unfounded fears of racial, ethnic,

[81] E Eshun, 'Soon Comes the Night', *Granta*, 8 August 2017, 2. An extract can also be read at: E Eshun, 'I dreaded going to sleep for fear of seeing him', *The Observer*, London, 11 June 2017. R Eddo Lodge writes about representation of black people on television, identifying the Cosby family as encompassing the idea of the successful black family which closely mirrored majoritarian stereotypes of the 'perfect family'. However, she notes that while the programme helped to challenge the other stereotypes of black people as lazy, it also reinforced the idea of a 'good black person' who is denied complexity. R Eddo-Lodge, 'Forming Blackness Through a Screen' in N Shukla (ed), *The Good Immigrant* (London, Unbound, 2016), n 76 above, 77–84.

[82] E Eshun (2017), n 81 above, 2.

[83] T Morrison, *The Bluest Eye* (London, Vintage, 1994).

[84] J Todres and S Higinbotham (2016), n 2 above, 59, 68.

> religious, cultural and linguistic or other forms of difference, the exploitation of prejudices, or the teaching or dissemination of distorted values. A reliable and enduring antidote to all of these failings is the provision of education which promotes an understanding and appreciation of the values reflected in article 29 (1), including respect for differences, and challenges all aspects of discrimination and prejudice. Education should thus be accorded one of the highest priorities in all campaigns against the evils of racism and related phenomena. Emphasis must also be placed upon the importance of teaching about racism as it has been practised historically, and particularly as it manifests or has manifested itself within particular communities. Racist behaviour is not something engaged in only by 'others'. It is therefore important to focus on the child's own community when teaching human and children's rights and the principle of non-discrimination. Such teaching can effectively contribute to the prevention and elimination of racism, ethnic discrimination, xenophobia and related intolerance.[85]

The Black child's right to an education is inadequately realised in many Western jurisdictions. The psychic harm of exclusion cannot be overestimated. This cannot be said to be in the child's best interests. Again, echoing Morrison's *Bluest Eye*, Reni Eddo-Lodge, commentator and author, writes about what it was like being the only black child in a class of 30 living in suburban South London in the early nineties:

> I have memories of my little white girl classmates trying to convince me that because my skin was black, my tongue was black too. I have memories of an art teacher encouraging my class to draw our 'beautiful blue eyes' whenever we got the crayons and sugar paper out. Everything around me was so starkly white that I began to believe that I would turn white sooner or later. I was quietly being written out of the narrative of humanity in my immediate surroundings.[86]

Books that have Black children as central characters are often 'issue' books discussing suffering and endurance. Inadvertently they may help to reinforce stereotypes. Rarely do Black children just get 'to be' or to have fun adventures. Occasionally a school collection will have the obligatory 'Anansi' story to tick its 'African' box. Other 'African folklores' can, at a push, be found in the reading schemes, but these allegorical tales may be as alien to the child as literature in another language. Happily this is changing and more stories for black children are being written and published.[87] Children with disabilities, and those from

[85] CRC General Comment No 1 on the Aims of Education, CRC/GC/2001/1 (2001) para 11.

[86] R Eddo-Lodge (2016), n 81 above, 77, 79. Living in suburban South West London with two young daughters, I am happy to confirm that schools have learned and changed and now children are given a palette of colours with which to draw themselves. Eddo-Lodge is also the author of the seminal *Why I am no Longer Talking to White People about Race* (London, Bloomsbury, 2017).

[87] In London, there are now bookstores and publishers devoted to selling books featuring black and other under-represented children (disabled, neuro-diverse and LGBT characters). These include Round Table Books and New Beacon books. See BBC 'BAME: The children's bookshop selling diversity', BBC, 11 May 2019. African-focused publisher Cassava Republic has expanded and started publishing children's books to address the black invisibility problem. New publishing houses such as Knights Of and Merky Books were established with the express aim of addressing the structural blockages that lead to the dearth of books for black and other children and, in the case of Merky books, adults too. They do this by 'creating a better pipeline: working with writers, illustrators, agents, retailers and other publishers to make books better'. From: http://www.knightsof.media.

diverse family settings or who are themselves not comfortable in the gendered binaries that are the stock in trade of children's books, must feel even more isolated. This may help to explain the phenomenon of Palacio's novel *Wonder* about disfigurement and its follow up which has resonated and is much read, discussed and loved by teachers, young readers and their parents.[88] It is my younger daughter's favourite book.

Uzodinma Iweala also captures the difficulties faced by children with migrant parents – they may be born in the 'new' country, and be citizens, but they are constantly reminded that they are not like the other (for which read white) children. They are reminded that their racial difference means that any infractions will be judged more harshly. 'You're not like these white children, my mother says, so don't go and follow their foolishness. But according to my father, I am already foolish, irredeemably foolish.'[89]

The girl child is further policed to ensure that she knows that girls must maintain their purity and learn to be 'good women'.[90] Although growing up in the West, they are constantly reminded of their 'culture' and told that they are 'lucky' relative to the children left behind. This creates dilemmas for the children of migrants – not having lived 'at home', how can they be expected to understand that they have this good fortune? They experience frustration because their parents expect them to abide by the behavioural rules which govern children 'at home'; yet they are in a different home, where children relate to each other and to adults in a less deferential way. Moving is Vietnamese-American Ocean Vuong's auto-fictional *On Earth We're Briefly Gorgeous*, a breathtakingly beautiful account of his inter-generational household with his loving grandmother and exhausted mother and how they look after each other.[91] His is a meditation on migration, race and love. He writes eloquently about coming out as a gay man.

Like Vuong, the children in fiction and biography often feel that they do not belong anywhere. Trips back home are not the balm that their parents think; rather they serve to highlight the distance between the child and the 'homeland', further reinforcing their sense of alienation.[92] Niru, the teenage son of two Nigerian

[88] RJ Palacio, *Wonder* (London, Corgi, 2012). Todres and Higinbotham (2016), n 2 above, 74–77. On family diversity see E Donoghue (illustrated by C Hadilaksono), *The Lotterys Plus One* (London, Macmillan Children's Books, 2017).

[89] U Iweala, *Speak No Evil* (London, John Murray, 2018) 93. Earlier his older brother had also reminded him: 'You aren't like these people, he says, they can do things that you and I can't.' (at 8). Makumbi has almost the same dialogue for her young protagonist being brought up by his Ugandan parents in Manchester, England. M Makumbi, 'Christmas is Coming' (2019), n 77 above, 1, 18.

[90] P Gappah, 'Before Tonde, After Tonde' in C Brazier (ed), *One World: A Global Anthology of Short Stories* (London, New Internationalist, 2009) 115, 117. 'Is this the way that a girl of your age talks to her father? Why does your mother not teach you some manners?'

[91] O Vuong, *On Earth We're Briefly Gorgeous* (London, Jonathan Cape, 2019).

[92] A notable exception is Makumbi's young protagonist who is desperate to leave Manchester to return to Uganda. J Makumbi, 'Christmas is Coming' (2019), n 77 above, 1, 8.

doctors in Iweala's *Speak no Evil* skewers his father's much professed love of his Nigerian homeland despite choosing to live in the United States:

> I've always felt weird about coming to Nigeria. Everything is always so overwhelming and aggressive from the moment we step out of the airport and into a country that my father loves so deeply he had to run away from it. But I've never had a choice. No one ever asked me.[93]

Sometimes, as captured in Chimamanda Adichie's short story, 'My Mother, the Crazy African', the children feel ashamed of their parents' seeming failure to integrate.[94] Why do they have to wear those clothes, why do they have to eat that food? In many ways all children feel sensitive about their parents and want them to be 'normal', but migrant children seem to feel it more sharply.

> When people ask where I am from, Mother wants me to say Nigeria. The first time I said Philadelphia, she said, 'say Nigeria.' The second time she slapped the back of my head and asks, in Igbo, 'is something wrong with your head?'[95]

Marjorie, Yaa Gyasi's teenage protagonist in *Homegoing*, also growing up in the US, has a different dilemma. Her teacher invites her to discuss what it means to her to be an African-American. She is conflicted. Is she, a child of Ghanaian descent, African or African-American? She longs to tell her teacher of the distinction between the two and to explain that Ghanaians call African-Americans *Akata*. She wants her teacher to understand:

> That *akata* people were different from Ghanaians, too long gone from the mother continent to continue calling it the mother continent. She wanted to tell Mrs. Pinkston that she could feel herself being pulled away too, almost *akata*, too long gone from Ghana to be Ghanaian.[96]

Mrs Pinkston soon puts Marjorie straight:

> Listen, Marjorie, I'm going to tell you something that maybe nobody's told you yet. Here, in this country, it doesn't matter where you come from first to the white people running things. You're here now, and here black is black is black.[97]

Children, particularly adolescent children, struggle with peer pressure and desire to conform and belong. This may sometimes lead to the angry rebellion manifested by teenage Katassi in Makumbi's 'Manchester Happened', where she details the struggles of Ugandan teenagers trying to integrate by changing their accents,

[93] U Iweala (2018), n 89 above, 53. At 54 Niru observes, 'No matter how many times we came "home," everything was so uncomfortable for me.'

[94] CN Adichie, 'My Mother, the Crazy African' in Adichie, *One World: A Global Anthology of Short Stories* (London, New Internationalist, 2009) 53–59.

[95] CN Adichie (2009), n 94 above, 53.

[96] Y Gyasi, *Homegoing* (London, Vintage, 2016) 273.

[97] Y Gyasi (2016) 273. See also C Obioma, 'The Naked Man' in N Shukla and C Suleyman (eds) (2019), n 76 above, 155, 165. See also T Cole, 'On the Blackness of the Panther' in N Shukla and C Suleyman (eds) (2019), n 76 above, 36, 39–41.

anglicising their names and denying any link to the African continent. Makumbi identifies the disconnect experienced by middle-class children who cannot understand their own status downgrade and who also struggle with the fact that the Britain that they imagined from media is not the one that they encounter. The rebellion, as detailed by Katassi's older sister with whom she lives, results in Katassi becoming:

> a contradiction, like multiple personalities. The more I tried to help the more she lashed out … I think the harder she tried to sound and act like them, the more the kids at school rejected her … She brought all the pain of school home to me. She would not lift a finger to do chores. She wanted designer gear. I bought winter woollies from charity shops for her and she was like, *E mivumba? I am not wearing second-hand clothes in Britain.* And by the way, she needed to go to France with her friends in summer. I was the obstacle to her happiness – strict, stingy, mean and patronising.[98]

Tendai Huchu's Magistrate in *The Maestro, The Magistrate & The Mathematician* tries to bond with his daughter, Chenai, by suggesting that they grow vegetables in their Edinburgh garden and offers to show her how. Her response is to tell him that they can buy vegetables from the supermarket. Coaxing her, he tells her about the joy in turning the soil to which she points out 'Ew, there's beasties in it', followed by a very Scottish, 'I dinnae ken nothing about growing stuff,' leading him to consider sending her for elocution lessons. He does not give up and tells her about the joy of tending a plot and watching the produce grow, to which she responds: 'It sounds like hard work.'[99] She concedes eventually.

Novels and short stories also capture that universal and inter-generational conversation about how 'things weren't like this in my day' which loom larger in conversations between migrants and their diaspora-born children and indeed between parents and children in general. Donkor's *Hold* throws up added poignancy of differences in privilege between the Ghanaian girl taken from her job as a family help and brought as a companion to Amma, the London-based daughter, and Amma who is seen as becoming a little wayward. Complaining about her parents and her situation results in Belinda (the maid) telling Amma that, compared to others, she is privileged and that she should thank her god and be grateful.[100]

Beverley Naidoo's *The Other Side of Truth* also explores an issue that is seldom discussed – that of intra-group tensions and discrimination. Specifically, on starting school, the daughter is paired with another 'African girl', whose family has fled Somalia and who have been given refugee status. Both girls suffer bullying and harassment from two black girls who think of themselves as 'properly' British and

[98] JN Makumbi, 'Manchester Happened' in *Manchester Happened* (London, Oneworld Publications, 2019) 62, 74.
[99] T Huchu, *The Maestro, The Magistrate & The Mathematician* (Edinburgh, Parthian Books, 2015) 103.
[100] M Donkor, *Hold* (London, 4th Estate, 2018) 120–21.

thus superior.[101] Their families come from the Caribbean and are part of an earlier migration. They have integrated, whereas the two African girls are still seen as outsiders. The deference to authority (teachers) and their eagerness to learn also marks the two 'new' girls as outsiders. The deference to teachers is a nod to the African Charter on the Rights and Welfare of the Child, 1990, article 31 injunction that children should respect their elders *at all times*. The girls have been brought up to abide by this injunction.[102]

In Gappah's story 'Before Tonde, After Tonde' the young daughter Patience, confronted by warring parents and a drop in their standard of living, longingly recounts what she misses and writes about in her school essay:

> I miss things like the sun always being there, or having a garden to run around in. I miss Blakiston, my old school, and answering questions in class without worrying if Kylie and her friends are going to make fun of me afterwards for knowing the right answers. I miss walking home with my friend Mandy … Most of all though, I miss our swimming pool, and that is what I wrote about.[103]

Her teacher thinks she has made up the swimming pool. It is important to acknowledge that some migrant families resort to violence within the family. Some, such as the abused husband in Makumbi's 'Christmas is Coming', attributes the wife's behaviour to stress and says things will get better. She is clearly an alcoholic. Wives and children may also be subjected to psychological violence, particularly, as in the case of Gappah's 'Before Tonde, After Tonde' where the husband-father is unable to find work that is commensurate to his former position at home. This causes him to lash out at the family.[104]

In her 2019 Caine prize short-listed story, 'It Takes a Village some Say', Ngwa-Mbo Nkweti, explores the issue of trafficking of children. We first come across the bustling Mrs Dukong when she comes to the family home. We learn that mother of the house has gone all out to buy the best meat to prepare a delicious stew for Mrs Dukong who is there to 'help her' by taking one of her daughters to live with a good family in America who want a child and will look after her and send money back to Cameroon. The girl, aged 13, is sent to the United States to live with an infertile couple who are materially successful and are only missing a child to complete the tableau of the perfect family. The couple take it upon themselves

[101] Cultural commentator Ekow Eshun, whose parents came as diplomats from Ghana, recounts regular beatings from his British-born, but Jamaican heritage, peers. They taunted him for coming from 'Africa' calling him 'Kunta Kinte' from the Alex Haley book, *Roots* and asked if he lived up a tree. Unlike his gauche, outsider status, for his peers, 'being West Indian and British brought with it an ineffable cool. They were the school trendsetters.' E Eshun, *Black Gold of the Sun: Searching for Home in England and Africa* (London, Penguin, 2006) 97.

[102] However, the siblings in *The Other side of truth* break the rules when it is for a positive end – for example they travel to central London, without permission from their foster carers, to seek out a famous broadcaster so that they can tell him their story.

[103] P Gappah (2009), n 90 above, 115, 118. Former President Barack Obama also details how, in order to fit into his new school in Hawai, he 'learned to speak less often in class.' B Obama (2007), n 71 above, 62.

[104] P Gappah (2009) 115, 119,121.

to change her name. In truth, Mrs Dukong, also called Aunty Gladys, would take advantage of the people in the village whom she would make sign contracts that they, being illiterate, could not possibly understand. She promised that their children would go to school and that they would receive money for their upkeep.[105] Aunty Gladys' trafficking operation in the United States is unmasked and then we learn of the victims:

> The courts contend that none of the children were sent to school. That they were little more than indentured servants, at their employers' beck and call day in and day out. The nominal pay they received (a pittance really at $30/week) was funnelled back to their parents only after Aunty Gladys received her 50-per-cent processing fee.[106]

The denouement, which I will not spoil, involves the girl at the start of the story reclaiming her name and wondering if she should write about her life and imagining a film being made about her.

The real-life case of Victoria Climbié in England is reminiscent of Nkweti's story, but with a tragic ending. Victoria was an Ivorienne girl whose parents had entrusted her to an 'aunt' figure who lived in England. They had done this believing that it would improve Victoria's life chances. The aunt promised to look after Victoria and treat her as if she were her own daughter. This is not what happened. The aunt beat her, burnt her with cigarettes, starved her and allowed her boyfriend to also mistreat her. The word torture was used to describe what she had endured. Social services were aware of the family. They visited but reasoned that there were different standards of child-rearing and that black people tended to be 'tougher' on the issue of parental authority. At least one social worker was black. Victoria eventually died, leading to an inquiry which led to changes in policy and practice.[107] The 432-page Laming Report, which is dedicated to the memory of Victoria, opens with a quote translated from de Saint-Exupery's *Little Prince*: 'I have suffered too much grief in setting down these heartrending memories. If I try to describe him, it is to make sure that I shall not forget him.'[108]

There is, however, still an on-going transnational and cross-cultural debate about whether smacking children constitutes abuse. Although the stereotype, including amongst many Africans, is that it is a parental right to 'chastise' their children, they are not alone in this. English Family law specialist Jonathan Herring notes that 88 per cent of people interviewed thought it right that a parent should retain the right to smack their child.[109] By way of contrast, many European states

[105] N-M N Nkweti, 'It Takes a Village Some Say' in *The Caine Prize for African Writing 2019 shortlist* (London, New Internationalist, 2019) 81, 91.
[106] N-M N Nkweti (2019) 81, 92.
[107] HMSO, The Victoria Climbié Inquiry, Report of an inquiry by Lord Laming (London HMSO, Cm 5730, 2003).
[108] J Hirabayashi from Y Kawahara's translation of *The Little Prince* by Antoine de Saint-Exupery, in Victoria Climbié Inquiry Report (2003) preliminaries.
[109] J Herring, *Family Law*, 8th edn (London, Pearsons, 2017) 515. See generally 512–15. Herring cites L Bunting, M Webb and J Healy, 'In two minds – Parental attitudes toward physical punishment in the UK' (2010) 24 *Children and Society* 359.

have outlawed physical chastisement of children, including by parents. The challenge, including for proponents of a parent's 'right' to discipline their child, is that the line between mild chastisement and abuse is not always clearly drawn. In her short story, 'On Monday of Last Week' Adichie writes a conversation between the white father of Josh, a biracial seven-year-old boy and his Nigerian babysitter on the issue of discipline. The father is of the view that one should reason with children and not smack them. For him smacking was abusive, while reasoning with the child would result in a change in behaviour. The child-minder, however, distinguishes discipline from abuse. She sees abuse as the equivalent of the cruelty that leads parents to stub out cigarettes on their children. However, mindful of her employer's sensibilities and wanting to keep her job, she goes along with his views about smacking.[110]

The fear of many African parents is that social services will come to their homes and threaten their fragile families and livelihoods. For this reason, they are careful about how they treat their children. In Makumbi's 'Christmas is Coming' there is an interesting scene where social workers visit the family home. They come because the son has secretly called social services to report his parents in the hope that they will intervene and send him back to Uganda. The father is both apoplectic and upset that anyone could accuse him of having abused his own children. The social worker is embarrassed and apologises for the intrusion saying that as her department had been contacted anonymously, there was a legal obligation to ascertain that all was in order.[111]

The case of *Abdi Ibrahim v Norway*[112] provides a good example of the challenges facing African parents who may themselves be damaged by their experiences. A Somali woman arrived in Norway and claimed asylum. She had been in Kenya and arrived with her one-year-old son. She was given a temporary residence permit and refugee status. She was not able to care properly for the child, leading to the intervention of social services. The child was placed in foster care with the mother being permitted short supervised visits six times a year. She wanted the child to be cared for by her cousin. Eventually it was decided to apply for an adoption order for the child to live permanently with a Christian Norwegian family who ate pork. The mother was Muslim. This, she argued was a violation of the freedom of religion. The mother challenged the adoption order, noting that it would terminate all her parental rights, including contact with the child. The Norwegian courts and social workers were of the view that there was no reasonable prospect of the mother ever being able to properly raise this child, or indeed to contribute meaningfully to the child's life and upbringing. The child had shown reluctance to spend time with the mother during the rare visits. The authorities argued that it was in

[110] CN Adichie, 'On Monday of Last Week' in *The Thing Around Your Neck* (London, 4th Estate, 2009) 74–94, 78.
[111] JN Makumbi, 'Christmas is Coming' (2019), n 77 above, 1, 10.
[112] *Abdi Ibrahim v Norway* [2019] ECHR 914.

the child's best interests to be adopted. The mother argued that the child's cultural background was important. Her claim that her article 8 rights to family and private life would be violated if the adoption were allowed to proceed was upheld. Her views and interests had not been adequately taken into account.

Of increasing concern in England is the rise in knife crime involving young black boys and men, explored in both Kelman's *Pigeon English* and Naidoo's *Web of Lies.* African names are now prevalent in the lists of names of murder victims released by the police. The occasional newspaper photo montages of people killed by knife crime invariably feature a gallery of the faces of young black men. The violence is often between groups of young black men, labelled 'gangs' by the police and media. Reasons given for the rise in black-on-black knife crime include drugs and the control of older drug dealers who recruit young teenagers to deliver or act as look-outs for their drug deals. This may lead to a criminal conviction which may lead to deportation.[113] Kayo Chingonyi ends his poem about a boy they called Grief by reminding us how in death the nameless young man/boy is reduced to yet another story about youth crime. He notes how the boy died selling drugs, 'so the white kids could say they *bun high grade.*' By reducing him to a statistic, Chingonyi poignantly reminds us of a mother's loss. She had her own name for her son, the boy commonly known as Grief.[114]

Invariably, family life and the absence of fathers or mothers due to multiple-jobs are highlighted as a factor. Seldom acknowledged is the high rate of black male exclusion from schools, the low rates of employment, including for qualified black men, and the stereotyping of young black men as being prone to violence, hyper-masculinised and irresponsible, particularly around sex and fatherhood.[115] Also not factored into the analyses has been the rolling back of state and local authority provision for youth centres and training programmes, all of which leave young people vulnerable to external influences and coercion. Young black men lead lives of intense oversight, more likely than others to be stopped and searched by police on suspicion of carrying drugs or having committed, or about to commit a crime. All these factors, which were recognised by the UN Special Rapporteur on anti-racism, E Tendayi Achiume, in her visit to the United Kingdom, can break the strongest willed.[116] This is captured in Belinda Zhawi's poem 'Deptford (*of masculinity*)' where the poet recounts a conversation with a lover who, accused of growing marijuana in his mother's garden, has been taken for a ride by the police who have beaten him up, leaving him with purple bruises. The way he sees it, '*I'm gonna end up in jail anyway*'.[117]

[113] J Bhabha (2014), n 28 above, 88–90. See also Home office guidance, 'Deporting Families of Foreign Offenders': GOV.UK, updated 4 February 2019; UK Visas and Immigration, 'Criminality guidance in article 8 ECHR', UK Gov, guidance of 14 May 2019.

[114] K Chingonyi, 'Grief' in K Chingonyi (2017), n 74 above, 40.

[115] See Akala, *Natives: Race & Class in the Ruins of Empire* (London, Two Roads, 2018) 15–22, 38–48.

[116] UN Special Rapporteur on anti-racism, visit to the United Kingdom, A/HR/41/54/Add.2, 27 May 2018, paras 25, 37, 39, 40.

[117] B Zhawi, 'Deptford (*of masculinity*)' in B Zhawi, *Small Inheritances* (Oxford, Ignition Press, 2018) 13.

Some parents seek to circumvent the travails of the 'Western' teenage years by sending them back 'home' for discipline and protection. This in turn sometimes results in alienation between parent and child.[118] Those that allow the children to stay have to navigate changing norms. Huchu's, Magistrate returns early from work to find his daughter Chenai fellating her Scottish boyfriend. The boyfriend stages a speedy exit. The relationship progresses until she falls pregnant, leading to an amusing cross-cultural conversation. The Magistrate's Zimbabwean friend, Alfonso, explains to the Scottish boy's father, Peter, that 'their' daughter has been 'damaged' and explains that to make good the damage, the young Scot or his father will have to give seduction damages which are a part of customary law. He adds the *lobolo* (bridewealth). Alfonso explains to Peter that they will have to proceed the 'traditional way' which will involve a payment of at least £5,000. To this the astonished Peter retorts that the girl is pregnant, not damaged. Alfonso is insistent on the need to make right the damage by way of monetary compensation.

The conversation descends into farce:

> 'I've had enough of this. You would try to sell your own child?' Peter stood up. Alfonso rushed towards him and grabbed the leg of his trousers.
>
> …
>
> 'Get off me, man,' Peter cried out.
>
> 'You must pay for our daughter. There is nothing for it. You've used her and now you want to cheat us. Statutory. She is underage. Five thousand pounds you owe. It's our culture. It's the law.'[119]
>
> Peter gets up to leave:
>
> 'You bloody scoundrels, trying to sell a little girl like this,' he said …
>
> Peter opened the door and called back to them, 'I am going to report this to the police, you blooming eejits.'[120]

This interaction opens up an interesting discussion about how to reconcile competing narratives about sexuality and marriage. The age of marriage in Scotland is 16. In England it is 16 but any marriage before the age of 18 requires the consent of the parent or guardian or legal permission to marry if the parental agreement cannot be given.[121] The most notorious child marriage case in England is that of *Mohamed v Knott* involving a migrant 26-year-old Nigerian student joined in England by his 14-year-old wife. He had married her in Nigeria when she was 13. The authorities became involved when she presented at the doctors with a sexually transmitted infection.[122] There were many questions asked, including about the validity of the marriage. As the parties were domiciled in Nigeria when the marriage was

[118] U Kufakurinani, D Pasura and J McGregor, 'Transnational Parenting and the Emergence of "Diaspora Orphans" in Zimbabwe' (2014) 7(1) *African Diaspora* 114, 121, 125–34.
[119] T Huchu (2015), n 99 above, 197.
[120] T Huchu (2015), 197.
[121] Marriage Act 1949 ss 2 and 3; Marriage (Scotland) Act 1977, s 1.
[122] *Mohamed v Knott* [1969] 1 QB 1.

contracted and Nigerian law recognised it, the English courts upheld its validity. This was 50 years ago. She would not have been given a spousal visa now.

While there are a number of African states with high rates of early and child marriages, it is the case that many now theoretically follow the injunction in article 21 of the African Charter on the Rights and Welfare of the Child, 1990 setting the age of marriage at 18.[123] Nevertheless migration, especially of people seeking refuge from war, can throw up challenging issues for the receiving state. This phenomenon is discussed by Nina Dethloff who explores the challenges posed by varying national ages of marriage, the different religious and cultural underpinnings of marriage and the fact that parents in conflict situations may elect to marry their daughters off early as a protection against violence and sexual violation. Dethloff's examination of Western responses to the marriage practices of incomers highlights different outlooks, from Canada's use of its provocatively titled law, 'Zero Tolerance for Barbaric Cultural Practices Act' to the debates in Germany about the validity of marriages contracted in Syria involving young girls, which would have been null and void in Germany.[124] Some countries set different minimum ages of marriage for family reunification applicants than for those marrying 'locally'.[125]

IV. Laws and 'Cultural Practices'

Migrants and other cultural minorities can also find themselves subjected to changing attitudes of police and state. An example is that of female genital cutting, or mutilation (FGM). There are differing ways in which the law deals with FGM. One is the criminalisation aspect, the other is how this relates to refugee status (particular social group) and the other is as a broader human rights issue. The human rights dimension is covered in the Istanbul Convention which expressly prohibits it, as do a myriad other human rights documents.[126] The refugee dimension has been addressed in Chapter four when I discussed the *Fornah* case which

[123] See also art 6 of the African Women's Protocol, 2003; UN Committee on the Rights of the Child (CRC), General Comment No 13 (2011): The right of the child to freedom from all forms of violence, 18 April 2011, CRC/C/GC/13; Joint General Recommendation No 31 of CEDAW and General Comment No 18 of the Committee on the Rights of the Child on Harmful Practices, CEDAW/C/GC/31-CRC/C/GC/18, 14 November 2014.

[124] N Dethloff, 'Child Brides on the Move: Legal Responses to Culture Clashes' (2018) 32(3) *International Journal of Law, Policy and the Family* 302, 303. See also EU Agency for Fundamental Rights, 'Addressing Forced Marriage in the EU: Legal Provisions and Promising Practices' (Brussels, EU Publications, 2014). Istanbul Convention, 2011, art 37.

[125] *R (Quila and another) v Secretary of State for the Home Department* [2011] UKSC 45. J Moses, 'Foreign Ideas about "Child marriage"? Diversity, the Family and Legal Reform in Contemporary Europe', Verfassungsblog on Matters Constitutional, 20 September 2019 https://verfassungsblog.de/foreign-ideas-about-child-marriage/.

[126] Istanbul Convention, 2011, art 38. Joint General Comment CEDAW 31 and CRC 18, CEDAW/C/GC/31-CRC/C/GC/18 (2014). African Women's Protocol, 2003, art 5.

led to the granting of asylum to a Sierra Leonean woman on the grounds of persecution due to social origin.[127]

In Britain, the practice was outlawed under the Prohibition of Female Circumcision Act 1985 but no prosecutions were ever brought. There were debates about the efficacy of a criminal law approach. Arguments were advanced against criminalising families who had their daughters cut because it would result in imprisonment, resulting in family breakdown. There was also the view that criminalisation would result in the practice going underground. These sensitivities meant that the police were reluctant to arrest parents, and social workers were hesitant about targeting minority families, not least because of the perception that this may be seen as racist.

By 2003 the mood music, influenced in part by the Climbié case, had changed and it was held to be more important to protect the rights of the children than to 'pander to' the feelings of cultural minorities. Neighbouring France was held up as an example of good practice. It has always taken a strict stance, prosecuting family members and practitioners. Controversially, children could also be examined by medical professionals. The result was that the UK Parliament passed the Female Genital Mutilation Act 2003. In addition to renaming the practice female genital mutilation, it became a crime to take a child out of the jurisdiction for the purpose of having FGM performed.[128] Border officers were to receive training to identify girls who were travelling and who may be perceived to be at risk. Schools were to be encouraged to discuss FGM within their Personal, Social, Health and Economic (PSHE) classes and to alert authorities as part of their safeguarding duty should they suspect that a child may be getting prepared for cutting.[129]

The 2003 Act has been buttressed by the addition of female genital mutilation protection orders under the civil law.[130] In 2015, the Serious Crimes Act made it an

[127] *Fornah (FC) v Secretary of State for the Home Department* [2006] UKHL 46.

[128] House of Commons Home Affairs Committee *Female Genital Mutilation: abuse unchecked*, Ninth Report of Session 2016–17, HC 390, 15 September 2016.

[129] An account of such a scenario is given by a solicitor called in to act for a mother who wanted to challenge an application for an FGM Protection Order made by the local authority to prevent the removal of a five-year-old Gambian girl by her parents who said they were taking her and her 10-year-old brother on holiday. The parents said that they were from non-practising communities and that Gambia had outlawed the practice in 2015. They also noted that they had gone to Gambia in 2014 and returned with an intact child. They agreed to a medical examination of the child which did not find any interference. Patronisingly, the German expert, who recommended that an FGM Protection Order be made for the duration of the girl's minority, and the solicitor both refer to the possibility that the parents may have been 'modernised or westernised' as pointing to the possibility that they may indeed not have their children cut on the proposed family holiday. The ignorance and failure of the local authority child services to investigate the actual likelihood of FGM before bringing action against the parents is explained away. A compromise was reached whereby travel would be permitted if undertakings were given. B Clulee, 'FGM Protection Orders: A Case Study', Family Law Group, 3 January 2017 at: www.familylawgroup.co.uk/site/blog/flg-news/fgm-protection-orders-a-case-study.

[130] Section 5A(2)(a) and Schedule 2, Part 1 of the Female Genital Mutilation Act 2003. HM Government, *Multi-agency statutory guidance on female genital mutilation*, Government UK, 2016, updated 23 October 2018.

offence to fail to protect a girl from FGM.[131] There was one, ill-advised and unsuccessful prosecution of a doctor whose defence was that he sewed a woman up after she had given birth, not to re-infibulate her, but to repair the trauma caused by birthing her child.[132] In February 2019, the Crown Prosecution service in London, finally secured its first conviction for FGM against the Ugandan mother of a three-year-old girl.[133]

FGM protection orders have been used more extensively to protect girls perceived to be at risk from being cut. Courts have also indicated a willingness to commit children to the care system if necessary. In a case of FGM – *Re B and G (Care Proceedings: FGM) (No 2)*[134] – the judge described FGM as a gross breach of human rights which would automatically trigger the threshold criteria for proving significant harm as laid out in the Children Act 1989. Male circumcision, being seen as less damaging, does not come in for the same opprobrium in Britain.

V. Conclusion

The chapter began by considering Todres and Higinbotham's thesis on how literature written for and by children can help to teach children about their human rights. Reflecting the raised interest in issues of migration is the increase in literature on the lives of children who travel alone, or who come with their families. What is it like to navigate the legal system alone? How does it feel to be a first-generation citizen child of a migrant? The normative frameworks guiding how states should treat minors are clear. However, we noted how, in practice, states were increasingly likely to breach or ignore those obligations. We learned too that the legal system is forced to reckon with different understandings of what it means to parent a child, in a new country where different cultural norms for raising children may apply.

The Conclusion follows.

[131] R Gaffney-Rhys, 'From the Offences against the Persons Act 1861 to the Serious Crimes Act 2015 – The Development of the Law Relating to Female Genital Mutilation in England and Wales' (2017) 39(4) *Journal of Social Welfare and Family Law* 417–34.

[132] S Laville, 'First FGM prosecution: how the case came to court', *The Guardian*, London, 4 February 2015. In 2018 another unsuccessful prosecution was brought against a Somali father alleging that his six-year-old daughter had been subjected to FGM. Medical evidence failed to establish this fact and the judge dismissed the case. S Morris, 'Police promise to learn lessons after collapse of FGM trial in Bristol', *The Guardian*, London, 22 February 2018. See also S Paterson, 'Britain's third FGM prosecution failure: African lawyer, 50, who was accused of cutting his nine-year-old daughter as a punishment is cleared after telling jurors "I'm Catholic, I don't believe in it"', *Daily Mail*, 22 March 2018. The UK Home Affairs Committee contrasted the UK's failure to prosecute with the rest of Europe where: 'there have been 40 FGM related trials in France, and European Commission figures to January 2012 show that there had been six in Spain; two in Italy and Sweden; and one each in the Netherlands and Denmark.' House of Commons Home Affairs Committee, *Female Genital Mutilation: abuse unchecked* (2016) para 51.

[133] BBC 'FGM: Mother guilty of genital mutilation of daughter', *BBC News* online, 1 February 2019.

[134] *Re B and G (Care Proceedings: FGM) (No 2)* [2015] EWFC 3.

Conclusion

In 2019 two fictional accounts both entitled 'The Wall' were published. The first was a novel by John Lanchester which was long-listed for the Booker Prize.[1] The second, a short story by Meron Hadero was short-listed for the 2019 Caine Prize for African Writing. A dystopian novel, Lanchester's *The Wall* is set in a fictional country which is walled. The protagonist is a guard, or defender, whose job it is to patrol the wall to ensure that the 'others' do not breach it. All the citizens within the wall are chipped to identify them. If a breach occurs, then the defender can be tried, executed or exiled. They become the 'other'. Lanchester's use of this wall as a metaphor for 'Fortress Europe' and the hostile environment which has resulted in the 'othering' of all those who are 'unalike' who seek to come, is startlingly apt. It echoes Christine Delphy's analysis, discussed in Chapter two, of how in France, the population is divided into 'the ones' who hold positions of power and privilege and the 'others' who are marginalised.[2] The 'others' are connected by their outsider status in both Lanchester and Delphy.

By way of contrast, Hadero's 'The Wall' is a tender exploration of the friendship that develops between a young girl who arrives in Iowa in the United States with her family who have fled Ethiopia via Germany, and Herr Weill, an elderly German man who had fled Germany in the 1940s. The 10-year-old protagonist only speaks Amharic and German and is therefore unable to interact with people outside of her family unit. She meets Herr Weill at a community potluck meal and they strike up a friendship, as they can communicate in German. He befriends and mentors her, gives her a diary to record her thoughts, teaches her English. The young girl has a second friendship with a Chinese girl in her class who also does not speak English. Their fragmentary communication occurs via symbols – our 10-year-old protagonist shows Yi her diary from Herr Weill; in turn, Yi gives her a pack of panda pens 'for her book'. As with Herr Weill, theirs is a friendship of equals, grounded in their shared experience of being refugees.

Herr Weill is sensitive to her family's poverty and sends parcels of food home with her. He takes her to the library for his annual Armistice Day visit to look at the German collection. They spend their day exploring German art, film, literature and opera. They also look at maps and try to pinpoint their old neighbourhoods. The maps also speak to the divisions that created boundaries separating people

[1] J Lanchester, *The Wall* (London, Faber & Faber, 2019).

[2] C Delphy (translated by D Broder), *Separate and Dominate: Feminism and Racism after the war on terror* (London, Verso, 2015).

that eventually led to the erection of an actual physical wall dividing Berlin in 1961. 'He pointed out the borders of the Jewish ghetto that he said had walls of its own when Germany was called something else, the Third Reich, but he did not call it that himself he said.'[3] Hadero also paints a picture of pre-Wall West Berlin, surrounded by the Communist bloc, leading Herr Weill to comment, 'It is a very uneasy thing to live life surrounded by enemies.' Our protagonist recalls how Herr Weill always quoted back to her, her observation:

> You say you lived with your family 'in the shadow of the Wall on the Western side, which looked the same as the shadow that fell on the East'. In this, you have pointed out the main aspect of a wall that these damn architects never seem to grasp: no matter which side you're on, its shadow is cast on you.[4]

I understand Herr Weill to be saying that the division hurt both sides. In the context of this book and Herr Weil and the young protagonist's discussion about their experiences of flight and exile, I also see the wall as highlighting how unjust laws and policies that unfairly restrict freedom of movement and fail to offer security to those under threat or in need, demean both the denied and the person or people who refuse to accede to the plea for help. The shadow cast by hostile immigration and refugee laws and policies leave us all cold. Similarly, Lanchester's darkly allegorical *The Wall* points to a joyless, 'empty' existence experienced by those protected behind the wall.

This book, which was started before their publication, has reflected the two 'Wall' stories: Lanchester's moral allegory about the impact of paranoia and what it does to a people who build walls to keep others out, is countered by the kindness of Herr Weill in Hadero's 'The Wall'. For me, Herr Weill stands for all those who have intervened as writers, poets and in the practice of law to humanise the 'other'. This in turn has led me to recall Maya Angelou's poem 'The Human Family' which reminds us how alike we are.[5] Our humanity connects us and acts as a universalising force.

I adopted and adapted Robert Mnookin and Lewis Kornhauser's 'Bargaining in the Shadow of the Law' and Sally Falk Moore's semi-autonomous social fields as my theoretical legal frameworks.[6] The shadows have been cast by immigration and refugee law. Using multiple narrative sources, the book followed the journeys of those who seek to navigate their ways around the law to reach places of safety. The walls have risen higher due to the incremental use of laws and policies by states keen on creating impregnable fortresses. However, what Chapter three showed is

[3] M Hadero, 'The Wall' in *Caine Prize for African Writing 2019 Shortlist* (London, New Internationalist, 2019) 41–63, 54.

[4] M Hadero (2019) 54–55.

[5] M Angelou, 'The Human Family' in M Angelou, *The Complete Collected Poems* (London, Virago, 1997) 224–25.

[6] RH Mnookin and L Kornhauser, 'Bargaining in the Shadow of the Law: The Case of Divorce' (1979) 88 *Yale Law Journal* 950–97 and SF Moore, Law and Social Change: The Semi-Autonomous Social Field as an Appropriate Subject of Study' (1973) 7(4) *Law & Society Review* 719–46.

that however high they build the walls, people will find a way to come. They will navigate their precarity using all the means at their disposal, including subjecting themselves to economic and psychological exploitation. If the state law does not give them any endowments with which to bargain, they will rely on other sources which may involve subjecting themselves to 'laws' administered by smugglers, employers and others met along the way. These are the semi-autonomous social fields of transnationalism.

The chapters which followed explored the ways in which different groups migrate and their experiences at the point of arrival. Chapter four on women showed how the structural inequalities that blight many women globally deny them economic opportunities and restrict their migration options. They often do not have the education that would entitle them to move as highly-skilled migrants, therefore they tend to come as domestic workers or to do other caring work. These jobs do not come with entitlement to family reunification, resulting in the women having to live separately from the children whose life chances they are working to improve. With few exceptions, the fictional and non-fictional literature shows how women who work as maids are treated as inferior or with suspicion. Case law throws up the uncomfortable truth that diplomats are over-represented among those mistreating domestic workers. The workers are denied basic employment law rights including fixed hours of work, regular and fair pay, paid holidays and the right to rest and leisure. The position of migrant domestic workers is made particularly difficult by the visas which tie them to their employers, making escape almost impossible. The fictional literature did throw up shafts of light including humour and examples of kindness.

Chapter four also explored trafficking and noted how for women, trafficking tends to lead them (disproportionately) into forced prostitution. The many human rights protections offered by the UN Trafficking Convention and regional conventions including that of the Council of Europe, do not seem to help most women who are exploited and who live in the shadows.[7] They are often afraid to come forward to seek assistance, fearing that their traffickers will target and harm the families left behind. Moreover, receiving states, far from taking the promised protective human rights approach, often resort to a more punitive criminal or immigration approach which leaves the women terrified of discovery.

Migration brings a shift in gender relations within the heterosexual family. The fictional literature highlighted the 'masculinity crisis' and status loss experienced by migrant men. They seem to struggle to re-adjust to their new conditions where they may not be able find employment in their former occupations and have to 'downgrade' to do work that they regard as beneath them, including paid work in

[7] UN Convention on Transnational Organized Crime; Protocol to Prevent, Suppress and Punish Trafficking in Persons, Especially Women and Children; Protocol against the Smuggling of Migrants by Land Sea and Air (2000); Council of Europe Convention on Action against Trafficking in Human Beings, 2005, CETS No.197.

the care sector. In the home they find that they have to do work that they would previously have classified as 'women's work' such as cleaning or cooking. For some this leads to enlightenment and a recognition of the uneven burden undertaken by their spouses in the home. Women, as mothers and wives, appear to cope better. They work hard to keep the family financially and emotionally intact. This is thankless work which takes its toll. There is also the issue of gender-based violence which impacts women disproportionately. Again, laws and policies conspire to make help-seeking difficult for migrant women, especially those who do not have the correct papers. Their access to resources, including information and help in navigating complex legal, housing and social security systems, is severely constrained. The lack of funding for groups which work with migrant communities, and which focus on Black and other minority ethnic women experiencing violence, further exacerbates an already desperate situation.

Chapter five highlighted the increase in both fictional and non-fictional literature on the lives of lesbian, gay, bisexual, transgender and intersex (LGBTI) communities on the African continent and in the diaspora. The journey here is a metaphorical one, from being invisible to being seen as the bearers of rights. The chapter reflected on the conversations, or controversies that have erupted over the status of LGBTI individuals in national laws on the continent. Colonial laws criminalising 'homosexuality' which had lain dormant for decades were dusted off and revived, ready for use or misuse. Some new laws, such as the Nigerian Same Sex Marriage (Prohibition) Act, 2014, were created to deal with perceived threats to social order and morality. As the late Binyanvanga Wainaina once noted, the rise in politicians' interest in homosexuality (the focus of much of the acrimony) coincided with elections and was 'seasonal'.[8] In their exhortations 'to reject this imported evil', the colonial roots of the legislation were forgotten and the message became 'Homosexuality was un-African and not part of African culture.' The fact is that African cultures were never unitary, and the denial of the existence of sexual and gender diversity in African societies was striking. Disturbing was the invocation of religion in support of the political message, and again, the near universal erasure of the fact that Christianity and Islam, the dominant religions, were themselves imports or imposed, depending on one's religiosity. The human rights practices of states in the Global North were examined in light of their responses to asylum seeking from those claiming persecution on grounds of sexual orientation. They were found wanting.

The increase in novels, biographies and ethnographies of the lives of LGBTI people on the continent and in the diaspora is helping to challenge the one-sided political rhetoric. I believe that reading builds empathy. The rise in case law is also indicative of an attempt to demand that states live up to their constitutional and human rights obligations on equal protection for all before the law. These advocacy efforts have had mixed results, but the fact that the cases were brought at all

[8] T Adams, 'Binyavanga Wainaina interview: coming out in Kenya', *The Observer*, London, 16 February 2014.

speaks to greater confidence in and impatience for the recognition and realisation of LGBTI rights. Charles Ngwena's plea for an Africanness based on inclusivity, democracy and equality for all is bearing fruit.[9]

The final substantive chapter, Chapter six, was on children. Using Jonathan Todres and Sarah Higinbotham, the chapter explored the educational power of literature to promote the values incorporated into the UN Convention on the Rights of the Child, 1989 and its regional counterpart, the African Charter on the Rights and Welfare of the Child.[10] Looking at the Concluding Reports of the CRC, supplemented by academic and fictional literature, one begins to understand that the promises of protecting the vulnerable are not honoured by states. This is most clearly seen when examining how unaccompanied minors are treated by both states of transit and also of arrival. Like adults, unaccompanied minors are subjected to scepticism, suspicion and scientifically-challenged age-determination tests. Chapter six also examined the lives of children in their new homes. Through poetry, autobiography and the fictional literature, we learned that black children in particular, face exclusion and feel alienated in school and society. This is in part because of educational curricula which do not reflect them or their experiences. Black children are subjected to stereotypes about their parents' countries which portray them in negative ways. As one needs money to go overseas and to navigate the visa regime, it is particularly galling for middle-class children to be confronted with these versions of their supposed inferiority. Children are also impacted by the status-downgrade of their parents, so may sometimes find themselves economically poorer. Additional pressures are put on them by parents who are fearful of losing their children to the 'wicked ways of the West' and therefore want to put in place restrictions for their protection. The children chafe at these and find that they want to belong, but find themselves caught between the parental pull to the 'old home' and the demands to integrate into the only home many of them have ever known. The chapter concluded by looking at how receiving states have dealt with practices such as Female Genital Mutilation and early marriage.

I. Law and Migration

The UN Special Rapporteur on contemporary forms of racism, Tendayi Achiume is clear that sovereignty entitles a state to set its own immigration policy. However, the Special Rapporteur goes on to qualify this by noting:

> However, where the strategy for immigration enforcement is so overbroad, and foreseeably results in the exclusion, discrimination and subordination of groups and

[9] C Ngwena, *What is Africanness?: Contesting nativism in race, culture and sexualities* (Pretoria, PULP, 2018).

[10] J Todres and S Higinbotham, *Human Rights in Children's Literature: Imagination and the Narrative of Law* (Oxford, OUP, 2016); UN Convention of the Rights of the Child, 1989, 1577 UNTS 3; African Charter on the Rights and Welfare of the Child, 1990, CAB/LEG/24.9/49 (1990).

> individuals on the basis of their race, ethnicity or related status, such a strategy violates international human rights law and undermines the Government's stated commitment to racial equality.[11]

Throughout the book we have seen the effects of these over-zealous and restrictive immigration laws and policies on people of African descent and others from the Indian sub-continent. Visas are near impossible to obtain, even for highly-educated individuals wanting to travel for work. The lack of options for legal travel leaves people at the mercy of smugglers and traffickers. The literature, both fictional and non-fictional, also shows that people resort to self-help measures to leave their countries of origin to travel. The hostile environment that greets those who make it to their intended countries makes for miserable living. Those without the right papers cannot work, those *with* the papers often find that they experience discrimination and are therefore forced to take jobs that are not consonant with their qualifications and experience. Accommodation is hard to source as is access to health care outside that provided by voluntary doctors and other medically-qualified staff. They cannot access state benefits and this impacts their quality of life and impacts the life chances of any accompanying children. Indirectly impacted by these hostile policies, are visible minorities who may already hold citizenship. They are seen as 'other' and thus not entitled to the rights and benefits that are given to other citizens. The Windrush scandal showed how difficult it is to reverse the mislabelling of citizens as unentitled aliens. These hostile policies create work for lawyers, who bring endless cases challenging the compliance of government policies with human rights law. However, lawyers and those who work in the voluntary and advice-giving sectors find that their resources to assist have also been cut.

II. Looking Ahead

There is cause for hope. Recent research in the UK suggests that the public's antipathy to immigration has peaked. There are multiple reasons for this. There is now emerging a more public discourse about why migrants choose the countries that they do. The colonial links between incomers and those early colonialists are now starting to percolate. There are recommendations that school curricula reflect the long histories of colonialism, contact between regions and also the contribution made by the forebears of those now labelled 'immigrants' to the safety, security, growth and prosperity of Western states.

[11] (A/HRC/41/54/Add.2, 27 May 2019, para 56. Khosravi is eloquent on the issue of hospitality, not least the need for unconditional hospitality which entails 'recognizing the other's right to have rights – the basic right of human rights.' S Khosravi, *'Illegal' Traveller: An Auto-Ethnography of Borders* (Basingstoke, Palgrave Macmillan, 2010) 129. On hospitality more broadly and the distinctions between the haves and the have nots, see 125–29.

Nevertheless, it remains a concern that it takes photographs of dead children (Alan Kurdi or more recently the El Salvadorean father Oscar Martinez Ramirez lying face down in a river, his two-year-old daughter, Angie Valeria, clinging to his neck, both dead) for outrage to be triggered. It is worth noting that the death of Alan Kurdi was marked, in part, by the naming of a rescue ship run by the not-for-profit, Sea Eye, after him. In August 2019, the crew of the *Alan Kurdi* rescued African migrants from a small sinking ship. They headed for the closest port, Lampedusa. However, the Italian government refused to accept the migrants and recommended that the *Alan Kurdi* transport them to Libya instead. The captain refused, asserting: 'We will obey international law and will not bring anyone back to a civil war country … Libya is not safe.'[12] The rescued were taken to Malta for dispersal within the European Union, for the Maltese government only accepted the landing on the basis that Malta would not take a single one of the rescued migrants.

In a radio discussion, a former British Labour government minister who had been in charge of immigration, noted: 'The problem with migration is that no one wants the door completely open, but nobody wants it completely shut.'[13] The proposed 'solutions' to the issue of the global movement of people vary from Trump's wall-building to keep the 'wrong people' out, to the utopian vision of open borders where people can wander freely. Gary Younge, a journalist and commentator, in a series on utopian ideas, wrote a piece advocating absolute freedom of movement, arguing 'why dream small?'[14] His reasoning is seductive and echoes the views expressed by Amir Heidari, the *dal lal* or 'smuggler' in Shahram Khosravi's ethnography.[15] However, neither Trump's policies nor Younge's uplifting vision are likely to be acceptable or seen as workable. Global financial and opportunity inequalities are always likely to determine who wants to move (those seeking opportunities) and where they want to move. Those in the richer countries have been reluctant to share the wealth, whatever the basis of its provenance (colonialism in many instances). The desire of those in possession of wealth to retain it is greater than any claim to a common humanity and sharing of resources. Our inter-connected histories demand that we honour our obligations, one to the other.

The attempts to improve the conditions in the countries of departure have been half-hearted and insufficiently resourced. Western states have made cynical use of regimes too poor and broken to look after their own citizens, let alone those who are turned away and denied entry. Western regimes have spoken with forked tongues, condemning human rights violations in the very states to which

[12] Reuters, 'Migrants land in Malta after Berlin brokers deal for EU to take them in', *The Guardian*, London, 5 August, 2019.

[13] Liam Byrne, 'Who Should be Let in?', *BBC World Service*, broadcast Friday 22 June 2018.

[14] G Younge, 'End all Immigration controls-they're a sign we value money more than people', *The Guardian*, London, 16 October 2017. The article was written in a series entitled 'Utopian Thinking, Human Rights'.

[15] S Khosravi (2010), n 11 above, 108–9.

they send people that they do not want. The results have been catastrophic: reports of widespread violations, including detention and being caught in the midst of a civil war in Libya; mass drownings; and treatment that fully meets the legal definition of degrading and inhuman treatment. The use of detention to hold migrants in Western states is also replete with contradiction between assertions of fairness, tolerance and equality for all before the law, and the procedural violations and denial of the detainees' rights to liberty and security of the person.[16] A significant number of states have expressed reservations about the Global Compact on Migration to lead one to wonder about its efficacy and whether it will ever be implemented.

It is not only states, both sending and receiving, that need to reflect on their approach to immigration. Much of the public backlash has been grounded in inaccurate and often inflammatory media accounts of the alleged predatory and anti-social behaviour of a group of people called 'immigrants'. Their multi-generational contributions, economic and cultural, to the development of the recipient states have been minimised or ignored. There have been counter-narratives which speak to the benefits of migration and which seek to honour the promise of human rights as inhering in and requiring the protection of all people.[17]

Fictional literature also provides us with hopeful endings. Chimamanda Adichie's *Americanah* ends with the protagonist voluntarily leaving the United States to return home to Nigeria. She reignites her relationship with her old love, and one is left with the sense that happiness follows.[18] Similarly, Babukar in Imbolo Mbue's *Behold the Dreamers*, refuses his boss's offer to hire an expensive immigration lawyer to help him and his family stay on in America.[19] My heart soared with joy at the end of Sunjeev Sahota's *The Year of the Runaways* where we glimpse Tochi, who has self-segregated throughout the book because he is a *chamaar*, or Dalit, with his new family back home in India.[20] There is pride and dignity in returning home. Babukar and Tochi remind us that the diminution of self and the loss of dignity that migration with its attendant humiliations, may not be a price worth paying after all.

And for me? Well, I remember how my father always said that when he died, he wanted to be buried 'at home'. Home for him meant his parents' village. He died in Harare, Zimbabwe on a Tuesday evening in January 2017. Early on Friday morning of the same week, a convoy of cars left for the drive back to his family village in Kasungu, Malawi. It passed through Mozambique, retracing his original journey. On Sunday, he was buried in a grave next to those of his mother and father. A

[16] J Wittenberg, 'You have no voice in there', *The Guardian*, London, 28 June 2019. See also D Herd and A Pincus (eds), *Refugee Tales II* (Manchester, Comma Press, 2017) and *Refugee Tales III* (Manchester, Comma Press, 2019).

[17] J Portes, *What do we know and what should we do about immigration?* (London, SAGE, 2019).

[18] CN Adichie, *Americanah* (London, 4th Estate, 2014).

[19] I Mbue, *Behold the Dreamers* (London, 4th Estate, 2016).

[20] S Sahota, *The Year of the Runaways* (London, Picador, 2016).

year later, a headstone was placed on his grave under majestic trees which let the dappled sunshine through, reminding me of Maya Angelou's 'Elegy' which starts:

> I lie down in my grave
> and watch my children
> grow
> Proud blooms
> above the weeds of death.[21]

He is home, and I must end my journey. But first, a last word with my father: 'Look Dad, a book on law and literature – it did not have to be a choice between one or the other; you can do both.'

Writing this book has felt like an on-going conversation with him. There are so many books that I have longed to share with him. I miss him still and probably always will.

And for my first country, my mother, who nurtures me still and whose love and self-sacrifice move me to tears, thank you.[22]

Through years of reading together and writing this book, I have connected with my children. This book is dedicated to Azera and Shamiso, my two extraordinary daughters. You are my 'proud blooms'. Inscribed in my heart forever. Mummy.

[21] M Angelou, 'Elegy' in M Angelou, *The Complete Collected Poems* (London, Virago, 1997) 115. Read the rest of the poem, it is beautiful.

[22] The reference to my mother as my first country is based on the poem 'Lands' by N Waheed in *Salt* (London, CreateSpace Publishing, 2013) 182 with which I opened the book.

AFTERWORD

As this book will be born into a world that is radically different to the one in which it was conceived, nurtured and written, it seemed worthwhile to try to take in a little of what has happened since it went to press. This afterword, like the capsules that are buried in new buildings or to mark momentous years, tries to explain what is happening now and to offer one's thoughts and hopes for an imaginary tomorrow.

I have often reflected on how the COVID-19 pandemic has highlighted so many of the themes raised in this book. The diaspora of slavery in the United States and the diaspora of colonialism have been disproportionately impacted by the virus.[1] They have contracted it in larger numbers and are over-represented in the death statistics.[2] In the United Kingdom all but one of the many doctors that have died have been of African, Caribbean, Arab or Asian descent. Members of the large migrant nursing community from the Philippines has joined the statistics of Black African and British Asian nurses who have died. The caring staff who work in nursing homes have also seen an over representation (in relation to their numbers) of people from Africa and the Philippines. Various reasons have been put forward to explain this disproportionate impact: the fact that people from Black and Asian (particularly South Asian) communities are more likely to suffer from type two diabetes and hypertension and from the lack of vitamin D, which is produced by exposure to the sun. Racism was cited by Black and Asian commentators as a major contributory factor. This was rejected, rebuffed, condemned as divisive and unhelpful, until the evidence became too overwhelming to ignore.[3] Using Standardised Mortality Ratio (the ratio of observed deaths in the study group to expected deaths in the general population) researchers who took a snapshot over seven weeks found:

> Specifically, adjusting for age and region, the risk of death from C-19 for Black African groups was 3.24 times higher than the general population; Pakistani was 3.29 times

[1] OHCHR, 'Disproportionate Impact of COVID-19 on Racial & Ethnic Minorities Needs to Be Urgently Addressed – UN High Commissioner for Human Rights', OHCHR Press Release, 2 June 2020 at: www.ohchr.org/EN/NewsEvents/Pages/DisplayNews.aspx?NewsID=25916.

[2] E Pilkington, 'Black Americans dying of COVID-19 at three times the rate of white people', *The Guardian*, 20 May 2020. It is worth noting that in some countries migrants from the Global South, asylum seekers and refugees have been all but invisible. Y Divakis 'Greece: locals "stay at home", while migrants stay invisible' LIDC Migration Leadership Team at: https://blogs.soas.ac.uk/lidc-mlt/2020/05/19/greece-locals-stay-at-home-while-migrants-stay-invisible-part-iii/.

[3] S Sanghera, 'Coronavirus and ethnicity: black and Asian NHS medics on the frontline, *The Times*, 24 April 2020.

higher; Bangladeshi was 2.41 times higher; Black Caribbean was 2.21 times higher; and Indian was 1.7 times higher.[4]

The researchers' recommendations point to the cause of the problem:

> Actions to reduce these inequities include ensuring an adequate income for everyone so that low paid and zero-hours contract workers can afford to follow social distancing recommendations, reducing occupational risks such as ensuring adequate PPE (personal protective equipment), reducing barriers to accessing healthcare and providing culturally and linguistically appropriate public health communications.[5]

As noted in Chapters three and four, migrant workers, especially those who are undocumented, are likely to have lower paid jobs in cleaning and caring, less negotiating power and feel unable to challenge unsafe working conditions including working without protective equipment. Zero hours contracts, where you are only paid for the hours that you work, heighten precarity and compel people to work even when ill. Their families, here and 'at home', depend on them for support so they have to keep going.[6] Also severely impacted were bus drivers and security staff, again disproportionately of Black or Asian descent. They too were exposed to unsafe working conditions.

The figures revealed that even highly skilled staff like doctors and consultants were not protected by their status. If anything, the public learned to their surprise that all these migrant health workers had to pay an NHS surcharge to enable them and their families to access the very health service for which they were paying with their lives. This was in addition to the exorbitant annual visa renewal fee that those who had yet to establish residence were asked to pay.[7] Initially the British government refused to remove this surcharge for health staff but public opinion forced a reversal of policy. The British government also eventually set up a review to look into the disproportionately high death rates of Black and Asian people. The government which had starved the NHS of funding suddenly found a seemingly inexhaustible supply of cash. In light of the British prime minister's own brush with death via a severe bout of COVID-19, the NHS will probably be better funded after the immediate crisis, though its staff may not be better paid.

[4] I am grateful to the kind and generous Jo Choulerton who not only copy-edited this entire book, but provided references such as this one – thanks Jo! R Aldridge et al, Black, Asian and Minority Ethnic groups in England are at increased risk of death from COVID-19: indirect standardisation of NHS mortality data [version 1; peer review: 3 approved with reservations] At: https://wellcomeopen-research.org/articles/5-88/v1; or UCL News, BAME groups two to three times more likely to die from Covid-19 at: https://www.ucl.ac.uk/news/2020/may/bame-groups-two-three-times-more-likely-die-covid-19 at: www.ucl.ac.uk/news/2020/may/bame-groups-two-three-times-more-likely-die-covid-19.

[5] UCL News (2020).

[6] L Bryant, 'As Coronavirus hits European Economies, Remittances Plummet, *Voice of America News*, 23 April 2020 at: www.voanews.com/covid-19-pandemic/coronavirus-hits-european-economies-remittances-plummet.

[7] N Malik 'Foreign NHS workers are risking their lives for us-and paying for the privilege' *The Guardian*, 19 April 2020.

The same government had voted down a pay increase for the poorly paid nursing staff two years previously. NHS staff and other 'keyworkers' have been showered with public affirmations of appreciation (the 8pm Thursday collective applause where people stand outside), and daily donations of meals and cakes from grateful companies and individuals. It has been telling and troubling that the public have felt compelled to raise extra money to fund the NHS to purchase protective equipment and other necessities. This should be the job of a responsible state and not passed back to citizens who have already contributed through their taxes.

In Chapter six I discussed children and specifically what it is like to be the child of a migrant, or even a citizen child. COVID-19 closed schools early, exams were cancelled and parents were provided with online links and resources to help home school their children. Again multiple inequalities were revealed. In Britain, the cancellation of public exams to be replaced by teacher assessments raised red flags for Black students and their parents who well understood the workings of bias and the downgrading of expectations of outcome for Black children. The provision of links and the introduction of online teaching revealed class inequalities – not all children and indeed families had access to multiple computers and tablets on which to complete work. Frankly some of them had neither and many had limited or no internet connection. It was a choice between paying the phone bill to obtain data to do school work or buying food or feeding the electricity meter.

The furloughing of staff including previously middle class people saw pressure on foodbanks which struggled to cope with demand and which had to start asking for donations to buy food because the food donations given by the public and supermarkets were insufficient. Some schools in poor areas took to making weekly food drops to the poorest and most vulnerable children. The lock down and the limits of one hour outside for exercise left many stuck in crowded high rise flats with no escape. There was an increase in violence against women – a global phenomenon. Vulnerable children and children at risk were not always monitored adequately because of the lockdown. Anxiety increased in both children and parents. Poverty and ethnicity are closely connected so that Black people are over-represented in poor, overcrowded housing without gardens. They were also more likely to be stopped and fined by police for violating lockdown when they did go out.[8] It is estimated that children from poor families will have fallen back significantly in attainment during this time. Not for them nights of camping in the garden, artwork and subscriptions to National Geographic.

At the opposite end of the age spectrum are older people. In Britain they were asked to shelter meaning they should not leave their homes at all. Groceries, medicine and all their necessities would be brought to them. Forgotten were those in residential facilities. Yes, they too could shield, but they were exposed to incoming staff and fellow residents returning from hospital stays. There were no testing

[8] M Busby and M Gidda, 'BAME people fined more than white population under coronavirus laws', *The Guardian* 26 May 2020.

facilities for staff or returnees to check if they had contracted COVID-19 and should self-isolate. There was no protective equipment provided for care staff. The result was chaos – a high death rate in residential care, late provision of protective equipment and delayed testing of staff and residents. Exposed was the government's long term failure to create a joined up policy linking social care and health. To add to the agony of the avoidable deaths was the ban put on family contact with those infected and in hospital. Funerals, like hospital goodbyes were lonely affairs watched through phone screens, Zoom or some other device held up by tired, but kind nurses and funeral directors.

As all this was happening another racism was rearing its head. Chinese people, and indeed anyone who "looked" Chinese (most Asians to the undistinguishing eye) were attacked in the street and called names for being the bearers and bringers of disease. They were told to go home. It did not help that President Trump took to calling COVID-19 'The Chinese Virus'.[9] In a surreal twist, it emerged that in Guangzhou, China, African migrants were being subjected to similar taunts and invitations to return to their homes by their Chinese hosts. They were said to be the carriers of the disease and found themselves evicted from their homes and excluded from public spaces including restaurants. McDonalds put up a sign saying black people were not allowed in. While in some countries, such as Britain, one could not get tested for love or money, in Guangzhou black people were compulsorily tested and forced to quarantine. African Americans living in Guangzhou were lumped in with their African kin and evicted or denied tenancies. Their first world passports did not protect them from third world treatment.[10] Chinese ambassadors in African countries were summoned for a rare dressing down by governments lobbied by their angry populations.

Meanwhile the head of the World Health Organization (WHO) whose daily press briefings were usually calm and reassuring disclosed that he had been the subject of a racist campaign. (Dr Tedros Adhanom Ghebreyesus is Ethiopian and the first African to head the WHO). He said that was only speaking out because his tormentors had now broadened their attacks to all Africans and Black people. While he was able to ignore personal attacks, he could not let these wider provocations go. Dr Tedros also identified a colonial mentality in two French scientists who had discussed, on a television programme, that vaccine safety trials could be moved from Europe and Australia to Africa where HIV vaccines had previously been tested.[11]

[9] S Tavernise and R Oppel Jr, 'Spit on, Yelled at, Attacked: Chinese-Americans Fear for their Safety', *The New York Times*, 23 March 2020; C Thien, 'I'm Chinese. That doesn't mean I have coronavirus', *The New York Times*, 7 May 2020.

[10] Human Rights Watch, 'China: Covid-19 Discrimination against Africans', *Human Rights Watch*, 5 May 2020; G York, 'African diplomats protest alleged racism and inhumane treatment of migrants in China', *The Globe and Mail*, 12 April 2020; E. Williamson and V Wang, '"We need help": Coronavirus fuels racism against Black Americans in China', *The New York Times*, 2 June 2020.

[11] W Feuer 'WHO chief addresses death threats, racist insults: "I don't give a damn"', CNBC, 9 April 2020.

Adding to the tale of woe, on 25 May 2020, just as this book was going to press, an African American man named George Floyd was asphyxiated to death (murdered) by a policeman kneeling on his throat in Minnesota USA. As he did this, his three colleagues watched but did not intervene leaving it to the crowd of people that gathered to plead with the policeman to remove his knee from George Floyd's neck. Floyd, who had his hands cuffed and was lying on the floor so not a flight risk, repeatedly told the policeman that he could not breathe. His arrest, his pleas and death were all captured on the mobile phones of the bystanders. Protests, handwringing and pledges to learn lessons and do better are underway simultaneously. Protestors noted that racism was as harmful and injurious a virus as the COVID-19 pandemic that was killing Black people in disproportionate numbers. The policemen were fired and all have been charged. However, as Nicola Rollock notes: '… the truth is Floyd's murder sits at the chilling end of a continuum of racism that many of us have been talking about, shouting and protesting about for decades.'[12]

At the start of the pandemic, there was much hand wringing about how Africa would cope. For now, fingers crossed, the COVID-19 induced African collapse, anticipated in apocalyptic terms, has not materialised. This may be because, unlike the US and UK, African governments took seriously the lessons learned from Asia and went into early lockdown. They also did their best to remember the lessons learned from previous epidemics like Ebola.[13] Senegal has done particularly well in containing the virus, testing and tracking and generally keeping on top of things. Also praised has been South Africa, although the absence of alcohol has led to some homebrewing initiatives of gin in the posh suburbs and regular brew in the townships. Class inequalities in South Africa have again been highlighted – lockdown and physical distancing in a big house in the suburbs is a luxury few people have as is working from home. Many in urban areas live in overcrowded townships. Those in the informal sector have to go out to earn their daily bread.

In Chapter one I cited Alex de Waal's observation that human rights organisations present the first draft of history.[14] These organisations have managed to continue to provide updates about human rights violations that are ongoing.[15] I shudder to think how big the COVID-19 academic production of blogs, comments, special issues, grant applications and webinars will have grown by the time you read this. It is already starting to feel overwhelming and unwieldly,

[12] N Rollock, 'It's time for white people to step up for black colleagues', *Financial Times*, 4 June 2020.

[13] A Hirsch, 'Why are Africa's coronavirus successes being overlooked?', *The Guardian*, 21 May 2020.

[14] A de Waal, 'Writing Human Rights and Getting it Wrong', *Boston Review*, 6 June 2016, available online at: http://bostonreview.net/world/alex-de-waal-writing-human-rights.

[15] 'Africa's Covid-19 Response Should Focus on People's Needs, Rights', *Human Rights Watch*, April 16, 2020 at: www.hrw.org/news/2020/04/16/africas-covid-19-response-should-focus-peoples-needs-rights. See also 'Africa: We must act now to avoid a catastrophe, say rights chiefs' *African Commission*, 20 May 2020.

although there have been some insightful pieces.[16] Frankly, I did wonder about fanning the flames with this afterword but felt it important to highlight how the challenges presented in the book are real and ongoing. Racism is real and it constitutes violence. Before I close the capsule, a few thoughts on what I hope will be happening by the time of publication and beyond.

My hopes are those of most people; that a vaccine will be found quickly; that its distribution will be global, that the African continent will not be an afterthought and that it will be given freely to those without the means to purchase it. I hope that the environment continues to regenerate in the way it has during lockdown. I hope that our children can resume their interrupted childhoods. I hope that we will never forget those whose lives have been lost, many of whom have died in service to others. I sincerely hope that we will always honour them so that the children and grandchildren that they left behind will know what extraordinary people they were. I hope that the disproportionate deaths of Black and Brown people in the Global North will not be in vain – a forgotten footnote, much like their service in wars for which they received neither acknowledgement nor full citizenship or rights. I hope that we will not shy away from naming racism when we see it and, more importantly, acting to change it. I hope that my people on the African continent are continuing to contain the virus – showing that having the humility and wisdom to learn from others and listening to what the science is saying can yield fruit. I hope that our socio-structural challenges have not overwhelmed us and that children have returned to school, that all people have nourishing food and access to adequate health care. I hope that the neighbourliness and care for each other that has emerged will be more than a phase. I hope for the continued good health of my family, friends and everyone's else's. I hope for the continuation of the clear head and peace of mind that being centred within the love of my family has given me – free from outside distractions, hurts and harms. I wish you well.

[16] Great blogs include: P Cullet, 'Learning from coronavirus to tackle climate change: the imperative of solidarity and equity', SOAS blog, 11 May 2020 at: www.soas.ac.uk/blogs/study/coronavirus-solidarity-equity/; T Haissan 'Education and Covoid-19 in Nigeria: tackling the digital divide', SOAS blog 28 April 2020 at: www.soas.ac.uk/blogs/study/covid-19-nigeria-digital-divide/; L Oette, 'How is Covid-19 impacting human rights?' SOAS blog, 30 March, 2020 at: https://www.soas.ac.uk/blogs/study/covid-19-human-rights/. The Centre for Human Rights, University of Pretoria has hosted some excellent webinars on COVID-19 and human rights discussing topics including police overreach and economic, social and cultural rights violations. It has a COVOID-19 portal: https://www.chr.up.ac.za/covid19.

BIBLIOGRAPHY

Books

Abel, R, *Politics by Other Means: Law and the Struggle Against Apartheid* (Abingdon, Routledge, 2002).
Abdelnabi, M (translated by J Wright), *In the Spider's Room* (Cairo, Hoopoe, 2018).
Achebe, C, *Arrow of God* (London, Heinemann, 1964).
Adichie, CN, *Half a Yellow Sun* (London, Harper, 2009).
Adichie, CN, 'My Mother, the Crazy African' in C Brazier (ed), *One World: A Global Anthology of Short Stories* (London, New Internationalist, 2009) 53–59.
Adichie, CN, *Purple Hibiscus* (London, 4th Estate, 2013).
Adichie, CN, *That Thing around your neck* (London, 4th Estate, 2009).
Adichie, CN, *Americanah* (London, 4th Estate, 2014).
Addonia, S, *The Consequences of Love* (London,Vintage, 2009).
Addonia, S, *Silence Is my Mother Tongue* (London, Indigo Press, 2018).
Aggleton, P and Parker, R, *Routledge Handbook of Sexuality, Health and Rights* (Abingdon, Routledge, 2010).
Akala, *Natives: Race & Class in the Ruins of Empire* (London, Two Roads, 2018).
Alexandrov, V, *The Black Russian* (London, Head of Zeus, 2013).
Alibhai Brown, Y, *Who do we think we are?* (London, Penguin, 2001).
Alibhai Brown, Y, *No Place Like Home* (London, Virago, 1995).
Ama Ata Aidoo, *No Sweetness Here and Other Stories* (Kumasi, Isaac Books and Stationery Service, 2013 [1970]).
Anderson, B, *Us and Them? The Dangerous Politics of Immigration Control* (Oxford, OUP, 2015).
Anderson, R, *Illegality Inc.: Clandestine Migration and the Business of Bordering Europe* (Richmond CA, California University Press, 2014).
Angelou, M, *The Complete Collected Poems* (London, Virago, 1995).
Angelou, M, *The Heart of a Woman* (London, Virago, 1986).
Appiah, KA, *In My Father's House* (Oxford, OUP, 1993).
Appiah, KA, *Cosmopolitanism: Ethics in a World of Strangers* (New York, Norton, 2006).
Appiah, KA, *The Honour Code: How Moral Revolutions Happen* (New York, Norton, 2011).
Appiah, KA, *The Lies that Bind: Rethinking Identity* (London, Profile Books, 2018).
Applegate, K, *Wishtree* (New York, Feiwel and Friends, 2017).
Arbel, E, Dauvergne, C and Millbank, J (eds), *Gender in Refugee Law: From the Margin to the Centre* (Abingdon, Routledge, 2014).
Arendt, H, *The Human Condition* (Chicago IL, University of Chicago Press, 1958).
Asante, M, *It's bigger than hip hop: The rise of the post hip hop generation* (New York, St Martin's Griffin, 2008).
Atuahene, B, *We Want What's Ours: Learning from South Africa's Land Restitution Program* (Oxford, OUP, 2014).
Atwood, M, *Hag-Seed* (London, Vintage, 2016).
Atwood, M, *The Penelopiad* (London, Canongate, 2018).
Ba, M, *So Long a Letter* (Oxford, Heinemann, 1989).
Banda, F, *Women, Law and Human Rights* (Oxford, Hart, 2005).
Banda, F and Fishbayn Joffe, L, *Women's Rights and Religious Law: Domestic and International Perspectives* (Abingdon, Routledge, 2016).
Bawden, N, *Carrie's War* (London, Puffin, 1974).

Bawden, N, *The Runaway Summer* (London, Penguin, 1969).

Beard, M, *SPQR: A History of Ancient Rome* (London, Profile 2016).

Beard, M, *Women and Power* (London, Profile Books, 2017).

Betts, A and Collier, P, *Refuge: Transforming a Broken Refugee System* (London, Penguin, 2017).

Beyani, C, *Protection of the Right to Seek and Obtain Asylum under the African Human Rights System* (Leiden, Brill, 2013).

Bhabha, J, *Children without a State: A Global Human Rights Challenge* (Cambridge MA, MIT Press, 2011).

Bhabha, J (ed), *Child Migration and Human Rights in a Global Age* (Princeton NJ, Princeton University Press, 2014).

Bhabha, J, Kanics, J and Senovilla-Hernandez, D (eds), *Handbook on Childhood Migration* (Cheltenham, Edward Elgar, 2018).

Biko, S, *Steve Biko 1946–1977: I Write What I Like*, A Stubbs (ed) (Oxford, Heinemann, 1988 [1978]).

Bindel, J, *The Pimping of Prostitution: Abolishing the Sex Work Myth* (London, Palgrave Macmillan, 2017).

Bindman, G (ed), *South Africa and the Rule of Law* (London, ICJ, Pinter Publishers, 1988).

Black, L, and Sinha, S, with Bryan, C, Baraku, V and Yembi, M, *Migrant City* (Abingdon, Routledge, 2015).

Boehmer, E, *Postcolonial Poetics: 21st Century Critical Readings* (London, Palgrave Macmillan, 2018).

Bohmer, C and Shuman, A, *Political Asylum Deceptions: The Culture of Suspicion* (London, Palgrave Macmillan, 2018).

Boochani, B (translated by O Tofighian), *No Friend but the Mountains: The True Story of an Illegally Imprisoned Refugee* (London, Picador, 2019).

Brian, F and Lazcko, F (eds), *Fatal journey tracking lives lost during migration* (Geneva, International Organization for Migration 2014).

Brink, A, *A Dry White Season* (London, Vintage, 1992 [1979]).

Bruner, J, *Making Stories: Law, Literature, Life* (Boston MA, Harvard University Press, 2002).

Bulawayo, N, *We need new names* (London, Vintage, 2014).

Carbado, D and Gulati, M, *Acting White? Rethinking Race in 'Post-Racial' America* (New York, OUP, 2013).

Chanock, M, *Law, Custom and Social Order: The Colonial Experience in Malawi and Zambia* (Cambridge, CUP, 1985).

Chariandy, D, *I've been meaning to tell you: a letter to my daughter* (London, Bloomsbury, 2018).

Chigumadzi, P, *These Bones will Rise Again* (London, Indigo Press, 2018).

Chikwava, B, *Harare North* (London, Vintage, 2010).

Chin, R, *The Crisis of Multiculturalism in Europe: A History* (Princeton NJ, Princeton University Press, 2017).

Chinkin, C and Freeman, M, 'Introduction' in M Freeman, C Chinkin and B Rudolph (eds), *Commentary on the Convention on the Elimination of all Forms of Discrimination against Women* (Oxford, OUP, 2013), 1–33.

Chingonyi, K, *Kumukanda* (London, Chatto and Windus, 2017).

Clanchy, K (ed), *England, Poems from a School* (London, Picador, 2018).

Clanchy, K, *Some Kids I Taught and What They Taught Me* (London, Picador, 2019).

Clemmons, Z, *What we Lose* (London, 4th Estate, 2017).

Cock, J, *Maids and Madams: Domestic Workers Under Apartheid* (The Women's Press, 1989).

Coetzee, JM, *Disgrace* (London, Vintage, 2000).

Cole, E, *House of Bondage* (New York, Random House, 1967).

Colfer, E and Donkin, A (with illustrations by G. Rigano), *Illegal* (London, Hodder, 2017).

Collier, P, *Exodus: Immigration and Multiculturalism in the 21st Century* (London, Allen Lane, 2013).

Cook, R and Cusack, S, *Gender Stereotyping* (Philadelphia PA, Penn Press, 2010).

Cornell, D *et al* (eds), *The Dignity Jurisprudence of the Constitutional Court of South Africa Volumes I & II* (New York, Fordham University Press, 2013).

Costello, C, *The Human Rights of Migrants and Refugees in European Law* (Oxford, OUP, 2016).

Couto, M (translated by D Brookshaw), *Woman of the Ashes* (New York, Farrar, Straus and Giroux, 2018).
Cox, F, with Brown, A (illustrator), *There's a boy just like me*(London, Little Tiger Press, 2018).
Crawley, H, *Refugees and Gender: Law and Process* (Bristol, Jordan Publishing, 2001).
Crush, J, Chikanda, A and Skinner, C (eds), *Mean Streets: Migration, Xenophobia and Informality in South Africa* (Johannesburg, South Africa Migration Programme, 2015).
Dahl, R, *Charlie and the Chocolate Factory* (London, Puffin, 2016).
Dangarembga, T, *Nervous Conditions* (London, The Women's Press, 1988).
Day, E, *Paradise* City (London, Bloomsbury, 2015).
Delphy, C (translated by D Broder), *Separate and Dominate: Feminism and Racism after the war on terror* (London, Verso, 2015).
Dembour, M-B, *When Humans become migrants* (Oxford, OUP, 2015).
De Prince, M and E, *Ballerina Dreams: From Orphan to Dancer* (London, Random House, 2014).
Desai, K, *The Inheritance of Loss* (London, Hamish Hamilton, 2006).
Desai, A and Vahed, G, *The South African Gandhi: Stretcher-Bearer of Empire* (Stanford CA, Stanford University Press, 2015).
Dickens, C, *Oliver Twist* (London, Penguin Classics, 2012).
Dolin, K, *A Critical Introduction to Law and Literature* (Cambridge, CUP, 2007).
Donkor, M, *Hold* (London, 4th Estate, 2018).
Donoghue, E (illustrated by C Hadilaksono), *The Lotterys Plus One* (London, Macmillan Children's Books, 2017).
Dove, R, *Sonata Mulattica*, (New York, WW Norton & Company, 2010).
du Preez Bezdrop, AM, *Winnie Mandela: A Life* (Cape Town, Zebra Press, 2003).
Earle, TF and Lowe, KJP, (eds), *Black Africans in Renaissance Europe* (Cambridge, CUP, 2005).
Eddo-Lodge, R, *Why I'm no Longer talking to White People about Race* (London, Bloomsbury, 2017).
Edozien, C, *The Lives of Great Men* (London, Team Angelica, 2017).
Edugyan, E, *Washington Black* (London, Serpents's Tail, 2018).
Eekelaar, J, *Family Law and Personal Life* (Oxford, OUP, 2017).
Eekelaar, J, 'Moral Failure and the Law' unpublished (2020).
Eekelaar, J and Maclean, M, *Family Justice: The Work of Family Judges in Uncertain Times* (Oxford, Hart, 2013).
Eggers, D, *What is the What* (London, Penguin, 2008).
Ehrenreich, B, *Nickel and Dimed: On (Not) Getting by in America* (New York, Metropolitan Books, 2001).
Eisenstein, Z, *Against Empire: Feminism, Racism and the West* (London, ZED Books, 2004).
El-Bisatie, M, (translated by Denys Johnson-Davies) *Hunger* (Cairo, American University in Cairo Press, 2014). (Published in Arabic as *Ju* (2007)).
El-Enany, N, *(B)Ordering Britain: Law, Race and Empire* (Manchester, Manchester University Press, 2020).
El Feki, S, *Sex and the Citadel: Intimate Life in a Changing Arab World* (London, Chatto and Windus, 2013).
Elkins, C, *Imperial Reckoning: The untold story of Britain's Gulag in Kenya* (New York, Henry Holt, 2005).
Ellis, S, *This Present Darkness: A History of Nigerian Organised Crime* (London, Hurst, 2016).
Eltahawy, M, *Headscarves and Hymens: Why the Middle East Needs a Sexual Revolution* (London, Orion Books, 2010).
Emenyonu, E (ed), *Diaspora & Returns in Fiction, African Literature Today 34* (Oxford, James Currey, 2016).
Emezi, A, *Freshwater* (London, Faber and Faber, 2018).
Emezi, A, *Pet* (London, Faber and Faber, 2019).
Endamne, A (translated by C Toman and her team of students), *Afropean* (CreateSpace Publishing, 2015 [2008]).

Epprecht, M, *Sexuality and Social Justice in Africa: Rethinking Homophobia and Forging Resistance* (London, ZED Books, 2013).
Epprecht, M, *Hungochani: The History of a Dissident Sexuality in Southern Africa,* 2nd edn (Montreal, McGill-Queen's University Press, 2013).
Eshun, E, *Black God of the Sun: Searching for Home in England and Africa* (London, Penguin, 2006).
Evaristo, B, *The Emperor's Babe* (London, Hamish Hamilton, 2001).
Evaristo, B, *Mr Loverman* (London, Hamish Hamilton, 2014).
Evaristo, B, *Girl, Woman, Other* (London, Hamish Hamilton, 2019).
Farah, N, *Hiding in Plain Sight* (New York, Riverhead Books, 2014).
Feldner, M, *Narrating the African Diaspora: 21st Century Nigerian Literature in Context* (Cham, Palgrave Macmillan, 2019).
Fiddian-Quasmiyeh, E, Loescher, G, Long, K and Sigona, N (eds), *The Oxford Handbook of Refugee and Forced Migration Studies* (Oxford, OUP, 2016).
First, R, *117 Days* (London, Bloomsbury, 1988).
Foulds, A, *The Broken Word* (London, Penguin, 2011).
Francis, S, Rugmore, H and Rico, *The Madam and Eve Collection* (Cape Town, David Phillips, 1998).
Friedan, B, *Feminist Mystique* (London, Penguin, 2010).
Fryer, P, *Staying Power: The History of Black People in Britain* (London, Pluto Press, 2018) (reissued from 1984).
Gallagher, A, *The International Law of Trafficking* (Cambridge, CUP, 2012).
Gappah, *An Elegy for Easterly* (London, Faber and Faber, 2009).
Gates, HL (ed), *'Race', Writing, and Difference* (Chicago IL, University of Chicago Press, 1985).
Gatrell, P, *The Making of the Modern Refugee* (Oxford, OUP, 2013).
Gatz, A, *Refugee* (London, Scholastic, 2017).
Gee, M, *My Cleaner* (London, SAQI, 2005).
Gentleman, A, *The Windrush Betrayal: Exposing the Hostile Environment* (London, Guardian, Faber, 2019).
Gikandi, S (ed), *The Novel in Africa and the Caribbean since 1950* (New York, OUP, 2016).
Gilbey, E, *The Lady: Life and Times of Winnie Mandela* (London, Vintage, 1994).
Gilligan, C, *In a Different Voice: Psychological Theory and Women's Development* (Boston MA, Harvard University Press, 1982).
Ginkere, R, Lubkemann, S and Steiner, C (eds), *Perspectives on Africa A Reader in Culture, History and Representation* 2nd edn (Oxford, Wiley Blackwell, 2010).
Goldberg, D, *The Mission: A Life for Freedom in South Africa* (Lexington KT, University of Kentucky Press, 2015).
Golding, W, *Lord of the Flies* (London, Faber & Faber, 1997).
Goodfellow, M, *Hostile Environment: How Immigrants became Scapegoats* (London, Verso, 2019).
Gopal, P, *Insurgent Empire: Anti Colonial Resistance and British Dissent* (London, Verso, 2019).
Gourevitch, P, *We Wish to Inform you that tomorrow we will be killed with our families* (London, Picador, 2015).
Gordon, L, *What Fanon said: A Philosophical Introduction to his Life and Thought* (New York, Fordham University Press, 2015).
Gordimer, N, *Burger's Daughter* (London, Penguin, 1981).
Gordimer, N, *July's People* (London, Bloomsbury, 2005).
Gordimer, N, *The Conservationist* (London, Bloomsbury, 2005).
Grosz, S, *The Examined Life: How we lose and find ourselves* (London, Vintage, 2014).
Gumede, W, *Thabo Mbeki and the Battle for the Soul of the ANC* (Cape Town, Zebra Press, 2005).
Gutierrez-Rodriguez, E (ed), *Migration, Domestic Work and Affect: A Decolonial Approach on Value and the Feminization of Labor* (Abingdon, Routledge, 2010).
Grove, V, *A Voyage Round John Mortimer* (London, Viking, 2007).
Gyasi, Y, *Homegoing* (London, Vintage, 2017).
Habila, H, *Travellers* (London, Hamish Hamilton, 2019).

Hall, S, *There Ain't no Black in the Union Jack: The Cultural Politics of Race and Nation* (Michigan IL, University of Chicago Press, 1991).
Hamid, M, *Exit West* (London, Penguin, 2017).
Hamid, M, *The Reluctant Fundamentalist* (London, Penguin, 2008).
Han, E and O'Mahoney, J, *British Colonialism and the Criminalisation of Homosexuality: Queens, Crime and Empire* (Abingdon, Routledge, 2018).
Hansberry, L, *A Raisin in the Sun* (New York, Random House, 1959).
Herd, D and Pincus, A (eds), *Refugee Tales* (Manchester, Comma Press, 2016).
Herd, D and Pincus, A (eds), *Refugee Tales II* (Manchester, Comma Press, 2017).
Herd, D and Pincus, A (eds), *Refugee Tales III* (Manchester, Comma Press 2019).
Herring, J, *Family Law*, 8th edn (London, Pearsons, 2017).
Hirsch, A, *Brit-ish: On Race, Identity and Belonging* (London, Jonathan Cape, 2018).
Hirsch, A and Beaumont, H, *Equal to Everything Judge Brenda and the Supreme Court* (London, LAG Education and Service Trust Limited, 2019).
Hirsi Ali, A, *Infidel: My Life* (London, Simon and Schuster, 2008).
Hobsbawm, E and Ranger, T, *The Invention of Tradition in Colonial Africa* (Cambridge, CUP, 1983).
Hochschild, A, *King Leopold's Ghost: A Story of Greed, Terror and Heroism in Colonial Africa* (London, Pan, 2012).
hooks, b, *From Margin to Centre* (Boston MA, South End Press, 1984).
Hosseini, K, *Kite Runner*, (London, Bloomsbury, 2011).
Hosseini, K, *Sea Prayer* (London, Bloomsbury, 2018).
Huchu, T, *The Hairdresser of Harare* (Harare, Weaver Press, 2010) (London, Freight Press, 2013).
Huchu, T, *The Maestro, The Magistrate & The Mathematician* (Edinburgh, Parthian Books, 2015).
Ibrahim, S (in Arabic *al-Lajna* [1981]) (translated by Mary St Germain and Charlene Constable), *The Committee* (Cairo, American University in Cairo Press, 2002).
Iweala, U, *Speak No Evil* (London, John Murray, 2018).
Jacobson, H, *Shylock is my name* (London, Penguin, 2016).
Jalloh, C, Clarke, K and Nmehielle, V, *The African Court of Justice and Human and Peoples' Rights in Context: Developments and Challenges* (Cambridge, CUP, 2019).
Jama, A, *Being Queer and Somali* (Oracle Releasing, 2015).
Jansen, E, *Like Family: Domestic Workers in South African History and Literature* (Johannesburg, Wits University Press, 2019).
Jeater, D, *Marriage, Perversion and Power: the Construction of Moral Discourse in Southern Rhodesia, 1890–1930* (Oxford, Unpublished D. Phil. dissertation, University of Oxford 1990).
Jones, H, Gunaratnam, Y, Bhatacharya, G, Davies, W, Dhaliwal, S, Forkert, K, Jackson, E and Saltus, R, *Go Home? The Politics of Immigration Controversies* (Manchester, Manchester University Press, 2017).
Kambalu, S, *The Jive Talker or, How to Get a British Passport* (London, Jonathan Cape, 2008).
Kaufmann, M, *Black Tudors: The Untold Story* (London, Oneworld, 2017).
Kaufmann, E, *Whiteshift: Populism, immigration and the future of white majorities* (London, Penguin, 2018).
Kay, J, *Red Dust Road: An Autobiographical Journey* (London, Picador, 2010).
Keaton, T, Sharpley-Whiting, R and Stovall, T (eds), *Black France/France Noire: The History and Politics of Blackness* (Durham NC, Duke University Press, 2012).
Kelman, S, *Pigeon English* (London, Bloomsbury, 2012).
Kerr, J, *When Hitler Stole Pink Rabbit* (London, Harper Collins, 2017).
Khosravi, S, *'Illegal' Traveller: An Auto-Ethnography of Borders* (Basingstoke, Palgrave Macmillan, 2010).
Khumalo, S, *You have to be Gay to know God* (Cape Town, Kwela Books, 2018).
Kingsley, P, *The New Odyssey: The Story of Europe's Refugees* (London, Guardian Books and Faber & Faber, 2016).
Kingsolver, B, *The Poisonwood Bible* (London, Faber and Faber, 2013).

Kristoff, K and WuDunn, S, *Half the Sky* (New York, Virago, 2009).
Lahiri, J, *The Interpreter of* Maladies (Boston MA, Houghton Mifflin, 1999).
Lahiri, J, *The Namesake*, (London, Harper Perennial 2004).
Lamche, P, *Winnie* (Netherlands, Pumpernickel Films, 2017).
Lanchester, J, *Capital* (London, Faber, 2013).
Lanchester, J, *The Wall* (London, Faber and Faber, 2019).
Land, S, *Maid: Hard Work, Low Pay and a Mother's will to Survive* (London, Trapeze, 2019).
Laundau, L (ed), *Exorcising the Demons Within: Xenophobia, Violence and Statecraft* (Tokyo, UN University Press, 2012).
Lawrence, C, *The Roman Mysteries* (London, Orion, 2001).
Lawrence, C, *The Thieves of Ostia* (London, Orion, 2002).
Lennon, J, Ono Lennon, Y, Amnesty International (illustrated by J Jullien), *Imagine* (London, Frances Lincoln Children's Books with Amnesty International, 2017).
Le Thi Diem Thuy, *The Gangster We Are All Looking For* (London, Picador, 2004).
Lessing, D, *Nine African Stories* (London, Longman, 1968, 1980 reprint).
Lessing, D, *The Grass is Singing* (London, 4th Estate, 2013).
Lugard, F, *The Dual Mandate in British Tropical Africa: Methods of Ruling Native Races* (Edinburgh, Blackwood, 1922).
Lutz, H, *Migration and Domestic Work: A European Perspective on a Global Theme* (Abingdon, Routledge, 2008).
Lutz, H, *The New Maids: Transnational Women and the Care Economy* (London, ZED Books, 2011).
Mabanckou, A (translated by H Stevenson), *Broken Glass* (London, Serpent's Tail, 2009/2011).
Mabanckou, A (translated by S Ardizzone), *Black Bazaar* (London, Serpent's Tale, 2012).
Maclean, M and Eekelaar, J, *Lawyers and Mediators: The Brave New World of Services for Separating Families* (Oxford, Hart, 2016).
Maclean, M and Eekelaar, J, *After the Act: Access to Family Justice after LASPO* (Oxford, Hart, 2019).
Mackinnon, C, *Towards a Feminist Theory of State* (Boston MA, Harvard University Press, 1989).
Magnanti, B, *Sex, Lies and Statistics: The Truth Julie Bindel Doesn't Want you to See*, Self-published, 2017.
Magorian, M, *Goodnight Mr Tom* (London, Puffin, 2014 [1981]).
Maharaj, M and Kathrada, A, *Mandela: The Authorised Portrait* (London, Bloomsbury, 2006).
Makumbi, JN, *Kintu*, (London, One World, 2018) Originally (Nairobi, Kwani, 2014).
Makumbi, JN, *Manchester Happened* (London, Oneworld Publications, 2019).
Mamdani, M, *When Victims become killers: Colonialism, Nativism and the Genocide in Rwanda* (Princeton NJ, Princeton University Press, 2001).
Manby, B, *Citizenship Law in Africa* (Oxford, Hart, 2018).
Mandela, N, *Conversations with Myself* (London, Macmillan, 2010).
Mandela, N and Langa, M, *Dare not Linger: The Presidential Years* (London, Macmillan, 2017).
Mathabane, M, *African Women: Three Generations* (London, Hamish Hamilton, 1994).
Matthews, P and Harley, T, *Refugees, Regionalism and Responsibility* (Cheltenham, Edward Elgar, 2016).
May, J, *Changing People, Changing Laws* (Gweru, Mambo Press, 1987).
Mbue, I, *Behold the Dreamers* (London, 4th Estate, 2016).
McGregor, J and Primorac, R (eds), *Zimbabawe's new Diaspora: Displacement and the Cultural Politics of* Survival (Oxford, Berghahn Books, 2010).
Mills, CE, *The Racial Contract* (Ithaca NY, Cornell University Press, 1997).
Mkandawira, T (ed), *African Intellectuals: Rethinking Politics, Language, Gender and Development* (London, ZED Books, 2005).
Modood, T, *Multiculturalism*, 2nd edn (London, Policy, 2013).
Mohamed, N, *Black Mamba Boy* (London, Harper Collins, 2010).
Mohammed, A, Nagarajan, C and Aliyu, R (eds), *She Called me Woman: Nigeria's Queer Women Speak* (Abuja/London, Cassava Republic, 2018).
Mohanty, C, Russo, A and Torres, L, *Third World Women and the Politics of Feminism* (Bloomington IN, Indiana University Press, 1991).

Morris, HF and Read, JS, *Indirect Rule and the Search for Justice* (Oxford, Clarendon Press, 1972).
Morrison, T, *The Bluest Eye* (London, Vintage, 1999).
Morrison, T, *Beloved* (London, Vintage, 2011) (includes her Foreword).
Mortimer, J, *Clinging to the Wreckage: A Part of Life* (London, Weidenfeld and Nicolson, 1982).
Mortimer, J, *The Collected Stories of Rumpole* (London, Penguin, 2013).
Naidoo, B, *Journey to Jo'burg* (London, Harper Collins, 2008).
Naidoo, B, *Web of Lies* (London, Puffin, 2004).
Naidoo, B, *The Other Side of Truth* (London, Puffin, 2000).
Namwase, S and Jjuko, A (eds), *Protecting the Human Rights of Sexual Minorities in Contemporary Africa* (Pretoria, PULP, 2017).
Narayan, U, *Dislocating Cultures, Traditions and Third World Feminism* (London, Routledge, 1997).
Naro, N, *A Slave's Place, A Master's World: Fashioning Dependency in Rural Brazil* (London, Bloomsbury, 2016) (new edition).
Naro, N, Sansi-Roca, R and Treece, D (eds), *Cultures of the Lusophone Black Atlantic* (London, Palgrave, 2007).
Nazer, M and Lewis, D, *Slave* (London, Virago, 2004).
Ncgukaitobi, T, *The Land is Ours: South Africa's First Black Lawyers and the Birth of Constitutionalism* (Cape Town, Zebra Press, 2018).
Ndebele, N, *The Cry of Winnie Mandela: A Novel* (Banbury, Ayebia Clarke, 2003).
Newberry, D, *Defiant Images: Photography and Apartheid South Africa* (Pretoria, UNISA, 2009).
Ngugi, WT, *Decolonising the Mind* (Oxford, James Currey, 2009).
Ngugi, M Wa, *The Rise of the African Novel* (Michigan, Michigan University Press, 2018).
Nguyen, VT (ed), *The Displaced: Refugee Writers on Refugee Lives* (New York, Abrams Press, 2018).
Nguyen, VT, *The Refugees* (London, Corsair, 2017).
Ngwena, C, *What is Africanness?: Contesting nativism in race, culture and sexualities* (Pretoria, PULP, 2018).
Noah, T, *Born a Crime: Stories from a South African childhood* (London, John Murray, 2017).
Nussbaum, M, *Poetic Justice: The Literary Imagination and Public Life* (Boston MA, Beacon Press, 1995).
Nussbaum, M, *Women and Human Development: The Capabilities Approach* (Cambridge, CUP, 2000).
Nyathi, S, *The Golddiggers* (London, Macmillan, 2018).
Nwaubani, A, *I do not come to you by chance* (London, Phoenix, 2010).
Oakley, A, *Housewife* (London, Pelican, 1976).
Obama, B, *Dreams from my Father: A Story of Race and Inheritance* (Edinburgh, Canongate, 2007).
O'Brien, R (ed), *Telling Stories Out of Court: Narratives about Women and Workplace Discrimination* (Ithaca NY, ILR Press, 2008).
Ofili, S (with illustrations by B Weyhe), *German Calendar, No December* (London, Cassava Republic, 2018).
Okafor, O, *Refugee Law after 9/11: Sanctuary and Security in Canada and the United States* (Vancouver, University of British Columbia Press, 2020).
Okojie, I, *Butterfly Fish* (London, Jacaranda, 2016).
Okparanta, C, *Under the Udala Trees* (London, Granta, 2017).
Olusoga, D, *A Black History of Britain* (London, Macmillan, 2016).
Olusoga, D, *The World's War: Forgotten Soldiers of Empire* (London, Head of Zeus, 2015).
Olusoga, D and Erichsen, C, *The Kaiser's Holocaust: Germany's Forgotten Genocide and the Colonial Roots of Nazism* (London, Faber and Faber, 2011).
Oomen, B, *Rights for Others: The Slow Home Coming of Human Rights in the Netherlands* (Cambridge, CUP, 2013).
Osondu, EC, *Voice of America* (London, Granta, 2010).
Oyewumi, O, *The Invention of Women: Making an African Sense of Western Gender Discourses* (Minneapolis MN, University of Minnesota, 1997).
Painter, NI, *The History of White* People (New York, W.W. Norton, 2010).
Palacio, RJ, *Wonder* (London, Corgi, 2012).
Palley, C, *The Constitutional History and Law of Southern Rhodesia* (Oxford, OUP, 1966).

Parekh, B, *Rethinking Multiculturalism: Cultural Diversity and Political Theory* (Boston MA, Harvard University Press, 2002).
Park, LS, *A Long Walk to Water* (New York, Clarion Books, 2010).
Pasura, D, *African Transnational Diasporas: Fractured Communities and Plural Identities of Zimbabweans in Britain* (London, Palgrave Macmillan, 2014).
Paton, A, *Cry the Beloved Country* (London, Vintage, 2002).
Perry, KH, *London is the Place for Me: Black Britons, Citizenship and the Politics of Race* (Oxford, OUP, 2018).
Phan Thi Kim Phuc, *The Napalm Girl's Journey through the Horrors of War to Faith, Forgiveness, and Peace* (Illinois, Tyndale Momentum, 2017).
Phillips, B, *Another Man's War: The Story of a Burma Boy in Britain's Forgotten Army* (London, Oneworld, 2014).
Phillips, C, *The Atlantic Sound* (London, Faber and Faber, 2000).
Phillips, L (ed), *The Swarming Streets. Twentieth-Century Literary Representations of London* (New York, Rodopi, 2011).
Pitts, P, *Afropean: Notes from Black Europe* (London, Allen Lane, 2019).
Popsescu, L (ed), *A Country of Refuge* (London, Unbound, 2016).
Portes, J, *What do we know and what should we do about immigration?* (London, SAGE, 2019).
Posner, R, *Law and Literature*, 3rd edn (Boston MA, Harvard University Press, 2009).
Poulter, S, *English law and Ethnic Minority Customs* (Oxford, Butterworths, 1986).
Quayson, A, *Diaspora Literary Studies* (Oxford, Wiley Blackwell, 2010).
Quayson, A and Daswani, G (eds), *A Companion to Diaspora and Transnationalism* (Oxford, Wiley Blackwell, 2013).
Raffield, P and Watt, G (eds), *Shakespeare and the Law* (Oxford, Hart, 2008).
Raffield, P, *The Art of Law* (Oxford, Hart, 2017).
Rankine, C, *Citizen* (London, Penguin, 2015).
Rauf, O (illustrated by P Curnick), *Boy at the Back of the Class* (London, Orion, 2018).
Rawlence, B, *City of Thorns* (London, Portobello Books, 2016).
Reich, D, *Who we are and how we got here: Ancient DNA and the new science of the human* past (New York, Pantheon Books, 2018).
Rodney, W, *How Europe Underdeveloped Africa* (Oxford, Pambazuka Press, 2012).
Rosenblatt, P, *The Impact of Racism on African American Families: Literature as Social Science* (Abingdon, Routledge, 2014).
Rundell, K, *The Explorer* (London, Bloomsbury, 2018).
Rundell, K, *The Girl Savage* (London, Faber and Faber, 2011).
Sachs, A, *The Strange Alchemy of Life and Law* (Oxford, OUP, 2011).
Sahota, S, *The Year of the Runaways* (London, Picador, 2016).
Sands, P, *East West Street: On the Origins of Genocide and Crimes against Humanity* (London, Weidenfeld, 2016).
Sarkin, J, *Colonial Genocide and Reparations Claims in the 21st Century. The Socio-Legal Context of Claims under International Law by the Herero against Germany for Genocide in Namibia, 1904–1908* (Santa Barbara, Praeger, 2008).
Schmidt, E, *Peasant, Traders and Wives: Shona Women in the History of Zimbabwe, 1870–1939* (Oxford, James Currey Ltd, 1992).
Selasi, T, *Ghana must go* (London, Penguin, 2014).
Sen, A, *Identity and Violence* (London, Allen Lane, 2006).
Sen, A, *The Idea of Justice* (Cambridge, Belknap Press, 2009).
Shah, A, *Tales from the Bazaars of Arabia: Folk Stories from the Middle East* (London, Tauris Parke Paperbacks, 2008).
Shah, P, *Refugees, Race and the Concept of Asylum in Britain* (London, Cavendish, 2000).
Shah, P, *Against Caste in British Law: A Critical Perspective on the Caste Discrimination Provision in the Equality Act 2010* (London, Palgrave Macmillan, 2015).
Shah, P and Menski, W (eds), *Migration, Diasporas and Legal Systems in Europe* (Abingdon, Routledge-Cavendish, 2006).

Shah, P, Foblets, M-C and Rohe, M, *Family Religion and Law. Cultural Encounters in Europe* (Farnham, Ashgate, 2014).
Shamsie, K, *Home Fire* (London, Bloomsbury, 2018).
Shaldberg, J, *Ernest Cole* (Surrey, Journeyman, 2006).
Shire, W, *Teaching my mother how to give birth* (London, Flipped Eye, Mouthmark series (No 10), 2011).
Shukla, N (ed), *The Good Immigrant* (London, Unbound, 2016).
Shukla, N and Suleyman, C (eds), *The Good Immigrant USA* (London, Dialogue Books, 2019).
Shuster, L, *A Burning* Hunger (London, Jonathan Cape, 2004).
Sikkink, K, *Evidence for Hope: Making Human Rights Work in the 21st Century* (Oxford, Princeton University Press, 2017).
Sisulu, E, *Walter and Albertina Sisulu* (Cape Town, David Philip, 2002).
Slimani, L (translated by S Taylor), *Lullaby* (London, Faber & Faber, 2018).
Smart, C, *The Ties that Bind: Law, Marriage and the Reproduction of Patriarchal Relations* (London, Routledge, 1984).
Smith, C, *Robben Island* (Johannesburg, Struik, 1997).
Smith, Z, *The Embassy of Cambodia* (London, Hamish Hamilton, 2013).
Snyckers, F, *Lacuna* (Johannesburg, Picador, 2019).
Soyinka, W, *You Must Set Forth at Dawn: A Memoir* (London, Random House, 2006).
Stewart, A, *Gender, Law and Justice in a Global Market* (Cambridge, CUP, 2011).
Stubbs, A (ed), *Steve Biko 1946–77: I Write What I Like* (Oxford, Heinemann, 1988).
Tamale, S (ed), *African Sexualities: A Reader* (Oxford, Pambazuka Press, 2011).
Tambo, A, *Preparing for Power: Oliver Tambo Speaks* (New York, George Braziller/Heinemann, 1987).
Thiam, C, *Return to the Kingdom of Childhood: Re-envisioning the Legacy and Philosophical Relevance of Negritude* (Columbus OH, Ohio State University Press, 2016).
Thornberry, P, *The International Convention on the Elimination of all Forms of Racial Discrimination: A Commentary* (Oxford, OUP, 2016).
Todres, J and Higinbotham, S, *Human Rights in Children's Literature: Imagination and the Narrative of Law* (Oxford, OUP, 2016).
Trilling, D, *Lights in the Distance: Exile and Refuge at the Borders of Europe* (London, Picador, 2018).
Twain, M, *The Adventures of Huckleberry Finn* (London, Penguin Classics, 2003).
UNESCO, *Njinga Mbandi: Queen of Ndongo and Matamba* (Paris, UNESCO and Collins, 2015).
Unigwe, C, *On Black Sisters' Street* (London, Vintage, 2010).
Unigwe, C, *Better Never Than Late* (London, Cassava Press, 2019).
Van Klinken, A, *Kenyan, Christian, Queer* (Pennsylvania, Penn Press, 2019).
Viljoen, F, *International Human Rights Law in Africa*, 2nd edn (Oxford, OUP, 2012) 416–17.
Villavicencio, K, *The Undocumented Americans* (New York, Penguin Random House, 2020).
Vuong, Ocean, *On Earth We are Briefly Gorgeous* (London, Jonathan Cape, 2019).
Wa Ngugi, M, *The Rise of the African Novel* (Ann Arbor, University of Michigan Press, 2018.
Waheed, N, *Salt* (London, CreateSpace, 2013).
Wakatama Allfrey, E (ed), *Africa39. New Writing from Africa South of the Sahara* (London, Bloomsbury, 2016).
Wakatama Allfrey, E, *Safe House: Explorations in Creative Nonfiction* (London, Cassava Republic, 2016).
Ward, I, *Law and Literature: Possibilities and Perspectives* (Cambridge, CUP, 2008 [1995]).
Ward, I (ed), *Literature and Human Rights: The Law, The Language and the Limitations of Human Rights Discourse* (Berlin, De Gruyter, 2017).
West, E, *What we got wrong about immigration and how to get it right* (London, Gibson Square, 2015).
Wiles, E, *The Invisible Crowd* (London, Harper Collins, 2017). Ellen Wiles at: https://www.ellenwiles.com/.
Wilson-Lee, E, *Shakespeare in Swahililand* (London, William Collins, 2016).
Williams, P, *The Alchemy of Race and Rights* (Boston, Harvard, 1992).
Williams, P, *The Rooster's Egg: On the Persistence of Prejudice* (Boston MA, Harvard, 1997).
Williams, P, *Seeing a Color-Blind Future: The Paradox of Race* (New York, Farrar, Strauss & Giroux, 1997).

Williams, P, *Open House* (New York, Picador, 2004).
Wrong, M, *I didn't do it for you: how the world used and abused a small African nation* (New York, Harper Perennial, 2005).
Yousafzai, M, *We are Displaced: My Journey and Stories from Refugee Girls around the World* (London, Weidenfeld & Nicolson, 2019).
Yoshino, K, *Covering: The Hidden Assault on our Civil Rights* (New York, Random House, 2007).
Yoshino, K, *A Thousand Times More Fair: What Shakespeare's Plays Teach Us about Justice* (New York, Harper Collins, 2012).
Zephaniah, B, *Refugee Boy* (London, Bloomsbury, 2017).
Zhawi, B, *Small Inheritances* (Oxford, Ignition Press, 2018).

Journal and News Articles (print and online)

Abebe, T, Abebe, A and Sharpe, M, 'After 50 years, Africa's refugee policy still leads', *ISS Today*, 21 June 2019.
Achiume, T, 'Reimagining International Law for Global Migration: Migration as Decolonization?' (2017) 111 *AJIL Unbound* 142–46.
Achiume, T, 'Migration as Decolonization' (2019) 71 *Stanford Law Review* 1509–76.
Adams, T, 'Binyavanga Wainaina interview: coming out in Kenya', *The Observer*, London, 16 February 2014.
Adichie, C, 'The Master' (2005) 92 *Granta* 17–41.
AfriClassical.com, 'George Augustus Polgreen Bridgetower (1789–1860)' at www.AfriClassical.com.
Agence France-Presse, '"I will never support legalizing homosexuality", Ghana's President Says', *National Post*, Accra, 2 November 2011.
Ahmed, A, '"Exploitation Creep" and Development: A Response to Janie Chuang', *AJIL Unbound*, 11 June 2015.
Ahmed, F, 'Remedying Personal Law Systems' (2016) 30(3) *International Journal of Law, Policy and the Family* 248–73.
Ahmed, N, 'A Look at LGBTI Literature in Sub-Saharan Africa' posted on 6 April 2012, at http://www.genderacrossborders.com.
Akbar, A, 'Akwaeke Emezi "I read everything, even the cereal box"', *The Observer*, London, 21 October 2018.
Allahyari, K and Rae, P, 'Behrouz Boochani's literary prize cements his status as an Australian writer', *The Conversation*, 1 February 2019.
Almendral, A, 'Heroes of the Philippines', *National Geographic*, December 2018, 138–49.
Amnesty International, 'South Africa: Ten years after xenophobic killings, refugees and migrants still living in fear' (London, Amnesty International, 2018).
Anderson, J and Doyal, L, 'Women from Africa living with HIV in London: a descriptive study' (2004) 16:1 *AIDS Care* 95–105.
Anyangwe, E, 'Why is travelling with an African passport so difficult?', *The Guardian*, London, 11 September 2015.
Appiah, KA, 'On the Kidnapped African Boy who Became a German Philosopher', *Literary Hub*, 29 August 2018.
Aris Escarcena, JP, 'Expulsions: The Construction of a Hostile Environment in Calais' (2019) 21 *European Journal of Migration and Law* 215–37.
Associated Press, 'Denmark withholds aid to Tanzania over gay rights', 16 November 2018, at: news.24.com.
Atuahene, B, 'Dignity Takings and Dignity Restoration: Creating a New Theoretical Framework for Understanding Involuntary Property Loss and the Remedies Required' (2016) 41(4) *Law and Social Inquiry* 796.
Ax, J, 'Strauss-Kahn countersues NY hotel maid for $1 million', Reuters, 15 May 2012.
Banda, F and Eekelaar, J, 'International Conceptions of the Family' (2017) 66 *International and Comparative Law Quarterly* 833–62,

Batchelor, T, '"Guilty until proved Innocent:" The trial of LGBT Asylum Seekers' Detention in the UK', *The New Statesman*, London, 10 March 2015.

BBC, 'Strauss-Kahn reaches legal settlement with hotel maid', *BBC News* online, 10 December 2012.

BBC, 'Ugandan archbishop responds to Welby on anti-gay laws', *BBC News* online, 1 February 2014.

BBC, 'Italy's Matteo Salvini Shuts Ports to Migrant Rescue Ships', *BBC News* online, 11 June 2018.

BBC, 'Trevor Noah defends "Africa won the World Cup" joke'. *BBC News* online, 19 July 2018.

BBC, 'FGM: Mother guilty of genital mutilation of daughter', *BBC News* online, 1 February, 2019.

BBC, 'Chagos Islands dispute: UK obliged to end control – UN', *BBC News* online, 25 February 2019.

BBC, 'Windrush Scandal', *BBC News* online, 12 October 2018.

BBC, 'France summons Italian envoy over Africa remarks', *BBC News* online, 22 January 2019.

BBC, 'Kenyan flight "stowaway" body found in Clapham garden', *BBC News* online, 2 July 2019.

Begum, R, '#MeToo, Say Domestic Workers in the Middle East', Human Rights Watch, 8 December 2017.

Berneri, C, 'Family Reunification between Static EU Citizens and Third World Country Nationals' (2018) 20 *European Journal of Migration* 289–313.

Berry, J, Kim, U, Power, S, Young, M and Bujaki, M, 'Acculturation attitudes in plural Societies' (1989) 38 *Applied Psychology: An International Review* 185–206, cited by J Eekelaar, 'Children between Cultures' (2004) 18(2) *International Journal of Law, Policy and the Family* 178–94.

Bidisha, 'Tudor, English and black – and not a slave in sight', *The Guardian*, 29 October 2017.

Birhanu, N and Han, B, 'Africans in China: The Pivot Back', Council on Foreign Relations, 25 July 2016.

Black, L and S Sinha, S, 'Stealing a Dream: young migrants living through anti-immigrant times', Open Democracy blog, 8 August 2018.

Bogner, D, Brewin, CR, and Herlihy, R, '"Refugees" Experiences of Home Office Interviews. A Qualitative Study on the Disclosure of Sensitive Personal Information' (2014) 36 *Journal of Ethnic and Migration Studies* 519.

Bowcott, O, and Jones, S, 'UN ruling raises hope of return for exiled Chagos islanders', *The Guardian*, London, 19 March 2015.

Bozic, M, Barr, C, McIntyre, N and Noor, P, 'Revealed: immigration rules in UK more than double in length', *The Guardian*, London, 27 August, 2018.

Breant, H, 'What if diasporas didn't think about development? a critical approach of the international discourse on migration and development' (2013) 6(2) *Africa and Black Diaspora: An International Journal* 99–112.

Brems, E '"Strong Women don't need Asylum" (The European Court on FGM)', *Strasbourg Observers*, 19 August 2010: https://strasbourgobservers.com/2010/08/19/%E2%80%98strong-women-don%E2%80%99t-need-asylum%E2%80%99-the-european-court-on-fgm/.

Brennan, D, 'Statelessness and the Feminist Toolbox: Another Man-made Problem with a Feminist Solution?' (2019) 24 *Tilburg Law Review* 170.

British Newspaper Archive, 'The Obscenity Trial of Miss Radclyffe Hall's novel, "The Well of Loneliness" – 16 November 1928' in *Headlines from History*, 15 November 2013.

Brittain, V, 'Ken Saro-Wiwa: A Hero for our Times' (2015) 56(3) *Race and Class* 5–17.

Bugan, C, 'Wole Soyinka's Poetry: The insistence on liberty', *English PEN*, 4 June 2015 at: https://www.englishpen.org/pen-atlas/wole-soyinkas-poetry-the-insistence-on-liberty/.

Bunting, L, Webb, M and Healy, J, 'In two minds – Parental attitudes toward physical punishment in the UK' (2010) 24 *Children and Society* 359.

Burke, J, 'Winnie Madikizela-Mandela dies aged 81', *The Guardian*, London, 2 April 2018.

Caldwell, P, 'A Hair Piece: Perspectives on the Intersection of Race and Gender' (1991) 2 *Duke Law Journal* 365–91.

Cassel, M, 'Alf Kumalo: the anti-apartheid photographer', *Al Jazeera*, 7 December 2013 at: https://www.aljazeera.com/indepth/features/2013/12/alf-kumalo-anti-apartheid-photographer-201312641847953345.html.

Chakaya, B, 'ECOWAS Court challenges vagrancy laws that target women', Reproductive health blog, 2017 at: https://reprohealthlaw.wordpress.com/2017/11/30/africa-nigeria-ecowas-court-challenges-vagrancy-laws-that-target-women.

Channel 4 News, *Yarl's Wood interactive: inside the immigration centre*, 2 March 2015.

Chanock, M, 'Neither Customary, nor Legal: African Customary Law in an Era of Customary Law Reform' (1989) 3 *International Journal of Law and Family* 72.

Charlesworth, H, Chinkin, C and Wright, S, 'Feminist Approaches to International Law' (1991) 85 *AJIL* 613.

Chigumadzi, P, 'Why I am no longer talking to Nigerians about Race', *Africa is a Country*, 7 April 2019.

Chigumadzi, P, 'Voices as powerful as guns: Panashe Chigumadzi on Dorothy Masuka's (w)ri(o)ting woman-centred Pan-Africanism', *Johannesburg Review of Books*, 6 May 2019.

Chinkin, C, 'Remembering Chrystal Macmillan: Women's Equality and Nationality in International Law' (2001) 22 *Michigan Journal of International Law* 523–85.

Chrisafis, A, 'France admits systematic torture during Algeria war for first time', *The Guardian*, London, 13 September 2018.

Chitando, A and Manyonganise, M, 'Saying the Unsaid: Probing Homosexuality in *The Hairdresser of Harare*' (2016) 63(4) *Journal of Homosexuality* 559–74.

Chuang, J, 'Exploitation Creep and the Unmaking of Human Trafficking Law' (2014) 108 *American Journal of International Law* 609.

Classicfm, 'George Bridgetower (1779–1860) and Beethoven: a troubled relationship' at: https://www.classicfm.com/composers/beethoven/guides/key-people-beethovens-music-and-life-george-bridge/.

Clulee, B, 'FGM Protection Orders: A Case Study', Family Law Group, 3 January 2017 at: www.familylawgroup.co.uk.

Cohen, D, 'Hidden Treasures: What's so Controversial about Picasso's Guernica?', *Slate*, 6 February 2003.

Coomans, F, 'The Ogoni Case Before the African Commission on Human and Peoples' Rights' (2003) 52(3) *International & Comparative Law Quarterly* 749–60.

Cooper, Y, 'On the anniversary of the Kindertransport, we should reflect on why we're failing child refugees today', *The Independent*, London, 21 November 2018.

Crenshaw, K, 'Demarginalizing the Intersection of Race and Sex: A Black Feminist Critique of Anti-Discrimination Doctrine, Feminist Theory and Antiracist Politics' (1989) 1 *University of Chicago Legal Forum* 138–69.

Crerar, P, 'Theresa May says she deeply regrets Britain's legacy of anti-gay laws', *The Guardian*, London, 17 April 2018.

Curry, A (with photographs by R Benali), 'Who were the first Europeans?' (2019) 236 (2) *National Geographic*, August 2019, 94–113.

Daily Mail, 'Lying asylum seeker can stay here – because she had two children by an HIV alcoholic', London, 1 February 2011.

Daily Mail, 'Guards at Asylum seeker centre unmasked as BNP members', London, 14 January, 2009.

Daley, P, 'Refugees, IDPS and Citizenship Rights: the perils of humanitarianism in the African Great Lakes Region' (2013) 34(5) *Third World Quarterly* 893–912.

Daley, P, Kamata, N and Singo, L, 'Undoing Traceable Beginnings' (2018) 1(1) *Migration and Society* 22–35.

DasGupta, S, '"Your Women are Oppressed, But Ours are Awesome": How Nicholas Kristoff and *Half the Sky* use women against each other' at: http://www.racialicious.com, 8 October 2012.

Davies, L, 'Lampedusa Victims include Mother and Baby attached by umbilical cord', London, *The Guardian*, Thursday 10 October 2013.

Dawes, K, 'Passport Control: "please can I be a Jamaican?"' (2005) 92 *Granta* 61–75.

de Oliveira, E, 'Myths about Migrants', *First News*, Issue 656, 11–17 January 2019.

de Vos, P, 'A Brilliant Court Victory for LGBTI people in Botswana Lays the Ground for Further Legal Activism', *Constitutionally Speaking*, 12 June 2019 at: http://www.constitutionallyspeaking.co.za.

de Vries, KM, 'Rewriting Abdulaziz: The ECtHR Grand Chamber's Ruling in *Biao v. Denmark*' (2016) 18(4) *European Journal of Migration and Law* 467–79.

de Waal, A,'Writing Human Rights and Getting it Wrong', *Boston Review*, 6 June 2016, available online at: http://bostonreview.net/world/alex-de-waal-writing-human-rights.

Demone, B, 'LGBT Rights in Malawi: One Step Back, Two Steps Forward? The Case of *R v. Steven Monjeza Soko and Tiwonge Chimbalanga Kachepa*' (2016) 60 (3) *Journal of African Law* 365–87.

den Heijer, M, 'Visas and Non-discrimination' (2018) 20 *European Journal of Migration and Law* 470–89.

Dethloff, N, 'Child Brides on the Move: Legal Responses to Culture Clashes' (2018) 32(3) *International Journal of Law, Policy and the Family* 302–15.

Devji, ZZ, 'Forging Paths for the African Queer: Is There an "African" Mechanism for Realizing LGBTIQ Rights?' (2016) 60(3) *Journal of African Law* 343–63.

Diallo, R, 'France's Dangerous Move to Remove 'Race' from its Constitution', *Washington Post*, 13 July 2018.

Dimova, M, Hough, C, Kyaa, K and Manji, A, 'Intimacy and inequality: local care chains and paid childcare in Kenya' (2015) 23(2) *Feminist Legal Studies* 167–79.

Doherty, B and Hurst, D, 'UN accuses Australia of systematically violating torture convention', *The Guardian*, 10 March 2015.

Dorward, J, 'Families torn apart as visa misery hits Britons with foreign spouses', *The Observer*, London, 19 August 2018.

Dotto, C, '"Little Africa" in China', *New Internationalist*, 11 March 2019.

Doyal, L, 'A Decade of Researching the Social Aspects of HIV and AIDS' (2014) 384 *The Lancet* 2102–3.

Doyal, L, 'Challenges in researching life with HIV/AIDS: an intersectional analysis of black African migrants in London' (2009) 11(2) Culture, Health & Sexuality 173–88.

Doyle, J and Fernandez, C, 'Lying asylum seeker can stay here – because she had two children by an HIV alcoholic', London, *Daily Mail*, 1 February 2011.

Duffy, N, 'The UK has rejected thousands of gay asylum seekers', *Pink News*, 30 November 2017.

Dunton, C, 'Sara Baartman and the Ethics of Representation' (2015) 46(2) *Research in African Literatures* 32–51.

ECOWAS, 'ECOWAS moves to promote free movement and tackle trafficking in persons in the region', ECOWAS News, 29 April 2019, at: https://www.ecowas.int/ecowas-moves-to-promote-free-movement-and-tackle-trafficking-in-persons-in-the-region/.

Edwards, C, 'Refugee who joined my son's school trip', *Evening Standard*, London, 21 June 2018.

Edwin, S, '(Un) solving global challenges: African short stories, literary awards and the question of audience' (2016) 28 *Journal of African Cultural Studies* 359–71.

Eekelaar, J, 'Children between Cultures' (2004) 18(2) *International Journal of Law, Policy and the Family* 178–94.

Ejorh, T, 'Modern African Migrations to Ireland: Patterns and Contexts' (2012) 38 *Journal of Ethnic and Migration Studies* 577–93.

Elgot, J, 'Family of Syrian Boy washed up on the beach were trying to reach Canada', *The Guardian*, 3 September 2015.

Ellis, S, 'The Origins of Nigeria's Notorious 419 Scams', *Newsweek*, 5 September 2016.

Epprecht, M, 'Black skin, "cowboy" masculinity: A genealogy of homophobia in the African nationalist movement in Zimbabwe to 1983' (2006) 7(3) *Culture, Health and Sexuality* 253–66.

Eshun, E, 'Soon Comes the Night', *Granta*, 8 August 2017, 2.

Eshun, E, 'I dreaded going to sleep for fear of seeing him', *The Observer*, London, 11 June 2017.

Farcy, J-B and Smit, S, 'Status (Im)Mobility and the Legal Production of Irregularity: A Socio-legal Analysis of Temporary Migrants' Lived Experiences' (2019) XX (X) *Social and Legal Studies* 1–21.

Financial Times, 'Lviv Diary: Philippe Sands on law, music and a city of history', 18 December 2017 at: https://www.ft.com/video/30739bf6-d2bc-4bd7-8c5b-b69c2433e45b.

Ford, R, 'How have attitudes to immigration changed since Brexit?', *The UK in a Changing Europe*, 1 June 2018, at: ukandeu.ac.uk/how-have-attitudes-to-immigration-changed-since-brexit/.

Ford, R, 'Zimbabwe asylum seekers can be sent back after ruling on persecution risk', *The Times*, London, 3 August 2006.

Frampton, S, 'In Search of Shakespeare's dark lady', *The Guardian*, 10 August 2013.

Furness, H, 'Has Shakespeare's dark lady finally been revealed?', *The Daily Telegraph*, 8 January 2013.

Gaffney-Rhys, R, 'From the Offences against the Persons Act 1861 to the Serious Crime Act 2015 – the development of the law relating to female genital mutilation in England and Wales' (2017) 39;4 *Journal of Social Welfare and Family Law* 417–34.

Gallagher, A, 'Human Rights and the New UN Protocols on Trafficking and Migrant Smuggling: A Preliminary Analysis' (2001) 23(4) *Human Rights Quarterly* 975–1004.

Gammeltoft-Hansen, T, 'International Cooperation on Migration Control: Towards a Research Agenda for Refugee Law' (2018) 20 *European Journal of Migration* 373–95.

Garbin, D and Godin, M, '"Saving the Congo": Transnational social fields and the politics of home in the Congolese diaspora' (2013) 6(2) *Africa and Black Diaspora: An International Journal* 113–30.

Garside, J and Osborne, H, '"Golden Passports" threaten European Security, warns EU Commissioner', *The Guardian*, London, 16 October 2018.

Gates Jr, HL, 'The Truth Behind '40 Acres and a Mule', *The Root*, 7 January 2013.

Gathii, J, 'Beyond China's Human Rights *Exceptionalism* in Africa: Leveraging Science, Technology and Engineering for Long-Term Growth' (2013) 51 *Columbia Journal of Transnational Law* 664.

Gentleman, A, 'Yarl's Wood Women feel Desperate Says Diane Abbott', *The Guardian*, 23 February, 2018.

Gettleman, J, 'Somalia, Pirates tell their story: They only want money', *New York Times*, 30 September 2008.

Goldberg, S, 'For Decades our Coverage was Racist. To Rise Above our Past, We Must Acknowledge it', 233(4) *National Geographic*, April 2018: https://www.nationalgeographic.com/magazine/2018/04/from-the-editor-race-racism-history/.

Gqibitole, K and Bello, S, 'Identity, politics and restriction in Athol Fugard's art: Writing and liberalism in apartheid South Africa' (2018) 39(1) *Literator* (online).

Greenwood, G, 'Home Office citizenship fees "scandalous"', BBC News online, 13 February 2018.

Grierson, J and Marsh, S, 'Slash "obscene" Home Office fees, say MPs and campaigners', *The Guardian*, London, 24 June 2018.

Grounds, M, 'Systemic prejudice in the UK, and visa refusals for African academics', *Mail and Guardian*, Johannesburg, 10 July 2019.

Guardian, '25 Years of the Refugee Crisis', *The Guardian*, London, 20 June 2018.

Haaretz Editorial, 'Israel's African Asylum seekers can't go "home" to Rwanda', *Haaretz*, 25 January, 2018.

Hales, L, 'The Criminalisation and Imprisonment of Migrant Victims of Trafficking' (2018) 8(1) *Onati Socio-Legal Series* 50–70.

Hall, R, 'Kenyan domestic worker assaulted by mob in Lebanon faces deportation', *The Guardian*, London, 5 July 2018.

Hall, R, 'Deportation reprieve for Kenyan domestic worker attacked in Lebanon', *The Guardian*, London, 6 July 2018.

Hall, R, 'The secret networks saving Lebanon's migrant maids from abuse', *The Guardian*, London, 1 August, 2018.

Halley, J, Kotiswaran, P, Shamir, H and Thomas, C, 'From the International to the Local in Feminist Legal Responses to Rape, Prostitution/Sex Work and Sex Trafficking: Four Studies in Contemporary Governance Feminism' (2006) 29 *Harvard Journal of Law and Gender* 335.

Halliday, I, 'MPs publish damning indictment of UK visa process for African visa' at: https://www.freemovement.org.uk/mps-publish-damning-indictment-of-uk-visa-process-for-african-visitors/.

Hamid, M, 'We are all Migrants' (2019) 236(2) *National Geographic* 15–20.

Hans, V, 'Dignity Takings, Dignity Restoration: A Tort Law Perspective' (2017) 92 *Chicago-Kent Law Review* 715, 716.

Hassim, S, 'Winnie Madikizela-Mandela: revolutionary who kept the spirit of resistance alive', *The Conversation*, 3 April 2018.

Henley, J, 'Citizenship for sale: how tycoons can go shopping for a new passport', *The Guardian*, London, 2 June 2018.

Hilsum, L, 'We Love China' (2006) 92 *Granta* 233.

Hirsch, A, 'Winnie Mandela was a hero: If she'd been white, there would be no debate', *The Guardian*, London, 3 April 2018.

Hirsch, A, 'When is an immigrant not an immigrant? When they're rich', *The Guardian*, 10 April 2019.
Hirsch, A, 'Africa's colonisation of the English language continues apace', *The Guardian*, 29 January 2020.
Hirsch, A, 'We need to talk about the British empire' (Podcast, Audible, 2020).
Hosseini, K, 'Refugees are still dying: How do we get over our news fatigue?', *The Guardian*, London, 17 August 2018 at: https://www.theguardian.com/books/2018/aug/17/khaled-hosseini-refugees-migrants-stories.
Howden, D, Fotiadis, A and Campbell, Z, 'Revealed: The secret European plot to keep migrants out', *The Guardian*, 13 March 2020.
Hull Daily Mail, 'The Banned Book. Magistrate Decides it is an Obscene Libel', 16 November 1928.
Human Rights Watch, 'Nigeria: Anti-LGBT law Threatens Basic Rights', Abuja, 14 January 2014.
Human Rights Watch, 'Israel: Detained Asylum seekers pressured to leave' (Human Rights Watch, News, 13 March 2013).
Hussey, A, 'Macron should be praised for facing France's last great taboo-torture in Algeria', *The Observer*, London, 16 September 2018.
Hyland, K (Anti-slavery Commissioner), 'Britain must address the root causes of sex trafficking from Nigeria to Europe', London, *The Guardian*, 12 August 2016.
International Labour Organization, 'New ILO Figures show 164 Million people are migrant workers', ILO Newsroom, 5 December 2018 at: https://www.ilo.org/global/about-the-ilo/newsroom/news/WCMS_652106/lang--en/index.htm.
Imoagene, O, 'Being British v. Being American: Identification among second-generation adults of Nigerian descent in the US and UK' (2012) 35(12) *Ethnic and Racial Studies* 2153–73.
Inge, S, 'Academics asked to check visas of international visitors', *Times Higher Education Supplement*, 8 March 2018.
Isaack, W, 'African Commission tackles sexual orientation, gender identity', *Pambazuka News*, 1 June 2017.
Iweala, U, 'Alain Mabanckou's Masterfully Unstructured Novel of Addiction', *The Paris Review*, 1 October 2018.
Jansen, E, 'Black authors, maids and madams', *Africa is a country*, 1 August 2019.
Jansen, E, 'Like Family', *Africa is a Country*, 30 July 2019.
Jones, J, 'The BAWSO Diogel Project. An Interview with Imogen Gunner, BAWSO Trafficking Senior Support Worker' (2018) 8(1) *Onati Socio-Legal Series* 71–84.
Jones, J and Winterdyk, J, 'Human Trafficking: Challenges and Opportunities for the 21st Century. Outcomes and Proposals' (2018) 8(1) *Onati Socio-Legal Series* 165–73.
Jones, T, *An American Marriage* (London, Oneworld Publications, 2019).
Johnson, M, 'Matteo Salvini accuses France of 'stealing' Africa's wealth', *Financial Times*, London, 22 January 2019.
Joiner, S, Lombardi, A, O'Neill, S, 'Hostile environment: Home Office makes 500m (sterling) from immigration fees', *The Times*, London, 11 August 2019.
Jordan, M, 'The Overlooked undocumented immigrants from India, China, Brazil', *New York Times*, 1 December 2019.
Jordan, T, 'The Experiences that Inspired "An American Marriage"', *New York Times*, 23 February 2018.
Kahn, J, et al, 'How not to talk about race and genetics', *Buzzfeed Opinion*, 30 March 2018.
Kakutani, M, 'A Child of Two Lands', *New York Times* book review, 15 May 2013.
Kanagmugire, J, 'African Countries in a fix as Rwanda Refugee Status Ends', *The East African*, 20 January 2018.
Karethi, M and Viljoen, F, 'An argument for the continued validity of woman to woman marriage in post-2010 Kenya' (2019) 63(3) *Journal of African Law* 303–28.
Kellaway, K, 'Claudia Rankine: "Blackness in the white imagination has nothing to do with black people"', *The Guardian*, London, 27 December 2015.
Kelly, A and Tondo, LO, 'Trafficking of Nigerian Women into prostitution in Europe "at crisis level"', *The Guardian*, London, 8 August 2016.
Khosravi, S, 'An Ethnography of Migrant "Illegality" in Sweden: Included yet Excepted' (2010) 6(1) *Journal of International Political Theory* 95–116.

Kington, K, 'Italian Mayor who welcomed migrants is Arrested', *The Times*, London, 3 October 2018.

Kirkpatrick, D, 'Europe wanted migrants stopped. Now some are being sold as slaves', *New York Times*, 30 November 2017.

Kleist, N, 'Flexible Politics of Belonging: Diaspora Mobilisation in Ghana' (2013) 72 *African Studies* 285–306.

Koka, E and Veshi, D, 'Irregular Migration by Sea: Interception and Rescue Interventions in light of International Law and the EU Sea Borders Regulation' (2019) 21 *European Journal of Migration and Law* 26–52.

Konsta, A-M, 'Is there a right to human dignity? The Example of the Right to Education of Refugees' (2019) 21 *European Journal of Migration and the Law* 261–79.

Kufakurinani, U, Pasura, D, McGregor, J, 'Transnational Parenting and the Emergence of 'Diaspora Orphans' in Zimbabwe, (2014) 7 *African Diaspora* 114–38.

Kunzig, R (with photographs by R Hammond), 'The New Europeans: Voices from a changing continent', *National Geographic*, October 2016.

Kuwonu, F, 'China's "Little Africa" losing its allure', *Africa Renewal*, August–November 2018.

Landau, LB, 'Xenophobia in South Africa: why it's time to unsettle narratives about migrants', *The Conversation*, 6 September 2018.

Landau, L and Amit, R, 'Decolonization's Borders', *Africa is a Country*, 21 February 2020.

Lawal, S, 'Ghana Must Go: The ugly history of Africa's most famous bag', *Mail & Guardian*, Johannesburg, 4 April 2019.

Laville, S, 'First FGM prosecution: how the case came to court', *The Guardian*, London, 4 February 2015.

Leader, D, 'The Mau Mau Litigation – Justice at Last' (OxHRH Blog, 3 November 2015).

Le Duc, J, Salvadoreno y su hija mueren ahogados en intent por llegal a EU', *La Jornada*, 24 June 2019.

Lee, H, *To Kill a Mockingbird* (Philadelphia PA, Lippincott & Co, 1960).

Leigh Day, 'Historic judgment as UK Government loses court battle on Kenyan colonial torture', 21 July 2011, at: https://www.leighday.co.uk/News/2011/July-2011/Historic-judgment-as-UK-Government-loses-court-battle.

Lentin A and Amiraux, V, 'Francois Hollande's Misguided Move: Taking "Race" out of the Constitution', *The Guardian*, London, 12 February 2013.

Lindsay, F, 'Sudan Unrest Led EU to Suspend Funds for Migration Control, but Khartoum Process Should End for Good', *Forbes Magazine*, 6 August 2019.

Luker, T, 'Decision-making Conditioned by Radical Uncertainty: Credibility Assessment at the Australian Refugee Review Tribunal' (2013) 25(3) *International Journal of Refugee Law* 502 at: http://classic.austlii.edu.au/au/journals/UTSLRS/2013/7.html.

Mckie, A, 'British Professor quits as external examiner over passport check', *Times Higher Education Supplement*, 21 January 2020.

Malik, K, 'White Identity is meaningless. Real dignity is found in shared hopes.', *The Observer*, London, 21 October 2018.

Malik, M, 'Family law in diverse societies' in J Eekelaar and R George (eds), *Routledge Handbook of Family Law and Policy* (New York, Routledge, 2014) 424–38.

Maloney, R, 'Trudeau on defensive for not publicly calling out Senegal's anti-gay law', *Huffington Post*, 14 February 2020.

Manji, A, '"Like a Mask Dancing": Law and Colonialism in Chinua Achebe's Arrow of God' (2002) 27(4) *Journal of Law and Society* 626–42.

Manji, A, 'Of the Laws of Kenya and Burials and all That' (2002) 14 (3) *Law and Literature* 436–88.

Manji, A, 'Law, Literature and the Politics of Culture in Kenya' (2003) *Law, Social Justice & Global Development Journal* (an electronic law journal hosted by Warwick University).

Manji, A, 'Law, Labour and Resistance to French Colonialism in Sembene Ousmane's *Les Bouts de Bois de Dieu* (2005) 25(2) *Legal Studies* 320–36.

Marini, F, 'Immigrants and transnational engagement in the diaspora: Ghanaian associations in Italy and the UK' (2013) 6 *African and Black Diaspora: An International Journal* 131–44.

Martin, G, 'Stop the boats! Moral panic in Australia over asylum seekers' (2015) 29 *Journal of Media & Cultural Studies* 304–22.

Martin, L and Penasa, S, 'Migration Crises and the Principle of Solidarity in Times of Sovereignism: Challenges for EU Law and Polity' (2020) 22(1) *European Journal of Migration and Law* 1.

Masters, T, 'Nelson Mandela Death: Film examines power of music', *BBC News* online, 6 December 2013.

McDonald, D, 'Credibility Assessment in Refugee Status Determination' (2014) (26) *National Law School of India* 116–26.

McGregor, J, '"Joining the BBC (British Bottom Cleaners)": Zimbabwean Migrants and the UK Care Industry' (2007) 33 *Journal of Ethnic and Migration Studies* 801–24.

McKinney CJ, 'Home Office loses a quarter of asylum decision-makers in six months', *Free movement*, 28 November 2017 at: www.freemovement.org.uk/asylum-staff-turnover/.

Melin, P, 'The Global Compact for Migration: Lessons for the Unity of EU Representation' (2019) 21 *European Journal of Migration and the Law* 194–214.

Mighetto, I, 'The Contingency of Credibility: Gender Related Persecution, Traumatic Memory and Home Office Interviews' (2016) 3 *SOAS Law Journal* 1–37.

Millbank, J, 'From Discretion to Disbelief: Recent Trends in Refugee Determinations on the Basis of Sexual Orientation in Australia and the United Kingdom' (2009) 13(2/3) *International Journal of Human Rights* 391–414.

Mensah, J, Williams, C and Aryee, E, 'Gender, Power and Religious Transnationalism among the African Diaspora in Canada' (2013) 32 *African Geographical Review* 157–71.

Mnookin, RH and Kornhauser, L, 'Bargaining in the Shadow of the Law: The Case of Divorce' (1979) 88 *Yale Law Journal* 950–97.

Mohdin, A, 'Destitute Children "Unlawfully denied aid" because of focus on parents' status', *The Guardian*, London, 27 May 2019.

Moore, SF, 'Law and Social Change: The Semi-Autonomous Social Field as an Appropriate Subject of Study' (1973) 7(4) *Law & Society Review* 719–46.

Morris, S, 'Police promise to learn lessons after collapse of FGM trial in Bristol', *The Guardian*, London, 22 February 2018.

Moses, J, 'Foreign Ideas about "Child marriage"? Diversity, the Family and Legal Reform in Contemporary Europe', Verfassungsblog on Matters Constitutional, 20 September 2019 https://verfassungsblog.de/foreign-ideas-about-child-marriage/.

Msimang, S, 'Belonging – Why South Africans Refuse to let Africa in', *Africa is a Country*, 15 April 2014.

Mugisha, IR, 'Deported from Zambia: Former Rwandan Refugees Choose to Stay', *The East African*, 15 September, 2018.

Mumford, G, 'Rafiki review – ground breaking lesbian romance aims to change Kenyan hearts and minds', *The Guardian*, 9 May 2018.

Murphy, J, 'Rationality and Cultural Pluralism in the Non-recognition of Foreign Marriages' (2000) 49 *International and Comparative Law Quarterly* 643–59.

Mutua, M, 'Savages, Victims and Saviors: The Metaphor of Human Rights' (2001) 42 *Harvard International Law Journal* 201.

Nagarajan, C, 'Culture/Religion/Tradition v. Modern/Secular/Foreign' (2018) 3 *Feminist Dissent* 114–46.

Nature Editorial on 'Sex and the Law' (2015) 522 *Nature* 127.

NBC News, 'Kenya lifts ban on lesbian film, making it eligible for Oscars', *NBC News*, 21 September 2018.

Nkosi, M, 'Winnie Mandela – the young mother who refused to be broken', *BBC News* online, 4 April 2018.

Nordling, L, 'African academics challenge homophobic laws' (2015) 522 *Nature* 135–36 (11 June 2015).

Noor, P, 'What do experts think of revoking Shamima Begum's Citizenship?', *The Guardian*, London, 20 February 2019.

Nussbaum, M, 'Women's Capabilities and Social Justice' (2000) 1 *Journal of Human Development* 219.

Nyoka, N, 'Amended Refugee Act restricts fundamental rights', *Mail and Guardian*, 20 February 2020.

Nwaubani, A, 'We spoke English to set ourselves apart', *The Guardian*, 14 March 2019.

Nzegwu, N, 'Gender Equality in a Dual Sex System: The Case of Onitsha' (1994) 7 *Canadian Journal of Law and Jurisprudence* 73–95.

Observer, 'The Audit; Attitudes to Immigration', *The Observer*, London, 21 October 2018.

Odugbemi, J, Rammala, O and wa Kamonji, W, 'Searching for Africa in African Studies: An open letter to teachers of Africa at UCL' on *Medium*, 29 July 2019 at: https://medium.com/@jodugb/searching-for-africa-in-african-studies-an-open-letter-to-teachers-of-africa-at-ucl-29a3a9d20eee.

Odugbemi, J, Rammala, O and wa Kamonji, W, 'Searching for Africa in African Studies' on *Africa is a Country*, 15 August 2019. at: https://africasacountry.com/2019/08/there-is-no-africa-in-african-studies.

Oette, L and Abdelsalam Babiker, M, 'Migration Control á la Khartoum: EU external engagement and human rights protection in the Horn of Africa' (2017) 36(4) *Refugee Survey Quarterly* 64–89.

O'Grady, S, 'Tanzania walked back on a claim that it was going after LGBT people. Now Amnesty says 10 men have already been arrested', *The Washington Post*, 6 November, 2018.

OHCHR, 'United Kingdom: UN expert condemns entrenched racial discrimination and inequality' OHCHR News, Geneva, 14 June 2019 at https://www.ohchr.org/EN/NewsEvents/Pages/DisplayNews.aspx?NewsID=24698&LangID=E.

Oloka-Onyango, J, 'Debating love, human rights and identity politics in East Africa: The case of Uganda and Kenya' (2015) 15 *African Human Rights Law Journal* 28–57.

Olsen, G, 'De-Americanizing Law and Literature Narratives: Open Up the Story' (2010) 22 *Law and Literature* 338–64.

Oludare Idowu, H, 'Assimilation in 19th Century Senegal' (1969) 34 *Cahiers d'Etudes Africaines* 194–218.

Onwwuemezi, N, 'Alarming Study reveals only 4% of books feature a BAME character', *The Bookseller*, July 2018, at: www.thebookseller.com/news/representation-childrens-literature-827841.

Pasura, D, 'Towards a Multisited Ethnography of the Zimbabwean Diaspora in Britain' (2011) 18 *Identities: Global Studies in Culture and Power* 250–72.

Paterson, S, 'Britain's third FGM prosecution failure: African lawyer, 50, who was accused of cutting his nine-year-old daughter as a punishment is cleared after telling jurors "I'm Catholic, I don't believe in it"', *Daily Mail*, 22 March 2018.

Perraudin, F, 'Home Office held "illegal interview" with asylum seeker', *The Guardian*, 20 March 2019.

Perraudin, F, 'Home Office faces legal cases over Zimbabwean asylum seekers', *The Guardian*, 5 January 2020.

Peroni, L, 'Violence against Women: The Istanbul Convention through a Post-Colonial Feminist Lens' (2016) 24 *Feminist Legal Studies* 49–67.

Poon, J, 'How a body becomes a Boat: The Asylum Seeker in Law and Images' (2018) 30 *Law & Literature* 105–21.

Rao, R, Re-membering Mwanga: same-sex intimacy, memory and belonging in post-colonial Uganda' (2015) 9 *Journal of Eastern African Studies* 1–19.

Ranger, T, 'The Narratives and Counter-narratives of Zimbabwean Asylum: female voices' (2005) 26 *Third World Quarterly* 405–21.

Rankin, J, 'Greece £2000 on offer for migrants to return home', *The Guardian*, 13 March 2020.

Raymond, AK, 'The story behind the viral photo of a migrant father and toddler', *New York* magazine, 26 June 2019 at: http://www.nymag.

Rawlinson, K and Dodd, V, 'Shamima Begum: Isis Briton faces move to revoke citizenship', *The Guardian*, London, 19 February 2019.

Reid, G, 'Egypt Doesn't Speak for Africa on LGBT Issues', Human Rights Watch, 1 November 2017.

Reid, G, 'Victory for Gender Identity in Botswana: Country's High Court Rules in Favour of Transgender Man', Human Rights Watch, 3 October 2017.

Reuters, 'Saudi prince killed servant at luxury London hotel', London, 5 October 2010.

Reuters, 'Director of banned Kenyan film about lesbian romance sues government', *The Guardian*, 14 September 2018.

Reuters, 'Migrants land in Malta after Berlin brokers deal for EU to take them in', *The Guardian*, London, 5 August, 2019.

Sanders, J and Campbell, M, 'Ernest Cole's photographs reveal America's apartheid', *The Sunday Times*, London, 22 October 2017.

Santer, K, 'Governing the Central Mediterranean through Indirect Rule: Tracing the Effects of the Recognition of Joint Rescue Coordination Centre Tripoli' (2019) 21 *European Journal of Migration* 141–65.

Sarkar, A, 'By demeaning refugees, Tories have caused a hunger strike', *The Guardian*, 1 March 2018.

Sarson, J and McDonald, L, 'No Longer Invisible: Families that Torture, Traffic and Exploit their Girl Child' (2018) 8(1) *Onati Socio-Legal Series* 81–105.

Sawyer, L and Habel, Y, 'Refracting African and Black Diaspora through the Nordic region' (2014) 7 *African and Black Diaspora: An International Journal* 1–6.

Schlüter, A, '*Biao v. Denmark*: Grand Chamber Ruling on Ethnic Discrimination Might Leave Couples Seeking Family Reunification Worse Off.' Guest blog *Strasbourg Observers*, 13 June 2016.

Selasi, T, 'The Sex Lives of African Girls' in (2011) 115 *Granta* 129–162.

Selasi, T, 'Bye-Bye Babar' at: http://www.thelip.robertsharp.co.uk/?m=200503, 3 March 2005, accessed 10 September 2015.

Sen, A, 'Human Rights and Capabilities' (2005) 6 *Journal of Human Development* 151.

Sevenzo, F, 'Britain's African Migrants who backed Brexit', *BBC News* online, 28 June 2016.

Sevenzo, F, 'Viewpoint: Boris Johnson and his 'colonial views' on Africa, *BBC News* online, 14 July 2016.

Sherwell, P, 'Dominque Strauss-Kahn accuser builds restaurant and a new life in New York', *The Telegraph*, 12 June 2015.

Shoko, T, '"Worse than dogs and pigs?" Attitudes towards homosexual practice in Zimbabwe' (2010) 57(5) *Journal of Homosexuality* 634–49.

Smith, D, 'They fought for Britain. In return they were given £10', *The Guardian*, 2 September 2006.

Snyder, F, 'Colonialism and the Legal Form: The Creation of Customary Law in Senegal' (1981) 19 *Journal of Legal Pluralism* 49.

Souter, J, 'Asylum decision-making in the UK: disbelief or denial?', Open Democracy, 4 April 2011 at: https://www.opendemocracy.net/en/5050/asylum-decision-making-in-uk-disbelief-or-denial/.

Sowale, A, 'Economic Community of West African States' Protocol on Free Movement and the Challenges of Human Trafficking in West Africa' (2018) 10(2) *Insight on Africa* 215–25.

Steemers, V, '*Broken Glass* or Broken Text?: The translatability of Alain Mabanckou's *Verre Cassé* (2005) into English' (2014) 45(1) *Research in African Literatures* 107–24.

Stewart, A, 'Who do we care about? Reflections on Gender Justice in a Global Market' (2007) 58(3) *Northern Ireland Legal Quarterly* 358–74.

Summers, C, 'A Case of Modern-day Slavery in the Suburbs', *BBC News* online, 17 March, 2011.

Tabengwa, M, 'Dispatches: Judgment Day Looms for Botswana LGBT Group', Human Rights Watch, 13 November 2014.

Tamale, S, 'A human rights impact assessment of the Anti-Homosexuality Bill' (2009) 15 *East African Journal of Peace and Human Rights* 509–19.

Tamale, S, 'Exploring the Contours of African Sexualities: Religion, Law and Power' (2014) 1 *African Human Rights Law Journal* 150–77.

Tan, NF, 'The Manus Island Regional Processing Centre: A Legal Taxonomy' (2018) 20 *European Journal of Migration* 427–451.

Taylor, D and Mason, R, 'Home Office staff rewarded with gift vouchers for fighting off asylum cases', *The Guardian*, London, 14 January 2014.

Taylor, D and McIntyre, N, 'Revealed: sick, tortured immigrants locked up for months in Britain', *The Guardian*, London, 10 October 2018.

The Times, 'Home Office is "institutionally racist" said report into Windrush scandal', London, 21 February 2020.

Timmons, P, Hodgson, M and Agren, D, 'Shocking photo of drowned father and daughter highlights migrants' border peril', *The Guardian*, 26 June 2019.

Tinarwo MT and Pasura, D, 'Negotiating and Contesting Gendered and Sexual Identities in the Zimbabwean Diaspora' (2014) 40, *Journal of Southern African Studies* 521–538.

Tofighian, O, 'Truth to Power: my time translating Behrouz Boochani's masterpiece', *The Conversation*, 15 August 2018.

Travis, A, '"Go home" vans resulted in 11 people leaving Britain, says report', *The Guardian*, London, 31 October 2013.
Travis, A, 'Tory immigration bill to curb right of appeal against deportation', *The Guardian*, London, 2013.
Turkewitz, J, 'South African Riots Kill Five and Spur Cries of Xenophobia', *New York Times*, 3 September 2019.
Tutu, D (Archbishop). See Leigh Day (above).
Underwood, A, 'So many ways of knowing: An interview with Jennifer Nansubuga Makumbi, author of "Kintu"', *Los Angelos Review of Books*, 31 August 2017.
Viljoen, F, 'Botswana court ruling is a ray of hope for LGBT people across Africa' in *The Conversation*, 12 June 2019.
Vogel, D, '"Kill the Lawyers" A Line Misinterpreted', *New York Times*, 17 June, 1990.
Warrell, H and Pilling, D, 'Africans twice as likely to be refused UK visa, say MPS', *The Financial Times*, 16 July 2019.
Waldrop, M Mitchell, 'Diversity: Pride in Science' (2014) 513 *Nature* 297–300 (18 September 2014).
Wanaina, B, 'I am a homosexual, mum', *The Guardian*, London, 21 January 2014.
Webster, T, 'China's Human Rights Footprint in Africa' (2013) 50 C*olumbia Journal of Transnational Law* 626.
Wessels, J, 'The Boundaries of Universality – Migrant Women and Domestic Violence before the Strasbourg Court' (2019) 37 *Netherlands Quarterly of Human Rights* 336–58.
Williams, AJ, 'James Baldwin's Black Queer Legacy', 23 March 2017, at: www.electricliterature.com.
Wilsher, K, 'My father's mother shaped my life. That's why Macron's apology is so important', *The Observer*, London, 16 September 2018.
Wittenberg, J, 'You have no voice in there', *The Guardian*, London, 28 June 2019.
Wright, JB, 'George Polgreen Bridgetower: An African Prodigy in England 1789–99' (1980) 66(1) *The Musical Quarterly* 65–82.
Woolley, A, 'Narrating the "Asylum Story": Between Literary and Legal Storytelling' (2017) 19(3) *Interventions: International Journal of Postcolonial Studies* 376, 386–91.
World Economic Forum, 'African migration: what the numbers really tell us', World Economic Forum 7 June 2018.
Yoshida, K, 'Towards Intersectionality in the European Court of Human Rights: The Case of *BS v. Spain*' (2013) 23 *Feminist Legal Studies* 195–204.
Younge, G, 'End all Immigration controls – they're a sign we value money more than people', *The Guardian*, London, 16 October 2017.
Younge, G, 'My Year of Reading African Women', *The Guardian*, London, 15 December 2018.

Book Chapters

Adichie, CN, 'On Monday of Last Week' in CN Adichie, *The Thing Around Your Neck* (London, 4th Estate, 2009) 74–94.
Adichie, CN, 'The American Embassy' in CN Adichie, *The Thing Around Your Neck* (London, 4th Estate, 2009) 128–41.
Adichie, CN, 'The Arranger of Marriages' in CN Adichie, *That Thing Around Your Neck* (London, 4th Estate, 2009) 167–86.
Adichie, CN, 'Shivering' in E Wakatama Allfrey, *Africa39, New Writing from Africa South of the Sahara* (London, Bloomsbury, 2016) 1–14.
Afolabi, S, 'Monday Morning' in S Afolabi, *A Life Elsewhere* (London, Jonathan Cape, 2006) 1–15.
Ambani, JO, 'A Triple Heritage of Sexuality? Regulation of Sexual Orientation in Africa in Historical Perspective' in S Namwase and A Jjuuko (eds), *Protecting the Human Rights of Sexual Minorities in Contemporary Africa* (Pretoria, PULP, 2017) 14–50.
Ama Ata Aidoo, 'Everything Counts' in *No Sweetness Here and Other Stories* (Kumasi, Isaac Books and Stationery Service, Reprinted 2013) 1–8.

An Na'im, A, 'State Responsibility under International Human Rights Law to Change Religious and Customary Laws' in R Cook (ed), *Human Rights of Women: National and International Perspectives* (Philadelphia PA, Penn Press, 1994) 167.

Angelou, M, 'Human Family' in M Angelou, *The Complete Collected Poems* (London, Virago, 1997) 224–25.

Angelou, M, 'Elegy' in M Angelou, *The Complete Collected Poems* (London, Virago, 1997) 115.

Arac de Nyeko, M, 'Jambula Tree' in *Jambula Tree and Other Stories: The Caine Prize for African Writing, 8th Annual Collection* (London, New Internationalist, 2008) 9–19.

Arnfred, S, '"African Sexuality"/Sexuality in Africa: Tales and Silences' in S Arnfred (ed), *Rethinking Sexualities in Africa* (Uppsala, Nordiska Afrikainstitutet, 2004) 59–77.

Ayeni, VO, 'Human Rights and the Criminalisation of Same-Sex Relationships in Nigeria: A Critique of the Same-Sex Marriage (Prohibition) Act' in S Nwamase and A Jjuko (eds), *Protecting the Human Rights of Sexual Minorities in Contemporary Africa* (Pretoria, PULP, 2017) 203–37.

Banda, F, 'Changing the Constitution and Challenging Attitudes: Recent Developments in Kenyan Family Law' in B Atkin (ed), *International Survey of Family Law* (Bristol, Jordans, 2014) 255–72.

Bellamy, C, 'Preface' in J Todres and S Higinbotham, *Human Rights in Children's Literature* (Oxford, OUP, 2016).

Bennoune, K, 'Law of the Republic vs. Law of the "Brothers": A Story of France's Law Banning Religious Symbols in Public Schools' in D Hurwitz, M Satterthwaite and D Ford (eds), *Human Rights Advocacy Stories* (New York, Foundation Press, 2009) 155–90. (Reprinted in Women Living Under Muslim Laws (WLUML), Dossier 30–31, The Struggle for Secularism in Europe and North America pp 11–42 (July 2011).

Bhaba, J, 'From Citizen to Migrant: The Scope of Child Statelessness in the Twenty-First Century' in J Bhaba (ed), *Children without a State* (Cambridge MA, MIT Press, 2011) 1–39.

Blitz, BK, 'Neither Seen nor Heard: Compound Deprivation among Stateless Children' in J Bhabha (ed), *Children Without a State* (Cambridge MA, MIT Press, 2011) 44–66.

Burman, S, 'First World Solutions for Third World Problems' in L Weitzman and M Maclean, *Economic Consequences of Divorce: International Perspectives* (Oxford, Clarendon Press, 1992) 367–80.

Chingonyi, K, 'Grief' in K Chingonyi, *Kumukanda* (London, Chatto & Windus, 2017) 40.

Chuang, J, 'Article 6' in M Freeman, C Chinkin and B Rudolph (eds) *Commentary to CEDAW* (Oxford, OUP, 2013) 169–196.

Cole, T, 'On the Blackness of the Panther' in N Shukla and C Suleyman (eds), *The Good Immigrant USA* (London, Dialogue Books, 2019) 36–51.

Collis, S, 'The Lawyer's Tale' in D Herd and A Pincus (eds), *Refugee Tales* (Manchester, Comma Press, 2016) 107–24.

Cousins, H and Dodson-Katiyo, P, 'Zimbabweanness Today: An Interview with Tendai Huchu' in E Emenyonu, *Diaspora & Returns in Fiction, African Literature Today 34* (Oxford, James Currey, 2016) 200–10.

Deyi, B, 'First class Constitution, second class citizen: Exploring the adoption of the third-gender category in South Africa' in S Namwase and A Jjuko, *Protecting the Human rights of Sexual Minorities in Contemporary Africa* (Pretoria, PULP, 2017) 128–50.

Dunsby, S, 'The Path' in K Clanchy (ed), *England, Poems from a School* (London, Picador, 2018) 67.

Eddo-Lodge, R, 'Forming Blackness through a screen' in N Shukla (ed), *The Good Immigrant* (London, Unbound, 2016) 77–83.

Edozien, CF, 'Forgetting Lamido' in E Wakatama Allfrey, (ed), 2016, *Safe House: Explorations in Creative Non-Fiction* (London, Cassava Republic, 2016) 289–307.

Eekelaar, J, 'Principles of Revolutionary Legality' in A Simpson (ed), *Oxford Essays in Jurisprudence* (Oxford, OUP, 1973) 22–43.

Ellams, I, 'The Unaccompanied Minor's Tale' in D Herd and A Pincus (eds), *Refugee Tales* (Manchester, Comma Press, 2016) 17–24.

Fanon, F, 'On Culture' from F Fanon, *The Wretched of the Earth*, extract reproduced in R Ginkere, S Lubkemann and C Steiner (eds), *Perspectives on Africa A Reader in Culture, History and Representation*, 2nd edn (Oxford, Wiley Blackwell, 2010) 484–97.

Gappah, P, 'My Cousin-Sister Rambanai' in P Gappah, *An Elegy for Easterly* (London, Faber and Faber 2009) 207–36.
Gappah, P, 'The Housemaid from Lalapanzi' in P Gappah, *An Elegy for Easterly* (London, Faber and Faber, 2009) 153–72, 159.
Gappah, P, 'My Cousin–Sister Rambanai' in P Gappah, *An Elegy for Easterly* (London, Faber and Faber, 2009) 207–236
Gappah, P, 'Before Tonde, After Tonde' in C Brazier (ed), *One World: A Global Anthology of Short Stories* (London, New Internationalist, 2009) 115–25.
Gevisser, M, 'Walking Girly in Nairobi' in E Wakatama Allfrey (ed), *Safe House: Explorations in Creative Non-Fiction* (London, Cassava Republic, 2016) 103–25.
Golakai, HJ, 'Fugee' in E Wakatama Allfrey (ed), *Safe House: Explorations in Creative Non-Fiction* (London, Cassava Republic, 2016) 25–46.
Goonesekere, S, 'Article 9' in M Freeman, C Chinkin and B Rudolph (eds), *CEDAW: A Commentary* (Oxford, OUP, 2013) 233–49.
Hadero, M, 'The Wall' in *Caine Prize for African Writing 2019 Shortlist* (London, New Internationalist, 2019) 41–63.
'Helen', as told to Women for Refugee Women adapted by Colfer/Donkin/Rigano, *Journey: Helen's Story* addendum to Colfer, Donkin and Rigano, *Illegal* (2017).
Herd, D, 'Afterword: Calling for an End to Indefinite Detention' in D Herd and A Pincus (eds), *Refugee Tales II* (2017) 113–24.
Higgins, M, 'Luck of the Irish' in N Shukla and C Suleyman (eds), *The Good Immigrant USA*, (London, Dialogue Books, 2019) 104–15.
Holtmaat, R, 'Article 5' in M Freeman, C Chinkin and B Rudolph (eds), *CEDAW: A Commentary* (Oxford, OUP, 2013) 141–67.
John, E, 'The Keepers of Secrets' in E Wakatama Allfrey (ed), *Safe House* (London, Cassava, 2016) 130–50.
Kandie, C, 'Sew my Mouth' in *The Caine Prize for African Writing* (London, New Internationalist, 2019) 65–80.
Kriger, N, 'The politics of legal status for Zimbabweans in South Africa' in J McGregor and R Primorac (eds), *Zimbabawe's new Diaspora: Displacement and the Cultural Politics of Survival* (Oxford, Berghahn, 2010) 77–102.
Kureshi, H, 'These Mysterious Strangers: The New Story of the Immigrant' in L Popsescu (ed), *A Country of Refuge* (London, Unbound, 2016) 27–30.
Lanzoni, L, '*The Trial of Jomo Kenyatta*, by Montague Slater: Oral Tradition and Fundamental Rights in the Trial' in I Ward (ed), *Literature and Human Rights* (Berlin, De Gruyter, 2017) 229–34.
Lessing, D, 'The Antheap' in D Lessing, *Nine African Stories* (London, Longman, 1968) 182–245.
Lessing, D, 'Introduction' in D Lessing, *Nine African Stories* (London, Longman 1968) 1–9.
Lopes, E, 'The Legal Status of sexual minorities in Mozambique' in S Namwase and A Jjuko (eds), *Protecting the Human Rights of Sexual Minorities in Contemporary Africa* (Pretoria, PULP, 2017) 183–89.
Magris, C, 'Who is on the Other Side? Considerations about Frontiers' in C MacLehose (ed), *Frontiers* (London, Harper Collins, 1994) 8–25.
Mahadew, R and Raumnauth, D, 'A Psycho-Legal Reflection on issues Surrounding the LGBTI Community in Mauritius' in S Namwase and A Jjuko (eds), *Protecting the Human Rights of Sexual Minorities in Contemporary Africa* (Pretoria, PULP, 2017) 159–82.
Mahfouz, S, 'Wearing Where you're at: Immigration and UK Fashion' in N Shukla (ed), *The Good Immigrant* (London, Unbound, 2016) 141–58.
Makumbi, JN, 'Christmas is Coming' in *Manchester Happened* (London, Oneworld, 2019) 1–28.
Makumbi, JN, 'Our Allies the Colonies' in JN Makumbi, *Manchester Happened* (London, Oneworld. 2019) 31–61.
Makumbi, JN, 'Manchester Happened' in JN Makumbi, *Manchester Happened* (London, Oneworld Publications, 2019) 62–85.
Makumbi, JN, 'Malik's Door' in JN Makumbi, *Manchester Happened* (London, Oneworld, 2019) 123–39.

Mazrui, A, 'Pan Africanism and the Intellectuals: rise, decline and revival' in T Mkandawira (ed), *African Intellectuals* (London, ZED, 2005) 78.

Mbugua, A, 'Gender dynamics: A transsexual overview' in S Tamale (ed), *African Sexualities: A Reader* (Oxford, Pambazuka Press, 2011) 238–46.

McGregor, J, 'Diaspora and Dignity: Navigating and Contesting Civic Exclusion in Britain' in J McGregor and R Primorac (eds), *Zimbabwe's new diaspora: Displacement and the cultural politics of survival* (Oxford, Berghahn Books, 2010) 122–43.

Mengistu, M, 'This is what the journey does' in VT Nguyen (ed), *The Displaced: Refugee Writers on Refugee Lives* (New York, Abrams Press, 2018) 129–35.

Minhas, P, 'How Not to Be' in N Shukla and C Suleyeman (eds), *The Good Immigrant USA* (London, Dialogue Books, 2019) 51–66.

Mohammad, A, 'The Deportee's Tale' in D Herd and A Pincus (eds), *Refugee Tales* (Manchester, Comma Press, 2016) 99–106.

Mozondidya, J, 'Migration, Citizenship and Identity among Zimbabweans in South Africa' in J McGregor and R Primorac (eds), *Zimbabawe's new Diaspora: Displacement and the Cultural Politics of* Survival (Oxford, Berghahn, 2010) 37–58.

Mudimbe-Boyi, E, 'Black France: Myth or Reality? Problems of Identity and Identification' in T Keaton *et al* (eds), *Black France: France Noir* (Durham NC, Duke University Press, 2012) 17–31.

Namwase, S, Jjuuko, A and Nyarango, I, 'Sexual minorities' rights in Africa: What does it mean to be human; and who gets to decide?' in S Namwase and A Jjuko (eds), *Protecting the Human Rights of Sexual Minorities in Contemporary Africa* (Pretoria, PULP, 2017) 2–12.

Nayeri, D, 'The Ungrateful Refugee' in VT Nguyen (ed), *The Displaced: Refugee Writers on Refugee Lives* (New York, Abrams Press, 2018) 137–50.

Nicolini, M, ''*n Droë Wit Seisoen in die Stormkaap:* Andre Brink and the Fundamental Rights of the Afrikaners in Apartheid South Africa' in I Ward (ed), *Literature and Human Rights* (Berlin, De Gruyter, 2007) 235–54.

Nkweti, N-M, 'It Takes a Village Some Say' in *The Caine Prize for African Writing 2019 shortlist* (London, New Internationalist, 2019) 81–103.

Obioma, C, 'The Naked Man' in N Shukla and C Suleyman (eds), *The Good Immigrant USA* (London, Dialogue Books, 2019) 155–68.

Obokota, T, 'Human Trafficking in Africa: Opportunities and Challenges for the African Court of Justice and Human Rights' in C Jalloh, K Clarke and V Nmehielle, *The African Court of Justice and Human and Peoples' Rights in Context: Developments and Challenges* (Cambridge, CUP, 2019) 529–52.

Oby Okolocha, H, 'Negotiating Race, Identity & Homecoming in Chimamanda Ngozi Adichie's *Americanah* & Pede Hollist's *So the Path Does not Die*' in E Emenyonu (ed), *African Literature Today* 34, *Diaspora & Returns in Fiction* (Oxford, James Currey, 2016), 143–62.

Olebile, LC, 'The Status of LGBTI rights in Botswana and its implications for social justice' in S Namwase and A Jjuko, *Protecting the Human Rights of Sexual Minorities in Contemporary Africa* (Pretoria, PULP, 2017) 190–202.

Olisakwe, U, 'This is how I remember it' in E Wakatama Allfrey, *Africa39, New Writing from Africa South of the Sahara* (London, Bloomsbury, 2016) 250–59.

Okwonga, M, 'The Ungrateful Country' in N Shukla, *The Good Immigrant* (London, Unbound, 2017) 224–34.

Onuora-Oguno, AC, 'Protecting Same-Sex Rights in Nigeria: Case Note on *Teriah Joseph Ebah v. Federal Government of Nigeria*' in S Namwase and A Jjuko (eds), *Protecting the Human Rights of Sexual Minorities in Contemporary Africa* (Pretoria, PULP, 2017) 238–42.

Osei-Nyame Jnr, K, 'Images of London in African Literature: Ama Ata Aidoo's *Our Sister Killjoy* and Dambudzo Marachera's *The Black Insider*' in L Phillips (ed), The Swarming Streets. Twentieth-Century Literary Representations of London (New York, Rodopi, 2011) 175–97.

Osundu, EC, 'Teeth' in Osundu, *Voice of America* (London, Granta, 2010) 165–75.

Osondu, EC, 'I will lend you my wife' in Osundu, *Voice of America* (London, Granta, 2010) 107–16.

Osundu, EC, 'Miracle Baby' in Osundu, *Voice of America* (London, Granta, 2010) 117–29.

Rao, A, 'The Politics of Gender and Culture in International Human Rights Discourse' in J Peters and A Wolper (eds), *Women's Rights, Human Rights: International Feminist Perspectives* (Abingdon, Routledge, 1995) 167.
Ranger, T, 'The Invention of Tradition' in E Hobsbawm and T Ranger, *The Invention of Tradition in Colonial Africa* (Cambridge, CUP, 1983) 211.
Reed, A, 'Diaspora Tourism: The Heritage of Slavery in Ghana' in A Quayson and G Daswani (eds), *A Companion to Diaspora and Transnationalism* (Oxford, Wiley Blackwell, 2013) 524.
Saro Wiwa, N, 'A Time to Lie' in L Popescu (ed), *A Country of Refuge* (London, Unbound, 2016) 128.
Senghor, L, 'Negritude: A Humanism of the Twentieth Century' (1970) extract reprinted in R Grinker *et al* (eds), *Perspectives on Africa A Reader in Culture, History and Representation*, 2nd edn (Oxford, Wiley Blackwell, 2010) 477–83.
Shah, A, 'The Queen of Saba and the Infidel' in A Shah, *Tales from the Bazaar of Arabia: Folk Stories from the Middle* East (London, Tauris Parke, 2008) 26–31.
Shire, W, 'Questions for Miriam' in W Shire, *Teaching my mother how to give birth* (London, Flipped Eye, Mouthmark series (No 10), 2011) 23.
Slovo, J, 'Introduction' to R First, *117 Days* (London, Bloomsbury, 1988).
Smith, B, 'The Truth that Never Hurts: Black Lesbians in Fiction in the 1980s' in C Mohanty, A Russo and L Torres, *Third World Women and the Politics of Feminism* (Bloomington IN, Indiana University Press, 1991), 101–29.
Souhami, D, 'Introduction' in R Hall, *The Well of Loneliness* (London, Virago Modern Classics, 1983).
Spivak, G, 'Can the Subaltern Speak?' in Cary Nelson and Lawrence Grossberg (eds), *Marxism and the Interpretation of Culture* (Illinois, University of Illinois Press, 2007) 271.
Tamale, S, 'Interrogating the link between gendered sexualities, power and legal mechanisms: experiences from the lecture room' in S Tamale (ed), *African Sexualities: A Reader* (Oxford, Pambazuka Press, 2011) 606–21.
Togue, M, 'The Status of Sexual Minority Rights in Cameroon' in S Namwase and A Jjuko (eds), *Protecting the Human Rights of Sexual Minorities in Contemporary Africa* (Pretoria, PULP, 2017) 245–57.
Tshuma, NR, 'New Lands, New Selves' in VT Nguyen (ed), *The Displaced: Refugee Writers on Refugee Lives* (New York, Abrams Press, 2018) 159–73.
Varaidzo, 'A Guide to being Black' in N Shukla (ed), *The Good Immigrant* (London, Unbound, 2017) 10–21.
Waheed, N, 'Lands' in *Salt* (London, Create Space, 2013) 182.
Wakatama Allfrey, E, 'Introduction' in E Wakatama Allfrey (ed), *Safe House: Explorations in Creative Nonfiction* (London, Cassava Republic, 2016) 15–20.
Watts, C, 'The Interpreter's Tale' in D Herd and A Pincus (eds), *Refugee Tales* (Manchester, Comma Press, 2016) 63–68.
Zeleza, P, 'The academic diaspora and knowledge production in and on Africa: what role for CODESRIA?' in T Mkandawira (ed), *African Intellectuals: Rethinking Politics, Language, Gender and Development* (London, ZED, 2005) 209–34.
Zephaniah, B, 'On Writing *Refugee Boy*' in B Zephaniah, *Refugee Boy* (London, Bloomsbury, 2017).
Zhawi, B, 'Deptford (*of masculinity*)' in B Zhawi, *Small Inheritances* (Oxford, Ignition Press, 2018) 13.

International Organisations – Reports, Guidance and Research

Amnesty International, *Mapping anti-gay laws in Africa* (London, Amnesty International, 31 May 2018).
African Union, 'Meeting of Experts on the Definition of the African Diaspora 11–12 April 2005 Addis Ababa, Ethiopia', paras 15, 18. at: http://www.dirco.gov.za/diaspora/fr/definition.html.
Australia Human Rights Commission, 'Information for List of Issues Prior to Reporting – Australia: Submission to Committee against Torture (2016), 27 June 2016.
Cheikh Ali, H, Querton, C and Soulard, E, *Gender Related Asylum Claims in Europe: A Comparative analysis of law, policies and practices in nine EU Member* States (European Parliament, Directorate for Internal Policies, 2012).

Council of Europe, *Gender Based Asylum Claims and Non-Refoulement: Articles 60 and 61 of the Istanbul Convention*, COE, December 2019, at: https://rm.coe.int/conventionistanbularticle60-61-web/1680995244.

Cusack, S, *Gender Stereotyping as a Human Rights Violation* (Geneva, OHCHR, 2013).

Edwards, A, CEDAW, 'Summary of background paper entitled "Displacement, statelessness and questions of gender equality and the Convention on the Elimination of All Forms of Discrimination against Women".' CEDAW/C/2009/II/WP.3, 11 July 2009.

EU Agency for Fundamental Rights, 'Addressing Forced Marriage in the EU: Legal Provisions and Promising Practices' (Brussels, EU Publications, 2014).

European Network against Racism (ENAR) *Racism and Discrimination in the Context of Migration in Europe* (Brussels, ENAR, 2016).

Human Dignity Trust, *The Criminalisation of Consensual Same-Sex Sexual Relations Across the Commonwealth-Developments and Opportunities* (London, Human Dignity Trust, 2015).

Human Dignity Trust, *Breaking the Silence: Criminalisation of Lesbians and Bisexual Women and its Impacts* (London, Human Dignity Trust, 2016).

Human Rights Watch, *In a Time of Torture: The Assault on Justice in Egypt's Crackdown on Homosexual Conduct* (New York, Human Rights Watch, 2004).

Human Rights Watch, *This Alien Legacy: The Origins of 'Sodomy' Laws in British Colonialism* (New York, Human Rights Watch, 2008).

Human Rights Watch, *Neighbours in Need: Zimbabweans Seeking Refuge in South Africa* (New York, Human Rights Watch, 2008).

Human Rights Watch, *Fast-Tracked Unfairness: Detention and Denial of Women Asylum Seekers in the UK* (London, Human Rights Watch, 2010).

Human Rights Watch, *Tell me where I can be safe: The Impact of Nigeria's Same Sex Marriage (Prohibition) Act* (New York, Human Rights Watch, 2016).

Human Rights Watch, 'No Longer Alone: LGBT Voices from the Middle East and North Africa' at: https://www.hrw.org/no-longer-alone.

Human Rights Watch, *Working like a Robot: Abuse of Tanzanian Domestic Workers in Oman and the United Arab Emirates* (New York, Human Rights Watch, 2017).

Human Rights Watch, *EU/Italy/Libya: Disputes Over Rescues Put Lives at Risk*, Human Rights Watch, 25 July 2018.

Human Rights Watch, 'Kenya Upholds Archaic Anti-Homosexuality Laws: Activists plan to appeal' Human Rights Watch, 24 May 2019.

Human Rights Watch, *You Pray for Death* (New York, Human Rights Watch, 2019).

International Court of Justice, Legal consequences of the separation of the Chagos Archipelago from Mauritius in 1965 (Request for Advisory Opinion, Press release 2017/32. 24 July 2017, https://www.icj-cij.org/files/case-related/169/169-20170724-PRE-01-00-EN.pdf.

International Court of Justice, Legal consequences of the separation of the Chagos Archipelago from Mauritius in 1964 (Request for Advisory Opinion), Press Release No. 2018/39, 1 August 2018.

International Court of Justice, Press Release 2019/9, 25 February 2019: https://www.icj-cij.org/files/case-related/169/169-20190225-PRE-01-00-EN.pdf.

International Dalit Solidarity Network, *ICERD Recommendations and Comments on Caste Based Discrimination* (IDSN November 2015) (covers the period 1996–2015). Available at: https://idsn.org/wp-content/uploads/2015/11/CERD-Recommendations-and-Comments-on-Caste-Compiled-Nov-2015.pdf.

International Labour Organization, *Domestic Workers across the world* (Geneva, ILO, 2013).

International Labour Organization and Walk Free Foundation, *Global Estimates of Modern Slavery* (Geneva, ILO, 2017).

International Labour Organization, *Employer-Migrant Worker Relationships in the Middle East: Exploring scope for internal labour market mobility and fair* migration (Geneva, ILO, 2017).

International Labour Organization, *Global Estimates on International Migrant Workers–Results and Methodology* (Geneva, ILO, 2018).

International Organization for Migration section on Migration Flows: Europe at: https://migration.iom.int/europe.

International Organization for Migration, *Towards Tolerance, Law, and Dignity: Addressing Violence against Foreign Nationals in South Africa* (Pretoria, IOM, 2009).

Kaleidoscope Trust, *Speaking Out* (London, Kaleidoscope Trust, 2013): https://kaleidoscopetrust.com/usr/library/documents/main/speaking-out-lgbti-rights-in-the-cw.pdf.

Mo Ibrahim Foundation and Afro Barometer, *Updata-ing the Narrative about African Migration* (London, Mo Ibrahim Foundation, 2019).

McQueen, R, *The Flowers of Progress: Corporations in the Colonies*, Griffiths Law School, Socio-Legal Research Centre, Research Paper Series 09–14.

Mlilo S and Misago, JP, *Xenowatch, Xenophobic Violence in South Africa: 1994–2018. An Overview* (The African Centre for Migration and Society, 2018). Available at www.xenowatch.ac.za.

Ndana, N, *Sol Plaatje's Shakespeare: Translation and Transition to Modernity* (Cape Town, Unpublished, PhD Thesis, University of Cape Town, 2005).

Oette, L and Hovil, L, 'Tackling the root causes of human trafficking and smuggling from Eritrea: The need for an empirically grounded EU policy on mixed migration in the Horn of Africa' (IRRI, SIHA, SOAS Centre for Human Rights Law, November 2017): https://www.soas.ac.uk/human-rights-law/reports-research-projects-and-submissions/file125174.pdf.

OHCHR, 'Fostering Cooperation between National Rapporteurs and Equivalent Mechanisms and Cooperation with International and Regional Organizations, Consultative meeting on strengthening partnerships with national rapporteurs on trafficking in persons and equivalent mechanisms 23–24 May 2013, at http://www.ohchr.org.

OHCHR, 'Migration, A Global Governance Issue', 2010 at: https://ohchr.org/EN/NewsEvents/Pages/MigrationGlobalGovernanceIssue.aspx.

OHCHR, *Protecting and Promoting the Human Rights of Domestic Workers in an Irregular Situation*, HR/PUB/15/4 (2015).

Plan International, London School of Health and Tropical Medicine (LSHTM) and IOM, *The Trafficking of Girls and Young Women in Nigeria* (London, PLAN, 2019).

Rhoades, A and Stein, D, 'Engaging Audiences through Visual Storytelling', IOM, 14 December 2017, web.log.iom.int.

SMART Volunteering for Migrant Women, 'Volunteering: Perceptions, Experience and Barriers among Migrant Women, NGOs and Private Sector in Six European Countries' (Brussels, SMART Volunteering for Migrant Women, 2018).

SOAS, Centre for Human Rights Law, together with Refugee Rights and WagingPeace, 'Sudan's compliance with its obligations under the International Covenant on Civil and Political Rights in the context of mixed migration from, and to Sudan' 124th session of the Human Rights Committee – Review of Sudan's State Party report (SOAS, Centre for Human Rights, 2018). Available on centre website at: https://www.soas.ac.uk/human-rights-law/reports-research-projects-and-submissions/file138868.pdf.

UN, '2015–2024 International Decade for People of African Descent', at: http://www.un.org/en/events/africandescentdecade/.

UN, *Transforming our World: The 2030 Agenda for Sustainable Development* A/RES/70/1.

UN Meetings Coverage and Press Releases, 'General Assembly welcomes International Court of Justice Opinion on Chagos Archipelago, Adopts text calling for Mauritius's complete Decolonization' GA Plenary, GA/12146, 22 May 2019.

UN Secretary-General, *In safety and dignity: addressing large movements of refugees and migrants* UN GA decision 70/539 of 22 December 2015.

UN Standard Minimum Rules for the Treatment of Prisoners (The Nelson Mandela Rules) A/RES/70/175, 17 December 2015.

UN Women, *Safe City and Safe Public Spaces: Global Results Report* (New York, UN Women, 2017).

UNAIDS, *Update on HIV in Prisons and other Closed Settings* (Vienna, UNODC, 2017) Written by M Beg. At: https://www.unaids.org/sites/default/files/media_asset/20171213_UNAIDS_PCB41_Update-HIV-Prisons-UNODC_PPT.pdf.

UNICEF, *A Child is a Child: Protecting Children on the Move from Violence, Abuse and Exploitation* (New York, UNICEF, 2017).
UNICEF, *A Right to be Heard: Young Migrants and Refugee Girls*, UNICEF, 2018.
UNICEF, *Harrowing Journeys* (New York, UNICEF, 2017).
UNICEF Rights Respecting Programme, see: https://www.unicef.org.uk/rights-respecting-schools/.
Union Juive Francaise pour la Paix, 'Manifeste des enfants cachés', 6 April 2017.
United States Department of State, *2018 Trafficking in Persons Report – Eritrea*, 28 June 2018.
UNODC *Global Trafficking Report 2018* (Vienna, UNODC, 2018).
Wenke, D, *Age assessment: Council of Europe member states' policies, procedures and practices respectful of children's rights in the context of migration* (Brussels, Council of Europe Children's Rights Division, 2017).
The Yogyakarta Principles plus 10, *Additional Principles and State Obligations on the Application of International Human Rights law in Relation to Sexual Orientation, Gender Identify, Gender Expression and Sex Characteristics to Complement the Yogyakarta Principles*, adopted Geneva, 10 November 2017 available at: www.yogyakartaprinciples.org.

UK Government Reports and Guidance and other UK documents and research

All-Party Parliamentary Groups on Africa, Diaspora, Development and Migration and Malawi with the Royal African Society, ASA UK, AFFORD, Scotland Malawi Partnership, on Africa, Visa Problems for African Visitors to the UK, APPG Africa, APPG Malawi, APPG for Diaspora, Development and Migration on Africa, *Visa Problems for African Visitors to the UK* (London, APPG Africa, APPG Malawi, APPG for Diaspora, Development and Migration 16 July 2019).
British Medical Association, *Locked up, locked out: health and human rights in immigration detention* (London, British Medical Association, 2018).
Collins, G, 'Feasibility Study, Literary Translation and Creative Writing Training in West Africa' (Bristol, University of Bristol, 2019).
Commission on integration, *Our shared future, the final report*, London, Commission on Integration, 2007 available at: http://www.integrationandcohesion.org.
Communities and Local Government (CLG) *The government's response to the Commission on Integration and Cohesion* (London, HMSO, 2008).
Detention Action, *Trafficked into Detention: How Victims of Trafficking are Missed in Detention*, November 2017.
Equality Network, Kaleidoscope Trust, University of Glasgow Human Rights Network, *LGBTI People of the Commonwealth* (Equality Network, 2014) 9–44. See also.
Ewins, J, *Independent Review of the Overseas Domestic Worker Visa*, Final report presented to the Home Office, 6 November 2015.
HM Government, *Revised Prevent Duty Guidance: England and Wales*, HMSO, 2015.
Hirabayashi, J (from Y Kawahara's translation of *The Little Prince* by Antoine de Saint-Exupery), in Victoria Climbié Inquiry Report (2003) preliminaries.
HMSO, The Victoria Climbié Inquiry, Report of an inquiry by Lord Laming (London HMSO, Cm 5730) 2003.
Home Office, *Asylum claims on the basis of sexual orientation: Experimental Statistics* (London, Home Office, 2017).
Home Office, *Country Policy and Information Note: Uganda: Sexual Orientation and Gender Identity and Expression*, at: https://assets.publishing.service.gov.uk/government/uploads/system/uploads/attachment_data/file/792036/CPIN_Uganda_SOGIE_EXT_April_2019.pdf (London, Home Office, 2016 updated 2019).
Home Office, 'Policy Statement: Section 67 of the Immigration Act 2016', 10 March 2017, updated 20 December 2018.
Home Office, 'Detailed Process Transfer of Minors to the UK from France under section 67 of the Immigration Act 2016' (Home Office, December 2018).
Home Office, Deporting Families of Foreign Offenders' Gov.UK, guidance updated February 2019.

Home Office, *Country Policy and Information Note Nigeria: Trafficking of Women*, Version 5.0, Home Office, July 2019.
Home Office, UK Visa and Immigration, *Family Life (as a Partner or Family) Private Life and Exceptional Circumstances*, Version 5.0, Home Office, December 2019.
Home Office, *Windrush lessons learned review: independent review by Wendy Williams* (London, Home Office, 2020).
Home Office, 'The UK's points-based immigration system: policy statement', Home Office, 19 February 2020.
House of Commons Home Affairs Committee, *Female Genital Mutilation: abuse unchecked*, Ninth Report of Session 2016–17, HC 390, 15 September 2016.
Judicial College, *Equal Treatment Bench Book 2018* (London, Judicial College, 2018).
Lacey, N, *Women, Crime and Character in Twentieth Century Law and Literature: In Search of the Modern Moll Flanders*, LSE Legal Studies Working Paper No 20/2017.
Lindley, A, *Injustice in Immigration Detention: Perspectives from Legal Professionals* (London, Bar Council, 2017).
London Borough of Croydon, Freedom of Information Team, 'Response to a Freedom of Information Request made by Ms Anna Mulchay, Our REF: F/10009648, 10 July 2018', available from: http://www.whatdotheyknow.com.
Lowles, N, 'Overview' Hope not Hate: *The State of Hate 2018*, Hope not Hate, available at: https://www.hopenothate.org.uk/research/state-of-hate-2018/overview/.
O'Connell Davidson, J, 'Gender, Migration, "Trafficking" and the Troublesome Relationship between Agency and Force' at: (2015). Available at: https://www.law.ox.ac.uk/research-subject-groups/centre-criminology/centreborder-criminologies/blog/2015/06/gender-migration.
Pyper, D, 'The Equality Act 2010: caste discrimination', 3 August, 2018 (House of Commons Library) at: http://researchbriefings.parliament.uk/ResearchBriefing/Summary/SN06862.
Refugee Council, *Between a rock and a hard place: the dilemma facing refused asylum seekers* (London, Refugee Council, 2012).
Ruiz, I and Vargas-Silva, C, *Differences in labour market outcomes between natives, refugees and other migrants in the UK*, COMPAS, Working Paper No. 137 of 2018.
Schengen Visa Info, 'Top Mistakes to avoid during a visa interview', 22 July 2016 at: https://www.schengenvisainfo.com/top-mistakes-to-avoid-during-a-visa-interview/.
Suresh, M, '"Terrorist" lives in Delhi's courts: An ethnography of the legal worlds of terrorism trials.' (London, Unpublished PhD Thesis, Birkbeck, London, 2016).
UK Border Agency, *Asylum Instruction: Considering the Protection (Asylum) Claim and Assessing Credibility*, Home Office, 2012.
UK Foreign and Commonwealth Office, *Human Rights and Democracy Report 2017 – Eritrea*, 16 July 2018.
UK Visa and Immigration, *Guidance: Spouses Set 03*, UK Government, 13 November 2013 at: https://www.gov.uk/government/publications/spouses-set03/spouses-set03.
UK Visas and Immigration, 'Criminality guidance in article 8 ECHR' UK Gov, guidance of 14 May 2019.
Wilkins, H and Macdonald, M, 'What is the Dublin III Regulation? Will it be affected by Brexit?' House of Commons Library, 4 November 2019.
Women for Refugee Women, *Detained* (London, Women for Refugee Women, 2014).
Women for Refugee Women, *I am Human* (London, Women for Refugee Women, 2015).

Radio and TV Broadcasts and Podcasts

BBC, 'From our Own Correspondent: Migration Special' presented by Kate Adie and Broadcast on *BBC Radio 4* on 9 September 2015 at 9am: https://www.bbc.co.uk/programmes/b068s1zs.
BBC, *In Our Time*: 'Picasso's Guernica', broadcast on *BBC Radio 4* on 2 November 2017.
BBC, *Inside Story* series. Episode TRC 99, 'Winnie Mandela and the Missing Witness' (Nicholas Claxton).
BBC World Service, *The Real Story*: 'Who Should be Let in?', BBC, Broadcast 22 June 2018.

BBC World Service, *Assignment*: 'The Man who Fell to Earth', BBC World Service online, broadcast on Thursday, 13 June 2013.
BBC World Service, *Assignment*, 'The Undercover Migrant', BBC, 26 May, 2019. The programme is also available as a Documentary podcast on the BBC website, dated 23 May 2019: https://www.bbc.co.uk/programmes/w3csy5cg.
BBC, 'Intrigue: The Ratline', *BBC Radio 4*, September/October 2018 (presented by P Sands).
Beard, M, *Ultimate Rome: Empire without limit* (DVD), Broadcast on *BBC 2*, April 2016.
Channel 4 News, 'Yarl's Wood: Undercover in the Secret Immigration Centre', 2 March 2015 at: https://www.channel4.com/news/yarls-wood-immigration-removal-detention-centre-investigation.
Channel 4 news, 'Underage girls sex trafficked into Italy', London, aired Monday, 19 August 2019.
Hard knock TV, 'K'naan on Somali Pirates – There is a Reason why this started', 30 December 2008. Available at: https://www.bing.com/videos/search?q=k%27naan+on+somali+pirates&&view=detail&mid=ECF363CCBA3C9E140A2DECF363CCBA3C9E140A2D&&FORM=VRDGAR.
Olusoga, D, 'Black and British: A Forgotten History: First Encounters', *BBC 4*, last aired 23 May 2018.

Photography and Film

Demir, N, 'Alan Kurdi', *Dogan News Agency*, September 2015. Featured in *Time* Magazine, '100 Photographs: The Most Influential Images of All Time.' At: http://www.100photos.time.com, site visited 20 August 2019.
Kahiu, W, *Rafiki*, released 23 September 2018, Kenya.
McQueen, S, *Twelve Years a Slave*, Fox Searchlight Pictures, 2013.
Nzima, S, 'Hector Pieterson photograph', taken on 16 June 1976: http://100photos.time.com/photos/sam-nzima-soweto-uprising.
Sands, P, 'Lviv diary: Philippe Sands on horror, law and music', 18 December, 2017 at: https://www.ft.com/video/30739bf6-d2bc-4bd7-8c5b-b69c2433e45b.
Ut, N, 'Napalm Girl', taken on 8 June 1972 available at AP Images.
Weir, P (director), *Green Card*, Touchstone Pictures, 1990.
Whittle, N and McGuirk, O, 'Lviv diary: Philippe Sands on horror, law and music', *Financial Times*, 18 December, 2017 at: https://www.ft.com/video/30739bf6-d2bc-4bd7-8c5b-b69c2433e45b.

Lectures and Exhibitions

Appiah, KA 'The Reith Lectures: Mistaken Identities' lecture on *Country*, delivered in Glasgow, Scotland, 2016. Available on: https://www.bbc.co.uk/programmes/b07zz5mf. Broadcast on the BBC World Service on 25 and 29 October 2016.
Cole, E, *Ernest Cole: Photographer*, Exhibition, Grey Art Gallery, NYU, Washington Square, organised by the Hasselblad Foundation, Sweden, 2014.
Lester, A, '*East-African Asians v. The United Kingdom*: The Inside Story' Odysseus Trust, Lectures, 23 October 2003 at: http://www.odysseustrust.org/lectures/221_east_african_asians-sharma.pdf.
Redfern, R, 'The Surprising Diversity of Roman London' Museum of London Docklands, *Roman Dead Exhibition*, 1 July 2018 at: https://www.museumoflondon.org.uk/discover/surprising-diversity-roman-london-docklands.
Wiesel, E, 'Hope, Despair and Memory', Nobel Lecture, 11 December 1986 at: https://www.nobelprize.org/prizes/peace/1986/wiesel/lecture/.

Music

Bob Marley and the Wailers, *Zimbabwe* (album) Island Def Jam Music Group 1979, re-released, Universal Music Group, 2014.
Clem Tholet, 'Rhodesians Never Die' from the album *Songs of Love and War*, released in 1973. See: https://sonichits.com/video/Clem_Tholet/Rhodesians_Never_Die.

Hugh Masekela, *Pure Sounds of Africa*, Sony Music, 2015. Copyright SME Africa (Pty) Ltd 2015.
John Lennon, 'Imagine'. Lyrics at http://www.genius.com.
Julia Fordham, 'Happy ever after' on her album *China Blue*, 1988.
K'Naan, 'Somalia' from the album *Troubadour*, Current Media, 2009.
Miriam Makeba, 'Pata Pata' Strut Records, remastered 2019, from her album *Reprise* [1966].
Michael Jackson and Lionel Ritchie, 'We are the World' for USA for Africa, produced by Quincy Jones and Michael Omartian, Los Angeles, A&M Records, 1985.
Nina Simone, *The Very Best of Nina Simone: Sugar in my bowl 1967–1972*, RCA Records Label, 1998.
Peter Gabriel, 'Biko', Real World Productions 2018, Copyright Peter Gabriel Ltd 2003.

Websites

Pablo Picasso–Guernica- https/www.pablopicasso.org/Guernica.
Africa Museum at: http://www.africamuseum.be/en/discover/renovation.
Amnesty International, 'Refugees, Asylum-Seekers and Migrants' at https://www.amnesty.org/en/what-we-do/refugees-asylum-seekers-and-migrants/.
Dr Yusuf Mohamed Dadoo at: sahistory.org.za.
GovUK, 'View a Job Applicant's Right to Work Details' at: https://www.gov.uk/view-right-to-work.
Guardian, 'The Windrush Scandal', *The Guardian*, 2018 at: https://www.theguardian.com/uk-news/windrush-scandal.
Henley and Partners Ltd (Henley Global), *2020 Henley Passport Index*, 7 January, 2020 at: www.henleyglobal.com.
International Organisation for Migration (IOM) at http://www.iom.int.
Investment Migration Forum: http://www.investmentmigrationforum.org.
Knights Of – children's book publishers: http://www.knightsof.media.
London international Development Centre Migration Leadership Team at: https://www.soas.ac.uk/lidc-mlt/.
Migration data portal, 'Migration data for the SDGs' at www.migrationdataportal.org.
Migration Observatory: http://www.migrationobservatory.ox.ac.uk.
Mohandes Karamchand Gandhi on sahistory.org.za.

INDEX

Please note that cases can be found under the entry 'Cases of Interest.' References to Notes are denoted by page number followed by the number of the Note.

www.ingramcontent.com/pod-product-compliance
Ingram Content Group UK Ltd.
Pitfield, Milton Keynes, MK11 3LW, UK
UKHW020233290926
15470UKWH00002B/516

9 781509 93834